Democratic Policymaking

An Analytic Approach

This introduction applies analytic models to policymaking challenges, equipping students with tools to evaluate core policymaking dilemmas. Students are introduced to the approaches of game theory, social choice theory, research design, and causal inference. Key terms, along with current research, are highlighted to build an understanding of public policy study. Exercises and thought questions enable students to develop skills to assess public policy dilemmas. The analytically rigorous style of the text is accessible and avoids lengthy descriptions. Supplementary resources for instructors include extensive notes, ancillaries, and online resources, including a test bank, quizzes, and editable lecture slides for all chapters that can be modified to fit particular courses. This textbook is suitable for introductory public policy and public administration courses at both undergraduate and postgraduate level.

Charles Barrilleaux is LeRoy Collins Professor and Chair in the Department of Political Science at Florida State University. His research and teaching focus on public policy and US state and local government and politics. He is the author or co-author of numerous articles, most recently in journals including *Economic Inquiry*, *Political Research Quarterly*, *Social Science Quarterly*, and *State Politics and Policy Quarterly*.

Christopher Reenock is an Associate Professor in the Department of Political Science at Florida State University. His research interests include comparative public policy, environmental regulatory policy, and regime dynamics. His articles have appeared most recently in journals including *Journal of Politics*, *Journal of Public Administration Research and Theory*, and *Political Research Quarterly*.

Mark Souva is Professor of Political Science at Florida State University. His research interests include the causes of interstate conflict, military spending, and economic sanctions. His most recent publications include articles in journals such as the *Journal of Conflict Resolution*, the *Journal of Peace Research*, *International Studies Quarterly*, and *International Interactions*.

Democratic Policymaking
An Analytic Approach

Charles Barrilleaux
Florida State University

Christopher Reenock
Florida State University

Mark A. Souva
Florida State University

CAMBRIDGE
UNIVERSITY PRESS

CAMBRIDGE
UNIVERSITY PRESS

University Printing House, Cambridge CB2 8BS, United Kingdom

One Liberty Plaza, 20th Floor, New York, NY 10006, USA

477 Williamstown Road, Port Melbourne, VIC 3207, Australia

314-321, 3rd Floor, Plot 3, Splendor Forum, Jasola District Centre, New Delhi - 110025, India

79 Anson Road, #06-04/06, Singapore 079906

Cambridge University Press is part of the University of Cambridge.

It furthers the University's mission by disseminating knowledge in the pursuit of
education, learning and research at the highest international levels of excellence.

www.cambridge.org
Information on this title: www.cambridge.org/9780521122764

© Charles Barrilleaux, Christopher Reenock, and Mark A. Souva 2016

First published 2017

A catalogue record for this publication is available from the British Library

Library of Congress Cataloging in Publication data
NAMES: Barrilleaux, Charles, author. | Reenock, Christopher, author. | Souva, Mark A., author.
TITLE: Democratic policymaking : an analytic approach / Charles Barrilleaux, Florida State University ;
    Christopher Reenock, Florida State University ; Mark A. Souva, Florida State University.
DESCRIPTION: New York, NY : Cambridge University Press, 2016. | Includes bibliographical references
    and index.
IDENTIFIERS: LCCN 2016015780| ISBN 9780521192873 (Hardback) | ISBN 9780521122764 (Paperback)
SUBJECTS: LCSH: Political planning–United States. | Public administration–United States. | United States–Politics
    and government–Decision making | BISAC: POLITICAL SCIENCE / Government / General.
CLASSIFICATION: LCC JK468.P64 B36 2016 | DDC 320.60973–dc23 LC record available at
    https://lccn.loc.gov/2016015780

ISBN 978-0-521-19287-3 Hardback
ISBN 978-0-521-12276-4 Paperback

Contents

5 The Economy and Income Security   *148*

6 Environmental Policy *194*

9 Crime and Punishment *316*

Figures

Tables

Preface: *Democratic Policymaking*

Public policy is the core of politics. Understanding how public policy is created is an essential component of a liberal education. In this book we challenge students to think critically about why policies are the way they are. Developing such an understanding among students can help them work to demand and create better public policies.

We wrote this book as a result of our experience teaching introductory public policy courses over the course of a decade. Our goal was to combine the dense policy description that often is provided in undergraduate texts with the analytic rigor that is available in more advanced policy analysis books and research that draws from academic and scientific sources. We taught from a blend of descriptive texts and more analytic texts and found it difficult to hit the right note: the books were typically too much of one and too little of the other, too much of both, or too little of both. We believe this book strikes a good balance between the descriptive and analytic. We've taught versions of the book to large classes over the past four semesters and have received positive reviews on it from students. We hope you have the same experience.

Democratic Policymaking assumes that students have a rudimentary understanding of political systems, on the level of a good high school civics course. Students who have completed an introductory American or comparative government course should be able to understand the text with little difficulty. We have taught the text to under-graduate students from a variety of majors, including the social sciences, business, natural sciences, and liberal arts, and we have encountered little difficulty in their ability to comprehend the materials.

We apply a broad theoretical framework that allows students to analyze core challenges in the formation and implementation of all public policies; we apply the scientific method to evaluate empirical evidence on public policies; and we draw on contemporary professional public policy scholarship. We believe this distinguishes our approach in *Democratic Policymaking* from that of the majority of texts that are available for general public policy courses.

Our analytical approach focuses on what individuals want and how institutions, interactions with others, and the context in which individuals operate affect the policies that are produced. We highlight the value of the scientific method, which is critical for evaluating and improving public policy. The scientific method leads to better policy evaluation because its process is transparent. Students who understand the scientific method will have a better understanding of the key questions to ask when someone presents evidence in support of a position. Those students will understand that not all evidence or all data is equal. Discriminating between good data and bad data is a key part of a liberal education and aids the creation and implementation of public policy. We pursue these goals by drawing on contemporary scholarship. We draw on recent, scientifically based works as the evidentiary base for our substantive evaluations of policy because such research forms the foundation of public policy as an academic field and the motivation for many real-world public policies.

The first four chapters provide the theoretical and analytic foundation for the text. Following those chapters, instructors may choose among substantive policy topics they wish to teach in a given semester. Each of the substantive chapters incorporates one or more of the analytic tools, and we note which tools are being emphasized in the beginning of each chapter, so instructors may choose based on substance or analytics what they wish to teach, or may teach the entire text over the course of the semester.

To summarize, *Democratic Policymaking*

- Introduces and applies a few models that are helpful for students learning about public policy.
- Helps students to learn by example by applying the models that are included in substantive chapters.
- Provides a more rigorous analytic framework than most introductory texts.
- Provides students and instructors with a full set of slides for use with each chapter.
- Provides instructors with a test bank.
- Uses examples from existing scientific and public policy studies to illustrate important concepts.
- Blends elements of introductory and more advanced public policy texts so that instructors who wish to instruct students on elements of critical thinking may do so in a single text.
- Enables instructors to pick and choose among the substantive topics they wish to cover in a class.

Introduction

Outline

Questions

- What is public policy?
- What are the opportunities and challenges of democratic policymaking?
- Why is public policymaking often inefficient?
- What is an analytic approach to public policy?
- What is a scientific approach to public policy?
- What is the scientific method?

Overview

- Public policy is government decisions (including not deciding) on societal rules.
- Core opportunities in policymaking include preference identification, agenda setting, alternative specification of an issue, implementation, and evaluation.
- Core challenges in policymaking include preference aggregation, delegation dilemmas, credible commitment problems, bargaining problems, cooperation, and coordination.
- This text uses an analytic approach to understanding public policy. An analytic approach uses models, game-theoretic, and political economy to understand how

individuals' choices are shaped by the policy context and rules that characterize their decision-making environment.
- This text uses the scientific method for evaluating public policy.
- The scientific method requires theory construction, research designs that rule out alternative explanations, testing, and replicability.

Introduction

Public policy encompasses a wide range of topics (for example, health care, tax policy, defense policy, environmental policy, and more), and public policy decisions have a wide range of effects. Many policy topics are complex, making them difficult to understand, as well as hard to improve or solve. Is deficit spending by governments desirable? Is it equitable for some citizens to pay a larger percentage of their income in taxes or for some not to pay income taxes at all? Why does the United States spend so much on health care, yet have such poor health outcomes? To enhance the prospects of peace between countries, is it better to focus on a strong defense or international organizations? Does getting tough on crime reduce crime? If Americans prize liberty so much, why do we have the USA Freedom and Protect America Acts? Why do US students lag behind students of other wealthy nations in educational attainment? Each of these questions reflects a salient and complex public policy question.

This book introduces readers to a set of simple tools that are useful for understanding public policy problems. We believe that by the end of this book readers will have a better understanding of how public policy is made, why we observe some of the policies that we do, and why improving or even changing public policy is often very difficult.

0.1 What Is Democratic Public Policy?

The focus of this book is on public policy developed within a democratic framework. Let's consider each of these concepts in turn.

What Is Public Policy?

Public policy is a challenging concept to define. Perhaps it is best thought of as the framework of governmental formation and deliberation, the intentions of decision-makers, the formal statement of public activity, or the consequences of that activity for the public (Hofferbert 1974). Public policy represents government decisions on the rules that affect our lives. Public policy may involve *doing* something or may involve *letting something (or nothing)* happen – it includes both government-in-action and government inaction. In brief, the study of public policy is concerned with explaining why government acts (or fails to act), when it does, and what the consequences of such actions are.

What Is Democracy?

All states, whether democratic, autocratic, or anocratic, enact public policies. In this text, however, we will exclusively focus on public policymaking within the United States. Democracy is rule by the people or representatives elected in free and fair elections by the people. Democracy takes many forms. In some democracies, the leader of the government is a president (for example, the United States or France) and in some the leader is a prime minister (for example, Great Britain or Canada). Some democracies have two legislative chambers (for example, the United States and Canada), while others have just one (for example, New Zealand). In addition to these institutional differences, there is a difference between a republic and a direct democracy. The United States, for example, is a republic, meaning that the nation is governed by elected representatives. It is not a direct democracy, a system in which citizens vote on all major policy issues themselves, instead of those issues being voted upon by their elected representatives. Compared to unelected dictators, elected representatives have incentives to be responsive to citizen preferences. Yet, doing so in practice can be quite challenging. Why? Because not all citizens agree on how government ought to act. A central problem faced by governments, democratic or not, is contending preferences. Some citizens want universal, publicly provided health care; some do not. Some citizens want lower taxes; some prefer the services provided by the current tax levels. Some citizens want more defense spending; some want less. Some citizens want common education standards; some do not. Worse still – for several issues, preferences are cross-cutting, meaning that groups of citizens do not share similar preferences across a variety of policy issues. Because of these cross-cutting pressures, any elected politician is likely to have preferences that differ from some people at least some of the time.

The problem of contending preferences is one we all face daily. You and a group of friends, for example, may be choosing which movie to see on Friday night. Some of you want the latest comedy, others prefer an action movie, while still others prefer an intense drama. How do you resolve these different preferences? The problem of contending preferences is exacerbated by resource constraints. If you had lots of money and time, you and your friends may decide to just watch each movie over the entire weekend (although there is still the problem of which to watch first). Most of us, however, do not have enough money and time to satisfy the contending preferences we face. Individuals and families, subject to budget constraints, often have to choose between steak or beans and rice. Worse still, families sometimes have to determine that some children get expensive things that they *need*, like allergy treatments, and this choice keeps another child from getting something that they *want*, like the ability to play on a travel sports team. Governments also do not have enough resources to satisfy all preferences. Governments, like families, then must make difficult choices among wants and needs. In addition, some contending preferences, such as views on same-sex marriage or Common Core education standards, are not simply about resources for implementation, but competing views of justice.

What Is Democratic Public Policy?

Democratic public policy is government action that is responsive to majority preferences. Government action can manifest either as process or outcome. Democratic public policy processes are decisions by elected officials or their agents. Democratic outcomes are public policy results that reflect majority preferences. There seems to be general agreement that public policies should be the products of democratic processes, whose outcomes adhere to the majority will. Elections have consequences. Winners get to rule and losers must live with those consequences until the next election.[1] Even where there are severe differences of opinion, the agreement that the choice was made via democratic methods ameliorates losers of political contests. However, enacting the majority's preferences on an issue is not so easily accomplished. A central purpose of this book is to help readers understand why public policy may not always reflect the majority's preferences.

0.2 The Opportunities and Challenges of Democratic Policymaking

In this text, we think of public policy in terms of opportunities and challenges for elected officials to respond to majority preferences. Public policy opportunities are arenas where citizens and government have the potential to preserve what is valuable, enhance life, and address new issues. These arenas include opportunities to identify citizen preferences over public policy, to set the agenda, to identify alternatives/policies, to implement public policy, and to evaluate policy performance.

As we will see in the following chapters, public policy decisions in any of these opportunity areas can affect citizens' lives. However, while these arenas generate opportunities to affect public policy, each also faces fundamental challenges that may shape, hinder, or alter the ways in which policies develop or change.

[1] John Dunn (1979: 2) describes democracy as "the moral Esperanto of the nation-state system." Democracy, like Esperanto, is the language everyone believes they speak and thinks of as a universal term.

Table 0.1 Areas of Opportunity for Making Public Policy

- Preference Identification (What do citizens want?)

- Agenda Setting (What is government paying attention to?)

- Alternative Specification (Which policy will government pursue?)

- Implementation (Once passed, how will government carry out the policy?)

- Evaluation (How can we know whether policies are successes or failures?)

The real-world pursuit of opportunities within democratic public policy is inefficient. The public policy process does not always live up to the ideal that many citizens have come to expect. To be fair, real-world policy differs considerably from what most citizens learned in grade school about the functioning of government. When policies fall short of idealized standards, popular consensus for such inefficiencies may cite varying usual suspects, including: corruption, career politicians, and/or ignorant politicians/citizens. While some combination of these potential causes are ever present, we believe that there is a set of deeper analytic challenges that are more often than not at the center of public policy inefficiencies.

In this text, we suggest that democratic policymaking inefficiencies may arise due to a set of core theoretical challenges that all democratic states face in developing and implementing public policy. Based on a large literature of scholarship over diverse disciplines such as economics, political science, and public policy and administration, several core problems have been identified as prime suspects for policy inefficiency.

Each of these core challenges can shape the manner, direction, and success of policy pursued in any of the opportunities identified above. We believe that this interplay between policy opportunities and challenges has been undervalued in previous introductory public policy texts. As a direct consequence, students of public policy have been denied an early introduction to the core theoretical challenges that exist in the policy world. Our approach here is to introduce students to these core challenges in a meaningful and accessible way. We do so, highlighting at least one challenge and often more than one, in each substantive chapter.

0.3 Our Approach: Analytics and the Scientific Method

Our approach is based on a simple and we hope non-controversial observation: public policy students should be treated no differently than students embarking on training in other fields. In our view, nearly all public policy textbooks operate from a view that students should not be exposed to the models, empirical analyses, and

Table 0.2 Core Social Interaction Challenges

- Preference Aggregation Dilemmas (How to extract a group's preference from individuals?)

- Delegation Dilemmas (How to hire and incentivize the right agent?)

- Credible Commitment Dilemmas (How to credibly signal intentions when there is an incentive to renege?)

- Bargaining Dilemmas (How to achieve efficient outcomes when all parties must consent?)

- Cooperation and Coordination Dilemmas (How do self-interested members of groups overcome incentives to undersupply group goals?)

scholarship produced by academics and practitioners of public policy. Rather, these texts tend to cover public policy in a descriptive manner, placing heavy emphasis on describing a variety of substantive public policy areas and less emphasis on the theories and analyses used to understand those areas. This approach is unique to public policy and political science and we believe it is unfortunate.

Introductory courses in Biology, Chemistry, Economics, Accounting, and Physics, to name a few, begin with an assumption that their students can readily negotiate the core elements of what professionals pursue in those fields. We believe that public policy should not be any different. To deny students access to real-world theories and analysis denies them the very tools with which they may be able to contribute successfully in the field of public policy. Just as in these other fields, public policy analysis is a scientific endeavor – an endeavor that seeks to apply rigorous theoretical models in conjunction with scientific methods of investigation to understand how and why policies develop in the way that they do and what impact such policies have on society.

Accordingly, our approach with this text is to engage students with substantive areas of public policy *in conjunction with* the core theoretical challenges that every area of public policy faces. To understand the opportunities and challenges of public policy we will: (1) apply a broad theoretical/analytic framework that will allow us to investigate each of these challenges and how they influence the formation and implementation of public policy; (2) employ the scientific method to evaluate empirical evidence; (3) draw on the most appropriate contemporary examples from professional public policy scholarship.

An Analytic Approach

This book presents public policy via the insights of analytic models of public policy. Many of these models are game theoretic and have their origins in economics or political economy and are applied to the study of politics. Within the domain of public policy, perhaps the most famous political economy thinker is the 2009 Nobel-Prize-winning political scientist, Elinor Ostrom. (To date, she is still the only woman to have won the Nobel Prize in Economics.) She was also a President of the Public Choice Society. Ostrom termed her approach to studying public policy Institutional Analysis and Development (IAD). As the name of her approach indicates, it is an analytic approach. Our approach is similar to hers, so we highlight the main aspects of it.

An analytic approach, such as Ostrom's IAD, attempts to understand how rational individuals' choices are shaped by the policy context and rules that characterize their decision-making environment. Several elements are key to this approach. First, individuals are the foundational decision-making agents (as opposed to groups or collectives) and they are rational actors. A rational actor is one who pursues her or his interests, whatever those interests happen to be. This approach does not assume that all individuals are trying to maximize economic welfare. Some individuals some of the time aim to do this, but we do not assume that this applies universally. In public policy, or politics, individuals are often trying to maximize their political standing. For a politician this may mean that one is trying to secure one's hold on office. For a bureaucrat, this may mean that one is trying to maximize one's bureaucratic power.

Second, institutions create incentives that influence individual choices. Institutions are the rules or norms that govern processes and choices in an issue area. There is a set of rules, for example, that governs how the United States selects its president. The winner of the presidential contest is the candidate who receives the most electoral votes. Among other things, this means that the winning candidate does not necessarily receive a majority of votes cast. If enough people wish to change this institution or rule, it is possible, but there are rules that must be followed to do so. To change the Electoral College rules requires passing a Constitutional Amendment. To pass a Constitutional Amendment, it is necessary for the proposal to pass the House of Representatives and the Senate with a majority two-thirds vote (or for two-thirds of State Legislatures to call a Constitutional Convention) and then three-quarters of the States must ratify the proposal. This is a high hurdle to cross and that is why there are few Constitutional Amendments. Of course, it is possible for the rules governing the amendment process to change as well. Our point is that institutions influence the public policy process and outcomes. For Ostrom, institutions have such a large effect on public policy that she titled her approach Institutional Analysis and Development. Not surprisingly, much of her work examined how institutions influence behavior and how institutions develop.

Third, individuals make choices with limited information. Information is knowledge. Some individuals have lots of knowledge and some have little. Some have accurate knowledge and some have very poor knowledge. Differences in information quality and quantity is one of the central reasons individuals hold different preferences about the world. An individual's interests are influenced by her or his information or knowledge about a topic. Public policy involves not only learning about the preferences of others, but also the melding or choice between contending preferences.

In turn, this whole process is significantly influenced by individuals' information, its quantity and quality.

The scientific method is especially useful for evaluating and generating information on most public policy issues. In this way, the scientific method is central to understanding and improving public policy. For this reason, this book emphasizes the scientific method. Because of its centrality to this book, we elaborate on the scientific method in the next section.

Fourth, public policy outcomes are a product of social interactions. Interaction is a process that leads to an outcome from the choices of two or more individuals. Individuals do not make choices in isolation, like Robinson Crusoe before Friday came along; they interact. This means that an individual's choices, as well as the public policies we observe, are partly a function of one's expectations about how others will act in response to our choice. To understand a person's choice, we need to understand not only his or her interests on the topic, information about the issue, and the institutions in place, but also the interaction context. With whom is one interacting to produce the outcome? Who else may respond to the choice made?

Once we recognize that public policy is generated when individuals with interests and information interact with other individuals within institutional constraints, we can see that there are a small number of core problems that permeate the making of public policy. These are the problems mentioned above: preference aggregation, delegation (or principal–agent problems), cooperation, which includes collective action and coordination problems, making credible commitments, and bargaining. Almost all public policy issues involve at least one of these core social interaction problems. It is perhaps for this reason that the famous public choice scholar and winner of the Nobel Prize in Economics in 1986, James Buchanan, refers to the political economy approach as "politics without romance" (Buchanan 2003: 8).

Emphasis on the Scientific Method

The scientific method is a system for producing work that is rigorous, unbiased, and replicable. In using the scientific method, researchers work collectively, often over long periods, to attempt to construct a reliable, consistent, and non-arbitrary representation of the world. There are many ways that scientific method is applied in the study of public policy. There are *also* times in which existing beliefs are overturned by the development of new knowledge, which, in turn, may ultimately be falsified. The important point is that we acknowledge that information about policy is crucial, that our understandings of facts and truths may change as other information is revealed, and that the goal is to be open to rethinking issues as new evidence arises. This is the basis of the scientific method: discoveries are made, new discoveries may threaten or amend them, and, most importantly, people learn from those discoveries and embrace the idea that new results may force reconsideration of earlier discoveries. Accordingly, this text will focus on public policy scholarship that is representative of these aspects of the scientific method. Our treatment does not place great emphasis on historical case, process tracing, or qualitative research. There are many other texts that provide excellent reviews of these alternative research methodologies.

The steps in the scientific method are:

1. Ask a question. Think of an outcome, which varies, that you wish to explain.
2. Form a theory that is able to explain variation in the outcome.
3. Derive a hypothesis, or a testable statement, from the theory.
4. Test the hypothesis.
5. Analyze the data to assess the hypothesis's validity.

First, the investigator must observe or describe a phenomenon or group of phenomena of interest. Implicit in this is that the observer should have a research question, that is, something that motivates curiosity. Second, the researcher formulates a theory that generates a hypothesis to explain the phenomenon of interest. A hypothesis states a relationship between an independent variable and a dependent variable. For example, as one's wealth increases, consumption increases. A theory explains why the hypothesis should hold. Next, one creates a research design or experiment for testing the hypothesis. This step also involves measuring the variables and gathering the data. Finally, one analyzes the data. This step often involves the use of statistical methods. We expand significantly on these ideas in Chapter 4.

Contemporary Scholarship

We believe that part of our charge as professors is to impart the most recent accurate knowledge of our subject material to our students. To do this, we believe that there is value in introducing students to the primary sources of knowledge production – academic and practitioner research. Accordingly, this text draws heavily on scholarship, presenting students with real-world analysis and professional work product. We believe it is important to know how it is that knowledge about public policy is produced so that citizens can be more intelligent and critical consumers of such information when they consume it.

0.4 Textbook Overview

The textbook will proceed with the following structure of chapters. The text is divided into two sections. Section I introduces students to the tools academics use to study public policy. Section II covers a variety of specific policy areas noting the core challenges that each may face.

Section I includes Chapters 1, 2, 3, and 4. Chapter 1 is an overview of the processes of public policy. Chapters 2 and 3 highlight several core theoretical challenges that every public policy process must confront and considers the role that institutions like markets and governments play in these challenges. Chapter 4 is an overview of the scientific method, highlighting scientific inquiry and uncertainty. Each of these chapters provides students with essential tools that they will employ in the remaining substantive chapters of the text.

Section II includes Chapters 5 through 13. Each of these chapters highlights a particular substantive area of public policy, as well as one or more fundamental theoretical challenges integrating contemporary scholarship as it applies. Chapter 5 covers the economy and income security, Chapter 6 covers environmental policy, Chapter 7 covers health policy, Chapter 8 covers education policy, Chapter 9 covers crime, Chapter 10 covers civil rights, Chapter 11 covers homeland security, Chapter 12 covers immigration policy, and the last chapter, Chapter 13, covers foreign policy.

We emphasize several analytic insights in each chapter that map onto our core theoretical challenges outlined above:

- **Chapter 2: Individuals and Social Dilemmas**
  - Collective action/Coordination problems
- **Chapter 3: Public Policy as a Solution to Social Dilemmas**
  - Market/Government failures
- **Chapter 4: Scientific Inquiry and Uncertainty**
  - Causation/Policy uncertainty
- **Chapter 5: The Economy and Income Security**
  - Redistribution/Bargaining (e.g. Ultimatum and Dictator games)
- **Chapter 6: Environmental Policy**
  - Externalities/Delegation
- **Chapter 7: Health Policy**
  - Externalities/Delegation
- **Chapter 8: Education**
  - Delegation
- **Chapter 9: Crime and Punishment**
  - Decision theory
- **Chapter 10: Civil Rights**
  - Credible commitment problems
- **Chapter 11: Homeland Security**
  - Delegation/Strategic allocation/Coordination problems
- **Chapter 12: Immigration Policy**
  - Comparative advantage/Collective action/Commitment problems
- **Chapter 13: Foreign and Defense Policy**
  - Delegation/Bargaining/Comparative advantage

1 Public Policy Models

Outline

Questions

- What are the expected benefits of studying public policy?
- What are the major areas of the policymaking process?
- How are policy "problems" and "solutions" defined?
- Do policy problems always precede policy solutions?
- How do political interests place items on the policy agenda for consideration?
- Why do some policy issues never seem to make it onto the agenda?
- Why do some policies register little change over lengthy periods, only to then give way to a rapid burst of change?
- What are the critical features of a theoretical model of public policy?

Overview

- Public policy is the study of government activity, including laws, regulations, and funding priorities, and its influence on society.
- We study public policy to satisfy three basic needs: our desire to ensure that government actions are accountable to the public, whether government expenditures are efficient, and that government is fair or equitable in its application.

- The policy process can be characterized, albeit not perfectly, by a "stages of the policy process" model.
- A good model of public policy will be multivariate, probabilistic, parsimonious, generalizable, falsifiable, clear, logically consistent, and ideologically neutral.
- Public policy outputs and outcomes can be understood via the interplay of actors, incentives, and rules of operation.

Introduction

Public opinion on public policy is often based less on rigorous evidence and more on what many citizens view as their own form of common sense. If you scan the television, you are likely to land on a person sharing his or her opinion about some public policy, and how he or she thinks the world ought to be. Personal blogs are scattered throughout the web. Individuals, often with very little training, share their insights on various topics hoping to expand their readership. The popularity of social media outlets like Facebook, Twitter, and Snapchat offer further evidence that in addition to sharing photographs and anecdotes, many people are also interested in sharing their opinions. Yet, we have reason to be skeptical of many of these broadly distributed opinions. To what degree are opinions and beliefs about public policy based on fact? As Mark Twain is believed to have said, "I am not one who in the formulation of my opinions restricts myself to the facts." This attitude may run deep among individuals – rarely is someone reluctant to share their opinion about politics or world events even when their knowledge base is quite low. Moreover, when it comes to public policy, many individuals have relatively unstructured thinking, or thinking that is biased, distorted, uninformed, and prejudiced. But when these relatively uninformed opinions enter the domain of public policy, we, as members of a democracy, have reason to care.

Political psychology research shows that individuals vary widely in their prior beliefs about politics, the proper role of government, markets, and public policy (see Taber 2003). Moreover, we know that when confronted with new information or evidence that contradicts a person's prior belief, that person is likely to stay relatively fixed on their prior belief, once it is established. This feature of human psychology presents a challenge for public policy practitioners and scholars alike. It is well and good that all citizens have the freedom to develop and express their opinion about public policy (indeed, this is a critical component of democracy). But, at some point, it would be beneficial for society to determine whether certain ideas, opinions, or attitudes about how and when government ought to act, empirically, have the policy effects that individuals believe they do. In the absence of such evidence, one could imagine public policies being developed, implemented, and maintained in the absence of any evidence of their effectiveness. Of course, just as individuals have opinions about public policy, so too can they generate their own statistical evidence. Twain once claimed that the former Prime Minister of the United Kingdom, Benjamin Disraeli (although some believe Twain to be the legitimate author), once said, "There are three kinds of lies: lies, damned lies and statistics." So the dilemma for public policy analysis and research is a challenging one. Analysts must sift through opinions and evidence that may be motivated by political ambition to generate an analysis that is grounded firmly in objective scientific policy analysis. The late Aaron Wildavsky described the task of the policy analyst as one of "speaking truth to power." In his book (1979) of that title, he describes policy analysis as an ongoing task in which analysts constantly revise and update their conclusions to match the changing opinions and ideas that are presented by the public and policymakers. Citizen observers are also looking at a constantly shifting landscape and it is difficult and time consuming to keep up with developments.

In this chapter, we will examine how scholars attempt to understand policymaking. We begin first by considering what public policy is and why it is in our individual and common interest to study and better understand public policy processes. Next, we examine the public policy process model, highlighting its relevant uses, and then we briefly review the academic application of theoretical models to public policy. We conclude this chapter by describing the elements of public policy analysis that we believe are most fruitful for providing a framework for students to understand public policy and that we will use throughout the course of this book.

1.1 Studying Public Policy

We define the **study of public policy** as the systematic, scientific analysis of government activity, including laws, regulations, and funding priorities, and its influence on society. In public policy we are interested in the questions of what the government is doing, what impact it is having upon its citizens, and how efficient and effective are its programs. We can define **public policy** as government action designed to address the demands of a set of citizens to resolve a social issue. To fully understand public policy, we must consider each aspect of this definition. Let's take each of these in reverse order.

First, notice that there is a social issue that some set of citizens is looking to the government to resolve. What exactly constitutes a social issue, what constitutes whether it is perceived as a problem, and whether citizens ought to ask the government to attempt to address it are all fundamental questions related to the study of public policy. We will see below that the definition of a social issue or a social problem has important ramifications. Very often, critical battles are fought on whether a social issue ought to be cast as a social problem desiring government attention. Given that the very definition of a social issue as a problem to be solved may have important ramifications for whether it receives government attention, you can imagine that organized interests are incentivized to shape how the public views a social issue. Much of what government does is prioritizing social ills. Some social problems rank higher on a government action priority list than others, while others never even make the list. It is impossible to understand public policy without understanding the forces and pressures that influence government priority.

Second, recognize that we refer to a set of citizens placing demands on the government. More often than not, public policy deals with subsets of citizens advocating for a given policy, while another subset is asking the government to pursue a different policy. Importantly, these policies very often are mutually exclusive, meaning that they cannot be pursued simultaneously. Someone will win, and someone will lose. Occasionally, compromises can be made. However, in other instances this is not possible. For example, each of us generates garbage. At the end of a given week we collect our garbage, carry it out to our trash can, and put our trash can out to be hauled off. For most of us this is the end of the process. We likely give little thought to what happens after that trash is hauled off. We probably do not consider where that landfill is located. But it must be located somewhere. In an ideal world, the landfill would not be located by anyone's home. But of course that's not possible. Someone must win and someone must lose: the landfill has to be near someone's home. So an essential part of public policy is trying to understand whose interests are represented in government action and whose are ignored or downplayed.

Third, we will consider what it means for government action to address or attempt to address a social ill. Evaluating public policy requires an understanding of what constitutes an action to remedy a social ill and the standards by which such actions' success will be evaluated. Last, what do we mean by government action? Do we mean spirited debate of a publicly contested issue? Do we mean the passage of a piece of legislation? Do we mean the rigorous enforcement of the provisions of a bill? We can imagine a government's action can consist of essentially two types: symbolic and purposeful. Symbolic actions may be geared toward appeasing certain interests seeking government resolution of an issue, and yet be very likely to have only minimal effects on the social issue. Purposeful actions, on the other hand, have a high probability of meaningful impact on a social issue. A scholar of public policy would do well to recognize the difference between the two.

1.2 Why Study Public Policy?

Public policy analysis is the study of governmental action or inaction. When the government acts with the intention of addressing a societal problem or elects to not act, many stakeholders are affected. Depending upon the issue of public policy, some stakeholders may be equally affected by government *action* as they may be by government *inaction*. As a result, citizens of all political, economic, and vested interests have incentives to know what their government is doing, why it does what it does, and what effects its action has upon them. Therefore, policy analysis can originate from a rather instrumental desire to know how a policy will affect you or people who share interests with you. However, it can also be used to determine whether government actions are accountable, efficient, and whether they are delivered equitably. Analyzing public policy is therefore a way to carefully evaluate policies with a view toward improving them. We will discuss each of these in turn.

Accountability

Agreeing on the goals of the policy is important. Perhaps the first and most obvious reason to study public policy is an instrumental one. Namely, precisely whose interests are being served by the government? It is useful to know what the government is doing and whether you, as a member of a democracy, approve of the government's actions. One of the foundations of democracy is "the consent of the governed" or the **accountability** of elected officials to the people. But the consent of the governed may be difficult to imagine in the absence of the governed not understanding precisely what it is that the government is doing in their name. A logical imperative to understanding how society, governments, markets, or other social institutions choose policies demands attention to at least three critical tasks. We must first understand the process by which policy choice sets are determined or shaped. Second, we must assess the precise trade-offs that any policy choice represents relative to another. Last, we must be able to communicate the information revealed by each of the prior tasks in a clear objective manner.

Box 1.1

Accountability can be pursued by government and non-government entities alike. The US Government Accountability Office or GAO is an independent non-partisan agency that examines how the federal government manages taxpayer dollars. At the direction of Congressional committees, the GAO can evaluate and audit federal agencies to determine how well they are administering government programs. Non-government entities provide this function as well. Taxpayers for Common Sense is a non-partisan non-government organization that watches over federal tax expenditures and generates databases of all legislative earmarks, or provisions designed to benefit specific projects or constituencies.

Efficiency Gains

A second reason to study public policy is to assess the means by which the government is attempting to achieve the ends of its action. By **efficiency**, we mean whether the resources, time, and energy of a program are delivering the greatest policy outcomes, for a given level of resources. It could very well be that a public policy, which is designed to pursue a goal that most Americans agree upon, could be better obtained through an alternative policy or program. Only by examining the relative performance of policies, either in comparison to each other or in comparison with themselves over time, can one gain the data necessary to make judgments on relative efficiency.

Box 1.2

The National Performance Review (NPR) was a Clinton–Gore administration initiative to streamline the federal government. It had three first order objectives: (1) downsize the federal government; (2) reduce administrative costs; and (3) reform the administrative system (Thompson 2000). Academic evaluations have varied in their scoring of the NPR's success.

An example of such an efficiency evaluation was the performance review initiated by the Clinton administration in 1993 and 1994. This initiative was designed to analyze the overall government efficiency and effectiveness of agencies and programs. The initiative's goals were to streamline policy performance and delivery. This evaluation tracked a series of measures of agency performance for nearly every major agency in the federal government across several years.

At the conclusion of each evaluation window, Congress would communicate with agency officials to relay their relative performance. Both through informal communication via public hearings and occasionally through formal budget and legislative initiatives, Congress encouraged the heads of agencies to improve their performance (Carpenter 1996; Huber and Shipan 2002; McCubbins *et al.* 1987, 1989).

Equitable Policy Delivery

In addition to accountability, another characteristic that many citizens may value is equity in policy delivery. By this we mean that a government should deliver the benefits of a policy evenly across all communities. This suggests that for those policies that are not means tested, there should be no correlation, in the ideal, between the services that the government provides and a community's wealth, economic class, ethnic make-up, or political clout. A long line of research and political science theory suggests that active, mobilized interests are more likely to be served by government institutions. If those active, mobilized interests do not share the preferences of the average or median citizen, then how government responds to those interests may have implications for not only government behavior, but also deeper concepts of democracy and accountability.

This is a difficult line for policymakers to walk. In the political world it is common and perhaps reasonable that in the relatively competitive environment of political pluralism, where interest groups compete for attention and policy benefits, those that are mobilized and better organized are more likely to receive greater attention. Yet, in the extreme, if the same groups consistently benefit from policies, alternative stakeholders may attempt to raise the cost for policymakers.

Box 1.3

The Great Recession presented a particular challenge on the issue of equitable policy delivery. Every day American citizens make decisions about their economic lives. They make decisions on whether to invest assets, how to invest, and what level of risk to do so. Generally speaking, most citizens acknowledge that any risk associated with their personal investment decisions are theirs to bear. As a result, it was difficult for most citizens to understand why the government might want to sponsor a wholesale bailout of investment firms and banks in the wake of the 2008 financial collapse. For many citizens, this Bush–Obama administration decision was viewed as unfair assistance to banks that had made unnecessarily risky bets on financial investment – and many believed that the banks ought to pay the price. While this logic is sound when investment losses are relatively small, at larger losses, the entire economy may be put at risk. This potential resulted in the "too big to fail" defense. Both the Bush and Obama administrations defended their bail-out practice with the logic that the banking losses were simply too large to allow every major bank to go under. What do you think? How big is "too big" to allow to fail?

Democratic Policymaking

Policymaking in a democratic system is complicated. You are likely familiar with some elements of the US system. One of the greatest complications of American politics is the federal system. **Federalism** is a system of shared powers in which the state governments shifted some of their original powers to the national government (through their ratification of the US Constitution in 1789) and in which local governments receive charters from the state. Hence, we will refer to each level of government by its correct name in the federal system – national, state, and local – and will reserve the term federal to refer to the full system.

The US Government operates under a Constitution, and each state has its own constitution. The states' constitutional powers are weaker than those of the national government. States may not coin money, may not declare war, and may not enter into treaties with other nations. Sometimes states and the national government disagree over what constitutes the appropriate division of authority between them, and the federal courts act as the arbiter of their disputes. The local, state, and national governments sometimes cooperate and sometimes are in conflict. For example, in 2012, a group of states joined in a lawsuit led by the National Federation of Independent Business to sue the national government as an objection to the adoption of the Patient Protection and Affordable Care Act (PPACA) (popularly known as Obamacare) of 2010. The US Supreme Court ruled 5:4 that the PPACA was legal under the Constitution, but gave the states the ability to opt out of a provision in the law that ordered them to expand their Medicaid programs, which are funded jointly by the national and state governments. That decision led some states to expand health care and others not to, which created an unforeseen difficulty for the policy's designers. The point of this is that federalism can complicate decision.

The United States also has a bicameral legislature, as do all but one of the states (Nebraska). In addition, the United States has a system of separation of powers that makes it difficult for the executive, be it the president, a governor, or a mayor, to gain acceptance of his or her policy choices. The president must contend with Congress, control of which may or may not belong to his or her party, and who may or may not support elements of the president's agenda. President Obama succeeded in passing the Health Reform Act of 2010 in large part because his political party controlled both the House and Senate. From 2010 to 2012, Democrats controlled the Senate, but not the House. Since 2012, Republicans have controlled both the House and the Senate. President Obama has had a progressively more difficult time gaining support for his preferred policies over the course of his presidency.

The states' bicameral legislatures work in much the same way as the national government's. All are affected by the division of partisan control and different constitutencies. The state governments also vary in their capacity to govern. Some are more professional than others, with better administrative and legislative staffs, greater capacity to do policy research, and so on. These variations in capacity lead to wide variation in state policy, some of which is a function of the states' ability to govern and the other of which is a function of state preferences.

The national, state, and local governments all have judiciaries, with the responsibility for prosecuting violations determined by the respective constitutions. Each level of government has a broad array of criminal, civil, and administrative courts.

The courts are a crucial part of the separation of powers plan in the United States because they adjudicate among the branches of government.

Democracy makes policymaking difficult. It would be simpler to make optimal decisions without the difficulties that public opinion, political disagreement, and differing institutional prerogatives introduce. Famously, Winston Churchill shared his thoughts on the relative appeal of democracy compared to other systems of government before the House of Commons in 1947:

> Many forms of Government have been tried, and will be tried in this world of sin and woe. No one pretends that democracy is perfect or all-wise. Indeed it has been said that democracy is the worst form of Government except for all those other forms that have been tried from time to time.
>
> (James 1974: 7566)

Despite its inherent challenges, we think democratic decision-making is the best choice given the need for accountability, efficiency, and equity.

1.3 The Policymaking Process

Scholars have studied policymaking formally for over sixty years. Throughout this period academic models attempting to understand various aspects of the policymaking process have come and gone. Perhaps the most used, and regrettably abused, model grew out of Harold Lasswell's "stages process" of the policy process (1951). The use of the stages was to provide a heuristic for analysts to understand the types of decisions that are ongoing in the policymaking process. The stages reflected the pathways by which policies are identified, proposed, evaluated, implemented, and terminated. While this heuristic to understand the policy process was useful early in academic research, its utility began to wane as critics weighed in on its rather unrealistic linear top-down assumptions of how policies are produced.

While many policy scholars have been critical of the stages model, we neverthe-less find it useful as an informational short cut to understand the *types* of decisions that are made in policy rather than their *causal ordering*. Accordingly, we will use the stages of policymaking analogy to describe various aspects of the policymaking process. Academic endeavors are largely oriented around answering questions that hew to each of these decision types. By and large, most scholars are concerned with answering questions of either why problems get onto an agenda, once on the agenda why certain solutions are more likely to be selected, what are the factors that condition implementation of a program, and how ought we to evaluate a program's effectiveness. Therefore, despite the fact that the policy process does not unfold in a linear way, we believe it nevertheless does describe the holistic approach of most academic work.

In the following sections, we take each of the stages and describe the dynamics inherent in each, the importance of these dynamics, and any appropriate theoretical applications that social scientists have applied to understand these questions. We would like to caution the reader, however, that at no point should we consider these stages to be unidirectional. Rather, each of the stages represents an important question that is likely to be asked about various aspects of the policy process.

Problem and Solution Identification

Perhaps the most interesting question about the policy process is: What is the genesis of social problems? Also, how do social issues become defined as social problems? Moreover, once social issues have been defined as social problems, how are solutions to those problems identified? A common belief among the general public is that there is a market of ideas that governs the supply and demand of problems. Under this market analogy, individuals mobilize to portray societal problems and solutions. If the market for these solutions is sufficiently large, individuals will be successful in "selling" their solutions to policymakers. While such a rough analogy is well intentioned, it fails to capture the reality of most policy systems. In particular, the common wisdom approach assumes that the association between **problem definition** and **solution definition** is best characterized as a linear, unidirectional relationship. Yet, most policy subsystems do not support this characterization.

How so? First, policy problems and solutions often do not exist in proportion to each other. There may very often be policy problems with few solutions or alternatives, or a single problem that faces several competing solutions. Consider climate change as an example. The consensus among climate scientists is that the world climate is changing and will likely have consequences for human behavior. In the absence of near-term responses to these changes, humans will likely experience cultural and economic conflict. Yet, this is a policy area that increasingly does not have consensus over the extent of the policy problem and for which there exists a wide variety of possible policy solutions. These solutions range from (1) no action to (2) international treaties over greenhouse gas emissions to (3) carbon taxes, etc. This is a policy problem that lacks a clear or obvious policy solution.

A second way in which common beliefs about the problem/solution definition relationship deviate from reality is that the relationship is rarely unidirectional. As we will see below, policy advocates often are incentivized to define problems or to search out problems to which their solutions can be applied. Let's look at energy policy again. The idea of a carbon tax, or a tax on the use of energy derived from fossil fuels, has a long history dating back to at least the Clinton administration. The idea behind the tax is that polluters or people who purchase energy derived from fossil fuels ought to pay for the externalities associated with them. The carbon tax is clearly beneficial on economic efficiency grounds. Yet, the idea is not popular with the average citizen or the fossil fuel lobby. As a result, policy supporters have often sought to frame the carbon tax solution in conjunction with other problems. It has been proposed as a solution to closing budget deficit holes, weaning us off foreign oil, and, more recently, helping us address global climate change. In each of these cases the solution (a carbon tax) generally preceded the problem (closing the deficit, weaning off foreign oil, global warming), suggesting a more complicated bi-directional relationship between the definition of policy problems and solutions. However, to better understand this process, we must first consider the individuals who are active within a given policy area and the incentives that motivate their behavior.

At the core of any policy area exists a set of individuals whose interests are at stake or affected by a given policy; let us call these individuals **stakeholders**. Within any set of stakeholders, there may be subsets of individuals who will be differentially affected by a policy problem or a proposed policy solution. Some individuals will benefit from the solution of a problem, while others will be harmed by a particular solution. This suggests that both sets of stakeholders have individual incentives to advocate or resist particular policy solutions. To secure these individual benefits, however, individuals must represent themselves as collective interests. The probability of successfully delivering a group benefit rises as the number of individuals in the group increases. But such advocacy is not costless. Forming a group, raising a budget, and lobbying for policy change requires time, energy, and resources. Moreover, if the group is successful in securing a policy solution, they may not be able to exclude group members who otherwise did not contribute to the group cause. As a result, not all stakeholders have individual incentives to pay the costs associated with forming a group and advocating for the policy change. As we will see in the next chapter, there are micro-level incentives that prevent individuals from organizing to advocate for benefits individually even though they may extract those collectively; we refer to such situations as **collective action dilemmas**.

The general solution to solving these collective action dilemmas is to provide individuals with selective incentives for participating in a group's activities (Olson 1965). Within the context of public policy, John Kingdon (1984), a well-known political scientist who studied policy processes, offered a potential solution to this dilemma. Kingdon pointed out that individuals with selective incentives, or benefits that only accrue to them individually, may have sufficient incentive to lead groups of stakeholders. Whether small business associations or citizen action groups, selective incentives may be sufficient to offset the costs of group organization for some individuals. Kingdon refers to such individuals as **policy entrepreneurs**. Policy entrepreneurs can be any individual who advocates, organizes, or attempts to define a policy problem or solution. For the policy entrepreneur, being an advocate is part of the pay-off of being involved in policy. Simply put, we can think of it as receiving a benefit from working with individuals to either advocate for them to help define a social issue as a problem. Policy entrepreneurs can be involved in shopping around policy solutions from which their stakeholders would benefit if enacted. When we allow for the existence of policy entrepreneurs, we can better understand the interplay between policy problems and solutions. Policy entrepreneurs are continually at work in the policy world, attempting to define, redefine, shape, and reshape policy issues as policy problems. They attempt to define problems by employing a variety of tactics.

One critical tactic is to shape a policy problem or solution's image. Every policy problem (or solution) has a series of images that individuals conjure up in their mind when activated (Baumgartner and Jones 1993). However, a policy problem's **dominant policy image** is that image that most citizens think of when a phrase or policy is mentioned. This dominant policy image can be quite useful in shaping how citizens think about an issue, vote about an issue, and otherwise interact politically with an issue. As a result, policy entrepreneurs have incentives to attempt to shape this dominant policy image. Entrepreneurs will pursue a variety of tactics, including political rhetoric, communications, and campaigns to shape this image. For example, clear your mind. Go ahead, clear it. Now, be honest, think about the first thing that comes to your mind when you see the phrase, Welfare Recipient.

What image came to your mind? Whatever came to your mind may very well be a by-product of the political battle to shape your view and the dominant policy image of a welfare recipient. The dominant image of a welfare recipient varies with the ebb and flow of different political coalitions in the United States. Arguably, the dominant policy image of a welfare recipient in the 1960s was a poor white family from Appalachia. By the 1980s, this dominant policy image shifted to a poor black family from the inner-city. While not all individuals will agree on this policy image, the dominant policy image may be very useful as a political tool in the definition of a social problem. If the dominant policy image is a positive one, in other words, if it is one whose social problem and stakeholders are held in positive esteem, it will be easier for a policy entrepreneur to advocate for resolution of this issue by government. Alternatively, if the dominant policy image is a negative one, where either the problem or the stakeholders are held in negative esteem, it may be easier for a policy entrepreneur to block changes to the status quo. The potential to manipulate how individuals think about and perceive a policy underscores the importance of policy entrepreneurs and their fight to shape what issues are and are not perceived to be problems.

Box 1.4 Dominant Policy Image

Shaping the dominant policy image of a policy initiative is a powerful political tool. With minor rewording, a non-controversial policy initiative can be converted into one that divides or attracts great political support. For example, a tax on inheritance wealth for estates above a certain threshold was fairly popular

Box 1.4 (*cont.*)

when it was referred to as an estate tax. This dominant policy image conjured up notions of landed estates where the sons and daughters of billionaires received large inheritances tax-free. But when this tax was reworded to be a death tax, or a tax that the government seeks out simply from the act of dying, popular support began to wane. These semantic battles have been waged by both sides of the political spectrum. Here are just a few examples that have shifted over time:

- Illegal Aliens shifted to Undocumented Immigrant.
- Civilian Casualties shifted to Collateral Damage.
- Torture shifted to Enhanced Interrogation.
- Affirmative Action shifted to Race-Based Preference.
- Social Justice shifted to Wealth Redistribution.

Similarly, policy entrepreneurs working for certain stakeholders have incentives to shop solutions around to those who make decisions on policy. These solutions may be expanding concealed weapons rights in a state or advocating for drug testing among state employees. One view of these solutions is that there is a legitimate policy problem that needs to be resolved, and policy entrepreneurs are sincere about solving them. Another perspective is that strategic policy entrepreneurs representing the gun industry or the medical testing industry are not primarily motivated by solving these policy problems. Rather to enhance sales of their products, representatives of the gun industry or medical testing industry identify policy problems that fit their products or solutions. In this respect, the causal relationship between policy solutions and policy problems is not necessarily unidirectional. Rather, crafty policy entrepreneurs can strategically use the creation of a problem to push through a policy solution that they had been shopping around for years.

Box 1.5

A Policy Window is an opportunity in time where political and policy pressures align momentarily to allow some set of policy problems and solutions to meet. The meeting of the solutions and problems as well as the political and policy pressures of the moment allow for the opportunity of an actual policy change. For example, in the wake of the Great Recession, it was easier for policymakers to vote for a massive regulatory overhaul of the Security and Exchange Commission's oversight of the financial system. Without the policy window of the Great Recession, vested interests on Wall Street would have been likely able to prevent any such legislation from moving to the floor of the House and Senate.

Consider for a moment many of the aspects of the USA Patriot Act that were passed in the wake of September 11. This piece of legislation, signed into law by President Bush on October 26, 2001, included a variety of controversial provisions that among other things: allowed for the indefinite detention (suspension of *habeas corpus*) of immigrants suspected of terrorism, the expansion of law enforcement search and seizure powers without a warrant, roaming wiretaps, "sneak and peek" warrants, dramatically increased border security personnel, and National Security Letters, which require an organization to turn over personal records of individuals without judicial review and prohibit the organization from revealing the issuance of the letter, even to their own lawyers. A subset of political interests (conservative and liberal) had been shopping around these policy provisions for years, but for any number of reasons, had never been able to convince enough policymakers that these solutions were necessary to solve an existing policy problem. September 11 changed everything. September 11 represented what John Kingdon calls the opening of a **policy window**. When such windows open, an opportunity arises to merge policy solutions with policy problems, sparking an actual policy change. Indeed, in less than one month, the Patriot Act provisions, which had lingered in the policy world for decades, were enacted as law.

When groups fight to define problems through policy advocacy, the question becomes: Which of the many competing problems being pursued by a variety of policy entrepreneurs are the ones that grab the attention of policymakers? This involves the delicate interplay that goes on with agenda setting.

Policy Demands

Policy demands are those pressures placed upon elected leaders and policymakers that change the costs of their inaction. What do we mean by this? Anyone can make a demand of you. Your parents may ask you to do well in your college coursework. Your romantic partner may ask you to treat him or her better than you have been. But among any of these demands, the ones you are likely to pay attention to are the ones that, if you ignore them, are most likely to generate some kind of benefit (or cost) for you. So, your parents can ask you to try harder in your college coursework, rewarding you for good performance or threatening to cut off your funding for poor grades. Or, your partner can ask you to treat him or her better, rewarding you with affection or threatening you with cutting off the relationship in the absence of change. Depending on how much you value these proposed benefits, fear the threatened sanction, and believe that the promise or threat is credible, you will be more likely to meet their demands. Policy demands are similar. Any number of demands can be made of our elected officials, or agency officials. But from an institutional actor's perspective, they will be more likely to respond to incentives, whether they are carrots or sticks, when actors sufficiently value either the benefit or the cost being offered or threatened and believe it to be credible.

A **credible action** is a promised or threatened action that the action's target believes will be carried out with a high probability. Threats made to policymakers, while possible, are less productive, frequently less credible, and therefore less used. Credible benefits, on the other hand, are ubiquitous. Competing groups offer these benefits as information subsidies to enhance policymakers' ability to advocate for policies that they generally already favor (Hall and Deardorff 2006). These benefits may include either direct financial support for electioneering, but, more frequently, include policy support in terms of subsidizing legislative or administrative information search costs. By providing legislators with additional resources in the form of information, strategic groups can subsidize legislators' "policy information, political intelligence and legislative labor" (Hall and Deardorff 2006: 69) with an eye toward maximizing their desired policy goals.

Agenda Setting

Agenda setting refers to the process by which formal institutional centers of power will take up and potentially act on a policy solution. Standard models may consider agenda setting a primarily elite domain. This elite domain is made up of three standard institutions: the executive, the legislature, and the courts. It is possible to also add within Federalist frameworks the level of governed as an additional venue within which formal decision-making can occur. This view of the critical actors in agenda setting, however, seems to assume that each institutional actor stands separate and divided not only from themselves, but also from other non-institutional actors. A competing view is one laid out by Paul Sabatier and later by Sabatier and Jenkins-Smith. Sabatier and Jenkins-Smith argue that policy agendas are more likely shaped by what they call advocacy coalitions (1988; 1993). **Advocacy coalitions** are policy subsystems that consist of a variety of interests, including actors within administrative agencies, legislative committees, researchers, policy analysts, etc. These advocacy coalitions share policy beliefs and coordinate their activities in attempting to achieve similar policy goals. To obtain their policy objectives, advocacy coalitions pursue strategies that attempt to alter the behavior of government authorities. Prior to examining the sets of factors that help to shape agendas in policy, we first must take special note of the role of the media in this process.

The Media and Agenda Setting

The media deserves special attention here. Early in the media's lifetime, radio and television media dominated US political communication. Newspapers and the evening news broadcast by the three major networks dominated news distribution from the

1950s to the 1990s. Along with newspapers and radio, Americans received their political information from television news. This has changed dramatically in the past twenty years. With the expansion of choices due to cable and satellite television as well as the Internet, news consumption has fundamentally changed how Americans interact with politics and with the media. Independent political news organizations that exist purely on the web, such as the Drudge Report or Slate or Politico, offer Americans access to political information 24/7. In addition, personal blogs offer information not only on public opinion, but also on news dissemination. As a result, the news cycle has become, in some sense, easier to manipulate. However, the background noise of the entire political news cycle has increased. While it is easier to broadcast your own signal, it is more difficult to have it heard above all of the background noise.

Policy entrepreneurs are, of course, aware of all this. And they have as their goal the manufacturing of media events. Each and every day policy entrepreneurs face the troubling question of ensuring that not another day goes by during which their policy issue goes unmentioned in the media. While one way to drive media attention is simply to purchase advertising, this method is expensive and likely to go unnoticed by individuals who are quick to fast forward through commercials and relegate such communication to background noise. Policy entrepreneurs must be creative in manufacturing a news event that is likely to draw the attention of the traditional media and provoke conversation among the non-traditional-web- or blog-driven media. Such free coverage is the goal of most media-driven campaigns. The tricky part is coming up with a controversial idea that can simultaneously be heard above the noise, but not be so controversial that it drives away supporters.

Factors That Drive Agenda Setting

How might these coalitions shape the policy agenda? There are essentially three distinct factors: (1) formal institutional actors can shape agendas; (2) actors external to formal institutions can help shape agendas; and (3) external shocks can impose a shift in emphasis.

First, agendas derive much momentum from key institutional actors. Presidents and legislators have their own policy agenda. When they run for office they run on policy platforms making promises to their constituents on the types of policies that they would like to enact once in office. These policy platforms are some mixture of sincere and strategic calculations. On the whole, research demonstrates that while the strength of public-policy-opinion congruence may ebb and flow over time, elected leaders are generally sincere in their pursuit of policy that closely aligns with their constituents (Erikson *et al.* 1993). In fact, legislative policy initiatives are driven by some mixture of individual legislator preferences and constituency interests (Kingdon 1989). This represents perhaps one of the more curious features of US politics. Most Americans, if you ask them, seem to believe that their elected leaders are more interested in pursuing their own agendas than pursuing what their constituents prefer. While a popular belief, research simply does not support it. Most elected representatives do pursue policies that are in line with their constituents' preferences (Page and Shapiro 1983; Erikson *et al.* 1993).

Second, actors external to these institutional actors can shape the agenda. Advocacy coalitions oriented around certain policies can attempt to shape external demand for policies to be taken up. These coalitions can be made up of subsets of the US public, interest groups, non-governmental organizations, businesses, and even members of specific administrative agencies. Essentially, such coalitions are interested in altering the public discourse in such a way that elected leaders in formal institutions have all but no alternative to take up the issue at hand. This goal is usually accomplished via a multi-pronged attack, including a popular movement, mass media, and internal advocacy. By attempting to manipulate the news cycle, advocacy coalitions can strategically use information releases, press releases, or press conferences to attempt to force an issue onto the agenda.

Box 1.6 Agenda Setting and the Affordable Care Act

As the Great Recession wore on into 2009 and 2010, President Obama had a choice: pursue a jobs agenda or pursue health care reform. He chose the latter. For many observers, this was a curious choice. At the height of the worst recession the United States had seen since the Great Depression of the 1930s, the president chose to put his political capital in pursuing health care reform rather than an aggressive jobs package. This choice underlines the Chief Executive as an important player in agenda setting. The president and key supporters in his political coalition believed that the political window that had opened in the wake of his historic 2008 election (providing a Democratic majority in both the House and Senate) would allow for movement on health care reform that had been unachievable for over fifty years. This moment in the policy–politics nexus is another example of John Kingdon's policy window opening.

Last, external shocks can also shape the agenda. In the spring of 2014, President Obama likely had on his domestic agenda a redoubling of effort to expand jobs and economic activity in the United States, but a variety of events shifted executive attention from the domestic economy to other events. The president was facing an aggressive move by President Putin of Russia in the Crimea and Ukraine, a scandal with Veterans Administration hospitals, and aggression by the Islamic State of Iraq and Syria (ISIS) throughout Iraq, among many other issues. Every president faces a series of competing issues on their agenda. But external shocks can exogenously strike the system, reshuffling any well-intentioned leader's agenda.

Any of the three factors can impact the types of issues that make it onto the policy agenda. But let's remember, equally important as deciding what gets onto the agenda in politics is the power to decide what is to be left off. The power to block or prevent certain issues from ever making it onto the agenda is for some groups half the political battle. Quite frankly, it's a much easier task. The more difficult task as a policy entrepreneur would be to promise my advocacy coalition that I can deliver their policy issue to the president and guarantee them that he takes up their issue in the first 100 days in office. That would be a tall order, particularly, if it was, for example, opposed to the president's original agenda. On the other hand, it is a relatively easier task to throw up roadblocks, barriers to a policy issue whose solution your coalition opposes.

Policy Formulation

Policy solutions come in many forms. There may exist, at any one point in time, a few alternatives or several dozen. A policy area's technical complexity, political salience, and area-specific features may each contribute to the variation in the number of policy alternatives generated. As the number of policy alternatives increases, policymakers face an increasingly complex decision over how to evaluate the pros and cons of each alternative against another. Why are some policy areas more prone to many diverse alternatives? Who formulates these alternatives and how do policymakers choose from among them? We take each of these questions in turn below.

Policy Areas and Incentives for Action

Policy areas have certain characteristics that either attract or deter political attention. Two characteristics in particular, technical complexity and policy salience, political scientist William Gormley (1984) argued, combine to structure not only the level of attention that elected officials give to a policy, but also whether they are more likely to even attempt to intervene with a policy solution. **Technical complexity** refers to the level of knowledge that is required to understand a policy area. Nuclear power and regulation is an example of a highly technically complex policy area. To even understand the basic science behind nuclear power requires a fairly high level of policy-specific knowledge. Banking regulation, as well, is an area that requires a high level of knowledge on the status quo and potential ramifications of the policy change. Technically speaking, a decision about abortion policy, cigarette taxes, or even the decision to go to war requires less technical knowledge and is therefore less complex. **Policy salience** refers to the number of citizens that are likely to be affected by the policy in a significant way. Environmental regulation, Social Security policy, and health care policy are all examples that affect a large swathe of the American public and are therefore highly salient policy areas. Billboard regulation and motor vehicle licensing are examples of areas that are less salient. We can then imagine a policy area being high or low on both of these dimensions simultaneously. Environmental regulation is an example of a policy area that is both high salience and has high technical complexity, while billboard regulation is an example of a policy area that is both low salience and low complexity. Interesting policy areas may also have unique characteristics of being low on one dimension while high on another. Consider civil rights policy. Clearly, this is a policy area that has high salience, but is not particularly technically complex. Alternatively, insurance regulation is fairly high in its technical complexity and yet low in public salience. Citizens are likely not very attracted to the issue of insurance regulation despite their potential benefits and being affected by policies in this area.

Each of these dimensions of policy is important, and how they combine present decision-makers with different incentives to participate in the policy process. A policy area's location in this two-dimensional salience-complexity space will shape the number and form of elected leaders who desire to participate in the policy area, as well as whether they prefer to allow other actors like business groups of bureaucrats to dominate policymaking. If we imagine these two dimensions in a Cartesian coordinate system, it allows for the possibility of four ideal types of policymaking arenas.

Politicians are generally drawn to any policy areas that have high salience. To do otherwise is to risk electoral prospects. However, politicians are also reluctant to tinker with policy in high complexity policy areas. The average elected official is reluctant to be held accountable for creating a policy disaster in an overly complex and technical area. As a result, politicians are attracted to high salience low complexity policy areas. Gormley refers to such areas as "Hearing Room Politics," where politicians are excited to be involved in policymaking in the bright lights of media coverage and grandstanding. Elected officials are drawn to the hearing room, but are reluctant to get involved with high salience high complexity policy areas. Gormley refers to these areas as functioning with an "Operating Room Politics," since to change policy in these areas requires a surgeon's precision. Accordingly, these types of policy areas tend to be dominated by upper-level bureaucrats who have both the political acumen and technical knowledge to hopefully make informed decisions about policy. In policy areas that are low salience, politicians are less likely to be involved. In low salience high complexity policy areas, ones that Gormley terms "Board Room Politics," the public is less likely to be involved, as is the media, and as a result policymaking is dominated by what Gormley refers to as a power elite. In these areas, members of key legislative subcommittees with a smaller subset of the business community, including key executives and representatives, are likely to dominate policymaking. Last are those policy areas that are both low salience and low complexity. Gormley refers to these as being dominated by "Street-Level Politics." In this policy area, neither elected officials nor the public have a great incentive to be involved. Nor does the media view a large audience for stories about these policies. As a result, these policy areas are dominated by lower-level bureaucrats who follow strict standard operating procedures to carry out their tasks.

While Gormley's typology is not without its limits, it is a useful heuristic to think about the types of actors that are active in a given policy area. These actors are at the core of the policy areas agenda setting alternative formulation and policy selection.

Alternative Formulation

For most policies, policy solutions are drawn from a set of competing alternatives. These alternatives often grow out of a competitive policy advocacy where subsets of organized interest groups, think tanks, and legislative subcommittees generate specific policy recommendations for adoption. Elected officials like choice. They generally desire to consider their options, even if they have no intention of pursuing most of them. To this end, decision-makers, including elected leaders or agency heads, often prefer to have varied interests to present different policy alternatives in order to evaluate the advocacy of each. This suggests that the ability to be "in the room" is a fairly important power. The groups, think tanks, and lobbyists who are invited to offer or supply specific policy alternatives have in some sense already won an early battle in the policy process simply by being invited to be in the room.

What got them in the room? Politics plays a role. But so do their ideas. To the extent that these groups can formulate policy alternatives that are likely to be adopted by elected officials, they must be able to offer precise recommendations that detail the mechanisms of the policy implementation and the likely effects on stakeholders. Alternatives most often take the form of so-called white papers or policy positions that outline, in executive summary form, the broad strokes of a policy alternative's central features and expected goals. Alternatively, drafts of legislation are also another work product that advocacy groups and think tanks will shop around to policy leaders for their consideration.

Who are these groups? You likely have heard about them or have seen them in passing if you scan a print or online story in the *New York Times, Washington Post, Wall Street Journal,* or via a broadcast news outlet like a major network like ABC, NBC, or CBS or a niche network like Fox News or MSNBC. They are groups with names like the Heritage Foundation, the Progressive Policy Institute, the American Enterprise Institute, or the AFL-CIO. There are too many to list exhaustively, but there are numerous groups and institutions that are dedicated to thinking seriously about policy alternatives.

Groups vary in the extent to which they have the ear of decision-makers. The Heritage Foundation represents conservative ideas and they are more apt to have the ear of Republican lawmakers than the Progressive Policy Institute, which is a liberal-leaning organization that is more likely to have the ear of Democrats. The American Enterprise Institute, in the past, had a reputation as a right-leaning organization that commanded attention from both Republican and Democratic legislators because its experts were credible on both sides of the aisle. A change of directors in the past few years has seen AEI shift to a more pronounced right-ideological leaning, which was done as a conscious attempt to garner more contributions from donors, as AEI had seen its donations erode as Heritage and the libertarian Cato Institute gained donors and influence. The Brookings Institution and the Urban Institute are known to be more left-centrist, but retain credibility among Democrats and Republicans given their publication of legitimate research documents.

It is important to distinguish the type of information that is being provided by information-producing organizations. The Cato Institute, for example, publishes *Reason* magazine, the *Cato Journal*, and, as do most of these organizations, an enormous stream of online material. Cato is clear that its mission is to provide information that supports its core goals of supporting "... individual liberty, limited governments, free markets, and peace" (Cato 2015). The Brookings Institution was founded in 1916 by Progressive Era reformers whose goal was to provide fact-based information for government policymakers. Brookings has a broader organizational mandate than Cato: to strengthen democracy, foster economic welfare, and encourage international cooperation. Because Brookings is a center-left think tank, they produce less narrowly focused work than Cato or the Progressive Policy Institute, and work that is less directed toward a specific policy or political agenda. Readers of policy analyses must be wary consumers of information and distinguish between expert and editorial opinion. The AFL-CIO engages in lobbying and provides expert information to elective officials, but, given that it represents organized labor, provides information that is especially favorable for labor's interests. Cato at times provides information that argues against the interests of organized labor. Citizens and (ideally) decision-makers should take into account those biases.

Professional and technical organizations like the American Society of Civil Engineers (ASCE) and the American Public Health Association (APHA), among others, make fact- and expertise-based recommendations on policy issues that may or may not reach the ear of policymakers. Those organizations' statements are less likely to contain information with ideological political content than are those of, for example, Heritage or the Progressive Policy Institute. A panel representing the American Society of Civil Engineers issues an "infrastructure report card" on the states and the nation every five years. The 2013 report assigned the United States a "D+" grade for the state of the nation's infrastructure: roads, bridges, parks, dams, ports, waterways, energy, and the like. The APHA publishes state-by-state health rankings annually, and advocates for healthy lifestyles. Each of these organizations has a political aim – the ASCE seeks funding for infrastructure development and maintenance and the APHA supports universal access to health care, gun regulation, and smoking bans – but they are not partisan and their positions are evidence based. Groups whose claims are based on unbiased information are able to make broader appeals to policymakers than are those whose claims are based on ideological or otherwise biased claims.

There is some evidence that some information-providing organizations have undue influence on legislative policymaking. Legislators, especially in the states, are confronted with hundreds of votes within a session, some of which involve highly technical information. Some state legislatures are not very professional, that is, the sessions do not last very long, members are paid poorly, and they have only a limited number of professional staff members to help them manage the session's demands. Some states, like California, have year-round legislatures with large, full-time staffs. Others, like Texas, meet only every other year (biennially) and have smaller staffs. The less professional states are more likely subject to undue influence by organized interests. For example, mining interests dominated Montana politics for years, as that single industry had the largest presence in the state's politics. More recently, the American Legislative Exchange Council (ALEC) has emerged as an especially potent conservative interest in state politics. ALEC is a membership organization of state legislators and business people that was established in 1973 by corporations to gain access to state legislators. It receives most of its funding from corporate sources, and its most influential members include Exxon-Mobil Corporation, Koch Industries, and other large businesses. ALEC staffers write policy position papers and model legislation, some of which appears verbatim in proposed state legislation (Garrett and Jansa 2015). Critics of ALEC claim that the organization exerts undue influence on state legislation via its construction of model legislation.

Policy entrepreneurs and organized interests engage in a variety of standard lobbying tactics to advocate for their preferred decisions. At the broadest level, lobbying can be broken into electoral or legislative tactics. The first electoral tactic focuses on advocating for or against specific candidates for office who agree or disagree with the group's policy alternatives. A more common tactic, the legislative tactic, focuses on rhetoric and analysis to convince legislators of a group's position. While the common wisdom appears to be that lobbyists buy legislators' votes with campaign contributions, this is not supported by empirical research. What then are lobbyists getting for their donations? Most recent research suggests that lobbyists are subsidizing legislators' time and research. Rather than focusing on changing legislators' policy positions, lobbyists instead focus on educating current supporters and providing them with the information to advocate for preferred initiatives.

Policy Selection/Adoption

Given all of the political activity that precedes a policy adoption (problem recognition and definition, media campaigns and alternative formulations), at some point elected officials or appointed members of the bureaucracy must evaluate their options and make a policy choice. These choices are driven by both political and policy concerns. Policymakers must evaluate whether a policy they wish to propose will pass muster with others who are involved in policy adoption or with the public. They must consider *policy effectiveness, cost, technical feasibility*, and *political feasibility* prior to pursuing policy adoption. Of course, there may be disagreements among the public and policymakers over which of these criteria is the most important.

The relative weight assigned to each of these inputs varies by decision-maker. For some decision-makers, namely particular elected officials, politics will play a more important role than policy analysis. This suggests that for certain elected officials, political ideology will drive their decision behavior regardless of what any rigorous empirical evidence or lobbying efforts may suggest to the contrary. Other elected officials may assign more weight to policy analysis, preferring to get the policy right even if that means trading off some of their political preferences. Similar calculations exist with members of the bureaucracy. Higher-level political appointees are more likely to place greater weight on political preferences than what policy analysis may suggest. Lower-level civil servants, however, have been found to pursue public policy interests despite potential conflicts with their own politics.

Consider, for example, the risk management/risk analysis process. This process applies to policy areas that attempt to quantify the risks that human populations as well as their possessions are likely to face when they are exposed to any number of toxins or potential hazards. However, this process has been distinctly divided into two elements. The first one represents risk analysis, which is conducted by bureaucratic scientists and specialists, based on empirical evidence, peer-reviewed to the highest standards of scientific inquiry. The end goal of this process is to characterize, to the best of their ability, the statistical risks that a population may face when exposed to a hazard. This information is then passed onto higher-level political appointees in the agency, who then are responsible for the second stage of this process – risk management. Risk management entails explicitly stating the political considerations of the economic and political costs of whether a given risk ought to be managed with regulation or restrictions. This phase allows for politics to play a greater role in determining whether or not, given some risk, they ought to attempt to do something about it.

The costs of a policy, even if it is successful, are a crucial concern for policymakers, implementers, and the public. Policymakers and constituent groups assign some financial value to a policy before they support or reject its adoption. If a policy is too costly to pursue, it may be rejected. What is too expensive depends on citizen and legislator tax preferences and other concerns, like whether the policy is highly salient. Technical feasibility may be linked to cost concerns as well. Some policies may be technically feasible – like desalination of drinking water in areas that have water shortages – but are expensive due to their complexity. The determination of what is too expensive may change over time as needs change. For example, the long-term drought in California may require investment in more expensive solutions to the water problem, and the price of those solutions will be more acceptable as need grows.

There are a number of formal and informal ways to go about this. One commonly used formal method is **cost-benefit analysis** (also called benefit-cost analysis). Cost-benefit analysis, as the name implies, involves identifying all of the costs of a proposed policy or project, all of its benefits, and calculating a ratio to determine whether benefits exceed costs. Cost-benefit analysis sounds straightforward, but demands extensive information collection and establishment of preferences and values. The steps in a cost-benefit analysis are outlined in Table 1.1 below.

Cost-benefit analysis requires several steps that may be controversial. Establishing costs and benefits is not difficult vis-à-vis declaring something to be a cost or a benefit, although there may be discussion about whether something is truly a benefit. The more difficult task is to assign monetary values to those costs and benefits. For example, let us return to the example of political risk management above. In that case, assigning risk was done first by experts who assign a political risk, and then the more difficult task falls to political appointees whose job is to assign risks. They may conduct a cost-benefit analysis to determine whether risks should be taken.

Table 1.1 Cost-Benefit Analysis

Identify the project	May require choice among policies, or comparison
List all benefits/costs	Include physical, psychological, financial, emotional, etc. and establish them as costs or benefits.
Assign value to benefits/costs in a common metric (usually money)	This is often difficult because some non-financial benefits require monetization. Be certain to include opportunity costs as well as financial costs.
Apply discount rate	Adjust for present value over time using a discount rate, which assigns values over time.
Sum costs and benefits, determine whether benefits outweigh costs, choose among alternatives.	The analysis is only as good as the inputs, and it is difficult to establish costs and benefits exhaustively. For a cost-benefit analysis to be accepted requires that all relevant stakeholders are aware of the process and have input.

Consider the case of establishing acceptable levels of risk for hydraulic fracturing, also known as fracking, which is the technique of using high pressure to inject sand and chemical-laden water into pipes drilled below the ground's surface to extract natural gas and oil. Fracking is controversial: the film *Gasland* (2011) showed frightening images of contaminated well water burning in taps, being useless for farming, undrinkable, and filled with particles. Some scientists claim that fracking is unhealthy and urge its ban. Others claim that the problems in some fracking operations are due to user error and that the technique is safe. The US Environmental Protection Agency (EPA) reported that the incidents of contaminated water are isolated and that the majority of hydraulic fracturing operations are safe (US EPA 2015).

Hydraulic fracturing has had an enormous economic impact on the United States. The nation's most rapidly growing state economy is in North Dakota, where energy production via fracking is producing a boom economy. Gasoline prices have gone down dramatically as one result of this boom, which leads in turn to more economic activity in other sectors of the economy as cheaper fuel reduces the price of getting products to market, and consumers spending less money on fuel provides greater opportunities for spending in other sectors, thus having an economic spill-over effect. However, the costs of fracking are uncertain, especially over time, and this uncertainty makes it difficult to assign monetary values to the costs of fracking activities. The downstream effects of having more and less expensive energy may have great effects over time. If we learn that the chemicals used in fracking, which some state governments do not force the companies doing the work to reveal because doing so violates their ability to protect their confidential information, are dangerous, that affects the discount rate as well. It is necessary to assign values to the risk of fracking, as well as to the opportunity costs (for example, land used for fracking is no longer useful for farming or ranching). Thus, cost-benefit is more complex than would be ideal.

Policy Implementation

Implementation is any activity related to carrying out a duly passed policy. By duly passed policy we mean any policy that has been passed by both houses of the legislature and signed by the Chief Executive. Implementation activities may consist of a variety of activities, but there are three basic services that most agencies fulfill for their political principles: rulemaking, regulation, and clientele service.

First, the bureaucracy engages in rulemaking. Very often, legislative policy will express the policy intent of the political coalition that passes the policy and will leave the finer details of implementation to bureaucratic specialists. As you might imagine, this is quite empowering to the unelected bureaucrats that staff the relevant administrative agency. While they are tasked with writing administrative rules, they are not without constraint. Bureaucrats must operate within the guidelines of not only the main legislation in question, but also their agency's current operating procedures, as well as the federal administrative procedures act, which outlines the manner and procedures by which administrative rules are promulgated.

A recent example is the Dodd–Frank Wall Street Reform and Consumer Protection Act. This piece of legislation was passed in July 2010 and was designed to regulate the financial system of the United States with an eye toward preventing another financial collapse similar to the Great Recession. The bill would require the Securities and Exchange Commission (SEC), the administrative agency in charge of implementing the legislation, to issue specific rules on how to administer the nearly ninety separate provisions of the bill. As of the writing of this text, in 2015, the SEC was still publishing notifications of its intent to issue rules relevant to the bill. Some of these rules were four years in the making. Why so long? Two reasons: technical complexity and politics. Financial regulation is inherently complex. The regulators at the SEC want to be sure to generate rules that will strike a balance between regulatory necessity and undue economic hardship. Moreover, elected leaders and regulated clientele (Wall Street, banks, etc.) wanted to lobby the SEC to ensure that their interests were looked after.

Second, the bureaucracy enforces rules and regulations. Thousands of bureaucrats are employed by the US federal government, state governments, and local governments to enact legislation and public policy. Whether it be a federal employee of the Environmental Protection Agency who inspects a facility to determine whether they are within their permit on air pollution, or a federal employee of the Food and Drug Administration who may conduct inspections of our meat supply, or a local police officer checking whether you have the proper driver's license vehicle registration and insurance information, members of the bureaucracy play a central role in carrying out the policies that our elected representatives pass. Similar to rule promulgation, however, these actors do not operate without constraint. In fact, their discretion is contingent upon the specific rules and procedures that have been developed both for and by the agency. The Environmental Protection Agency has established internal procedures that their regulatory officers must follow when inspecting and deciding whether to penalize a non-compliant firm. Similarly, a local police force must operate within the bounds of fair standard operating procedures. Of course, this suggests that an important component of policy implementation is the level of discretion or constraint with which a bureaucrat operates.

Last, non-regulatory agencies service clientele. For these agencies, their clientele, or the subset of citizens who benefit from their agency, are their primary service targets. This clientele may consist of individuals seeking to renew their driver's or fishing license, elderly citizens attempting to remedy an issue with their Social Security account, or citizens in need of medical care, taking advantage of government health care insurance such as Medicare or Medicaid.

In each of these areas of agency service, members of the bureaucracy are very often most citizens' only interaction with their government. Most citizens have never met their mayor, city councilman, legislative representatives, or the president. However, most have interacted with city inspectors, police, park rangers, and any number of line officer bureaucrats. Citizens, on average, do not like being told what they can and cannot do. Moreover, when citizens want something from government, they want it accomplished quickly and efficiently. For each of these reasons, the average citizen may not have very positive feelings toward the bureaucracy, especially when it is considered in the abstract, that is, if they have not met directly with officials. When people have face-to-face contacts they often are personally pleasant enough, but the types of things they are doing – getting the driver license renewed, getting permits, and the like, are not especially pleasant. You have probably heard more than once from a friend or family member complaining about government "red tape." This phrase is often used to characterize the slow-moving pace of bureaucratic work. But if most citizens do not prefer bureaucratic red tape, and on the surface none of our elected officials seems to prefer it either, then why does it exist?

Contracting Out to the Bureaucracy

When a law is passed with the intention of addressing a policy issue, most citizens simply assume that the law will be enacted efficiently and effectively. But decades of study of the bureaucracy suggest that such an assumption is invalid. In fact, the success of any legislative initiative may very well hinge on a variety of factors that shape the policy area's technical complexity, public salience, and bureaucratic capacity. This is because to implement any policy that a legislature or executive passes, political coalitions must contract out the services to the bureaucracy. Individual legislators can certainly not implement their own policies. However, in contracting out this service, legislators face a few dilemmas. We will see in later chapters that any time a principal contracts out with an agent they face two fundamental challenges: selecting the right agent; and incentivizing the agent. The fundamental problem for any legislative body is that the individuals who staff the bureaucracy may not share the policy interests of the legislative coalition that produced the policy. Moreover, unlike legislative coalitions, members of the bureaucracy are more likely to have career civil service positions. So the question for any legislative coalition is: How do we get the bureaucracy to do what we want them to do and preserve our policy into the future?

We will see in later chapters that this problem is best addressed either through reward and punishment strategies or through the strategic design of agency operating procedures. Reward and punishment strategies generally require the agency to act first and for the legislature to decide whether they would reward or punish the agency for what policy is delivered. Alternatively, a legislative coalition can attempt to restrain an agency's behavior prior to their making policy choices. They can do so with the creative use of operating procedures. If legislators can design an agency structure and procedures in such a way that they can minimize the agency's ability to deliver surprise policies, then legislators will be better able to guarantee that policies are implemented in the way that they prefer. This tactic sheds some light on the bureaucratic red tape issue. It suggests that bureaucratic red tape may indeed be a by-product of the contracting relationship that exists between principals and agents or legislators and bureaucrats.

Why Red Tape?

Bureaucratic red tape is a phrase often used to describe the rules and procedures for government action. Such red tape can describe the numerous steps and procedures that a government official may need to follow before they are able to take an act, even one that is in the service of a citizen. Or, red tape may describe the procedures that citizens must follow before they are able to apply for a government benefit or to pursue an activity that requires government approval. An unrefined view of government may simply conclude that such inefficiencies are inevitable. But such a conclusion ignores the fact that some government agencies are less bureaucratic than others. Some state governments, for example, are more efficient than others. Some federal agencies are more efficient and better run than other government agencies. So the answer "all government is inefficient" cannot explain variance between government agencies.

Political scientists have suggested at least one explanation for variation in government red tape. Matthew McCubbins, Roger Noll, and Barry Weingast, writing as McNollGast, argue that in the search for public policies that will benefit their political coalition, policy entrepreneurs will occasionally try to pursue bureaucratic procedures and rules that will lock in political bias in administration (1987, 1989). The idea here is that bureaucratic red tape serves political purposes. Rather than being a necessary by-product of government administration, bureaucratic red tape is actually a strategically useful tool for political coalitions seeking to either lock in their policy preferences or prevent their opponents from doing the same.

Let's consider an example. One of the classic complaints against government bureaucracy is that it is slow. It is slow to issue new rules. It is slow to pursue enforcement of those rules. It is just all around slow. What might be a political explanation for this? After a piece of legislation is passed, regulatory agencies are given the task of issuing new rules to carry out the intention of the legislation. To the frustration of many advocacy groups, often these new rules are delayed for quite a long period. In fact, the federal government and many state governments have mandated public notice and comment windows, often ninety days in length, during which the public and any number of stakeholders are allowed to file public comments about the agencies' proposed new rules. Under the common wisdom explanation, this procedure looks like government dragging its feet. Private businesses don't ask the public what they think of new proposals for ninety days, they simply just enact them. Why is government different? What McNollGast suggest is that the application of a rule like a ninety-day notice and comment period supplies political coalitions with a valuable resource, namely time. Such time delays allow the coalition to respond to any action that an agency may pursue against the coalition's interests. So what political coalitions are doing with this rule is protecting themselves and their policies. They are protecting themselves against bureaucratic action that they may not agree with. So even though every elected official will bemoan slow government action, in reality, they may very well be extracting a benefit from the government taking its time in making a timely decision. Evidence suggests that these delays are most valuable for business interests, whose comments receive more attention than those of non-business interests (Yackee and Yackee 2006).

Policy/Program Evaluation

In the end, citizens, policy entrepreneurs, elected officials, and bureaucrats have an interest in knowing whether proposed or enacted policies are likely to deliver the promised social changes. **Policy evaluation** is the systematic investigation of the effects of a policy on its intended social target, prior to action. **Program evaluation** is the systematic investigation of the effects of a program on its intended social target, once enacted. For all intents and purposes we will treat each of these types of evaluations as the same thing. The goal of theoretically based policy or program analysis is to analyze and evaluate policy with a view toward improving it. Both are concerned with the fundamental question of "what effect will policy X have on social phenomenon Y?" In this respect, the ideal policy evaluation is not concerned with political ideology or stakeholders' interest – although it can certainly be used to those ends. Rather, policy evaluation attempts to uncover, to the best of the analyst's ability, an objective assessment of a policy's impact on society.

The intended goal of a policy or program evaluation is to issue this assessment in the form of a formal or informal report. After a policy assessment is produced, political interests can intervene to make use of the results of the report as they see fit. To conduct an objective policy evaluation, an analyst must make an honest effort at being policy neutral. By **policy neutral**, we mean the analyst must guard against injecting their own political beliefs into the analysis process. How might an analyst's personal political views come into play in conducting a policy evaluation? To answer this, let's consider the technical elements of a formal program evaluation.

Program evaluation consists of primarily two parts. First, the analyst must decide whether X had an effect on Y. To systematically evaluate the effect of X on Y is a complicated scientific endeavor. As it turns out, causality, while more readily observable in the context of a controlled experiment, is more difficult with messy field data. To establish a causal relationship between two variables, four conditions must be met: a theory to explain how one variable induces a response in the other, X and Y must be correlated, X proceeds Y in time, and no other variables can account for the correlation between X and Y. Second, the analyst must decide whether the estimated effect of X on Y is at, below, or above the program's initial projected performance criteria. To do this, the analyst must define what is meant by successful performance. Is success a dichotomous concept that consists of either successful or not successful? Or should success be conceived as a continuum, where a program is simply more or less successful? At what point may an analyst declare a program to be a "success" or a "failure?" These are difficult choices for an analyst to make and to justify to others. By choosing which policy to evaluate and how to evaluate it, an analyst is essentially defining the standards of success. To be thorough and value-neutral, in reporting findings, analysts use well-specified criteria and standards. And if the goal of the policy analysis is not to be value neutral, then the analyst should at least be clear about their personal biases and assumptions. There is nothing necessarily wrong with a conservative or liberal policy analysis, provided that the analysis is upfront about its assumptions. If analysts believe that there is a trade-off between economic growth and environmental protection, for instance, then whether the analyst is conservative or liberal, he or she ought to be clear about their personal political assumption or beliefs. By clearly identifying these assumptions, the individual who consumes the information will be better able to put in the proper context.

Does Policy Cause Politics?

Theodore Lowi (1979) argued that traditional systems of policymaking had been supplanted by what he called "interest group liberalism." One component of interest group liberalism is a constant feedback in which policy decisions are processed by groups and create new political demands and, ultimately, new policy demands. Suzanne Mettler and Joe Soss (2004) pursue the logic of Lowi's argument further and develop an explanation of how policies affect the public. They find that existing policies help frame how people think about politics, suggesting that policy causes politics to some extent. Suzanne Mettler (2011) describes this phenomenon in light of the politics of the Patient Protection and Affordable Care Act of 2010 (aka Obamacare): Medicare recipients responded negatively to that policy with cries of "Keep the government out of Medicare," which is odd because Medicare is funded by the government. The existence of the Act, and the publicity that surrounded it, helped create a visceral but poorly informed set of policy demands that led some people to demand things that were contrary to their interests.

1.4 Models of Public Policy

Public policy holds a fairly unique position in academic research. The types of questions in which scholars and practitioners are interested in asking in public policy span a number of traditional academic disciplines. These areas include political science, public administration, international relations, economics, and sociology, as well as any number of policy-specific disciplines (i.e. health policy administration or environmental policy). While each of these disciplines is pursuing answers to policy questions in the public domain, they have slightly different focuses. Common to each, however, is the application of a theoretical model to explain and facilitate empirical examination of the policy process. A **model of public policy** is a simplified representation of the causal relationships that link any number of policy inputs with a policy output of interest. In the following sections, we will discuss the utility of such models and their common characteristics, and finish with a brief overview of what we believe to be a particularly useful theoretical framework that we will employ throughout the text.

The policy world is a complex place. Despite the simplistic treatments that some elected leaders may offer us or even those that policy textbooks present us, including this one, real-world policy problems and solutions are rarely simple or well behaved. Policy problems are multi-dimensional and complex, with many moving parts and causes. In actuality, there are more moving parts and causes behind our policy outcomes than we will ever know. As a result, as we attempt to understand public policy, we must recognize from the outset that our theoretical understanding of, as well as our ability to predict, policy outputs are layered with varying levels of uncertainty. And these are limitations which nearly every science must confront.

Despite these challenges, we cannot shy away from attempting to understand what we can of the policy process. We must endeavor to simplify a complex world – to make manifest what is latent and to shine a light on those causal processes that may be difficult to see at first. The goal of the policy scholar is to use careful logical construction of theoretical arguments to understand the most important elements of the causal process. These various elements can then be represented in a unified or generalized model of the policy process question. What does it mean to identify a causal process or mechanism? And what is a theoretical model and how can we distinguish between a good model and a bad one? We take each of these questions in turn below.

Positing a Causal Relationship

Public policy is interested in identifying causal relationships between variables and in specifying the mechanisms by which these causal relationships operate.

A **causal relationship** is one *between an input variable and an output variable, where an outcome variable has changed due to an exposure to an input variable.* Whether examining poverty, economic recessions, pollution, or inflation, public policy analysts are interested in the factors that cause these phenomena to vary. In addition, analysts are also interested in specifying the precise mechanism or process by which an input induces a change in an output. A thorough discussion of a causal relationship between an input variable and an output variable will therefore explain not only the nature of this relationship, but also the process or means by which this relationship operates.

In your lifetime, you have probably posited many causal relationships. Whether in politics, economics, sports, or your personal life, you at one point or another have probably made a claim of, "I think X (fill in the blank) causes Y (fill in the blank)." That is the easy part of specifying a causal relationship. The more challenging part is to specify the precise mechanism or process by which this causation occurs. You have likely had practice doing this. Occasionally, after we make a claim, a friend may have challenged you by asking, "And why is that?" We believe this question gets to the heart of exploring causal mechanisms and processes. Let's explore how.

And Why Is That?

Consider a relatively simple act – turning on a light in a room. What would you say was the cause of the light turning on? The first thought in your head may have been, "It was me, because, when I flipped the light switch, the light turned on." This is a perfectly reasonable response. What if we wanted to push further on what the precise mechanism or process by which the light turning on was induced? You can often zero in on the precise causal mechanisms or processes by repeatedly asking a series of questions that take the form: "And why is that?" So a perfectly acceptable answer may be that *you* caused the light to turn on. But let's push a bit further with our "And why is that?" questions.

Q: What caused the light to turn on?
A: When I flipped the light switch, the light turned on.
Q: And why is that?
A: Because, when I flipped the switch I completed the electric circuit within which the light is located and then the light turned on.
Q: And why is that?
A: Because, when I flipped the switch, I completed the electrical circuit, creating a voltage or an electrical potential in the electrical wire, which induced a current in the wire, and then the light turned on.
Q: And why is that?
A: Because, when I flipped the switch, I completed the electrical circuit, creating a voltage potential in the electrical wire, which induced a current in the wire,

which exerted a force on the free electrons in the copper wire, which agitated the energy level of bound electrons in the atoms within the incandescent bulb's filament. When the atom's bound electrons' energy levels fall back down to normal, they release this extra energy in the form of a photon, which we see as visible light.

Now we would likely consider any of these individual answers to be a "correct" causal account of the mechanisms or processes by which the light turned on. But with each successive answer to our "and why is that?" question we gained a more nuanced and better understanding of the precise mechanisms by which the causal process operates. This suggests that an analyst must be careful to think about what level of causal precision he or she wishes to examine when proposing causal mechanisms in public policy. Pushing hard on this process and drilling deeper into the causal mechanisms may be useful for theory construction even if the eventual causal story is not told at the most precise level. Let's consider a policy example.

A consistent finding in education policy is that a parent's socioeconomic status (SES) has a large impact on a child's k-12 school performance – children whose parents have higher SES tend to perform better than children whose parents have lower SES (Sirin 2005). But what is a potential causal story linking these variables? Why might poorer children perform less well in school? What is the precise causal process by which this comes about? Let's try applying our "and why is that?" approach. One potential story could be that a poor child's parent(s) spends less time working with their child on schoolwork.

Q: And why is that?
A: Because poor parents are less well-equipped to help their child with schoolwork.
Q: And why is that?
A: Because poor parents have less free time to work with their children.
Q: And why is that?
A: Because poor parents may *both* work 9–5 jobs, and may even work multiple jobs.
Q: And why is that?
A: Because poor parents didn't receive a good education.
Q: And why is that?
A: Because this causal process has a high potential to be cyclical.

By repeatedly asking ourselves "and why is that?" we can push further into the causal process to identify the different mechanisms by which the proposed causal link occurs. To be clear, this technique is useful for identifying a potential causal process. There is nothing to say that there cannot be multiple processes at work, competing processes at work, or conditional processes at work. And different analysts may have answered our "and why is that" questions differently – and that would be just fine.

The point of these series of questions is to spur you to think carefully about the mechanisms that might be at work behind a social process.

Necessary and Sufficient Causality

Policy analysts often speak of causal relationships as being of two fundamental types: necessary and sufficient. If X is a **necessary condition** to cause some outcome, Y, then whenever we observe the presence of Y, we must also observe X. Alternatively, if X is a **sufficient condition** to cause some outcome, Y, then if we observe the presence of X, we must observe Y. If a causal relationship is both necessary and sufficient, then Y will only ever be present if and only if X is present.

Continuing our parent SES and child school performance example, if we claimed that low parental SES was a necessary condition for low-performing students, then we would expect that all cases of low-performing students (our outcome – Y) would have lower SES parents (our cause – X). Of course, this leaves open the possibility that some lower SES students could have performed well at school, it only requires that of the students who did perform poorly, all of them were low SES. Alternatively, if we claimed that low parental SES was a sufficient condition for low-performing students, then we would expect that all cases of low SES would result in low-performing students. This leaves open the possibility that some students performed poorly on the exam, but were not low SES students.

Conditional Causality

Policy analysts may also face relationships that are conditionally causal. **Conditional causality** exists when the effect of one variable, X, on Y is moderated by the effect of another variable, Z. For example, a conditional relationship could describe a situation where X only has an effect on Y for sufficiently high or low values of Z. Alternatively, a conditional relationship may suggest that X has an increasingly positive or negative effect on Y and Z increases or decreases. In our parental SES and student performance example, it may be the case that a parent's educational achievement may condition the effect of their income on their child's educational performance. If this were the case, we may expect that only at sufficiently low values of a parent's educational level, Z, will their income, X, have an effect on the student's performance. Why might this be? We assume that poor parents are less well equipped to help their children with schoolwork, perhaps as a function of their own education. However, if parents were reasonably well educated, but poor (think graduate students), then the effect of their higher education may be sufficient to offset the negative impact of their poverty on a child's performance.

Deterministic vs. Probabilistic Relationships

Social processes are generally better captured by a probabilistic rather than deterministic relationship. What does this mean? A **deterministic relationship** is one that will always produce the same output from a treatment or initial state. A **probabilistic**

relationship, on the other hand, is one that will produce an output from a treatment or initial state, with some probability. Probabilistic relationships allow for random chance to alter their outcomes. We refer to such relationships as being stochastic, meaning that some portion of their variability is simply random.

These expressions of causality, however, tend to operate with deterministic relationships of causality. With the deterministic sufficient condition, in 10,000 cases if we observed one case where Y was present and X was not, then we could declare that sufficient condition could be said to not exist. This is a fairly high standard. As a result, some individuals refer to probabilistic causation, or the increased likelihood of observing Y in the presence of X. Let's consider this more carefully. In any relationship in which some phenomenon, X, is believed to cause another phenomenon, Y, we must recognize that there will always be some amount of error in predicting the precise nature of this relationship. In equation form, this is often done by adding a term epsilon, ε, to represent the stochastic or unpredictable error that is common to any social process. So, rather than discussing an equation, $Y = X$, we instead refer to $Y = X + \varepsilon$, where epsilon represents all of the unknown features that may randomly affect Y. Moreover, social processes are also multivariate, meaning that they have multiple causes. The idea of recognizing that a social process may have multiple causes, for most people, is not a natural one. Ask anyone you know what they believe causes some phenomenon and they will likely give you a single answer. Rarely will you have someone say, "well, it depends, that's a very complex process. It likely is a result of any number of factors" – unless of course your friend is a scientist. The drive for individuals to settle on one cause of a phenomenon is no less likely in public policy – indeed, it may be more prevalent. Political ideologues are very likely to believe that some policy outcome of interest has a single cause. Conservatives may believe that Y is caused by X_1, while liberals believe that Y is caused by X_2. Yet, a more accurate description of a given policy outcome, Y, is that it is likely caused by X_1, X_2, X_3, X_4, X_5, and X_6 in addition to some random error, ε. Each of these variables may affect Y with different magnitudes. One may be more important than another in how it shapes some policy outcome. But each of them may play an important role in determining why we see the variable Y distributed in the way that we do.

What policy analysts are interested in is identifying precisely which variables play a role in shaping a policy outcome and what are the sizes of their effects. Prior to examining this empirically, analysts must know which variables ought to be even included in this equation; an analyst must have a theoretical basis for their inclusion. This is the underlying goal of a theoretical model of public policy.

What Is a Model of Public Policy?

As noted above, a model of public policy is a simplified representation of the causal relationships that link any number of policy inputs with a policy output of interest.

Nearly all social phenomena have multivariate causes, meaning that they are caused by a finite but large set of factors. A model is a theoretical representation of a reduced set of these factors or inputs that are thought to play the most important role in influencing an outcome. Moreover, some of these factors may interact with each other or condition the effect of other factors, making the complete causal story even more complex. Nevertheless, despite the rather daunting task of explaining how and why public policies vary, it is useful for us to simplify our theoretical accounts of these processes. Doing so provides us not only with a stronger understanding of why policies vary, but also allows us to both predict future variations and propose policy interventions to improve performance. In this respect, a theoretical model is not unlike a model car. In many respects, a model car captures the most important elements of a real automobile trading off certain characteristics like size, functionality, etc. A model is most useful when it captures the basic essence of a real-world phenomenon that it is attempting to explain, without being as complex as the real-world phenomenon itself.

For example, any number of reasons may explain why regulated firms under the Clean Air Act violate the law. We can logically produce a set of factors that likely influence a firm's compliance records, including the firm's ability to comply with the law (how often they are inspected), its willingness to comply with the law (economic pressures to violate), and its knowledge of the law. We could also produce a set of factors that likely influence a regulatory officer to pursue non-compliant firms. Regulatory officers may lack motivation (low pay or incentive), oversight, or proper resources to secure high compliance rates from firms. We could produce theoretical justifications for including any of the aforementioned factors as variables in our theoretical model – and doing so would likely yield great benefits in our general understanding of why firms break the law.

However, we could also imagine additional more obscure factors that may also play a role, albeit minor, in whether a firm violates the law. Perhaps an internal firm auditor simply made a mistake in record-keeping. Perhaps a minor random technical malfunction caused a portion of the plant to emit slightly higher pollution than their permit allowed. Or perhaps the owner of the firm had an affair with the husband of a regulatory officer. These three factors: mistakes, random technical malfunctions, and marital affairs, while possible in influencing our outcome of interest, are not equally likely explanations of why firms violate the law. Accordingly, we would not likely include a variable "is having an affair" in our theoretical model simply because the benefits of doing so would not outweigh the complexity of adding such minor variables to our model.

Of course, by not including less important variables that precisely characterize all possible contexts, we lose the ability to understand *perfectly* or predict every instance of our outcome. Instead, we will have a model that represents the most important general features that influence our policy output across many contexts – in other words, we will have a **generalizable** model. A generalizable model is one that is not context-specific. Continuing our example using firm compliance, if we propose a sufficiently thoughtful generalizable model, it ought to be able to explain firm compliance in any context. It ought to do well explaining firm compliance in rural Kentucky as well as downtown Manhattan. It ought to do well explaining firm compliance in the 1980s as well as the 1990s. Generalizable models, however, will not be able to explain changes in outcome based upon trivial, highly specific, or random factors that are case-specific. There may be a single firm in Montana for which our model fails to explain why they are or are not breaking the law due to some random factor. This is the trade-off that we face when constructing a generalizable model.

Michael Coppedge (2012) offers the metaphor of the whale and the octopus to explain this trade-off. Imagine a whale swimming through the world's oceans. This whale has a very broad appreciation of what the oceans offer. It understands breadth, general characteristics of the ocean, and a broad understanding of ocean currents, food supplies, and topographical features, but only from a high depth from the ocean floor. It has no appreciation for variations in small ocean plants, coral, or granules of sand. An octopus, on the other hand, knows its immediate environment extremely well. It can sense and observe fine variations in the sea floor, vegetation, coral, and even miniscule aquatic life. However, its knowledge may be confined to a 10 square-foot area, where the octopus spends most of its life. In constructing models of public policy, it is good to be aware of this trade-off.

Why Do We Need Models of Public Policy?

A strong theory enables us to identify causal relationships. A strong theory or model can help explain why regular as well as irregular relationships exist in our data. A good theory must be more than simply descriptive. It must move beyond answering the "what?" question. It must also address "why," "how," or "by what means" variables are related to each other. If we are to focus on the precise mechanisms by which one variable *causes* another variable to change, we must be very clear about what we mean by causality. To establish causality, four essential components must be present. First, we must have a reasonable theoretical story for why one variable is able to induce a response, or change in another variable. Second, the causal variable must precede the outcome variable in time. Third, the two variables must be empirically correlated with each other. Last, the empirical correlation between the two variables cannot be explained by a third variable that causes both of them.

Second, a strong theory enables us to use our understanding of current relationships and current data to forecast future relationships and developments. Theoretical models explain not only why we observe what we do in the policy world, but they also potentially have use in predicting what we might observe in the future. We model processes not only to understand current events, but also to learn as we proceed to push into new policy areas. The basic idea here is to learn from the past so as to not repeat mistakes. Policy knowledge based on anecdotes and individual stories are less likely to be able to make accurate predictions about what the future holds. Logically consistent theoretical models, on the other hand, while clearly vulnerable to external shocks, if well developed, ought to be able to accommodate new events.

Last, a strong theory can serve as the basis for political or policy action. We increasingly live in a data-driven world. Governments, corporations, small businesses, parents, and students all seek out the best information in order to make the most well-informed decisions possible. Public policy is no different – well, it's slightly different. It is certainly the case that scientific models can be used by elected leaders and bureaucrats to inform their policy choices. But, of course, elected leaders also have political goals. For some elected leaders, no amount of empirical evidence could change their minds about a public policy. Nevertheless, scientifically valid policy models based on well-implemented empirical research have great value in lobbying and advocating for normatively good public policy.

Elements of a Good Model

Policy models may be evaluated or compared on a series of dimensions. At a minimum, a good model will be multivariate, probabilistic, parsimonious, generalizable, falsifiable, clear, logically consistent, and ideologically neutral. Models that fail to include one or any of these characteristics are likely to be indicted by academics or policy practitioners as being in need of improvement.

Multivariate

Good models recognize that outputs have **multivariate**, or multiple causes. While casual observers of politics or politically dedicated ideologues believe that public policy outputs are driven primarily by their pet causes, social scientists recognize that all social phenomena have multiple causes. The challenge for building a strong model is sorting through the variety of potential causal factors to identify the most important or relevant ones from the least relevant.

Probabilistic

Closely linked to the first characteristic, good models recognize that we live in a **probabilistic world**. In other words, when we attempt to explain a policy output, we must recognize that there exists a set of factors (both systematic and unobserved and random) that are likely to impact our outputs of interest. What does this mean practically speaking? It suggests that when we make scientific claims about causal relationships, we should use probabilistic rather than deterministic language. So, an input variable, X, will "increase the likelihood" or "propensity of observing" an output variable Y, rather than X guarantees Y.

Parsimonious

Good models strive to be **parsimonious**; they seek to explain much with very few moving parts. In terms of the example above, a good model will produce a theoretical expectation of the important relevant variables to include in a causal model of a policy outcome, Y. And it will ignore irrelevant or less relevant causal factors. Scientific parsimony entails a trade-off. Parsimonious models, by definition, will be unable to account for every context-specific nuance of a policy area. A given model may be able to explain, with a high level of accuracy, the causal relationship between several variables and some policy outcome in forty-eight of the fifty states. But for reasons specific to Alaska and Hawaii, the model may fail to capture their state-specific dynamics. To some, this neglect of the finer details is a weakness of the scientific approach. But, the gains made on generalizability and theoretical understanding offset these trade-offs. In addition to parsimony, good theories are able to explain phenomena. In other words, they must be able to answer the "why" question. When we observe a phenomenon in a policy area, a good theory will be able to answer "and why do we see that?" Moreover, it will be able to do this for a wide range of questions. Weaker models are more time-, policy-, or scope-bound; they are highly constrained in the breadth and depth of questions that they are able to answer. Indeed, theoretical advances in the social and natural sciences are often characterized by a new theoretical model providing all of the answers that its predecessors could provide, in addition to a few more. So in evaluating models, scholars will often compare which model is better able to offer a simpler explanation for the most phenomena.

Generalizable

A good model is generalizable, or can produce hypotheses across a broad range of contexts. This quality contrasts with anecdotal models, or stories about how particular individuals, actors, or institutions are believed to be associated with specific policy outcomes. Advocates of anecdotal stories believe that public policy is best understood by digging into individual anecdotes. Such advocates resist attempts to generalize about the policy process, believing that there are few or no generalizable theories or hypotheses that apply to public policy. This is generally based upon the fact that it is always possible to identify one person or case to whom the general theory may not extend. We could all conjure up anecdotes about individuals that we have encountered throughout our lifetime whose experiences we believe tell us something about a particular public policy. And these fine details have great value in fleshing out the logic of a theory or the assumptions associated with a theory; however, they have little value in hypothesis testing. In a probabilistic, multivariate world in which measurement error exists, one or even a few cases are not sufficient to falsify a theory-driven hypothesis. Good theories accommodate contextual changes. But they cannot possibly accommodate all contexts lest they become so narrowly oriented as to explain very little.

Falsifiable

Despite what you may have learned in grade school, the scientific method is not geared toward proving any claims. Rather, scientific theory is used to produce hypotheses that can be put to the test using logic or observations from the real world. This notion, that a hypothesis or a claim can be potentially falsified, is a critical feature of scientific theory. Karl Popper (2002), a famous scientific theorist, argued for the validity of **falsifiability** as the foundation for the advancement of scientific knowledge. The basic logic is that if a scientist proposes a theory or hypothesis, any number of observations or arguments in support of this hypothesis, while generally confirming, would never be sufficient to suggest that our theory is valid. This is because it would always be possible that another set of observations, yet to be made, may be inconsistent with our hypothesis. As a result, additional confirmatory evidence does little more than increase the confidence in our hypothesis – by no means does it prove it. On the other hand, it is possible to reject a hypothesis or theory based upon a set of inconsistent observations. With inconsistent observations, we would have to declare that our hypothesis or theory must be incorrect. Hence, Popper suggests that scientific knowledge truly advances upon logical falsification rather than verification. Expressing support for the importance of falsification to scientific progress, Einstein noted that, "No amount of experimentation can ever prove me right; a single experiment can prove me wrong."

Imagine that a scientific theory generates a hypothesis, let's call it H_1, which claims a relationship between two variables. For this hypothesis to be falsifiable, it must at least be possible for us to either (1) gather data or (2) logically demonstrate that this hypothesis is not valid. So, if a social science model predicts that state speed limit laws having a maximum speed of 55mph have fewer annual motor vehicle deaths, it is possible for us to consider some subset of states that possess these laws, and another subset that do not, and compare their relative annual motor vehicle deaths.

Can you think of a non-falsifiable hypothesis? Non-falsifiable hypotheses tend to be either normative in their prediction or deal with unmeasurable or unobservable concepts. An example of the first, a normative hypothesis, would be something like, "Good people support the death penalty." The problem with this hypothesis is that it is difficult for us to objectively define what a "good" person is. As a result, this hypothesis is not falsifiable. An example of the second, a hypothesis with unmeasurable or unobservable concepts, would be something like, "Upon death, my soul will go to heaven." This may very well be true and certainly many individuals believe it to be true, but scientifically speaking, we do not have the technology to assess this outcome. We cannot measure the presence or absence of the soul, nor can we assess the status of the soul after death. As a result, this claim is non-falsifiable – it cannot be put to empirical testing.

More formally, when scientists test a hypothesis, they compare the prediction of a theory-generated hypothesis, H_1, to a null hypothesis, H_0. A **null hypothesis** is one that predicts no relationship between two variables. In this respect, all hypothesis testing is relative. Using our speed limit and motor vehicles example from above, the null hypothesis would be that there is no relationship between speed limit restrictions and annual motor vehicle deaths. So, when we look at the evidence, if we find that there is a statistical relationship between these two variables, then we would conclude that we have evidence to reject the null hypothesis. In other words, the null hypothesis cannot be true, given the data before us. Alternatively, if we found evidence of no difference between states with and without speed limit restrictions on annual motor vehicle deaths, we would have no evidence to reject the null hypothesis. In the absence of any evidence to reject the null, we must continue to accept it as valid.

Clear and Logically Consistent

By **clear**, we mean that a strong model will introduce a clear question and will be transparent with respect to its assumptions and presuppositions. It will be **logically consistent**, by defining its concepts and carefully relating each concept to another with a logical causal story of how these concepts are related. This feature has value for two reasons. First, imprecise causal logic will undoubtedly not lead to a stronger theoretical understanding of a causal process; it will obfuscate rather than clarify. Second, a clear and precise theory is useful not only for consumers of the theory to understand the process at work, but also to effectively critique and build upon theoretical modifications or additions. In the absence of clarity and precision, replication and extension become difficult, if not impossible.

Ideologically Neutral

To be taken seriously as a scientific theory, a good theory will be **ideologically neutral**. If a theory is laden with political assumptions, either liberal or conservative, scientists and objective consumers will be more likely to reject the theory out of hand. To have the widest appeal, therefore, good theory must be careful to not inject personal political opinion in the place of carefully constructed theoretical logic. For some, this is a challenging feature – they simply cannot see the policy world through objective lenses. Much like any skill, to theorize and write in an ideologically neutral way takes practice. The greatest challenge may be for analysts to recognize their own political biases. If you come from an ideologically homogenous culture, family, or background, you may have never had anyone question your fundamental political assumptions and biases. On this feature, policy students must be their own worst critic, often asking themselves: what do I believe and why do I believe it?

Elements of a Useful Model for Public Policy

In a series of different pieces, 2011 Nobel prize-winning political scientist Eleanor Ostrom developed a framework for analyzing questions related to public policy.

Termed the **Institutional Analysis and Development** framework (or IAD), Ostrom's approach attempts to understand how rational individuals' choices are shaped by the policy context and rules that characterize their decision-making environment. Ostrom's framework is sufficiently generalizable that it can be used or adapted to study policy choices in any number of venues. Moreover, it is a framework that scholars can use to develop specific theories for specific policy outcomes. As a result, it is a very attractive, flexible framework that can be used to generate any number of models and hypotheses about a policy area of interest. Below, we review the critical components of the IAD framework in a student-friendly version.

To be able to understand and explain policy outcomes, Ostrom centers on what she calls an action arena. An **action arena** entails that the "social individuals interact, exchange goods and services, solve problems, dominate one another, or fight (among the many things that individuals do in action arenas)" (p. 42). For policy scholars, the action arena is a domain within which the policy decisions of interest are made. The action arena consists of any number of variables that give structure to and influence the policy process. These may include "the set of participants, the specific positions to be filled, the set of allowable actions, the potential outcomes that are linked to these actions, the level of control each participant has over choice, the informational information available to the participants, and the costs and benefits assigned actions and outcomes" (Sabatier *et al.*: 43). Simply put, an action arena includes relevant actors, the rules that structure the actors' available actions and incentives, and how these features interact with each other.

Actors

Actors refers to the individuals who are central to understanding the potential policy outcomes of interest. These actors may include formal – those with established institutional roles in the policy process – and informal actors. They may include a class or group of actors (for example, farmers) or individuals. The critical point is for the analyst to include any actor who is attempting to influence the outcome at hand. This suggests, of course, that one of the first steps an analyst must take to begin analyzing a policy is to understand who the potential important actors may be. Next, the analyst must make a series of assumptions about what it is that an actor values or desires, the level and type of information that the actor possesses, the actor's belief structure, and whether or not the actor has any constraints on their information-processing capabilities.

Rules

Rules refer to formal or informal agreements between actors regarding what actions are "required, prohibited, or permitted." Rules within these arenas can be of both the formal and informal types. Formal rules are those that generally occur in written documents and are accompanied with the threat of formal organized sanction for their violation.

Informal rules are those that need not occur in written form, but perhaps are passed on verbally or orally by tradition and are accompanied with the threat of sanction for violation by social punishment or ostracizing. These rules can also be characterized as institutions in that they structure the allowable interactions between actors.

Actors Interacting with Rules

Much of political science is concerned with the origin of such rules. Policy analysis, on the other hand, is often concerned with how such rules structure interactions with actors within the action arena to influence policy outcomes. Rules can have profound effects on a policy action arena. They can structure the number of actors involved, who gets to participate, in what order, and with what power. They can, for example, determine burdens of evidence, or informational requirements needed to move, alter, or pass a regulatory initiative.

Throughout this text, we will employ a rationalist institutional framework to understand public policy. While applying a rational-institutional analysis in the style of the IAD, we will not refer explicitly to IAD or its particular lexicon. However, we will regularly refer to important actors, rules, and institutions and the way in which these interact to change incentives and shape policy outputs and outcomes.

1.5 Conclusion

Whether due to concerns over accountability, efficiency, or equitable delivery, we have incentive to study and better understand how public policies develop and perform. Every citizen possesses beliefs about public policy. More often than not, these beliefs are unstructured, based more upon personal biases and political philosophies than upon careful causal argumentation and empirical evidence. This chapter has discussed the mechanisms that public policy scholars have employed to answer these critical concerns.

To introduce students to the varied questions in public policy, we've built upon Lasswell's "stages of the policy process" heuristic. While policy does not proceed in the unidirectional deterministic fashion that the stages heuristic implies, it nevertheless identifies the major themes of political interest and research effort in public policy. Each of these stages characterizes not only a salient area of public policy, but also a substantive subset of academic research dedicated to better understanding how policy develops.

Within each of these research areas, scholars endeavor to identify valid causal processes to explain how or why a given process occurs. A set of inter-connected causal processes is referred to as a model of some aspect of the policy. Good models will be multivariate, probabilistic, parsimonious, generalizable, falsifiable, clear, logically consistent, and ideologically neutral. When a model meets all of these conditions, it will be most capable of producing scientifically valid predictions and hypotheses about the public policy process.

Key Terms in This Chapter

Study of public policy
Public policy
Accountability
Efficiency
Federalism
Problem definition
Solution definition
Stakeholders
Collective action dilemma
Policy entrepreneur
Dominant policy image
Policy window
Policy demands
Credible action
Agenda setting
Advocacy coalition
Technical complexity
Policy salience
Cost-benefit analysis
Policy evaluation
Program evaluation
Policy neutral
Model of public policy
Causal relationship
Necessary condition
Sufficient condition
Conditional causality
Deterministic relationship
Probabilistic relationship
Generalizable
Multivariate
Probabilistic world
Parsimonious

Falsifiability
Null hypothesis
Clear
Logically consistent
Ideologically neutral
Institutional Analysis and Development framework
Action arena
Actors
Rules

CHAPTER EXERCISES

1. Can you think of examples of equitable policy delivery? How about examples of less than equitable policy delivery? What explains that?

2. The tragedy in Newtown Connecticut provided a policy window in the United States on gun control. What was the result of that policy window opening? Explain.

3. Try to identify examples of agenda setting across different media outlets (for example, newspapers, TV, talk radio). What was the policy issue being discussed in the media? Did you find examples of how the same topic may be addressed from a different view point?

4. Why does bureaucratic "red tape" exist? What facts could you present to someone who was complaining about bureaucratic "red tape?"

5. The "And why is that?" question is a tool to uncover a detailed analysis of a public policy area. Consider the following statements and use at least three iterations of the "And why is that" question:

   (a) The inner city is dangerous and filled with drug dealers.

   (b) Beverly Hills High School has excellent standardized test scores.

6. Characterize the difference between Deterministic and Probabilistic relationships.

7. Rank order the elements of a good model. If you could only secure three of these elements, which would you retain? Explain.

REFERENCES

Baumgartner, Frank and Jones, Brian. 1993. *Agendas and Instability in American Politics*. University of Chicago Press.

Carpenter, Daniel, P. 1996. "Adaptive Signal Processing, Hierarchy, and Budgetary Control in Federal Regulation." *American Political Science Review* 90(02):283–302.

Coppedge, Michael. 2012. *Democratization and Research Methods*. Cambridge University Press.

Erikson, Robert, Wright, Gerald C., Jr. and McIver, John P. 1993. *Statehouse Democracy: Public Opinion and Policy in The American States*. New York: Cambridge University Press.

Garrett, Kristin and Jansa, Joshua N. 2015. "Interest Group Influence in Policy Diffusion Networks." *State Politics and Policy Quarterly*, in press.

Gormley, William. 1986. "Regulatory Issue Networks in a Federal System." *Polity* 18(4):595–620.

Hall, Richard L. and Deardorff, Alan V. 2006. "Lobbying as Legislative Subsidy." *American Political Science Review* 100(1):69–84.

Huber, John D. and Shipan, Charles. 2002. *Deliberate Discretion?: The Institutional Foundations of Bureaucratic Autonomy*. Cambridge University Press.

Kingdon, John W. 1989. *Congressman's Voting Decisions*, 3rd edn. Ann Arbor, MI: University of Michigan Press.

  1996. *Agendas, Alternatives and Public Policy*, 2nd edn. Boston, MA: Little, Brown & Co.

James, Robert Rhodes (ed.). 1974. *Winston S. Churchill: His Complete Speeches, 1897–1963*. New York: Public Affairs Press.

Lowi, Theodore. 1979. *The End of Liberalism*. New York: Norton.

Lasswell, Harold D. 1951. "The Policy Orientation," in Daniel Lerner and Harold D. Lasswell (eds.), *The Policy Sciences*. Stanford University Press.

McCubbins, Mathew D., Noll, Roger G., and Weingast, Barry R. 1987. "Administrative Procedures as Instruments of Political Control." *Journal of Law, Economics, and Organization* 3:243–77.

  1989. "Structure and Process, Politics and Policy: Administrative Arrangements and the Political Control of Agencies." *Virginia Law Review* 75:431–82.

Mettler, Suzanne and Soss, Joe. 2004. "The Consequences of Public Policy for Democratic Citizenship." *Perspectives on Politics* 2(1): 55–73.

Mettler, Suzanne. 2011. *The Submerged State: How Invisible Government Policies Undermine American Democracy*. University of Chicago Press.

Ostrom, Elinor. 1990. *Governing the Commons: The Evolution of Institutions for Collective Action*. New York: Cambridge University Press.

Page, Benjamin I. and Shapiro, Robert Y. 1983. "Effects of Public Opinion on Policy." *American Political Science Review* 77(1):195–190.

Popper, Karl. [1934]. 2002. *The Logic of Scientific Discovery*, 2nd edn. New York: Routledge.

Sabatier, Paul. 1988. "An Advocacy Coalition Framework of Policy Change and the Role of Policy-Oriented Learning Therein." *Policy Sciences* 21:129–68.

Sabatier, Paul and Jenkins-Smith, Hank. 1988. *Policy Change and Learning: An Advocacy Coalition Approach*. Boulder, CO: Westview Press.

Sirin, Selcuk R. 2005. "Socioeconomic Status and Academic Achievement: A Meta-Analytic Review of Research." *Review of Educational Research* 75(3):417–53.

Taber, Charles S. 2003. "Information Processing and Public Opinion," in David O. Sears, Leonie Huddy, and Robert Jervis (eds.), *The Handbook of Political Psychology*. New York: Oxford University Press, pp. 433–76.

Thompson, James R. 2000. "Reinvention as Reform: Assessing the National Performance Review." *Public Administration Review* 50(6):508–21.

US Environmental Protection Agency (EPA). 2015. "Assessment of the Potential Impacts of Hydraulic Fracturing for Oil and Gas on Drinking Water Resources (External Review Draft)." EPA/600/R-15/047.

Yackee, Jason W. and Yackee, Susan. 2006. "A Bias Toward Business? Assessing Interest Group Influence on the U.S. Bureaucracy." *Journal of Politics* 68(1):128–39.

2   Individuals and Social Dilemmas

Outline

Questions

- Why do economic and political systems of all stripes regularly come up short with their attempts to find effective solutions to social problems?
- Under what conditions does the individual pursuit of self-interest fail to generate socially optimal outcomes?

Overview

- Individual pursuit of self-interest is a powerful motivator that generally is sufficient to improve one's position.
- Under certain conditions, pursuit of self-interest is not sufficient to improve one's position.
- Cooperation and coordination dilemmas are unique conditions that undermine individual abilities to secure improvements. In fact, under certain circumstances, individuals pursuing their own self-interest can lead to deteriorations in all individuals' positions.
- Analytic models assist us in understanding solutions to cooperation and coordination dilemmas.

Introduction: Origins of Social Problems

Society faces numerous problems on the public policy landscape. Whether under-education, environmental hazards, malnutrition, economic malaise, or rising health care costs, the policy palette is infused with a rich spectrum of challenges. Most individuals would agree that many of these areas would benefit from a healthy dose of improvement. But that is likely where citizen consensus ends. Opinion polling suggests that there is often plurality consensus on what citizens believe to be the most important policy problems facing their country. However, there is less consensus on what citizens believe to be the proper solutions to these problems and who precisely ought to address them. One thing appears certain: elected leaders are willing to respond to citizen concerns. Political parties offer a variety of what they believe to be the most appropriate solutions to society's problems. But why look to government or political parties for answers to society's problems? Couldn't individuals, seeking a mutually agreeable goal, simply agree to work on a solution together?

In some cases, individuals each pursuing their own interest can be beneficial for others in a community (or at a minimum their pursuit may not harm anyone). For example, if a homeowner in a neighborhood puts sweat equity into his or her house in the form of new paint, better landscaping, and greater attention to detail to overall upkeep, that person's individual actions will likely benefit other landowners in the neighborhood. But, given this potential positive benefit to all members of the community, should the community *require by coercion* each homeowner to dedicate some minimum effort and resources to the upkeep of their home, or should such decisions be left to the personal domain of each homeowner? Alternatively, what if the interests of the individual are not necessarily aligned with those of the community? Consider a private landowner who desires to develop a portion of his or her land to construct a new high-density housing development. While this project may generate new employment opportunities for the community, it may also contribute to suburban sprawl, increased congestion on the local roads, heavier enrollment pressures for the local school, and increased pollution in the form of storm water run-off. How should the community evaluate this trade-off? Should the community have a say in how the landowner puts his land to use?

While definitive answers to social problems are beyond the scope of this (or perhaps any) text, in this chapter, we highlight the outlines or boundaries within which answers to these questions are generally sought. Here we consider the limits on individual self-interest and its ability to uniformly deliver socially optimal outcomes. We introduce students to the micro-foundations of the rational actor approach to behavior, game theory, and a few core analytic models that offer profound insights into public policy.

2.1 Game Theory as a Tool

Game theory is a mathematical analytic tool to study **strategic** decision-making. It is a tool to understand the choices an actor makes when his or her preferences depend upon the choices of other actors. Game theory was developed as a field by John Von Neumann and Oskar Morgenstern (1944). Over the past decades, it has grown into a powerful analytic tool to understand how humans interact with each other. Game theory consists of a collection of models that are abstractions used to understand our observations and experiences (Osborne 2004: 1). We apply game theory to help us understand why we might be observing certain outcomes or behaviors in the policy world.

Game theory is distinct from **Decision theory**, the study of how actors make choices, *absent interactions with other actors*. Consider the following example. Upon waking, you look out the window and see that it is a cloudy day. You must decide whether to bring an umbrella to work. You will likely assess the probability of rain by gathering information about the day's weather forecast and then make your choice. This is a decision theoretic situation. The probability of rain is said to be **exogenous**, or externally determined, to the actor. Now consider the same scenario, but in this case, after you make your choice, your neighbor, who controls a weather machine, gets to choose whether to make it rain or not. This is now a game theoretic situation because the introduction of another competing player introduces **endogenous** probabilities of rain, which are determined by the interaction of the two players (Tsebelis 1989). In public policy, nearly all choice is interactive. There is nearly always some other actor or set of actors whose choice depends on the choice of some other actor or set of actors. Given this, actors must choose what to do based upon their expectations or their beliefs about what will improve their lot, conditioned on what other players are likely to do. Game theory models help us understand how players respond to various situations.

As you will see in this chapter, and throughout the other chapters of the book, game theory models are based upon a set of clear assumptions of human behavior. These assumptions are the building blocks upon which a model can be constructed to explain some experience in the world. As we noted in the previous chapter, assumptions and models are simplifications of reality. The value of a given model is generally weighed by its ability to explain some phenomenon with a simple set of assumptions and propositions. Often, these assumptions are relatively non-controversial. However, you may encounter some assumptions about human behavior in game theory that you may find questionable – good.[1] You *should* question the assumptions of any model, not just

---

[1] Criticisms of rational choice models target several dimensions of the approach (see Green and Shapiro 1994). Some highlight the potential of the mathematical applications of game theory to erect cost-prohibitive barriers to potential critics that lack the mathematical background. Early critics focused on the theoretical exclusivity of game theory, indicting models as being divorced from empirical testing – this criticism has waned in light of the

those of game theory. But, keep in mind, even a questionable assumption may not be sufficient to throw out all of the insights from a model. We must always ask ourselves, "While this model's assumption(s) may not be perfect, is there an alternative model that is simpler and more accurate that can generate equal or stronger explanations?" Indeed, in the Economic Policy chapter we review a set of game theory models, the Dictator game, and the Ultimatum game, for which experimental subjects do not respond in the way that standard models would suggest.

2.2 Individual Action

Individuals are the building blocks of game theory and understanding any social problem – both the problem's origins and its potential solutions. This chapter will consider how individual choices help to generate socially undesirable outcomes and will highlight the limits on individuals' ability to resolve these problems. Prior to doing so, however, we must establish some ground rules on how we are going to think about individual choice. We are going to adopt a perspective called rational choice to understand individual decision-making. This perspective assumes that individual choice is purposeful. We introduce the essential elements of this framework in the following sections.

Box 2.1

Utility is a measure of the relative satisfaction that a person receives from possessing or consuming a good or service. A **utility function** produces a numeric value to each good in a given set of consumption sets, allowing them to be ranked. If two items hold the same value in this function, the individual is said to be **indifferent** between the two items.

Personal Utility Maximization

To understand how society, governments, markets, or other social institutions choose policies, we have two tasks. We must first understand the outlines of individual choice. Second, we must demonstrate that individual choice and individual preferences have implications for group decisions (as it turns out a non-trivial matter). We begin by first offering a model of individual choice based upon the assumption that citizens or actors in society are *rational* in their decision-making. But there are a few foundations upon

more recent trend to encourage empirical tests of game theoretic insights (e.g. The Empirical Implications of Theoretical Models (EITM) movement). Last, the rationality assumption itself has been questioned on its applicability and generalizability (see Lupia *et al.* 2000).

which rationality is based. First, all individuals must be allowed some choice over alternative courses of action. To talk about a person making a rational choice, an individual must actually face a choice among different alternatives. Second, the individual must recognize that associated with each choice are basic costs and benefits that are the consequences of selecting any course of action. When an individual pursues a given action, there is a consequence. An action will improve their situation, worsen it, or have no impact. Third, given an array of choices an individual must be able to express a preference over the consequences attached to each action. Last, the individual must be able to rank these preferences and then, when given the opportunity, must choose actions that are more preferred. If all of these foundations hold, then we can refer to individuals as being rational or as engaging in rational choice. What does this look like in practice?

Imagine an individual possesses preferences on a variety of elements within a set of goods or services. It would be useful for us to know how much value an individual assigns to each individual element within any of those sets. If we had such information we could derive a host of predictions about how an individual might behave if given the opportunity to choose from a set of actions. A utility function is a mathematical relation that assigns a number to each element in a set of options in terms of individual ordered preferences. The particular number assigned to each element can be thought of as reflecting the relative subjective value that an individual attaches to each action or outcome. We can assign numbers to these outcomes. The standard approach is to allow elements to be assigned "unit-less" values, reflecting the overall relative utility or enjoyment that each action provides to the individual. You will often see the utility of a specific action, A, expressed as the following: U(A) or u(A). Either of these expressions is read aloud as "the utility of A is . . .".

For example, imagine a set of three options regarding some government program, X: decrease spending, do not change spending, or increase spending. Citizen A's choice set is {decrease spending, no change, increase spending}. Citizen A's utility function over these choices maps her preferences into utility units. So, citizen A's utility function could be: u(decreased spending) = 3, u(no change) = 2, u(increased spending) = 1. This suggests that, for citizen A, decreased spending is most preferred relative to no change or increased spending. However, the citizen does prefer no change relative to increased spending. It is important to recognize that the actual values assigned to these outcomes convey meaning of relative rank among outcomes, but do not reveal any information on strength of preference between outcomes. **Ordinal preferences** are preference orderings that assign values to outcomes that convey only relative order; the values assigned tell us nothing about the absolute magnitude of the preferences over outcomes. In the example above, given ordinal preferences, we can only say that citizen A prefers decreased spending more than increased spending. Since the numbers mapped onto these different outcomes have no intrinsic value we cannot, for example, say that citizen A prefers decreased spending three times as much as increased spending. Ordinal preferences differ from **cardinal preferences**, which do reveal the magnitude of relative preferences.

Between any two items in a set, ranked preferences can either be strictly preferred, weakly preferred, or indifferent. A **strict preference** suggests that an individual prefers option A to B, which we can write as A≻B, or aPb. A **weak preference** suggests that an individual prefers A at least as good as B, which we can write as A ⪰ B. An **indifferent preference** suggests that an individual prefers A equally to B, or A=B, or aIb. The utility function makes use of this information and assigns a number to each element of the set, reflecting also the relative position of each element in the set.

What are the implications of such utility functions? We need to introduce two additional features prior to introducing a rational choice among outcomes. First, an individual's preferences over their options must be complete (or **comparable preferences**). This means that for any two outcomes, the individual either prefers A to B (aPb), prefers B to A (bPa), or is indifferent between the two (aIb). This simply requires the individual to be able to express a preference (or lack thereof) between any two options. Second, an individual must have **transitive preferences**. Preferences are transitive if the individual holds strict preferences over a set of alternatives, say A, B, and C, such that if ApB and BpC, then ApC. In practical terms, if these two conditions are present, then given the choice between a set of ranked options or elements, rational individuals would choose those items that are ranked higher by their utility function compared to those that are ranked lower. This process is personal utility maximization, or the process by which a rational individual seeks to obtain the greatest amount of utility, or personal satisfaction, by choosing their most preferred and available option.

With this tool, it is possible to conceive of citizens as being involved in a series of personal utility decisions whether in politics or everyday life. Whether referring to preferences over different health care reform packages or the choice between different tax reforms, we can imagine individuals as having a personal utility function over a series of different sets of information. And we can refer to individuals' selection or pursuit of various activities, goods, or services as attempts to increase their utility. For the individual, then, we would refer to the outcome of such a selection process, where an individual made the best choice, given certain constraints and stable preferences, as being **rational**.

Let's be clear. We cannot confuse one individual's rational choice for one that is socially acceptable to others. Rational choices are not necessarily normatively good choices. A racist individual that values the separation or elimination of other races above other actions may rationally choose to support a pro-slavery candidate for Congress in the 1850s (or today). Similarly, a terrorist that values the destruction of the United States' center of financial power may rationally choose to hijack an airplane and fly it into the World Trade Center. Yet, no reasonable person would argue that such choices, albeit rational by our definition, were anything other than disgusting acts. In fact, some have often referred to racists or terrorists as being "crazy," suggesting that to engage in an overtly racist or terrorist act an individual would have to be a raving lunatic – detached from reality. This of course is not required by the definition of rationality used here. "Rational action" refers to nothing more than individuals maximizing their own utility by selecting their most preferred option.

Box 2.2 Rational Choice and Altruism

A frequent criticism of rational choice theory is that it cannot account for altruism, or "the willingness to act in consideration of others without the need of ulterior motives" (Nagel 1970: 79). Recent work in behavioral economic theory suggests at least one interpretation of altruistic behavior within a rational choice framework (Camerer 2003). When individuals are observed donating or being charitable to another, without concern of whether that donation will benefit them in turn, some scholars believe that this behavior is driven by "warm glow" theory (Andreoni 1990) or positive utility that occurs from the positive feelings of helping others. Of course, by the strictest definitional standards, this utility may appear to violate the definition of altruism, which requires no ulterior motives on behalf of the donor. This dilemma motivates recent research on altruism and has even led cognitive scientists to investigate how the brain responds to charitable giving.

While interesting to examine how individuals attempt to maximize their utility, the study of politics is concerned with collective choices, or the aggregation of individual choices. But what mechanisms should society use to determine collective preferences over social issues and problems? This is no small question. Indeed, this question most often revolves around a fundamental political issue of the proper role of markets and government (a question we take up in the next chapter).

Challenges in Resolving Social Problems

Individuals in society do not exist on an island unto themselves. Rather, most individuals are integral parts within a social fabric, inextricably linked to other individuals. Whether within families, neighborhoods, communities, or some other social entity, we do observe individuals exhibiting social cooperation, or behavior that benefits others. This may lead some to wonder, why can individuals not simply come together to solve our social dilemmas collectively? Are individuals uninterested in solving these dilemmas? Or are they simply not equipped to do so? This creates two interesting puzzles to answer. First, in the case of social problems, are the individuals who are seemingly unable or unwilling to cooperate with each other to resolve these social ills simply stupid or somehow unequipped intellectually to resolve these problems? On more than one occasion you have probably heard a friend or family member opine that "if only politicians weren't so corrupt/stupid/self-interested they could solve our society's problems." But is this really what is at the core of some of our most nagging social ills? Are the most inept among us truly the most motivated to run for office? Perhaps. But there may be a more interesting explanation. Second, when collective effort is observed to work, under what conditions does it thrive? How is it that individuals come together to produce some social good? Is this only possible in the presence of deeply held familial bonds? Do individuals require a third party to essentially force them to do what is otherwise not in their immediate interest?

2.3 Cooperation and Collective Action

We will see that both of the puzzles outlined above are best understood as cooperative and collective action dilemmas. As we note above, we base our understanding of the success or failure of social cooperation (and collective action) dilemmas on the assumption that individuals are interested in pursuing their own self-interest. However, under certain specific conditions, the pursuit of self-interest can indeed generate positive outcome for other individuals as well and can contribute to the solution of social problems. Under other conditions, rational individuals pursuing their self-interest can generate suboptimal outcomes; indeed, they can generate outcomes in which all individuals are *worse off*. How could this be?

Cooperation Dilemmas

To understand why individuals may find it difficult to choose to act collectively to generate a social benefit, let's consider a familiar problem: exploiting a renewable resource. This renewable resource could be fish or oyster stock, potable water, or forest goods. Each of these goods is renewable, meaning that below some critical level of consumption, the good will regenerate. Beyond a critical level of consumption, however, the good will be exhausted. Let's use a game theoretic approach to consider this problem.

Below we will introduce the normal form, or strategic form, game table. This table displays two players each with two choices and the outcomes that occur upon each player making his or her choice. Notice that in the table each player makes a move simultaneously with the other player. Sequence is not allowed in this form of a game. Figure 2.1 displays the empty table for the resource exploitation game (i.e. this is also

	B Defect	Cooperate
Defect	D, D	D, C
Cooperate	C, D	C, C

(Left side label: **A**)

Figure 2.1 Possible Outcomes in a Simple
Resource Allocation Game

the common Prisoner Dilemma game). Each player has the choice whether to cooperate with the maximum withdrawal limits that the community has agreed upon or to defect against these withdrawal limits. Depending upon what action each player takes, we see four possible outcomes of the game: (Defect, Defect), (Defect, Cooperate), (Cooperate, Defect), and (Cooperate, Cooperate). To set up the game we must assign a preference ordering for each player over these four outcomes. Let's consider these from each player's perspective. Essentially, any player would benefit most from withdrawing above the maximum limit while the other player refrained (Defect, Cooperate). The next second preferred outcome is one where both players abide by the limits (Cooperate, Cooperate). Each player's worst preferred outcome is the exact opposite of their most preferred, or where one agrees to refrain and the other defects (Cooperate, Defect). This leaves the situation where each player's defect choice is the second-to-least preferred outcome. We can represent these preference orderings accordingly. Player A's preference ordering is: (Defect, Cooperate) > (Cooperate, Cooperate) > (Defect, Defect) > (Cooperate, Defect). And let's further assume that Player B's preference ordering is: (Defect, Cooperate) > (Defect, Defect) > (Cooperate, Cooperate) > (Cooperate, Defect).

Now we need to assign pay-offs to each of these preferred outcomes. Given that these preference orderings are strict preferences, each can be represented as $A \succ B$, which mean that outcome A is strictly preferred to outcome B and does not allow for indifference between any two options. To make this easy, we will assign ordinal pay-offs to these orderings to convey relative rank only. We have four outcomes, so let's use pay-offs 1 through 4, with 4 representing the most preferred outcome. We will assign each pay-off to the relevant outcome for the relevant player. In the normal form game, by convention the pay-offs in each cell will be ordered (Player A, Player B). When we fill in these pay-offs we get the normal form game in Figure 2.2.

We can now use the information displayed in the normal form game to determine how each player would act if given the opportunity. Our goal is to identify the **strategy profile**, or complete set of **best responses**, for each player given the action of all other players. To solve this game, we must apply a specific solution concept that conveys the

B

	Defect	Cooperate
Defect	2, 2	4, 1
Cooperate	1, 4	3, 3

A

Figure 2.2 Choice Values in a Resource Allocation Game

B

	Defect	Cooperate
Defect	2, 2	4, 1
Cooperate	1, 4	3, 3

A

Figure 2.3 Player Responses in a Resource Allocation Game

conditions under which a player will have a best response. The solution concept that we will employ is the Nash Equilibrium (Nash 1951). A **Nash Equilibrium** is a set of strategies such that no player can unilaterally improve their position given the other player's action. Essentially, the Nash Equilibrium reveals both players' best response given the other's action. So let's use this solution concept to solve the game.

To solve the game, we begin by picking one of the players, A or B, and examining how they would respond to the other's actions. As we consider each Player's best response to the other's action, we will set these strategies aside as candidates for a Nash Equilibrium – we will denote each of these in Figure 2.3 with an underline. An outcome for which both players have best responses will be a Nash Equilibrium.

So let's begin with Player A. From Player A's perspective, if Player B chooses "Defect," then Player A can either receive a 2 if Defect, or a 1 if Cooperate – so Player A will prefer Defect. If, however, Player B chooses "Cooperate," then Player A can either receive a 4 if Defect, or a 3 if Cooperate – so Player A will prefer Defect. Essentially no matter what Player B chooses, Player A always has an incentive to "Defect." When a player has a single strategic response regardless of what another player does, this is referred to as a dominant strategy. Now let's pick the other Player. From Player B's perspective, if Player A chooses "Defect," then Player B can either receive a 2 if Defect, or a 1 if Cooperate – so Player B will prefer Defect. If, however, Player A chooses "Cooperate," then Player B can either receive a 4 if Defect, or a 3 if

Cooperate – so Player B will prefer Defect. Player B has a dominant strategy to "Defect." Each of these best responses is underlined in Figure 2.3.

Notice that, while there are several best response strategies for any one player underlined in Figure 2.3, only in one of the outcomes do *both players* have best responses – (Defect, Defect). Given that both players have best responses to each other's actions for the outcome (Defect, Defect), this outcome is a Nash Equilibrium. What does this mean? This means that if we allowed the players to actually carry out this game, we would expect them to both play the "Defect" strategy against each other and in this situation each player would ignore the established limits on the exhaustible good and would seek to cheat against the other.

An important implication of this game is that despite each player pursuing their own rational self-interest, each is worse off compared to if they both agreed to cooperate with the maximum limits. This result underscores the difficulty of how individual actions might lead to suboptimal outcomes for society. We can also think of this as a **commitment problem** where one or both parties cannot credibly commit to a strategy despite its high utility. (We will return to commitment problems in Chapter 10 on Civil Rights.) Notice we did not have to introduce any elements of either player being irrational, stupid, or ignorant of any aspect of the game to generate a relatively worse outcome. Rather, given the unique set of actors and preferences involved we were able to show how two players each trying to better their own position could both wind up worse off than if they had cooperated with each other. Scholars in a wide range of disciplines have been concerned about the outcome of this Prisoner's Dilemma (PD) game for decades. Taken at its worst, the results of the standard PD game suggest a rather bleak prospect for cooperation among people. Yet, if society is likely to produce suboptimal outcomes when citizens pursue their own self-interest, then why do we observe relatively large amounts of cooperation among citizens all around the world?

Overcoming Barriers to Cooperative Behavior

The general solution to the cooperation dilemma essentially requires a revision to the basic PD game by altering the pay-offs to the players. In other words, if we want people to behave differently, we have to incentivize them differently. We have to alter the pay-offs of the game such that the individual no longer has an incentive to pursue the immediate benefit of defecting against the other player. Social science has revealed three basic ways in which individuals' incentives can be structured to avoid the suboptimal outcome that we observed above.

Repeated Interaction
One of the less realistic assumptions of the classic PD game that we solved above is that it assumes that each player only has one shot to "get it right." In other words, the game

does not allow for any additional interactions between the players. What is the direct consequence of this? For all practical purposes, this restriction does not allow individuals to *learn* about what to expect from others if they are provided opportunities to interact on a continual basis. Indeed, for some sets of citizens repeated interaction more closely reflects their experiences. Family members interact frequently, citizens within community organizations interact with each other frequently, and members of small towns know essentially everyone in town and have regular interaction with each other. This suggests that perhaps the set-up of a one-time interaction between two players is a bit too artificial – at least under certain conditions. But how might allowing for repeated interaction alter the possibility of sustaining cooperation between the players?

To understand whether repeated interaction can induce sustained cooperation we must first consider an important implication of playing a game long into the future with another player – that is, how much does the player value the future? Imagine that not all individuals value the future similarly. Consider a person who has received a negative prognosis about their health; they have been given a year to live. That person is likely going to place greater value on the near term and very little value on the future – given that they are not likely to be around to enjoy any benefits earned in the future. This idea reflects the basic notion of discounting. Individuals discount the future at varying rates. To add some precision to this discussion, we can make use of a **discount factor**, or the degree which people discount future benefits relative to current ones. This discount factor ranges from 0 to 1. If you are someone who does not value the future at all, your discount factor would be 0 – in other words, the future is worth nothing to you. If, on the other hand, you value some benefit received years from now precisely as you value the same benefit delivered to you today, then your discount factor would be a 1 – you value the future benefit precisely as you value the present benefit. Another way to think about discounting is that a person's discount factor essentially tells us how patient a person is in waiting for some benefit. A high discount factor suggests that that person is quite patient, while a low discount factor suggests that the person prefers to be compensated in the near term. Once we know a person's discount factor, we can calculate precisely how much they will value today any long-run stream of benefits that they may accrue in a repeated interaction with another player.

Box 2.3 Axelrod's Computer Experiment

In the early 1980s, Robert Axelrod invited people to solicit strategies for a computer-simulated tournament of Prisoner's Dilemmas. A strategy describes a complete set of actions for a player in response to any other actions from their partner. The tournament pitted players against others in repeat-play, implementing whatever strategies the players sent in, with no communication between

Box 2.3 (*cont.*)

players. Players submitted a variety of strategies, including some that contained hundreds of lines of code. The winner, however, was one of the simplest strategies submitted: Tit-for-Tat (TFT). TFT strategy calls for the players to cooperate on the first round and then mimic the other player's move on the last round played. Axelrod suggested that the reasons for TFT's success was that it was sufficiently nice (cooperating on the first round), retaliatory (is willing to punish others who defect), forgiving (did not punish defectors who return to cooperation for more than one round), and clear (the strategy was clear enough for another player to decode).

Let's consider an example. You are all college students, investing in your education so that you can one day earn a good living and not have to live on Ramen noodles and Natty Light. This suggests that with respect to a monthly additional stipend of $100, a college student likely has a fairly low discount factor. Why? Because while you are a student, that $100 a month would make quite a difference in your day-to-day life. Ten years from now, however, when you are earning $4,000 a month, an extra $100 will have less relative value for you. So, as time passes, each additional $100 monthly payment contributes less and less value to you today – because you need it most today! We call this estimate of how much your future stream of benefits is worth to you today the **present value**. How can we figure this out mathematically?

Let's look at your income over time. In the first month, you receive $100. Since this $100 is realized in the present day, there is no discount factor – you value it at $100. In the second month, you are to receive $100, but to find out how much you value this future payment in the present you must discount it by your discount factor, d. To do this we simply multiply them together 100*d. In the third month, you are to receive $100, but you must discount it by, d, essentially twice since you already discounted it once, or $100*d*d. We repeat this process for as many time periods, t, that we would like to consider. To consider an infinitely repeated interaction, mathematically, we have the following series:

$$PresentValue\ (FutureMonthlyPayments) = 100 + 100d + 100d^2 + 100d^3 \ldots 100d^\infty$$

Luckily, this series corresponds to the geometric series: $a + ad + ad^2 + ad^3 \ldots ad^{t-1}$, which converges to $a/(1-d)$. So, for our example, the present value of $100/month payments long into the future would be $100/(1-d)$. So if you were a very patient person and highly valued the future, your discount rate would be $d \approx 1$ and the present value of these life-long monthly payments would be $100/(1-.9999999)$ or nearly infinitely valuable to you. On the other hand, if you were very impatient and valued those future payments very little, your discount rate, d, would be 0, and the present value of these life-long monthly payments would be 100/(1-0) or worth $100 to you in the present.

How does this help us understand whether cooperation can be sustained if we allow repeated interactions? In repeated interactions, each player must decide what strategy they would like to play. For example, there are a variety of strategies a player could adopt. A player could play Always Cooperate or Always Defect, where the player never changes their play regardless of what the other player does. Alternatively, players can adopt a grim trigger strategy. With a grim trigger strategy, Player A decides to begin by cooperating with Player B. However, if Player B ever defects, then Player A will defect for the rest of the interaction. Another popular strategy is tit-for-tat, where a player begins by cooperating and then echoes the other player's last move. If the other player defected in the previous round, then you defect in this round. If they cooperated in the previous round, then you cooperate in this round. If we are given the combinations of these strategies for our two players and their discount factors, we can use the information derived from the calculation of present value above to determine whether a combination of strategies is a Nash Equilibrium. For a player to cooperate, the present value of cooperation must be greater than the present value of "stealing." When this condition is met for both players, we would have a mutual best response and therefore a Nash Equilibrium.

Cooperation between both players can be sustained in the long run with certain strategies if each player's discount factor is sufficiently high. The precise value of the sufficient discount factor varies by strategy. But essentially the message is the same. Individuals pursuing their own self-interest are not necessarily doomed to the sub-optimal world of everyone defecting. Cooperation in repeated interactions can be sustained with certain strategies as long as each player sufficiently values the future. Also important to note is that this equilibrium is self-enforcing, meaning that each player can improve their situation without the necessity of a third party to enforce the bargain. Rather, the equilibrium is enforced by the very incentives that are internal to the game – no third party is required to make the players behave.

This finding sheds light on any number of policy dilemmas that citizens face. Crime may be in part explained as the result of citizens discounting the future. Citizens whose life circumstances provide little hope over the longer term are more likely to discount the future and judge short-term defection, in the form of theft or crime, to be attractive. The dilemma of relatively low citizen concern about climate changes may be in part a function of discounting the future. When climate driven events are predicted to impact us hundreds of years from now, it might be challenging to incentivize those who discount the future to care today. Poor health choices as well may be linked to a citizens' risk propensity toward a long life. An individual with a higher genetic propensity toward a life-shortening disease may opt to live life differently than someone without such a propensity.

Internalized Norms/External Enforcement

We saw above that cooperation among individuals pursuing their own self-interest was possible given repeated interaction and sufficiently low discounting of the future and that such cooperation was self-enforcing. But, of course, many interactions in society are anonymous, one-shot interactions. If you pull off the interstate and visit a town for the first time and try to purchase a car with a third party, out-of-state check without any forms of identification, you are going to be denied. There is no opportunity to form a reputation with this car dealer (you are anonymous) and you will likely never see him or her again (he or she discounts their future interaction with you). So the owner has no incentive to cooperate with you. All is not lost in these situations. There is another way to encourage cooperation between two parties, and that is to alter the pay-offs of the cooperation game. We can accomplish this by one of two ways: internalized norms and third-party enforcement.

Internalized norms are beliefs or values that derive from a variety of sources, including family, religion, or non-religious based morals. These internalized norms represent a form of psychological cost that the player feels they would suffer for engaging in defection. **Third-party enforcement** entails the introduction of a third party to the game. This third party could be the state, the government, the police, or a privately hired party that is granted coercive power over the two original parties in the game. This third party has the ability to offer a punishment for defecting behavior.

Whether by internalized norms or by third-party enforcement, the cost associated with defecting is important in how it alters the pay-offs of defecting to the players. Figure 2.4 displays the same cooperation game from above, but this time integrates a cost parameter, c, that each party would pay if they defect. What we need to determine is whether there is any value of, c, or the punishment that might be sufficiently high to incentivize our players to cooperate in a one-shot game.

So let's begin with Player A. From Player A's perspective, if Player B chooses Cooperate, then Player A can either receive a 4-c if Defect, or a 3 if Cooperate. Now notice what is different from that last time we solved this game. In the one-shot game without a cost parameter, Player A simply compared the pay-offs of Defect (4) vs. Cooperate (3) and

		B	
		Defect	Cooperate
A	Defect	2-c, 2-c	4-c, 1
	Cooperate	1, 4-c	3, 3

Figure 2.4 Resource Allocation Game with Defection Costs

chose accordingly – Defect. However, now we want to know how large our cost parameter must be to incentivize Player A to choose Cooperate. In our current game, if Player B chooses Cooperate, then Player A will choose Cooperate when $3 > 4\text{-}c$, or when $c>1$ (you should work out this algebra on your own). Of course, this finding is also similar (because of the symmetric pay-offs) for Player B. If you work through the rest of the possible outcomes you will see that only (Cooperate; Cooperate) is a set of mutual best responses and hence a Nash Equilibrium. These results show that in society, we can encourage cooperative outcomes even in the absence of repeat play, but to do so we need a bit of help from either internalized norms or from a third party. When either of these institutions are present and generates sufficiently high costs for defecting for both parties, the parties will cooperate.

There are of course a few issues to consider with either internalized norms or third-party enforcement solutions. Norms can be effective in encouraging cooperative behavior. But recognize that both parties must be similarly motivated by the cost generated by internalized norms. This suggests that if some parties share different norms and the cost parameter associated with defection varies in size across different norms, then cooperative outcomes may be more difficult to maintain. We see scenarios like this emerge in society regularly with different cultures exhibiting different norms. In some societies, being kind, sharing, and helping others is a well-established norm. An individual may feel intense internal pressure to behave in line with societal norms that emphasize these values. Yet, in a society in which norms are not similarly shared, cooperation will be harder to sustain. If we introduced a contagion, a subset of selfish individuals into the generous community above, with sufficient time and numbers they may actually be able to affect the eventual evolution of that community.

On the third-party enforcement solution, we must consider the sources of the punishment mechanism. To pursue a third-party enforcement solution, we would have to contract with a third party, incentivize them to behave appropriately, and then raise revenue and dedicate payment for the monitoring and enforcement of the various players. It is due to these various costs that third-party enforcement is less efficient than the self-enforcing equilibrium above. Three types of specific problems arise with third-party contracting.

First, we must contract with a third party and incentivize them to behave appropriately. Ideally our third party should be a neutral third party, one that has incentives to enforce the societal rules dispassionately without regard to any one party's interest. In reality, this is more complicated. It is very likely that a third party will often have a conflict of interest with a scenario involving two or more parties and have an incentive to sway enforcement in a biased direction. To avoid these scenarios, we have to be quite particular about our screening and selection methods for hiring our third party and also incentivizing him or her to behave appropriately in their office.

Such incentive packages could include performance indicators or quotas regarding enforcement, tenure in office – to mitigate external interference, or any number of various perks to encourage impartiality.

Second, **monitoring and enforcement** will be costly. Sufficient numbers of third-party enforcers must be hired to monitor the actions of our parties and be able to enforce these actions once caught. Moreover, we must also set aside enough funding to provide support resources to compensate them for their health and retirement benefits (should we provide dental?), we must identify, purchase, and set up physical office buildings to house our enforcers. Any number of individual line-item expenditures must be allocated for our third-party enforcement to function.

Third, monitoring and enforcement will be imperfect. The probability, p, of getting caught for an act that violates a societal rule hardly ever approaches 1. That is, in most cases, even with the best-funded third-party enforcement, p $<$1, which means that some number of individuals will also get away from a societal defection. How many of you have ever broken the speed limit in your car and gotten away with it? There is some distribution over risk-taking in society. Some of you are simply more willing to enter the lottery surrounding getting pulled over than others. Moreover, cottage industries will evolve to help individuals evade societal rules. Radar detectors can be purchased. Radio stations may alert citizens about the location of police speed traps. Oncoming traffic may flash their high-beam lights to alert you of an impending speed trap. For a variety of reasons, enforcement of any societal rule is not perfect.

Given all of these costs, does third-party enforcement still make sense? It depends upon the relative gains made given the costs of enforcement. But the relative gains can often be difficult to assign a specific numerical assessment. The costs of hiring a police force, paying for their retirement and health benefits, and insuring them against injury on the job may be readily calculated. But how do we assess the precise value of having them on the job? Is the total number of prisoners caught a preferable measure? If not, what then?

There are a number of important lessons from this investigation. First, cooperation dilemmas emerge everywhere in society. Whether in environmental settings, labor relations, or in getting your roommates to occasionally clean out the refrigerator, the cooperation dilemmas of the Prisoner's Dilemma abound in society. Second, such cooperation dilemmas exist even though individuals are pursuing their own self-interest. For some social scenarios, the pursuit of self-interest is not sufficient to solve societal cooperation dilemmas. Last, societies are not doomed to suffer from cooperative dilemmas. They can resolve in a number of ways. Whether through repeated non-anonymous interaction, the presence of strong informal norms, or via third-party enforcement, societies are not doomed to suffer suboptimal outcomes that harm all involved.

Barriers to Collective Action

A related but slightly different perspective to the cooperative dilemma is the issue of collective action. Why can't individuals who appear to have a shared preference about fixing a perceived social dilemma simply organize themselves to take action against either other citizens, groups of other citizens, or the government? On first pass one answer to this question may be, well they do – sometimes. For example, when individuals disagreed with the individual mandate in President Obama's health care package, they took to Congressional members' town halls to register their complaints and then moved further to embolden a newly organized political organization called the "Tea Party." So we do observe collective action responses to political situations. But surely, we could all conjure up an example from the policy world where a great number of citizens apparently prefer change, but are either unwilling or somehow unable to assemble collectively to challenge the status quo. So why do we observe collection action as a response to some suboptimal policies, like civil rights or the anti-abortion movement, but not others? And when we do observe collective action, why does it occur in one time and place, but not elsewhere? Are there necessary or sufficient conditions for collective action to emerge?

Multi-Person Cooperation

Let's consider under what conditions it might be rational for an individual to join in protest with his or her fellow citizens. To better understand this analytic lesson, we will use the Civil Rights Movement of the 1960s as an example. Nearly all blacks had a shared preference to undo the Jim Crow laws of the South that denied them equality of access to schools, lunch counters, buses, and the ballot box, to name just a few. Yet, for many decades, few blacks took to the streets to protest these laws. In the late 1950s, this began to change. Protest activity increased. By the 1960s, there were numerous active protests taking place in the streets all across the South (and the North), large percentages of blacks participated, yet a few did not. At the height of the American Civil Rights Movement in the mid to late 1960s, scholars estimate that the percentage of African-Americans participating in street protests varied from town to town and from state to state. This raises two interesting theoretical questions: Why did some blacks not join in to protest? Why did others decide to join in? After all, every African-American citizen had a shared interest in undoing these unjust laws and every citizen would benefit from their repeal, even if they didn't take to the streets to protest. As it turns out, this last notion that everyone would benefit even if some did not partake is part of this answer.

Let's consider the following model. Imagine that you were a young African-American considering participating in a street protest in 1964. Now imagine that your community has as its goal the repeal of Jim Crow laws in your state. Let's imagine that you value this benefit, at some level B. But participating in the street protest is not costless. After all, you have seen the police reaction to other street protests – the batons, the attack dogs, the fire hoses, and the like. So let's imagine that you have assigned all of these potential threats to your physical well-being some cost, c. Now, should you take to the streets? Well, we forgot to consider what your other friends and members of the community might be doing. It is unlikely that you and you alone will be able to deliver the benefit, B, of all Jim Crow laws being repealed. You will need help. But you also likely do not need every single other member of your community to take to the streets to have the government listen to your demands. Let's imagine that there is some minimum number of your friends that must show up, k, to deliver the group benefit, B. So we can imagine that you can be facing three basic scenarios: your group has far below the minimum number, your group only needs one additional person to deliver the benefit, and your group already has sufficient people to deliver the benefit. What should you do in each of these scenarios?

Let's assemble the model of individual participation within a group based upon the features that we discussed above. Figure 2.5 presents this basic model. You face the decision to either participate or not participate (the little ~ symbol means "not"). And you face the three scenarios that we discussed above. Under which conditions should you participate? If your group already has enough members participating to secure the benefit, with either k or more members, then if you elect to participate you will receive the Benefit minus any costs of participating, B-c. Alternatively, if you stay at home, you will only receive the Benefit, B. This suggests that if your group already has enough members participating, then you should not participate. Let's consider the other extreme. What if you have very few members participating, less than k-1? This suggests that even if you participate the number of total people participating will still not reach the necessary k people to achieve the Benefit and therefore you will be left with only –c. On the other hand, if you stay at home, you will forego the Benefit, but not have to pay any costs associated with participating. So you should not participate. Now, let's consider what happens when k-1 people are participating. When k-1 people are participating, then if you choose to participate, you will be the exact person to help the group achieve k people, thereby supplying the Benefit, B. You will have to pay the costs of participating, but it will still be better than staying at home where you will receive no Benefit, since you didn't put your group over the top.

	<k-1	k-1	k or more
Participate	-c	B-c	B-c
~Participate	0	0	B

Figure 2.5 Other Members Participating

The outcome of the Group participation game over many members suggests that we would likely observe two outcomes to this game: either no one participates or just k members do. What is the impact of the size of the parameter, k? Suppose we allowed the size of k to grow significantly larger? What would this mean substantively? A large k would suggest that you would need many African-Americans to participate in the movement for it to be successful. Alternatively, a very small k would suggest that just a few African-Americans could participate and secure the Benefit for all in the group. This would appear to suggest that as the size of k relative to the size of the overall group decreases, any individual members will likely discount their sense of having to be involved to make a difference and will choose to not participate. But, as k increases, each member feels a greater sense of the need to contribute to the group's effort, since without their participation the goal will fail. As the size of k declines, particularly to the total size of the group, N, it will be increasingly more difficult to incentivize members to participate. This suggests that to be successful in securing their benefit, leaders of the Civil Rights Movement had a critical task: to convince each of their constituents (and even others) that their individual participation was critically important for the success of the movement. Perhaps the most powerful weapon in Dr. Martin Luther King's arsenal throughout the Civil Rights Movement was his ability to inspire civic action. Through public speeches, letters, and personal interactions, Dr. King's inspirational message fell upon many ears that were convinced they were uniquely required to help secure a victory for civil rights.

Box 2.4

Dr. Martin Luther King's "Letter from a Birmingham Jail" attempted to give all Americans the sense that they were critical players in the fight for civil rights – perhaps as an attempt to increase the relative size of k. By reminding Americans that "Injustice anywhere is a threat to justice anywhere," Dr. King sought to expand to every American the sense of duty to participate in the struggle for civil rights. He went on to write, "We are caught in an inescapable network of mutuality tied in a single garment of destiny. Whatever affects one directly, affects all indirectly ... Anyone who lives inside the United States can never be considered an outsider anywhere within its bounds." For much of the letter, Dr. King gently chides those who have been complacent and conformist.

Group Organization

Another barrier to collective action is the ability of individuals to form together into groups to advance their policy preferences. Throughout much of the first half of the twentieth century, assumptions about the regular representation of various political interests at the policy table were informed by the interest group pluralism perspective. Interest group pluralism assumed that if individuals had shared preferences on some political or policy issue, they could simply form interest groups that could advocate for the specific policies that they preferred (Truman 1951). As it turns out, however, there are some strong disincentives to group formation and maintenance that act as barriers to equal representation of political interests.

These insights were best articulated by Mancur Olson in *The Logic of Collective Action* (1965), in which he highlighted the difficulties that interest groups should have in both forming and maintaining their memberships. He countered the classic assumption that individual interests would naturally form into organizations. By Olson's thinking, organized groups face a particular problem – under what conditions will members join and remain members of a group? This problem is similar to the one we analyzed in the previous section. Essentially, attracting members to join a group and to contribute to the group's goals is particularly challenging when the group offers indivisible benefits that are likely to accrue to either non-group and group members alike or to non-participating group members. This **free-riding** behavior describes any situation where an individual knows that she or he may be able to enjoy a group benefit whether or not they join the group or whether, upon joining the group, they fail to contribute to the group's goals. In these situations, organized groups will be difficult to maintain. This problem is particularly acute among large organized groups because any individual's lack of effort toward the group goal is likely to go unnoticed by other members – as a result, non-participation is not likely to suffer any sanction. Smaller group settings may be able to avoid this problem, since anonymity is more difficult to maintain.

Consider any group project or study group that you have ever been a part of. The smaller the group, the easier it is for you to observe and attempt to sanction non-participation. However, as the size of your group grows, it becomes more difficult for you to observe each member's contributions perfectly. Indeed, your effort in this very class is likely affected by the size of the class. If you are enrolled in a policy class that is relatively small in size, your professor can likely identify you by name, can call on you in seminar, and can sanction your lack of knowledge or participation in the class. Moreover, in group work you can observe others' behavior. As a result, you have greater incentive to behave accordingly.

2.4 Conclusion

To understand public policy, we must have an appreciation of the micro-level origins of policy demands. Often, policy demands grow from the inability of individuals to obtain a position-improving social outcome. In this chapter, we reviewed basic game theoretic analytic applications of a few common social dilemmas faced by individuals. You will see references to these dilemmas in later chapters throughout the text. There are several important lessons to keep in mind from this review of key social dilemmas. Individuals can generally improve their position by pursuing self-interest. However, under certain conditions, the pursuit of self-interest is not sufficient to guarantee self-improvement. In fact, with cooperation dilemmas, despite each actor's pursuit of self-interest, both can be left worse off than they would have been had they been able to forego the temptations of short-term improvements. In the next chapter, we will examine whether institutions, like markets and governments, offer any solutions to these social dilemmas and, if they offer solutions, assess the way they attempt to do so.

Key Terms in This Chapter

Game theory
Strategic
Decision theory
Exogenous
Endogenous
Utility
Utility function
Indifferent
Ordinal preference
Cardinal preference
Strict preference
Weak preference
Indifferent preference
Comparable preference
Transitive preference
Rational
Strategy profile
Best response
Nash Equilibrium
Commitment problem
Discount factor
Present value
Internalized norms
Third-party enforcement
Monitoring and enforcement
Free-riding

CHAPTER EXERCISES

1. Which of the following are strategic vs. decision theoretic scenarios? Explain.
   a. A legislator considering voting for a bill.
   b. A bureaucrat attempting to shirk.
   c. A regulated firm contemplating the benefits of violating the law.
   d. A research service conducting a cost-benefit analysis.
2. An economist has argued that it is perfectly rational that poor individuals spend their scarce money on consumables (i.e. cigarettes, alcohol, cell phones, etc.) rather than save their money. Can you think of a possible explanation for why this behavior may be rational, given a poor person's situation? Explain. (Hint, think about discount factors.)
3. Describe a cooperation dilemma within the public policy arena. Carefully explain the incentives that have created this cooperative dilemma. How might these incentives be altered to resolve the dilemma and incentivize actors to cooperate?
4. Think carefully about the notions of present value and discount factors. Identify a choice or decision that you have had to make that involved these concepts. Would you say you had a relatively high (or low) discount rate? Why?

REFERENCES

Andreoni, James. 1990. "Impure Altruism and Donations to Public Goods: A Theory of Warm-Glow Giving." *Economic Journal* 401(June): 464–477.

Axelrod, Robert. 1984. *The Evolution of Cooperation*. New York: Basic Books.

Camerer, Colin F. 2003. *Behavioral Game Theory*. Princeton University Press.

Green, Donald P. and Shapiro, Ian. 1994. *Pathologies of Rational Choice Theory: A Critique of Applications in Political Science*. New Haven, CT: Yale University Press.

Lupia, Arthur, McCubbins, Matthew D., and Popkin, Samuel. L. 2000. *Elements of Reason: Cognition, Choice, and the Bounds of Rationality*. Cambridge University Press.

Nagel, Thomas. 1970. *The Possibility of Altruism*. Princeton University Press.

Nash, John F. 1951. "Non-Cooperative Games." *Annals of Mathematics* 54(2): 286–295.

Olson, Mancur. 1965. *The Logic of Collective Action*. Cambridge, MA: Harvard University Press.

Osborne, Martin J. 2004. *An Introduction to Game Theory*. New York: Oxford University Press.

Tsebelis, George. 1989. "The Abuse of Probability in Political Analysis: The Robinson Crusoe Fallacy." *American Political Science Review* 83(1): 77–91.

Truman, David. 1951. *The Governmental Process*. New York: Knopf.

Von Neumann, John and Morgenstern, Oskar. 1944. *Theory of Games and Economic Behavior*. Princeton University Press.

3 Public Policy as a Solution to Social Dilemmas

Outline

Questions

- What role do markets play in creating and solving social dilemmas?
- What role does government play in creating and solving social dilemmas?

Overview

- In this chapter, we examine the role of markets and governments as devices to solve social dilemmas. While markets provide efficient solutions to certain kinds of social problems there are certain features that handicap markets' ability to provide effective solutions.
- Institutions, like markets and governments, help facilitate individual and collective action. But these institutions have limitations.
- Markets can efficiently allocate resources when certain conditions are met.
- In the absence of these conditions, markets are said to fail.
- Market failure derives from certain characteristics: lack of competition, incomplete information, and transaction costs.
- Government was originally intended to provide citizens with security. However, government itself can also be a threat to security.

- To harness the support and productivity of their citizens, governments must alleviate citizens' fears of predation by other citizens, while simultaneously alleviating their concerns about government predation of their assets.
- To credibly commit to not predating upon their citizens, governments must effectively bind their hands with institutional devices that citizens believe limit state power.
- Governments can also experience failure.
- Government failure includes the dilemma of majority rule, market distortions, and principal–agent delegation problems.
- Analytic models assist us in understanding the role of markets and government in public policy.

Introduction: Institutions and Social Problems

In the last chapter, we saw that individuals each pursuing their own interest can sometimes be beneficial for others in a community. But sometimes the pursuit of self-interest may lead to suboptimal outcomes for all parties. Where might citizens look for solutions to such social problems? For some Americans, it is almost natural to look to government for a solution to many if not all of these problems. For others, the market is seen to offer the best hope of solving society's most nagging dilemmas. But what does it mean for government or the market to solve a social problem? What larger social dilemmas are these institutions, government, and markets thought to resolve? And are these institutions, whether government or markets, similarly equipped to solve all types of social problems? Does the introduction of a market or government institution create new social problems? These are a few of the questions that we take up in this chapter.

In this chapter, we consider how markets and governments offer potential remedies to organizational and representation dilemmas in resolving social problems. We then use analytic models to examine the limits or failures of each of these institutions. We end the chapter with a discussion of the rather optimistic prospect that rather than an either-or choice between market and government solutions to social dilemmas, some combination of market and government institutions is often optimal for solving societal problems.

3.1 Institutions as Facilitators of Individual and Collective Action

Left to their own devices individuals may not always be able to secure optimal outcomes. Cooperation dilemmas, coordination problems, and collective action difficulties are common and lead to suboptimal outcomes. Certain institutions, however, may be able to resolve or at least mitigate these social problems. In a political economy framework, institutions are important features of our environment. They structure the number of actors, the order of play, constrain actions available to various actors, impose costs on certain actions, and winnow the set of options available.

But to understand how institutions might improve social outcomes we must clarify what we mean by improvement. What criteria should we apply to determine whether an institution improves individuals' positions? Two basic sets of criteria are normative and positive. **Normative criteria** focus on what the state of the world *should be*. **Positive criteria** focus on what the state of the world *is*. An important and ubiquitous criterion for policy analysis is the **Pareto criterion**. Vilfredo Pareto (1848–1923) was an engineer and economist who introduced the concept of Pareto efficiency to describe the relative levels of performance among alternative states of allocating goods. Imagine some allocation of goods among a set of individuals. If we can change this allocation in some way to make at least one individual better off without making any other individuals worse off, then we have a **Pareto improvement**. If we obtain an allocation, to which no further Pareto improvements can be made, then we say that we have a **Pareto efficient** or **Pareto optimal** outcome. Very often in policy analysis when you hear people talk about more or less efficient outcomes, they are referring to Pareto efficiency.

Consider a few examples. Imagine that an underdeveloped beach front exists on the Panhandle of Florida. The area remains underdeveloped because of the difficulty of accessing this particular beachfront. However, with the construction of a new highway connecting to Interstate 10, economic development may bring a greater social benefit to the Panhandle. Could such a policy be a Pareto improvement? Probably not. Although such a project may produce greater social benefits compared to social costs, and therefore a net social gain, some individuals are likely to be worse off. Individuals living near the area and enjoying the lack of development, for example, may be worse off after the highway is built. Therefore, the project would not be a Pareto improvement. It is also important to recognize that a Pareto efficient outcome does not necessarily imply equitable or fair outcomes. Imagine four classes of individuals in society: the rich, the middle class, the working class, and the poor. Assume that wealth is distributed in the following way across the four classes: 70, 15, 12, and 3 percent, respectively. Imagine that the economy grows by some percentage, x, every year. Assuming zero inflation, if we were to adopt a policy that divided all of the gains of economic growth among the rich and the middle class, would this be a Pareto improvement? While perhaps not fair or equitable, such a policy represents a Pareto improvement because the policy would not make the working or poor classes worse off. With no inflation, they would retain their original wealth. The policy would, however, improve the positions of the rich and middle classes. Now if we assume that individuals care not only about their personal wealth, but also the current distribution of wealth, then this policy of dividing all of the gains between the rich and middle classes would not be a Pareto improvement.

Let's consider one final example. Imagine that a neighborhood is considering adopting a voluntary neighborhood crime watch program. Interested individuals can participate and if they do, the probability of crime in their neighborhood may decrease by some amount. This decrease in crime will have a non-negative impact on housing prices – there might be an increase in housing prices, or no change, but they will at least not fall. Might such a program be Pareto efficient? Yes, it likely would be. Why? Most, if not all, individuals would benefit from the presence of the program and as long as the program is voluntary, no tax was required to be raised to pay for the program, leaving no individuals worse off because of it (assuming the neighborhood benefit was greater than the individual cost of participating in the program).

These examples outline the usefulness of the Pareto criterion for comparing different social allocations or policies. The last example, however, does raise a potential difficulty. As you might imagine, Pareto optimality might be difficult to maintain in the presence of complicated institutions, or policies over a large set of individuals. Requiring that no individual suffer a loss by a policy change is indeed a tall order and in reality nearly impossible. As such, Pareto optimality is a stringent criterion for efficiency. How might this criterion be relaxed? Two economists, Nicholas Kaldor and John Hicks, offered a potential solution. The **Kaldor-Hicks criterion** suggests that if the beneficiaries of a proposed alternative could hypothetically compensate those who are likely to be made worse off, then we may obtain a **Kaldor-Hicks improvement**. Such a criterion offers a more realistic application to the policy world. The notion that beneficiaries of some alternative are able to hypothetically compensate those worse off is known as the **compensation principle**. Critically important is the notion that while it is hypothetically possible to compensate a party for its loss, no such compensation is actually required.

With these criteria in mind, we are now better equipped to talk about how institutions may improve individuals' lots. It is through institutions that out of an otherwise complicated and chaotic setting emerges relative stability. Two institutions that have helped human beings organize their activities and improve their utilities are markets and governments. We consider each of these in the next two sections.

3.2 Markets

One social mechanism that allows individuals to express their preferences over different goods and services is a market. When we hear people suggest that we should "let the market handle" some social goods provision, what precisely do they mean by this? What are markets, how do they operate, and under what conditions do they fail to provide efficient outcomes? In this section, we consider each of these questions in turn.

A **market** is any institution or operation wherein individuals can trade goods, services, or information. In a market, the relative pressures of supply and demand determine the prices of goods and services. Consumers vary in their demand for particular goods and services and sellers vary in their production of particular goods and services. In a competitive market, consumers seek goods and services at the lowest possible price, while suppliers attempt to sell at the highest possible price. Let's consider the standard supply-and-demand framework from economics.

For any good or service we can describe the level of supply that exists for that good or the level of demand of that good. Supply refers to the amount of a good for which sellers are willing and able to produce and sell it. The level of supply for a good is driven by a variety of factors, including: the price of the good, technology, factor prices, productive capacity, and a host of other factors. All of these factors *except the price of the good* are referred to as **determinants of supply**. The Law of Supply states that holding all else constant, or *ceteris paribus*, as the price of a good increases, the quantity of that good that suppliers will produce will increase and vice versa. Figure 3.1 displays a supply curve (although economists call it a curve, it is just a straight line) which relates the quantity of the good or service, Q, to the price for that good or service, P. For a given price, p_0, the amount of the good supplied will be q_0. At a higher price, say p_1, we would expect more sellers to be willing to increase supply and so we would expect a **change in the quantity supplied** to q_1. To be clear, this type of change only characterizes the relationship between price and the quantity of the good supplied. Recall that in addition to price there are determinants of supply that also shape the price of a good. When we allow a determinant of supply to change we refer to such a change as a **change or shift in supply**. Rather than representing movement along the supply curve, changes in supply actually shift the entire curve. This is because a determinant of supply can increase or lower the entire supply curve by

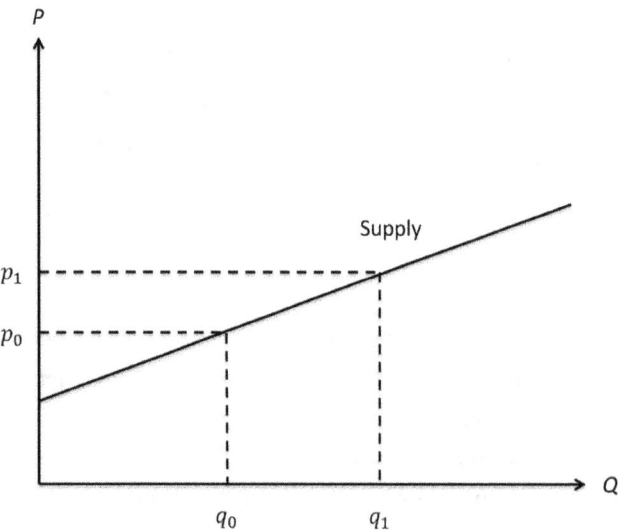

Figure 3.1 Supply Curve

changing the price of production or changing technology. Figure 3.2 displays a change in supply where the entire supply curve has shifted to the left. The supply curve was represented by S_1, but some determinant of supply has changed, and is now represented by S_2. Let's imagine that labor costs have increased industry-wide. This would result in a leftward shift as seen in Figure 3.2. What does this mean for the market? It suggests that for the same quantity of the good supplied, q_0, suppliers will no longer be willing to sell it for the price, p_0, but rather will have to raise the price to p_1. Shifts in supply to the left suggest higher prices for goods and services. The opposite is also true. Shifts in supply to the right, due to a technological advance, reduction in factor prices, or lower labor costs lead to suppliers being able to sell the same quantity of good or service for lower prices.

Demand refers to the amount of a good for which buyers are willing and able to pay. The level of demand for a good is driven by a variety of factors, including: the price of the good, the buyer's income, the value of other substitutes, and a host of other factors. All of these factors, *except the price of the good*, are referred to as **determinants of the demand**. The Law of Demand states that holding all else constant, or *ceteris paribus*, as the price of a good increases, the quantity of that good that buyers will demand will decrease and vice versa. A change in price will affect a change in the quantity demanded. The lowest price at which the demand for any amount of the good is zero is the choke price of the good. Figure 3.3 displays a Demand curve which relates the quantity of the good or service, Q, that consumers are willing to buy to the price for that good or service, P. For a given price, p_0, the equilibrium amount of the good demanded will be q_0. At a higher price, say p_1, we would expect a reduction in the number of consumers willing to demand the good

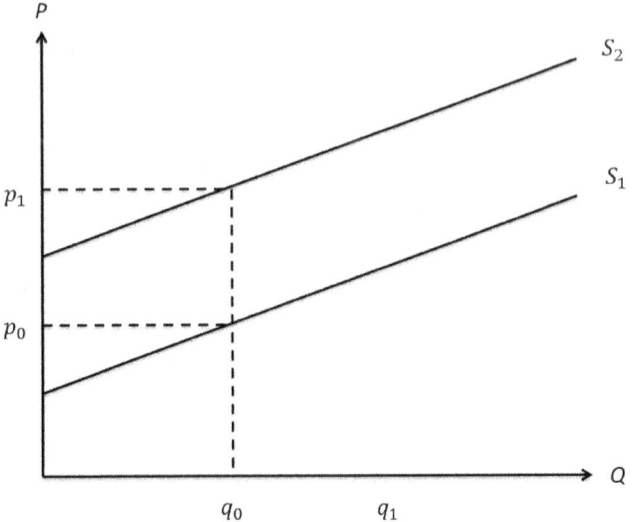

Figure 3.2 Supply Shift

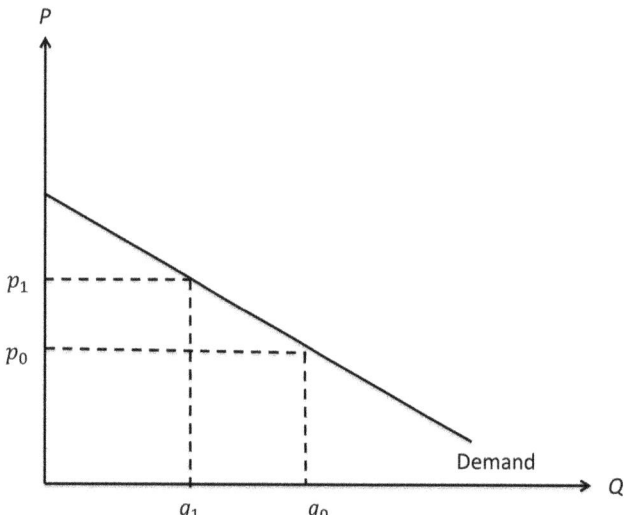

Figure 3.3 Demand Curve

and so we would expect a **change in the quantity demanded** to q_1. To be clear, this type of change only characterizes the relationship between price and the quantity of the good demanded. Recall that, as with supply, in addition to price there are determinants of demand that also shape the price of a good. When we allow a determinant of demand to change, we refer to such a change as a **change or shift in demand**. Rather than representing movement along the demand curve, changes in demand actually shift the entire curve. This is because a determinant of demand can increase or lower the entire demand curve by changing the price of substitutes or buyer's income. Shifts in demand have the opposite effect on prices compared to shifts in supply. Shifts in demand to the left suggest lower prices for goods and services. At every point on the demand curve, the price will be lower than before. The opposite is true for a demand shift to the right. Shifts in supply to the right increase the quantity of the good or service demanded at every price. Using Figure 3.3 as a template, see if you can sketch out the impact of a shift in demand in prices.

Now that we have discussed supply and demand curves, we are ready to put them together to understand the concept of market equilibrium. When the price of a good or product is established via perfect competition under the condition that the demand for the good exactly equals the supply of the good, there is said to exist a **market equilibrium price**. At this price, the market will "clear," meaning that there will not exist any over- or under-production of the good or service. Why is this the case? Let's look at our supply and demand curves together.

Figure 3.4 displays a supply-demand plot. Where the two curves (i.e. lines) meet we have an equilibrium price. At this price, suppliers can sell all of the goods or services that they have to sell and consumers are able to acquire all the goods and services that

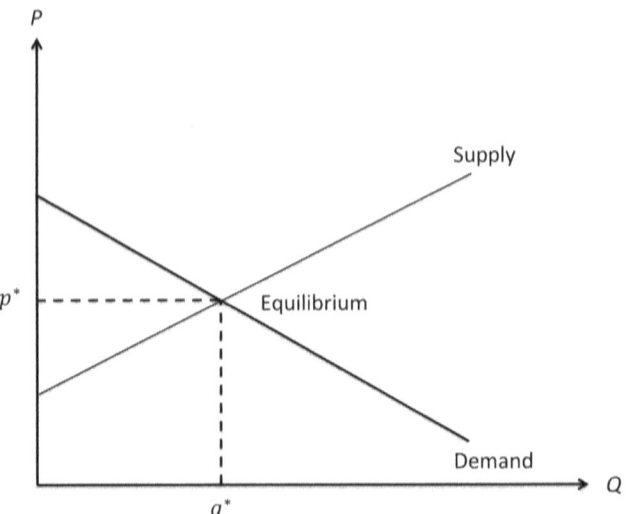

Figure 3.4 Supply and Demand Curves

they desire. This is an efficient outcome. The quantity of goods and services supplied is exactly equal to the quantity of goods and services demanded. Neither party has an incentive to change their situation. The market equilibrium price will obtain at the intersection of the Supply and Demand curves.

Why does this equilibrium price obtain? Certainly, it is not magical. The answer is market forces. To understand how this price obtains, let's consider how suppliers and consumers would behave under different price conditions. We will use Figure 3.5 to illustrate this relationship. If a price is set below the market-clearing price, say p_2, then a **shortage of supply** exists. The total amount or size of the shortage is represented by the lighter shaded triangle in Figure 3.5. Under a shortage, excess demand for the good exists, but suppliers are unwilling to produce the good at this price. However, given excess demand, consumers will bid up the price of this under-supplied good, eventually up to p^*. Suppliers will then have an incentive to produce more. So the price will move upward in the direction of the market equilibrium price. You can also see that as the price, p_2, approaches the equilibrium price, p^*, the size of the shortage, represented by the lighter shaded triangle, will decrease, eventually reaching zero.

But, what if suppliers, seeing this pent-up demand, get greedy and set their prices much higher than the market equilibrium price? If a price is set above the market-clearing price, say p_1, then a **surplus of supply** exists. The total amount or size of the surplus is represented by the darker shaded triangle in Figure 3.5. Consumers are unwilling to buy the good at this price and so supply builds up. Suppliers now have an incentive to lower the price of the good to reduce the supply of their inventory of the good. The result is downward pressure in the price of the good toward the equilibrium

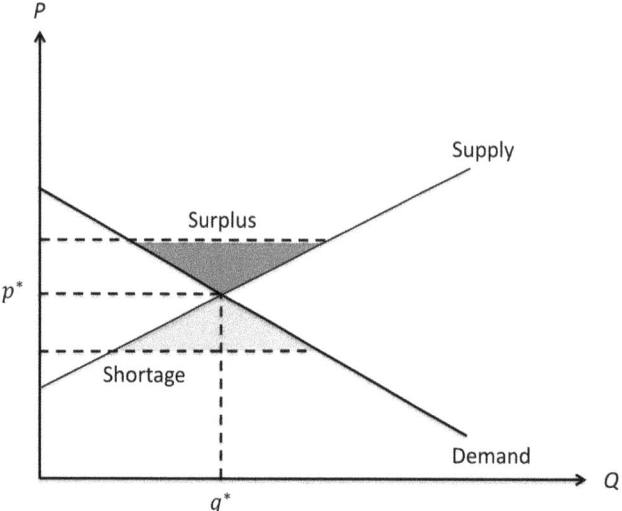

Figure 3.5 Surplus and Shortage

price. You can see that as the price, p_1, approaches the equilibrium price, p^*, the size of the surplus, represented by the darker shaded triangle, will decrease, eventually reaching zero.

Notice that in this highly idealized scenario, a market price was obtained without the existence of a centralized organization. No government or non-government entity was required to exist to set prices; rather, the market is said to have determined these prices seemingly automatically. Moreover, the market was able to operate and satisfy both consumer and supplier alike, with each pursuing their own self-interest. Neither party was required to be motivated by a deeper philosophical concern for the other. By merely pursuing their own self-interest, both parties benefitted. This notion is what many believe Adam Smith, an early economic theorist, was referring to in his classic treatise, *The Wealth of Nations* (1776), as the "invisible hand of the market." The idea was that the common interest or common good was likely to benefit from individuals pursuing their own self-interest. Of course, we just saw in the previous section that this idea does not always hold. In fact, there are several situations where individual pursuit of self-interest in fact harms all parties involved.

We will see below that the efficient operation of the market rests on several critical conditions that must be met in order to deliver mutually preferable outcomes via market exchange. When these conditions are not met, the ability of the market to produce an efficient solution is threatened. So, any good economist would suggest that a *perfectly competitive market* can be efficient, *ceteris paribus* – which recalls the old joke: "How many economists does it take to change a light bulb? Two: one to change the light bulb and the other to hold everything else constant." Unfortunately, every-thing else is rarely held constant and ideal conditions are rarely met in the real world.

Under these conditions markets are not efficient, but it is possible that they could be more efficient than some alternatives.

In the ideal case, a free market describes exchange completely devoid of regulation, interference by a third party, central government, or other institutions external to the transactions occurring within the market. Essentially, no economic market meets these conditions. For this reason, it is better to characterize markets by the level of government intervention or regulation that exists in the market. In this way we can say that some markets are more "free" than others, and the debate centers around relative differences between systems rather than a debate on absolute differences.

How might we measure how free one market is relative to another? Scholars have considered a variety of plausible measures of so-called economic freedom. One measure developed by the Heritage Foundation is the Economic Freedom Index (Miller *et al.* 2014). This index includes four components: Rule of Law (which measures property rights and freedom from corruption); Limited Government (which measures fiscal freedom and government spending); Regulatory Efficiency (which measures business freedom, labor freedom, and monetary freedom); and Open Markets (which measures trade, investment, and financial freedom). These components assess different aspects of critical features of whether a market would be characterized as "free" or not. Each of these dimensions reflects similar information about countries' overall free-market tendencies.

Consider the map in Figure 3.6, which shows the world's Economics Freedom scores. Darker green countries reflect the freest markets, while darker red countries reflect the least free countries. The first item to note is the wide variance in the world's economies. The world is populated with a great diversity of national economic models. Second, most of the world's economies are not particularly free. In fact, approximately 19 percent of the world's countries' markets are considered "free" or "mostly free" compared to 81 percent that are either "moderately free," "mostly unfree," or "repressed." In terms of population, approximately 13 percent of the world's citizens or nearly 890 million live in "free" or "mostly free" economies, while the other 5.9 billion do not. Most of human history can be characterized as a struggle between more-free and less-free economic systems. Moreover, this struggle has stark consequences for both the residents of these countries and their neighbors. Quality of life, individual wealth, the absence of war, and violent domestic conflict tend to all be positively associated with freer economic systems. But if this is true, then why don't more countries adopt free market operations? This question begs a complicated answer, but at a minimum, it likely revolves around a country's ability to resolve a critical problem that is inherent in all market operations: private property and credible commitment.

Property Rights/Credible Commitment

Fundamental to any well-functioning market is the existence and maintenance of property rights. By **property rights**, we mean the exclusive right to determine how a

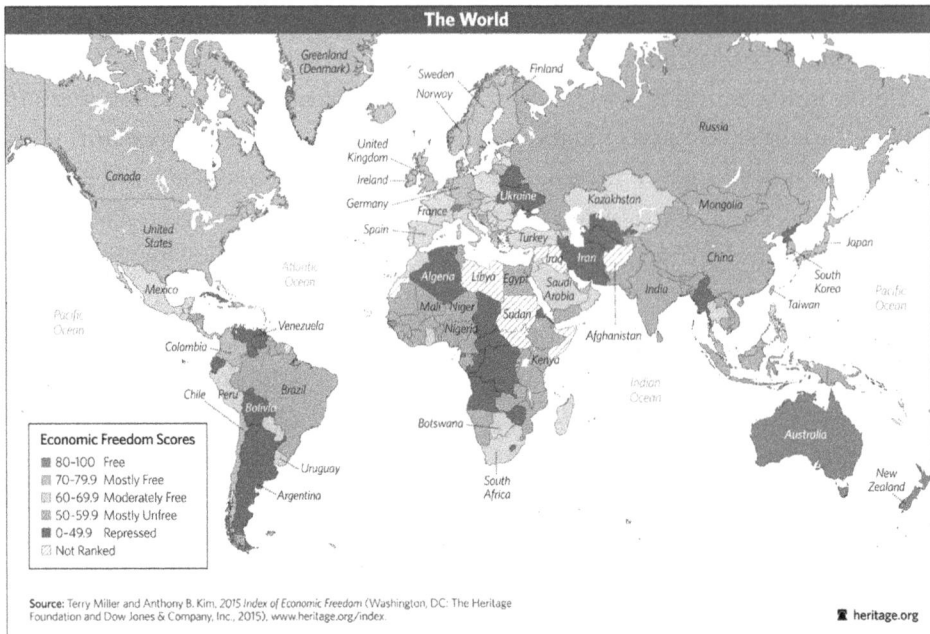

Figure 3.6 Heritage Foundation's Economic Freedom Scores

resource or property is to be used. When property rights are absolute, the owner has sole and unlimited authority to make decisions over property access, use, exclusion, and management, without interference from other parties. When property rights are relaxed, abrogated, or violated, non-owners exercise a level of authority over property that they do not own.

What are the benefits of property rights? First, property rights are necessary to encourage future investment in economic activity. Without guarantees of property rights protection, it would be rather difficult to convince a set of investors to risk their assets for the benefit of growing the economy. Second, private property is also useful for resolving a variety of resource difficulties faced in society. Elinor Ostrom (1990) dedicated much of her work to understanding how private property rights contribute to the management of scarce resources. Individuals who possess property rights over small areas of a common pool resource, like a forest or a fishing ground, are incentivized to better manage their resource. Third, private property is useful as a check against political power. By scoring off an area that the state or sovereign has no authority to manage, property rights delineate boundaries to the state.

How are property rights violated? Essentially there are two ways in which property rights are violated. *Citizens* can violate the property rights of other citizens, or the *state* can violate the rights of its citizens. If we include a person's physical integrity as a dimension of their property rights as well as the actual possessions that they own, then murder, burglary, or theft are all examples of one citizen violating another's property rights. Some rights violations are codified under criminal law, meaning that they are deemed to be acts which are, in a sense, offences against all of society, while others are codified under civil law, which deals more with disputes between private parties. For example, citizens who harm the health or welfare of other citizens may be thought of as having violated the laws of society against pollution (potential criminal violations) as well as other citizens' private property rights (potential civil violations). So pollution, whether in the realm of air, water, or even noise, may, to the extent that it damages another person's ability to enjoy their property, be cast as both a criminal and a civil violation.

How can we encourage citizens not to violate each other's rights – to deter property violations? Clearly, incentives often exist for one party to transgress another's rights. Social philosophers like Thomas Hobbes proposed a solution in the form of a third party. Written during the English civil war, Hobbes recognized that citizens in the state of nature, where all individuals war with each other, are likely to face difficult times in the absence of a strong hand to govern. He famously argued that in the state of nature, without the protections afforded by a "common power to keep them all in awe" they [individuals] will experience "continual fear, and danger of violent death; and the life of man, solitary, poor, brutish, and short." Seeking to avoid such a difficult existence, Hobbes laid the groundwork for "social contract theory," which considers imagining that individuals enter into a contract with a third party for their own protection. Hobbes referred to the third party as the Leviathan. Hobbes suggested that the Leviathan possessed all-encompassing power so that it could compel, by force if necessary, individuals' mutual respect of private property rights. The Leviathan would protect citizens from each other and in turn they would cede to the Leviathan a subset of their liberty.

Of course, the solution of the Leviathan, while potentially successful in solving citizen-against-citizen property rights violations, does nothing to remedy the potential of the state to violate the rights of the citizen. The difficulty of course with this view of government's role was made clear in Madison's concern over the potential threat of government:

> Government is instituted to protect property of every sort; as well that which lies in the various rights of individuals, as that which the term particularly expresses. This being the end of government, that alone is a just government which impartially secures to every man whatever is his own.
>
> (James Madison, Essay on Property, March 29, 1792)

> If men were angels, no government would be necessary. If angels were to govern men, neither external nor internal controls on government would be necessary. In framing a government which is to be administered by men over men, the great difficulty lies in this: you must first enable the government to control the governed; and in the next place, oblige it to control itself.
>
> (James Madison, Federalist No. 51, February 8, 1788)

Madison's brilliance, in part, was his recognition of the inherent difficulties in constructing a third party (e.g. a government, a Leviathan, etc.) to oversee the protection of property and the enforcement of contracts. He recognized that government could *simultaneously* represent a means of protection against property rights violations *and* a threat to citizens' property rights. In this respect, government faces a very delicate balancing act: they must find a way to induce citizens to invest in their states and economies, while not presenting so much of a threat to citizens' well-being that they fail to be productive and creative members of society and economy. Political scientists have spent many years pondering over the ways for governments to credibly commit to such a position.

Effectively what governments must be able to do to constrain themselves credibly is to bind their own hands. Of course, by offering to bind their own hands, we arrive at the same problem: how exactly does a government police itself? Even if a government can creatively design a set of institutional constraints on its power, under what conditions would these institutions function in the way that they are designed to? Consider, for example, Montesquieu's suggestion. Montesquieu, a French political philosopher, was the earliest supporter of the principle of the separation of power, where lawmaking, enforcement, and adjudication powers would be separated and each office used as a check on the other's power. In some respects, this solution is not quite satisfying. Different branches of government may not have the coercive ability to enforce a judgment against another branch. Traditionally, only the executive has a police force with which to enforce the law. Why would we believe a court to be a credible protection against state violations in the absence of its ability to enforce its own decisions?

One potential answer is that these institutions are credible constraints on power when a sufficient number of citizens believe that the institutions are effective constraints on government power. Barry Weingast, a political scientist, suggested that when a sufficient number of citizens can agree that a state's violation of a fundamental right occurs and a sufficient number of them are willing to take action against an abusive government, then the government will be incentivized to obey its constraints, essentially making such constraints credible (Weingast 1997). The difficult question for citizens, of course, is what government actions constitute fundamental violations and under what conditions should citizens coordinate a response to these violations? Weingast suggests that this is precisely what constitutions provide for citizens. Constitutions are focal points that provide citizens with cues as to what may constitute government trespass and provide guidance on when and how to react to such trespasses. When a sufficient number of citizens believe that government constraints are real, then such commitment devices can be thought of as being credible. If institutional constraints are present, but citizens fail to recognize or believe that these institutions are likely to constrain state power, then such devices are not likely to be credible devices.

Market Limitations or Market Failure

Markets are useful institutions for allocating resources in ways that benefit individuals while generally not harming others. Yet, there are limitations on a market's ability to deliver efficient outcomes. These limitations derive from a variety of specific problems, including: externalities, public goods, asymmetric information, and market power. Each of these represents a necessary though not sufficient condition to generate an inefficient market. In the presence of one or more of these limitations, markets are less able to operate effectively and may deliver goods or services that are inefficient. To better understand the conditions under which markets may struggle to provide efficient outcomes, we must first consider two characteristics of goods or services.

Rivalrous and Excludable Goods

Goods are any product or service capable of consumption by others. Economists find it useful to speak of two basic attributes of goods produced in society: rivalrousness and excludability. The distribution of a given good on each of these two dimensions has wide implications for understanding the efficiency of a market producing that good.

Rivalrousness refers to whether a good can be used or consumed by one person while another person is using or consuming that good. In other words, a **rivalrous good** is one whose use or consumption will limit or eliminate the supply of that specific good to others. For example, an automobile, a gallon of gasoline, or a firearm are all examples of rivalrous goods. An individual's use or purchase of these goods prohibits another individual from simultaneously enjoying that specific good at the same time. A **non-rivalrous good** is one whose use does not deplete the availability of the good. For example, clean air and cable television are both non-rivalrous. I can breathe clean air and watch my favorite TV episode while another citizen simultaneously does the same. There is nothing inherent in either of these goods that would deprive another from consuming these goods, while I do the same.

Excludability refers to whether access to a good can be restricted by its owner. In other words, an **excludable good** is one whose use or consumption by others can be restricted by the owner of the good. For example, classes at a private university, a rental property, or a toll road are all examples of excludable goods. An individual's use or purchase of any of these goods allows that individual to restrict others' access to the good. A **non-excludable good** is one whose access cannot be or is exceedingly difficult to deny, regardless of who owns the good. For example, national defense, clean air, and fishing are all non-excludable. It is effectively impossible to deny national defense or clean air to a citizen of a state or territory who may have not contributed to the effort. Similarly, there are rather large bureaucratic implementation difficulties associated with restricting access to all fishing grounds.

When taken together, these two attribute dimensions suggest a basic framework for understanding why markets may poorly, or inefficiently, provide certain goods and why those goods may be better produced by government.

Consider Figure 3.7. When we imagine the intersection of each of these characteristics we have four ideal-types of goods as the product. **Private Goods** are those goods with which we are most familiar. These goods are both rivalrous and excludable: one person's use of the good prevents the simultaneous use of the good by another and excludes others who have not paid for the good from enjoying it. If a good is non-excludable but rivalrous, we refer to it as being a **Common Good**. Common Goods or common pool resources are those whose consumption cannot be prevented or excluded, but whose consumption eliminates others from enjoying the good. **Club Goods** describe goods that are excludable and non-rivalrous. A club good is one that requires a membership to enjoy the good. A classic example is a private hunting club or membership in a subscription-based service. Last, **Public Goods** are those goods that are both non-rivalrous and non-excludable.

The distinction between different goods is important from the perspective of whether such goods are likely to be delivered efficiently in a market. It turns out that Private Goods and Club Goods possess characteristics that are amenable to markets. These goods are likely to be produced at efficient levels where the amount of the good supplied meets the amount demanded. Non-excludable goods, on the other hand, whether Common Goods or Public Goods, are likely to be under-produced and under-supplied. Why might this be the case? With either Common or Public Goods, given that the good is non-excludable, once the good is produced its consumption cannot be limited to paying customers only. Rather, a positive externality exists, such that individuals not party to the transaction will benefit from the transaction. However, unlike some positive externalities that may be a by-product of transactions involving excludable goods, in the case of non-excludable goods, these positive externalities lead to the inefficient outcome of the good being under-produced – since no producer could make a profit by supplying them.

	Excludable	Non-excludable
Rivalrous	Private goods (food, clothing)	Common goods (forest/fish stocks)
Non-rivalrous	Club goods (Netflix, private park)	Public goods (clean air, national debt)

Figure 3.7 Goods Characteristics

Non-Competitive Markets (Monopolies)

In any given aspect of the economy there generally are a host of suppliers of goods and services. If you are feeling peckish for a hamburger, in most cities you would have quite a few choices to satisfy your needs. You could select among any number of national chains or your favorite local mom-and-pop burger stand. Your disappointment would likely be quite high if there were only one business in town that sold hamburgers. But of course you would likely find out that limited choice was not the only consequence of having no competition for your single supplier. You would likely also face an inflated burger price, relative to other more competitive markets.

In situations where a market only has a single supplier of a good or service there are profound consequences. Such situations are known as a **monopoly**, or a situation where a single seller of a good or service faces many buyers. Why might monopolies arise? Of the many circumstances that may contribute to the origin or maintenance of a monopoly, all have a common feature – they erect barriers to entry by other firms. These circumstances can grow out of market or government origins. On market origins, monopolies may derive from the pursuit of large economies of scale, intense capital demands, or even customer loyalty. Businesses pursue larger scales of operation not only to grow their customer base, but also to take advantage of the relatively lower cost of operation as the scale of their business increases. As the scale of a business increases, the cost per unit generally declines as the business is able to capitalize on gains in various dimensions, including: technology, speed of delivery, purchasing, and managerial advantages. The gains of economies of scale, however, can be sufficient to ward off competition from new entrepreneurs, potentially heightening the prospects of monopoly formation. Intense capital demands may also be a barrier to new investment. Consider the capital demands of constructing a new nuclear reactor to produce commercial electricity. The capital demands are tremendous, the construction delays are notorious, and the time required to recoup the initial capital investment may be on the order of decades. These costs are likely sufficient to set up a barrier to new investment. Last, on customer loyalty, consider the following: Could you start a new professional baseball franchise in Boston in the shadow of Fenway Park? Probably not. Loyal Red Sox fans would be highly unlikely to defect to your new team, even in off years when the Sox are underperforming. Such barriers do not always derive from the market, however.

Barriers to entry may also have government as their origin. Legal patents or copyrights may effectively ban other competitors from the marketplace for a certain number of years. Consider drug patents. In the United States, new drugs can be patented against competitive copy for a period of no longer than twenty years (although extensions are occasionally granted). The actual coverage of the drug on the market may be less than twenty years given that many drug patents are applied for before clinical trials even begin. Pfizer released its cholesterol-lowering pill LIPITOR®

to the public in 1997. With the aid of aggressive direct-to-consumer publicity, Pfizer was able to market the advantages of LIPITOR® over other market competitors and soon became the market leader. In the fall of 2011, the patent for LIPITOR® expired. Other companies were now free to market their own version of the drug – so-called "generics." In the absence of this legal barrier, generic drugs were offered for a considerably lower monthly cost to the patient. Indeed, many health insurance companies may require their patients to purchase generics when available. The steep loss of market share that a specific drug faces when a patent expires is often referred to as the "patent cliff." LIPITOR® may have never held a complete monopoly on the cholesterol-lowering market, but their market performance was greatly enhanced by the barrier to entry that their patent protection supplied.

Governments may also ban entry to markets by anointing a single supplier of a good or service in the marketplace. Many US towns have a single supplier of electricity. These publicly sanctioned utilities are either wholly private or public-private partnerships that have strong pricing power in their respective markets. Given that the costs of another firm entering the utility market are prohibitively high, the utility operating there essentially possesses monopoly pricing power. It is because of this pricing power that many utilities are regulated by a publicly controlled utility commission that reviews price increase requests by utility companies.

Negative Externalities

When individuals choose to purchase a good or service in a market setting, we assume that both the provider and the consumer do so freely and willingly. To this end, each party can improve their utility. If they can agree on the terms of exchange, one party can sell their good or service and the other can buy it, increasing utility for both. However, in some instances, a market transaction between two parties may affect a third party not involved in the transaction. If this third party is harmed or otherwise negatively affected by a transaction to which they are not a party, we refer to any costs borne by that party or parties as a **negative externality**. This cost is referred to as an externality precisely because the affected third party was not a party to, or was outside of, the transaction that produced the cost.

A standard example of a negative externality is pollution. Consider a transaction between a company that makes lawn fertilizer and a homeowner. The homeowner suffers from lawn envy and would like his or her lawn to be the greenest and healthiest lawn on the block. The lawn fertilizer company sells a product that promises to do exactly this. If this company and homeowner can meet on a price, this would likely be a productive exchange for both parties. A dilemma arises, however. Lawn fertilizers are high in nutrients like nitrogen and phosphorous and may contribute to ground water pollution in a watershed – pollution that the rest of society may have to spend resources on to reduce. In this instance, all citizens who do not purchase lawn fertilizer but do want clean drinking and surface waters may suffer costs (either in the form of pollution clean-up or health effects) for the otherwise private transaction between the homeowner and the lawn fertilizer company. This cost will show up either in the form of higher property taxes, local sales taxes, or higher state income taxes to pay for pollution control measures or, in extreme cases, higher health care costs.

The critical feature of a negative externality is that the organization(s) or individual(s) responsible for producing the externality do not bear the total cost of it. Rather, the parties externalize or **socialize** some portion of those costs to others who were not involved in the transaction. Accordingly, the price of the transaction does not reflect these total costs. In other words, the market price of lawn fertilizer may not reflect either the costs of the potential damage to health or welfare that pollution may cause or the costs of cleaning up that pollution. As a result, fertilizer producers have no incentive to reduce the pollution deriving from their transaction. Moreover, the lower prices of these goods mean that they will be relatively more attractive to consumers on the market. These lower prices encourage greater consumption of the good and an in-turn greater production of negative externalities. In economic terms, this suggests an **inefficient outcome**, meaning that too much of a certain good (in this case lawn fertilizer) will be produced or consumed relative to the overall costs and benefits to society. If, however, the total societal costs were included in the price of the transaction, producers would have incentive to lower the externality and consumers would purchase less of the good, lowering the overall costs to society.

Incomplete Information

Markets are better able to perform efficiently if a consumer is able to understand perfectly the differences in the quality of the good or service provided. The logic for this is fairly straightforward. If consumers falsely believe an objectively inferior good or service to be a superior one, they will over-consume this good relative to what their ideal preference would be. Similarly, if consumers have errors in their preferences over an objectively superior good or service, they are more likely to under-consume the good or service. This is inefficient given that in such an exchange the consumer is made worse off due to the exchange. In the presence of more information about the true quality of the product the consumer would have likely made a different choice that would have improved his or her utility. In such situations, we say that there exists an **information asymmetry** between the two parties to the exchange. One party has a great deal more information than the other about the quality characteristics of the good or service to be exchanged. As a result, there is likely to be an inefficient exchange. If the buyer is more poorly informed, demand for the good or service will be higher than it would be if the buyer were better informed about the product.

Box 3.1 Information Asymmetry and Medical Care

A classic case of information asymmetry between two parties to an exchange is medical care. Well-trained medical professionals are likely to possess more information on a given patient's current health status than the patient themselves. Moreover, most doctors have a financial incentive to provide additional medical services, given that their incomes are a direct function of the number of services and tests provided. This situation is fertile ground for the inefficient allocation of medical care. Doctors have incentive to prescribe more medical care than their patients may in fact require and the typical patient does not have adequate information to know how to evaluate this choice. The result is that too much of the service, medical care, is produced, compared to what would have been otherwise in the presence of symmetrical information.

Consider the standard example of the used car market. If you step onto a used car lot, you likely face a formidable incomplete information problem. Namely, the previous owners of the set of cars for sale have knowledge about their cars that they may be unwilling to share with the car lot owner. The previous owners know whether the car has been in an accident, whether they have driven mostly city miles or highway miles, whether they have had the car regularly serviced, etc. Moreover, the previous owners have no incentive to share any of this information with the car lot owners. Why? Because if they were to share this information it might lead to the car lot owner either offering much less for the car or, in the worst case, not even buying the car. Similarly, the car lot owner (even if he or she is aware of such negative information) has no incentive to share this information with you. In smaller towns, this problem is less daunting, since used car salesmen are known to the citizens in the town. As a result, citizens are likely to have formed beliefs about the reputation and reliability of a particular used car salesman based on prior interactions. So people may say, "That Bob is a decent guy, he's always willing to be honest about his cars." Whereas, you may also hear that, "Richard is a total @%&$, he sold me a lemon that broke down not even one month later." This information may offset some inefficiency. In larger cities, where anonymity is prevalent, reputation is more difficult to establish. There are, however, solutions to such information failures.

Both market and government solutions exist. One such market solution might be a third party selling information on automobiles. Private companies such as Consumer Reports® or Carfax® offer information to consumers, usually for a membership fee, that is designed to lower the informational barriers between consumers and either general classes of goods (all makes or models of cars) or individual cars (identified by their vehicle identification numbers). And as we will see below there are also government solutions to this market failure.

Transaction Costs

Markets perform efficiently in the absence of transaction costs that one or the other party to a transaction must pay. A **transaction cost** is a cost associated with the eventual provision of a good or service, but not directly related to the creation of the good or service. Examples of such transaction costs may include search and information costs, bargaining and decision costs, or policing and enforcement costs. **Search and information costs** include any expenditure in time or other resources dedicated to learning about some aspect of the transaction. These costs might reflect time lost researching a potential choice over the best automobile. **Bargaining costs** include all resources spent on negotiating an acceptable agreement with all parties involved and drawing up the relevant terms of the contract between the parties. Policing and enforcement costs include the resources that are spent ensuring that the parties to an agreement or transaction are adhering to the terms of the agreement. These costs would also include any resources spent on litigation or any other ex post attempts to enforce the contract.

Transaction costs are present in nearly every market exchange. What tends to vary is the nature and size of the costs that are present. To the extent that such transaction costs exist they may sufficiently encourage inefficient allocation of resources. For example, in the fall of 2013, as the US economy continued to recover from the Great Recession, the US unemployment rate was ~7.7 percent; roughly 8 million Americans were seeking employment and yet unable to secure a job. However, at this same time approximately 3 million jobs were available nationally and continued to go unfilled. Why? There are any number of possible reasons, including a mismatch between worker skills and job training, but one factor contributing to this pattern was the search and information costs that individuals and firms face. Consider that an unemployed worker in Michigan may never learn about a potential job for him or her in South Carolina, given search costs. Moreover, even if the worker learned of the job, he or she may be unable to pay the costs to move his or her family across the country to begin work. The end result of these transaction costs (search and moving in this case) is an inefficient outcome: a willing employer and a willing employee are unable to improve their positions due to transaction costs. Both market and government solutions, for example private headhunters and government work programs, are designed to address these costs, but such programs are not always present for every exchange or do not fully compensate for the transaction costs in all cases.

3.3 Government: Legitimate Coercion and Institutional Collective Action

Government is a societal institution that organizes the legitimate use of power over those that reside within a set of geographic borders. Put another way, government is the institution that legitimizes the use of coercion over the ruled. Governments can be democratic or autocratic. Democratic governments lead with the "consent of the governed" through the use of competitive elections. Autocratic governments, on the other hand, lead with the consent of a much smaller support coalition without the use of competitive elections (Bueno de Mesquita and Smith 2005). In either case, however, government is the only legitimate entity that has the power to coerce individuals to engage in an activity that they prefer not to do.

For example, a government can demand compulsory military service of its citizens, and many countries in fact do. Alternatively, governments can ban child labor and have done so. It is precisely this notion of coercion that predisposes many against having positive evaluations of government. Many citizens do not like the idea of their government coercing them to do something. Unlike other organizations, government is unique in this characteristic. If a religious organization attempts to coerce an individual, he or she may quit the group. If a business attempts to coerce an employee to accept a reduction in pay, he or she may quit his or her job. If the professor teaching this course attempts to coerce you into reading this book, you can elect to take another course. But if the government issues a ruling (i.e. passes a law or issues a court order) on a matter, you must obey that ruling or risk sanction, including fines, penalties, and even jail (you can opt to exit the country, but this is a high hurdle and in many cases you would still need to settle your penalties prior to exit).

With market institutions, decision-making is decentralized – individuals make choices. With government institutions, decision-making is centralized – leaders make choices on behalf of individuals. For this reason, in many instances citizens prefer market mechanisms over government to allocate scarce resources. But as we will see in this section, under certain circumstances market institutions cannot allocate resources efficiently. When these conditions are met, government action is often turned to as a potential corrective measure. In addition, government allows for institutional collective action. As we saw earlier, even when individuals may benefit from collective action individual incentives may prevent a set of individuals from securing a higher social outcome. Government institutions help to overcome the sorts of collective action and free rider problems that stymie individual pursuit of these outcomes.

Response to Market Failures

Government interventions in the economy are often oriented to correct a market failure that has created inefficiency, leading to a misallocation of a scarce resource. In essence, government interventions are attempts to address the market failures covered above: under- or inefficient provision of common or public goods, monopoly, information asymmetries, externalities, or transaction costs. Standard government responses to these market failures are for the government to directly provide a good or service, to provide tax subsidies to discourage or encourage behavior change, and to provide regulation to structure acceptable versus unacceptable behavior. In some instances, these government actions can remedy market failures; in others they can lead to another set of unforeseen consequences.

Provision of Goods and Services

One solution to the inefficient provision of goods and services by a market is for government to provide those goods and services directly. This decision is generally a function of the relative gains/losses in efficiency across these different institutions. For example, in the production of a smart phone, the profit motive is a necessary condition for an efficient allocation of resources in a market setting. Private firms have incentive to produce this good and sell it for a price, which will be determined by the relative levels of supply and demand in the market. It would be less efficient for government to enter the smart phone market given the relatively efficient allocation of these goods by the market. On the other hand, consider the elderly medical insurance market. Do private companies have incentive to operate a medical insurance company for the elderly? The elderly are fairly likely to require medical care and therefore will be very likely a net drain on a private company's revenue. In the absence of the ability to gain other customers, a private insurer's net costs are likely to outpace their net revenues, making it rather challenging to maintain a competitive firm. The end result would be the undersupply of firms offering coverage to elderly customers. Most would likely consider the wholesale underinsurance of elderly medical care a suboptimal societal outcome. One remedy to this situation is government provision of these services. In the United States, the Medicare program is an example of a government provision of a service: health insurance.

Medicare is a government health insurance program for seniors age 65 and over. The program is a "pay as you go" program, which means that current taxpayers pay for current retirees. This is quite different from how most citizens believe Medicare works. It is not, for example, as many citizens believe, a health account from which retirees draw as they need medical treatment. Rather, this program is funded through a payroll tax, or a tax that is assessed on current wage and salary earners' pay stubs. The next time you cash a pay-check look carefully at your pay stub. You will notice a line that says MC/EE. This line reflects the amount that has been deducted to pay for the Medicare program and amounts to 1.45 percent of your earned wage. With this deduction, you are paying for the medical insurance of the elderly currently relying upon the program. When you are older and need to rely upon Medicare, younger adults' payroll taxes will pay for your insurance. We discuss Medicare in more detail in Chapter 7.

Taxation Subsidy

Another tool of government is the tax subsidy. The **tax subsidy** can be either a direct or indirect payment from the government to an individual or business with the purpose of altering the behavior of that individual or business for some societal goal. Direct subsidies can be made in the form of direct financial assistance via grants-in-aid. For example, the next time you take advantage of your Pell Grant you are taking advantage of a government subsidy – taxpayers are allowing some portion of their state and federal tax dollars to subsidize your college education. Direct subsidies can also be made to businesses whose product or service the government would like to encourage. In the 1970s, under the Nixon administration, the federal government began to heavily expand a corn subsidy program to encourage the production of bountiful amounts of cheaper corn. The original idea stemmed from the goal of making affordable food more abundant. Cheaper corn would translate into cheaper feed for farm animals (cattle, cows, chickens, etc.), which would translate into cheaper meats for the American citizen. Over the past forty years, corn subsidies have reduced the cost of corn greatly such that it can now be found in nearly every food item in your local grocery store, whether as an indirect ingredient (as feed) or as a direct ingredient. Perhaps the most controversial recent application is the production of high fructose corn syrup (HFCS) as a cheaper sweetener derived from corn.

Indirect subsidies also exist in the form of tax breaks or deductions and insurance programs. Look at IRS form 1040. This is the standard form that individuals fill out to determine their income tax bill each year. There are two sections on this form, the Adjusted Gross Income and the Tax and Credits sections. The latter contain tax breaks for various individuals who qualify. For example, when you have graduated, if you make sufficiently little income, you may be able to deduct the interest that you pay each year on any outstanding student loans that you may have (line 33).

The impact of both direct and indirect government subsidies is to alter the price of a good or service in the marketplace to encourage its consumption. For example, the use of high fructose corn syrup has become controversial with obesity becoming an ever-important health issue in the United States and food with higher sugar content contributing to both diabetes and obesity. It is rather ironic that this government subsidy that was originally intended to benefit citizens by providing cheaper food may be contributing adversely to individuals' long-run health and economic costs. This example highlights one of the potential drawbacks of government interventions in the market place – **unintended consequences**. Unintended consequences include any set of changes that adversely affect policy outcomes resulting from a policy intervention that were not anticipated by the policy's advocates. In the two examples above, an unintended consequence could be the over-consumption of a good, or literally the policy version of "too much of a good thing." Almost all policies have unintended consequences.

Regulation

Regulation is another attempt by government to remedy an otherwise inefficient market outcome. **Government regulations** are rules of operation that either ban a particular good or service, or proscribe the manner in which goods or services will be provided. Regulations can be designed to remedy any number of market failures, including: monopoly, information asymmetries, and negative externalities. Regulations can be designed to prohibit monopoly formation or to facilitate break-up of a consolidated industry once it has formed. They can aim to reduce information asymmetries to encourage more efficient allocation of resources by empowering consumer choice. For example, the Food and Drug Administration requires nutritional labels on food products regarding calories and nutritional breakdowns, with an eye toward consumers making "more informed choices." Last, and probably the most familiar form of regulation, are those rules that are designed to address negative externalities in the market place. The Federal Register, which is the federal government's registry of all rules and regulations, contains hundreds of thousands of rules designed to remedy market externalities. These regulatory remedies may include everything from the health procedures on how to slaughter animals for human consumption, to environmental pollution control measures on how a coal-fired electricity plant must operate, to work place safety rules, to whether a certain species ought to be protected against further de-population.

Of course, the stated goal of these regulatory interventions is to remedy market failures. To gauge the success of a regulatory program, however, can be tricky. Let's consider the nutritional labels example. The Food and Drug Administration requires nutritional labels to be present on all packaged food in the United States. The goal of this regulation is for the consumer to make more informed choices. In the ideal, more informed choices ought to lower over-consumed harmful food products and increase under-consumed healthful food products. But how might we measure the benefits of this regulation? We would want to know not only how food-related purchasing behavior has changed as a result of the regulation, but also what impact it has had on healthful eating and eventual health outcomes. Quantifying these benefits, however, can be challenging, given the rather onerous data collection required to draw an inference about individual eating habits and health outcomes. While quantifying the benefits of this regulation is challenging, less so is quantifying the costs of the regulation. A business must spend a fixed amount of resources to alter these labels and to affix them on their packaging – a relatively easy quantity to estimate. This example highlights a standard difficulty with evaluating the pros and cons of regulations. While relatively easy to quantify the costs of enacting a regulation, it is relatively more challenging to quantify the precise benefits of a regulation. Regulations also often fall short of their stated goals.

Nutrition Facts

8 servings per container

Serving size   2/3 cup (55g)

Amount per 2/3 cup

Calories   230

% DV*

12%	**Total Fat** 8g
5%	Saturated Fat 1g
	Trans Fat 0g
0%	**Cholesterol** 0mg
7%	**Sodium** 160mg
12%	**Total Carbs** 37g
14%	Dietary Fiber 4g
	Sugars 1g
	Added Sugars 0g
	Protein 3g

10%	**Vitamin D** 2mcg
20%	**Calcium** 260mg
45%	**Iron** 8mg
5%	**Potassium** 235mg

* Footnote on Daily Values (DV) and calories reference to be inserted here.

Figure 3.8 Nutrition Facts

Government Limitations

Government interventions in the economy that aim to correct market failures may either be unable to successfully achieve their goals or may actually create a new set of inefficiencies that may rival the very market inefficiency that they were set up to address. When government introduces such inefficiencies, we refer to this as **government failure**. The difficult choice that societies face is not whether markets or governments create inefficiencies – they both can under certain circumstances. Rather, the difficult calculation is whether an inefficiency created by a government intervention is worse than the original market inefficiency that it was designed to address. Your general attitude on this relative calculation probably maps onto your underlying political ideology. Conservatives are more likely to believe that government interventions are not worth the inefficiencies that they may generate even if they resolve an aspect of a market failure, while liberals are more likely to accept some government-derived failure if it mitigates a market failure.

Social Choice and Majority Rule

Solutions to social dilemmas often arise from the give and take between individuals on the perceived proper balance between the individual and the community in society and competition between communities. Whether such communities exist in the form of neighborhoods, organizations, cities, states, countries, or the like, several questions arise when considering the role of the individual within these aggregations. In particular, a critical element of government is to determine: What is the general will of the community? And how can we determine what it is?

Politics consists of citizens debating their relative visions of how to make their country a better place. Clearly, what is meant by better is in the eye of the beholder. One person's policy solution is another's policy nightmare. But how might we take the great variety of individual preferences across any number of policy options and somehow translate them into an aggregate ranking over these various social states? A **social welfare function** provides precisely this information – it does in the aggregate what the individual utility function does at the level of the individual. A social welfare function translates individual preferences over a set of policy visions or social states into a social ordering. This process of determining a social welfare ordering from a set of individual orderings is studied under an umbrella of academic work called social choice theory.

One of the dilemmas in social choice theory is determining precisely who "the majority" is and what policies they prefer. This may seem to be a trivial problem upon first glance. You are likely thinking: well, just take a vote, count up the majority and you know the majority's preference. But determining what the majority prefers is a bit more challenging depending upon certain conditions.

Imagine that three legislators, Smith, Johnson, and Williams, must decide on a funding bill in front of their sub-committee. There are three priorities for the funding bill: Defense, Health Care, and Environmental. Each of the legislators has complete and transitive preferences over these three programs and which they would prefer to see prioritized by the administration. Figure 3.9 displays these preferences. So let's see if holding a majority vote would generate a "will of the majority." If you inspect the table, you will see that no two people (a majority) share the same first preference. Each has a different first preference from the other. What now? A common tactic would be to pair off each proposal against the other working through a round robin tournament. By simple majority rule we look to see which program wins with two legislators supporting it. If we start with Defense vs. Healthcare, Defense wins. Smith prefers Defense, Johnson prefers Healthcare, and between these two options, Williams prefers Defense. Now we have to pair off the winner, Defense, against the remaining program, Environment. When we examine the table, we see that in this pairing, Environment

Legislator

	Smith	Johnson	Williams
1st Preference	Defense	Health care	Environment
2nd Preference	Health care	Environment	Defense
3rd Preference	Environment	Defense	Health care

Figure 3.9 Ranked Funding Preferences by Legislator

wins. Smith's first preference is Defense, Williams' is Environment, and between these two programs, Johnson prefers Environment.

Now, we may be tempted to declare Environment the majority winner. But if this is a proper expression of the majority will, it ought to not matter how we decided to begin the pairing. Let's try this again, but this time let's begin with another program. If we start with Healthcare vs. Environment, we see that in this pairing, Healthcare wins. And then if we pair this winner against the last program, Defense, that Defense wins. What are we to make of this? With the *same* voters and the *same* rational preferences among these voters we managed to get a completely different answer to what the majority prefers by simply reordering the pairings. Depending upon how we pair off the alternatives, we can produce different majority preferences from this three-person electorate. A profound problem arises from this example. Note that we began the example with complete and transitive preferences for each of the individual legislators. Despite these individual-level rational preference orderings, we could not successfully translate these preferences into a stable, transitive group choice. Rather, the group choice here was cyclical, meaning that the group's preferences are not transitive, despite the individual legislators' preferences being so. This rather bizarre outcome is known as Condorcet's paradox.

Condorcet's paradox (named after eighteenth-century French mathematician Marquis de Condorcet) observed that under certain conditions group preferences might not be transitive despite each individual member of the group possessing transitive preferences. In the ideal situation, we would like to identify a policy that would defeat all other policies in pairwise majority contests, or what is known as a **Condorcet winner**. But, as we saw above, depending on the conditions, a Condorcet winner may not exist. What then? As we did above, we can impose order on this group choice if someone has the authority to organize the voting procedure. If we allow for an agenda setter to order the pairings, *as he or she sees fit*, we see that the group's preferences will not cycle. Of course, this is only because the agenda setter, by looking down the decision tree, has essentially picked which majority outcome will be the winner. So a rather disturbing outcome of Condorcet's paradox is that to avoid the cycling over various majorities we may need to appoint an agenda setter who has the power to select among competing majorities.

Number of Alternatives	Number of Voters					
	3	5	7	9	11	limit
3	0.056	0.069	0.075	0.078	0.080	0.088
4	0.111	0.139	0.150	0.156	0.160	0.176
5	0.160	0.200	0.215			0.251
6	0.202					0.315
limit	~1.0	~1.0	~1.0	~1.0	~1.0	~1.0

Figure 3.10 Probabilities of a Cyclical Majority

This is indeed a disturbing outcome about democratic choice. But perhaps it is not one that we are likely to face all that often. Indeed, it may be the case that in our construction of Figure 3.9 we artificially rigged the heterogeneous preferences of the voters simply to suit our needs in making this point. This is true – but it does not necessarily imply that cycling is a rare event. What conditions contribute to the propensity of cycling? As we saw above, it must be related to either the number of voters, or the number of alternatives, or both. William Riker, a political scientist and game theorist, examined this precise question (1982). He determined that the probability of a cyclical majority increases as we increase either the number of voters or the number of alternatives. To see this, Figure 3.10 reports the probabilities of a cyclical majority over both the number of voters and alternatives. As we see in the table, the probability of group cycling indeed increases in both the number of voters and the number of alternatives, but at different rates. The probability of cycling increases much faster in the number of alternatives. What does this tell us? It suggests that between these two conditions, the number of alternatives from which a group must choose is more likely to contribute to the failure of a group making a rational choice than the number of voters in the group. Indeed, with a nearly infinite number of voters and only three alternatives, the probability of not finding a Condorcet winner is 0.088, or roughly one chance out of eleven. This is quite different from what we see when we increase the number of alternatives. With a nearly infinite number of alternatives, and only three voters, we are essentially guaranteed to not find a Condorcet winner. The takeaway point seems to imply a trade-off. If we have a fairly large set of voters, for all practical purposes any community larger than a town, the way to avoid cyclical majorities is for someone, perhaps an agenda setter, to limit the number of alternatives presented to the voters. We simply cannot have both. If we attempt to pursue unrestricted alternatives in the setting of large social groups we cannot gurantee a rational translation of individual preferences into group preferences.

To be fair, such restrictions may be related to the specific voting procedure that we elected to use in the above examples. Could it be that our use of a round robin tournament generated this unsettling account of democratic voting? The work of a Nobel Prize winning economist, Kenneth Arrow, suggests otherwise.

In his seminal work, *Social Choice and Individual Values* (1951), Arrow considered whether any procedure that could simultaneously satisfy a few desirable conditions regarding group choice and still deliver a coherent translation of individually rank-ordered preferences into group preferences existed. Arrow laid out a few minimal fairness conditions that he argued ought to be preferable for any such procedure. In addition to individual preferences being complete and transitive, Arrow also added four fairness conditions:

1. Non-dictatorship: No single individual can determine the group's preference, without considering the preferences of the other group members.
2. Unanimity: If every member of the group prefers a single alternative to every other alternative, then the group's ordering of preferences must do so as well.
3. Independence of Irrelevant Alternatives: A group ranking between two alternatives must not be sensitive to an individual's re-ordering of other irrelevant alternatives.
4. Universal Admissibility: Any individual is allowed to adopt any rational preference ordering that they prefer.

These fairness conditions are likely uncontroversial. If you examine each carefully, you will see reasonable benefits of a preferable voting procedure equipped to deliver all of these conditions. These conditions are also not unnecessarily thick, but rather minimalist – they set a fairly low bar for a voting procedure. So what is the result of Arrow's investigation? He shows with a rigorous mathematical analysis that any rank-ordered voting procedure that intends to translate individuals' complete and transitive preferences into a complete and transitive group preference ordering *cannot simultaneously satisfy all of the fairness conditions above.*

This finding is quite shocking. It underlines a restriction in social choice that is unappealing and perhaps troubling. If we want fairness in our decision-making, we must trade off stability in outcomes. Alternatively, if we value stability, we must trade off fairness. We cannot have both. Essentially, if we want a voting procedure to translate individual preferences into reasonably coherent transitive group preferences, we must be willing to trade off at least one of the conditions above. Alternatively, if we want all of the conditions above, then we must be willing to trade off group transitivity, or well-behaved, stable group preferences. The critical feature to recognize about Arrow's theorem is that it underscores the importance of political arguments in highlighting which of these conditions may be more palatable for a society to violate. For some, violating fairness might be preferable, while for others violating stability may be more so. In any case, governments seeking to advance policies preferred by the majority will face these challenges regardless of form, type, or quality. If government is to be used to resolve the collection action challenges that individuals face, it will inevitably face other challenges along the way.

Market Distortions

Nearly all of the government interventions that are outlined above, including government provision, subsidies, and regulation, may in turn distort market exchanges beyond what is desired or expected. A **market distortion** is a situation where some incident has caused the market price to be either higher or lower than the price that would have been obtained in the presence of a perfectly competitive market (i.e. when demand meets supply in the presence of a "perfectly competitive market"). When a market is distorted with an artificially low price, a good or service will be over consumed beyond what would have been consumed without the distortion. So, if student grants-in-aid were available for all students regardless of academic achievement or effort, the price of a college education would be artificially lower than otherwise and would encourage over consumption of college education. Alternatively, when a market is distorted with an artificially high price, a good or service will be undersupplied compared to what would be supplied in the absence of the distortion. So a government regulation requiring a minimum wage may artificially raise the price for the lowest skilled labor in an economy, which will reallocate resources away from others who might have been employed and direct them toward those who are now making a higher (the legally mandated minimum wage) wage. The end result of a minimum wage regulation is increased earnings for those at the bottom of the income scale with the trade-off of some number of potentially employable workers remaining unemployed. As you might imagine, whether this trade-off is evaluated in a positive or negative light is a function of one's political ideology.

Principal–Agent

When government decides to regulate a sector of the market, it must do two things: hire a set of agents to actually carry out the regulation; and ensure that the agents act as the government wants them to act. On hiring a set of agents, we face many of the limitations of third-party enforcement that we discussed above. We have to contract with a third party, incentivize them to behave appropriately, and then raise revenue and dedicate payment for the monitoring and enforcement of the various players.

The first problem, contracting and incentives, taps into the fundamental problem of a principal–agent relationship. When a principal offers an agent a contract to perform some action on the principal's behalf, the principal faces two basic problems: adverse selection and moral hazard. Adverse selection refers to the principal's problem of not knowing whether he or she has hired the right person for the job. Moral hazard refers to the difficulty of how to properly incentivize the agent to perform dutifully after the contract has been offered. As we will see in later chapters, a principal will need to address both of these issues to reduce the agent's ability to shirk, or not perform their contracted duties as specified.

3.4 Markets and Government in Combination

Up to this point, we have considered markets and governments as mutually excludable solutions to social dilemmas. We have been operating with the rather unreasonable assumption that communities face a stark choice between either using a market or a government to resolve social dilemmas. But this is rarely the case. In reality, many communities have found efficient solutions to their problems by combining the strongest elements of marketing solutions with those of centralized or government institutions. Elinor Ostrom (1990) analyzes such cases by considering how communities manage common pool resources throughout the world.

Common pool resources (CPRs) are natural or human-made goods that are renewable or replenishable, but can be exhausted from overuse. Recall from earlier in the chapter that CPRs are goods whose consumption cannot be prevented or excluded (or for whom exclusion is costly to enforce), but whose consumption may eliminate others from enjoying the good. CPRs include resources such as forests, fisheries, aquifers, etc. Due to their good attributes, such resources are notoriously difficult to manage. Purely privatized market institutions have less incentive to invest in CPRs given the challenges that excludability can present in the form of free riding. Purely centralized government institutions are inefficient, as well, presenting challenges in the form of preference aggregation and enforcement. Accordingly, Ostrom set out to understand how communities throughout the world have successfully managed CPRs.

Over her career, Ostrom analyzed several communities throughout the world to better understand what types of institutional arrangements traditional and contemporary communities used to solve CPR management. Whether analyzing grazing land policy, ancient forests, or modern irrigation techniques, Ostrom found that communities were most effective in managing their CPRs when they were able to creatively design hybrid institutions that borrowed the best components from market institutions and combined them with some of the attractive components of centralized government institutions. In fact, after viewing the results of her research, Ostrom was able to present us with a set of principles to guide the efficient allocation of CPRs. These eight principles were:

1. Define clear group boundaries.
2. Link rules governing the provision of common goods to local conditions.
3. Those affected by the rules must be able to participate in modifying the rules.
4. Use an effective participatory monitoring system.
5. Sanction rule violators with graduated penalties.
6. Disputes ought to be resolved via low-cost accessible mechanisms.
7. Outside authorities must respect the rulemaking rights of community members.
8. For sufficiently large CPRs, nested organizational design is preferred, with small CPRs constituting the lowest level.

Each of the above principles has clear implications for encouraging property rights, facilitating cooperation, and sanctioning negative actions. In many respects, these eight principles reflect the fundamental insights underlying the tit-for-tat strategy. Be nice, don't be afraid to punish poor behavior, be forgiving, and learn from one's mistakes. It borrows critical features of market institutions, namely the value of property rights and properly incentivizing individuals. And yet, they recognize the critical role that government institutions play, the development and enforcement of rules of behavior.

Ostrom's research highlighted a potential third path for individuals to solve their cooperation and collective action dilemmas. She cautioned all of us to be careful of falling prey to dichotomized, black-and-white thinking between market and government solutions to public policy dilemmas. Despite our rather fundamental urge to see policy problems through a polarized lens, where individuals only perceive solutions that fit their predetermined political persuasions, Ostrom reminds us that compromise and institutional creativity may be a more productive step in solving some of the world's most stubborn policy problems.

3.5 Conclusion

In the previous chapter, we introduced several conditions under which the pursuit of self-interest is not sufficient to guarantee self-improvement. Such social dilemmas may be avoided with the implementation of certain institutions. In this chapter, we saw that institutions, like markets and governments, offer important solutions to many social dilemmas. They help to organize resources efficiently and incentivize behavior that may help to solve many social dilemmas. Such institutions, however, are not without their own challenges. Under certain conditions, both markets and governments can both suffer potential failures. When they do fail, these institutions may leave citizens worse off. Indeed, they may leave citizens worse off than they might have been prior to the institutions' installation. Last, we saw that markets and governments need not be mutually exclusive solutions to social dilemmas. Ostrom's research highlights the cooperative, piecemeal approach of hybrid institutional settings which utilize the best elements of each.

Key Terms in This Chapter

Normative criteria
Positive criteria
Pareto criteria
Pareto improvement
Pareto efficient
Pareto optimal
Kaldor-Hicks criterion
Kaldor-Hicks improvement

Compensation principle

Market

Determinant of supply

Change in quantity supplied

Change or shift in supply

Determinant of demand

Change in quantity demanded

Change or shift in demand

Market equilibrium price

Shortage of supply

Surplus of supply

Property rights

Rivalrousness

Rivalrous good

Non-rivalrous good

Excludability

Excludable good

Non-excludable good

Private Good

Common Good

Club Good

Public Good

Monopoly

Negative externality

Socialize

Inefficient outcome

Information asymmetry

Transaction cost

Search and information costs

Bargaining cost

Government

Tax subsidy

Unintended consequences

Government regulations

Government failure

Social welfare function

Condorcet's paradox

Condorcet winner

Market distortion

Common pool resources

CHAPTER EXERCISES

1. Imagine a proposal for a tax on candy and soda. What types of externalities are associated with junk food that the tax might be aimed at reducing? Who would like the idea of a junk food tax? Who might not?

2. Let's continue with the junk food tax. Identify a few normative criteria to evaluate such a policy. Now, identify a few positive criteria to evaluate this policy.

3. Using an example, explain the difference between a change in the quantity supplied vs. a change or shift in supply.

4. Give several examples of rivalrous and non-rivalrous goods not listed in this chapter. Next, give several examples of excludable and non-excludable goods not listed in this chapter. How do these examples fit into a 2×2 table such as the one in Figure 3.7?

5. Why do you sometimes choose to have food delivered to your house versus picking it up from the restaurant? It is likely that you unconsciously calculate transaction costs entailed in each of these choices. What are some of the transaction costs associated with each option? At what point are you willing to accept the transaction costs?

6. Three people, Gretchen, Chris, and Cole, would like to see a movie. There are four movies in the running. Gretchen prefers m_1 p m_2 p m_3 p m_4. Chris prefers m_2 p m_1 p m_4 p m_3. Cole prefers m_4 p m_3 p m_1 p m_2. What are the prospects that these three people will experience "cycling" over these outcomes? How can you determine this? How might these people avoid cycling?

REFERENCES

Arrow, Kenneth. 1951. *Social Choice and Individual Values*. New York: John Wiley & Sons.

Condorcet, Jean-Antoine-Nicolas de Caritat. 1994. *Foundations of Social Choice and Political Theory*. Northampton, MA: Edward Elgar Publishing, Inc.

De Mesquita, Bruce Bueno and Smith, Alastair. 2005. *The Logic of Political Survival*. Cambridge, MA: MIT Press.

Hobbes, Thomas. [1651] 1991. *Leviathan*, ed. Richard Tuck. New York: Cambridge University Press.

Madison, James. [1788] 1961. "The Structure of the Government Must Furnish the Proper Checks and Balances between the Different Departments" in Clinton Rossiter (ed.), *The Federalist Papers*. New York: Penguin Putnam.

Miller, Terry, Kim, Anthony, and Holmes, Kim. 2014. *Index of Economic Freedom*. Washington, DC: The Heritage Foundation and Dow and Jones & Company, www.heritage.org/index.

Montesquieu, Charles-Louis de Secondat. 1752. *The Spirit of Laws*, ed. Anne M. Cohler, Basia C. Miller, and Harold S. Stone. New York: Cambridge University Press.

Ostrom, Elinor. 1990. *Governing the Commons*. New York: Cambridge University Press.

Riker, William H. 1982. "The Two-Party System and Duverger's Law: An Essay on the History of Political Science." *American Political Science Review* 76(December): 753–766.

Smith, Adam. [1776] 2012. *The Wealth of Nations*. Hollywood, FL: Simon and Brown.

Weingast, Barry R. 1997. "The Political Foundations of Democracy and the Rule of the Law." *American Political Science Review* 91(2): 245–263.

4 Scientific Inquiry and Uncertainty

Outline

Questions

- How do policy analysts evaluate causal claims empirically?
- What are acceptable levels of uncertainty in scientific research?
- What is the difference between scientific uncertainty and ill-informed skepticism?
- How is ill-informed skepticism used as a political tactic to achieve policy goals?

Overview

- The counterfactual model of causal inference is a useful tool to understand causation.
- To isolate a causal effect between an input and a policy output, analysts must rule out other confounding factors.
- In experimental designs, random assignment of subjects to treatment and control helps rule out confounding factors.
- In observational studies, statistical control helps to rule out confounding factors.
- Scientific uncertainty derives from sampling error, measurement error, and random error.

- Scientists use probabilities to express their uncertainty about specific scientific claims.
- For a scientific claim to be considered valid, it must have less than a 5 percent chance of not being successfully replicated.
- Ill-informed skepticism is not scientifically rigorous and does not assign probabilities to assessments of doubt.
- Despite these weaknesses, ill-informed skepticism is a powerful political tool to advance or block policy initiatives.

Introduction

Science is an evidence-based endeavor. Only through rigorous empirical evaluations can scientific claims be pitted against one another to reveal which, if any, are valid. Public policy analysis is no different from other sciences. Academic models of the policy process, bureaucratic evaluations of new regulations, and legislative analysis of program evaluations all depend upon rigorous empirical evaluation to sort out legitimate from illegitimate empirical claims. The promotion of scientifically sound public policies faces several challenges, including demonstrating that the policy has the purported causal effect as well as persuading people to accept a policy when it goes against their self-interest or prior belief on the topic.

Consider child car seat policy in the United States. Many of you probably grew up in a time when car seats were mandatory for infants and toddlers. But this was not always the case. In the 1950s, 1960s, and well into the 1970s, car seats for children were not required. However, with each passing decade, scientific evidence began to accumulate revealing that infants, toddlers, and young children were being exposed to risk of injury due to not being restrained in their car. As the evidence mounted, pressure increased for politicians to enact laws to require car seats to be used. Politicians began to respond in the late 1970s. While the passage and strength of car seat laws varied by state, Tennessee was the first state to require parents to put infants and toddlers in car seats in 1979. Within ten years of Tennessee's action, all states had some form of child car seat legislation on the books.

Despite these laws, parents continue to resist using child seats and restraints. As a result, children are still found to be at risk. The Centers for Disease Control and Prevention estimates that car seat use can reduce the risk of death in a car accident by 71 percent for infants less than 1 year old and by 54 percent for toddlers between the age of 1 and 4 (Durbin 2011). The use of a booster seat for young children reduces the risk of serious injury by more than half (54 percent) compared to the use of the seatbelt alone (Arbogast *et al.* 2009). Despite these risks, parents are still resistant to this protective measure. Of the children who died in car accidents in 2011, nearly half (45 percent) of all 8 to 12 year olds were not buckled up, compared to 33 percent of toddlers and 25 percent of infants (National Highway Traffic Safety Administration 2013). In fact, a strong predictor of whether a child or infant is restrained in the car is whether the driver of the car uses seatbelts regularly.

Why, despite the overwhelming scientific evidence that restraining a child in an automobile could prevent his or her death or serious injury, do some parents resist? Parental resistance derives from a variety of concerns. A primary concern is cost. Some parents simply cannot afford baby seats and as a result go without them. Other concerns derive, perhaps counterintuitively, from a deep love and traditional familial concern for the infant. Family members from older generations tend to maintain the belief that they could better protect their children if they held them in their arms while in the car than if the children were placed into a car seat. Unfortunately, these parents are not well acquainted with the physical laws of momentum, which no amount of good intention can overcome in an accident. Others simply do not believe the scientific evidence, opting to base their beliefs on the ubiquitous but rather flawed logic of anecdotal evidence. This logic is usually accompanied with a statement closely resembling, "I wasn't put in a car seat when I was younger and I grew up just fine."

This anecdote about child car restraints underlines two particular challenges of public policy. First, how does one scientifically demonstrate evidence for a public policy claim? Science uses a rigorous method of testing and retesting over hundreds if not thousands of cases in order to understand general patterns of causality. It does not rely upon anecdote or unsystematic argument. When scientists are uncertain about the precise nature of their causal claims, they assign probabilities to express the exact level of this uncertainty. Second, given scientific evidence for a claim, how do you persuade the public of its validity? Unlike the scientific method, many citizens engage in what we will call **ill-informed adherence** or **ill-informed skepticism**, which reflects a non-systematic anecdotal assessment of evidence. These two forms of uncertainty, scientific uncertainty and ill-informed skepticism, occasionally exist in tension with each other.

In this chapter, we consider how policy scholars, practitioners, and analysts examine hypotheses empirically. We begin with a primer on causal inference in the counterfactual model of causal inference. We then discuss a sample of the most commonly used descriptive statistics and measures of association in policy analysis. Next, we discuss the origins of scientific uncertainty and how policy analysts assign specific probability estimates to their uncertainty. We end with a discussion of the differences between scientific uncertainty and what we term ill-informed skepticism, noting the potentially powerful political use of the latter to call into question the former.

4.1 Scientific Inquiry

It is difficult to understand the role of uncertainty in policy analysis without a brief review of the fundamentals of scientific inquiry. In Chapters 1 and 2, we covered academic and analytic models of common public policy problems. These models and theories put forward any number of causal relationships believed to link policy inputs and outputs. But theory is only one part of the scientific endeavor; the other part is empirical analysis. Scientific inquiry is perhaps best thought of as a method or a process of investigation in which the analyst develops a theory to produce empirically testable or falsifiable hypotheses and then tests these hypotheses with data. You probably were exposed to the scientific method as early as grade school, conducting simple experiments in science class. Whether conducting a backyard experiment, examining the effectiveness of a social program, or conducting research into the deepest mysteries of the universe, the scientific method at its core is universal. Scientific inquiry is concerned with accurately describing and/or explaining a natural or social phenomenon through empirical observation and hypothesis testing.

Policy analysis is concerned with drawing a conclusion about causal relationships between various inputs and policy outputs and outcomes. This process is referred to as **causal inference**. In this chapter, we will focus our primer on the scientific method as it pertains to empirical causal inference. Simply put, once you have your theory and hypotheses, how do you go about testing them? To be clear, entire books and college courses are devoted to the topic of causal inference (see Kellstedt and Whitten (2008) for a more thorough treatment of research design). In the following sections, we aim to provide students with a fundamental but brief overview of the counterfactual model of causal inference and the central concerns of scientifically estimating a causal effect (with uncertainty) in public policy analysis.

Counterfactual Model of Causal Inference

An easy way for us to try to understand the scientific investigation of causality is to consider the simple counterfactual model of causation (Morgan and Winship 2007). This is a model of causation with which you probably are very familiar given its abundance in elementary and high school science classes. The counterfactual causal model of inference is the basis of what is known as the classic experiment. In the classic experiment, we are interested in testing for the causal effect of some treatment, X, on some outcome, Y. In other words, if we expose a case or data point to our treatment, X, how will the outcome, Y, change relative to a case or data point that did not receive our treatment?

To give you a better sense of how this works, we are going to operate with a running example: texting while driving. Texting while driving has risen on the public policy agenda. The argument is that texting while driving is distracting and disorientating to a driver and heightens the propensity to lower driver performance and cause accidents. In fact, a recent study suggests that texting while driving poses similar risks to other causes of poor driver performance like alcohol consumption (Drews *et al.* 2009). How do policy analysts come to such conclusions? In order to examine this, let's consider the following.

If you have ever been in a car accident, you probably spent at least some time rerunning the events in your head. You likely tried to figure out what went wrong and how it could have been avoided; this is natural. Were you texting? Were you distracted? Did you turn around to get something from the back seat? Or were you lost in thought or expression as you listened to your favorite song? What you are doing when you engage in these thoughts is conducting a "thought experiment" of counterfactual analysis. You are attempting to compare the conditions of the factual outcome (the car accident) with the imagined conditions (the thought experiment) of the counterfactual outcome (the avoided car accident).

We conduct these types of counterfactual analyses all the time. Whether attempting to analyze why a relationship ended badly, or why someone did poorly on a test, or why someone did not get into their first college of choice, people are naturally given to running these types of thought experiments. The problem is that we can never *actually* run this experiment. We cannot turn back time and drive down that road again under a different set of conditions to see whether we can change the course of events. Fundamentally, the logic that we use in a thought experiment is the foundation of the counterfactual model of causal inference. Let's see how we could examine the relationship between texting while driving and driver performance in an actual experiment that takes advantage of the counterfactual model of causal inference.

Imagine that we want to study the causal effect of "texting while driving" on driving performance. We would now like to move from the context of a thought experiment to an actual controlled experiment using a real human subject. In this example, our relevant outcome variable, Y, is a subject's *driver performance*, on a controlled-environment driving course. The relevant treatment variable is "texting while driving." Ideally, we would have a subject drive through the course without texting and score his or her driving performance, noting any accidents or deviations from the course. In the ideal, we would then rerun the same subject through the course, but this time he or she would be required to answer texts that we send and we would re-score their driver performance. We would then compare the two driver performance scores and attribute any observed difference to a causal effect of the treatment variable "texting while driving." Of course, this is not ideal. It is possible that the subjects could have experienced a so-called "repetition effect." A **repetition effect** is any change in a subject's performance due to repeating the experimental condition. Repetition effects can interfere with valid causal inference. In our experiment, a repetition effect may be registered if our subjects were better driving through the course the second time around, since they were already familiar with some of the obstacles. If their driving improved in the second iteration of the course, the repetition effect might be strong enough to wash out any negative change in their driving due to the texting condition.

Ideally, we would like to be able to magically rerun the second experiment with the subject having no memory or knowledge of having run the first experiment. This is of course difficult to achieve in most experimental settings. When we apply this type of research design, what we are essentially attempting to do is to compare the **factual outcome** of how the subject performed without texting to the **counterfactual outcome** of how the subject *would have performed* while texting had they been exposed to the treatment. But, we are never able to know how a subject *would have behaved* in the counterfactual because they did not, in fact, receive the treatment. This problem is often referred to as the **fundamental problem of causal inference**. The fundamental problem of causal inference refers to the difficulty that we face in experimental situations where we cannot expose the same individual to both treatment and control *at the exact same moment in time*. But if this comparison is never possible, how then can we ever assess causality?

Luckily, the classic experiment allows us a way out of this difficulty. In the classic experiment, we assign participants in our experiment to two groups. One group is called the **treatment group** and the other group is called the **control group**. The treatment group consists of subjects who would drive the course while texting. The control group consists of subjects who would drive the course without texting. To assess whether texting while driving is causally related to driver performance, we would compare the average performance scores of the subjects in the control group to the average scores of the subjects in the treatment group. We could then attribute any difference in these average grades to texting while driving. So how does this classic experimental design solve the fundamental problem of causal inference? The answer is that rather than comparing an individual's factual exam performance with no texting with their theoretical counterfactual exam performance as if they had been texting, we compare the average scores of those who drove without texting with the scores of those who drove with texting. What we are unable to do at the individual level of the subject, we can do by aggregating across all of their scores. But there is a catch.

Minimum Conditions for Drawing Valid Inferences

Of course, in order to draw a valid causal inference with a classic experiment a few conditions must be met. First, *there can be no differences between the subjects in the treatment group and the control group that are also correlated with our potential outcome.* Imagine that we had selected our subjects for treatment by identifying which subjects enjoyed texting while they drive. If a subject enjoys texting while they drive, we assigned them to the treatment group. If the subject does not text while they drive, we assigned them to the control group. And then we ran the experiment. This non-random selection into treatment would very likely interfere with our ability to draw a valid causal inference and would generate a **selection effect**. Why? There are a variety of reasons why people may not enjoy texting while they drive. They may be impatient, wanting to know what their friends are doing at the moment. They may be risk-acceptant, willing to take chances with their and others' lives, or were simply down-playing the risks that texting while driving play. Subjects who prefer not to text while driving may be cautious, patient, and risk-averse. The critical issue here is that these same characteristics that are correlated with whether someone likes to text while driving or not (and are correlated with our assignment of subjects to treatment or control) are also very likely correlated with whether someone is a careful driver – someone who is likely to do better or worse on a driver performance course.

So, if we ran our experiment and found a difference in driving performance between the treatment group and the control group, could we be confident to attribute that difference to a texting while driving effect? It is doubtful. It is more likely that, instead, we might be measuring a "cautious driver effect" or a "patient driver effect" or a "risk-averse driver effect." If this were the case, then we very likely would have observed differences in driving performance between our two groups even if there had been no texting treatment. When we have a set of variables that are correlated with *both* our treatment and our potential outcome, so-called **confounding variables**, our experiment will be unable to reveal a valid causal effect.

The classic example used to illustrate a confounding variable is to imagine an empirically verified correlation between ice cream consumption and violent physical assaults throughout the year. Why might such a correlation exist? We could twist ourselves into theoretical knots attempting to come up with explanations for this correlation. Perhaps after raining blows down upon their victims, violent criminals seek to let off some steam with a soft-serve cone. This is silly, of course. A better explanation for this correlation may be that there is another variable that is correlated to both ice cream consumption and violent physical assaults throughout the year and is making it appear as if there is a causal relationship between our two original variables. When a relationship between two variables appears to exist, due to the confounding presence of a third variable, we refer to this as a **spurious relationship**. Can you think of what this third variable might be? Well, it turns out that both ice cream consumption and physical assaults are highest during the summer when it is hot. So, "summer months" or average monthly temperatures would be a confounding variable to our originally posited causal relationship. This example underscores the oft-uttered observation that correlation is not causation. The intention behind this admonition, of course, is that in the absence of sufficiently careful theoretical work that is able to explain how or why variables are causally related and empirical work to rule out confounders, we must be careful to attribute causation to correlations.

To reiterate, when we have a set of variables that are correlated with *both* our treatment and our potential outcome, our experiment cannot reveal a valid causal effect. This is a critical point to recall as we move through the various chapters in this text. So we emphasize the **minimum conditions** for drawing valid causal inferences here:

> *To estimate a valid causal inference with the classic experiment, we must ensure that all other variables that are correlated with both our treatment and our outcome are randomly distributed across the groups.*

To satisfy this condition, when assigning individuals to a treatment or control group, we must assign individuals randomly, so that we minimize any systematic differences between treatment and control groups with respect to our potential outcome variables. The difficulty with public policy analysis is that very often we cannot conduct a classic experiment. It may be that conducting an experiment is simply impractical. Given the policy issue in question, running a classic experiment may be challenging or impossible. If we were investigating the question of social programs aimed to alleviate poverty, it may be difficult to induce "poverty" experimentally among a set of subjects. Alternatively, it may be that conducting such an experiment is unethical. If we were interested in investigating the effects of air pollution on lung disease, it would be unethical for us to expose subjects in the treatment group to high levels of air pollution and then assess them at some later date for the presence of lung disease.

In situations where a classic experiment is not feasible, possible, or ethical, policy analysts can employ an **observational study**. In an observational study, the assignment of subjects to the treatment and control groups is not under the analyst's control. This makes it more difficult to draw a valid causal inference. So, instead of attempting to run a classic experiment to investigate the effects of pollution on lung disease, an analyst might gather data on individuals that have been exposed to varying levels of air pollution and then assess their level of lung disease. In this study, the health policy analyst did not assign subjects to receive lower or higher levels of air pollution. Rather, the analyst gathered data on air pollution and rates of lung disease in a number of communities. The analyst, then, attempts to draw a causal inference based on the variation, or differences, in air pollution and lung disease rates across the different communities.

Given that the assignment of cases to treatment is not under the analyst's control, it is particularly important for observational studies to rule out the presence of confounding variables. Unlike the classic experiment, the analyst cannot use randomization of assignment to minimize the presence of confounding variables. In observational studies, the analyst must account for any such potential confounding variables by including them or "controlling for" them in their statistical analysis. By "controlling for," we mean that the analyst uses a statistical technique to essentially match or balance the treatment and control group on the set of confounding variables. Let's consider an example to make this clear.

How might we conduct an observational study of the relationship between texting while driving and driving performance? Let's imagine that we had access to a cell phone carrier database of texting usage for all drivers and we had access to police records of driving citations. Nationally, these databases would contain millions of research subjects. The cell phone database would tell us the time stamp of exactly when a person was texting and the police records would tell us the time stamp of exactly when a driving citation occurred. If we had sufficient resources, we could conduct a statistical analysis to determine whether or not, in a given time window, someone was texting and if this behavior was correlated with their receiving a police citation. If we found a statistical difference between police citations for those drivers who were texting and those who were not, we may be tempted to conclude that there is a causal effect between texting while driving and driver performance.

However, recall that to draw a valid causal inference, we must ensure that all other variables that might be correlated with our treatment and our potential outcome are randomly distributed across the groups. Our proposed observational study assumed that any other factors that could be correlated with our treatment and our outcome were perfectly balanced between our two groups: those individuals who were texting while driving relative to the individuals that were not. This is a rather tenuous assumption. Can you think of a few reasons why this might be the case?

There are any number of other factors that could have been correlated with our treatment, texting while driving, and our potential outcome, police citation, that we did not control for in our analysis. As we noted above, cautious, patient, and risk-averse people may be less likely to text or to text and drive. For us to draw a valid causal inference between these two variables, we would have to gather additional data on any variables that we think are correlated to both texting while driving and receiving a police citation and include them in our statistical analysis.

Internal and External Validity

Different types of research designs have strengths and weaknesses in the validity of the causal inferences they are able to draw. There are two basic threats to the validity of a research design: internal and external. By **internal validity**, we mean the likelihood or level of confidence that a causal inference drawn from an analysis reflects the "true" underlying causal relationship. Threats to internal validity may derive from a variety of sources, including: biased samples, measurement error, and violations of the counterfactual causal inference model discussed above. For example, excluding a critical confounding variable from a research design or including a very poorly measured key concept could threaten a design's internal validity. Any inference drawn based on such a design would be suspect and criticized as such by other analysts or consumers. By **external validity**, we mean whether the findings from a study based upon a sample or an experiment can be extended or generalized to a larger population. Threats to external validity may derive from non-random sampling from a large population, which generates a non-representative sample. Or, it may derive from an experimental design, where the experiment-specific factors may have induced a unique response among the participants. Threats to external validity are the most common criticisms of classroom or laboratory experiments in the social sciences. Why? Given that college students may be systematically different from the average citizen on many features, critics may be skeptical whether the findings from an experiment about decision-making, for example, on forty college students can be validly extended to the population of all adults.[1]

4.2 Estimating Statistics of Interest

To test their expectations, policy analysts examine a variety of empirical quantities of interest. They are interested in quantifying descriptive statistics, measures of association, and statistics that test the likelihood of observing statistically significant relationships. These statistics go by many names, including: mean, standard deviation, Chi-squared, Pearson's correlation coefficient, regression parameters, and a host of others. As we mentioned above, scientific analysis of policy questions may use experiments or observational studies to estimate the association between two variables or causal effect of one variable on another. All of these statistics are in some sense a way of describing a population of interest or estimating how much one variable varies with another. In many respects, these parameters are what we are interested in learning in policy analysis; we would like to know how much one variable varies in response to another. While this is not a research design text, in the following sections we present an overview of the main statistics that you are likely to encounter in public policy.

Descriptive Statistics

Policy analysts often desire to learn critical information about various stakeholders and clientele. For example, education policy specialists may want to learn about the percentage of K-12 students who come from single-parent homes. Or, environmental policy specialists may need to know the attitudes of regulated firms toward command-and-control

---

[1] Campbell and Stanley (1966) provide the classic treatment of threats to validity in research.

regulation. Most recently, a scandal has erupted within the Veterans Affairs hospital in the servicing of veteran clientele. Members of Congress and administrators at the VA may desire to know how satisfied veterans are with their hospital service and how much these opinions vary within veteran groups. **Descriptive statistics** help describe both the average response and dispersion of opinion around the average for a given population of stakeholders or clientele.

Information about the **central tendency** and variation (or dispersion) of a population distribution is referred to as descriptive statistics. Descriptive statistics reveal information about the location of the middle and shape of the distribution. While there are several descriptive statistics that tell us about different components of a distribution, the two most common statistics that policy analysts use are the mean and standard deviation. Both of these quantities of interest are useful for policy analysis because they reveal not only where the "middle" of the distribution tends to be, but also whether many of the cases tend to cluster around this "middle" or whether they tend to be located further away from it.

The mean of the distribution is simply the arithmetic average of all case scores. The mean is designated by the simple equation $\sum x_i/N$, or the sum of x scores, indexed by the total number of cases, i, divided by the total number of cases, N. For example, if we wanted to know the average wait time of veterans at VA hospitals around the country, we would simply add up the wait time, x, that every veteran, i, has experienced at a hospital stay and divide by the total number of veterans, N. This statistic, the mean, is a useful metric to compare hospital wait time efficiencies across different hospitals, cities, or states.

The standard deviation of the distribution is the average squared distance between each case and the mean – it assesses the **variation** or **dispersion** of the data around the center of the distribution. The standard deviation is calculated by taking every individual case's score, subtracting it from the mean of the distribution, squaring each of these deviations, and then adding all of the squared deviations up and dividing by the total number of cases. But, what does this tell us about the distribution? The basic rule of thumb is that for any normal distribution, 68 percent of all of the cases will fall between plus or minus one standard deviation around the mean, 95 percent will fall between plus and minus two standard deviations around the mean. To give you a sense of what this statistic captures, let's imagine two scenarios.

Let's imagine that we have a feeling thermometer survey question on which respondents rate their opinions on a scale from 0 to 100 about their feelings toward the Veterans' Affairs hospital at which they have received service. We have these data for VA hospitals in two different states. In the first state, the sample, x_1, reveals that the average feeling thermometer score is an 80 and has a standard deviation of 5, while in the other state, the sample, x_2, reveals that patients had an average feeling thermometer score of 80 with a standard deviation of 20. What does the difference in standard deviations tell us about the differences between these two populations?

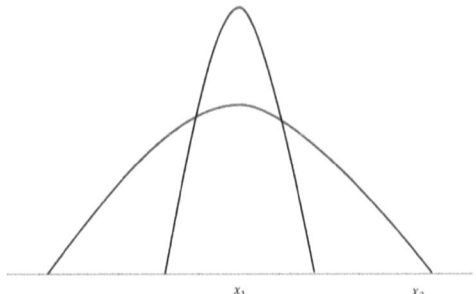

Figure 4.1 Central Tendency and Dispersion

These two distributions are displayed in Figure 4.1. The first thing we recognize is that both populations have the same average feeling thermometer reading, 80. This means that both sets of patients have similar mean evaluations of their Veterans Affairs hospitals and these evaluations are good, being further up on the thermometer and closer to 100. But what do the different standard deviations between these two samples tell us? The smaller the standard deviation, the tighter the distribution is around the mean. In other words, most of the people who responded to the survey or to use the rule of thumb that we talked about above, 68 percent of those veterans surveyed are between 75 and 85 in their evaluation of the hospital. On the other hand, for the second population, even though they have the same average feeling thermometer, there is more variance in people's evaluation of hospital care, with most people, 68 percent of the population, rating the hospital between 60 and 100. Therefore, despite having the same mean, the differences in the standard deviations suggest that hospital satisfaction in the second state is more variant or uneven than it is in the first state. The first state is consistently producing relatively high evaluations, while the second is less consistent. Standard deviations are useful because they tell us how consistent or inconsistent information from a distribution is.

When we are interested in a relatively small population, we can learn the descriptive statistics with great precision. For example, if we wanted to know the average satisfaction of the students in this class with your professor, we would simply ask each of you to fill out an evaluation and we could calculate the mean and standard deviation for this class. However, it is more typical that populations of interest in policy analysis are large enough that we cannot practically ask or survey every individual or case. In these situations, we must take samples in an attempt to learn about the population's mean and standard deviation. This process is called inferential statistics and we will discuss this more below.

Measures of Association

Descriptive statistics describe the shape of a given distribution. And this information can be very informative. But policy analysts are more often interested in describing how one variable co-varies or is associated with another variable. We may want to know whether the amount of money that we spend on air pollution control programs reduces the amount of air pollution, and if it does, by how much? Or, education researchers may want to know whether elementary school class size is associated with student performance, and if it is, what is the precise direction and size of this association? If we were to find that class size is negatively associated with student performance, then we would want to also know the magnitude of this effect. Do students in smaller classrooms have 5 percent, 10 percent, or larger improvements in class performance? To answer these types of questions, policy analysts make use of a class of statistics called measures of association. There are a great variety of statistics that measure the level of association between two variables. The two most common that you are likely to come across in public policy are correlation and regression analysis.

Correlation

Correlation tells us whether and how strongly two variables tend to co-vary. Correlation reveals whether two variables are positively associated, meaning that as one increases so does the other, whether they are negatively associated, meaning that as one increases the other decreases, or whether they are not associated or uncorrelated. The most common measure of correlation is the correlation coefficient. The correlation coefficient ranges between –1 and 1. At –1, the two variables are said to be perfectly negatively correlated and at +1 the two variables are said to be perfectly positively correlated. A correlation coefficient of zero suggests that the two variables have no association. An important limitation of a correlation parameter is that it does not reflect specific unit change in one variable in response to a unit change in another variable. Rather, a correlation parameter simply suggests a general strength of association.

Let's consider an example. One hypothesis from education policy is that a student's socioeconomic status is likely to be correlated to their academic performance. However, this correlation is thought to be reduced or mitigated in the presence of intensive small classroom instruction. Imagine reading a report that conducted correlation analysis between the SES scores of third grade students and their standardized test scores. Now assume that we gathered these data for two sets of students. The first set of students was randomly selected from classrooms of less than twenty students, while the second set of students was randomly selected from classrooms of more than thirty students. This analysis reported a correlation parameter of –0.70 between student SES scores and standardized test scores for the students in the larger class setting and a correlation parameter of –0.30 for the students in the smaller class setting. At least two pieces of information are conveyed by this report. First, the negative coordinate correlation parameters for both sets of students suggest that student SES varies negatively with student performance, suggesting that poorer students are more likely to also be students who perform less well on the standardized exam. Second, this correlation varies over the size of the classroom. In smaller classrooms the correlation drops from a strong –0.70 to a weak –0.30. In this respect correlation analysis has been useful in not only revealing a relationship between SES and student performance, but also a potential remedy for this association – smaller classroom size. The limitation of correlation analysis as a measure of association, however, is that it does not reveal the precise nature of the relationship between the two variables in question, or precisely how much a change in one variable induces a change in another. While we can talk about the relationship being "strong," "moderate," or "weak," we cannot know the precise nature of this relationship.

Regression

Regression analysis accomplishes exactly what correlation analysis does not. With regression, an analyst can determine the precise relationship between an input variable and an output variable of interest. Regression analysis is probably the most popular and ubiquitous measure of association that you will encounter in public policy analysis. Regression requires the analyst to write out a theoretically informed equation of the form, $Y = B_0 + B_1 x_1$, where Y is the outcome variable of interest and x_1 is the input variable of interest.[2] This equation should look familiar to you if you have had elementary geometry, algebra, or trigonometry – it is simply the equation of a straight line, which you likely learned in the form $Y = mx+b$. Recall that m was the slope of the line, or how rapidly y changes with changes in x, and b was the Y-intercept, or the value of Y when x equals zero. The regression equation is similar. B_0 is the Y-intercept or the value of Y when x is zero. And B_1 is the slope of the line, or how fast Y changes with changes in x. You may have heard this slope of the line referred to as the "rise over the run" in earlier classes – this refers to how rapidly y "rises" as we "run" over values of x. The slope of the line reveals how much our output variable is expected to change if we change our input variable by one unit.

Let's continue with our student performance example from above. If our education analysis reported the results of regression analysis between student exam performance (our y variables) and student SES (our x variable) of the following: $Y = 5 (x) + 50$, or Exam Performance $= 5 (SES) + 50$, what does this tell us? These results tell us that if we increase student SES by one unit, however measured, we will see an expected increase of ten units in our exam performance score, however measured. So, if our exam performance was measured on a scale of 0 to 100 and our SES scale was measured on a scale of 1 to 10, this would suggest that with each one unit increase in our SES scale we would expect to see the average student perform five points better on the exam. Take a minute to look at the equation above and prove this to yourself.

---

[2] Y may at times be referred to as the dependent or response variable, and x as the independent or stimulus variable.

We could also imagine a hypothetical situation where we want to compare students of different SES. Imagine one student with an SES score of 1 and another student with an SES score of 10. What difference, on average, would we expect between their two exam scores? To answer this, fill in their SES scores in the equation above and calculate the expected exam performance score for each student. For a student with an SES score of 1, we would expect, on average, students to have an exam performance of $5 \times 1 + 50$, or 55 percent. For a student with an SES score of 10, we would expect, on average, those students to have an average exam performance of $5 \times 10 + 50$, or 100 percent.

Note that with regression we are able to specify the precise relationship between our input and output variables. We can learn how student exam performance is driven by student SES. Rather than the vague relationship information conveyed by correlation analysis, regression analysis reveals exactly how many fewer points on an exam we might expect poor children to lose relative to wealthier ones. Policy analysts can then use this information to inform policy decisions on potential targeted interventions.

Much like the descriptive statistics discussed above, measures of association are also often used to draw inferences about populations larger than the set of data to which we had access. In other words, despite only having access to 1,000 students, an analyst would want to use the information learned from a correlation or regression analysis to draw conclusions about students in the larger population. Therefore, measures of association are in many ways our "best guess" as to the likely relationship that exists in the larger unobserved population. Whenever analysts attempt to draw inferences about populations using smaller samples, they are engaging in a process called statistical inference, which necessarily contains within it some uncertainty.

4.3 Estimating Scientific Uncertainty

Uncertainty is ubiquitous in every natural and social scientific endeavor. Whether public policy, economics, physics, biology, or engineering, scientific research continually negotiates sources of error that give rise to uncertainty in scientific claims. One of the hallmarks of scientific research, however, is the rigorous methodology to evaluate the certainty of claims and the ability to express, with precise probabilities, the level of certainty associated with a given claim.

Sources of Uncertainty

Scientific uncertainty is the process of estimating a precise expression of uncertainty in some claim that derives primarily from three sources of error: measurement error, random error, and sampling error. We discuss each of these below.

Measurement Error

Every method used to measure a concept in public policy is prone to measurement error. Whether measuring student performance, bureaucratic efficiency, or pollution, the choices we make in operationalizing these concepts with actual measurable variables are always prone to measurement error. Measurement error can have conceptual or empirical origins. Conceptual measurement error occurs when individuals cannot agree that a proposed measure accurately assesses the concept of interest. Empirical measurement error occurs when the instrument or device used to assess the underlying concept does so imperfectly. Let's consider an example from health policy. For many decades a person's BMI or body mass index has been proposed as a proxy for a person's overall physical health, by measuring the percentage of body fat as a proportion of a person's overall mass. This measure, however, is prone to both conceptual and empirical measurement error. Conceptually, critics disagree that a person's BMI accurately reflects sufficient information about their overall health. Empirically, critics suggest that assessing an individual's BMI is difficult to measure, because the instruments used to assess fat content vary over different parts of the body. Analysts try to minimize conceptual measurement error with careful attention to prior work and logical argumentation. Empirical measurement error can be minimized through careful execution and instrumentation. In the end, however, some amount of measurement error is likely to exist in most analyses.

Random Error

Another source of scientific uncertainty is random error. **Random error** describes the stochastic or random probability that some events are simply not perfectly predictable. In other words, random error is that component of a causal process that reflects a probabilistic rather than a deterministic relationship. For example, in the regression equation that we used above, we assumed that a deterministic relationship existed between SES and Exam Performance – this is a very unreasonable assumption. It is more reasonable to assume that while SES differences matter, there are other components of student exam performance that randomly vary between every student in the population. This element of randomness is central to probabilistic processes. We can express the probabilistic (or stochastic) relationships by adding an error term symbolized by the Greek letter, ε, to the end of an equation. When we do so, the regression equation above becomes $Y = B_0 + B_1 x_1 Y + \varepsilon$. In this probabilistic expression of our regression equation, ε reflects all of the possible random reasons why individual students may vary in their performance on the exam – this may include any number of factors, for example: a student forgot their glasses and couldn't see the board, a student was sick that day, a student stole the exam key but forgot to bring it to class, etc. The existence of random error in any analysis decreases our ability to be perfectly precise about our scientific claims. As a result, an analyst must endeavor to take reasonable steps to reduce random error when specifying an equation relating a policy input to an output.

Sampling Error

Another source of scientific uncertainty is sampling error. Sampling error refers to the inaccuracies that may occur when we attempt to use a sample to draw inferences about a larger population. As we will see below, when we draw a sample we aim for it to be a randomly drawn representative sample of the larger population. Occasionally, this assumption is not met and the sample drawn from the population is subject to random error. If we proceed in the face of sampling error, our descriptive statistics or measures of association may be biased and thus may lead us to draw incorrect inferences. Consider a famous example from political polling. In 1936, the *Literary Digest*, a now-defunct magazine, published the results of their presidential poll that had been completed about a week before the presidential election between Franklin D. Roosevelt, the incumbent Democrat, and Alf Landon, the Republican governor of Kansas and nominee. Their poll predicted a victory for Landon, who lost in a landslide, 523 Electoral College votes for Roosevelt to 8 for Landon. The magazine had mailed cards to more than 10,000,000 people and received over 2,000,000 responses. There were problems with their mailing list: included were people with telephones, people who subscribed to the *Literary Digest*, people who belonged to clubs, and people with cars. It was a biased list: the majority of voters did not subscribe to the magazine, did not belong to clubs, did not have cars, and did not have telephones. Therefore, the sample drawn was not a random sample and was not representative of the larger voting population. This sample was biased toward higher income, more Republican voters and resulted in the magazine's ultimate failure. George Gallup predicted the 1936 outcome correctly with a much smaller but demographically representative sample and established the utility of drawing random samples. Researchers can estimate public opinion within 3 percent error in either direction with about 1,100 respondents. To minimize sampling error, scientists endeavor to draw randomly representative samples from the population of interest.

Inferential Statistics

Whether assessing descriptive statistics or using measures of association to attribute causality, analysts often use samples to learn something or draw inferences about larger populations. By **population**, we mean the entire set of individuals or cases with which an analyst is interested in examining or learning about. By a **sample**, we mean a subset of the population. Statistical inference is the process of using the characteristics of a randomly drawn representative sample to learn something about the

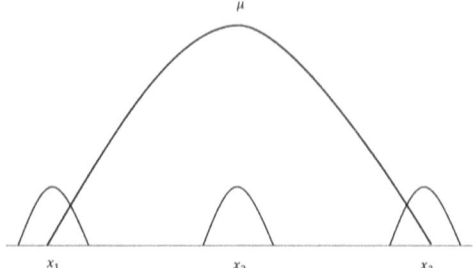

Figure 4.2 Inferential Statistics and Sampling Bias

characteristics of a larger population. Characteristics of a population are referred to as **parameters**, while the corresponding characteristics from a sample are referred to as **statistics**. Statistics that do not reflect the true value of a population parameter due to error are said to be **biased** statistics.

Consider Figure 4.2. This figure shows the population of all US citizens by income in blue. The population parameter, μ, the average income of all US citizens, is $32,000. But of course, as analysts, we have no way of knowing this – it is impossible to know what every American earns. Accordingly, we have to rely upon a sample of Americans to infer the population parameter. Imagine that we wanted to know the average income and standard deviation of American citizens. One approach to getting this information would be to survey a smaller subset or sample of this entire population. Also displayed in the figure are three different potential samples that we could have drawn from the population. One sample, x_2, has a mean of $32,500 and most closely reflects the "true" parameter or mean of the population. The sample on the far left, x_1, reflects a downwardly biased sample, with a mean of $20,000. Last, the sample on the far right, x_3, has a mean of $54,000 and reflects an upwardly biased sample. If we were to use the results from either the downwardly or upwardly biased samples, we would incorrectly infer that the average citizen in the United States is either substantially more poor or more wealthy, respectively, than they actually are. Only the middle sample reflects the "true" population mean about which we are trying to learn. The question for analysts is how to guarantee an accurate representation of the population when one draws a sample? Luckily for us, nature has provided us with a nice solution.

The "Magic" of Statistical Inference

Biased samples like the two that we drew in the income example above are always possible. Luckily for us, if we follow a few simple procedures, it turns out that severely biased samples are always possible, but not that probable. We must select cases at random to minimize the number of biased samples drawn. If we violate this randomization rule, we are likely to produce a biased sample.

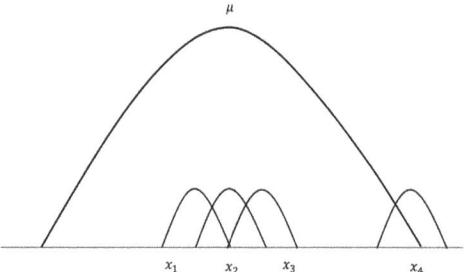

Figure 4.3 Inferential Statistics

Imagine that we took an infinite number of *random* samples from a population. Four of the samples are represented in Figure 4.3. Notice how the means from samples x1, x2, and x3 are all fairly close to the population mean, μ. Only one of our samples, x4, is far away from the population mean. Now imagine that we continued to draw an infinite number of samples. As we continued adding more samples to the figure, we would see more and more samples falling near or under the population mean, μ, with very few falling far away from μ. If we took the average of this infinite number of samples, the sample of samples or *sampling distribution*, we would see that the average of all of the samples would be a true or unbiased estimate of our population parameter, μ.[3] In other words, if we took enough samples and simply calculated the average of the samples, we would have a pretty good estimate of the unknown population parameter, μ.

In reality, it is expensive to draw one sample, let alone an infinite number of them. But, as it turns out, probability and statistical theory tell us that, on average, a great majority of the samples that we draw from the population are likely to fall very near the true population parameter, *provided that the samples are randomly drawn from the larger population*. In fact, 68 percent of any drawn sample will be within one standard deviation of the population mean. And, 95 percent of any drawn sample will be within approximately two standard deviations of the population mean. This is great news! This suggests that as long as we can assure that our sample is drawn randomly we have a very good probability of producing a sample mean that is very similar to the population mean. This reveals how it is possible to learn something about 100 million Americans by only surveying 1,000 of them (this is what George Gallup learned in the 1936 presidential election). As long as we draw our survey of 1,000 randomly from the larger population, our sample statistics ought to be unbiased estimates of the population parameters. If you want to know the precise mathematics and statistics behind this finding, you will need to take a course in research methods or statistics. This finding is the keystone of modern probability and inferential statistics, as well as

---

[3] The standard deviation of the sampling distribution is equivalent to the standard deviation of the population divided by the square root of n, where n is the number of cases in each sample drawn.

survey research. It allows anyone seeking to learn about large populations to do so with only a reasonably small sample. But estimates of population parameters from a sample are not perfectly precise.

Estimating Uncertainty with Probability

When we draw a sample and use it to make an inference about a population parameter, the statistic that we learn from the sample, whether it is a mean, standard deviation or some measure of association, is our best guess for what those quantities of information are for the entire population; we refer to such best guesses as point estimates. "Point" here refers to the fact that our best guess is represented by a single number. Yet, as we saw above we know that there are a variety of sources of uncertainty that are likely to exist when making any of the so-called best guesses. A trade-off that we make when we use samples from a population is that our estimates about the population parameter that we are interested in are not 100 percent precise. Our estimates of these causal effects are subject to uncertainty.

Scientists reference uncertainty by making use of probabilities. We can express the level of certainty or uncertainty that we have in making a scientific claim by attaching a probability to our statement. Recall that a probability ranges between zero and one. If an event has a probability of zero, then we are perfectly confident that the event will not occur. If an event has a probability of one, then we are perfectly confident that the event will occur. At the midpoint, p=0.5, an event has a 50–50 chance of occurrence; think of a flip of a coin.

Box 4.1 Probability as an expression of scientific uncertainty

Scientists view most events as having an underlying probability distribution. A probability distribution can be thought of as reflecting the likelihood of observing a particular outcome over a range of a random variable, X. In the distribution below the most likely outcome is centered on the distribution's mean, u. As we move in either direction away from the mean, the likelihood of that outcome becomes less and less probable. The least likely outcomes are represented by the distribution's "tails." You may often hear someone refer to someone or some case as being in the "tail of the distribution." What they are attempting to convey is that the case is a rare outlier, existing either far above or far below the meaning of the distribution. Using probabilities, policy analysts can represent the precise uncertainty associated with any of their claims.

In scientific inquiry, it is common practice when reporting a point estimate of a causal effect to also report how confident we are in this estimate. To do this we build a statistical confidence interval around our point estimate. This confidence interval recognizes that given the variety of sources of uncertainty in our scientific investigation, the actual value of the parameter may vary from the precise point estimate that we have produced. You are probably most familiar with a confidence interval from reports of surveys or public polling, as we mentioned in the discussion of the 1936 election. For example, a poll of 1,000 adults may report that the president has a 45 percent approval rating (+ or −3 percent) – this is an example of a statistical confidence interval. But what precisely is this confidence interval telling us? To answer this, we must first talk about statistical thresholds.

In nearly all avenues of science, researchers need to agree on what level of uncertainty they are willing to live with before they regard a strict scientific claim to be valid. The level that has been agreed upon purely by convention to denote a scientifically valid finding is a 95 percent threshold. This threshold is usually denoted with the notation, $p<0.05$. What does this mean? A popular, although slightly incorrect, interpretation of the 95 percent threshold is that we are confident with 95 percent certainty that a scientific claim is valid, leaving a 5 percent chance that the claim is invalid. A more accurate representation of the 95 percent threshold is that if we repeated an experiment an infinite number of times, the point estimate of the causal effect from our experiment would fall within our confidence interval 95 percent of the time – 5 percent of the time it would fall outside of our interval.

When we see a poll of 1,000 adults report that the president has a 45 percent approval rating (+or −3 percent), this means that if we sampled 1000 US adults over and over again, for an infinite number of times, then we would expect 95 percent of our sample means to be between 42 and 48 percent. How might our confidence change if we increased the size of our sample each time? Increasing the size of our sample will increase our confidence about guessing where the population parameter lies. So if we increase each sample to 3,000 adults, our margin of error may fall to 45 percent (+ or −2 percent), giving us a new confidence interval of 43 to 47 percent. Notice how our interval tightened up. We have a better guess with more individuals in our sample; however, we had to triple our sample size to reap this gain. This relationship flattens out over larger and larger samples. So while we do gain precision with a larger sample, we must use a very large sample for extremely precise estimates. To produce a confidence interval of 45 percent (+ or −0.01 percent), or a confidence interval of 44.99 to 45.01 percent, may require a sample of tens of thousands of individuals. Why then do most surveys you see report margins of error around + or −3 percent? Surveys are expensive. This margin is simply deemed reasonably precise and acceptable for the amount of resources that a polling firm must expend to put the survey in the field. Policy consumers, policymakers, and policy analysts should be cautious in consuming survey results.

Hypothesis Testing

Scientific uncertainty and probabilities also play an important role in how scientists test hypotheses. It is best to think of **hypothesis testing** as a process in which scientists attempt to determine whether sufficient evidence for the research hypothesis has been presented to reject the null hypothesis.

Standard Hypotheses for Descriptive Statistics

There are three standard hypotheses pertaining to most descriptive statistics. Most frequently, we want to know whether or not the mean of a given sample, μ_o, is greater than the population mean, μ, less than the population mean, or statistically different from the population mean. Each of these three research hypotheses can be represented with standard notation: $H_1: \mu_o \neq \mu$, $H_1: \mu_o > \mu$, and $H_1: \mu_o < \mu$. The null hypotheses for each of these research hypotheses is that $H_o: \mu_o = \mu$, $H_o: \mu_o \leq \mu$, $\alpha\nu\delta$ $H_o: \mu_o \geq \mu$, respectively.

Standard Hypotheses for Measures of Association

There are three standard hypotheses pertaining to most measures of association. Most frequently we want to know whether or not a measure of association is different from zero, greater than zero, or less than zero. This suggests three standard research hypotheses: $H_1: x \neq 0$, $H_1: x > 0$, and $H_1: x < 0$. The null hypotheses for each of these research hypotheses is that $x = 0$, or that the measure of association is no different from zero, that x is less than or equal to zero, or that x is greater than or equal to zero, respectively.

In both of these cases, the analyst is attempting to discover whether there is sufficient evidence to reject the null hypothesis. This means that we are perfectly content to have the null hypothesis be the best available scientific information until and unless we can produce sufficient evidence to suggest that it is likely not valid. Recall Karl Popper's falsification thesis. Scientists attempt to determine whether sufficient evidence has been presented to falsify or refute a null hypothesis. The tricky question is how much evidence is required to refute a null? This is where we make use of our 95 percent threshold.

Box 4.2 Substantively Interesting vs. Statistically Significant

Intelligent consumers of scientific information must be aware of the fact that substantive importance of estimated treatment or causal effects is a different concept from whether such effects are statistically significant. If an effect is not statistically significant, then we can conclude that we have no evidence of a

Box 4.2 (*cont.*)

substantively interesting effect. However, if a treatment effect is statistically significant, two possibilities may hold. First, we may have a statistically significant effect that is substantively interesting. For instance, texting while driving may be found to have a statistically significant effect on increasing the likelihood of an accident by 400 percent. This is a substantively interesting finding. On the other hand, we may have a statistically significant effect that is substantively uninteresting. For instance, texting while driving may be found to have a statistically significant effect on increasing the likelihood of an accident by 0.01 percent. In the second case, even though the effect is statistically different from zero, it is not exactly an effect that is likely to provoke public outrage. Whenever you read research in the media you should always ask yourself, "What is the size of the effect?" Manipulating a statistical finding for the benefit of advancing a political agenda is a very powerful political tool.

We can also think of the confidence interval we are willing to accept as a tolerance for risk in policy settings. If, for example, we learn that a fairly inexpensive teaching technique yields positive results for at-risk students, but we are only confident at the 90 versus 95 percent threshold, we may be willing to take a risk. If a person is told that she can be confident at 80 percent that she will win double her money if she bets ten dollars, there is a good chance she will take the bet. But if someone learns that a group that wishes to transport hazardous waste through their neighborhood is confident at 99 percent that nothing will go wrong, they will not be likely to accept that risk.

Why 95 Percent?

So why choose 95 percent? There is nothing magical about the 95 percent threshold. It is simply a convention that has been agreed to by the scientific community. In fact, as you will see throughout this text and in applied research articles, scientific authors are often encouraged to report the precise p-values for their statistics of interest so that the audience can be better informed of their statistical precision. But why not choose a lower number? Why not choose 80 percent, or why not make it really easy on ourselves and choose 50 percent? Well, these numbers may be too low for an acceptable scientific standard. Using a standard of 50 percent would be essentially like saying, "I am as certain about my scientific claim as I am in the outcome of a coin flip." With an extremely low scientific threshold, we would be likely to reject *true* null hypotheses. When one rejects a true null hypothesis, then we say that an analyst has committed a particular type of hypothesis testing error. This type of an error is referred to as a **Type I error**, an error of the first kind, or a **false positive**, and is represented by the Greek symbol, α. As we noted above, the scientific standard for certainty is 95 percent and this means that we have set a scientific standard of a Type I error at $\alpha=0.05$, or 5 percent. So, if we accepted scientific uncertainty of 50 percent, we would have an $\alpha=0.50$ and we would be very likely to find many claims to be scientifically valid, despite the fact that we would very likely be *incorrect* to do so.

Ok, so why not choose 100 percent for our threshold? This would mean that we would have to be perfectly certain about our claims. Simply put, 100 percent confidence is a threshold that is essentially unachievable in most scientific research. If such a threshold were to be required to declare a scientific finding valid, science would never make any progress. Essentially, with an extremely high scientific threshold, we would be unlikely to reject null hypotheses even when we should have. When one fails to reject a false null hypothesis, then we say that an analyst has committed a different type of an error. This type of an error is referred to as a **Type II error**, or an error of the second kind, or a **false negative**.[4] Essentially, with too high a threshold, we have now made the standard of scientific inquiry too difficult. We would likely bypass important scientific findings because our threshold requires 100 percent certainty.

Box 4.3 Thought Questions: Choosing between Different Statistical Errors

Consider a few additional instances where different types of hypothesis testing errors may impact social policy. For each of the following, which type of error is more important to minimize, Type I or Type II?

- HIV tests
- Death Penalty cases
- Special Needs/Gifted Assessments
- FDA drug testing
- Safe Air/Water Pollution Levels
- Mammogram Testing

Let's consider an example. Many social processes can be viewed through the lens of scientific hypothesis testing and the trade-offs between different types of errors. For example, imagine you were designing a pregnancy test. Would it be more important to minimize having a Type I or Type II error? In the case of pregnancy, a Type I error or

---

[4] While in this extreme case, a Type II error is linked to our α threshold, Type II errors have links to other research design features that also affect their precise level. Therefore, we can have varying probabilities of Type II errors even when we keep our α threshold fixed.

a false positive would mean that a potential mother would think she is pregnant when she actually was not. A Type II error would mean a potential mother would think she is not pregnant when she actually was. While there would likely be some psychological disappointment associated with a Type I error (false positive), for a variety of reasons, a Type II error with pregnancy is probably more concerning, given that the actually expectant mother would not be able to avoid cigarettes and alcohol and would likely not be paying close attention to prenatal nutrition, vitamins, etc.

The Non-Uniqueness of Scientific Uncertainty

Scientific uncertainty is not an artifact of public policy. Common wisdom seems to imply that there is nothing scientific about politics or public policy, and that politics cannot be studied scientifically. Such statements seem to be based upon at least two beliefs about politics or public policy. First, there is a belief that unlike chemistry or physics, public policy does not entail general propositions that characterize phenomena. Yet, public policy research is riddled with generalizable propositions about how policies develop, are implemented, and affect communities at which they are targeted. Second, there is a belief that public policy, given its relation to human interaction and politics, is simply too complex to submit to scientific inquiry. While it is certainly true that a fair portion of the scientific uncertainty inherent in policy analysis derives from the complexity of the policy process and the challenges inherent in predicting human social interaction, it is also not the case that scientific uncertainty is unique to politics.

Some of you taking this course may be majoring in another discipline. Indeed, many of you may be studying other fields of intellectual inquiry referred to as the "hard" sciences. Yet, even in those disciplines, scientific uncertainty abounds. If this were not the case, we ought not to expect to find scientific uncertainty featuring prominently in other research disciplines – and yet we do. Here are just a few examples of scientific uncertainty from other fields.

Medical Uncertainty

Medical research is often based upon small-N experiments, or experiments consisting of a small number of subjects. These experiments have a variety of sources of uncertainty, including confounding factors and measurement error. As a result, medical researchers report estimates of scientific uncertainty along with their results. For example, in the care of cancer patients, it is common to see probability estimates of survival rates at five-year intervals. These estimates contain scientific uncertainty. The survival rate for a particular type of cancer at a five-year interval may be 85 percent plus or minus 5 percent. Such an estimate reflects the inherent uncertainty in medical research.

Physics

Both in thermodynamics and in quantum mechanics, a variety of phenomena are best described by probabilistic rather than deterministic equations. In fact, a rather famous example of this uncertainty in quantum mechanics is the Heisenberg uncertainty principle, which, among other predictions, suggests that precise knowledge of one piece of information about an elementary particle may come at the expense of knowledge about another piece. If we know with certainty the momentum of an elementary particle, we cannot know much information about the location of that elementary particle.

Biology

In biological assessments and toxicity reports, we are often interested in the human response to exposure to toxic chemicals. Of course, this process is stochastic and riddled with uncertainty – it is difficult to predict the precise conditions under which each person will respond to a particular exposure of a particular toxin. So-called dose response assessments often contain expressions of scientific uncertainty, where the scientist expresses the likelihood or probability that a cancer will form given a particular exposure to a particular dose of a toxin.

Engineering

Scientific uncertainty can also be found in areas of civil and mechanical engineering. In the construction of skyscrapers, bridges, elevators, etc. engineers must take into consideration the accumulation of measurement error and material stresses that lead to estimates of tolerance or failure factors. The next time you get in an elevator look for somewhere on the control panel for an indication of the maximum number of persons (or weight) allowed on the elevator. This estimate of 3,000 pounds, or 10 people, is a parameter estimate that has a tolerance and a scientific uncertainty associated with it.

In many ways, preconceived notions that individuals bring to the study of public policy are based on the specific policy issue in question rather than the method used to study the question. Yet, as we stated earlier in this chapter, science is perhaps best characterized as a method or a means toward an end, not in the end itself. Scientific knowledge is nearly always in flux, improving, changing, being challenged and refuted. It is the method by which these improvements, changes, and challenges occur that uniquely situate science as a productive pursuit of knowledge. In many ways, the distinction between the old dichotomy of the "hard" and "soft" sciences is a remnant of a pre-scientific social science era, where the social sciences were more characterized by philosophical debates and normative arguments than they were scientific investigation. However, in the modern era, the social sciences apply many of the same rigorous standards of scientific investigation, laws of probability theory, and statistical models that any of the fields discussed above apply.

4.4 Statistical Uncertainty vs. Ill-Informed Skepticism

The basis of scientific advancement is for scientists to be skeptical or suspicious of their fellow scientists' findings. Only through rigorous criticism followed by unencumbered empirical testing and re-testing can we adjudicate competing claims with evidence. Scientists live in a probabilistic world. Recognizing this, they express their uncertainty in terms of likelihoods and propensities, assigning specific probabilities to reflect their level of uncertainty.

Ill-Informed Skepticism/Adherence

A conceptually distinct but closely related concept to scientific uncertainty is what we will refer to as ill-informed skepticism. Ill-informed skepticism is disbelief or distrust in a scientific claim that is based less upon rigorous evaluations of competing arguments and evidence and more upon political orientation or vested interest. We introduce this concept to distinguish between the rigorous scientific method that despite its rigor retains some small amount of uncertainty from the ill-informed disbelief that an observer may develop solely from personal convenience or their political orientation. The distinction here is slight but important and revolves around the intention of the critic. Rather than reflecting a sincere intention to advance scientific knowledge through rigorous criticism, ill-informed skepticism may reflect a detractor's strategic intention to question and even obscure scientific knowledge for personal or political purposes or may simply grow out of a low information environment.

In recent political discourse, particularly in the United States, scientific uncertainty and ill-informed skepticism have morphed into near synonyms. But as we will see in this section, this is a rather troublesome development. Why? Because it suggests that the basic standards of scientific uncertainty are similar to the standards of political doubt. Moreover, it provides an impression that skepticism regardless of its methodological rigor or expression of precise uncertainty is similar in all respects to scientific uncertainty.

The antonym of ill-informed skepticism is ill-informed adherence, or the adoption of, or belief in, a claim is based less upon rigorous evaluations of competing arguments and evidence and more upon political orientation or vested interest. Ill-informed adherents are those citizens who have adopted beliefs about public policy claims with little to no rigorous examination of the logic, theory, or evidence in support of their beliefs. Taken together, then, we can imagine how scientific certainty and uncertainty interacts with ill-informed skepticism and adherence. If we cross these two dimensions, they combine to present four particular combinations regarding the orientation of scientific uncertainty toward a claim versus ill-informed skepticism or adherence.

Scientific Certainty/Ill-Informed Adherence

This combination is the least politically interesting. It reflects uncontested beliefs between the scientific community and ill-informed observers. In this scenario, scientists are fairly confident about claims and ill-informed observers adhere to them as well. Modern physicists as well as ill-informed observers are confident in their theories of gravitation, as it applies in the macroscopic world. As a result, we rarely come across ill-informed observers expressing skepticism of gravity as they jump from the twentieth floor of a building. The critical point here is that the ill-informed observer, even though they may not understand the science behind gravity, ill-informedly adheres to the claim and the implications of the claim, nonetheless.

Scientific Uncertainty/Ill-Informed Adherence

Another combination is a situation where scientific knowledge is either newly developed or undeveloped and as a result has high uncertainty regarding its claims and, yet, ill-informed observers adhere to their own beliefs about the claim. A contemporary example of this could be individual beliefs about the benefits of certain natural extracts and supplements. Many of the natural supplements that are sold at your local vitamin and supplement store have not been rigorously tested by private or government facilities. As a result, the science on the effects of such supplements is highly uncertain. Yet, many individuals swear by the benefits of the supplements, claiming that they treat or cure ailments ranging from male pattern baldness, to depression, to memory loss. This combination of scientific uncertainty with ill-informed adherence is a potentially dangerous combination. For example, there is a potential for harm to the public good if the public ill-informedly adheres to a dangerous product or behavior. Given the lack of systematic testing of many natural supplements, it is not clear whether they may present risk in the form of a debilitating disease going untreated (because the person is placing faith in a natural supplement rather than traditional medical treatment) or in the form of a troubling side effect or interaction with other supplements or traditional medicines.

Scientific Certainty/Ill-Informed Skepticism

The third combination is a situation where scientific knowledge is very certain and yet ill-informed observers express high skepticism. This combination exists in many forms. Occasionally, it maps onto political ideology. One such combination that seems to cut across political ideology and appears to be gaining ground is preventive vaccinations. There is extremely low scientific uncertainty about the benefits of preventive vaccinations. The scientific evidence suggests that while there are minimal risks to such vaccinations, there is a great risk to society at large if individuals refuse to vaccinate their children. Yet, ill-informed observers, both liberal and conservative, perhaps for different reasons, have been increasingly skeptical of preventive vaccinations. This pattern presents society with a particularly nagging challenge. Individual action based upon ill-informed adherence rather than scientific knowledge may place society as a whole at risk. But it also presents a challenge for elected leaders. If sufficiently high numbers of individuals in society reject the accumulation of scientific knowledge, then elected leaders face a conundrum. Elected officials must decide between the evidence produced by the scientific community, ill-informed skeptics in the policy community, and their constituents.

Scientific Uncertainty/Ill-Informed Skepticism

This combination is essentially a politically uninteresting one. This scenario reflects scientists and ill-informed observers both acknowledging that they are uncertain or skeptical of a specific claim. One growing area of research is on behavioral adaptations early in life that may help stem the tide of developing Alzheimer's later in life. Early research suggests that Lumosity-type online cognitive activities may yield some benefit, but the science on this is in its infancy and therefore has relatively high uncertainty (Shute *et al.* 2015). Ill-informed observers as well are likely skeptical of specific recommendations at this stage.

Skepticism as a Political Asset

Ill-informed skepticism is a political resource. If political interests can develop skepticism or disbelief about a policy claim among a reasonable share of the population – even if that claim is supported with traditional levels of scientific rigor, then they may be able to convert that public uncertainty into gains at the ballot box or in legislation. If a segment of the population can be convinced that they ought to be doubtful of a policy claim, then it will be all the more easy to defeat policy initiatives or policy proposals that are built upon that claim. Given this potential political reservoir of power, political interests have incentive to manipulate, manage, and shape political doubt.

If a political interest desires a policy change or wishes to resist a policy change that reflects or is built upon a claim, supported by scientific evidence, a well-developed political strategy is one that would attempt to undermine public confidence in that scientific evidence. As Naomi Oreskes and Erik Conway (2010) point out in their book, *Merchants of Doubt*, there are two tactics to the strategy. Political interests can either attack the science, the scientists, or both. The appealing feature of this political strategy is that it does not require the advocate to necessarily produce their own evidence in support of any alternative claim. Rather, they must simply raise sufficient questions in the minds of the public about either the evidence supporting the claim or the scientists conducting the research for the public to begin to express ill-informed skepticism. At this point, the tactic is successful. The public is sufficiently doubtful even though they may know very little about the science or the scientists – they have doubts and elected leaders are incentivized to respond to these doubts. Let's look at these two tactics more closely.

With the first tactic, political interests attack the science. These critical evaluations have two targets: the scientific method (assumptions, analysis, data, etc.) and scientific uncertainty. Critics can highlight any aspect of the scientific method. By highlighting a shortcoming in any component of the method, critics level the charge that it follows that all of the inferences and conclusions rendered are invalid. Rarely is such a wholesale indictment of professionally published scientific research merited. This is true for several reasons. Professionally published scientific research in the best venues has gone through peer review. Peer review is the process whereby academic journals ask scientists to review the work of other scientists before publishing it. In all likelihood, reviewers would have already identified whether a piece suffers from major flaws in logic or analysis. When such flaws are identified, the pieces are rejected for publication. When minor shortcomings are identified, if the reviewers believe that such shortcomings do not rise to the level of undermining the causal inferences drawn in the piece, then they may allow it to move forward toward publication. Moreover, no research is perfect. We can certainly identify shortcomings in the areas of argument, measurement, and analysis that may not necessarily lead to a wholesale rejection of the scientific claim. The critical question that the skeptical consumer of scientific information must ask themselves is, "Is this shortcoming sufficient enough to unravel the entirety of the claim?"

Another popular target for doubt merchants is scientific uncertainty. Scientific uncertainty is inherent to all forms, modes, and manner of science. For political operatives marketing doubt, however, scientific uncertainty is a synonym for claiming that scientists are "unsure" or "don't know." These operatives point to scientific assessments of uncertainty and declare, "See, the scientific community is unsure. We simply don't know what to think about policy x." But as we saw above, no science operates with 100 percent precision, not even the scientific endeavors that many people think of as the "real" or "hard" sciences. To portray a claim that is supported with 95 percent confidence as being unsure is scientifically disingenuous but politically effective. Many Americans are scientifically illiterate when it comes to understanding the rigor of scientifically estimated uncertainty. So when they hear a political pundit tell them that scientists "aren't sure" about a finding, they process this information in the same way as they would hearing that bookies "aren't sure" who is going to win the Kentucky Derby – as if each of these uncertainties were equivalent, when, in fact, they are not. All scientific claims and policy recommendations have uncertainty associated with them. To criticize a claim or a policy simply because it contains an estimate of uncertainty is not sufficient to disarm the claim's scientific validity.

With the second tactic, political interests attack the scientists. Character assassination has a long political history. Raise enough questions in the minds of people about the messenger and they will pay little attention to his message. Savvy political operatives notice and will attempt to impeach the credibility of scientists who have conducted the research in question. By calling into question their motives, training, or financial sponsors, critics seek to raise doubts in the minds of the public as to the scientists' credibility. Beginning in the late 1950s, evidence began to appear questioning whether inhaled tobacco smoke played a role overall in the acquisition of lung cancer. As a counter to this research, some scientists received grants from some of the large tobacco companies to determine whether these claims linking inhaled tobacco smoke and lung cancer were valid. In the eyes of a savvy political operative, the evidence didn't matter either way. This was because anti-smoking interests could use the scientists' financial connection to the tobacco companies as grounds to impeach their scientific credibility.

4.5 Empirical Research and "Policy-Oriented Learning"

What is the end-goal of empirical policy research? Policy research enables us to learn about the inputs, outputs, and outcomes of policy interventions. Ostensibly, advocacy coalitions can use this knowledge to advance their agendas through coordinated activity; in other words, they can attempt to change policy. In the language of the Advocacy Coalition Framework (ACF), advocacy coalitions attempt to translate their core (fundamental normative views of the world) and secondary (instrumental decisions required to implement the core) beliefs into government action (Sabatier 1987). Policy change nearly always comes about from some external shock. This can occur when a new political coalition is elected or as the result of an emergency that necessitates a new policy. Rarely does policy change result due to one coalition convincing another coalition of correctness of their core ideas. Yet, we do occasionally observe coalition members revising their beliefs in the presence of new information. Sabatier refers to this process as **policy-oriented learning**.

Policy-oriented learning refers to "the relatively enduring alterations of thought ... that are concerned with the attainment or revision of the precepts of one's belief system" (Sabatier 1987: 672). Prospects for revising one's core beliefs are rather low, but individuals are able to more easily shift their secondary beliefs when they confront new information or data that conflicts with their prior beliefs. This is a lengthy process; one likely to occur on the order of years rather than days or weeks. Such learning across belief systems is more likely to occur under certain conditions. Learning is most likely due to both coalitions having technical resources to engage in a debate and the debate being between parts of their secondary beliefs system. It is also most likely to occur when both coalitions interact in a relatively apolitical forum that is dominated by professional, rather than political, norms. Last, policy-oriented learning is most likely to occur in areas where the policy problem is readily measured by quantitative indicators as compared to more normative or subjective measures (Sabatier 1987: 678–680). When all of these conditions are present, we would *expect the greatest potential for policy learning across belief systems*. In this way, high quality empirical analysis can change policy. By slowly altering the belief systems of the actors operating within a policy subsystem, beliefs are refined and policies changed.

4.6 Conclusion

In this chapter, we reviewed the foundations of scientific inquiry and uncertainty as they apply to public policy. Scientific inquiry is based on empirical evaluations of theoretical arguments. To know whether a theoretical claim has some empirical basis, we must test it against a control or a counterfactual condition, where the treatment condition was not present. A critical condition that must be met for this counterfactual model of causal inference to yield valid inferences is to control for any confounding factors that may be correlated to both our treatment and our potential outcomes of interest. By comparing outcome of interest in both the treatment and control conditions, we can gain an appreciation of the causal processes at work.

We also saw that all scientific inquiry has various sources of error. These sources of error, whether measurement, random, or sample based, contribute to our estimates of both descriptive statistics and measure of association. However, given the rigors of scientific inquiry, we are able to estimate the level of precision (or uncertainty) that we can assign to our scientific claims. This rigorous method and ability to assign probabilities to our uncertainty over claims distinguishes the scientific method from ill-informed inquiry of speculation. While a weaker form of knowledge production, ill-informed adherence (or uncertainty) is nevertheless a powerful political tool that strategic political operatives can use to manufacture doubt among citizens in order to pursue policy initiatives.

Key Terms in This Chapter

Ill-informed adherence
Ill-informed skepticism
Causal inference
Repetition effect
Factual outcome
Counterfactual outcome
Fundamental problem of causal inference

Treatment group
Control group
Selection effect
Confounding variables
Spurious relationship
Minimum conditions
Observational study
Internal validity
External validity
Descriptive statistics
Central tendency
Variation
Dispersion
Correlation
Scientific uncertainty
Random error
Population
Sample
Parameters
Statistics
Biased
Hypothesis testing
Type I error
False positive
Type II error
False negative
Policy-oriented learning

CHAPTER EXERCISES

1. Give an example of a public policy research question that is well suited for an experimental investigation. Provide another example of a research question that is well suited for an observational study. Justify your choices.

2. Explain what is meant by "normal distribution." Can you depict this graphically? How is the normal distribution helpful to policy analysts?

3. Identify two variables that you believe are likely to be correlated. Supply a justification for why these two variables might be causally related. Last, identify at least one

confounding variable that should be controlled for to rule out a spurious relationship.

4. What is scientific uncertainty? How does it differ from ill-informed skepticism?

5. What is the best interpretation of a finding that is reported to be statistically significant at $p < 0.05$? What would the best interpretation of a finding reported to be statistically significant at $p < 0.12$ be? Explain.

6. Scientific uncertainty and ill-informed skepticism are not synonyms. How are these two concepts distinct?

	Scientific Certainty	Scientific Uncertainty
Ill-informed adherence	Example	Example
Ill-informed skepticism	Example	Example

REFERENCES

Arbogast, Kristy, Jermakian, Jessica, Kallan, Michael, and Durbin, Dennis. 2009. "Effectiveness of Belt Positioning Booster Seats: An Updated Assessment." *Pediatrics* 124(5): 1281–1286.

Campbell, Donald T. and Stanley, Julian C. 1966. *Experimental and Quasi-Experimental Designs for Research*. Boston, MA: Houghton Mifflin Co.

Drews, Frank, Yazdani, Hina, Godfrey, Celeste, Cooper, Joel, and Strayer, David. 2009. "Text Messaging During Simulated Driving." *Human Factors* 51(5): 762–770.

Durbin, D. R. 2011. "Technical Report – Child Passenger Safety." *Pediatrics* 127(4): 2011–2015.

Kellstedt, Paul and Whitten, Guy. 2008. *The Fundamentals of Political Science Research*. Cambridge University Press.

Morgan, Stephen and Winship, Christopher. 2007. *Counterfactuals and Causal Inference: Methods and Principles for Social Research*. Cambridge University Press.

National Highway Traffic Safety Administration. 2013. Traffic Safety Facts, 2011 Data: Children. Washington, DC: US Department of Transportation, National Highway Traffic Safety Administration; available at www-nrd.nhtsa.dot.gov/pubs/811767.pdf.

Oreskes, Naomi and Conway, Erik. 2010. *Merchants of Doubt*. New York: Bloomsbury Press.

Popper, Karl. [1934]. 2002. *The Logic of Scientific Discovery*, 2nd edn. New York: Routledge Press.

Sabatier, Paul A. 1987. "Knowledge, Policy-Oriented Learning, and Policy Change: An Advocacy Coalition Framework." *Science Communication* 8(4): 649–692.

Shute, Valerie J., Ventura, Matthew, and Ke, Fengfeng. 2015. "The Power of Play: The Effects of Portal 2 and Lumosity on Cognitive and Noncognitive Skills." *Computers & Education* 80(2015): 58–67.

5 The Economy and Income Security

Outline

Questions

- Why is it difficult to arrange collective action institutions to support the widely agreed-upon idea that citizens should not fall below a basic income floor?
- Can governments manage their economies to achieve desirable goals?
- Is deficit spending by governments desirable?
- Is it equitable for some citizens not to pay income taxes?
- Can the Social Security program be redesigned to provide benefits more equitably and more affordably?

Overview

- The primary analytic concept we apply in this chapter is redistributive analysis via ultimatum and dictator games.
- Political management of the economy is difficult given strong external forces.

- Governments seek economic growth, full employment, low inflation, and a positive balance of trade.
- There is disagreement over austerity versus a Keynesian approach to managing the economy.
- Citizens appear to support the idea of there being an income floor beneath which people should not fall.
- Economic inequality is rising.
- Private savings rates have declined since the 1930s.
- Social Security is a large portion of many people's retirement savings.
- There are several forms of income redistribution practiced in the United States and elsewhere.
- Housing represents an important portion of many people's nest eggs.

Introduction

Barack Obama was elected president in 2008 largely due to voters' unhappiness with the state of the economy.[1] On September 22, 2008, Gallup surveys showed that Democratic nominee Barack Obama and Republican nominee John McCain were tied. One week later, Obama held a 7-point lead. This huge change resulted from the financial crisis that began in late September of 2008.[2] President Obama entered office with strong support from the public, and the Democratic Party also held the House and the Senate. By Obama's mid-term election in 2010, the Republican Party won the House and left the Democrats with a small majority in the Senate.

President Obama's mid-term losses were due to a number of factors, not the least of which is that incumbent presidents typically lose Congressional seats in mid-term elections. However, he went from high popularity to under 50 percent approval fairly quickly. He was hurt by weak economic growth, controversy over policies to manage the recession, and his passage of a health reform bill, of which only about 40 to 45 percent of citizens have supported at any time. The Republican Party leadership successfully criticized Obama and the Democratic Party's management of the economy to help build support for what appeared to be an unlikely Grand Old Party (GOP) turnaround in a brief period.

Although presidents typically win or lose office based on economic conditions (Lewis-Beck 1990), as do other national and even state and provincial leaders, there is little they can do to control economic outcomes. Domestic and world economies are

---

[1] www.gallup.com/poll/107674/gallup-daily-election-2008.aspx.
[2] For an excellent discussion of the Financial Crisis, see Raghuram Rajan's *Fault Lines: How Hidden Fractures Still Threaten the World Economy* (Princeton University Press, 2010).

influenced by processes that are largely random and for the greatest part beyond the control of governments or governmental leaders. Governments, nonetheless, attempt to manage economic outcomes despite there being little evidence of their being able to do so. At times, good fortune leads to especially strong economic performance. In the 1990s, the Clinton administration governed during a time of rapid rise in value of technology stocks, which, along with a protracted period of no wars and higher taxes, resulted in economic surplus. The 9/11 attacks had a major impact on the US economy. The Dow Jones Industrial Average dropped about 14 percent in the first week after 9/11, and it is estimated that US stocks lost about $1.4 trillion in value in this period.[3] Clinton had good economic circumstances due in large part to actions that were not his own, and Bush had bad economic circumstances due to an attack by an outside group. Managing a large economy is a difficult job, and one that requires skill, timing, and possibly most of all, good fortune.

In this chapter we discuss the economic goals of governments, the economic tools they use in their attempts to achieve their goals, the different economic philosophies that undergird their management of the economy, and a number of policies that are used to help people become and stay economically secure. We also discuss how citizens think about what's fair and unfair in how much money people may earn and keep, and we discuss income distribution in the United States and other nations. More broadly, this chapter is about taxes and redistribution. Some of the questions we address are: Is there an optimal tax rate? Who pays for government? Why do some people prefer more taxes than others? What social safety net programs exist and how do they operate?

5.1 The Political Marketplace: The Foundation of the Economy

To understand tax policy and preferences on redistribution, we need to first understand why the government is involved in the economy. To understand government involvement in the economy, we need to understand the foundations of politics and governments themselves. As will shortly become clear, without the government there is no well-functioning or flourishing economy.

Governments rule over societies, and a society is a group of families. No society can be productive if there is not order and peace. If a family can maintain some semblance of order, why can't fifty, 100, or 1,000 families together do so? It is a collective action problem. As group size increases, it is more difficult to act collectively because there is a greater incentive to free ride (Olson 1965). For example, imagine the group

---

[3] www.investopedia.com/financial-edge/0911/how-september-11-affected-the-u.s.-stock-market.aspx.

wants a leader. To take the job, the leader demands payment, which requires taxes. Each individual reasons that there will be enough in taxes if everyone except him contributes. But when everyone reasons this way, few people contribute and no one accepts the leader position. Although not our major focus at the moment, this example illustrates that one of the primary purposes of government is to compel people to pay taxes. That is, government exists in part to transform a Prisoner's Dilemma situation, where the optimal individual strategy is not to pay taxes, into a cooperation enterprise.

But how do we get a government? Individuals do not band together to empower and constrain a leader, at least not initially. Monarchy, or dictatorship, is the norm throughout human history. Rather, individuals band together to pay someone for protection from other predators; they prefer stationary bandits that provide order over roving bandits and their associated chaos (Olson 1993). More broadly, we can say that the political market involves the exchange of taxes for a distribution of benefits, where the primary benefits are order and establishing property rights (North 1989, 1990). With these benefits in place, economic production increases.

A leader may tax the subjects heavily, but will not confiscate everything. If he did, the subjects would have no reason to work and produce. But how do societies transition from dictatorship to democracy? Does it happen when people are fed up with their high taxes and oppression and overthrow the king? Not exactly. Olson (1993) tells us there are two reasons why democracy is not the typical outcome of oppression. First, the people face a collective action problem (Olson 1965). To overthrow the king, one individual's contribution has little effect, but conflict, battling the monarch, is costly. Second, if a successful revolution occurs, what keeps the new leader from becoming a monarch? Democracy emerges when there are competing power centers; when no one group is able to easily subdue all of the others. These groups, then, constrain the leader. In other words, democracy is the outcome of a political market where individuals pay taxes and receive institutions that make commitments credible (North 1989, 1990: 356–357).

In a democracy there is taxation, but it will be less than in an autocracy. All democracies have competing political parties. In the United States, multiple issues divide the parties, but economic policy has always been central to the difference between the parties (Poole and Rosenthal 1997). If one party wants to tax too much, voters will opt for the other party. If a party does not tax enough, meaning it provides fewer public goods, voters will opt for the other party again. Voters, then, balance paying taxes with the public goods they receive. In other words, individuals pay taxes and receive public goods. Among these public goods are security, infrastructure, credible commitment institutions, and redistribution. In summary, a well-functioning economy is the product of a political market. Among other things, this means the central actors in the political marketplace, politicians that run the government, have an incentive to manage the economy. The analytic techniques applied in this chapter include theories of redistribution, ultimatum, and dictator games.

5.2 Approaches to Managing the Economy

Economics is divided into two primary fields of study, microeconomics and macroeconomics. Microeconomics analyzes individual markets. For example, if a firm produces more of a product, what happens to the price of that product and demand for it. We covered a few microeconomics topics in Chapter 3. Macroeconomics analyzes the economy as a whole. When unemployment is high, what, if anything, can the government do to address the problem? In other words, macroeconomics focuses on how to manage the economy of a country. In this section, we will focus on macroeconomics.

Economic Goals

Although the economy is difficult to manage, governments have clear economic goals they attempt to achieve. Governments wish to promote economic growth, low inflation, full employment, and a positive balance of trade. **Economic growth** is crucial because a growing economy suggests expanding opportunities for people and businesses, which is more desirable than a stagnant or declining economy. The world economy has experienced relatively low growth since the recession of 2008, although the rate of growth has increased recently. **Low inflation** is desirable because inflation affects the price producers must pay to produce goods and services and also affects the price consumers pay for goods and services. Inflation occurs when there are too few goods and services (and labor supply) available in the market, making prices rise. Inflation is thought of as too little production or services pursuing money. Full employment is desired, but not really achievable. Typically, an employment rate of 4 to 5 percent is considered **full employment**, as some people are naturally between jobs, such as seasonal laborers and people who are changing industries or jobs for various reasons. Moreover, the drive to keep inflation low creates an unemployment floor, below which unemployment will not be allowed to move. A **positive balance of trade** is often politically desired because the average citizen believes it is better to be a net exporter and import a smaller portion of what they consume. Nations that are net importers are less independent than nations that import less. Yet, importing benefits consumers with cheaper and oftentimes better products. (Do you drive a foreign or American-made car?)

Box 5.1 Inflation and Unemployment: A Trade-off

To manage economic growth, inflation, and unemployment, governments sometimes manipulate both fiscal and monetary policy tools. A natural trade-off or tension exists between inflationary and employment goals. When the economy

Box 5.1 (*cont.*)

contracts, buying and selling falls off. In turn, suppliers try to cut costs by laying off workers. Having no or lower income, workers buy fewer goods. This cycle can continue, eventually pushing an economy into recession. To fight recessions, governments manipulate both fiscal and monetary policy tools to encourage consumers to buy more goods and businesses to hire more workers. Governments use fiscal policy to cut taxes or monetary policy to lower interest rates – both of which increase available money, encouraging people to borrow and spend. However, when fiscal and monetary policy are very generous, the economy can "overheat," with higher employment and a rising supply of money. These conditions lead to inflation, where the purchasing power of a dollar declines. If inflation rises too high, governments may use policies to push back on growth prospects by increasing taxes or raising interest rates. Higher taxes and interest rates give incentives to save rather than borrow and buy. Consumers buy fewer goods and suppliers draw back, laying off workers, and the "cooling" cycles begins. This implies a trade-off: at full employment, inflation runs high; at low inflation, unemployment runs high. Given US Government policy to pursue low inflation, the United States will always have roughly 4 to 5 percent unemployment rate (currently roughly 4 or 5 million out of ~100 million workers).

Classical Economic Model

There are two major approaches to macroeconomic policy: the Classical model and Keynesianism. The **Classical model** of economics holds that supply and demand are natural regulatory tools; thus, the economy regulates itself. This perspective is sometimes described as the *laissez-faire* model of economic governance. ***Laissez-faire*** is a French word that invokes a policy that there should be no interference by government or anyone else in the regulation of an individual's affairs. In the Classical model, significant macroeconomic problems, like high unemployment or high inflation, result from changes in technology and/or government interference in the economy. From the *laissez-faire* perspective, the best way to address these problems is to let the economy regulate itself. There are two problems with this completely hands-off approach. First, as we discussed above, it is not possible to have a large market economy without the government. The government establishes property rights and other institutions that allow the market to operate. To say the government should be completely hands-off is to call for a very small economy. Second, under a variety of conditions (information asymmetries, poor institutions, liquidity deficits, monopoly, etc.), markets operate inefficiently. In reality, there are few supporters of a pure *laissez-faire* approach. However, many inspired by this Classical model of the economy believe the government should spend less.

In recent years, there has been much discussion about austerity policies. Austerity means policies that reduce a government's budget deficit. These policies involve reducing government spending, raising taxes, or both. Those favoring the Classical approach tend to favor austerity in times of a recession. The argument for austerity in tight economic times goes like this. If the economy is weak and tax collections are down, then the government should rein in spending. Proponents of austerity often compare a country's economy to a household economy. They note that the solution to not having money is seldom borrowing money, which is "borrowing from Peter to pay Paul." A paper by economists Carmen Reinhart and Kenneth Rogoff provides one contemporary justification for the austerity approach. They wrote that economic growth is slowed dramatically as the ratio of public debt to **gross domestic product (GDP)**, which is the total monetary value of all goods and services produced within a country in a given time period, rises to 90 percent and above. That report provided policymakers with justification to pursue policies of low taxation and austerity. However, Reinhart and Rogoff (2013) themselves note that poorly done austerity policies result in more difficulties for the working and middle classes than for more affluent people.[4]

Keynesian Economic Model

Keynesianism is named after the twentieth-century British economist John Maynard Keynes who, writing in the midst of the Great Depression in 1936, argued that government could act as an employer and contractor of last resort, as in the Depression when there was too little money in the economy for producers to make things for consumers to buy, and too high unemployment for consumers to afford to buy much of anything. Keynes's solution was to conceive of aggregate demand as the product of consumption, government spending, and investment, and to argue that when demand lagged because of lags in those elements, it is appropriate for government to use deficit spending, that is, to spend more than is budgeted, to pay for public works and to pay workers. Thus, where the Classical model calls for less government spending during a recession, Keynesianism calls for more government spending.

---

[4] After its release, some minor errors were found in the Reinhart and Rogoff data. These errors do not significantly change their main conclusions. At very high levels of debt-to-GDP, economic growth decreases. However, the corrected data calls into question the 90 percent threshold emphasized by Reinhart and Rogoff in the original study. In other words, crossing the 90 percent figure does not automatically lead to economic unraveling. For a critique of Reinhart and Rogoff, see www.newyorker.com/news/john-cassidy/the-reinhart-and-rogoff-controversy-a-summing-up.

Box 5.2 The New Deal's Critics

Not everyone was positive about the move toward Keynesianism and deficit spending. The writer Jesse Stone wrote a song titled "WPA" (www.allmusic.com/song/wpa-mt0011524614/lyrics) that was recorded by Louis Armstrong and the Mills Brothers in 1940 and is tongue-in-cheek in its treatment of the WPA:

> Sleep while you work, while you rest, while you play
> Lean on your shovel to pass time away
> T'aint what you do; you can't die for your pay.
> The W.P.A.

Copyright J. Stone 1940

Keynesianism's most prominent practitioner was President Franklin D. Roosevelt (FDR), who used deficit spending and a Keynesian model to develop and pay for his **New Deal** program of economic recovery. Roosevelt, like most people, opposed deficit spending prior to his experience governing during the Depression. He created the National Recovery Administration (the NRA),[5] which was later ruled unconstitutional by the US Supreme Court, the Civilian Conservative Corps (CCC), the **Works Progress Administration (WPA)**, and other agencies designed to get people off the street and put them to work. Visitors to City Park in New Orleans can see roads with names and "NRA" molded in the cement and on park benches. The CCC hired young men to build roads and national parks, drain swamps, and complete other public works projects. The WPA engaged in building projects, but also hired writers, artists, producers, and musicians to produce in what some instances came to be lasting contributions. The writers included Zora Neale Hurston, Richard Wright, and John Steinbeck, each of whom contributed lasting work from their WPA employment. Orson Welles produced plays for the WPA. Thomas Hart Benton, Willem de Kooning, Lee Krasner, and Jackson Pollock, artists from differing schools, produced WPA murals. Woody Guthrie worked for the WPA for a month in 1941 and wrote songs like "Roll on Columbia" about the western dams that were being built under a contract with the Bonneville Power Authority.

Although the Depression-era programs provided sustenance to many people, and in the case of the dams and art works provided lasting effects, these government fiscal policies were less influential on ending the Depression than government monetary policy. The most important monetary policy was abandoning the gold standard. Former Chair of the Federal Reserve Ben Bernanke summarizes the research this

---

[5] Readers who see "NRA" emblazoned on public works projects like bridges today may be confused as to their origin. They are from the National Recovery Administration, not the gun rights organization.

way: "To an overwhelming degree, the evidence shows that countries that left the gold standard recovered from the Depression more quickly than countries that remained on gold" (Bernanke 1995: 4). Former Chair of the Council of Economic Advisors Christina Romer's research reaches similar conclusions. She finds that "any self-correcting response of the US economy to low output was weak or non-existent in the 1930s" (Romer 1992: 758). Her research shows that it was the increase in the money supply that led to increased economic growth and the end of the Depression.

In recent years, perhaps the most significant macroeconomic debates have been between Keynesians (or New Keynesians to be more precise). While all Keynesians embrace government deficits in a recession, they disagree about how large those deficits should be and how the government should produce them. Broadly speaking, those with a more liberal bent favor government spending and a significant monetary stimulus, while those with a more conservative bent have favored tax cuts and a less significant monetary stimulus. That is, both sides in this debate favor the use of fiscal and monetary policy, but in different ways.

5.3 Tools for Managing the Economy

Governments use a variety of policy tools to manage the economy. They fall broadly into the areas of **fiscal policy**, **monetary policy**, and **regulation**. Fiscal policy has to do with taxing and spending. Governments determine what to tax and tax rates in order to pay for government services and to spur economic growth. Monetary policy has to do with the supply of money. In the United States, the **Federal Reserve Board** (the Fed) is responsible for managing the supply of money in the economy. It operates with considerable autonomy from the executive and legislative branches of government and the members of the board and its chairman wield considerable power quietly. Regulations are rules that affect the incentives for undertaking various activities. All economic activities are influenced by regulations.

Fiscal Policy

Fiscal policy tools involve taxing and spending decisions. Although taxes generally are unpopular, they are required to pay for services that citizens demand and to spur some forms of economic behavior. Under some conditions, for example, one way to increase economic growth is to reduce taxes so that people have more money to spend, which they in turn can circulate through economic activity. A central reason for taxes is redistribution, the transference of wealth from the haves to the have nots. Redistribution reduces income inequality and can contribute to economic growth. Some in society want less redistribution and a less progressive tax system. **Progressive taxation** schemes involve the wealthier members of society paying a higher portion of their incomes as taxes, as with the progressive income tax. **Flat tax** proposals are less progressive. With a flat tax, all earners pay the same rate. The flat tax leads to a much higher incidence of taxes on low income people, making it a more regressive taxation scheme. **Regressive taxation** occurs when poorer persons pay a larger share of their income. Sales taxes and excise taxes on alcohol or tobacco are examples of regressive taxes. As we discuss in more detail below, in recent years, a less progressive income tax schedule and a changed job market have contributed to an increased concentration of wealth among the wealthiest in most industrialized countries.

In addition to tax rates, policymakers focus on tax incidence. **Tax incidence** refers to who pays the tax. For example, people who work pay a portion of their income into Social Security, about 6.3 percent up to $117,000 of earnings, an amount their employer matches. Although the employer is paying a share of that tax, the tax's incidence falls on the worker, as the employer pays the employee that taxed amount in lieu of income he or she would have received otherwise. The taxes are withdrawn when an employee is paid – the government is assured of receiving its money by withholding the money directly – but the incidence of the taxation falls squarely on the worker. This points to another issue in tax collection: the tax collector wants to be sure that taxes are paid. Schemes like Social Security, Medicare, or income taxes result in fairly certain collections. Use fees (like fees to use a park), sales taxes, and other taxes that must be collected via a mechanism less certain than automatic withholding are not so easily collected.

Income tax rates vary considerably by nation, although tax rates are complicated due to the variation in tax withholding across nations. In the United States, tax rates are complicated by a series of tax deductions that are used as incentives for certain types of behavior. For example, persons who purchase houses may take deductions for their interest payments and for closing costs. People receive tax deductions for investing in certain types of savings plans, like Individual Retirement Accounts. People receive tax deductions for paying tuition to a college or university. All of these deductions serve the dual purposes of encouraging certain types of behavior that are deemed valuable, and rewarding certain groups, like lenders who are able to promise a tax break to people who borrow money for houses.

Monetary Policy

Monetary policy involves managing the supply of money. The United States accomplishes this by having the Fed act semi-independently from the executive and legislative branches. The Federal Reserve Board consists of a chairperson, who is appointed by the president and approved by the Senate to a four-year term, and six other members of the Board of Governors, who are also appointed by the president and confirmed by the Senate and serve terms of fourteen years. A Chairman's service is independent of his or her service on the Board, although he or she is appointed to the Board before becoming Chairman, so chairs may serve more than fourteen years. The current Chairman is Janet Yellen, who was appointed in 2014. Her predecessor, Ben Bernanke, served eight years, and Bernanke's predecessor, Alan Greenspan, served nineteen years.

Service on the Fed is an especially influential position, and the Board's role in managing the economy is pronounced. The Board, for example, meets quarterly to set the discount rate for member banks; lower discount rates to banks translate into lower interest rates for consumers, which in turn affects borrowing and the cost of doing business. When interest rates are low and money is inexpensive to borrow, it is more likely that companies will expand facilities, people will build houses, buy cars, and otherwise spend money. More expensive interest rates constrain economic activity. Higher interest rates are desirable when inflation is too high: the cost of money goes up and people will have less money to buy products, which in turn should reduce inflation.

The Fed is sometimes criticized for wielding too much power that cannot be checked through regular political channels. The Federal Reserve is governed partly by the public, but partly by banks, and thus is not entirely free of the bank's influence. Some critics of the Fed claimed that by failing to raise interest rates in 2001, it helped create the financial collapse of 2008. Some Republican and Tea Party supporters call for the abolition of the Fed on the grounds that it is printing money without gold to back it in order to repay the debt, that it favors banking interests and extended the recession unnecessarily, and the like.

Regulation

Regulation involves government intervention in the decisions that firms make or in market outcomes. The economic rationale for most regulatory interventions is market failure. Market failures may take various forms, including natural monopolies or oligopolies, incomplete or missing markets, and information failures, for example, information asymmetries, transaction costs, and the like. Regulation may include legal regulation, social and environmental regulation, direct control of market outcomes by the use of tariffs, price regulations, and the like, by taxes, by providing subsidies (e.g. farm subsidies), and by government ownership and/or operation of production (e.g. Amtrak, the Corporation for Public Broadcasting, the North American Import–Export Bank, the Federal Deposit Insurance Corporation, among others). Regulation, along with redistribution and distributive policy, is among the core tools of government, and as such is controversial and often breeds conflict.

The government uses a variety of tools to regulate. It may use **price setting**, which may involve an outside source, like a government, to establish a price ceiling or floor on an industry with limited competition. For example, the US Government and the states set prices for Medicaid services, which helps to control spending. Producers setting prices is considered price fixing and is illegal. Another form of economic regulation is setting **entry restrictions**, like franchises, certificates of need, and license fees. States' governments require barbers to be licensed. In theory, that involves passing a test that, in some states, includes demonstration of knowledge of hygiene, infection control, and first aid, in addition to knowing how to cut hair. Entry restrictions may also serve as a form of economic protection for a trade by introducing a **barrier to entry**. For example, the requirement that physicians be certified by examiners creates a barrier to entry for unqualified persons seeking to practice medicine. Another form of regulation is the imposition of service obligations. Hospitals must provide care for people who are in need and are obligated to do so. Attorneys must provide a set amount of *pro bono* work. Finally, economic regulation involves oversight of costs and of investment decisions. Banks in the United States are subject to regulation in order to maintain transparency in their actions. That has not always succeeded; regulation is an ongoing process.

Regulation is controversial: some critics view it as a hindrance to economic growth and demand less regulation. For example, supporters of the plan to build the Keystone XL pipeline, which would run from eastern Alberta, CA to Port Arthur, TX claim that the environmental regulations that have halted it during the Obama presidency have had enormous effects on jobs and US independence from foreign oil producers. Regulations may be used in a number of ways to affect economic growth. Excise taxes, user fees, and subsidies to do or not do things are all forms of regulation that affect economic growth.

Regulation is often criticized as a hindrance to economic growth. Florida Governor Rick Scott (R) travels to states whose governors are Democrats to tout Florida's low business regulations and low taxes in a bid to convince companies to relocate. Early research on the politics of regulation (Stigler 1971; Peltzman 1976) depicted regulatory politics in which the regulated entity (e.g. business) usually received favorable treatment. The logic holds that politicians (the regulators) seek re-election, business interests provide support for re-election with more influence than voters, and regulation favorable to business interests ensues. More contemporary research on regulatory politics (e.g. Krause and Douglas 2005; Carpenter 2004) includes bureaucratic incentives to seek rents, as well as those of business and elected officials. Bureaucracy is an important participant in regulatory politics, with administrative design and implementation of regulatory policies ensuring its central role in regulatory politics. Complaints against bureaucratic red tape are often complaints against regulations that slow economic activity.

Taxes

Keynesians and those partial to the classical economic model disagree about whether the appropriate fiscal response to a recession is government spending or tax cuts because they disagree on the effects of tax cuts. Politically, one might contend that economists, and others, disagree on the effects of tax cuts because they favor different groups in society. We will return to that point later. First, we will focus on the analytic question.

The **supply-side** approach, sometimes called **trickle-down economics**, favors tax cuts. This approach leads to a less **progressive taxation** scheme with much lower taxes on wealthy earners and holders of capital. Progressive taxation schemes involve the wealthier members of society paying a higher portion of their incomes as taxes, as with the progressive income tax. In contrast, regressive taxation occurs when poorer persons pay a larger share of their income. Sales taxes are an example of a regressive tax. The logic motivating the supply-side approach is that excess taxation reduces the incentive to invest in the economy as holders of capital and dividends choose leisure over investment as a way to use their time. According to the **Laffer Curve** (see Figure 5.1), tax cuts can lead to an increase in tax collections. That is, moving from a tax rate of zero to some value t* leads to an increase in government revenue, but beyond t* government revenue decreases. If taxes are far to the right in this figure, there is an argument to be made that cutting them can increase government revenue. With lower taxes and more government revenue, everyone benefits. In other words, the effect of lower taxes on the wealthy "trickles down" to the less wealthy through an increase in government revenue, which resulted from an increase in economic growth.

One critical question about the Laffer Curve and supply-side approach is: Where is the tipping point? At what level of taxation does government revenue begin to decrease? Saez (2001) contends that the optimal marginal tax rate is between 50 and 80 percent. Currently, the highest marginal tax rate in the United States is 39.6 percent.

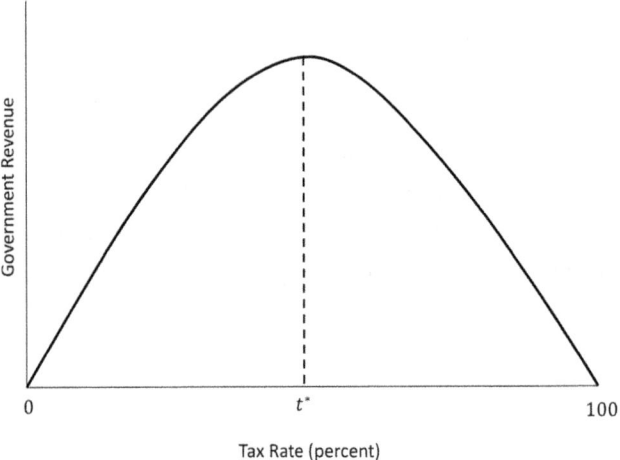

Figure 5.1 Laffer Curve

Another important question concerns the degree of dynamic scoring that should be used to assess the likely effect of a tax policy. Recall that in supply-side theory, reducing taxes increases government revenue. How is this paradoxical outcome supposed to occur? With lower taxes, it is argued, there is greater investment in capital and labor, and this in turn leads to greater economic growth than before taxes were lowered. With greater growth there is a larger pie. For example, if the size of the US economy was $100 and taxes were at 20 percent, then government revenue would be $20. If taxes were lowered to 19 percent, but the size of the economy grew to $120, then government revenue would be $22.80. In this scenario, tax cuts more than pay for themselves. Alas, neither economic theory nor data supports a dynamic effect to this degree. Two major supporters of dynamic scoring, Mankiw and Weinzeirl (2004), find that about 17 percent of a tax cut on labor is made up for with higher economic growth. In other words, a one-dollar cut in taxes does not necessarily lead to a one-dollar cut in government revenue, only an 83 percent cut in government revenue.

Before moving on, we caution readers that these are not settled topics. For example, in most contexts it is probable that a one-dollar cut in taxes will not lead to a one-dollar loss in government revenue, but it is not clear if the loss will be 50 cents, 95 cents, or some other number. A central reason for this is "that standard economic theory does not predict the response of labor supply to income taxation" (Manski 2013: 87). The basic economic model that applies here posits that individuals aim to maximize their utility, which is defined in terms of work/income and leisure. Supply-siders highlight that most people prefer more income to less. But individuals also prefer some leisure to no leisure. Generally speaking, an individual may have one of three types of preferences over the bundle of income and leisure. Preferences may be substitutes, complements, or a mix of the two. When one views labor/income and leisure as substitutes, it is said that the preferences are additive and more of one means less of the other. In other words, more of one perfectly compensates for less of the other. When preferences are complements (in economic jargon, these are Leontief preferences), an individual does not want to trade away one good for the other very easily. This means lowering taxes does not increase work and therefore income. In fact, because individuals want some leisure, an increase in taxes can lead to more work in order to secure enough income for leisure. When income and leisure are viewed as partial substitutes and partial complements, they are called Cobb–Douglas preferences; here, changing the tax rate has little effect on economic growth. All of this means that different preferences over the income and leisure bundle lead to different effects for how tax policy affects labor supply and economic growth. In other words, it is very difficult to predict precisely how tax policy will affect labor supply and economic growth (see Manski 2013: 86–93 for further discussion).

Tax Rates and Government Transfers

In the United States, tax rates are complicated by a series of **tax deductions**. For example, people who purchase houses may take deductions for their interest payments and for closing costs. People receive tax deductions for investing in certain types of savings plans, like Individual Retirement Accounts. People receive tax deductions for paying tuition to a college or university. All of these deductions serve the dual purposes of encouraging certain types of behavior that are deemed valuable and rewarding certain groups, like lenders who are able to promise a tax break to people who borrow money for houses.

Tax deductions are sometimes referred to as **tax expenditures**, for the government is essentially giving money back to individuals who meet the criteria and claim the credits. If you do not meet the criteria, then you do not receive this government transfer. In light of the fact that these tax deductions are not often viewed as government transfers, the Political Scientist Christopher Howard coined the term "hidden welfare state" (Howard 1997). They are a larger outlay than Medicare spending, Social Security spending, or Defense spending.[6]

Why tax expenditures are so large, however, is not a surprise. These benefits accrue disproportionately to the wealthy and other well-organized interests. As we have discussed previously, smaller groups are better able to solve the collective action problem, and politicians pay close attention to well-organized groups since their members are more likely to turn out to vote, contribute to political campaigns, and work to mobilize others to vote.

Who Pays for Government?

Table 5.1, from the non-partisan Congressional Budget Office, helps us understand who pays for the government. In Row 7, for example, we see that individuals with an income above $83,300 (the fourth quintile and the highest quintile) have a positive tax rate after government transfers are considered. Further, until one's income is around $234,000, one's net tax rate is not very large. This sheds some light on Mitt Romney's comment that 47 percent of Americans do not pay income tax. Broadly speaking, he is correct.[7] The reasons for the 47 percent number are that many Americans earn very little and others receive substantial government benefits, such as being able to deduct mortgage interest.

Unemployment

Unemployment remains a large problem in the post-recession economy. The amount of unemployment is measured and reported by the US Bureau of Labor Statistics. In

---

[6] www.realclearpolicy.com/blog/2013/05/29/the_hidden_welfare_state_is_regressive_530.html. CBO Figure 1, 2013.
[7] www.politifact.com/truth-o-meter/statements/2012/sep/18/mitt-romney/romney-says-47-percent-americans-pay-no-income-tax/.

Table 5.1 Who Pays for Government?

	Lowest Quintile	Second Quintile	Middle Quintile	Fourth Quintile	Highest Quintile
1. Average Market Income	$15,500	$29,600	$49,800	$83,300	$234,700
2. Average Government Transfers	$9,100	$15,700	$16,500	$14,100	$11,000
3. Market Income + Government Transfers (Before-Tax Income)	$24,600	$45,300	$66,300	$97,400	$245,700
4. Average Federal Taxes Paid	$500	$3,200	$7,400	$14,800	$57,500
5. Average Federal Tax Rates on Market Income + Transfers	2.0%	7.1%	11.2%	15.2%	23.4%
6. Federal Taxes Paid Minus Government Transfers Received	($8,600)	($12,500)	($9,100)	$700	$46,500
7. Average Net Tax Rates After Government Transfers	−35.0%	−27.6%	−13.7%	0.7%	18.9%
8. Dollars Received in Transfers per Dollar Paid in Taxes	$18.20	$4.91	$2.23	$0.95	$0.19

Source: Congressional Budget Office, *The Distribution of Household Income and Federal Taxes* (2011)

the United States, unemployment in December 2009 was 9.9 percent of the non-institutionalized civilian workforce, defined as people not in prison or other institutions aged 16 or over. In December 2013, the unemployment rate declined to 6.7 percent, and in May 2014, it dropped further to 6.3 percent. In July 2015, it was at 5.3 percent, although there was concern that the reduction represented people halting their job searches. Of course, unemployment is not distributed randomly and has greater effects on some portions of the population than others. In April 2014, the unemployment rate for white men and women aged 20 and over was 5.3 percent. For black or African-American men and women aged 20 and over, it was twice that – 11.6 percent. White of either sex aged 16 to 19 had an unemployment rate of 15.9 percent; blacks or African-Americans of that age had an unemployment rate of 36.8 percent. Given that rising employment is one component of economic growth, these unemployment numbers are not good news, and the variation by race points to long-term problems in the jobs sector.

The rates of unemployment also vary by educational attainment. Figure 5.2 shows educational attainment and earnings for persons aged 25 and older. Unemployment is highest and earnings are lowest among persons with no high school degree, and unemployment diminishes as education increases. Earnings increase with education, although professionals – attorneys, CPAs, physicians – earn more than those with

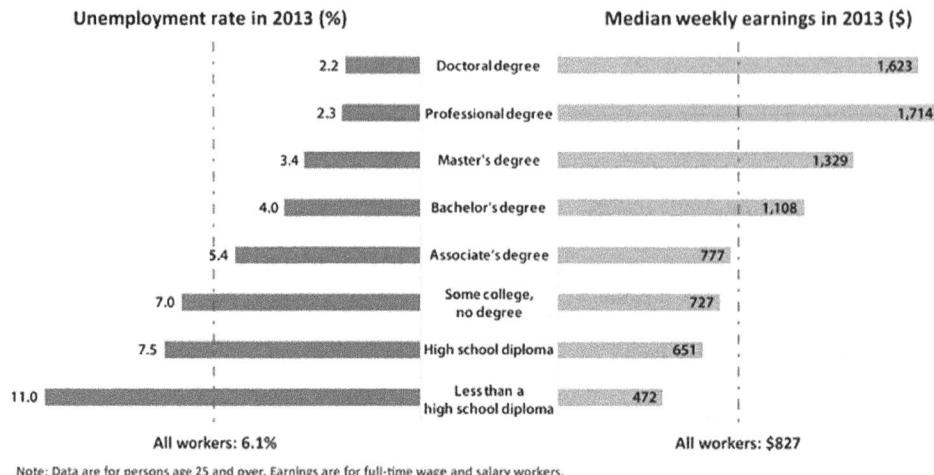

Unemployment rate in 2013 (%) **Median weekly earnings in 2013 ($)**

	Unemployment rate		Median weekly earnings
Doctoral degree	2.2		1,623
Professional degree	2.3		1,714
Master's degree	3.4		1,329
Bachelor's degree	4.0		1,108
Associate's degree	5.4		777
Some college, no degree	7.0		727
High school diploma	7.5		651
Less than a high school diploma	11.0		472

All workers: 6.1% All workers: $827

Note: Data are for persons age 25 and over. Earnings are for full-time wage and salary workers.
Source: Current Population Survey, US Bureau of Labor Statistics, US Department of Labor.

Figure 5.2 Earnings and Unemployment Rates by Educational Attainment

PhDs. Note that persons who have earned a bachelor's degree and are 25 years of age or older have an unemployment rate of 4 per cent and earn more than $1,000 weekly.

The economic recovery since 2009 has been described as a jobless recovery. The stock market enjoyed a boom in 2013 and, despite some fluctuations, the Dow Jones Index, which measures the performance of stocks and other investments, is over 16,000, which is an historic high. It is good that stock prices are rising, since that means the economy is growing. People with investments in the stock market, including people with funds invested in mutual funds as many working people do, are making money. However, less than 50 percent of Americans have investments in the stock market, and the interest received on bank accounts and certificates of deposit are very low, around 1 percent for CDs in April 2014. Checking and savings accounts earn less than that. The housing market, which has long been the source of many people's long-term wealth, is returning after the crash in 2008, but foreclosures remain and it is more difficult to get money to invest in housing now than in the period before the housing bubble burst, so this market is not a source of security for people.

Deficits and Debts

Americans do not like taxes or debt. They like public services. At times, their preference for low taxes, and for tax reductions, conflicts with their taste for public services. This causes difficulty for policymakers who wish to keep taxes low and provide generous benefits. The golden rule of public finance is that spending must not exceed revenue. If it does, the sole justification for debt is government investment (Yakita 2004). The US

Government has had a budget deficit for all but four years – 1998, 1999, 2000, and 2001 – since 1995. The public debt is the accumulation of deficits over the years. The deficit increased dramatically following the war in 2001 and even more with the bail-out in 2009. It has dropped each year since 2012, and is now $443.35 billion, the lowest amount since 2008 (US Office of Management and Budget 2016). In 2015, the US public debt was about $18.5 trillion. The US Congressional Budget Office (CBO) notes that the only way to reduce the deficit (and the debt) is to cut spending, raise taxes, or both. Neither the US Congress nor the executive branch is keen to do either, and citizens complain about the debt, but are reluctant to pay higher taxes or get fewer services.

The services–taxes trade-off is the problem that results in the deficit and in rising debt. The US Government is able to go into debt by selling bonds for which investors receive an established rate of interest. There are several types of treasury bonds, which are sold by the government and by brokers and banks. They typically pay fairly low interest, but are safe, that is, they are unlikely to default. They also are desirable because they are treated favorably for taxes – for example, they are not taxed before maturity. State governments do not have as much flexibility for managing their deficits as the national government; they cannot issue treasury notes, but must raise money by selling bonds on private markets. As their debt grows, so does the cost of borrowing, as they are charged higher prices to borrow when they are judged to be poorer risks.

There are disagreements among policymakers about the debt and deficit issue. Some argue that deficits are acceptable inasmuch as they represent an investment in the economy and spur growth. Others argue for belt-tightening, likening the behavior of states and nations to that of families, who spend when they have resources and spend less when times are hard. The urge to avoid debt is understandable, but the investment argument, especially for the national economy, is as well. There is a well-documented need to repair and rebuild roads, bridges, and other infrastructure in the United States. Some observers argue that an investment in infrastructure would solve the problem of crumbling roads, as well as create an economic boost for citizens. Those who call for budget austerity, that is, belt-tightening during hard times, claim that that provides greater benefits in the long term. There is no agreement on which approach is more desirable, so we can expect to continue to muddle through.

5.4 How Do Societies Ensure That Their Members Have Economic Security?

Rawls's "Veil of Ignorance"

How can we arrange collective action institutions so that people may earn as much as they wish, but others do not fall below an income floor, which the majority of citizens consider to be a desirable outcome? The philosopher John Rawls, in *A Theory of Justice* (1971), creates a thought experiment in which he asks readers to imagine a world in which they are born in an original position behind a "**veil of ignorance**." By "original position," Rawls means that people would enter the world in some set way of being, disregarding their intelligence, and the veil of ignorance means they would not know the circumstances into which they would be born. Rawls argued that the most desirable way to organize the world would be to maximize the resources – benefits, rights, and so on – available to the least well off in society so as to ensure a floor for the poorest in society, which may be described as a maximin plan. By contrast, John Harsanyi argued that the best way to organize society is by following the utilitarian principle, in which the highest average benefit should be accorded to citizens.

The Mixed Solution

Two researchers sought to test the competing explanations. Norman Frohlich and Joe Oppenheimer (1992) conducted laboratory experiments using students from several nations as subjects. They arranged tests of both the maximin and utilitarian positions, but others as well. Their experiment led them to conclude that the most frequently preferred arrangement is one in which individual earnings may be maximized, but a floor beneath which no person will fall exists. That circumstance is analogous to what exists now in the United States: earnings taxes are lower than in most developed democracies, and taxes on capital gains are lower still. A modest floor exists in the form of various religious, private, and public charitable organizations, although there is constant tension over the extent to which the floor should exist and the extent to which persons should be shielded from bad economic outcomes.

The difficulty with this set of circumstances is that few people voluntarily contribute enough to insure a floor for persons who do not earn enough. In addition to that, there is conflict over what constitutes a reasonable floor. Should everyone be able to buy a house or clothing as part of that floor? Should they be able to buy food to sustain themselves and their families? Should education and health care be considered part of that floor? Clearly, society provides a good number of these benefits, but the extent to which that is desirable is contested. For example, in the wealthiest US states, the distance between the earnings of the rich and poor is the greatest, yet redistributive benefits are more generous in real terms than they are in less affluent states. That is, low income people who live in Massachusetts, a wealthy state, receive more generous benefit payments than low income people who live in Mississippi, a low income state. Income inequality is greater in Massachusetts than in Mississippi, yet low-income people in Massachusetts receive more generous benefits than low-income people in Mississippi. Some people argue that income inequality is a problem that requires policy action. Others argue that income distribution is not the appropriate concern, but that the real benefits provided to secure the income floor is the key. This is the collective action problem that defines income security policy.

5.5 How to Provide Income Security?

Taxes and earnings are the concerns of most people, and much political activity surrounds questions of taxing and income redistribution. Taxation gets to many people's core concerns with government: they often disagree about what share of their earnings government should be able to claim for taxes, and there are also disagreements about how taxes should be levied. Of course, there are similarly disagreements about how government should use tax money, especially if it involves income redistribution of any sort, which is a source of tremendous disagreement among citizens.

How do people plan for their future earnings? The most obvious way is to earn money while at their most productive times, and to save money for the future, when earnings may decline. In societies in which physical labor is the best way to earn money, the need to set something aside for the future is clear. Also, the saying that you should "set something aside for a rainy day" says just that: It is difficult to be productive when it is rainy, so be sure to save. The connection between labor and sustenance is not so direct in developed nations, and the "rainy day" is now for the most part figurative. Nonetheless, financial analysts warn regularly of the failure of many citizens to set aside as much as they should.

Saving

How much do people save? Data from the Organization for Economic Co-operation and Development (OECD) reveal substantial variation in household savings rates among member nations. In 2013, US households saved 4.5 percent of earnings, while the Swedish saved nearly 12 percent. Citizens of some nations, like Poland, were in the red, losing 0.5 percent of earnings. Clearly, there is variation, some of which is surprising – for example, the high savings rates of highly taxed Swedes, who save a high portion of earnings despite paying taxes to pay for a socialized health system, generous family leave and child care, well-financed public education, and the like. The United States, with its Yankee ethic of self-sufficiency, shows a lower commitment to savings among its citizens.

The Income Inequality Problem

One issue that has become increasingly central to discussions about earnings is the rise of **income inequality** in the United States, as well as in other industrialized democracies. Income inequality is defined as the extent of the difference in total earnings between the highest income people in an area, say the top 5 percent, and those with the lowest incomes, say the lowest 30 percent. As the amount of total wealth among the one group rises (lowers), income inequality rises (lowers). The political scientists Evelyn Huber and John Stephens (2014) argue that the primary determinant on how well people do economically is education, and public investment in that education.

Table 5.2 shows Americans' earnings rankings by income level in 2012. People who earn $5,000 per year are in the bottom 2 percent of earners; people who earn $383,001 or more are in the top 1 percent. Perhaps more revealing is the percentage of the population in those income categories. In 2012, the year for which these data are reported, the median family income in the United States was $51,000, which places the median just below that amount. The data are disproportionately distributed on the lower end of the distribution, suggesting that incomes are distributed in a manner in which lower earners represent a much higher portion of the population than high earners. This is no real surprise, since there have always been more moderate and low

Table 5.2 Household Incomes in the United States

Household Income	Rank
$5,000	Bottom 2%
$10,000	Bottom 7%
$25,000	Bottom 24%
$50, 000	Bottom 49%
$75,000	Top 33%
$100,000	Top 21%
$125,000	Top 13%
$150,000	Top 9%
$175,000	Top 6%
$200,000	Top 5%
$250,000	Top 3%
$300,000	Top 2%
$383,001	Top 1%

income people than high income people, but the distribution has nonetheless changed over the past forty-odd years, with the amount of earnings accruing to the most wealthy rising more rapidly than earnings of the less wealthy.

Another way to think of income distribution is to consider what portion of income in a year is accrued by which block of earners. The top 1 percent of earners account for about 36 percent of all income in 2009. The group from 2 to 10 percent of people accounts for another 36 percent of income, bringing the top 10 percent to about 72 percent of all wealth in that year. The bottom 40 percent of earners claimed less than 10 percent of total income in that year.

Why is there so much income inequality? A few factors seem to be central. First, in a now famous work, Piketty (2014) puts forward the following inequality: R > G. R refers to the rate of return on capital (e.g. interest, dividends, rent, etc.) and G refers to economic growth. To explain, in the normal course of events, incomes for most workers will rise at about the same rate as economic growth. If R is greater than G, however, then the incomes of those with substantial amounts of capital will see their incomes and wealth rise at a greater rate than others. This leads to an increase in inequality. Further, Piketty contends that the primary way this inequality has been broken in the past is with significant increases in top tax rates (e.g. World Wars I and II) or economic depressions. Second, there has been a reduction in tax progressivity. The need for resources to pay for war led nations to increase their rates of progressive taxation during World War I, which decreased economic inequality (Scheve and Stasavage 2012). Since the end of World War II, the richest members of society have seen their tax rates decrease. Piketty and Saez (2006: 201) show that inequality "declined during WWI, recovered during the 1920s and declined again during the Great Depression and WWII." In each of these periods of decline, the wealthy paid more in taxes and earned less on their capital. Analogously, they find that it was not until significant changes in tax rates in the United States in the 1980s that inequality sharply increased. Third, Piketty and Saez's (2006) data also suggest that, beginning in the 1970s, incomes in English-speaking countries began to become increasingly skewed toward the wealthy, but that the gains came from wages earned by the highest earners. Increased wages and earnings for those at the top incomes stems from changes in technology. Because of globalization, for example, someone like Bill Gates can earn much more now than in the past. While there is significant disagreement about how to address income inequality, there is significant agreement that these three factors have contributed to it.

Americans are aware of and concerned about inequality, but it is not clear that much will change. A Gallup poll from January 2014 showed nearly two-thirds of US adult citizens to be concerned with the present distribution of income. In Figure 5.3, Americans' satisfaction with their perceived opportunities to get ahead are arrayed from 2001 through 2014. The darker lines on the bottom of the chart show a secular increase in the percentage dissatisfied over the course of the series. The changes began

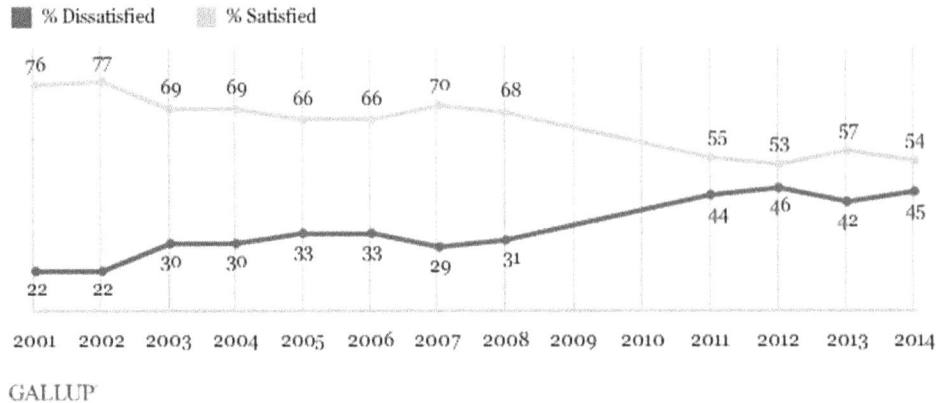

Figure 5.3 Satisfaction with Americans' Opportunities to Get Ahead by Working Hard, 2001–14 Trend

in 2002 and have moved steadily upward, from about 30 percent in 2004 to 45 percent in 2014. Some of that was brought on by the economic crash in 2008, and has stayed around 45 percent over the past three years. Even with these reports, the majority of Americans do not have favorable opinions about welfare or redistribution, when it is expressed as "welfare," which has a racial connotation (Gilens 1999). Recall our discussion of dominant policy images from Chapter 1. When George W. Bush won election to the presidency in 2000, he quickly moved to reinstate lower income tax rates that had been imposed by the Reagan administration. The majority of US citizens responded that their taxes were "just about right" in a 2012 CBS/*New York Times* poll. Higher taxes on higher earners, which were removed by the Reagan tax reforms, might be expected to assist people's abilities to earn more money, but the response to polls suggests that they do not believe anyone is not paying a fair share of the tax burden. Without tax increases or enormous growth in jobs or income, the falling opinions about the ability to get ahead are unlikely to change soon. Thus, a quick solution to the income distribution problem is not likely to come easily.

Research by Nathan Kelly shows that which party is in control of the government affects the income distribution. Kelly estimates a series of over-time regression models that test the effects of liberal (Democratic) party control, union strength, labor market factors, and demographic factors on the amount of pre-redistribution inequality in the United States. Pre-redistribution inequality, the dependent variable, is the state of income distribution prior to policy adjustments. He finds that liberal party control and union strength are each associated with less income inequality, and the results hold over time (Kelly 2009: 115–116). Thus, Kelly's research suggests that politics and political organization matter. There is contentious ongoing debate about income distribution in the United States; these results help explain why interest groups that hope to affect the distribution of income focus on the parties they support and on easing or making more difficult union organization.

Box 5.3 Kelly's (2009: 112–113) Estimates of Pre-Redistribution Inequality, 1947–2000

Dependent variable:

Δ Pre-Redistribution Inequality

Independent variables:

Δ Democratic President$_{t-1}$	-0.30^* (0.09)
% Unionized $_{t-1}$	-0.09^* (0.02)
% Unemployed$_{t-1}$	0.10^* (0.03)

Note: $^* = p<0.05$, two-tailed.

The model contains five additional controls and explains about 57 percent of the variation in the dependent variable. We are interested in the three key measures, which suggest that the presence of liberal (Democratic) party and stronger unions is associated with lower unemployment. Here, one unit change in the percentage of time the president is a Democrat reduces inequality by 0.30 units. The −0.30 is the regression coefficient. The figures in parentheses are standard errors. To be statistically significant at the 0.05 level, dividing the regression coefficient by the standard error should equal 2. All of the measures in this table are statistically significant, meaning we can reject the null hypothesis of no relationship. The lagged measure of union membership (t-1 denotes a one-year lag in the data, that is, if the dependent variable represents 2000 the lag is for 1999) indicates the pre-redistribution inequality declines by 0.09 units, with each unit change in the percent unionized. The coefficient for unemployment states that rises in unemployment produce rises in income inequality.

Social Insurance

One way to insure against poverty is to provide social insurance. Social Security, which is discussed in a section below, is a form of social insurance. Workers who are legally in the country pay social security taxes and receive benefits at the end of their working lives as a form of insurance policy. Social insurance is generally more popular among citizens than income redistribution because the beneficiary pays something for the benefit regardless of whether he or she uses it.

Redistribution

Redistribution involves taking from the people who have income and giving to the people who do not have enough income. It is controversial. Redistribution most often flows from the "haves" to the "have-nots," although there are instances where the direction goes the other way. Redistribution takes place in many ways: it may involve progressive taxation or it may be charitable giving. Regardless of the source, the redistributive sector contributes a huge amount to the creation of an income floor for people.

Most economic policy revolves around questions of whether society should help others who may need assistance. When we observe an individual helping another individual, however, it is unclear why they may be doing so. If you see a person standing at an intersection, holding a sign that reads "Hungry," and observe another person give him money, what do you think motivated that donation? If the passer-by's utility function was solely driven by a simple self-interested pay-off, then we should not have observed that person donate any money. So why did we observe a donation? Was the passer-by's action altruistic? Did she gain utility from the other person's pleasure? Or was it out of a sense of fairness? Did the person donate based on the belief that it is only fair that she share some of what she has with this person who is less fortunate? Or was it out of a sense of reciprocity? Did she donate to the man in the belief that if she ever needs assistance her behavior will spur others to act similarly? What does political economy suggest we ought to observe in this situation? Let's consider an experiment.

Ultimatum Game

Imagine two players. Player 1 has $10 and faces a decision. She must choose how much of this $10, if any, to share with a second player. For convenience, let's assume that she can only subdivide her total amount into whole dollars. Player 1 keeps the remainder of what is not offered to Player 2. However, after Player 1 decides how much of the $10 to offer Player 2, Player 2 can either accept the offer or reject it. If Player 2 accepts the offer, then the pay-offs are made in accordance with Player 1's original offer. If Player 2 rejects the offer, then both players receive $0. This game is displayed in Figure 5.4.

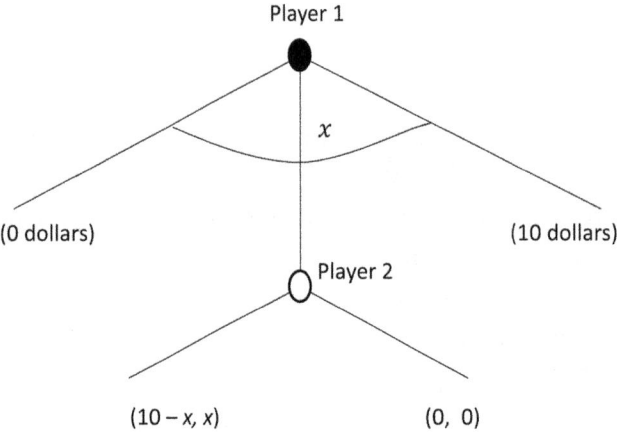

Figure 5.4 Ultimatum Game

The arc displayed under Player 1 denotes the fact that a range of choices, between 0 and 10 dollars, constitutes her first move. Player 2 then can accept or reject. If Player 2 accepts, the players receive the pay-offs, 1-x and x, respectively. If Player 2 rejects the offer, neither player keeps any money.

How can we solve this game? We can apply a Subgame Perfect Nash Equilibrium solution concept. Recall from Chapter 2 that this means we are searching for equilibriums that represent each player's best responses to the other at each node in the game tree. We begin at the end of the game and work backwards, using backward induction to determine each player's best response.

The challenge here is that we have a variable in the pay-off on the left node of the game. So we must consider all possible values of x. Let's consider Player 2's best move if Player 1 offers any non-zero value of x. Under this circumstance, Player 2 will receive at least a dollar, maybe more, if he accepts and nothing if he rejects. So, if there is any non-zero offer from Player 1, then Player 2 will accept. Knowing this, what should Player 1 do? Let's start with the lowest amount. If Player 1 offers \$1, she knows that Player 2 will accept. But let's consider other possibilities. Could Player 1 improve her position by offering more? In short, no. She could offer more than \$1 and we see that Player 2 would accept any of these offers, since they are all improvements for Player 2. But, Player 1's best response to Player 2 is to offer the lowest non-zero amount – in this case \$1. Therefore, (\$1, Accept) is a Subgame Perfect Nash Equilibrium of this game.

Our solution suggests that if we move this game into the experimental context, we ought to observe players sharing the least non-zero amount possible with the second player. What do we actually observe? This experiment has been run thousands of times and hundreds if not thousands of scientific papers have been published on the results of the Ultimatum game. When conducted among university students, the modal offer is 50/50 with a mean of between 40 and 50 percent (Camerer 2003). These numbers are generally consistent albeit with large variance when conducted across a variety of cultural contexts (Henrich *et al.* 2005). In either case, these results are not consistent with the prediction from our classic model. We are observing more giving than we ought to have. Moreover, Player 2 frequently rejects offers that fall below 20 percent. Our model suggested that this should not occur. Anything is more than nothing, and as a result Player 2 should not reject a non-zero offer – but they do if the offer is sufficiently low.

Is this evidence of individuals' affinity for fairness? Perhaps. Or perhaps it is evidence that Player 1 is making decisions out of fear of rejection by Player 2. To consider this possibility, we analyze the Dictator game.

Dictator Game

If we believe that Player 1's motivation to be more generous with Player 2 is perhaps driven by her fear of being rejected by Player 2, then we must remove that fear of rejection. We can do this, in part, in the Dictator game. Imagine two players. Player 1 has $10 and faces a decision. She must choose how much of this $10, if any, to share with a second player. For convenience, let's assume that she can only subdivide her total amount into whole dollars. Player 1 keeps the remainder of what is not offered to Player 2. However, unlike the Ultimatum game, after Player 1 decides how much of the $10 to offer Player 2, Player 2 has no move. He simply receives whatever offer Player 1 has put forward. In this way, we have removed Player 1's motivation to act out of fear of rejection. What do we observe when we run this experiment? When run on student populations, modal offers center on 0 percent, with a mean offer between 20 and 30 percent. Among non-student populations in industrialized populations, the modal offer is nearly 50 percent and the mean ranges between 40 and 50 percent (Henrich *et al.* 2005). These results seem to suggest that even when fear of rejection is ruled out, some players are still motivated to assist others.

What might explain the generous pro-social behavior that we observe in the Dictator and Ultimatum games? Scholars have investigated several possibilities. A reasonable conclusion is that our assumptions about the inputs of a player's utility function are too simplistic. Players are clearly maximizing multiple dimensions. Academic debate exists over what these dimensions may be. These may include an explicit desire to improve another person's welfare or altruism, or to pursue a vision of "fairness." Esarey *et al.* (2012) report results of production experiments in which student participants who are asked to assign redistribution amounts to fellow participants respond more strongly to fairness concerns when players lose earnings based on "disasters" or other bad luck than when they have low earnings as a result of poor performance. The results are stronger for participants who express liberal ideology, but they exist across ideologies. They are disposed toward providing social insurance, but not social welfare, that is, they are willing to insure against risk, but not against poor performance. (Their results comport with those of Alesina and La Ferrara (2005), which are discussed below.) In either case, we have clear evidence that economic models based *solely* on material motivations fall short in explaining behavior in economic experiments. Self-interested material gains clearly matter, but so too do other motivations.

What is the origin of these alternative motivations? There is scant evidence that individual differences play important roles. Factors like ideology, political party, gender, age, etc. tend not to offer ready accounts of the patterns observed. Across many of these factors players tend to behave similarly in the games. Rather, institutional features like a player's family background (e.g. parental orientation) or cultural environment offer more promise. Players raised in a family or cultural environment of strong individualism tend to make fewer offers and when they do the offers are smaller (Camerer 2003). Players raised in more cooperative environments that encourage community and reciprocity tend to make more frequent and generous offers (Henrich *et al.* 2005). Simply put, context matters.

Does Our Analysis of These Games Provide Insights?

These games offer some interesting insights. Evidence suggests that patterns of fairness or pro-social behavior likely vary based on the environment in which one was raised, whether parental, community, or cultural. People have learned what behavior is considered to be "appropriate" and act accordingly. Norms of generosity and stinginess appear to be learned behavior from regular interactions within institutional settings that have implications for future generations. Cues taken from one's family, church, or larger cultural settings are important in that they not only shape the behavior of current players, but also the behavior of future generations of players. Evidence from evolutionary game theory, where individuals are placed into different aggregate communities and allowed to repeatedly interact, suggest that generosity (or stinginess) is contagious. In other words, players can reshape communities with their behavior. One thing seems certain. Given that this behavior is learned, it is also teachable. Individuals have choices to make about their lives and the communities in which they live. This is the essence of politics – individuals have different worldviews and beliefs about how society ought to operate. The policy world is the applied context in which these worldviews collide with consequences for all. Economic policy evidences this debate as clearly as any other policy area. Below, we describe some empirical, observational research that helps further our understanding of people's preferences for redistribution.

5.6 Programs Designed to Provide Income Security

In this section we focus on programs that are based in the US national government that are designed to help provide income security. They involve a mix of social insurance and redistributive programs. Two of the programs, Social Security and Temporary Assistance for Needy Families (TANF), are **cash transfer** programs in which eligible persons receive checks each month. They differ because Social Security is a social insurance program and TANF is a means-tested redistributive program. Other programs provide cash transfers, but others provide other forms of benefits, all of which adds up to construct the network of income support.

Social Security

In June 2011, in a debate among contestants for the 2012 Republican presidential nomination, Texas Governor Rick Perry claimed:

> People who are on Social Security today, men and women who are receiving those benefits today, are individuals at my age that are in line pretty quick to get them, they don't need to worry about anything. But I think the Republican candidates are talking about ways to transition this program, and

it is a monstrous lie. It is a Ponzi scheme to tell our kids that are 25 or 30 years old today, you're paying into a program that's going to be there. Anybody that's for the status quo with Social Security today is involved with a monstrous lie to our kids, and it's not right.

Perry's statement was contradicted by former Massachusetts governor Mitt Romney, the eventual Grand Old Party (GOP) candidate, and by many observers from both political parties. However inaccurate his statement may be vis-à-vis the facts of what constitutes a Ponzi scheme, the sentiment resonates for a number of people, many of whom believe that continuing the Social Security program in its present guise is unsustainable in the United States. Others disagree, and point to the system as a hallmark program, the continued existence of which is a crucial portion of the country's long-term commitment to social security among American citizens.

The Social Security Act of 1935 is the foundation of the modern US welfare state. Officially, the federal social security program is called the Old-Age, Survivors, and Disability Insurance (OASDI) program. It provides social welfare (income) for retirees, widows, and widowers, and those with disabilities. The OASDI program is only one of several programs administered by the Social Security Administration. Others include Temporary Assistance for Needy Families (TANF), State Children's Health Insurance for low income citizens (SCHIP), Supplementary Security Income (SSI), Medicare (Health Insurance for the Aged and Disabled), and Medicaid (Medical Assistance Programs for low income citizens). In this section, we focus on the OASDI program, what most people think of as **social security**. In subsequent sections, we discuss TANF and SCHIP. In the chapter on health care, we go over Medicare and Medicaid.

Social security is a social insurance program. **Social insurance** is motivated by two general principles. First, some individuals (e.g. disabled people, widows, elderly people) may not be able to provide adequately for themselves. This was especially common during the Great Depression, but is relevant in any time period. Second, a majority in society believe it is better for all in society if those who cannot provide for themselves receive some assistance. Social insurance, like any other form of insurance, operates by spreading the risk. For example, if an individual becomes disabled, it would be a significant financial burden on one's family and friends to provide for that person. With social insurance, there is still a burden on one's family and friends, but it is lessened because others have contributed to the insurance pool.

Here's how the US social security system works. Workers and employers make mandatory contributions to the system. The contribution is in the form of a tax paid to the government. Individual income up to $117,000 is taxed at the rate of 6.2 percent. Employers match this percentage. If you are self-employed, then you pay 12.4 percent for OASDI. When a person retires, they receive an amount based, roughly, on the number of years they contributed and their average monthly earnings. Now a retiree does not receive his or her full monthly earnings, only a percentage. From the beginning, social security was designed to help low income individuals. With this principle in mind, the system was constructed to give a low income individual a higher percentage of their income in retirement than a high income individual, although the latter will likely receive a larger amount in absolute dollars. For example, if a person's average monthly earnings are about $3,000, they will receive roughly 45 percent of that in retirement. If a person's average monthly earnings are about $10,000, they will receive roughly 25 percent of that in retirement. In summary, the social security system takes in money from workers and pays out money to retirees, with specific pay-outs determined by a number of factors, including, but not limited to, the number of years one has worked, how much one made during those years, when one retires, and marital status.

Some people think that their social security contributions go into an account. When they retire, they receive back what they contributed. As the previous discussion makes clear, this is not how social security operates. In fact, most people receive more in social security than what they put in. For example, over thirty-five years a person making $36,000 a year pays about $65,100 in taxes. If they start collecting social security at age 65 and live until age 78, they will collect about $206,491. Now if the individual invested this money and earned 3 percent interest, they would have about $138,461 after thirty-five years. Not everyone, of course, receives more in social security than what they contribute, but with more people living longer, this is becoming more common.

It is projected that the social security administration will not have enough funds to meet its current obligations by 2033. The primary reasons for this are twofold. First, people are living longer and therefore collecting more social security in retirement. Second, in the near future more people are retiring. In 2015, about 15 percent of the US population was over 65. In 2050, it is estimated that this will increase to 21 percent. These demographic changes are making social security an important public policy issue. Before discussing some potential changes to social security, let's return to erstwhile presidential candidate Rick Perry's likening social security to a Ponzi scheme.

To consider Governor Perry's statement, it is necessary to understand what a Ponzi scheme is. The moneymaking plan is named after Charles Ponzi, a clerk in Boston who created the plan in 1919 to buy stamps internationally and redeem them for higher value stamps in other countries. He initially earned a good bit of money doing that, which was legal, but he then began to take others' money with the promise of high returns, which he paid upon receiving investments from other unwitting investors. A newspaper investigated him in 1920, which created a run on his investments. He owed more than $7 million, and he was eventually arrested, convicted, and served fourteen years in prison. The allure of Ponzi schemes lives on: Bernard Madoff established a fund with unbelievable profits that led to people losing enormous amounts of money. He is currently in prison.

A Ponzi scheme is defined as a financial arrangement in which investors are paid high amounts of interest, but those payments come from the investments of new investors and not from any real earnings that accrue. The claim that social security is a Ponzi scheme suggests that employed persons will cease to make contributions to social security and that the US Government will stop making social security payments. Neither of these is likely. In other words, as long as individuals pay their taxes and the government honors its obligations, social security is not a Ponzi scheme. However, this does not mean there will not be any changes to social security. Indeed, in a 2014 Pew Foundation survey, no groups, including those aged 50 and older, believe that social security payments should be stopped.

There are legitimate concerns about how to organize social security for the future, and policymakers and policy analysts recognize that the present benefits scheme is not sustainable without tax increases, increases in the amount of wages taxed (which occurred beginning in 2014, when the highest level of wages taxed was raised to $117,000), changes in benefit payments, full or partial privatization, or other possible changes. In the past, the age for receipt of benefits was increased from 65 to 67, and increasing it again would reduce the number of people claiming benefits and the duration of receipt of benefits. The Pew survey mentioned previously also found that a large majority of persons between the ages of 18 and 34 – 61 percent – believe that social security payments should not be reduced. Thus, despite even the prospect of the young paying for support of the old, survey responses still suggest strong support for continuing social security.

Privatizing social security either in part or entirely is one possibility that has been tried with social insurance programs in other nations, but has not received a positive response in the United States. The best example in the United States is in three Texas counties, Galveston, Matagorda, and Brazoria, all of which took their employee retirement systems out of Social Security before doing so was made illegal in 1983. The Social Security Administration conducted a policy analysis of the effects of the change in Galveston, and the results show a mixed set of effects, although in the long term employees seem to be protected best under the social security system mainly due to their not being able to make as many choices about payment frequency as are available in Galveston. In Galveston, employees agree to pay 6.13 percent of wages into what is called the Alternative Plan (it became the sole plan in 1987 and hence there is no alternative retirement plan other than not working for Galveston County) and the county pays 8.765 percent (Galveston County, TX 2014). Unlike social security, employees of Galveston County have no vesting period, meaning they are immediately eligible for benefits. They may choose to take lump-sum payments, may set their payments over a given number of years (e.g. ten years, fifteen years, etc.), or may take a lifetime annuity. Social security does not provide that discretion to determine when benefits begin, or how they are paid. A private firm makes low-risk investments for the

Galveston program that guarantee payments of 3.75 to 4 percent per year. Benefits payments are not indexed to the cost of living like social security; the 1999 policy analysis indicates that the Galveston plan protects lower income persons less well than higher income persons, while social security provides better overall benefits to low income persons than the Galveston plan (Wilson 1999).

Conservative observers view the Galveston plan as a boon, a plan that provides better benefits than social security and is tied to the individual and does not have the social insurance characteristics of social security. There is a minimal social insurance plan included, however, as a term life policy is provided to all employees at a rate of two times their annual salary. That is a modest pay-out, especially for persons who earn low incomes, but social security provides no such benefit, but does provide life benefits for widows and survivors when a beneficiary dies. The social security benefits do not accrue to male survivors of a female spouse, nor do they accrue to working female survivors of a male spouse, so they are designed to protect female homemakers who otherwise would receive no benefits due to non-participation in the system.

The best-known privatized pension system was created in Chile in 1981, and reformed again in 2008. The Chilean system is entirely privatized, and wage-earners may choose among five investment plans to buy into. In the system's initial guise the payments received as fees by the financing companies were higher than desirable, and investments by workers were low. The former problem has been fixed, but still workers put only about 10 percent of their earnings in the plans, so returns are not as close to replacement income as would be desirable. The reason for this is that retirees' payments are based on their lifetime earnings, and the system has paid a high rate of return for the past several years, over 8 percent (OECD 2013). However, people's early earnings are much lower than their later-in-life earnings, so the return on investment is sound, but not up to the level that retirement-aged workers desire.

The private retirement system in Chile and the system in Galveston, TX are relatively successful. Chile's system was created in 1981 by a president who was listening to a group called "The Boys from Chicago," young economists trained under Milton Friedman at the University of Chicago who were excited about pursuing the free market models espoused by Friedman and others of the Chicago School of Economics. Despite these moderately successful programs in Texas and Chile, the majority of US citizens do not support privatization of the social security system. Recall the survey results cited above that show even young people who expect not to receive benefits support continuing the existing system.

Unemployment Insurance

Unemployment insurance (UI) is a federal-state program in which benefits are paid to workers who have lost their jobs through no fault of their own. The benefits are lower than those workers would normally receive, and they are for a set time, after which they expire regardless of whether workers have found replacement jobs. The lower wages and time limit on benefits are considered necessary incentives for workers to return to normal work. Critics argue that if pay was equal to usual wages, and there was no limit on the time workers could receive benefits, workers would have an incentive to shirk rather than work. In some nations, workers pay a portion of their UI expenses, but in the United States all contributions are from the employer.

In Sweden, for example, unemployment insurance is paid under the Ghent system, in which the nation's unions manage unemployment benefits. Workers receive a set of benefits that decline over time, but the administration by the union has the effect of encouraging people to return to work as soon as they are able.

The US unemployment insurance program was created initially as part of the Social Security Act in 1935. Benefits are based on payroll taxes paid by employers to state governments and the national government. In 2010 to 2012, the average weekly benefit was about $300 (Stone and Chen 2013). Workers with full eligibility generally are granted twenty-six weeks of eligibility. The usual duration of benefits is about six months, although the national government has extended benefits, at federal expense, when the economy has been weak. Not all workers are covered by UI in the United States, including those who are fired from their jobs, those who have not entered the workforce, or those that voluntarily leave their job and later decide to re-enter but are unsuccessful in doing so.

Temporary Assistance for Needy Families (TANF)

Temporary Assistance for Needy Families (TANF) was created in 1996 as part of the Personal Responsibility and Work Opportunity Act (PRWORA). PRWORA was a product of the Republican Party's Contract with America, and was introduced by a Republican legislator, but passed by Democratic President Bill Clinton. TANF's predecessor program was Aid to Families with Dependent Children (AFDC), which was the primary cash transfer program for the non-elderly created during the war on poverty in 1965. AFDC was widely criticized because it required no work or training from its recipients and, when pre-transfer earnings were considered, had not alleviated poverty in the United States. Some observers claimed that AFDC and other pre-TANF War on Poverty programs had created a culture of dependency in which people came to depend on long-term public assistance to alleviate their poverty rather than using assistance for the short term while they developed skills necessary to rise above poverty. TANF differed from AFDC because it set limits on the amount of time that people could receive cash transfers, it required recipients to partake in job-training, and it placed limits on the amounts and duration of benefits to be received.

Critics of TANF claimed that the program was overly punitive in its treatment of the needy. However, critics of AFDC claimed that it was necessary to strengthen the work requirements of that program, and so welfare reform made work a necessary but not sufficient requirement for receipt of benefits.

Temporary Assistance for Needy Families is a **redistributive** program for which enrollees must be **means tested**. Means testing involves officials determining whether persons have income low enough to qualify for benefits. The states and the national government jointly manage TANF, and states have latitude to set income levels for eligibility, thus providing variation in the amounts of earnings people may have and receive benefits at the same time. The goals of TANF, according to the Department of Health and Human Services, are to:

- provide assistance to needy families so that children can be cared for in their own homes;
- reduce the dependency of needy parents by promoting job preparation, work, and marriage;
- prevent and reduce the incidence of out-of-wedlock pregnancies; and
- encourage the formation and maintenance of two-parent families (US Dept. HHS 2014).

The national government provides **block grant** funds to states to accomplish these goals. The institution of block grants was a major departure from the design of TANF's predecessor program, AFDC, in which states were provided benefits under a **categorical grant** program. The presence of block grants provides the states more discretion in program design than exists under categorical grant programs. State governments prefer block grants, but the national government is less able to exercise control over program design decisions under a block grant system. Thus, the decision to provide block grants rather than categorical grants cedes power over program design to the states. AFDC was often criticized because of the importance of the national government in program design and control, and TANF represents a shift toward state-based influence.

The 1996 welfare reform included the adoption of a clearer distinction between the deserving and undeserving poor. The distinction comes from English Poor Law, and distinguishes between people who are poor due to misfortune, illness, or unfortunate circumstance, including some disabled people, women with children, and the elderly, all of whom are described as "deserving." The "undeserving poor" are those who are able to work and decide not to, those who are incapable of work due to alcohol and/or drug addictions, and the like. The politics of providing benefits to the deserving and undeserving differ; even the most reluctant-to-spend politicians agree that the indigent aged deserve some assistance, but that agreement is not so easy to gain for people who are healthy and have no job training, for example. TANF requires that persons seek work within two years of receiving assistance, establishes a five-year lifetime

limit on the receipt of federally paid benefits, encourages the creation and maintenance of intact families by discouraging out-of-wedlock childbirths, enforces child
support payment, and makes it illegal for undocumented aliens to hold service
licenses in a state.

Supporters of the reformed welfare program claim it reduced poverty, which was
not the case under AFDC. Early evaluations of reform pointed to the effectiveness of
work incentives for former AFDC recipients, noting that enrollments declined almost
immediately following the reform adoptions (Blank 2002). Rom (2013) describes the
programs as more about changing behavior than about providing cash assistance, and
the core of the reforms focused on exactly that. More recent reviews suggest that the
reform did have the effect of decreasing the welfare roles, but has had little effect on
the extent of poverty among the target populations (Blank 2006; Ben-Shalom et al.
2011). Blank (2006) argues that early evaluations of welfare reform, including her
earlier work, were flawed in that they did not control adequately for the effects of
the booming economy of the late 1990s in their assessment, and even in those cases
missed the reality that spending and enrollments were declining, but poverty was not.
Ben-Shalom et al. (2011), in a later evaluation, note that enrollments have declined, as
has spending, but the most successful antipoverty effects have been on disabled and
elderly people – the "deserving poor" – while the younger, more deeply impoverished
citizens' situations have worsened.

Ben-Shalom and his colleagues note that the reformed system is paternalistic and
biased toward the highest income groups of poor. Joe Soss, Richard Fording, and
Sanford Schram (2011) echo this observation, and describe a highly paternalistic
and racially biased and motivated system of benefit eligibility determination and
administration in a case study of local and state administration in Florida. Their
work focuses principally on Florida, but they also show a relationship between race
and the extent of sanctions, which are punishments that remove recipients from
eligibility for benefits, across fourteen states with high percentages of sanctions.
Their simple correlation between the TANF Sanction Rate (a percentage) and the
percentage of the TANF caseload which is black or Hispanic is 0.66, indicating a
fairly strong positive relationship, which suggests the relationship between race and
sanctions in TANF is not limited to one state. Belinda Davis, Michelle Livermore,
and Younghee Lim (2011) studied who gets assigned to work training under TANF
in Louisiana and report that the race of the administrators of parish (county)
programs in Louisiana has an impact. They report evidence that race helps black
clients get access to training services, and this is especially true when they are
served by a black parish administrator who is well networked in the community
(2011: 502–503). The implication of this is that the results reported by Soss et al.
may be moderated by the inclusion of blacks in the cadre of managers in welfare
programs. The overwhelming message of these studies is that welfare reform

accomplished the goals of reducing spending and increasing state and local control, but it did not improve the situation of the people it was designed to help, the most impoverished, and has failed to replace poverty through the implementation of incentives to work.

Earned Income Tax Credits (EITC)

During the 2012 presidential election, the Republican candidate Mitt Romney was recorded on video saying that "forty-seven percent of Americans pay no taxes" and arguing, further, that that bloc of voters were solidly in President Obama's corner because of their self-interest. He made disparaging remarks about non-taxpayers being part of a group that "... believes they are entitled to health care, to food, to housing ..." and went on to argue that those voters would not respond to his platform of tax cuts. Romney was widely criticized for his comments, which were presented to a partisan audience at a fundraiser in Boca Raton, Florida, and were geared to the audience's anti-tax biases. However, despite the criticism, a good bit of what he said was true. A large portion of US citizens pays no federal income taxes, but they do pay a large burden of taxes through sales taxes, property taxes (even those that are passed through via rent), and other various taxes and fees. Thus, it is fair to say that nearly half of American citizens pay no income taxes, but it is not accurate to say that nearly half pay no taxes.

One large tax break that is available to low income people is the **earned income tax credit (EITC)**. The EITC is a form of "negative income tax" in which people are given tax credits as an inducement to work. To explain, the negative income tax, as the name implies, may provide payments to persons who earn less than an established amount (in the 2013 tax year, from $37,870 to $51,567 for working families depending on the number of children) and less generous payments for persons without children ($14,340 for single people; $19,680 for married people). The EITC pays people a tax credit when they file their taxes. For example, a married couple with two dependent children that earned $40,000 in 2013 would earn a tax credit of about $6,000. That is, the taxpayers would calculate what they owed in income taxes for that year and then would be able to credit their payments against the EITC amount. If their tax liability exceeded their tax payments, they would receive the entire amount as a payment. The idea is to give people the incentive to work by reducing the tax disincentive for earnings. Candidate Romney is correct to say that a large percentage of people pay no federal income taxes, but a large portion of that group benefits from the EITC, which was created to reduce work disincentives among the poor.

The idea of a negative income tax was initially presented by Milton Friedman in 1962, was discussed but rejected in the Johnson Administration's "War on Poverty" discussions, and was attempted in 1968 under the Nixon Administration's "Family Assistance Plan." The negative income tax experiment was first attempted in sites in New Jersey that were assigned randomly to experimental and control groups to allow researchers to determine whether establishing an income floor, as had been suggested by Friedman and others, and was part of what people thought most fair in economics experiments of the 1990s, led people to work toward income self-sufficiency. The New Jersey experiments proved difficult to evaluate due to problems with the overlap of existing public assistance benefits affecting subjects' behavior. The US Congress adopted a form of negative income tax in 1975 in the form of Earned Income Credits.

The EITC has survived over the decades and is now among the largest means-tested entitlements in the US budget. It is easy to complain about people who pay income taxes and argue that everyone should have "skin in the game" vis-à-vis paying income taxes. But at the same time, it has been supported by both conservative and liberal economists and reflects an apparent preference for citizens being provided a floor beneath which they do not fall. Some forms of EITCs exist in several western democracies, including England, Canada, Finland, and Austria, and twenty-six US states have mini-EITCs for their state taxes.

The Minimum Wage

The **minimum wage** is established by the national government in the Fair Labor Standards Act of 1937; states and cities may set wages higher than the federal amount. In 2014, the US minimum wage was $7.25 and, in states with no state law, the federal minimum applies. However, in some states, for example, Georgia and Minnesota, rates less than the federal rate may be paid to employees of small employers or of employers who are not covered by the Federal Fair Labor Standards Act.

Critics of the minimum wage claim that it dampens employers' willingness to employ additional people, especially those, like high school students, who are inexperienced, have poor job skills, or both. The minimum wage's supporters claim that it is necessary to allow people to earn a wage they can live on. The McDonald's Corporation, in a 2014 memo to employees showing them how to budget, suggested they have two minimum wage jobs to create a liveable income; the website upon which it was originally published is no longer available. There has been long debate over the employment effects of the minimum wage, but recent work suggests that the trade-off exists. That is, there is a trade-off between offering higher wages and more employment, and the effects are most pronounced among the young and poorly trained (Neumark *et al.* 2013). In 2014, the city of Seattle raised its minimum wage to $15.00, making it the nation's highest, which the city justified on the grounds of its economic boom and a desire to ensure that people receive a living wage.

Card and Krueger (1994, 2000) studied the effects of the state of New Jersey increasing the minimum wage in 1992 on employment in the fast food industry in New Jersey and Pennsylvania. They survey 410 fast food stores in New Jersey and eastern Pennsylvania before and after the policy change. They assessed patterns of expansion, hiring, reduction of hours, impacts on hiring teen workers, and other issues. They conclude that the increase in the minimum wage did not reduce employment, but show evidence that it increased employment. Their findings are contrary to most economic expectation and prediction. Even with strong empirical evidence for the benefit of higher minimum wages, their adoption is controversial.

Food Security

The Supplemental Nutrition Assistance Program (SNAP) is the principal provider of food assistance for the poor in the United States, although a number of additional programs exist at the national level, and there are also a number of volunteer and faith-based programs that provide nutrition assistance. SNAP is a national government program that is run by the US Department of Agriculture. The USDA link to SNAP is clear: SNAP is designed to provide food, and because USDA regulates and otherwise works with the agricultural constituency, it was established (as the Food Stamp program) in 1939 and initially operated until 1943. The program was revitalized in 1961, and the name was changed to SNAP in 2008. The program is administered at the state level by state governments' departments of family services or children's services.

SNAP is the most visible portion of a larger program of food security supported by the US Government. Along with SNAP, the national government provides support for free or subsidized school lunches and/or school breakfasts, support for adults and children, and other specialized programs of nutrition support. In 2012, persons in more than 22,000 households participated in SNAP, with a total cost of about $78.45 billion dollars, or about $278.50 per household. The school lunch program provided meals and snacks, either free or subsidized, to more than 31.5 million children at a cost of nearly $11.6 billion. The stand-alone school breakfast program served over 2 million meals to more than 128,000 children at a price just under $3.3 billion. Other programs served thousands more adults and children and cost an additional $2.6 billion. In sum, the national government provides considerable in-kind assistance via food and nutrition programs.

Housing Security

Housing is a crucial component of most people's economic security. Renters pay large portions of their incomes for housing, and homeowners treat their homes as significant portions of their financial plans. In fact, housing is often the largest asset in people's portfolios when they plan for retirement or the future. The **recession** of 2007 to 2011 included enormous drops in home values, with significant consequences for many people's income security. Given that people save relatively little, and that social security payments to retirees are modest, people often rely upon home appreciation to finance their eventual retirement.

The housing crisis that was part of the recession of 2007 to 2009 affected savings in two ways. First, given that interest rates were low and house values had been increasing, large numbers of people bought more expensive houses as investments on the belief that prices would continue to rise. The problem was exacerbated by their taking risky mortgages with large lump-sum payments due in a set time, often five years, or interest-only loans which allowed them to buy houses with low or at times no down payment. Interest-only loans are inexpensive because the purchaser needs no capital to make a purchase, only evidence of income. Buyers expected to use short-term interest-only loans to buy houses, which they then expected to appreciate in value, which they then would use to roll the house over, that is, to sell it, for a quick profit. When the loan payments were due, many people were unable to pay and their homes were foreclosed upon. When a house is foreclosed, the lender reclaims the property. In other cases, the values of the homes declined and people were paying for an asset the value of which was less than they agreed to pay before. In either case, the value of housing as a retirement asset declined, and values have not returned to pre-recession levels. The high rate of foreclosures, bankruptcies, and subsequent losses to banks contributed to the worldwide recession.

Box 5.4 Hurricane Katrina and Public Housing in New Orleans

New Orleans had several public housing projects that were in some ways models of what planners now view as the "new urbanism," which places housing in the center of the city near places where people work. The public housing projects closest to downtown, where there is a high demand for service workers, were once models of well-constructed, well-maintained housing in which work, schools, and social services were integrated into the community. The best built public housing projects were constructed during the New Deal era, and were built with individual entrances with small porches, open areas with room for gardens and playgrounds, and were developed with the idea of creating a community.

After Katrina hit in September 2005, a number of the projects were flooded, but were well made and could have been renovated. The St. Thomas projects, in an area located near downtown, were mostly demolished to make way for subsidized single-family rentals that were of lesser quality than existed before Katrina. Prior to Katrina, the St. Thomas Housing Project, known to be among the most violent in the nation, had been taken over by the Department of Housing and Urban Development due to malfeasance by the New Orleans Housing Authority and, as part of that, relocated more than 3,000 residents to other parts of town. The overall effect of relocations of residents from St. Thomas and other (less crime ridden) housing projects was to displace low income people from the central city and easy access to jobs and to place them further out of the city in lower quality housing with poorer access to jobs.

The housing crisis affected where people were able to live, as well as their retirement planning. For low-income people, housing security is often difficult to gain. The United States has a limited commitment to providing public housing or housing support. Public housing is often scarce due to a preference for providing housing via the private market. In the United States, housing subsidies are provided via grants from the US Department of Housing and Urban Development (HUD). Some city governments are reluctant to provide public housing within their borders due to its obvious attraction of low-income citizens. City governments prefer to attract higher income persons, who can afford to buy more expensive houses, pay higher property taxes, and be a strong economic force in the community. As a result, there is little support for the construction of new public housing, and even high quality public housing is not viewed favorably when it competes for land that may be of greater value in the private real estate market.

5.7 Individual Preferences on Taxes and Redistribution

Why do some individuals prefer more taxes and more redistribution than others? To provide some insight on this important question, we turn to an analysis by Alesina and La Ferrara (2005). The conventional wisdom on views toward redistribution focuses on economic motivations. In broad terms, redistribution is a transfer of wealth from those with more (the wealthy) to those with less (the poor). Those who earn more want less redistribution and those who are likely to need government benefits want them. Alesina and La Ferrara's analysis supports this conventional wisdom. The wealthy, on average, want less redistribution. Economically speaking and in the short term, redistribution does not benefit the wealthy; more redistribution means higher taxes on the wealthy. Alesina and La Ferrara's research also shows that those with more than a four-year college education (e.g. those with a law, medical, Masters, or Doctoral degree) desire less redistribution. This group also tends to be better off economically than those with less education. Complementing this they find that those with less than a high school education desire more redistribution. Of course, this is the very group that has the most difficulty finding a well-paying job.

But pure present day wealth or need is not all that influences one's preferences on redistribution. Alesina and La Ferrara show that expectations about future wealth or need matters as well as beliefs about the extent to which equal opportunities exist for all. The dependent variable in this analysis is whether one agrees with this statement: the government should reduce income differences between the rich and the poor. The first independent variable of interest is a person's opinion about the ability of someone

Table 5.3 Factors Affecting Whether a Person Believes the Government Should Reduce Income Differences between the Rich and the Poor

	Coefficient (Standard Error)
Get Ahead: Hard Work	−0.081*
	(0.031)
Expected Income	−0.002*
	(0.001)
N	4,042

Note: * = $p<0.05$, two-tailed. Drawn from Table 12 in Alesina and La Ferrara (2005: 958). Estimates for control variables – age, married, female, black, educ. b12, educ.N16, children, ln(real income), self-employed, unemployed in the last five years, prestige of father's job, father's education, states, years – not shown.

to get ahead in the world with hard work. Specifically, the variable Get Ahead: Hard Work equals one if a person agrees that hard work is more important than lucky breaks or help from others to get ahead in the world, zero otherwise. The second independent variable is Expected Income. This is a measure of the probability that an individual will move from an income below the mean to one above the mean in the next year.[8] In addition, Alesina and La Ferrara include a number of control variables: age, married, female, black, less than high school education, more than four-year college degree, children, ln(real income), self-employed, unemployed in the last five years, prestige of father's job, father's education, and fixed effects for each state and each year in the analysis. We show estimates from the multiple regression logistic model in Table 5.3.

First, we observe that the coefficients on the variables Get Ahead: Hard Work and Expected Income are statistically significant. Recall that the general rule of thumb for determining statistical significance is whether the coefficient is at least twice as large as the standard error. This is the case for the coefficient estimates shown in Table 5.3. Also recall that statistical significance means we are unlikely to observe this particular relationship by chance. In fact, the probability that the covariation between the variables is a result of chance is less than five in a hundred. Second, we examine the sign on the coefficient. In Table 5.3, all of the coefficients are negative. This means that an increase in each variable decreases the probability that an individual will agree with the following statement: the government should reduce income differences between the rich and the poor. For example, the more one believes that one can get ahead through hard work, then the less likely one is to support government redistribution.

---

[8] The actual measure of expected income is quite complex and we refer readers to the original article for more details.

Similarly, the greater one's expected income, then the less likely one is to support government redistribution.

Next, recall that regression estimates should generally be viewed as correlations, and correlation does not necessarily equal causation. Correlation, however, is necessary for establishing causation. With observational data, as we have here, the greatest threat to the validity of the analysis is that the relationship is spurious because there is an omitted variable. Given the array of control variables included in this analysis, that concern is not too great. In other words, the statistically significant relationships between beliefs in getting ahead and expected income and redistribution are all the more noteworthy given the inclusion of so many relevant control variables.

5.8 Conclusion

The goal to manage the economy to ensure prosperity, economic growth, and rising incomes is universal. There is disagreement on how to accomplish those interlocking goals. Since the 1980s, there has been a focus on tax reductions at the national level, with the justification for that being that lower taxes will lead entrepreneurs to make investments in the economy, which will result in the growth of jobs and income for the public and higher-end tax receipts for the government because of the income tax consequences of those higher earnings.

Governments use a number of policy tools in their attempts to regulate the economy to produce greater growth. They hold down interest rates to encourage investment and spending. They increase the supply of money to hold down inflation. They regulate industries domestically and abroad to encourage trade that will be valuable. They are limited in their ability to control economic performance and growth by a number of things, including the actions of other nations, military disputes, natural disasters, technological developments, and the availability of energy.

Regardless of their success or failure, attempts to manage the economy will continue, as even the most ardent supporters of free markets want to help as well as they are able. The problems facing the US social security program are great, but strong support for the program's continued existence remains even among young people who expect not to receive support in the course of their lifetimes. It remains to be seen how great the problem of income inequality becomes. The differences in incomes between the top and bottom quintiles of earners have grown enormously since the 1980s and the problem seems not to be lessening. The tools that are available for correcting the problem, increasing taxes for redistribution either through the EITC or TANF, or in some other way to transfer income, are not likely to be popular among the people whose taxes will rise to support the transfers.

Perhaps the greatest hope is to have renewed economic growth. Even with that, the differences in skills that exist among populations make it unlikely that the least educated will gain from those changes, which may increase the income distribution problem.

Key Terms

Economic growth
Low inflation
Full employment
Positive balance of trade
Classical model
Laissez-faire
Gross domestic product
Keynesianism
New Deal
Works Progress Administration
Fiscal policy
Monetary policy
Regulation
Federal Reserve Board
Progressive taxation
Flat tax
Regressive taxation
Tax incidence
Price setting
Entry restrictions
Barrier to entry
Supply-side
Trickle-down economics
Laffer Curve
Tax deductions
Tax expenditures
Unemployment
Veil of ignorance
Income inequality
Redistribution
Cash transfer
Social security

Social insurance

Redistributive

Means tested

Block grant

Categorical grant

Earned income tax credit

Minimum wage

Recession

CHAPTER EXERCISES

1. How do tax rates affect purchasing decisions? Can governments regulate taxes to induce certain behaviors?

2. The negative income tax is criticized because it leads to substitution effects among workers. Discuss the meaning of substitution effects in the economy and how it would affect behavior with a negative income tax.

3. The social security program functions as an entitlement program in the United States. What effect would creating a means test for benefits have on recipients of social security and on payers?

4. Rates of personal savings are low in the United States. What has led to the low rate of savings, and is there a way to alter that behavior?

5. The Supplemental Nutrition Assistance Program (SNAP) is run by the US Department of Agriculture, and several other programs that provide public income security benefits are run by different agencies. Is it desirable to have multiple government agencies providing benefits, or would it be desirable to house them all in a single agency?

6. Should public policy be used to provide an income floor beneath which people would not be allowed to fall? If so, how would that income floor be maintained?

REFERENCES

Alesina, Alberta and La Ferarra, E. 2005. "Preferences for Redistribution in the Land of Opportunities." *Journal of Public Economics* 89: 897–931.

Ben-Shalom, Yonathan, Moffitt, Robert A., and Scholz, John K. 2011. "An Assessment of Anti-Poverty Programs in the United States." NBER Working Paper no. 17042. Available online at www.nber.org/papers/w17042.

Bernanke, Ben S. 1995. "The Macroeconomics of the Great Depression: A Comparative Approach." *Journal of Money, Credit, and Banking* 27(1): 1–28.

Blank, Rebecca M. 2002. "Evaluating Welfare Reform in the U.S." *Journal of Economic Literature* 40(4): 1105–1166.

2006. "What Did the 1990s Welfare Reforms Accomplish?" in Alan J. Auerbach, David Card, and John M. Quigley (eds.), *Poverty, the Distribution of Income and Public Policy*. New York: Russell Sage Foundation.

Camerer, Colin. 2003. *Behavioral Game Theory: Experiments in Strategic Interaction*. Princeton University Press.

Card, David and Krueger, Alan B. 1994. "Minimum Wages and Employment: A Case Study of the Fast-Food Industry in New Jersey and Pennsylvania." *American Economic Review* 84(4): 772–793.

2000. "Minimum Wages and Employment: A Case Study of the Fast-Food Industry in New Jersey and Pennsylvania: Reply." *American Economic Review* 90(5): 1397–1420.

Davis, Belinda, Livermore, Michelle, and Lim, Younghee. 2011. "The Extended Reach of Minority Political Power: The Interaction of Descriptive Representation, Managerial Networking, and Race." *Journal of Politics* 73(2): 494–507.

Esarey, Justin, Salmon, Tim, and Barrilleaux, Charles. 2012. "Social Insurance and Income Redistribution in a Laboratory Experiment." *Political Research Quarterly* 65(3): 685–698.

Frohlich, Norman and Oppenheimer, Joe A. 1992. *Choosing Justice: An Experimental Approach to Ethical Theory*. Berkeley, CA: University of California Press.

Galveston County, TX. 2014. "Human Resources Manual." Available online at www.galvestoncountytx.gov/HmPg%20Information/HR%20Policy%20Manual.pdf.

Gilens, Martin. 1999. *Why Americans Hate Welfare*. University of Chicago Press.

Henrich, J., Boyd, R., Bowles, S., Camerer, C., Fehr, E., Gintis, H. *et al.* 2005. "'Economic Man' in Cross-Cultural Perspective: Behavioural Experiments in 15 Small-Scale Societies." *Behavioral and Brain Sciences* 28: 695–855.

Howard, Christopher. 1997. *The Hidden Welfare State: Tax Expenditures and Social Policy in the United States*. Princeton University Press.

Huber, Evelynne and Stephens, J. T. 2014. "Income Inequality and Redistribution in Post-Industrial Democracies: Demographic, Economic and Political Determinants." *Socio-Economic Review* 12(2): 245–267.

Kelly, Nathan. 2009. *The Politics of Income Inequality in the United States*. New York: Cambridge University Press.

Krause, George and Douglas, James W. 2005. "Institutional Design versus Reputational Effects on Bureaucratic Performance: Evidence from U.S. Government Macroeconomic and Fiscal Projections." *Journal of Public Administration Research and Theory* 15(2): 281–306.

Lewis-Beck, Michael S. 1990. *Economics and Elections: The Major Western Democracies*. Ann Arbor, MI: University of Michigan Press.

Mankiw, N. Gregory and Weinzeirl, Matthew. 2004. "Dynamic Scoring: A Back-of-the Envelope Guide." Cambridge, MA: National Bureau of Economic Research working paper 11000.

Manksi, Charles F. 2013. *Public Policy in an Uncertain World*. Cambridge, MA: Harvard University Press.

Neumark, David, Salas, J. M. Ian, and Wascher, William. 2013. "Revisiting the Minimum Wage-Employment Debate: Throwing out the Baby with the Bathwater?" Institute for the Study of Labor (IZA), discussion paper 7166. Available online at http://ftp.iza.org/dp7166.pdf.

North, Douglass C. 1990. *A Transaction Theory of Politics*. New York: Cambridge University Press.

1989. "Institutions and Economic Growth: An Historical Introduction." *World Development* 17(9): 1319–1332.

Olson, Mancur. 1993. "Dictatorship, Democracy and Development." *American Political Science Review* 87(3): 567–576.

1965. *The Logic of Collective Action: Public Goods and a Theory of Groups*. Cambridge, MA: Harvard University Press.

Organization for Economic Co-operation and Development (OECD). 2013. "Pension Markets in Focus." Available online at www.oecd.org/finance/PensionMarketsInFocus2013.pdf.

Peltzman, Sam. 1976. "Toward a More General Theory of Regulation." *Journal of Law and Economics* 19(2): 211–240.

Piketty, Thomas. 2014. *Capital in the Twenty-First Century*. Cambridge, MA: Harvard University Press.

Piketty, Thomas and Saez, Emmanuel. 2006. "The Evolution of Top Incomes: A Historical and International Perspective." National Bureau for Economic Research working paper 11955.

Poole, Keith T. and Rosenthal, Howard. 1997. *Congress: A Political-Economic History of Roll Call Voting*. New York: Oxford University Press.

Rawls, John. 1971. *A Theory of Justice*. Cambridge, MA: Harvard University Press.

Reinhart, Carmen and Rogoff, Kenneth S. 2013. "Financial and Sovereign Debt Crises: Some Lessons Learned and Those Forgotten." International Monetary Fund working paper WP/13/266.

Rom, Mark Carl. 2013. "State Health and Welfare Programs" in Virginia Gray, Russell Hanson, and Thad Kousser (eds.), *Politics in the American States*, 10th edn. Los Angeles, CA: Sage/CQ Press. "The Politics of Bureaucratic Structure" in John Chubb and Paul Peterson (eds.), *Can the Government Govern?* Washington, DC: Brookings.

Romer, Christina D. 1992. "What Ended the Great Depression?" *Journal of Economic History* 52(4): 757–784.

Saez, Emmanuel. 2001. "Using Elasticities to Derive Optimal Tax Rates." *Review of Economic Studies* 68(234): 205–229.

Scheve, Kenneth and Stasavage, David. 2012. "Democracy, War and Wealth: Lessons from Two Centuries of Inheritance Taxation." *American Political Science Review* 106(1): 81–102.

Soss, Joe, Fording, Richard C., and Schram, Sanford F. 2011. *Disciplining the Poor*. University of Chicago Press.

Stigler, Joseph J. 1971. "The Theory of Economic Regulation." *Bell Journal of Economics and Management Science* 2(1): 3–21.

Stone, Chad and Chen, William. 2013. "Introduction to Unemployment Insurance." Washington, DC: Center for Budget and Policy Priorities.

US Department of Health and Human Services. 2014. "About TANF." Available online at www.acf.hhs.gov/programs/ofa/programs/tanf/about.

US Office of Management and Budget. 2016. "Historical Tables." Available online at www.whitehouse.gov/omb/budget/Historicals.

Wilson, Theresa M. 1999. "The Galveston Plan and Social Security: A Comparative Analysis of Two Systems." *Social Security Bulletin* 62(1): 47–64.

Yakita, Akira. 2004. "Elasticity of Substitution in Public Capital Formation and Economic Growth." *Journal of Macroeconomics* 26(3): 391–408.

6 Environmental Policy

Outline

Questions

- What role do markets and government play in addressing environmental issues?
- What is public opinion on environmental issues and does it influence the policy process?
- What role do bureaucrats play in implementing environmental legislation?
- What different elements are involved in evaluating an environmental program?

Overview

- The primary analytic concepts we use to provide insights on environmental policy are negative externalities and agency theory.
- Environmental pollution is a negative externality generated as a by-product of market exchanges.
- A variety of corrective mechanisms can be used to deter the production of such negative externalities.

- Command and control regulation is the most often employed corrective mechanism in environmental policy.
- While individuals tend to support government intervention in the affairs of private enterprise to resolve pollution concerns, they are less supportive of regulation or taxes that affect them directly.
- Environmental issues tend to be less salient relative to other public policy issues.
- The success of any regulatory program depends in part on the ability of the chief executive or legislative principals to properly incentivize their bureaucratic agents to perform. In the absence of proper incentives, agents are more likely to deliver suboptimal outputs.
- Evaluating a regulatory program involves assessing both the total costs and benefits of the program. Total benefits are nearly always more difficult to quantify relative to costs, and this has both policy and political consequences.

Introduction

We often make decisions that have little consequence for others. For example, on any given day you can either choose to go for a walk or a run. And, while important for you, your choice likely has little consequence for other people. There are infinite examples of such decisions in our daily lives. However, we also make decisions that have great consequence for others, either positively or negatively. Consider the following example: at the encouragement of my passengers, I choose to speed in my car. I could potentially harm not only myself, but also my passengers if I were to crash the car. Now, someone may say, "Well, that's not a problem. All of the parties involved consented to my speeding, so there is no ethical conflict here." However, what if I had harmed a person walking down the street? What if I had crashed into an innocent bystander – a person who was not involved with me and my passengers' agreement – what then? This type of negative consequence to someone who was not a party to an agreement is at the core of this chapter on environmental policy.

When individuals choose to purchase a good or service in a market setting, we assume that both the provider and the consumer do so freely and willingly. To this end, each party can improve their lot. If they can agree on the terms of exchange, one party can sell their good or service and the other can buy it, increasing utility for both. However, our day-to-day transactions in the market may affect an individual or entity who is not a party to the transaction. If we affect them positively, we likely would not hear any complaints. For example, if I hire a contractor to renovate my dilapidated house and, as a result, the homes in my immediate vicinity increase in value, I likely will not be the subject of neighborhood ire. However, if we harm others not a party to some transaction and we fail to compensate them for their harm, then we have a dilemma. Those parties could claim that they had no role in the agreement and as a result should not be harmed in any way by its existence. We refer to the costs borne by parties external to a transaction as **negative externalities**. Recall that this cost is referred to as an externality precisely because the affected third party was not a party to, or was outside of, the transaction that produced the cost. How society addresses such externalities is the focus of this chapter.

In this chapter, we look at how pollution arises from market interactions, what people think about pollution, what has been done about it, and what remains to be addressed. We begin with a review of different possible responses to pollution as a market externality. We then consider the role of the public in formulating demand for regulatory initiatives. We review the major pieces of environmental legislation advanced over the last forty years and consider the challenges inherent in implementing command and control regulation. We end the chapter with an evaluation of the performance of these legislative initiatives.

6.1 Environmental Policy, Market Failure, and Negative Externalities

We can understand negative externalities within environmental policy in the following ways. Consider a factory that produces automobile tires and pollutes the air of the citizens living around the factory. The citizen living by the factory receives no compensation, and thus suffers from the negative externality of polluted air. When farmers fertilize their crops with nitrogen and phosphorous and these chemicals leach into the ground water and flow into surface waters, a negative externality (polluted water) may be imposed on other farmers or citizens who wish to use those waters. When citizens choose to drive older automobiles that lack modern pollution-reducing technology, a negative externality (polluted air) has been imposed on their fellow citizens without compensation.

In each of these cases, the critical feature is that the institution(s) or individual(s) responsible for producing the externality does not bear its total cost. Rather, the parties externalize or **socialize** some portion of those costs to others – others who were not involved in the transaction. Accordingly, the price of the transaction does not reflect these total costs. In other words, the prices of the tires produced, the fertilizer sold, or the older cars do not reflect either the costs of the damage to health or welfare that the pollution caused or the costs of cleaning up that pollution. As a result, the tire manufacturers, fertilizer producers, and used car lot owners have no incentive to reduce the pollution deriving from each. Moreover, the lower prices of these goods mean that they will be more attractive to consumers on the market. These lower prices encourage greater consumption of these goods and, in turn, a greater production of negative externalities. In economic terms, this suggests an **inefficient outcome**, meaning that too much of a certain good will be produced or consumed relative to the overall costs and benefits to society. Given that negative externalities in the form of air, water, and hazardous waste pollution are driven by whether their total costs are borne by private parties, such externalities are rather difficult to resolve in the absence of some form of price adjustment.

Let's consider negative externalities more formally. Using the supply and demand curves from Chapter 3, Figure 6.1 displays the relationship for some good. Let's imagine that it is lawn fertilizer. This figure displays the relationship between the private cost (suppliers' marginal cost curve) and the social cost (society's marginal cost curve) of lawn fertilizer with the demand curve for this good. Notice that the Social Cost curve is shifted left from the Private Cost curve. This reflects the fact that society will bear the costs of increased ground water pollution and that such pollution costs are not reflected in the market price, P_p, at the market equilibrium for demand, Q_p. Why? This result obtains because consumers make their choice based on where their marginal cost equals their marginal benefit and this obtains at point b in the graph. Consumers do not consider the cost of the negative externality in their decision. This means that at all demand levels the social costs of selling lawn fertilizer are higher than the actual price obtained in the market. Instead of obtaining the optimal production of lawn fertilizer, Q_s, at the optimal price, P_s, the market equilibrium holds at point b.

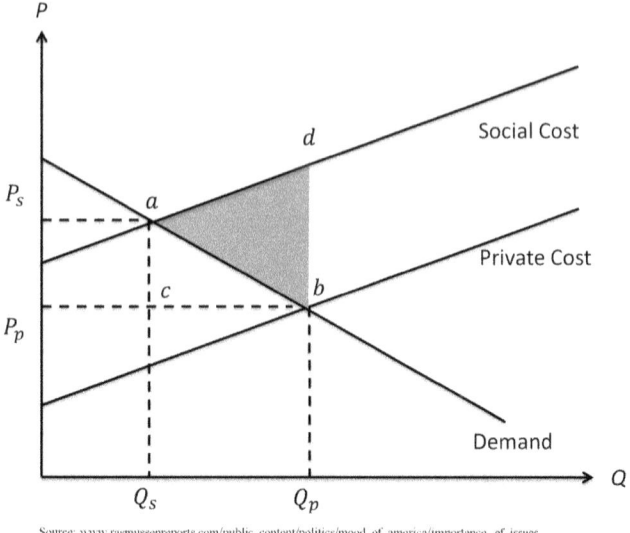

Figure 6.1 Negative Externalities and Dead Weight Loss

This results in a loss of economic efficiency. At Q_p, the social benefit of lawn fertilizer is less than its social cost. Society would be better off if the quantity of fertilizer between Q_p and Q_s had never been produced. Why? Consider the figure. As the social cost curve shifts further and further left, away from our private equilibrium at point b, an area of the figure, designated by the triangle a-b-d, grows in size. Alternatively, you can see that if we were able to decrease the negative externalities associated with lawn fertilizer then we would see a migration of the social cost curve rightward, decreasing the distance between our Social equilibrium, a, and our Private equilibrium, b, and shrinking the size of the triangle a-b-d. The area represented by the triangle a-b-d represents the **deadweight loss** generated by the negative externality. The deadweight loss is the negative surplus to society of generating too much lawn fertilizer at too low costs. Given the costs that the product is generating for society, for an efficient allocation of goods, the market price must reflect the total cost.

For a market to reduce the negative externalities produced by some good or service, the price of that good or service must be adjusted to reflect its total cost. The idea behind this is simple: producers must internalize the total costs of their products. By internalize, we mean they must share or pass on those costs to the consumer of the good or service. Once these "true" costs are reflected in its price, demand for the product will likely decrease since the product will be much more expensive. There are several mechanisms that can be used to correct negative externalities, including consumption taxes – also called **Pigouvian taxes**, subsidies (negative Pigouvian taxes), or output standards (regulations), which we discuss in more detail below. The utility of any one corrective mechanism can be evaluated on at least three dimensions – its costs of implementation, the expected return on the investment (the benefits supplied by the mechanism), or the political effort required to enact the mechanism. A highly beneficial mechanism may have little usefulness if the costs outweigh the benefits or if the current political regime does not support it. It is useful to consider these three dimensions when evaluating any corrective mechanism.

Box 6.1

Arthur Pigou (1877–1959) was an economist who worked on negative externalities and their solutions. In the presence of a negative externality, he showed that a market outcome would not be efficient; the market would overproduce a given item relative to the total cost and benefits to society. To correct for this externality, Pigou suggested that a tax be levied on the good or service. If the new tax was set at the level of the externality, the resulting new price of the item would then

Box 6.1 (*cont.*)

return efficiency to the market. While simple in theory, Pigouvian taxes face practical challenges, including determining and setting the size of the tax. Why might selecting the size of the tax be challenging?

The first corrective mechanism, the **consumption tax**, is an added cost applied to a good or service thought to be generating a negative externality. For example, such a tax could be applied to older (or less fuel-efficient) automobiles to increase the relative cost of the automobile to reflect its total cost on society, thereby pricing the externality into the total cost. The United States implemented such a tax, commonly referred to as the "Gas Guzzler" tax, in 1978 to discourage the purchase of cars with low fuel efficiency. The tax was required to be paid for certain car models that were deemed to be too fuel-inefficient. The Gas Guzzler tax only applied to cars. Trucks, vans, and SUVs were excluded from the tax because these vehicles were rare at the time. In 1978, only 22.7 percent of the light vehicle market consisted of vans, light trucks, and SUVs. In theory, compared to other more fuel-efficient cars, the less fuel-efficient (and now more expensive because of the tax) automobiles should be less preferable. Consumers should shift their preference away from the more wasteful and expensive cars. Consumption taxes, conditioned on the size of the tax, are generally believed to be effective at inducing lower consumption of targeted goods and services. Setting the optimal level of the tax is a delicate choice, however. If it is set too low, it will likely not induce a behavioral response. If it is set too high, it will likely incentivize the development of a black market, where citizens can purchase the goods at lower cost.

One difficulty associated with a consumption tax, or any tax for that matter, is the potential for political conflict. After 1978, political winds shifted toward deregulation and the average price of gasoline paid at the pump plummeted throughout the 1980s and 1990s. Lower gas prices removed the incentive to alter consumer behavior. As a result, Congress was less likely to update the Gas Guzzler tax to reflect growing consumer preference for light trucks and SUVs. This is especially important considering that the share of the light vehicle market consisting of vans, light trucks, and SUVs had more than doubled; by 2005 it was at 49.7 percent.[1] Yet, as of 2005, the Gas Guzzler tax applied only to cars like the 12-cylinder Ferrari and the 12-cylinder Rolls Royce, which were not widely purchased in the United States. The tax excluded, however, the Hummer, The Jeep Grand Cherokee, the Ford Explorer, and other frequently purchased SUVs because SUVs were not covered under the law.

[1] Source: US Environmental Protection Agency, *Light-Duty Automotive Technology and Fuel Economy Trends: 1975 through 2005*, July 2005

An alternative corrective mechanism to the consumption tax, which in essence penalizes choices that society deems undesirable, is the subsidy (or negative Pigouvian tax). Subsidies reward people for making choices that society considers desirable. Such taxes can be used to encourage private transactions that have **positive externalities**, or benefits to parties external to the agreement. In essence, these **subsidies** are transfer payments from society (the government) to an institution or individual in return for a behavioral choice. If governments wish to encourage businesses or individuals to make a particular behavior choice, they can offer a cash payment or a tax credit to offset some portion of the costs associated with that choice. For example, if the current market price of installing solar panels is too costly for the average small business or citizen, the government can offer a tax credit to lower the effective cost of the purchase. This type of a subsidy would encourage solar panel purchases – the behavior choice that the government sought to influence.

Box 6.2

The Cash for Clunkers Program, formally the Car Allowance Rebate System (CARS), was a temporary automobile purchase subsidy program that existed for approximately two months in the summer of 2009. The purpose of the program was to simultaneously stimulate the economy by encouraging owners of older, "dirtier" running automobiles to trade them in for newer, cleaner running, more fuel efficient models. Basic eligibility required the trade-in to be less than twenty-five years old and make less than 18 miles per gallon fuel efficiency. The new car needed to be less than $45,000 and make more than 22 miles per gallon. If these conditions were met, the program provided a direct subsidy (either $3,500 or $4,500) for the car's purchase to the owner. While the program officially registered sales on the order of ~600,000 vehicles, critics have argued over the precise benefits of the program, suggesting that a sizeable proportion of these sales would have occurred despite the program's incentives.

The third and more common corrective mechanism is the setting of **output standards**. Output standards are either outright bans or limitations on the amount of a given externality (air pollution) that may be produced. Some forms of output, such as the dumping of hazardous waste directly into a waterway, may be banned outright. Others, such as the emissions from a coal-fired electricity generating plant, are limited to some maximum amount. To implement an output standards mechanism, government bureaus are created and charged with setting the level of the output standard. They are also responsible for inspecting and punishing firms or individuals who exceed their output limitations. This approach to correcting a market externality is often referred to as **command and control** regulation.

The command and control approach to resolving market externalities has its critics. Opponents of command and control regulation argue that the resources that must be spent on the creation of a bureaucracy to implement such a regulatory system, including infrastructure (i.e. buildings and offices), personnel, pensions, fleets of vehicles, etc., can lead to an inefficient use of resources. As an alternative, opponents of command and control generally advocate consumption taxes or subsidies to manipulate the total costs of certain products or services. However, such taxes and subsidies are often difficult to achieve politically – mainly due to the ability of the consumer to identify the precise amount of the tax or subsidy in the purchase price. The costs of command and control regulation, on the other hand, are rarely represented on the sticker price or sales receipt of a good. For this reason, among others, command and control remains the primary tool that modern democracies use to address market externalities.

Whether society elects to pursue one of the specific corrective mechanisms mentioned here or elects to do nothing in response to negative externalities in the environment depends upon several factors. The most crucial of these factors is the level of expressed demand from the public and the willingness/ability of elites, both elected (chief executives and legislators) and unelected (lobbyists and interest groups), to pursue environmental initiatives. In the next section, we consider the role of the public and elites (political parties and elected officials) in environmental policy.

6.2 Public Opinion, Political Parties, and Environmental Policy

The relative impact of public opinion on public policy depends upon several critical features. First of all, citizens must have an opinion. In other words, they must be able to express their desires and have these desires understood and acted on by elected leaders. Therefore, to understand the role of public opinion in environmental policy, we must consider public opinion on environmental regulation, the relative salience of environmental concerns relative to other issues, and, finally, the barriers that may prevent citizens' environmental preferences from being translated into votes for particular elected leaders.

Public Attitudes on the Environment

Where does the typical US citizen stand on issues related to the environment? While this seems like a fairly simple question, upon further reflection we will see that it is actually quite complex. This is because when we dig below the surface of public opinion we may see conflicting, competing, or what appear to be nonsensical preferences. To better understand what the public believes or prefers about the environment, we first need to consider how to interpret public opinion generally. Public opinion can be thought of as having five critical characteristics that are useful in deciphering the public's attitude. These five characteristics of opinion are: direction, intensity, salience, knowledge, and stability. Direction refers to the level of support that a citizen assigns to a specific policy. Intensity refers to how strongly a citizen feels about a given issue. Salience registers the relative importance of a given issue relative to other issues. Knowledge refers to the level of information that a citizen possesses on a specific issue. Finally, stability refers to how much volatility we observe in citizen attitude over time. Only when we consider all of these features can we best understand where the public stands on a given policy. In the following section, we consider each of these characteristics and what they reveal about the public's relationship to environmental issues.

With respect to direction, upon first pass, it would appear as if most citizens are actually quite "green." The public seems to agree both with the idea of increasing spending on environmental protections and with maintaining high environmental regulatory standards. Moreover, these attitudes are generally intensely held and quite stable over time, meaning that citizens appear to hold strong beliefs regarding enhanced protection for the environment. Although these beliefs may fluctuate slightly over time, the public actually holds fairly stable attitudes in the aggregate over time.

However, while Americans seem to favor increasing regulations and taxes for the benefit of the environment, they appear to support doing so only when those regulations and taxes apply to others – not when they apply to themselves. For example, in the domain of air pollution, Americans overwhelmingly support the idea of imposing increased emission standards on the automotive industry. They support the idea of the government requiring car companies to dedicate more research and development as well as production resources to emission standard technology – perhaps assuming that these costs will not be passed on to the consumer in the form of a higher sticker price. When the question turns to what "sacrifice" the individual citizen is willing to provide, Americans are skeptical of government intervention in their lives in the form of regulations and taxes. Over half consistently suggest that they would not be willing to pay an additional gas tax for the benefit of reducing pollution.

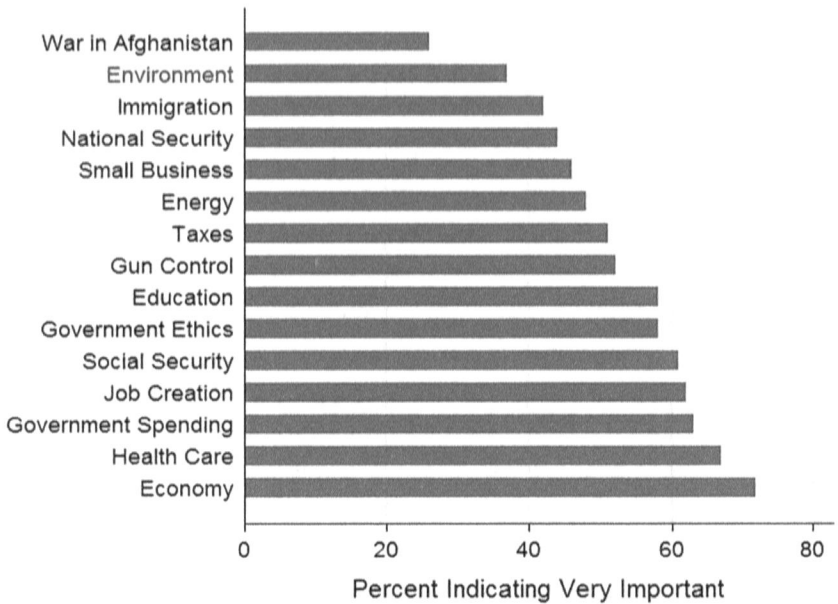

Source: www.rasmussenreports.com/public_content/politics/mood_of_america/importance_of_issues.

Figure 6.2 Salience of Environmental Regulation Relative to Other Issues

We see this pattern again and again in environmental policy. Americans are generally willing to have the government be more involved in the affairs of large corporations, yet are quite resistant to the government being more involved in their lives – even if to obtain the same end. This applies in air pollution, water pollution, and even recycling. Americans are more likely to approve of requiring businesses to bear more regulations and taxes for pollution control than individual citizens. Certainly, some portion of this behavior is cost shifting, or the idea that few of us prefer to pay for a good or service if we can find someone else to pay for it instead. Privatizing benefits and socializing costs to others has a long history in politics. But there may be another factor driving this result as well. We will return to this point further in the chapter.

With a large consensus among the public on environmental issues, it is surprising that resolving environmental issues continues to present such a challenge to elected leaders. There are at least two reasons for this. First, public support for environmental issues is a relatively soft issue compared to other issues. This means that when analyzing policy, we have to be mindful to not fall into the **saliency trap**. This refers to the logical fallacy of believing that, because a citizen has an opinion on some policy issue, this opinion is a salient or important issue to them relative to other issues. This is a rather tenuous assumption to make. Consider Figure 6.2. In a survey from 2009, citizens expressed their attitudes on several public policy issues. Notice that among the various policy issues included in the survey (the economy, terrorism, education, social security, crime, etc.), citizen concern over environmental issues ranks relatively low. This suggests, for example, that an elected leader would likely be incorrect to run a campaign primarily on the issue of the environment or to pursue comprehensive environmental legislation. Eventually, they may find themselves pursuing an issue that is not all that important to their constituents. This is not to suggest that legislators cannot pursue multiple issues at the same time. Rather, some issues are more pressing for constituents and, given finite resources, legislators are likely to allocate their time and energy accordingly. Polling research shows us that this saliency trap is particularly strong in times of economic distress. When citizens are struggling to find work and maintain their standard of living, their relative concern for environmental issues (Guber 2003; Scruggs 2003) and even their confidence over the threat of climate change (Scruggs and Benegal 2012) are lower than in times of economic boom.

Last, consider the knowledge that citizens may hold on a given policy question. Mark Twain once said, "I am not one of those who in expressing opinions confine themselves to facts." This humorous quote echoes a well-founded admonition about public opinion – we ought not to confuse opinion for knowledge. Many citizens express opinions on topics upon which they have little or no knowledge (Delli Carpini and Keener 1996; Barabas *et al.* 2014). Pollsters learned this lesson relatively late in the game. In early public opinion research, polls forced people to express opinions on issues that they may have had little familiarity with – resulting in biased results. Well-conducted contemporary polls provide respondents with an exit option in the form of "I don't know" or "I have no opinion." While this exit option helps to reduce the amount of bias in a survey, it is certainly not a perfect inoculation. People enjoy offering opinions, even when they may possess little or no information about the topic at hand.

When it comes to pollution, most Americans likely have not updated their information on the primary sources of air and water pollution today. Many still believe that the most troubling sources of air and water pollution are large factories spewing emissions and effluent into our air and water, respectively. The fact of the matter is that most (over 90 percent) of these factories have been operating in compliance of their permits for over thirty years. For the most part, these stationary air and point sources of water pollution are not the greatest culprits of today's lingering air and water pollution. Nor are they the sources of the greatest increases in air and water pollution that we have witnessed over the past thirty years. The largest increases in air pollution over this period derive not from factories, but from American citizens themselves. A large part of the increase is due to a drastic increase in vehicle miles traveled (VMTs). Since the 1970s, Americans have been driving farther and farther to commute between home and work and have been relying less and less upon mass transit. The result has been an explosion in mobile source air pollution.

A similar story exists with water pollution. The source of most lingering water pollution over the past thirty years is not the result of factory pipes spilling effluent into our rivers. Rather, it is often the result of non-point source pollution, or water pollution *not* derived from the end of a pipe. It is not only large agri-businesses and corporate farms that pollute our water. The use of herbicides, fertilizers, and pesticides on personal lawns also contributes to the growing level of pollution that leaches into our surface and ground waters. Yet, few Americans seem to recognize this. Surveys suggest that most Americans still believe that large factories are the primary reason to blame for our lingering air and water pollution. Despite this widespread opinion among the public, the data suggest that the actual source of contemporary air pollution is individual citizens themselves.

What, then, might explain this? There are two important possibilities. First, citizens may be wholly uninformed of their own personal responsibility in contributing to lingering pollution. As a result, they see no connection between their individual driving habits and lingering air pollution. Second, even if they recognized their own role in continuing pollution difficulties, citizens may be unwilling to pay those costs personally. They would prefer to increase the costs of driving cleaner automobiles to the car manufacturers in the form of higher auto emissions standards than to pay the costs themselves in the form of a tax on gasoline.

If knowledge on a given issue is relatively low, then an interesting question follows: Would citizens change their positions on public policy if they were better informed on the issues? Until a few years ago, this was a relatively challenging question, but the Center for Deliberative Democracy (CDD) at Stanford University has made significant advances in order to answer it. The difficulty in assessing the information-opinion linkage was that it was nearly impossible to ask a sufficiently large randomly selected sample of citizens about their opinion on a topic, expose them to at least two perspectives on the topic (while isolating any other changes), and then reassess their opinion to see if and how it changed. The CDD solved this issue by flying in a national sample and conducting the experiment on site. In one example of their work, the researchers assembled a random sample of voters from Michigan and polled them on issues relevant to the environment (CDD 2010). The researchers then exposed the citizens to in-group discussions led by trained moderators and had competing experts representing different opinions on the issue. After this treatment, the citizens were polled again. Figure 6.3 shows the results.

The effects of discussion and deliberation were stark. There was a consistent and fairly large increase in the amount of support that citizens were willing to provide to the various environmental issues in the experiment. It would appear that in this context, additional information, both in the form of citizens interacting with other citizens and in the form of hearing information from competing policy experts, had an

	Before	After	Change
Making Michigan a greener economy	55%	67%	+12
Increasing incentives for businesses to produce green products and services	60%	75%	+15
Designing and redesigning buildings to be more efficient	52%	61%	+9
Increasing tax credits for energy efficient homes and businesses	54%	66%	+12
Encouraging people to use less energy	61%	68%	+7
Creating and maintaining state parks	46%	52%	+6
Training people for green jobs	58%	72%	+14
Requiring a greater percentage of electricity to come from renewable energy	58%	66%	+8

Figure 6.3 Effect of Information and Discussion on Citizen Support for Environmental Policy

impact on public opinion. This suggests additional evidence in support of Twain's quote. While we should not confuse opinion for knowledge, we should also bear in mind that additional knowledge can affect and alter opinion.

The results of this study suggest that at least some portion of citizens hold opinions that may be resistant to deliberation, while others are more open to the prospect. This is important to the political realm of the policy process. The potential to influence citizens' opinions provides great opportunities for political parties, interest groups, and other interested stakeholders to affect how political debates are framed. If the debate over air pollution is framed as deriving from dirty polluting factories, citizens may support greater environmental regulation. If the debate is framed as deriving from citizens driving their cars too far/much, citizens may resist additional environmental regulation. In the end, for citizen attitudes to influence policy, they must be able to perceive a clear choice between the political parties on the issues that are important to them. Without such choice, the ability of citizens to translate their preferences into actual policy may be threatened.

Perceiving Policy Differences between Parties

For environmental issues, citizens must be able to match their policy preferences with those of competing party representatives in order to make the right choice in the voting booth. This leads to a simple question: do citizens perceive policy differences between the two major political parties on environmental issues? Most research suggests that strong partisans perceive the parties as offering a clear choice on the issue of the environment. Strong Democrats clearly view their party as superior and

Strong Republicans view their party as the better choice, albeit less starkly. This is not surprising. What is a bit more surprising is that independents and independent leaners (those who claim independence, but still lean toward one party or the other) generally perceive no difference between the two parties on environmental issues. From the perspective of democratic theory, this is troubling. This suggests that even if citizens were to hold clear policy preferences on environmental issues, they may have, or at least believe that they have, less clear choices on which party best represents these policy preferences.

Cross-Cutting Cleavages

Even if citizens held clearly distinct policy preferences on the environment and perceived clear differences between the platforms of candidates for office, there is still another reason why they might not see a connection between public opinion and electoral or policy outcomes. The reason is simply that politics consists of a variety of policy issues. When citizens hold preferences across many of these policy issues, it becomes more and more difficult to identify a candidate or a political party that will maximize their policy concerns across all issues. With each additional policy dimension, it becomes increasingly likely that a given candidate may take a position that a previous supporter will oppose. So while a citizen may share preferences with a candidate on the environment, abortion, and health care, they may hold opposing positions on foreign policy, immigration, and taxation. When this occurs, we say that the person is experiencing **cross-cutting cleavages**. Moreover, citizens have limited information-gathering capabilities, inhibiting their ability to learn about each candidate's positions on all policies. In a complex world, the average citizen may have to, as Herbert Simon (1955) suggested, **satisfice**. In other words, citizens must make the best choice that they can at any given moment, given the limited information and ability that they possess. Rather than making the *optimal* choice, citizens make the *adequate* choice, given their limited information.

In sum, the linkage between public opinion on a specific policy dimension (environmental, health, labor, etc.) and elected leaders may be weaker due to the salience trap, information shortfalls, perceptions of party differences, and cross-cutting cleavages of politics. Each of these items serves an important role in linking public opinion and elite action on environmental issues.

6.3 Legislative Initiatives in Environmental Policy

Despite the many threats to a strong linkage between public opinion and elected leaders' behavior on specific policy action, there have been several notable legislative initiatives in environmental policy over the last forty years. Public concern over environmental issues began to rise throughout the 1950s and 1960s. Pollution trends in the United States had been rising for decades. Yet, such pollution, while harmful and costly, was not primary in the public's mind. Without certain environmental crises that demanded the attention of the public and elected leaders, pollution growth may have continued.

The public's attention on environmental issues was focused by a few historic events that occurred throughout the 1960s. Rachel Carson's publication of *Silent Spring* (1962) is often thought of as marking the beginning of the contemporary environment movement. In her book, she documented the impact of pesticides such as Dichloro-DiphenylTrichloroethane (DDT) on birds and other animals in the food chain. Through exhaustive analysis, Carson demonstrated that not only did DDT kill insects far beyond the targeted group, but also it remained in the food chain, building up in the fatty tissues of animals, including human beings. This build-up of DDT was further linked to both genetic damage and cancers in the exposed animals. Carson's book was partially credited with the eventual ban on the production of DDT in 1972. Even more critically, however, her book sounded a warning bell on the consequences of the unregulated use of chemical pesticides, resulting in a wider public awareness of the possible risks of chemical use and abuse.

Another key focusing event of the 1960s was the Cuyahoga River's spontaneous combustion in the summer of 1969. Due to concentrated levels of oil and other water pollution, the Cuyahoga River in Cleveland Ohio caught fire. During this time, a river catching fire due to pollution was actually not an uncommon event. In fact, the Cuyahoga itself had caught fire ten times over a 100-year period. The 1969 fire, however, was different. It took place when the political context was ripe for environmental issues. This event, coupled with similar ones across the United States, gained and focused the public's attention. These were just a few of the events that opened a policy window for major public policy initiatives. Facing the public's growing concern over environmental issues, elected leaders felt pressure to respond. In the 1970s, they finally did.

Box 6.3

The Cuyahoga River Fire (1969) was a momentous occasion in the US environmental movement. The spontaneous combustion of the river due to inordinately high levels of water pollution helped shape public opinion on government involvement in regulating pollution. Political scientists, such as John Kingdon, refer to such occasions that allow for major public policy initiatives to move forward as **policy windows**. Kingdon suggests that when such windows open, they act as a lens focusing and combining previously existing policy solutions

Box 6.3 (*cont.*)

with political forces. This combination typically results in major policy reforms. Without such windows, large-scale reform is difficult to advance. What other historical events have acted as policy windows, enabling major policy reforms to pass?

Major Legislative Initiatives

Prior to the 1970s, the federal government's involvement in environmental affairs was primarily in land conservation, research and development, and financial assistance to the states. The setting and enforcement of air and water pollution standards, however, were generally reserved to the domain of the states. This state-dominated approach to environmental issues changed in the 1970s. Congress responded to the environmental issues of the 1950s and 1960s with several comprehensive legislative initiatives, which located primary authority to set and enforce environmental standards with the federal government. Not since the 1930s' New Deal initiatives under President Roosevelt had the United States witnessed such a large transfer of policy authority (in terms of scope) from the states to the national government. While these initiatives spanned a variety of policy areas including water, air, hazardous waste, and drinking water, each used a similar command and control approach to negotiate pollution concerns. Below, we summarize several of these initiatives.

The National Environmental Policy Act (NEPA) – In 1970, Congress passed and President Nixon signed into law a bill that included several important provisions. Namely, the law established national environmental priorities, required all federal agencies to prepare Environmental Impact Statements (EIS) to assess the environmental consequences of their actions, and created the Council on Environmental Quality (CEQ). The CEQ was located within the Executive Office of the President, and became the president's main advisory body on environmental issues.

EPA – In 1970, President Nixon issued an executive order, Reorganization Plan No. 3, to create the Environmental Protection Agency (EPA). With the creation of EPA, the national government now had an agency that would become the central regulatory body of environmental policy. The order identified the pollution control programs across a wide variety of agencies (i.e. air and solid waste programs within the Department of Health, Education, and Welfare and water programs within the Department of the Interior, etc.) and consolidated all of them under the authority of EPA. EPA was tasked with conducting research and disseminating information on pollution prevention, but also with the establishment and enforcement of pollution control standards.

Clean Air Act Amendments – In 1970, Congress passed and President Nixon signed a major overhaul of the nation's air pollution program (originally passed in 1963). The amended law included a new regulatory program that implemented pollution standards for six criteria pollutants (lead, carbon monoxide, nitrogen oxides, sulfur oxides, ozone, and particulate matter). This system of limitations was to be enforced through a new pollution permitting system (commonly referred to as Title V after the section of the bill that authorized it). Under this permitting system, the national government (and states working under national authority) would issue permits to **stationary sources**, or fixed emitters of air pollution, limiting the **emissions** of these and other hazardous pollutants. Violations of these permit limitations could result in firms being cited, fined, or even brought to civil or criminal cases. Legislation also allowed citizens to bring lawsuits against entities thought to be violating the terms of the law – a particularly innovative change in the approach to environmental issues. The law has since been amended in 1977 and 1990, with the greatest change being the creation of an emissions trading scheme added with the 1990 amendments.

Clean Water Act Amendments – In 1972, Congress passed and President Nixon signed a major reform of the nation's water pollution program (originally passed in 1948). These amendments used a similar approach to the Clean Air Act to address water pollution. The new act created a permitting system for **point sources**, or single identifiable sources of water pollution (i.e. a pipe), known as the National Pollution Discharge Elimination System (NPDES). These permits were used to set limits on the amount of point source pollution, or **effluent**, that a given facility could discharge to a water source. **Non-point source pollution**, however, was not regulated in this original bill. Only with the 1987 addition of Section 319 did it include non-point source regulation.

Resource Conservation and Recovery Act (RCRA) – In 1976, Congress passed and President Ford signed RCRA into law. This legislation's purpose was to regulate the creation, transportation, use, and disposal of hazardous waste. The innovation of this legislation was its "**Cradle to grave**" approach to regulation. It required a stringent tracking system that kept detailed records on each specific amount of hazardous material from its generation (cradle), to its transportation/use across the United States, and eventually to its disposal (grave).

Safe Drinking Water Act – In 1974, Congress passed and President Ford signed a reform of the nation's drinking water regulation. The SDWA gave EPA the authority to set standards for public community water systems and to enforce the maintenance of those standards. Public systems are required by law to meet federal standards for the Maximum Contaminant Level (MCL) for nearly 100 primary water contaminants, and are open to compliance sanctions for violations. The SWDA also includes a list of an additional fifteen recommended, but non-enforceable, secondary water contaminants, which includes such items as fluoride and pH.

Toxic Substances Control Act – In 1976, Congress passed and President Ford signed a bill that created a process to test and document the potential toxic effects of existing and new chemicals. Information on tested chemicals is stored in the TSCA Inventory. Upon notification by a firm of its intention to produce a new chemical, EPA must review the chemical's properties and assess whether it may present an "unreasonable risk." The TSCA permits EPA to regulate chemicals that may present such a risk.

Comprehensive Environmental Response, Compensation and Liability Act (CERCLA) – In 1980, Congress passed and President Carter signed a bill that established a procedure and a "polluter pays" funding source for the clean-up of sites contaminated with hazardous materials. The legislation, also called Superfund, establishes a process by which candidates for funding are ranked in order of potential risk to public health and welfare. If ranked sufficiently high, a site can be added to the National Priorities List (NPL) and will then be eligible for clean-up funds. The fund was originally financed by a tax on the petroleum and chemical industry. This tax was allowed to expire under President Clinton in 1996, and, since exhausting its reserve funds in 2003, has been funded through general revenue.

Each of these legislative initiatives represents a singular event in environmental regulatory policy, with each concentrating regulatory power away from the states and toward the federal government. Within one decade (1970 to 1980), the breadth of the federal government had expanded into what had traditionally been the domain of the states. The federal government would continue its traditional role in encouraging land conservation, providing research and development, and assisting states with funding, but now would be the lead government entity in setting and enforcing environmental standards across a host of policy domains. In fact, much of the contemporary debate over the proper role of the federal government and its relation to the states grew out of the regulatory expansion in the 1970s.

6.4 Implementing Environmental Policy

Each of the previously listed initiatives represents a major legislative accomplishment in environmental policy. Yet, passing legislation is only one step in the policy process. Once passed, legislative programs are turned over to the executive branch for implementation. Bureaucrats, most of whom are unelected, are charged with implementing the legislature's policy. This means that bureaucrats must interpret the legislature's "statutory intent," balance this intent with their own policy preferences, and then fashion specific regulatory rules that they believe are in line with the intended goals of the legislation. Toward this end, these bureaucrats are also empowered with inspecting and enforcing the standards laid out in regulatory rules. In short, the success of any piece of legislation is conditional on the cooperation, skill, and policy preferences of the agency charged with implementation. What is critical for our purposes here is to recognize that unelected bureaucrats are not neutral agents. Rather, they are political actors who have their own personal preferences and may seek to pursue those preferences despite legislative direction to the contrary. Under what conditions, then, will unelected bureaucrats follow the "will of the people" as opposed to pursuing their own policy agenda? Under what conditions will professional bureaucrats pursue policy choices dictated by their expertise as opposed to policy choices, however uninformed, that are consistent with their legislative principals? These are the questions that we take up in the following sections.

Box 6.4

Civil Service Reforms were developed in the early nineteenth century as a reform initiative of the Progressive Party. The reforms were aimed at limiting the purely partisan appointment of unqualified persons to important bureaucratic offices. These reforms were centered on the notion that citizens deserved "professional" bureaucrats to carry out government tasks, not partisan individuals who were selected purely on the basis of political allegiance rather than professional credentials. A reduced number of "political appointees" within each agency were generally permitted, but only at the highest levels of government.

Delegation Issues and Implementation

Political science has long been interested in questions about the responsiveness of the unelected bureaucracy. Such questions fall under a larger area of study in political science called delegation theory, or principal–agent theory. **Principal–agent theory** is the study of the challenges faced whenever one actor (the principal) delegates authority to another actor (the agent) to carry out some task. The core problem in principal–agent theory in the policy arena is rather simple: the principal (the legislature) must ensure that the agent (the bureaucracy) will dutifully implement the law as intended. This is particularly interesting, given that the bureaucrats may have different preferences from the legislature regarding whether, with what vigor, and how to implement the law. As a result, doing precisely what the legislature wants may be costly to the bureaucrat. Moreover, it is difficult for the legislature to motivate bureaucrats to act dutifully on its behalf without constant direct supervision. Such delegation dilemmas are ubiquitous in public policy. Our elected leaders have a great deal vested in whether unelected bureaucrats implement legislative initiatives dutifully. The specific reasons the delegation problem exists and the potential solutions to it are the focus of this section.

Recall from Chapter 3 that the fundamental problem faced by principals in any delegation dilemma is one of asymmetric information. Principals lack key information on two features of their agents: (1) whether the agent's preferences differ from the principals; and (2) whether the agent is dutifully carrying out his or her responsibilities. While agents possess this information about themselves, they often have little incentive to reveal it to the principal.

Adverse Selection

First, principals cannot be confident that the bureaucrats tasked with carrying out the policy at hand possess similar preferences. We refer to the problem of possibly selecting the wrong agent as **adverse selection**. For example, when Republican Ronald Reagan was elected President in 1980, he likely had a reasonable suspicion that the unelected bureaucrats who staffed EPA did not share his policy preferences on deregulating environmental laws. Professional bureaucrats are generally dedicated to their agency's mission, and likely sought employment with their given agency because of this commitment. In fact, surveys of environmental agency staff have shown that, while they are not necessarily more ideologically biased, they are professionally dedicated to the task of the agency – regulating against pollution (Hunter and Waterman 1996). As a result, a new President seeking deregulation may expect to receive pushback from the career staffers at EPA. This is precisely what B. Dan Wood (1988) found evidence of after President Reagan's first few budgets. In his first two fiscal budgets, President Reagan dramatically cut back EPA's enforcement budget. As expected, annual enforcement activity coming out of EPA fell precipitously. However, Wood also found evidence of pushback from EPA career bureaucrats. Eventually, after a series of political scandals rocked Reagan's choice for EPA head Anne Gorsuch, career bureaucrats at EPA responded to the president's efforts with *increased* regulatory activity – despite smaller budgets. The lesson from this research regarding preference asymmetry is clear. Chief executives, whether governors or presidents, cannot assume that simply because they have been elected to office their policy wishes will be automatically and precisely converted into policy outcomes.

In a perfect world, principals would always pick agents with precisely the same policy preferences. However, two features complicate this ideal scenario. First, we do not possess perfect information about an agent's preferences. We cannot know with certainty the preferences that one or more agents hold on air pollution regulation or hazardous waste. Indeed, some agents have incentive to hide their true preferences. Under a Republican President, a liberal bureaucrat seeking to pursue a different set of priorities has little incentive to reveal that they are more liberal than the president. As a result, the president risks hiring the wrong person for the job. A possible solution to this problem of adverse selection is **screening and selection**. Screening and selection basically refers to an intensive interview process that is meant to reveal an agent's true preferences. Presidents could require an intensive interview process through which they could sort through appointees, choosing to appoint only political allies for all posts in the bureaucracy. However, the second feature of bureaucratic politics complicates this solution. Most elected leaders cannot interview and hire all members of the bureaucracy. Many federal and state government employees are protected by civil service rules that limit the scope of items for which they can be dismissed from their positions – a newly elected chief executive who disagrees with their individual politics is not one of them. As a result of civil service reforms of the early nineteenth century, chief executives are permitted to make appointments only to the highest positions in a given agency. For example, the president can select the heads of many federal agencies as well as several deputies beneath the agency head. Out of approximately 1.4 million federal civil servants (excluding military members), the president can appoint only approximately 2,400 personnel to serve in "political" positions. In sum, restrictions on the efficiency with which screening processes reveal information, and on appointment powers, suggest that screening and selection devices are likely to be limited in their effectiveness. This is so because, despite their best efforts to select agents with similar preferences, there will be error in the process. When this occurs, principals must negotiate the second issue central to the delegation dilemma.

Moral Hazard

The second issue faced by principals is that agents may have inadequate incentive to perform their duties. When incompatible incentives are present, a problem of moral hazard may arise. As discussed in Chapter 3, **moral hazard** derives from the prospect of the agents not bearing the entire costs of their poor task performance. In the context of environmental policy, this might be observed when career bureaucrats who do not have to stand for election engage in an activity, shirking their enforcement responsibilities, which leads to costs borne in the form of increased pollution risks for the population. An elected official, a governor or a President, may then be held accountable for this underperformance at the ballot box. Yet, an unelected bureaucrat may not suffer at all, particularly because of civil service and/or union protections. Due to differences in policy preferences or to other divergent incentives, bureaucrats may not always dutifully carry out the policy wishes of their principals. When moral hazard is present, bureaucrats do not bear the full costs associated with their underperformance in their jobs. In turn, this incentivizes bureaucrats to resist performing in line with their elected officials' request.

When this problem is present, principals have two choices: (1) they can directly monitor their agent, watching their every move and then correcting/punishing agents for any deviations; or (2) they can construct outcome-based incentive packages for their agents in an attempt to align their agents' preferences with the principals. In either of these situations, if the incentives do not perfectly align with the principals, then bureaucrats will have some motivation to misbehave.

Direct monitoring of agent activity and punishing deviations after the fact is referred to as an **ex post control**. Ex post means "after the fact," and refers to a principal's strategy of monitoring agent activity; they wait for them to misbehave, and then punish agents after the misbehavior has been detected. Ex post controls are, however, not necessarily attractive solutions for the principal. First of all, it is often costly for principals to directly observe their agents all of the time, making this type of oversight challenging. In an agency of 3,000 personnel, guaranteeing that each bureaucrat is dutifully performing his or her tasks can be a challenge for any agency head. It would be folly for the head of EPA to believe that they alone, or even with the assistance of a few deputies, could ensure that all personnel are being held to account by direct monitoring of their actions. Second of all, even if it were possible to observe all actions, the very nature of ex post control tactics suggests that the principals must wait until after a deviation in policy has been observed. If we think of the legislature as the principal and EPA as the agent, it would be unacceptable for legislators to wait until EPA fails to perform some function, possibly harming stakeholders in the process, to seek to correct the problem. From a legislator's perspective, attempting to solve a major environmental disaster after the fact may present greater political costs than preventing it in the first place.

Let's consider an example of ex post control tactics. The Minerals Management Service (MMS) was the government agency created in 1982 that was tasked with permitting and enforcing offshore drilling operations. Within the agency, permitting decisions (the regulatory process of applying for and receiving permission to drill) and enforcement decisions (the regulatory process that oversaw inspections and punishment of non-compliance over offshore drilling locations) were made under the same roof – occasionally by the same people. Early critics warned that this combination worked at cross-purposes. They suggested that when large and politically powerful energy companies interact with agency officials who both grant permits and inspect rigs, it was likely to lead to a lax enforcement climate. On April 20, 2010, The Deepwater Horizon Platform exploded and sank, shearing its pipeline and opening up a constant source of oil flowing directly into the Gulf of Mexico. Fifty-six days and 4.9 million barrels of oil later, the blowout was capped. The damages from the spill were widespread: they affected ecology, fisheries, tourism, and health throughout the Gulf Coast. Estimates of the total damages are difficult to assess, but are believed to be in the tens of billions. Much of the damage is not quantifiable and cannot be reversed. In July 2015, BP agreed to pay a record $18.7 billion to the US Government to compensate for damages from the spill.

Box 6.5

Rent-Seeking (Regulatory Capture) refers to a situation where a regulatory agency advances policy decisions based not upon the public's interest, but on

Box 6.5 (*cont.*)

the narrow interest of the industry that it regulates. Given its role in regulation, government decisions can benefit some individuals at the expense of others. Rent-seeking behavior arises when, given their financial stake, members of a specific regulated industry attempt to extract extra benefits, or rents, for themselves from government actions. Given that individual members of the public possess a relatively low stake in a specific industry, they are likely to abstain from lobbying the agency. The result is the agency having a pro-industry bias "captured," and being more inclined to produce rents for the specific industry. If an agency's structure and procedures are designed to be politically independent from outside forces, then the prospects of rent-seeking may be lower compared to when the agency is designed to be politically dependent.

After the disaster, inquiries were made as to the various contributing causes of the explosion and oil release. A report by the MMS Inspector General suggested that at least one contributing factor was the lax enforcement environment at the MMS. In response to this disaster, President Obama used the ex post tactic of administrative reorganization, reorganizing MMS into the Bureau of Ocean Energy Management, Regulation, and Enforcement. Its functions were divided into three separate divisions: permitting (leasing), enforcement, and revenue collection. The obvious downside to such ex post tactics is the rather large costs that a principal must be willing to pay after the deviation (disaster) has occurred. A cheaper, more efficient method would have been to head off the disaster prior to its occurrence.

The alternative to ex post control tactics is **ex ante control tactics**. Ex ante tactics refer to any actions that a principal takes prior to an agent's action to incentivize a desired behavior. Ex ante tactics are essentially incentive packages that attempt to alter the costs and benefits of agents pursuing different behaviors. The utility of these techniques were best captured by three political scientists in a famous article that described the so-called "structure and process" solution to delegation; McNollGast (1987) argued that to avoid the costly and inefficient ex post control tactics, principals (legislators) could tinker with certain elements of an agency's structure and procedures to "encourage" agents to behave in the desired way. Legislators could therefore essentially "design" their policy preferences into the agency's organizational structure and standard operating procedures.[2] If legislators were creative enough, they could engineer administrative structures or procedures

---

[2] This article was particularly influential not only in that it suggested an additional control tactic for legislators or principals of organizations, but also in that it suggested a movement away from the perspective that public agencies are constructed with neutral political intent. This new "biased" structure and process perspective was controversial. It cut against legal or public administration scholarship that argued for a more neutral process-oriented public administration.

that could guarantee stronger (or weaker) regulatory stringency from an environmental agency. A particularly novel idea in McNollGast's work is the notion that structure and process is political and, therefore, has great consequence for the delivery of public policy. How might legislators use such design choices to get what they want out of an agency?

Box 6.6 Decentralization as a Control Device

Andrew Whitford (2002) argued that structural reforms are an important control tactic used to shape patterns of influence over bureaucratic outcomes. Between 1975 and 1983, the National Regulatory Commission's (NRC's) enforcement actions were processed through the national office. However, in 1984, the Reagan administration reorganized the office, decentralizing its enforcement structure and granting regional offices primary enforcement authority.

Whitford exploited this "natural experiment," in which the treatment and control values of the main explanatory variable changed due to actors in the policy arena, but not the research analyst. By comparing the NRC's enforcement activity prior to decentralization to that after decentralization, he could estimate the causal impact of the structural change not only on agency regulatory output, but also on how national vs. regional elected officials' relationship with the agency changed.

He found that post-decentralization, national elected officials either had no effect or had a smaller effect on the agency. Yet, the agency continued to be responsive to local ideology and actually increased its annual enforcement activity relative to the number of operators. In sum, the effect of decentralization was to insulate the regional offices from national political influence and increase the level of local regulatory activity. This research is useful in demonstrating that decentralization is a "political" design choice, which has both political and policy consequences.

Let's consider structure first. If you were setting up an administrative agency that was to oversee the enforcement of air pollution regulations for your state, would you use one physical location for the office or would you choose to use multiple regional offices? Why? At first when contemplating this decision you may have considered issues like cost, efficiency, and the user friendliness of such an organizational choice. You may have thought that you want to save taxpayers money and therefore you will only have one office located in the state capital. Or, you may have thought that you wanted to maximize the ease with which regulated firms can contact the relevant agency officers and therefore opted for a regional office arrangement. But McNollGast suggest that we need to think carefully about how such a choice is likely to affect what the agency does, its work flow, its ability to regulate, its annual production of enforcement actions, its responsiveness to elected officials, its likelihood of being *captured* by the very interests that it regulates. McNollGast suggest that members of a political coalition seeking a certain structural arrangement for the agency will likely be concerned about these types of issues. The number of regional offices, decentralization, and the location of an office within the larger bureaucracy are all examples of structural choices that may affect the agency's output. Can you think of other examples?

In addition to structural change, elected officials can also pursue policy desires with the strategic design of procedural mechanisms. If, for example, a legislature was seeking to encourage fewer enforcement actions from agents at EPA, this might be accomplished with a procedural requirement, such as requiring enforcement actions to be approved or signed off by at least three supervisors. While arguing that the main goal of such a procedural rule would be to enhance accountability, the coalition pursuing it could have another intention. Such an approval process, though tedious, when aggregated across thousands of regulated firms, would slow down the regulatory process and result in fewer annual enforcement actions – a laudable goal for an anti-regulatory coalition. On the other hand, if a legislative coalition was seeking to grant greater access to environmental interest groups to EPA's decision-making, it could require a ninety-day notice and comment period for any new proposed regulation. Such notice and comment periods have been shown to enhance environmental groups' access and level the playing ground between environmental groups and business interests (Reenock and Gerber 2008). The list of possible procedural requirements is endless, but there is one additional point to note. Any structural or procedural requirement that seeks to alter an agent's incentive structure can have unforeseen consequences.

Performance standards are an excellent example of this potential. Suppose that a liberal legislative coalition, seeking to enhance environmental outcomes, wrote into a piece of legislation that an agency must produce a minimum of 400 enforcement actions annually at the risk of punishment. Initially, this seems like a reasonably good idea to the liberal coalition. The law mandates a certain level of enforcement and legislators do not have to actively oversee the agency to ensure its performance. However, as with most quotas, if there is no incentive to move beyond the fixed level, in this case 400 actions per year, then field officers have incentive to shirk once they reach the legislative goal of 400. This type of problem is referred to as **goal displacement**; the process of attaining the goal becomes an end in itself. Although they were pursuing the grander outcome of a cleaner environment, when the liberal legislative coalition set a quota of 400 actions per year, the goal of producing a cleaner environment was displaced by the less aggressive goal of achieving 400 enforcement actions per year. When this occurs, agents can lose sight of whether or not their actions are aiding in the larger goal of cleaning the environment, because their incentive structure only provides them with punishment/reward for the goal of attaining 400. Of course, goal displacement is not guaranteed with the use of performance standards. It can be avoided with creative and artful design of the agent's incentive package.

Box 6.7 Bureaucratic "Red Tape": An Aside

Anyone who has ever worked for an organization, public or private, understands that bureaucratic red tape can be frustrating. The rules and procedures that dictate the actions and flow of information and the forms that are required to process a request can be mind boggling. From the discussion above, however, we now have a greater appreciation for the political purposes that such red tape serves. Despite their publicly decrying the inefficiency of bureaucratic red tape, elected officials are often the origin of such red tape. Seeking to keep public bureaucracies responsive to their interests, elected officials will draft legislation that spells out, often in tedious detail, the standard operating procedures that a public bureau must follow to ensure an output aligned with the legislature. This leads us to an important idea in the literature on public bureaucracy.

The political scientist Terry Moe (1989) noted that, given their need to balance accountability with effective service, legislature do not necessarily design public bureaus to be maximally effective at delivering public services. Rather, public agencies are designed to provide elected officials with the balance of accountability with which they feel comfortable. Under certain conditions, legislators may value accountability more than effectiveness. If this were the case, then public bureaus to some extent may actually be "designed to fail" or at least be designed to be less effective than we might expect. The next time you find yourself frustrated with an inefficient public bureau, try asking yourself the following: "Why might this agency be designed to operate this way, or, alternatively, who benefits from this design?"

Ex ante control tactics that use structural and procedural designs to achieve control over agents is attractive to principals on several fronts. First, ex ante tactics help to avoid the worst possible outcome – a policy disaster that must be corrected after it has failed. Most elected officials do not want to stand for re-election while having to explain why the bureaucracy experienced a policy disaster on their watch. Second, ex ante control tactics are low cost. Once set up, they require less active oversight than do ex post tactics. Legislators can set up the agency with these automatic control devices and then let the agency run on autopilot with less concern that it will fail.

How Much Discretion?

Regardless of the *tactics* used to constrain bureaucrats, we must still establish how much discretion officials should allow an agency. Before we can address this question, we must first recognize that there is a trade-off that elected officials face in setting discretionary levels. If they use structure and procedures to restrict agents' behavior too much, they risk losing the agency's policy effectiveness. If a disaster management bureaucrat must file five forms in triplicate and receive permission from four superiors before attempting to avert a disaster, his or her policy effectiveness will likely be compromised. This represents a fundamental trade-off for principals.

A political scientist named Kathleen Bawn (1995) recognized this trade-off. She argued that elected officials must balance their desire for political control of an agency against the technical accuracy of the agency's decisions. She suggested that elected officials could attempt to maximize political control of an agency *or* the technical accuracy of an agency's decisions, but not necessarily both. To exert maximum political control, the agency's effective discretion must be ratcheted down, providing it less ability to exercise its expertise. However, if granted great leeway in its decision-making, the agency's choices, while perhaps technically accurate, may be politically unpleasing to elected officials. Bawn suggests that elected officials' preferences regarding this choice are shaped by two types of uncertainty: technical and procedural. The first type, **technical uncertainty**, refers to the uncertainty the agency has in its estimate of the policy consequences of a given choice. The second type, **procedural uncertainty**, refers to the uncertainty about what type of choice the agency is likely to make. If elected leaders grant an agency greater independence, this will decrease the agency's technical uncertainty while increasing its procedural uncertainty and vice versa. One of the critical findings from Bawn's study is that we would expect elected officials to grant greater independence to agencies whose technical uncertainty is relatively higher. Higher technical uncertainty means that the agency has a much more difficult time knowing the real-world consequences of its actions. Bawn suggested that this type of uncertainty likely exists in policy areas such as environmental health (EPA) as opposed to workplace safety (OSHA). Her logic was that if a person is harmed on the worksite, there is likely a clear and readily knowable cause of the accident. On the other hand, if a person develops lung cancer or asthma, it is much more technically challenging to assess precisely why these health issues developed. According to this logic, Bawn found that legislators should grant the agency that regulates health issues greater independence than one that regulates workplace safety.

Literature suggests a host of other factors to determine elected leaders' preferences as to how much leeway to grant the bureaucracy, including: party competition, divided government, and policy salience. We know that regardless of the specific factors, legislators must balance their desires for influence over agency actions against limiting the agency's ability to actually perform its duties. To achieve this end, elected officials use structure and procedures to shape an agency's discretion.

6.5 Evaluating Environmental Regulation: Forty Years after EPA's Founding

Nearly forty years after President Nixon created EPA and ushered in a decade of expansive environmental regulatory programs, it is useful to take a moment to evaluate the effectiveness and efficiency of these programs. By **effectiveness**, we mean the change in environmental outcomes attributed to some regulatory program. By **efficiency**, we mean the relative total benefits provided by a given program weighted against the costs of the program. Any regulatory program can be evaluated along these dimensions. Effective regulatory programs deliver reductions in the negative externality that they were designed to address. Efficient regulatory programs deliver reductions in the negative externality, but at lower cost. To consider how a program performs, we must weigh the benefits and costs of a program, as well as its overall efficiency.

The Benefit of Environmental Regulation: Lower Pollution and Health Gains

Most people would probably agree that over the past forty years, the typical amount of pollution that the average American confronts has improved. But by how much, and at what cost? In this section, we aim to determine how much it has improved and the cost of the improvements that have been made. We consider the improvements in four specific areas: the air, water, hazardous waste, and drinking water policies.

Air Pollution

Of the six primary pollutants regulated by the Clean Air Act, all six have seen dramatic reductions since the 1970 Clean Air Act amendments. In fact, between 1970 and 2008, there was a 60 percent reduction in these six pollutants, with the greatest decreases occurring in the first 20 years of the program. Figure 6.4 shows the increasing trends in air pollution in the United States over time. Between 1940 and 1970, prior to the decade of national environmental legislation, the four pollutants shown (carbon monoxide, nitrogen oxide, volatile organic compounds, and sulfur dioxides) were all on the rise. This pattern was also present in other air pollutants as well as water pollution. While all six pollutants have been reduced dramatically, the greatest advances have been made against lead, particulate matter, and sulfur dioxide. Despite these advances, Americans continue to face pollutants in the air that they breathe primarily in the

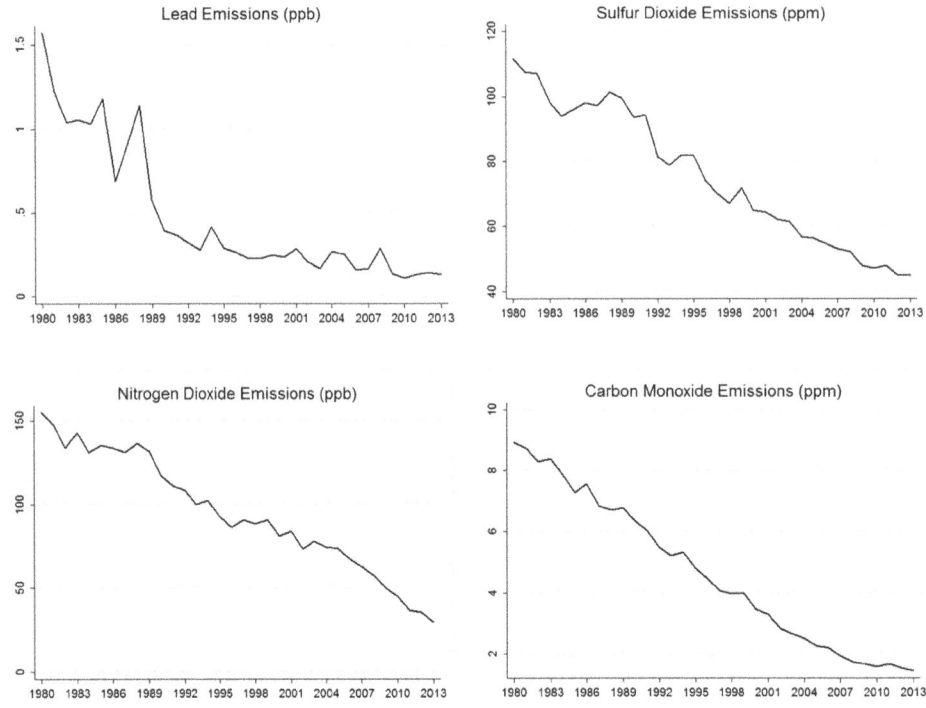

Figure 6.4 Trends in Air Pollution for Components Regulated by the Clean Air Act (1980–2013)
Source: http://epa.gov/airtrends/
Note: ppm denotes parts per million, ppb denotes parts per billion.

form of ground level ozone. In fact, nearly 120 million people live in counties across the United States where ground level ozone levels exceed the levels allowable under the Clean Air Act.

The primary reason for this is mobile sources of air pollution – trucks and cars. Over the past forty years, the number of vehicle miles traveled in the United States has increased by nearly 163 percent. With greater economic activity and more people driving further to commute to work, the amount of pollution has rapidly increased. As a consequence, while the legislative initiatives in air pollution regulation have made great strides against stationary sources of pollution (factories and regulated businesses), they have been less successful with the lingering mobile sources (individual cars, trucks, and SUVs).

In evaluating program effectiveness, aside from considering what is regulated by the Clean Air Act (CAA), we would be remiss if we did not also consider what is not regulated. For example, when the CAA was adopted, carbon dioxide (CO_2) was not included as a primary pollutant under the Clean Air Act. Yet, CO_2 emissions in the United States have increased dramatically since 1970. As a result, one of the primary greenhouse gasses produced domestically has remained essentially unregulated. The two primary sources of CO_2 emissions derive from electricity generation (fossil fuel-fired generating plants) and transportation (cars, trucks, trains, and planes). This pollutant, despite evidence of the dangers that unchecked emissions of it present, has proven difficult to regulate. Primarily, the difficulty has been one associated with political will rather than technical competence.

The second most prevalent greenhouse gas, methane, has also risen over the past decades. Methane's two primary sources are enteric fermentation (animal flatulence) and landfills. As Americans have consumed more meat in the form of cattle, chickens, and hogs, the amount of methane produced by these concentrated feeding operations has increased (not to mention the surface water pollution). Moreover, as we dispose of more of our waste in landfills, as that waste decays it produces methane gas that is released into our atmosphere.

In summary, where legislative initiatives have regulated businesses that produce negative externalities in the form of air pollution, there have been significant advances. On the other hand, when those externalities occur primarily at the hand of individual citizens heating and cooling their homes, driving their cars, and consuming greenhouse-intensive food, there has been less success.

Water Pollution

On average, industrial pollution of our waterways has decreased. However, assessing precisely where we are now with water quality is slightly more difficult for water than air. This is primarily because we simply do not have data on the many lakes and streams across the United States. Of the more than 3.5 million miles of rivers and streams in the United States, only 26 percent have actually been assessed for pollution impairment. Of those that have been assessed, about half have been designated as impaired.

In fact, in water pollution we see a mirror image of what we saw in air pollution. Industrial pollution from point sources that is regulated under NPDES of the Clean Water Act is nearly 97 percent compliant with the law. These sources are obeying the law, following their permits, and are generally not considered to be the sizeable source of continuing pollution. The top three causes of pollution or impairment of our current waterways are pathogens, sediment, and nutrients – less relevant here are the heavy metals and chemicals associated with industrial pollution. The more likely culprit behind the lingering surface and groundwater pollution is less point source pollution from industrial sites and more non-point sources that derive from the agribusiness of farming and cultivation, bio-industrial production of concentrated animal feeding operations, and to a lesser extent personal home use of fertilizers, pesticides, and herbicides. However, there is much uncertainty as to the specific sources of many water pollutants, simply due to the lack of data and difficulty of ascribing a source to a given pollutant. This increases the regulatory challenges of addressing non-point source pollution. For example, a sample of water drawn from the mouth of the Mississippi showing high levels of nutrients is rather difficult to track back to its source, given that the Mississippi is over 2,300 miles long, with thousands of potential sources along the way.

The Clean Water Act's Section 319 program attempts to deal with non-point source pollution and has been relatively successful. However, it also faces stark challenges. For non-point source pollution, the greatest challenge is educating resource users about the consequences of their actions and then offsetting the costs of addressing these actions. For example, golf courses use tons of fertilizers, herbicides, and pesticides each year. But, there are certain practices that when applied may mitigate the impact of these pollutants on surface and ground water supplies. A golf course could use less harmful substances (which are often more expensive), or they could construct buffer zones between the golf course and environmentally sensitive areas to reduce the amount of pollution run-off into surface waters. Such **best management practices**, however, increase costs to the user. Rather than issue a mandate that users employ these practices or face penalties, the Section 319 program uses a different approach. Section 319 provides grants designed to address these challenges. Specifically, these grants are used to transfer federal funds to state programs that in turn use the money to educate farmers and land owners to apply best management practices to reduce run-off into surface and ground waters. These grants can also be applied to defray the costs to farmers or other landowners of construction projects that might reduce run-off from their properties. In this way, users are incentivized to address pollution by reducing the total front end costs of employing more favorable practices. Critics, however, have pointed out that such grants always fall short of the total need of grant applicants, with annual funding holding steady at $200 million per year for the past ten years.

Drinking Water

Public and private water systems are regulated under the Safe Drinking Water Act. Private wells, serving only the immediate property, are not. There were approximately 153,399 public water systems in the United States in 2009 serving over 300 million citizens. For these public systems, the SDWA regulates nearly 100 primary water contaminants, including items like arsenic and lead. Public systems are required by law to meet federal standards for the Maximum Contaminant Level (MCL) for these contaminants and are open to compliance sanctions for violations. The SDWA also includes an additional fifteen recommended, but non-enforceable, secondary water contaminants, which include such items as fluoride and pH. The number of water systems that are currently within the compliance EPA guidelines for these substances has steadily grown over the past thirty years. As of 2009, 28 percent of these public water systems had at least one significant violation (either a health-based standard or a monitoring or reporting violation) and 7 percent had violations of health-based standards.[3] This means that on a daily basis fewer citizens are being exposed to the types of toxins that their parents and grandparents may have been exposed to as a result of the SDWA.

A particularly challenging aspect of drinking water regulation, however, is that the target is constantly shifting. The number and type of pollutants found in our water supplies have *increased* over the past forty years. More toxic substances are being manufactured annually than at any other time in our history. And, more of these pollutants and chemical by-products are making their way into our waters. These toxins include anything from lawn herbicides to various new chemical compounds to prescription drugs. As more citizens consume prescription drugs, these medications drugs are more likely to find their way into our water supply through direct or indirect means.

Politics often has difficulty keeping up with the technology. Perhaps more interesting than what is regulated under the SDWA is what is not. While the current SDWA regulates about 100 specific items, there are hundreds and hundreds of other contaminants in our drinking waters that are not currently regulated. Occasionally, EPA must publish a Contaminants Candidate List in which they list items that they would like to consider listing and regulating. Currently, the third such list from EPA, the CCL3, includes 116 contaminants, many of which are herbicides, pesticides, and lawn fertilizers. For many of these contaminants, whether the risk presented by each outweighs the costs of regulating it is a political question. And any attempt to add pollutants to this list is often a hotly contested political debate. Do you have a filter on your faucet?

The Costs of Regulation

Each of the programs considered above has been relatively successful in reducing pollution in its respective media. But the question that is important to policymakers and citizens alike is "at what cost?" For fiscal year (FY) 2009, EPA was budgeted at $10.5 billion. This is the total direct cost of all EPA programs as implemented by the federal government. Of course, this ignores the entire amount of money spent by the states on environmental protection. This adds up to another approximately $9 billion from state and other non-federal sources, bringing the total annual government expenditures to approximately $19.5 billion. If the entire federal budget was equivalent to $100, government expenditures on environmental regulation would equal ~39 cents. These government expenditures, however, pale in comparison to the private sector's

---

[3] EPA, 2009 National Public Water Systems Compliance Report.

annual expenditures to comply with federal environmental regulations each year. These can be thought of as the "regulation tax" that private companies pay to adhere to federal regulations. A 1999 study by the Organisation for Economic Co-operation and Development (OECD) estimated that in the United States the size of this regulation tax was approximately 0.3 percent of GDP or ~$80 billion. A rough estimate of the total costs spent on environmental regulation including both public and private expenditures is ~$100 billion per year. To give you a sense of this cost, it is equivalent to ~$300 for every man, woman, and child in the United States. Is this amount worth the benefits gained by these programs? Are there alternate ways to achieve the same benefits at lower cost? The political sphere will eventually negotiate answers to these questions.

Balancing Benefits vs. Costs: Risk Assessment and Risk Management

How much is a human life worth? How much is a child's not developing asthma worth? Try debating these questions late one night in your dorm room. While most elected leaders would be loath to offer a precise number for these types of questions, regulators must confront this issue on a regular basis. They must decide at what point the risks of exposing a portion of the population to some hazard outweigh the costs of regulating that hazard. From a public choice perspective, a reasonable standard is that a regulatory program ought to deliver benefits to society as a whole above and beyond the costs of achieving that goal. Figuring out where that tipping point lies, of course, is tricky.

Generally, EPA separates out the scientific assessment of a given substance's risk from the political assessment of whether and how much to regulate the substance. These two sequences are **risk assessment** and **risk management**, respectively. The first sequence of this process, risk assessment, is generally conducted by professional scientists within the agency. Risk assessment is a multi-step process that begins with the science of what we know about a given substance and attempts to end up with an objective estimate of the likelihood that humans will experience any of a series of negative reactions associated with a substance. The first step, Hazard Identification, gathers and evaluates data on the types of health injury or disease that may be produced by a chemical and on the conditions of exposure under which injury or disease is produced. Dose Response, the second step, describes the quantitative relationship between the amount of exposure to a substance and the extent of toxic injury or disease. This step attempts to statistically relate the change in the likelihood of negative health effects with changes in the levels of exposure to some substance. The third step, Exposure Assessment, describes the nature and size of the population exposed to a substance and the magnitude and duration of their exposure. Many citizens were exposed to lead from leaded gasoline prior to its regulation and therefore the exposure assessment for lead would be higher than granite, which may be only likely to expose the specific individuals who process the material at an industrial site. Risk Characterization is the final stage in which all of the information of the three previous stages are combined into one characterization of the threat involved with a particular substance. Total report on a given substance is then catalogued in EPA's database, the Integrated Risk Information System (IRIS), which includes the current risk assessments on all conducted assessments. Anyone can access this database online to review the reports on a given substance.

Once a risk assessment has been conducted the results are passed on to other individuals for risk management. Risk management is a process that more explicitly allows for the introduction of politics into its decisions. This process seeks to determine a fundamentally political question: Are the risks associated with the substance worth regulating despite the economic costs of doing so? We suggest that this is fundamentally political since it relies upon different individuals' assumptions about risk, "acceptable" costs, and "likely" benefits. Essentially, the benefits of regulating some substance or economic activity must be weighed against the costs of doing so. Despite what your liberal or conservative friends may suggest, there is rarely a "correct" answer on these sorts of decisions. Rather, each political interest is likely to approach these decisions differently.

Box 6.8 Cost-Benefit Analysis: An Example

In the summer of 2011, the EPA released its final rule on Cross-State Air Pollution. The new rule requires older electricity generating plants (which had been exempted from technology upgrades) in twenty-seven states to install new pollution scrubbing technology to reduce SO_2 and NOx pollution. This rule was justified, in part, based on a cost-benefit analysis that considered the aggregate health benefits expected to be gained from the pollution being removed from the air vs. the expected costs to implement the rule. According to EPA's analysis, the rule's expected benefits, measured in health cases avoided annually, include 15,000 fewer non-fatal heart attacks, 19,000 fewer bronchitis attacks, and 1.8 million fewer days of missed work, totaling an expected annual savings of between $120 and $280 billion. The expected costs of implementing the rule are expected to be $800 million annually. As a result, EPA determined that the rule was justified.

There was political resistance to this rule, particularly from the utilities for whom the rule would apply. Why? Part of the explanation lies in the difference between diffuse benefits and concentrated costs. The cost-benefit analysis conducted by EPA was at the societal level. EPA assessed the total benefits that

Box 6.8 (cont.)

society is likely to accrue (diffuse benefits) and the total costs that society is likely to bear (diffuse costs). Of course, an individual facility is concerned about *concentrated* costs and benefits. For example, one facility expected the new rule to cost their power plant approximately $500 million in new technology expenditures. When compared to the relatively small possible concentrated benefit to the company of the rule – a few workers experiencing fewer health problems over the year – it is easy to understand how the cost-benefit analysis looks quite different to an individual facility and may motivate them to resist the rule.

Assessing risk generally depends upon at least three critical components: cost-benefit analysis, risk orientation, and orientation toward scientific uncertainty. On the first component, cost-benefit analysis, regulators assess the total expected benefits and total expected costs of issuing a regulation. Critical in such analyses is what factors are included in the calculation and the economic valuation assigned to each, or a process called **monetization**. Politics can enter this process by deciding precisely what should be included as a benefit or cost and the value to be assigned to each. In this process, assigning precise values to the environmental and health benefits of a given regulation may be more challenging than assigning precise quantitative values to the expected costs of implementing the regulation. It may be relatively easy to estimate the costs of implementation in the form of increased business expenses, lost jobs, and the like. A relatively more challenging task is assigning a precise economic value to reduced health costs for asthma treatment or to the savings reaped from a decline in lung cancers. Other benefits are even more difficult to quantify. For example, what precise economic value should be assigned to preserving the bald eagle, or to protecting Old Faithful at Yellowstone Park, or to saving dolphins from tuna fishers' nets, or to reclaiming a haze-free view of the Smoky Mountains? How might we approach monetizing these benefits? These are inherently difficult benefits to assign precise economic values to and make cost-benefit analyses more challenging. It is the challenging quantification of environmental benefits and the relative ease of quantifying economic costs that result in many environmental activists to be opposed to explicit cost-benefit analyses.

Box 6.9 Risk vs. Uncertainty

Many people often confuse the use of these two terms. **Uncertainty** refers to our inability to know "with certainty" that an outcome will occur. We can measure the extent of our uncertainty over some outcome occurring with a probability,

Box 6.9 (*cont.*)

which ranges between 0 and 1. If we are perfectly certain an event will occur, it has a probability of 1. If we are perfectly certain that an event will not occur, it has a probability of 0. Uncertainty says nothing about whether we expect to gain or lose from the event. **Risk** generally refers to the expected utility or probability associated with a loss. It can be measured as the probability of some negative outcome or loss multiplied by the value of the negative outcome. Imagine being given the choice between two options: a 50 percent chance of gaining $1,000,000 or a guaranteed $500,000. Which would you choose? Different people have different tolerances for the risk of such "lottery" over outcomes. A risk-neutral person would think of the lottery over $1,000,000 (0.5 x 1,000,000=$500,000) as being the same as losing $500,000 with certainty (p=1). However, not all individuals are risk neutral. A risk-acceptant person would need a guaranteed pay-off much greater than $500,000 to not take the lottery. A risk-averse person would settle for a guaranteed pay-off much lower than $500,000 to not take the lottery. How much would you need guaranteed to not take the lottery over $1,000,000?

Another component of risk management is whether an individual is risk averse or risk acceptant when it comes to the possible costs and benefits of regulation. If I announced the odds of winning at some game of chance, there would likely be variation around the number of people who would like to bet on that game of chance. Even with the same odds, some people would prefer to place a bet and others would not, deeming it too risky. This variation around attitudes toward risk is similar with regulation. If one is risk acceptant, one is more likely to adopt the view that everything in life is risky and therefore we should be careful about rushing headlong into regulation. Such individuals are more likely to prefer postponing regulation until either better empirical evidence on the effects of the hazard or better technology is available to lessen the costs of implementing the regulation. Alternatively, if one holds a risk-averse stance, one is likely to believe that even relatively small amounts of a substance may present harm. Such individuals are more likely to prefer regulation, even in the face of uncertainty about the hazards effects or costs rather than risk exposure. Last, one's attitude toward scientific uncertainty will also contribute to one's orientation toward risk management. All scientific statements are associated with some level of uncertainty. As noted in Chapter 4, uncertainty can usually be represented as either a confidence interval around one's estimate or a probability associated with one's estimate. A confidence interval tells us the range around our point estimate within which we have a 95 percent chance of observing the value under repeated experiments. In other words, if we found that a proposed regulation has the potential to save 100,000 lives per annum, this point estimate may seem impressive. But how might your opinion change if we learn that, by including a measure of uncertainty to construct a confidence interval around the estimate, we learn that the rule could save 100,000 lives plus or minus 95,000? Would your opinion change if the estimate was 100,000 lives plus or minus three lives? The former has a wider confidence interval and the latter a tighter one. The tighter confidence interval means that we are more confident about our estimate (the actual saving is highly likely to be 100,000 lives, between 99,997 and 100,003 lives), while the wider one means that we are more uncertain (the actual saving could lie between 5,000 and 195,000 lives).

Alternatively, scientific uncertainty can be represented as a probability, or a p-value that the statement made could be false. For statements with low uncertainty, we would expect a small p-value. The earth is round ($p < 0.0000000000000001$). This suggests that the probability that the earth is not round is smaller than the number displayed. In other words, it is extremely unlikely (flat-earthers: don't give up yet!). Alternatively, a risk assessment report could state, "Low dose rates of aluminum sulfate to mice in controlled experiments is associated with increased occurrence of liver tumors ($p < 0.10$)." This suggests that there is less than a 10 percent chance that we might be wrong making this statement. Is this chance of being incorrect low enough? How do we determine when to accept an analyst's scientific statement as likely to be (not) supported by the data? The standard in the social sciences for both confidence intervals and p-values is a 5 percent threshold. In other words, for confidence intervals, we want to be 95 percent sure that the real value of the quantity of interest lies within the interval (or a 5 percent chance that it is outside the interval) and for probabilities we are willing to accept any statement that has a p-value smaller than 0.05. We reject, as not supported by the data, any statement that has a p-value larger than 0.05. Yet, attitudes toward such statements vary. Despite the fact that such statements of uncertainty are common through all of the sciences, natural and social, some believe that statements that acknowledge uncertainty are synonymous with admissions of flaws in research or that the research is not quite "scientific." Others believe that such statements reflect the best available information on the relationship in question and are more willing to accept that quite frequently the best available information on a question may have a degree of uncertainty associated with it. A person's attitude to questions of uncertainty may influence their orientation toward risk management.

Recall that cost-benefit analysis, risk orientation, and orientation toward scientific uncertainty all play important roles in the political process of risk management. Each of these components can be manipulated by political interests from all points on the spectrum. Pro-regulation interests will often accentuate the potential risks of a certain pollutant, while minimizing the benefits and costs that continued use of the pollutant would bring to society. Pro-regulation interests will also be more likely to be risk averse and are more comfortable with estimates of uncertainty. Anti-regulation interests emphasize the benefits to society of continued use of the pollutant and often highlight the costs of coming into compliance with the specific regulation, minimizing the risks that the pollutant presents to populations. At the same time, these interests are more likely to be risk acceptant and more skeptical of estimates of uncertainty.

Box 6.10 Fracking Federalism

Fracking or Hydraulic Fracturing is a controversial method of extracting oil and gas from deep shale reservoirs using high pressure water injectors. There are a variety of potential water pollution vectors, including, but not limited to: water extraction for use in the well, ground water contamination via injection, and waste water treatment and disposal. EPA has reported that although fracking accidents have occurred with pollution consequences for surface and ground waters, the number of incidents is rare relative to the number of wells operated (US EPA 2015). The economic benefits of fracking, however, for consumer and producers of natural gas is estimated to be an additional $48 billion per year (Hausman and Kellogg 2015). This controversial practice offers a case study into environmental federalism. Concerned about the potential effects of fracking on water pollution, in 2014, voters in the Texas town of Denton voted to outlaw fracking within its city limits. Fracking proponents vowed to fight back, suing the city and authoring several bills in the state legislature to prohibit cities from banning fracking. In May 2015, Texas Republicans in the state legislature, traditionally supportive of empowering local government, passed a law prohibiting cities in Texas from banning hydraulic fracking within their jurisdictions. Shifting the venue of political conflict is a long-standing resource practiced within environmental policy. Policy entrepreneurs often hunt for the most appropriate level of government within the federal system to pursue their initiatives. What constitutes a disadvantage within one venue may translate into an advantage within another.

Returning to the question with which we began: How much is a human life worth? While no document has been produced by EPA that suggests what a human life is worth, one can deduce what the number may be by considering their regulatory decisions on toxic substances. In one study of 132 decisions on regulating carcinogens, it was found that for every chemical that presented an individual cancer risk greater than 4/1,000, the chemical was regulated. No action was taken when a substance presented an individual cancer risk of less than 1 in a million. Moreover, it was determined that a substance was regulated if the cost per life saved was less than $2 million. However, when the cost per life saved was higher than $2 million, the substance was not regulated. According to this study, we could reasonably infer that for the cases considered EPA has assigned human life to be worth approximately $2 million.

Remaining Challenges: Climate Change

The greatest environmental challenge policymakers continue to face is climate change. Before we can understand the challenges of climate change we first have to understand the difference between changes in weather and changes in climate. Weather refers to the atmospheric conditions (measured by wind speed, temperature, precipitation) at a given place at a given time. Weather change refers to variations in weather over very short or even medium-range time periods. We have all experienced a particularly rainy week or a hot summer, or a cold and snowy winter. These are all examples of weather change or weather patterns. **Climate** refers to variations in average weather over long to extremely long periods of time. The World Meteorological Organization (WMO) uses three decades as the standard length of time to discuss climate change, but scientists may also refer to changes in climate over hundreds and even thousands of years. **Climate change** refers to long-term variations in weather patterns.

Consider Figure 6.5. For any measure of weather (temperature, precipitation, etc.), we can plot the long-term relationship of these measures on the y-axis over time on the x-axis. In the figure, the black line represents the long-term average of the series – think of it as a moving average over several decades. The orange line, however, represents daily, weekly, or monthly measures of our weather indicator. What is quite obvious from the figure is that a long-term increase in some weather indicator does not rule out short-term variations in weather. For example, the long-term temperature of the Earth has warmed approximately 1.5F over the past 100 years and is expected to continue to warm another several degrees over the next 100 years (US EPA 2014). But we can still expect local and short-term variations in weather – a cold winter or a

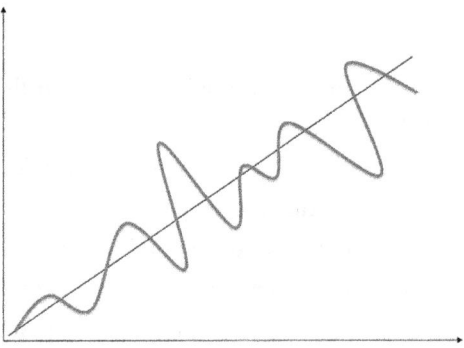

Figure 6.5 Weather Variations vs. Climate Change

moderate summer can occur on occasion – valleys and troughs occur throughout the orange curve. Only through a change in perspective, shifting our view toward long-term patterns, can we appreciate how climate (rather than weather) changes.

Why is the Earth on a warming trend? When sunlight penetrates the Earth's atmosphere, some of that energy is reflected back into space, some is absorbed by the atmosphere, and the remainder is absorbed by the Earth. The energy absorbed by the Earth then radiates back into the atmosphere. Some escapes back into space, but certain gases in the atmosphere reabsorb this radiation and then reflect it back toward the Earth's surface. At higher levels of these gases in the atmosphere, less radiation escapes the Earth and increasingly more radiation is absorbed by the Earth's surface – this cycle of increasingly trapped radiation and warming is known as the **Greenhouse Effect**. The gases that contribute to this effect include water vapor, carbon dioxide, methane, and ozone, and are known as **Greenhouse gases (GHGs)**. The Earth has experienced a geometric increase in GHGs. The Industrial Revolution together with the discovery and mass consumption of fossil fuels in the form of coal, oil, and natural gas in addition to other factors has contributed to a large increase in global GHGs. The correlation between the growth in GHGs and global climate change is quite high. Yet, the growth in temperature could be driven by various forces, some naturally occurring and some occurring due to human or anthropogenic activity. Variation in volcanic activity and solar activity are potential contributors among the naturally occurring drivers. However, when pitting these naturally occurring forces against human activity explanations for rising global temperatures against each other, evidence increasingly supports the conclusion that human activity is contributing to climate change (Hegerl *et al.* 2007). In a recent article, Miller *et al.* (2014) applied the most recent climate model from NASA's Goddard Institute for Space Sciences to estimate, among other goals, how well human vs. natural sources fair in estimating the observed rising global temperatures over the past 150 years. Figure 6.6 reports the results of their findings. In the figures, the black line represents mean global average temperature and the blue and red lines represent different estimated models, with a plus or minus two standard deviation uncertainty bar (shown in gray). The left panel reports the results of models based solely on human sources of warming, while the right panel reports the results of models based solely on natural sources. The evidence suggests that models estimated solely on human sources are able to explain the pattern in global warming, while the models based on natural sources are not.

What can be done about the Earth's warming trend? As with all potential policy interventions, elected leaders and policy experts must assess the expected costs and benefits of an intervention. Even if we assume some intervention is warranted, world leaders must overcome some rather daunting cooperation and collective action challenges. The Earth's climate is intertwined. Changes in human practices in one part of the globe can affect climate prospects in another. As such, this policy area is plagued by a classic

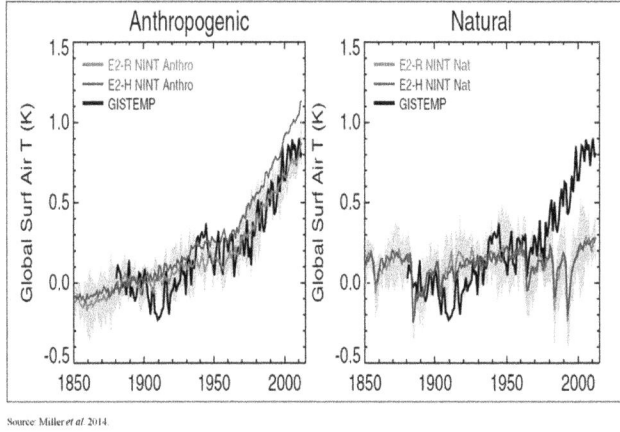

Figure 6.6 Human vs. Natural Sources of Global Temperature Increases
Source: Miller *et al.* 2014

cooperation dilemma. International efforts have generated treaties attempting to moderate GHG production. In 1992, the Kyoto Protocol was an international treaty designed to have countries commit to reducing their GHG production over several periods. Most of Europe, including Russia, signed on to binding reduction targets. The United States never ratified the treaty and Canada withdrew in 2012. Most of the developing world agreed to non-binding targets. The US position is skeptical of the treaty's potential success given that most of the developing world are not committed to binding targets.

Cooperating on climate change is more challenging for some countries and less for others. Some countries are in a stronger position economically to contribute to the solution, while others are not. The United States, the European Union, and Japan are three of the world's top ten global emitters of GHGs. However, they are relatively wealthy states and have the slowest growth rates in GHGs over the past decade among many of the other high-emitting countries. China, India, and Indonesia are also among the world's top ten global emitters of GHGs. However, they are economically developing states and are currently registering the greatest percentage increases in emissions over the past decade. So how much should each country contribute to reductions? Should wealthier states with lower rates of GHG growth contribute more than poorer states with higher rates of GHG growth? These questions cut to the core of the difficulties of international cooperation on climate change.

Nationally, the United States is deadlocked on climate change policy, with partisan differences in the post 2010 election era too wide to span. In the federal system, however, progress has been made at the state and local levels. Barry Rabe refers to a type of "Contested Federalism" existing between states and local government and the national government over climate policy (2011). Over the past decade, several states and hundreds of local governments have adopted climate change policies to lessen their impact on global climate change, overcoming the cooperation challenges of committing to a policy while others refrain.

6.6 Conclusion

What environmental challenges remain? Consider the following anecdote. If you were to travel out to an apple orchard to gather apples for an afternoon snack for your family, which apples would you pick first? You probably would start with the ones nearest the ground within arm's reach. And you would continue with this strategy until you had picked all of those lowest hanging fruit clean. To make any more progress you would now need a new skill or technology. In other words, you would have to make use of a stick with an extended arm to grab the higher fruit or a ladder to climb higher or the skill of climbing. The point is that the **lowest hanging fruit** is the easiest and cheapest to pick. To get at the other fruit requires new skills and new technology.

Environmental challenges are similar to the lowest hanging fruit anecdote. The "easiest" pollution has already been addressed. And by easy we mean those problems that require the least amount of political and technological capital. Consider drinking water. If we handed you a glass of putrid, dirty water, how might you attempt to purify it enough to drink? You might first try straining it through some cheap material, like a shirt or a piece of cheesecloth. This first step may remove significant amounts, let's say 70 percent, of the undesirable pieces of floating debris and dirt and may even make the water appear and smell a bit better – this was the lowest hanging fruit. But of course there are still pollutants, heavy metals, chemicals, and microbes, too small to be caught by your shirt, that remain in the water. Next, you may try filtering your water through sand or if you have additional funds, activated charcoal. While a little more costly, each of these techniques would remove even more pollutants from your water, let's say an additional 25 percent. You could next turn to costly chemicals, to treat the water, including chlorine and ozone gas. These would remove an additional 3 percent of the remaining microbes in your glass. In total, you have now removed nearly 98 percent of the undesirable materials from your water. What about the last 2 percent? The water in the glass by now is perfectly fine to drink, with minimal risk to your long-term health. But what if you wanted to push further? You could try more expensive filters, including reverse osmosis filters, which use advanced engineering and high-tech materials to remove most of the remaining materials – but for *considerably* more cost. You might have to purchase a $3,000 filtering system to remove completely the remaining materials from the single glass that I gave you. The point is simple: the costs of pollution removal increase exponentially as more pollution is removed from the system.

Many of the remaining pollution problems faced by Americans linger precisely because they are more costly. They are either politically costly, meaning public opinion has not quite embraced the need for sacrifice (economically or lifestyle-wise), or they are technologically costly, meaning the technology is not quite there to remove the remaining pollution at a "reasonable" cost. Regardless of the environmental dilemma at hand, whether it is incentivizing Americans to drive less, developing clean coal technology, or addressing climate change, one thing is clear, these challenges will require investments of political, technical, and economic capital.

Key Terms

Negative externalities
Socialize
Inefficient outcome
Deadweight loss
Pigouvian tax
Consumption tax
Positive externalities
Subsidies
Output standards
Command and control
Saliency trap
Cross-cutting cleavages
Satisfice
Policy window
Stationary sources
Emissions
Point sources
Effluent
Non-point source pollution
Cradle to grave approach
Principal–agent theory
Adverse selection
Screening and selection
Moral hazard
Ex post control tactics
Ex ante control tactics
Goal displacement
Technical uncertainty

Procedural uncertainty

Effectiveness

Efficiency

Best management practices

Risk assessment

Risk management

Monetization

Uncertainty

Risk

Climate

Climate change

Greenhouse Effect

Greenhouse gases

Lowest hanging fruit

CHAPTER EXERCISES

1. Think carefully about how other individuals' (or corporations') actions affect you on a daily basis. List five negative externalities that you have experienced. In addition to listing these, propose a market correction for each of these externalities. Estimate the policy and political effectiveness of each correction you propose.

2. Now list five positive externalities that you have experienced. List any subsidies that are currently encouraging the production of these positive externalities. Can you think of a positive externality that you would like to encourage? What form of subsidy would be appropriate to achieve the goal that you prefer?

3. Political Games with Numbers. Use the following numbers and construct two arguments (one pro and one con) for the Cash for Clunkers Program on whether the program was cost effective. Be sure to consider the costs and expected benefits of the program. Also be sure to mention the assumptions that you must make to make each argument.

   Statistics to include:

   - Total vehicles purchased under program
   - Total cost of implementing program
   - Expected gain/loss in aggregate fuel efficiency
   - Expected gain/loss in aggregate vehicle originated air pollution
   - Assumptions are made over how many of the cars were likely to have been bought. Assumptions must be made to determine benefits of each program.

4. A new regulatory rule to limit the amount of arsenic in drinking water has been proposed. The new rule is expected to provide benefits to health such as x, y, and z

at a saving of approximately $5b +or– a year. The total cost of implementing the rule in the form of x, y, and z is expected to be between 3 and 9. Take a side and promote the passage of the rule.

5. Imagine you are responsible for re-writing the Gas Guzzler tax today. What automobiles would you put on the list? What criteria would you use to establish the list of cars? What political difficulties do you foresee in creating your list of gas guzzling automobiles?

6. Design a small-scale survey related to the information-opinion linkage. Structure your questions such that the first questions elicit opinions regarding topic X, and then elicit information-based data from your participants. What are your results? What does this tell you about the information-opinion asymmetry?

7. To better understand ex-post and ex-ante tactics, imagine for a moment that you are a parent of a 5-year-old boy who is strong-willed and mischievous and does not want to do his homework. What sort of ex-post or ex-ante tactics might you employ? What are the costs and benefits of each approach? What would be more effective? Why?

8. Individuals tend to be risk averse or risk acceptant (or more rarely risk neutral) when it comes to scientific uncertainty about the state of knowledge on a given substance. Consider your own life, what things are you risk acceptant about, and to what things are you risk averse? How does that inform your policy beliefs?

REFERENCES

Barabas, Jason, Jerit, Jennifer, Pollock, William, and Rainey, Carlisle. 2014. "The Question(s) of Political Knowledge." *American Political Science Review* 108(4): 840–855.

Bawn, Kathleen. 1995. "Political Control versus Expertise: Congressional Choice about Administration Procedures." *American Political Science Review* 89: 62–73.

Carson, Rachel. 1962. *Silent Spring*. Boston, MA: Houghton Mifflin.

Center for Deliberative Democracy. 2010. *By the People: Hard Times Hard Choice Michigan Residents Deliberate*. Available online at http://participedia.net/en/cases/hard-times-hard-choices-mich igan-citizens-deliberate.

Delli Carpini, Michael X. and Keeter, Scott. 1996. *What Americans Know about Politics and Why It Matters*. New Haven, CT: Yale University Press.

Guber, Deborah. 2003. *Grassroots of The Green Revolution: Polling America on The Environment*. Cambridge, MA: MIT Press.

Hegerl, G., Zwiers, F. W., Braconnot, P., Gillett, N., Luo, Y., Orsini, J. M. *et al.* 2007. "Understanding and Attributing Climate Change" in S. Solomon *et al.* (eds.), *Climate Change 2007: The Physical Science Basis*. Cambridge University Press, pp. 663–746.

Hunter, Susan and Waterman, Richard W. 1996. *Enforcing the Law: The Case of the Clean Water Acts*. Armonk, NY: ME Sharpe.

McCubbins, Mathew D., Noll, Roger G., and Weingast, Barry R. 1987. "Administrative Procedures as Instruments of Political Control." *Journal of Law, Economics, and Organization* 3: 243–277.

Miller, R. L., Schmidt, G. A., Nazarenko, L. S., Tausnev, N., Bauer, S. E., Del Genio, A. D. *et al.* 2014. "CMIP5 Historical Simulations (1850–2012) with GISS ModelE2." *Journal of Advances in Modeling Earth Systems* 6(2): 441–477.

Moe, Terry. 1989. "The Politics of Bureaucratic Structure" in John Chubb and Paul Peterson (eds.), *Can the Government Govern?* Washington, DC: Brookings, pp. 267–329.

Rabe, Barry. 2011. "Contested Federalism and American Climate Policy." *Publius* 41(3): 494–521.

Reenock, Christopher and Gerber, Brian. 2008. "Information Exchange and Interest Group Enfranchisement through Agency Design." *Journal of Public Administration Research and Theory* 18(3): 415–440.

Scruggs, Lyle. 2003. *Sustaining Abundance: Environmental Performance in Advanced Democracies.* New York: Cambridge University Press.

Scruggs, L. and Benegal, Salil. 2012. "Declining Public Concern about Climate Change: Can We Blame the Great Recession?" *Global Environmental Change* 22(2): 505–515.

Simon, Herbert. 1955. "A Behavioral Model of Rational Choice." *Quarterly Journal of Economics* 69(1): 99–118.

US Environmental Protection Agency (EPA). 2014. "Climate Change Indicators in the United States, 2014." 3rd edn. EPA 430-R-14-004.

2015. "Assessment of the Potential Impacts of Hydraulic Fracturing for Oil and Gas on Drinking Water Resources (External Review Draft)." EPA/600/R-15/047.

Whitford, Andrew B. 2002. "Decentralization and Political Control of the Bureaucracy." *Journal of Theoretical Politics* 14(2): 167–193.

Wood, B. Dan. 1988. "Principals, Bureaucrats, and Responsiveness in Clean Air Enforcements." *American Political Science Review* 82(1): 213–234.

7

Health Policy

Outline

Questions

- How can we ensure access to care while controlling health spending?
- Can we provide health care that is affordable and available to all?
- How are individuals who have health insurance linked to those who do not?
- Why does the United States spend so much, yet have such poor health outcomes?
- Can Medicare and Medicaid continue to provide public insurance?
- Can we learn to manage health care efficiently?

Overview

- The primary analytic concepts we use to assess health policy are externalities, adverse selection, and moral hazard.
- The health economy is a case of market failure.

- It is possible to provide health insurance, but not to guarantee health outcomes.
- Health care is the fastest growing segment of the US economy.
- Health inflation has slowed, but still exceeds inflation in other sectors in the US economy.
- Health insurance is more affordable for the entire community if all members of the community are insured, but that may result in higher prices for the healthiest members of the community.
- Young people's health costs and health needs differ from those of older people.
- Moral hazard is a problem in health insurance.
- Health providers have more and better information than health consumers; there is information asymmetry in health care.

Introduction

Francis is a reasonably healthy 45-year-old man. He is a little overweight and smokes, but has not had any serious medical problems. Francis has health insurance. If Francis experiences a health crisis, who pays for his care? He will seek care from his primary physician and may require treatment in a hospital. In either case, Francis will bear some portion of the total costs to manage his crisis under the terms of his policy and his insurance company will pay the remainder. In contrast, Leo is a healthy 21-year-old man. He has no serious or chronic medical problems, is physically active, does not smoke, drinks infrequently, eats well, and is not obese. Leo does not have health insurance. If Leo experiences a health crisis, who pays for his care? Absent insurance, Leo may choose to ignore his crisis – possibly generating future complications and higher downstream health costs. If he seeks care for it, he likely does not have a primary care physician and will instead seek care from a hospital emergency room (ER). If Leo can afford it, he can pay for his health care out-of-pocket. However, given his lack of insurance, he will be responsible for 100 percent of any costs incurred. If he cannot afford it, he will still receive the care in an ER because it cannot be denied, but if he refuses to pay or is unable to pay it will ultimately be considered uncompensated care, and the public will pay for Leo's care with funds made available through public taxes.

On the surface, Francis's choice to purchase insurance and Leo's choice to not have insurance appear to be independent. If the consequences of these decisions had no bearing on any party outside of these transactions, then they would be independent. However, this is not the case. They are linked. One goal of this chapter is to explore how such choices are interdependent.

This vignette highlights what we believe are the three insights from the analysis of health policy – **externalities**, **adverse selection**, and **moral hazard**. Recall from Chapter 3 that externalities are those benefits or costs that a third party bears despite not being involved in the transaction. In health care, we are exposed to both positive and negative externalities of other citizens' choices on health. Citizens who care for themselves and maintain their health generate positive externalities for other citizens, through cheaper insurance and medical costs. Citizens who don't care for themselves or elect to not purchase health insurance but then expect taxpayers to cover their medical bills when they need care generate negative externalities in the form of higher taxes and higher insurance premiums. Francis's choice to purchase health insurance is an example of adverse selection. Those who are most in need of insurance purchase it; as a result, the set of insured people is not representative of society as a whole and is less healthy. One effect of adverse selection is that even healthy people who obtain insurance pay more for it than they would if the set of insured represented all members of society. Francis's behavior may also be a function of moral hazard: a choice for which you do not pay the full cost. Because of his health insurance, Francis will not pay the full cost for any smoking-related illnesses. His costs are partially transferred to other more healthy people with insurance. Each of these insights underscores how individual choices about health care and health insurance have serious implications for others not a party to the choice.

Given that these decisions are linked, should society require individuals to obtain health insurance? If the democratic will is that everyone should have access to an average amount of health care, how should it obtain this end? In other words, if society believes it is best for a citizen to obtain health insurance or access to health care, how should it ensure this outcome? Should there be a single-payer health care system, health insurance with a mandate to purchase the insurance, or some variation on one of these types of systems? Like the set of rules governing US healthcare provision prior to 2010, there are far-reaching consequences of any reorganization of the system. Some who did not have much access to health care will receive it. Some may have to pay more for their health care than before. Some employers may alter work schedules to shift health care costs from themselves to the government. Some doctors may provide more of one service than another, while other physicians will choose to specialize in one area versus another. Each of these and many other effects result from the rules governing health care. The important point for the moment is that any set of rules chosen has far-reaching implications. Because of these significant effects on who has access to health care, how much it costs, and who pays, bargaining over health care policy is intense. Political disagreement may be costly, but if one believes an agreement will have adverse effects, then an agreement to change the rules may be more costly.

In this chapter, we provide an overview of the major issues in health care policy in the United States. We focus principally on three analytic problems: adverse selection, moral hazard, and principle-agent. Substantively, we illustrate these problems with a discussion of the Affordable Care Act and changes it made to health policy, Medicare, Medicaid, prescription drugs, other health care programs in the United States, and innovations in health care policy.

7.1 Health Policy, Risk Pools, Adverse Selection, and Moral Hazard

In the United States, health care provision is organized primarily around health insurance. How much an individual pays for insurance is primarily a function of their risk profile, the risk pool, and their specific insurance plan (e.g. a Preferred provider organization versus a health maintenance organization). In this section we focus on the first two components: risk profile and risk pool.

All else equal, the price one pays for health insurance is based on one's risk profile and the risk pool. A **risk profile** is a general assessment of how much an individual will spend on health care in a given period of time. One type of risk profile is an experience rating, which is largely a function of age, gender, and health. From the perspective of an insurance company, young and healthy individuals are low risk, for they are not likely to consume much health care. Older and less healthy people are higher risk. They may need any number of expensive treatments such as chemotherapy, heart bypass surgery, organ replacement, etc.

Box 7.1 Expected Utility and Demand for Insurance

Imagine two people with different incomes, I_1 and I_2. Each person faces a risk of a health care incident, which will present costs to each person of c_1 and c_2, respectively. After their health crisis, each person's income will then be I_1-c_1 and I_2-c_2. Let's imagine that the health care incident c_1 represents a "health crisis," something akin to a heart attack, and that c_2 represents a "health event," something akin to a sinus infection, where $c_1 >> c_2$. The probability of c_1 is p_1 and c_2 is p_2. Health crises are more rare than health events, therefore, $p_1 << p_2$. Which event should a customer insure against? Recall from Chapter 3 that since we are dealing with uncertain events we must consider each person's expected utility attached to each event.

If these individuals are young, heart attacks are a relatively rare event, while sinus infections are a relatively more common event. Both individuals earn $40,000. The probability of health crisis, c_1, is 0.01 and is expected to cost $30,000, while the probability of health event, c_2, is 0.30 and is expected to cost $429. What is the expected income of each person as a result of these events?

$$E(I_1) = (1 - p_1)\, I_1 + p_1(I_1 - c_1) = 0.99 * 40,000 + 0.01 * 10,000 = \$39{,}700$$

$$E(I_2) = (1 - p_2)\, I_2 + p_2(I_2 - c_2) = 0.30 * 40,000 + 0.70 * 39,571 = \${\sim}39{,}700$$

Box 7.1 (*cont.*)

The expected outcomes in this case are the same. Why? Because, the relative risks imposed by these events are offset by the relative size of the probability and cost of the event. Assume that marginal expected utility is positive, but declining in income (i.e. a person is risk averse). Which event would a person desire to be insured against in the marketplace? Why?

The **risk pool** is the set of individuals covered by insurance. The more healthy the individuals covered, the lower the insurance company's expected costs, and vice versa if the risk pool contains an inordinate percentage of less healthy individuals. The riskiness of the pool depends on the risk profiles of those in the pool. To reduce risk and overall individual insurance costs, the goal is to make the pool less risky. One way to affect the risk pool is to base an individual's risk profile on expected costs over their lifetime, as opposed to the expected costs in a year. Insurance, generally, is an annual policy, suggesting that one should focus on the year. Doing so, however, gives more incentive for healthy individuals not to purchase insurance until they desperately need to. This leads to the pool of insured being relatively more risky. Basing costs on expected average lifetime expenditures might motivate more individuals to obtain insurance sooner and reduce the adverse selection problem. For similar reasons – to counter the adverse selection problem – some advocate that the price of health insurance should be based on the expected health costs of the larger population within which they live (e.g. a state or city). This is called a **community rating**. The choice of risk profiles – individual year, individual lifetime, average of individuals in a region – has a significant effect on the risk pool and the price of health insurance.

Some disagree with the idea that health costs should be purely a function of an individual's expected health expenditures in a given year. Doing so, they fear, will induce moral hazard. Insurance, recall, reduces an individual's cost should they need health care. When one does not pay the full cost of one's actions, more risky behavior may result. Perhaps people will engage in more smoking. At the same time, surveys of the US public indicate support for subsidized health insurance for individuals in poor health as a result of an accident or chronic condition (e.g. asthma) that is no fault of their own. Subsidizing their health insurance, however, means the adverse selection problem needs to be addressed, that is, more healthy people need to purchase insurance or healthy people with insurance need to pay more than they otherwise would. In some situations, one might be able to reduce the moral hazard problem with taxes. Taxes on cigarettes, for example, help deter smoking. Further, if the taxes collected from the sale of cigarettes are used prudently, they may further reduce smoking. This is the goal of cigarette tax policy in the state of California. Tobacco taxes are earmarked for anti-smoking campaigns, and research shows that these campaigns do reduce smoking. (World Health Organization 2012).

It is impossible to guarantee health outcomes. Societies can only provide access to health care so that people may seek treatments if they require them. Affordable access and decent health care, however, require one to address the adverse selection and moral hazard problems.

Moral Hazard

The **moral hazard** problem is especially crucial in the health care setting. Moral hazard exists when insurance leads a person to behave in ways that may be more risky than they might be in the absence of insurance. For example, a person may decide to eat less healthily than he or she should because of knowledge of having health insurance to provide care in the event of illness. Because of the presence of health insurance, people have the incentive to take more risks than they might in the absence of insurance. Moral hazard may also lead health service providers – physicians, clinics, and hospitals, among others – to provide more services than are needed in order to boost billings. Insurers have a strong incentive to provide coverage that is adequate, but is regulated in a manner in which overuse of services is not a regular problem.

The problem even extends to those without insurance: Much of the rationale for the controversial health insurance mandate that is the centerpiece of the **2010 Patient Protection and Affordable Care Act** (also referred to as the 2010 reform law or Obamacare) is based on this problem. The Act has a mechanism that requires people either to have health insurance or to pay a tax of $2,500 if they choose not to carry insurance. People are guaranteed some form of charity care even when they disavow responsibility for their health care. As a result, an incentive to take risks that may not be taken in the absence of some insurance coverage exists. To explain, physicians and hospitals are required to provide care to people regardless of their ability to pay. A person who is injured in an automobile accident will receive treatment regardless of their ability to pay. However, if they are not critically injured, their insurance may be checked before receiving treatment; their ability to pay may determine whether treatment is received in a private hospital versus a public or not-for-profit hospital. Moral hazard may give people the incentive not to enroll in an insurance plan because they know that they must be given care if they are in need. A large part of health spending in the United States covers **uncompensated care**, care that is given to people who do not pay.

Box 7.2 Uncompensated Care as a Negative Externality

In 2012, hospitals experienced approximately $46 billion in uncompensated care costs to pay for individuals who could not afford to pay for their own care. This accounted for nearly 6 percent of hospitals' total expenses. With approximately 200 million adult US citizens, this means that every adult would need to be taxed ~$230, or ~$460 per two-adult family, to pay for individuals who required care but did not have insurance or other means of paying. This is a **negative externality** of an individual's choice to not carry or inability to afford health insurance.

The moral hazard problem affects health care in a couple of ways. First, there is no strong incentive to try to seek less expensive treatments in the face of generous health insurance. This is true for individuals and for providers as well. Widespread concern with unnecessary use of expensive treatments by providers – called remunerectomies by some critics – shows the layers of the problem. Individual policyholders have incentives to seek possibly unnecessary treatments because of the existence of their policies. For example, a person may need a single blood test to diagnose his or her health problem. If that person has health insurance that will pay for a larger battery of tests, she may request them because it has no effect on her, although it will likely increase the costs borne by the insurer. Similarly, if a physician needs a single test to diagnose a problem, he or she may ask for more tests if the insurance company pays for them. The physician may justify it as practicing defensive medicine, i.e. being cautious, but the reality is that the existence of generous insurance allows him more discretion and thus provides an opportunity for moral hazard. In other cases, providers have incentives to over-treat patients or provide unnecessary tests in order to increase the price of care.

It is evident that moral hazard presents problems for the insurer and, ultimately, for the consumer. The insurer faces higher costs of service provision, which increases operating costs. Those cost increases are passed along to the consumer, which in this case means the price of insurance increases, which affects businesses that provide health coverage for their employees, governments that pay for health insurance, and individuals who purchase private plans.

The existence of incompatible incentives among individuals, providers, and insurers produces moral hazard in health care. Some early health insurance plans provided what is known as "**first dollar**" coverage, meaning that all of an individual's costs were covered regardless of the malady. In that case the individual assumes no risk of being uninsured regardless of how he or she behaves. In that case the sole cost of receiving a treatment is possible discomfort or loss of privacy, but not money. In the presence of full insurance coverage, the provider has no incentive to limit the services provided. As recently as the 1980s, providers were allowed to bill at "customary and prevailing rates," meaning that they were allowed to establish prices as they saw fit. Hence the price of equivalent services – say, for example, a medically uncomplicated childbirth – could vary greatly within and across geographic areas.

Asymmetric information also lends to the moral hazard problem. Some of this is largely uncontrollable: not everyone is at equal risk of being exposed to poor health. That is, some people are predisposed toward having high blood pressure, diabetes, and other chronic conditions that lead to long-term receipt of health treatments. Sometimes people choose not to behave in ways that might lessen their immediate and future need for care: they eat unhealthily, drink to excess, smoke, engage in risky behaviors, and the like. In either case, the insurer is uncertain about the individual's behavior and thus faces a risk in extending coverage. However, the individual likely is aware of his or her relative health risk and it is unlikely that he or she freely shares it with the insurer.

Adverse selection occurs when individuals seek insurance because they are of particularly high risk. For example, smokers are more likely to suffer illnesses over the life course and are more likely to take advantage of health insurance than non-smokers. If an insurer does not know that person seeking coverage is a smoker, there is **information asymmetry**: one has more information than the other. Insurers wish to guard against adverse selection through screening of applicants for coverage. There is a concern as well that insurers may screen applicants who may have genetic predispositions toward illness as they attempt to reduce the risk of paying large amounts for treatments.

Policy Solutions

The solution to moral hazard issues is to align incentives so that they no longer create the problem. Insurers now uniformly require that recipients of services contribute to the costs of their care. This may be done in a variety of ways. The most traditional is to have users pay the price for a **deductible**, a fixed percentage of the services they receive, say 20 percent, which is expected to lessen service use. Most of these policies have a fixed amount, for example, 20 percent up to a total expenditure of $20,000, after which the full amount is covered. This partially solves the moral hazard problem, but after the individual spends the full amount for which he or she is required to pay, the moral hazard problem re-emerges. For example, a person may have large medical bills and pay out his full deductible by October and may choose some elective surgery before the end of the calendar year to avoid paying an additional deductible in the following year.

Another approach is via charging co-payments for services received. **Co-payments** may be small amounts – as little as $5 per visit but more commonly $20 or $25 per visit – that are expected to make people realize that they are receiving services. There is strong evidence that cost sharing of this sort leads to reduced use of services and lessened spending. Researchers affiliated with the Rand Health Insurance Experiment, which was conducted from 1975 to 1984, reported that service use declined as out-of-pocket spending increased (Newhouse 1993). The researchers reported that the use of all types of services – physician visits, outpatient hospital visits, and inpatient visits – declined as co-payments increased. The effects of cost sharing had little effect on the health of the average person, but had adverse effects on the poor, whose already strained budgets were more greatly strained by higher costs.

Insurers may also monitor the insured as a method for regulating moral hazard. One way to do so is to lessen the extent of coverage. They may do this by conducting ex ante (before the event) evaluations of potential enrollees' health and behavior. They may require physical examinations to assess health status, although they may not discriminate according to potential health costs in offering coverage. That is, insurers may not determine, for example, that a person has a family history of heart disease and refuse to insure a person because of that risk. However, they may observe that people engage in unhealthy behaviors, like smoking, and try to mediate that behavior upon covering them. In truth, these ex ante (before the fact) attempts to regulate behavior are not especially effective inasmuch as people are the product of their backgrounds and may not be able to alter the probability that they will suffer a particular ailment. However, knowing of people's predilections may be useful for the insurer, who may be able to tailor a plan for that person's treatment.

Ex post (after the fact) observations are more likely better predictors of behavior. For example, if an insurer observes a person using the emergency room regularly, it may be possible to steer that person toward a less expensive venue for receiving services. Likewise, if a person places regular claims for respiratory ailments, and smokes, the insurer may use that information to steer him or her toward a smoking cessation program.

7.2 Principal–Agent Problems and Health Care Markets

Proponents of free-market health care solutions often invoke the expansion of the government's role in health care as a driving factor in price increases. However, there are underlying problems in the health market that produce a market failure (see Chapter 3, section 3.3) in which supply and demand does not operate efficiently. Kenneth Arrow's 1963 paper, "Uncertainty and the Welfare Economics of Medical Care," describes the problems inherent in a pure market model of health care. The uncertainty to which Arrow refers is the key to the problem: the use of health care is largely uncertain, especially to recipients, and this uncertainty contributes to substantial principal–agent problems in the relationship. When people need health care, and especially when they need care for serious and atypical conditions, they are at the mercy of providers for information. That is, there is an information asymmetry in which the provider – here, the physician – controls substantially more knowledge about the patient's needs than the patient. The patient has entered into an agency relationship with the provider, in which they concede less knowledge and agree to accept the providers' decisions regarding treatment to a large extent. This is akin to the agency relationship people enter into with attorneys or other professionals, but is especially strong in the case of health care because of the emotion that often attends illness. That is, persons in need of care or the relatives of persons in need of care face decision-making under substantial uncertainty and considerable emotional stress. Thus, the agent has considerable influence over decisions.

This problem is made stronger still by the presence of insurance. The person in need of care is often ill informed, possibly under emotional stress, *and* faces a low price constraint in the presence of insurance. This gives the provider the ability to establish what needs to be done to treat a particular malady. The recipient's uncertainty coupled with a low or non-existent payment concern gives the provider considerable power in the market transaction. In a sense, the provider is the ultimate determiner of what needs to be done to treat the problem. Hence, the provider is in a position to establish demand for the service and provide the service. This is contrary to a free market model for health care.

In fact, when people call for a free market for health care they are often not describing the classic free market of Adam Smith. They describe a market that is freed from government involvement, but has voluntary price controls and self-regulating mechanisms. Those mechanisms often fail, but their popularity among their supporters remains, causing demands for a free market for health care to continue. The health care free market has failed because of the information asymmetry that occurs in health care, and due to the presence of insurance, consumers face only small portions of the true prices of care.

A number of innovations have been put in place to improve upon the market-like characteristics of health insurance. One innovation is the use of co-payments, which we discussed above. In addition, the rise of for-profit hospitals and **health maintenance organizations** (HMOs) (where charitable or not-for-profit organizations/physicians once were) has led to a more market-like health care system. Regardless of those changes, the enormous information problems in health care continue to exist, even with greatly improved health information systems. Ultimately, health care still fails as a market good.

7.3 Health Outcomes in the United States and the World

The United States spends a larger portion of its income on health than any other country in the world. A 2013 study conducted by a group convened by the National

Academy of Sciences paints a distressing image of health care in the United States. The study is based on research on seventeen wealthy, developed nations – the group that is most similar to the affluence and development of the United States – and reports that the United States ranks at the bottom of that group on most meaningful health measures (Woolf and Aron 2013).[1] The most revealing item they note is that life expectancies are shorter in America than in other nations. Those differences are especially pronounced among women. The difference holds for all ages of the life course, until the age of 75 years.

The report lists a litany of problems for Americans in relation to people in the comparison group. The reviewers ranked populations on nine health characteristics, and the United States fared worse, or near the bottom, on each. The United States has a higher number of adverse birth outcomes and higher infant mortality rate than residents of other wealthy nations, and the likelihood of a child living to the age of 5 is lower in the United States than in other nations. Violent deaths by car crashes, gun injuries, and the like occur more often in the United States than in the other nations. Additionally, more US children die by violent death than do children in other parts of the world. Americans have more adolescent pregnancies, more STDs, and more HIV and AIDs cases than the other nations. Other nations have lower drug-related mortalities, and do not have the obesity, diabetes, and heart disease problems of US citizens. Finally, US citizens have worse chronic lung disease problems and more disabilities than residents of the other sixteen nations. Yet, the United States spends more per person on health care than the other nations . . . it does not appear to get a strong return on its investment.

A recent study suggests that the higher-than-average cost of health care in the United States versus other industrialized nations is due to higher prices and readily available technology (Squires 2012). Health care spending in the United States consumed over 17 percent of the nation's gross domestic product (GDP) in 2009. The average in thirteen of the seventeen wealthy nations listed previously was 9.5 percent. Health spending in the United States was nearly $8,000 per capita in 2009; the average for the thirteen Organisation for Economic Co-operation and Development (OECD) nations included in the study was about $3,200. In the United States, about $3,800 of that was public spending, nearly $3,200 from private insurers, and just under $1,000 was out-of-pocket spending. By contrast, the average for the thirteen OECD nations was $2,400 from public insurers, $193 from private insurers, and $553 out-of-pocket (Squires 2012: 3).

Spending is high in the United States, and the rate of growth in expenditures also exceeds that of most other nations. It is difficult to isolate the sources of the United

---

[1] The nations are the United States, Australia, Austria, Canada, Denmark, Finland, France, Germany, Italy, Japan, the Netherlands, Norway, Portugal, Spain, Sweden, Switzerland, and the United Kingdom.

States' high spending. Lifestyle choices and health behavior are factors that influence health usage and spending. Obesity is one problem that is linked to higher health spending, for Americans are more obese than people in other nations. The United States also has higher drug and physician prices than other nations. Also, health technology is a large contributor to health spending in the States. Americans are proud of their advanced health technology they are accustomed to using, but that access to technology is costly and produces higher health spending (Sloan and Hsieh 2012).

Americans pay more for health care than the citizens of other nations. They get collectively poor outcomes for that high expenditure. Despite this, they are skeptical about health reforms, and many believe the United States has the world's best system of health care. The price differences between the United States and the rest of the world are stark. Recent data show the United States to be much higher than most developed nations in daily hospital prices, the price for specific services (e.g. simple child birth), and for specialized drugs. For example, the average daily price for hospital care in the United States is nearly $4,300. Australia has the second highest average among the set of seventeen nations discussed above, yet is less than $1,500. The cost of an appendectomy in the United States is nearly $14,000; it is just below $5,500 in Australia, again the most expensive among the nations listed other than the United States (*Washington Post* 2013). Most nations have more stringent pricing mechanisms and regulatory schemes than the United States, and that results in lower prices and better health outcomes. The politics of health care in the United States make it difficult to change those conditions.

Health price inflation has been greater than inflation in the broader Consumer Price Index (CPI) for most of the past thirty years. That changed in 2013, when the price of health care rose at 1 percent as opposed to 1.4 percent in the index. Some observers are quick to claim that as a victory for the 2010 Health Reform Act, but others claim that it is due to the overall economy being down and a rise in price-shopping among consumers (Morath and Radnofsky 2013).

7.4 American Health Policy and US National Health Care Programs

The US health system is a mixture of programs that constitute a series of patches rather than a coherent whole. This is a function of the incremental way in which health insurance was developed in the 1930s (with expansion in the post-war United States). The initial creation of widespread insurance began immediately following World War II, and took the form of employment-supported programs that were paid for as a portion of benefits for returning veterans. During the war, wage and price controls led to there being a premium on labor. Employers responded by providing workers with pensions and health insurance in lieu of pay increases, which were not available as a way to retain workers. Those benefits were tax-deductible by employers and were not taxed as income for workers, which made them especially popular. After the war, when those controls were lifted, insurers, workers, and employers had come to accept the fact of employment-linked health insurance. That model of coverage continued into the post-war era (Starr 1982).

Political scientist Paul Pierson argues that the development of the US health system is a function of **path dependence** in which the system's initial developments – borne largely in the 1930s Great Depression – have established the path to health policy development and change in the current era. This is consistent with what has occurred in other nations. For example, the British National Health Service is what many US citizens view as the pinnacle of socialist health management. The majority of its physicians are government employees, citizens are subjected to waits for services, and services are scarce and in some cases are rationed or not provided if they are considered to be non-urgent. The NHS can be seen as an entirely reasonable response to the nation's circumstances when it was implemented in 1948. As the physician and author Atul Gawande notes (2009), Great Britain's move to the national health program was nearly guaranteed by the nation's declaration of war on Germany in 1939. The British, unlike the Americans, were subjected to evacuations from the city to the country, air raids, medical facilities that were destroyed by shelling, and poor health due to the absence of any health insurance for most citizens prior to the war. The government responded to the need for health care and health facilities with the creation of the National Health Service in 1945. Similarly, the French, under de Gaulle, established a national health service using a system of insurance based largely on voluntary contributions from union members – this was the best fit for their circumstances following the war. The French system was ranked as the world's best in a 2000 study by the World Health Organization. As Gawande notes, the English and French decisions were pragmatic and not based on some ideological predilection for collective decisions.

The idea of a path dependency affecting policy decisions helps explain the peculiar development of health care policy in the United States. In the States, private insurers and medical providers, the latter led by the American Medical Association and the American Hospital Association, likened early attempts to require universal coverage to collectivist sentiments that were popular in some parts of the nation during the 1930s and, later, to socialized medicine, long a potent rallying call in opposition to universal care in the United States (Poen 1996). This long-term opposition helps explain why it is so difficult to reform health care in the United States or in any nation. While most people can agree that being uninsured is undesirable, it is also the case that people who are insured are reluctant to support changes that might upset the status quo. That is, people may understand that health care is expensive, that insurance prices are rising, and so on, but they are not willing to risk worsening their own situations by supporting change.

The United States is unique among wealthy nations in its failure to guarantee universal health coverage. However, if someone is not insured, they are still able to get emergency care at some form of public or not-for-profit hospital or clinic. This care is often billed to the uninsured recipient and, if that person cannot pay, it is declared a tax loss by the provider and claimed as uncompensated care. Ultimately, it is billed to persons with insurance through various means, such as charging high rates for parking, or enormous amounts for a single aspirin. In either situation, the uninsured are less likely to receive care as quickly as those who are insured, and it is likely to be provided in an expensive emergency room setting. Thus, the claim that the United States has a large uninsured population is correct, but it does not necessarily mean that people cannot receive care.

Supporters of **health insurance mandates**, such as the Massachusetts Plan (also known as Romneycare) and the Patient Protection and Affordable Care Act of 2010 (known as Obamacare), point to the need for required health insurance coverage. These provisions require that persons purchase health insurance or pay a tax to support their care if uninsured. Supporters of these mandates claim that they are needed to lessen persons' ability to take a "free ride" on uncompensated care. To explain, insurance is guaranteed to fail if users are allowed to purchase insurance *after* an undesirable event occurs. For example, organizations that insure against floods are unlikely to allow people to buy flood insurance and seek claims after the flood occurs. To do so violates the model of insurance, and the only circumstance in which such coverage would be considered appropriate would be under the condition of an emergency or disaster. Given that a number of health care events are fairly predictable over the course of a lifetime and that there is a social norm of providing care to persons who require it, the insurance mandate seems a reasonable solution in many quarters. The insurance mandate is controversial, but people are purchasing policies as required, and it appears to be a moderate success in its initial stages, but it remains to be seen how well it will work in the future.

Forces in the economy and politics prohibited the United States from developing a system of universal coverage akin to that in other wealthy nations. This was not a function of ideology so much as one of circumstance, and to some extent, this continues to occur. Despite this, a continued move toward expanded coverage exists.

Box 7.1 Back and Forth with Health Mandates

In November of 1993, Senator Ron Wyden (R-OK) and twenty-four Republican co-sponsors introduced the Consumer Choice Health Security Act (SB 1743), which required employers to deduct health insurance premiums from employees' wages and pay those premiums to employees' chosen health insurance

Box 7.1 (*cont.*)

companies. It also required employers to notify employees of their right to seek tax credits for the premiums. On November 23, 1993, Senator Lincoln Chafee (R-RI) and twenty co-sponsors (two Democrats and eighteen Republicans) introduced the Health Equity and Access Reform Act (SB 1770), which called for universal health coverage, except in cases in which an individual opposed health plan coverage for religious reasons or relied on spiritual means for care. On January 18, 2007, Senator Ron Wyden (D-OR), along with seven Democratic, one Independent, and nine Republican co-sponsors, introduced the Healthy Americans Act (SB 335). This Act required each citizen to purchase a Health American Private Insurance Plan if they did not either have another plan or rejected insurance for religious reasons. Penalties were assessed if they did not enroll. On February 5, 2009, Senator Wyden again introduced the Health Americans Act (SB 391), this time with eight Democrats, one Independent, and five Republican co-sponsors. It was very similar to the 2007 Act, but expanded the acceptable insurers. On December 24, 2009, HR 3590, the Patient Protection and Affordable Care Act, was passed with no Republican votes. This was ironic, considering that it was originally a Republican bill disliked by Democrats. The mandate came full circle, and is now a large part of the Republican complaint with the Obama administration.

Americans are wary of government involvement in the provision of health care. The path of health care's development explains this fear. The existence of private office physicians, the presence of trade-group and employer-based coverage, and initially voluntary and now mixed voluntary and for-profit hospital industry largely shaped the discussion about how best to provide health care. The first attempt to gain universal coverage began with Theodore Roosevelt's call for the creation of a single national health service in his 1912 campaign. It was an important issue in his run for the presidency on the Progressive ticket after he had served as president from 1901 to 1909. However, Roosevelt's Bull Moose Party failed to win the election and the issue died.

A national goal of establishing universal health insurance coverage was reintroduced by Franklin Roosevelt in 1933. He sought to gain passage of a coverage bill within the broader Social Security Act, which passed in 1935. To his dismay, the health insurance bill was dropped, due largely to resistance from the American Medical Association and state-level medical associations. One result of this failed attempt, however, was the creation of Blue Cross and Blue Shield associations. They function as not-for-profit health care insurance organizations via, respectively, the American Hospital Association and the American Medical Association. In 1975, Blue Cross was described as "... an agent of the government, with the obligation to carry out the policies of Congress and administrative agencies" (Law 1976: 2). Thus, Blue Cross functioned as a quasi-governmental agency. To avoid the monopoly problem, each state has a least one independent BCBS organization (California has two, one for the north and one for the south). Although BCBS's market domination has diminished over the years, the company's market share is as high as 75 percent in some states. This suggests that, for those with private health insurance, BCBS serves as a de facto system of national health insurance, albeit one paid through earnings and employer contributions.

Following FDR's failed attempt to create a national health insurance program, President Harry Truman attempted to create some form of universal health care, but was also rebuffed. Despite Truman's failure to enact a large public program, President Lyndon Johnson used the basic design of Truman's program to create Medicare and Medicaid, each of which is discussed in more detail in the section that follows. Medicare is still in force and provides hospital insurance for senior citizens. Medicaid, which is also still in force, provides health insurance to the indigent and medically indigent.

Both Medicare and Medicaid have been greatly altered over the course of their histories, but stand as the most significant moves toward universal coverage in US history. In 1971, Senator Edward Kennedy (D-MA) proposed a national health insurance plan, which was to be financed through payroll taxes. President Nixon advanced his version of a bill, the National Health Partnership Act, which would preserve private insurance, yet require businesses to provide coverage to employees or make payments to a government-run fund. The bill failed, largely due to lack of Democratic support; Kennedy believed, incorrectly, that he could gain passage of his broader bill. Nixon later succeeded in expanding the presence of HMOs in 1973. Later attempts by President Jimmy Carter to expand health coverage were stifled in large part by Senator Kennedy's push for a more expansive set of policies. Kennedy, at the time of his death in 2009, voiced regret at not having worked with Nixon to adopt a policy.

The Reagan and George H. W. Bush administrations advanced health care access principally by expanding coverage for elderly and disabled people, but also expanded employees' assurance of coverage. In 1993, the Clinton administration sought to expand health care to ensure near-universal coverage as its first major domestic initiative, but the proposal failed due to weak support among Congressional Democrats and opposition from providers and insurers. However, Clinton did have some major health care successes during his presidency. In 1996, the Health Insurance Portability and Accountability Act (HIPAA) was passed, enabling the continuity of health insurance coverage for persons who lose their jobs and promoting the creation of medical savings accounts. Clinton's administration also improved access to long-term care services and coverage. These are not spending bills; unemployed persons who wish to maintain their insurance may do so at their *own* expense. This can be difficult to accomplish while unemployed, but in some cases it can be negotiated. In 1997, Clinton succeeded in establishing the State Children's Health Insurance Program (CHIP), which helped establish care for low-income children whose families earned too much to gain Medicaid eligibility. President George W. Bush's most significant health policy initiative was the creation in 2003 of a Medicare drug benefit. In all of these cases, failures of large-scale policy changes were met with incremental changes that built upon the established health system and the Medicaid and Medicare systems.

Obamacare

The Obama administration's passage of the Patient Protection and Affordable Care Act (ACA) on March 22, 2010 marked the most ambitious and far-reaching expansion of the federal government's role in ensuring access to health care since Medicare and Medicaid were created in 1965. The politics of the bill's passage were contentious: The bill was passed with Democratic control of the House and Senate with no Republican support. Republican lawmakers in the House and Senate participated in committee work that drafted the legislation, and 161 Republican-drafted amendments were added to the Senate bill in 2009; forty-nine Grand Old Party (GOP) amendments were not included (Strauss 2010). Nonetheless, no GOP members voted for the bill and moved immediately to condemn it after it was passed. Some Republican-led states brought suit, claiming that the law violated the Constitution because of the federal governments' requirement that citizens purchase insurance or pay a tax if they decide not to do so. The cases were heard in appellate courts in Florida, Virginia, and Georgia, and the rulings were 2–1 against the states' positions. The US Supreme court, in *National Federation of Independent Businesses v. Sibelius* (2012), ruled that the United States was within its rights to require the purchase of health insurance on the grounds that it was a tax and, as a result, within the rights of Congress to enact. However, the Court ruled that the national government could not require the states to expand their Medicaid programs, and that decision created additional difficulty for the Obama administration's attempt to expand health coverage.

The Act calls for Medicaid to be expanded so that the states pay no Medicaid share from 2014 until 2017. After that, the federal share declines slowly until it reaches 90 percent of total Medicaid spending in 2020. The Court decision in *National Federation of Independent Business v. Sibelius* (132 S. Court 602, 2011) came in a suit brought initially by the state governments, whose claim was that the legislation violated the constitution. The decision upheld the law's constitutionality, but the justices' ruling that states cannot be required to expand Medicaid (regardless of the promise of federal reimbursement) shifted the focus of the debate. By September 2013, twenty-nine states supported the expansion, sixteen opposed it, and five had not decided (Kaiser 2013). All of the states with Democrat governors supported the expansion, and all of the states that opposed the expansion had Republican governors. Republican governors who opposed the Medicaid expansion claimed they did so due to concerns about the expense of added Medicaid enrollees. Empirical evaluation of their claims suggests their refusal was grounded solely in partisan preference, with Republican governors refusing billions of dollars of national government aid by refusing expanded Medicaid (Barrilleaux and Rainey 2014). For the 2015 fiscal year, for example, the state of Florida refused more than $2 billion in national government assistance to pay for expanded Medicaid for low-income residents. Thus, Medicaid policy is a key element in the debate over health insurance expansion.

A second challenge to the Act involved another suit that was decided by the US Supreme Court. The *King, et al. v. Burwell, Secretary of Health and Human Services, et al.* (576 US (2015)) case hinged on the claim that the language in the 2010 Act stated that only *state governments* could establish health exchanges, which are the mechanism the national government uses to provide subsidies that make health insurance affordable to over 6 million Obamacare enrollees. When the policy was designed, states could establish exchanges or, if they decided not to do so, could default to use exchanges that were designed by the national government. Rigby and Haselswerdt (2013) model state choices to adopt or not adopt exchanges and find that it is driven mainly by partisanship, with Republican-led states more likely to rely on national government established exchanges. Thirty-four states did not design their own exchanges. The *King* plaintiffs argued that the national government-designed exchanges were not eligible for subsidies. The Supreme Court voted 6–3 that the exchanges established by the states and the national government are eligible for subsidies. If they had ruled otherwise, the foundation of the ACA would have crumbled. The cumulative effect of the 2012 and 2015 Court rulings is to cement the legality of the Affordable Care Act, and to make it unlikely that it will be subject to major change before the end of 2017 when a new president takes office.

Public opinion toward Obamacare has been divided, hovering around 42 percent in favor and 42 percent opposed over most of the years since it was passed, but polls from January until August 2013 showed public opinion toward the program tending to be more negative than in the past, with favorability averaging around 36 percent for the period and unfavorable views holding at around 42 percent (Hamel *et al.* 2014). The unpopularity of the ACA is due to the complexity of the policy and its opponents' success in criticizing it as unconstitutional, invasive, and a threat to policyholders' existing insurance coverage. Yet, survey respondents rate many elements of Obamacare, like the restriction on insurers' ability to block coverage due to pre-existing conditions and the rule that allows children to stay on their parent's coverage through the age of 26, favorably. The ACA is evidence that major policy change is hard to accomplish and comes with high political costs.

7.5 US Health National Government Health Care Programs

The two largest national government-sponsored health insurance programs are Medicare and Medicaid. The Children's Health Insurance Program, the Veterans Health Service, and other programs are also important parts of the US-Government-aided health system. Medicare is a federally funded program; citizens' earnings are charged Medicare taxes each year. Medicaid is funded jointly by the national government and the states. State government contributions are determined by median incomes; wealthier states pay a larger share of Medicaid than less affluent states. The wealthiest states receive a Medicaid match of 50 percent, meaning that for each dollar they spend on Medicaid services, they receive rebates of one dollar. Poorer states receive higher payments; the average for all states was 57 percent in 2012. The highest state reimbursement was 82 percent.[2] In some states, like New York, the state shares spending with its counties. In this case, counties pay one-quarter of the state's share.

The distinction between Medicare and Medicaid is important. Medicare is provided as an **entitlement** that is not means-tested, which means that citizens receive the payment regardless of their economic need. Medicaid is also an entitlement, but it is **means-tested**; this means that recipients must demonstrate evidence of low income as well as other factors in order to be enrolled. The distinction between the poor and the elderly in determining access to publicly supported health benefits is a function of the politics of health policy decision-making. The elderly, regardless of their income, are granted health insurance coverage as a right of citizenship because they are considered deserving by virtue of their age and their inability to participate in the able-bodied labor force. The able-bodied young poor are considered to be the undeserving poor because they are not working or have children to whom they are unable to provide health care without assistance. They are subject to means tests and Medicaid is paid with joint state-national funding, which allows states to vary in their eligibility, service provision, and payment standards. Those conditions were necessary to gain passage of the bill in 1965, where some states were reluctant to have the national government establishing uniform criteria.

Medicare and Medicaid have undergone substantial revision and reform in the years since they were initially implemented. Both were originally **fee-for-service (FFS)** programs, meaning that providers were paid an agreed-upon price for services rendered. The states and the national government initially set prices high in an attempt to gain physician and hospital participation in the programs. Additionally, they established generous eligibility standards for Medicaid, hoping that doing so

---

[2] See www.medicaid.gov/Medicaid-CHIP-Program-Information/By-Topics/Financing-and-Reimbursement/Financing-and-Reimbursement.html.

would encourage use. Their efforts were too successful; by the mid 1970s, it was clear that both Medicare and Medicaid were more expensive than expected and the search for cost control began. This led to the cost-access problem in health services: as access to services increased, the cost of services also increased, so policymakers continually search for ways to ensure adequate access to services while controlling spending. Given that both Medicaid and Medicare were intended to provide access to health care akin to that received by the general public, and not "welfare" or "cut-rate" care, there is a tension between access to services and the prices governments agree to pay for those services. As the amount of reimbursement declines in either program, providers may opt out of the programs, refusing to provide care for Medicare or Medicaid patients.

Refusing to participate is more practical for physicians or groups than for hospitals. Medicaid reimbursements to physicians are low, and most state governments have moved toward **capitated payment models**, in contrast to the old fee-for-service model. Capitated payments contract with a provider or group to insure a client for some period of time – a month, a year, or the extent of their eligibility for Medicaid – for a fixed price payment. The provider then has an incentive to provide care efficiently so that the organization receives a profit at the end of the capitation period. This is the health maintenance organization (HMO), **preferred provider organization (PPO)**, or otherwise capitated plan. Although there are complaints about such plans, evidence suggests that they are more efficient methods of providing services than FFS programs, although the presence of a co-pay, in which the recipient of services pays even a nominal amount for care, lessens service use (Newhouse 1993).

Box 7.2 Medicare, Medigap, and Medicare Advantage

Medigap policies are private insurance plans that pay for co-pays and other expenses that are not paid by **Medicare Part A** and **Medicare Part B**. A person must be enrolled in Medicare Parts A and B to be eligible for a Medigap policy. Persons with Medicare Advantage plans may not buy Medigap plans unless they cease to be enrolled in Medicare Advantage upon buying a Medigap plan.

Medicare Advantage plans are private plans that offer full coverage, that is, all Medicare Part A and B coverage, and **Medicare Part D**, drug coverage. They are called **Medicare Part C**.

Medicare is a national government program that provides health insurance coverage for persons aged 65 and over, persons under 65 with certain disabilities, and persons of any age with end-stage renal disease. Medicare is divided into four parts, each of which covers specific services and has different costs. Medicare Part A provides hospital insurance, inpatient hospitalization, skilled nursing facilities (i.e. nursing home care up to 100 days), hospice care, and home health care. Medicare Part A is "free" for people who have paid Medicare taxes through their payroll taxes and their spouses. People who have not paid those taxes may purchase Medicare insurance. Medicare Part B pays for medical insurance, fees for doctors, outpatient care services, durable medical equipment (e.g. wheelchairs, oxygen tents, etc.), home health care, and some preventive services. Medicare Part B coverage is purchased by the individual or by a third party, for example by a retirement program or by a state Medicaid program. Some people who want to improve the coverage of Part B purchase "Medigap" insurance policies (see Box 7.2). Medicare Part C is called Medicare Advantage, and provides the benefits of Medicare Parts A and B via a Medicare-approved private insurance company. It can also provide extra benefits depending on the specific policy. Most Medicare Advantage policies provide drug benefits, which are covered under Medicare Part D. Medicare Part D is the prescription drug benefit, which provides drug insurance from Medicare-approved private companies. Part D provides some discounts on drugs, but the drugs covered and discounts vary by private plan; the private plans are subsidized. Medicare is expensive; according to the US Congressional Budget Office (CBO), the program cost about $569.4 billion in 2012. Of that, Medicare Part A cost $264 billion, Part B $242.6 billion, and Part D $60.1 billion.

Box 7.3 Medicaid Spend Down

If a person is a minor or over 65 years of age and has income greater than the state's Medicaid eligibility amount, she or her guardian may be able to "spend down" to become Medicaid eligible. To do so, it is necessary to demonstrate that the difference between a person's income and a person's health expenses is large enough to make them "medically needy," which warrants Medicaid eligibility. It is legal to spend down as a way to protect assets for living spouses or descendants, whose care is then paid by the state Medicaid program.

Medicaid

Medicaid is administered by the national government under the Center for Medical Services. It differs from Medicare in that Medicaid requires state government participation to gain entry. The national government pays for at least one-half of each state's expenses and as much as 83 percent in states with the lowest incomes. Medicaid is a means-tested program, in which persons gain eligibility due to having low income and resources; eligibility is determined by state government rules that vary among the states.

Medicaid covers benefits for young and old alike, with a large portion of Medicaid spending being devoted to nursing home care for the elderly. Because Medicare covers only 100 days of skilled nursing facility care, a significant portion of elderly persons "spend down" to Medicaid eligibility after their Medicare benefits and other resources are depleted. Although most Medicare recipients are women and children, the largest amount of money is spent on elderly and disabled enrollees.

In 2012, federal Medicaid spending totaled about $258 billion; state spending in 2010 was about $97.5 billion. About $148 billion federal dollars was spent on Medicaid elderly and disabled enrollees during 2012, while only about $50 billion was spent on children and $35 billion was spent on adults. Elderly and disabled people accounted for about 17 percent of the population in 2012. The costs of care for elderly and disabled people far outstrip that of children and adult eligible enrollees: the average elderly enrollee received benefits valued over $11,300 in 2012, while the average child's benefits cost about $1,500. This spending discrepancy has led some people to question the benefit to cost ratio of spending on the elderly versus the young, with some claiming that higher investments in young people would likely provide better returns than investments in the elderly (Kaiser 2012).

State governments and the national government constantly seek ways to reduce Medicaid spending. One controversial recommendation that is gaining popularity among some Republican members of Congress is to move Medicaid from a **categorical grant** to a **block grant**. Categorical grants establish a formula that the recipient follows in order to get some agreed-upon payments. The Medicaid categorical grant is open ended: spending is regulated by eligibility, service coverage, and prices, but it has no cap. A block grant sets an amount of spending that is agreed upon and the grantee has flexibility, within limits, to spend the money as best fits the state's needs. Proponents of the block grant approach support it as the only way to set an established Medicaid budget. Critics claim that it will unduly cut access to services for people in need and increase the uncompensated care burdens that already strain not-for-profit hospitals. In the past, state governments have been leery of a block grant because Medicaid payments from the national government to the states have been generous, and even conservative governors viewed it as "free money" for their populations. It is unclear whether that view would hold with a unified Republican US House and Senate.

Child Health Insurance Program

Child Health Insurance Program (CHIP) is a program designed to provide benefits to children whose parents earn too much to gain access to Medicaid. Like Medicaid, it is funded by the state and national governments. Total funding for the program was $10.6 billion in 2009. Of that, the national government spent $7.5 billion and the states $3.1 billion. As with Medicaid, state governments determine how generous they wish to be through the establishment of financial eligibility levels; higher income for eligibility suggests more generous state decisions and higher costs per beneficiary.

Department of Defense and Veterans Administration

Department of Defense and **Veterans Administration** account for another large piece of US health care spending. Together, about $89 billion was spent on the two programs in 2009. Current estimates suggest that health care accounts for about 10 percent of the Defense Department budget in fiscal year 2012. The Veterans Administration (VA) provides health care through a network of VA Hospitals that exist across the country, but also via Tricare, a health insurance program for active duty service people, veterans, and their dependents. Insurance under Tricare is provided without charge to some active-duty service members and with modest co-payments to others. There are a variety of programs and co-payments available within Tricare.

Indian Health Service

The **Indian Health Service (IHS)** provides services through IHS-run clinics and tribal health services. IHS serves about 2 million Native American and Alaskan Native populations living on or near reservations and in some urban areas. Spending for the IHS totaled about $4.3 billion in 2012. While spending per capita for the entire US civilian population averaged about $7,239 in 2012, average expenditures for the IHS population were $2,741.[3]

7.6 The Search for Health Care Price and Access

The costs of health care are large and growing. The struggle for greater access and more effective cost control defines much of the post-Medicare and Medicaid experience in the United States. As noted previously, expanding access to care leads to higher spending – the cost-access problem remains. One problem with searching for cost control in the US system is that the method of providing access to care is fairly fixed; providers and recipients of care tend to avoid change, or at least to be wary of it. This is understandable: about 80 percent of US citizens have some sort of health coverage and are reluctant to accept changes that might upset their receipt of care. Much of the concern over health reforms focuses on people not wanting to lose the care they have. As a result, complaints about government intervention in programs can become near comical. See, for example, this *New York Times* commentary:

> At a recent town-hall meeting in suburban Simpsonville, a man stood up and told Rep. Robert Inglis (R-S.C.) to "Keep your government hands off my Medicare."

---

[3] See www.ihs.gov/PublicAffairs/IHSBrochure/Profile.asp.

> I had to politely explain that, "Actually, sir, your health care is being provided
> by the government," Inglis recalled. But he wasn't having any of it.

Citizens in the United States for the most part oppose "socialized" medicine. This is a misrepresentation, however, as a large portion of the nation's hospitalization is paid by a socially provided program (Medicare) and surveys show consistently that Americans think of Medicare as an important portion of the social contract. Studies of citizen attitudes toward Medicare show consistent support for the program and understanding that it is a government program. Therefore, the dislike of socialized medicine appears to be a dislike of socially *provided* medicine, or provision by some government entity or government employee, rather than government *payment* for health care.

Even though citizens are often displeased with the costs of medical care, they are pleased with the treatments they receive. The United States has a large number of citizens being uninsured. Below, we discuss efforts in Taiwan to provide universal coverage in ways that avoid some of the high costs that are associated with care in the United States, and also note the results of an experiment in the state of Oregon in which subjects were assigned randomly to Medicaid.

Taiwan's Reforms

There are no simple ways to provide generous access while reducing costs. One innovative approach was taken by the nation of Taiwan, which created a system of universal care in 1995. The health care situation in Taiwan was poor before the new system was created: about 45 percent of its citizens had no insurance. It was provided for government workers, soldiers, farmers, and employees of large firms, but others had none. Taiwanese President Lee Teng-hui wished to accomplish something that would be helpful and visible for all citizens and believed health care reform would do that. After initially appointing four Taiwanese professors to develop a program, which did not work because each had their own ideas about how best to provide care, Taiwan hired Harvard University health economist William Hsiao to design a program. Hsiao, an expert on health finance in the United States and internationally, determined that a Canadian-style single-payer plan would best fit Taiwan's needs. As in the Canadian system, Taiwan's system allows enrollees to choose between private and public providers and hospitals, but encourages competition among providers. Hsiao noted that satisfaction has been high among recipients of health care in Canada as it has been in Taiwan after adoption. Taiwanese rates of insurance coverage are around 99 percent, and the nation only spends about 6 percent of its GDP on health care; this compares favorably with the 16 percent spent by the United States.

Aside from the observational assessment linking improved access and outcomes to the creation of a single-payer system (as was done in Taiwan), research that applies experimental methods to study health access, outcomes, and payments has proved to be valuable and compelling in some policymaking circles. The Rand Health Insurance Study began in 1971 in response to a proposal from the US Office of Economic Opportunity and later by the US Department of Health, Education, and Welfare (now the Department of Health and Human Services). The study sought to assess the effects of **cost sharing**, or co-payments, which were new at that time and required people to pay for a portion of the care they received, in contrast to the first dollar coverage that existed at the time. First dollar coverage means that the full price of a medical episode will be paid without a co-pay or deductible. In addition, the experiment was designed to determine whether HMOs provided care comparable to that of fee-for-service plans and whether it was at a comparable price. The Rand Experiment is also important because it was the first widespread health reform experiment in existence. The research group sampled 2,000 non-elderly families in six areas of the country; those families participated for three to five years in health plans with differing designs. The Rand group found that co-payments mattered – they reduced the use of services, while having no negative effects on care. This led to the widespread adoption of the co-pay model in health care.

Oregon's Medicaid Experiment

An experimental study in Oregon demonstrated that uninsured persons get better care, but with a higher cost than they would if left uninsured. The researchers created a lottery in which people who wished to gain access to Medicaid could apply to participate. The lottery resulted in Medicaid coverage for about 10,000 households in 2008. Thus, the Oregon study is especially instructive because assignment to the insurance pool was based on a random draw, thereby allowing researchers to make inferences about the causal effects of the policy without worry over the **selection effects** that influence non-experimental studies. As we discussed in Chapter 4, section 4.1, selection effects occur when subjects are assigned treatment by some method other than random assignment. When this occurs, the internal validity of the research design is threatened – calling into question the ability of drawing valid causal inferences.

The Oregon study looked at the average treatment effect of participating in Medicaid on a series of dependent variables. Recall from Chapter 4 that a dependent variable is the outcome variable of interest – it is the thing that we are trying to explain. The authors of the Oregon health insurance experiment conducted regression analysis on a variety of different variables using the treatment of participating in the Medicaid program as the main independent variable. We report several of the dependent variables in Table 7.1, along with the estimated average treatment effect from their regression analysis. Across from each of the dependent variables are two numbers. The first is the estimate of the regression coefficient that describes the relationship between

Table 7.1 Oregon Health Insurance Experiment Treatment Effects

	Average Treatment Effect
Dependent Variables	
Hospital Admissions	
through ER	0.70
	(0.62)
~through ER	1.6*
	(0.51)
Received all needed care	23.9*
	(2.2)
# of days of good mental health	2.1*
	(0.64)

Source: Estimates are taken from Finkelstein *et al.* (2012). Standard errors are in parentheses.
* = p<0.05, two-tailed.

participating in Medicaid and each dependent variable. The size of the coefficient will indicate how different average recipients of the Medicaid treatment were from individuals in the control group that did not participate in Medicaid. In addition, the sign on the coefficient indicates the direction of this effect. For each of the coefficients in the table, positive coefficients suggest that, for a given dependent variable, participants in the Medicaid program scored higher than those in the control group. Below each of these coefficients, in parentheses, are the standard errors of these regression estimates. Recall from Chapter 4 that a standard error reveals how confident we can be that our regression estimate is different from zero. A rule of thumb is that a coefficient that is at least twice the size of a standard error is likely large enough to be statistically different from zero. Any estimate that is statistically significant is indicated in the table by a star next to it. In this case, all of the estimates with stars are statistically significant at the 99 percent level. This means that if we reran this experiment 100 times, we would expect to find that this coefficient is different from zero 99 times out of 100. If there is no star next to a coefficient, this means that we cannot be confident that our estimate is different from zero and we should not attach any substantive interpretation to it.

Before we can figure out how to interpret the results of the study, we must know how the dependent variables were measured. The first three variables are yes/no, dichotomous variables. For example, these variables measure an individual's response to the question "Were you admitted to a hospital through the ER?" The coefficients have been scaled to represent the expected change in the percent of recipients responding in the affirmative. The last variable, *Days of good mental health*, is measured as the number of days.

So what do the results of the analysis suggest? First, let's consider the impact of Medicaid participation on Hospital Admissions either through the ER or not through the ER. One expected benefit of health insurance coverage is to encourage individuals to seek out healthcare from their primary doctor before going to the ER. Look at the results in Table 7.1 and see if you can find evidence of whether or not this is the case. To do this, first find the two coefficients that tell us the effect of hospital admissions through the ER and hospital admissions not through the ER. These coefficients are 2.1 and 1.6, respectively. To know whether or not we should attach any substantive interpretation to these coefficients, we first look to see whether they are statistically significant. We can see that, given the absence of a star, there is no difference between those enrolled in Medicaid and those who were not on direct hospital admissions through the ER. Therefore, we can essentially think of our estimate of 0.7 as being equivalent to zero. On the other hand, the estimate of 1.64 hospital admissions not through the ER is statistically significant at the 99 percent confidence level. This suggests a positive difference of 1.6 percentage points among Medicaid enrollees who sought out advice from their primary care doctor before heading to the ER. In addition to hospitalization, Medicaid enrollment also appears to have positive effects on both health outcomes and the mechanisms behind improved health. Both of the coefficients for the *Received all needed care* variable and the *Number of days of good mental health* variable are statistically significant and positive. The substantive effects suggest that individuals who enrolled in Medicaid were nearly 24 percentage points more likely to have received all of the needed care that they required over the past six months. In fact, this may be linked to the positive health outcome of Medicaid recipients reporting, on average, to additional days of good mental health relative to individuals who did not receive coverage.

On the whole, the Oregon study showed that people who were selected into the health insurance pool (a) were more apt to use services than those who were not, (b) had better health outcomes than the uninsured, (c) their service use resulted in higher public spending than those without health services accrued, and (d) had better self-reported mental and physical health than in the control group. The latter result is interesting inasmuch as the 2010 Patient Protection and Affordable Care Act claimed that health spending would be lessened after coverage was implemented. The Oregon results suggest that health care would improve for the uninsured, but that the cost to the public would increase. This suggests that health care is a choice that involves considerations of equity and public spending preferences that are difficult to make in political situations.

7.7 The Health Information Explosion

The arguments over Obamacare have focused primarily on the plan's health insurance mandate and reliance on community rating. One major change that has attended the administration's health reform efforts is a massive investment in health information systems. HMOs and **medical service organizations** (MSOs) have received billions of dollars to digitize their health records. The move to electronic records is a massive undertaking, one that represents an employment growth area in the slow post-recession economy.

Digital Records

Beginning in 2009, and for five years thereafter, the Obama administration invested $10 million annually into the digitization of health records (Wogan 2012). That initial funding was via the 2009 Budget Stimulus. Additionally, Medicare and Medicaid programs made investments in health data technology. As a result, there has been a shift toward digital recordkeeping, which is expected to increase the information available to health policymakers and practitioners. One unintended consequence of the new records is that medical billings are now more complete. The data allow more comprehensive billing, so spending has increased as a result of its implementation.

The health data collection efforts also play into some critics' fears of government having an overabundance of information about citizens' health needs, their use of services, and their choice of providers. One of the criticisms of the Obama health reforms is that physicians would lose their influence over medical care, and that that influence would be replaced by faceless bureaucrats who would determine who gets what vis-à-vis health treatments; the rise of a large health data system feeds those fears. More specifically, critics complain that the data collection efforts violate the Health Insurance Portability and Accountability Act (HIPAA) of 1996, which, among other things, requires the Secretary of the Department of Health and Human Services (HHS) to publicize standards for the privacy security of electronically exchanged health information. While those specific complaints appear to be unwarranted, public skepticism about the national government collecting and storing large amounts of health care data are understandable, especially in light of revelations about the extent of US intrusions into telephone and online privacy.

Medical Corporatization

Regardless of concerns, the digitization of health care records may prove to be among the most lasting elements of the Obama administration's health care reform efforts. Electronic recordkeeping further strengthens the ability of large health providers, HMOs and MSOs, to better manage and streamline service delivery. Electronic records will also contribute to greater centralization of health management functions. In 1973, the health economists Mark Pauly and Michael Redisch described the not-for-profit hospital as a "physician's cooperative," in which income-maximizing physicians worked within charitable organizations in ways that maximized their incomes. By the mid 1980s, not-for-profit hospitals were competing with newly emerging for-profit hospitals, and perhaps more importantly the role of the physician as the hospital's chief decision-maker eroded as non-physician administrators gained more influence over hospital decision-making. These changes have also affected the status of the single hospital; the movement toward larger hospital chains, some of which serve as health insurers as well as hospitals, continues. Thus, health care is changing, and will continue to change. Additionally, the movement toward more information being collected and digitized will continue, potentially lessening patient privacy.

7.8 Should We Ration Health Care?

One solution to the health care problem is simply to use less of it. Health prices in the United States are high. There is significant price variation among providers, regions, and medical/surgical specialty groups. Furthermore, there is widespread reluctance to regulate those prices, at least among legislators. Richard Lamm, who was governor of Colorado from 1975 through 1987, suggested the idea of health care rationing in the 1980s. Lamm claimed that ill and infirm elderly people had a moral obligation to younger people to accept death so that they did not place too great a burden on health care spending. Lamm's statement was controversial, and he remains an advocate of rationing health expenditure.

The idea of rationing care is unpopular inasmuch as it suggests that people who desire care may be told "no." There are some who suggest providing care based on the extent to which that care is likely to have a positive effect on health; that can be extended further to consider how *long* a person can be expected to enjoy the benefits of treatment. For example, if a medical procedure that costs 2X will extend a person's life by two days, but giving that person relief through other means costs X, but will extend their life by only one day, we can ask whether it is worth spending twice the amount for an additional day of life in a world of finite financial resources. We can also consider whether it is more valuable to provide a limited financial resource to a young person with a long life expectancy than to an older person with a shorter life expectancy. In 1994, the State of Oregon expanded Medicaid eligibility to all persons at or below the poverty line, but also established a form of service rationing in which services were to be provided to the persons who were expected to benefit most from them. Oregon devised a list of seventeen medical services and ranked them from "essential" to "very valuable" to "valuable to certain people" (Oberlander *et al.* 2001). The plan was to provide those services in order of value. All enrollees would receive "essential services" and fewer would receive the other categories. Policy evaluators suggest that the rationing was more apparent than real: Oregon got a tremendous amount of publicity for the decision, but very little true rationing occurred (Oberlander *et al.* 2001).

Rationing health care is unattractive to most people, but access to health care is rationed daily. Rationing can come in the form of limitations on prescription refills, limits on the number of hospital days a person may have, etc. Other rationing occurs when people are not given access to care, as with the uninsured. In that case, the rationing is not especially effective because people may become chronically ill and, as discussed previously, become expensive users of health care – treatment of chronic illnesses are often more expensive than preventive care.

The health economist Victor Fuchs described all health systems as forms of rationing, whether or not we are willing to describe them as such (1983). In a pure market system or an insurance system as in the United States, health care is rationed based on income. Those with more money have more access to health care and more health care options than those with less wealth. In a national single-payer system, government plays a larger role in rationing care.

7.9 Conclusion

Health care is the fastest growing segment of the US economy. Health spending per person in the United States surpasses that of all other nations. The outcomes of exceedingly high health care spending are mixed. The United States leads the world in some technologically intensive treatments, and also does a much better job of treating heart disease than most nations. The United States does less well in providing basic health services, especially to the uninsured, therefore getting a mixed review on the efficacy of its exorbitant health spending.

The United States is unique among industrialized democracies in that large numbers of its citizens are uninsured. Most agree that this is an unfortunate situation, but there is disagreement over how to fix the problem. Most attempts and large-scale reform have failed, and the plans that succeed come with high financial and political costs. Despite complaints with the 2010 reforms, there are elements of the bill that are widely popular, even among Republicans; insurers now cannot deny coverage based on pre-existing conditions or force dependents off of their parents' insurance plans until the age of 26.

Finally, struggles with health care reform illustrate the difficulties of widespread policy change and the power of past decisions over current policy issues. The US system has some clear advantages and disadvantages, many of which are influenced by decisions made before World War II. Health coverage in the United States is broadening, but it is doing so incrementally.

Key Terms

Externalities
Adverse selection
Moral hazard
Risk profile
Risk pool
Community rating
Patient Protection and Affordable Care Act of 2010
Uncompensated care
Negative externality
First dollar coverage
Adverse selection
Information asymmetry
Deductible
Co-payment
Health maintenance organization
Path dependence
Health insurance mandates
Entitlement
Means-tested
Fee-for-Service
Capitated payment model
Preferred provider organization
Medigap policy
Medicare Part A
Medicare Part B
Medicare Advantage
Medicare Part D
Medicare Part C
Medicare
Medicaid
Categorical grant
Block grant
Child Health Insurance Program
Cost sharing
Selection effects
Medical Service Organization

CHAPTER EXERCISES

1. Should health care risk be based on experience or on community rating? What are the consequences of each for equity and efficiency? What trade-offs, if any, are desirable?

2. Is health rationing desirable? If so, how should we choose what to ration?

3. Is a national health care system desirable? How is a private insurance program better than a public program? In what ways is a public program better?

4. Is it desirable to block grant Medicaid? What costs and benefits might come from that choice?

5. Do new developments in health technology hold promise to reduce health costs? Do they create concerns over privacy?

6. How can societies guard against moral hazard issues emerging in their health insurance systems? Is it possible to have a voluntary system of insurance coverage without some element of moral hazard?

REFERENCES

Arrow, Kenneth J. 1963. "Uncertainty and the Welfare Economics of Medical Care." *American Economic Review* 53(5): 941–973.

Barrilleaux, Charles and Rainey, Carlisle. 2014. "The Politics of Need: Examining Governors' Decisions to Oppose the 'Obamacare' Medicaid Expansion." *State Politics and Policy Quarterly* 14(4): 437–460.

Finkelstein, Amy, Taubman, S., Wright, B., Bernstein, M., Gruber, J., Newhouse, J. *et al.* 2012. "The Oregon Health Insurance Experiment: Evidence from the First Year." *Quarterly Journal of Economics* 127(3): 1057–1106.

Fuchs, Victor. 1983. *Who Shall Live?* New York: Basic Books.

Gawande, Atul. 2009. "Getting from Here to There." *The New Yorker*. January 26.

Hamel, Liz, Firth, J., and Brodie, M. 2014. "Kaiser Health Tracking Poll, August–September 2014." Kaiser Family Foundation. Available online at http://kff.org/health-reform/poll-finding/kaiser-health-tracking-poll-august-september-2014/.

Kaiser Health Forum. 2012, 2013. "Medicaid." Available online at http://kff.org/medicaid/.

Law, Sylvia. 1976. *Blue Cross: What Went Wrong?* New Haven, CT: Yale University Press.

Morath, Eric and Radnofsky, Louise. 2013. "Medical-Price Inflation Is at Slowest Pace in 50 Years." *Wall Street Journal*. September 17. Available online at http://www.wsj.com/articles/SB10001424127887323342404579081312680485476.

Newhouse, Joseph. 1993. *Free for All? Lessons from the Rand Health Insurance Experiment*. Cambridge, MA: Harvard University Press.

Oberlander, Jonathan, Marmor, Theodore, and Jacobs, Lawrence. 2001. "Rationing Medical Care: Rhetoric and Reality in the Oregon Plan." *Canadian Medical Association Journal* 164(11): 1583–1587.

Pauly, M. and Redisch, M. 1973. "The Not-For-Profit Hospital as a Physician's Cooperative." *American Economic Review* 63: 87–99.

Poen, Monte. 1996. *Harry Truman versus the Medical Lobby*. Columbia, MO: University of Missouri Press.

Rigby, Elizabeth and Haselswerdt, Jake. 2013. "Hybrid Federalism, Partisan Politics, and the Early Implementation of State Health Insurance Exchanges." *Publius: The Journal of Federalism* 43(3): 368–391.

Starr, Paul. 1982. *The Social Transformation of American Medicine*. New York: Basic Books.

Sloan, Frank and Hsieh, Chee-Ruey. 2012. *Health Economics*. Cambridge, MA: MIT.

Squires, David A. 2012. "Explaining High Health Care Spending in the United States: An International Comparison of Supply, Utilization, Prices, and Quality." Commonwealth Fund pub. 1595 Vol. 10. Available online at www.commonwealthfund.org/~/media/Files/Publications/Issue%20Brief/2012/May/1595_Squires_explaining_high_hlt_care_spending_intl_brief.pdf.

Strauss, Ethan E. 2010. "Fact Checking the GOP on Healthcare Reform." *Salon*, February 23. Available online at www.salon.com/2010/02/23/hcr_amendments/.

Wogan, J. B. 2012. "Invest in Electronic Health Data Systems." *PolitiFact*. Available online at www.politifact.com/truth-o-meter/promises/obameter/promise/59/invest-in-electronic-health-information-systems/.

World Health Organization. 2012. "Tobacco Taxation and Innovative Health Financing." Available online at www.searo.who.int/tobacco/documents/2012-pub1.pdf.

Washington Post. 2013. "21 Graphs that Show America's Health-Care Prices Are Ludicrous." Available online at www.washingtonpost.com/blogs/wonkblog/wp/2013/03/26/21-graphs-that-show-americas-health-care-prices-are-ludicrous/.

Woolf, Steven H. and Aron, Laudun (eds.) 2013. *US Health in International Perspective: Shorter Lives, Poorer Health*. New York: National Academies Press.

8

Education

Outline

Questions

- How is education provided and paid for in the United States?
- Why is the public dissatisfied with US education?
- Why do US students lag students of other wealthy nations in educational attainment?
- Is a national standard for education scores desirable?
- Can the states manage education adequately?
- Are charter, choice, and other reforms a solution to education problems?
- Who should decide what's to be taught in schools?
- Can we provide higher education effectively online?
- Can we reduce the debts accrued by college students?

Overview

- The primary analytic concept we use to provide insight on education policy is agency theory.
- There is a strong commitment to public education in the United States, but disagreement over how best to organize and provide that education.
- Despite showing strong support for public education and their local schools, citizens are critical of the state of public education.
- Educational performance among students educated in elementary and secondary schools in the United States lags behind that of most advanced industrialized nations.
- There is a strong reform movement in US education, although there is disagreement about which reforms are most desirable or promising.
- The school choice movement has strengthened over the past thirty years and choice has become institutionalized in most public school systems.
- There is controversy over what is to be taught in schools.
- State legislatures are pushing schools in their states to reduce the price of education.

Introduction: Education Choices, Reforms, and Persistent Problems

Americans have more choice in public education than at any time in the history of public schools. In the past thirty years, the range of choices available to families has increased, and schools now compete for students. Families may choose among specialized schools for the arts and sciences, charter schools, magnet schools, and other varieties of programs. Schools and school districts are innovating with curriculum, evaluation, teacher training, and even in how they manage the school day.

These education reforms are the product of concerns with the quality of education and with the desire to make schools better. The greatest problems are in urban schools, where test scores are persistently lower than in rural and suburban schools. The United States lags behind a number of industrialized democracies in the test scores of its students. There is also a problem with violence in US schools, which affects them at all levels but is most prevalent in urban schools. Despite these problems, there is strong commitment to public education in the United States.

If everyone is for education, why are there so many problems with education policy? The political economy framework is especially helpful for shedding light on this question. Education policy, just like many other policy areas, has to address difficult principal–agent and bargaining problems. One principal–agent problem in this area is the relationship between the community (e.g. parents, children, school boards, society at large) and teachers. How does the community, the principal, ensure the agent, teachers, do their job well? As is often the case in principal–agent relationships, the agents, here the teachers, have more knowledge about the situation than the principal. Yet, teachers, like all other people, face moral hazard temptations. Education policy also involves significant bargaining problems. For example, who decides the curriculum? Should there be national standards or local standards? The parties in these debates recognize that there are long-term effects to the choice made, and that makes it all the more difficult to reach an agreement today. These political economy problems are at the heart of this chapter.

In addition, it is often difficult to identify the effectiveness of policy innovations. Do smaller class sizes contribute to student learning? Does school choice in the form of charter schools improve educational outcomes? Is color-blind affirmative action more effective than affirmative action at helping under-represented groups achieve a college education? Do teachers make a substantial educational difference or are educational outcomes almost exclusively a function of a child's environment (e.g. income level, neighborhood crime, parental education, etc.)? Answering these and other education questions is not easy. In this chapter, we discuss some of the best research on these topics.

We use a delegation model to illustrate the negotiations and trade-offs that occur in education policymaking. Educators must respond to the demands of legislators, but have more information and expertise than legislators. Legislators may have specific spending targets or other ways in which they express policy preferences, but legislators also are less certain about the quality of their recommendations and may defer to educators in an agency relationship.

8.1 Why Public Education?

The United States was created during the **Enlightenment**, a period during which republicanism, religious tolerance, scientific method, and learning emerged as the most desirable way to establish a society. Benjamin Franklin created free public libraries and a free school. Thomas Jefferson supported the ideal of free public education as the best means to foster democracy among citizens.[1] Most US citizens have received some amount of public education. Education is thought of as a great equalizer: support for public education remains strong despite objections to other forms of income redistribution, like income transfers, because education is thought to provide people with the skills they need to improve their ability to earn money and to rise in the economic system. Education spending in US local municipalities, states, and

---

[1] Of course, Franklin and Jefferson confined their concerns about education to free men.

the national government exceeded $944 billion in 2013; education spending follows only pensions and health care among the nation's largest expenses. Thus, taxpayers make a large investment in education, and expect to receive a good return on their investment.

The Value of Public Education and an Enlightened Citizenry

One justification for the investment in public education is that it increases economic productivity, and it does (Barro and Lee 2001). More educated persons are better equipped to compete in the market economy. In this way, providing access to public education equalizes opportunity for people of widely disparate economic backgrounds. Of course, not everyone, even if educated, is assured of being accomplished or successful, but in the absence of a widespread preference for income redistribution, the belief that educational opportunity helps reduce the gap between rich and poor is reassuring.

Long-term public support for free public education does not mean that education is without its critics. Public school systems are often criticized for doing a poor job of training students, especially in inner city areas, and for being heavily bureaucratized and unable to respond quickly to changing educational needs. For the past thirty years, there has been a movement that demands school choice, which is designed to enhance parental power to determine how their children will be educated, but has been criticized for failing to ensure that all economic, racial, and ethnic groups are equally able to take advantage of educational choice.

8.2 The Governance Structure of Education in the United States

The absence of mention of education in the US Constitution led it to be treated as a state and local concern. The fact of state and local control of education funding and curriculum decisions led to tremendous variation in the quality and content of education in the United States.

Traditionally a State and Local Function

Education traditionally has been a state and local government function. However, there is conflict among the levels of government in the US federal system, as each wishes to control public education to the extent it can, and each typically wants some other level of government to pay to educate its citizens so as to avoid tax expenditures.

The struggle between the nation and states for control of education is pronounced and long-lived. It is evident today in the Heritage Foundation's warnings that a federal role in education is contrary to Constitutional principles, in the administrations of Republican and Democratic presidents who try to impose national testing standards on the states, and in the ongoing struggle over how to fund public schools. There are also conflicts over the content of schools' curricula, including treatment of subjects like evolution and social studies.

US school districts are public systems that provide educational services, including regular, special, and vocational education for children in pre-kindergarten through the twelfth grade. They are locally administered, but their geographic organization and structure varies according to state and region. Most districts are arranged according to regional and state custom, with districts in the Mid-Atlantic and New England states organized according to county, city, or township boundaries and those in the Midwest and West more likely to be laid out independent of municipal boundaries. In 2012, the United States had over 14,000 public school districts and federal, state, and local governments combine to spend more than $500 billion on public elementary and secondary education each year. State governments are also involved in education in universities and colleges, but often without local government participation.

There are nearly 100,000 elementary and secondary schools in the United States (Table 8.1), a figure that has grown since the 1980s. In addition, the number of private schools grew by more than half between 1980 and 2010. The row labeled Postsecondary Title IV institutions refers to trade schools, community colleges, and four-year colleges and universities whose students are eligible for Title IV federal financial assistance, which is to say most accredited schools. There are about 4,495 colleges and universities, a substantial increase since 1980–81, and a new category, "non-degree granting" institutions, which includes various private job-training institutions for which students may receive financial aid. The large number of schools and colleges, and their variety, points to the large number of education choices that are available at all levels. Of course, access to schools varies by where people live and their economic status, with some states and cities having stronger education systems than others.

Beginning in 1997, the national newspaper *Education Week*, a national not-for-profit publication (501-c) that is funded by charitable giving and was established to report on education issues in 1957 after the Sputnik launch, has published a ranking of states called *Quality Counts*. The annual ranking evaluates states' schools on three broad categories: policies, inputs, and outputs. In 2013, Maryland was the top-rated state, and North Dakota received the lowest ranking. By contrast, a ranking from StudentsFirst, an organization that places parental choice issues like parent triggers, which enable parents to take over some failing schools, educational vouchers, charter schools, and similar items, gives Maryland a grade of "D." Hence, there is disagreement about what constitutes good schools.

Table 8.1 Number of Educational Institutions 1980–81, 1990–91, 2009–10

Level and control of institution	1980–81	1990–91	2009–10
Public schools	**85,982**	**84,538**	**98,817**
Elementary	59,326	59,015	67,140
Secondary	22,619	21,135	24,651
Combined	1,743	2,325	5,730
Other	2,294	2,063	1,296
Private schools	**20,764**	**24,690**	**33,366**
Postsecondary Title IV institutions	–	–	**6,742**
Degree-granting institutions	3,231	3,559	4,495
Two-year colleges	1,274	1,418	1,721
Four-year colleges	1,957	2,141	2,774
Non-degree granting	–	–	2,247

Source: National Center for Education Statistics, IPEDs Data (2013)

Variations in School Governance Finance

This variation in scores illustrates that school districts and states vary in a number of important ways with respect to education. Some states are aggressive, with a variety of educational reforms like the development of **charter schools**, the creation of student **high-stakes tests**, and changes in **teacher testing and qualifications**, each of which will be discussed below. They also differ in their allocations of school funding, with some paying a larger share than others. In the past, schools were funded principally with local **property taxes**, which are assessed against the value of residential and commercial property. Property taxes are a good source of revenue inasmuch as they are a dependable source, but they are also a problem in at least two ways. First, they are based on property values, so changes in property values produce changes in school revenues. A property tax is based on a **millage rate**, which is tax rate per $1,000 value of a property. For example, if a property is worth $100,000, and the millage rate is 0.25, the tax would be 0.25 X 100 = $250. If property values decline, then property taxes decline, meaning less revenue for schools. In addition, property taxes are sometimes a source of political conflict. Some people want more revenue for schools and support higher property taxes. Others want lower taxes. Sometimes, the outcome of this political battle is a reduction of property taxes, by state legislatures or municipalities, and consequently less money for schools. Second, when school revenue depends

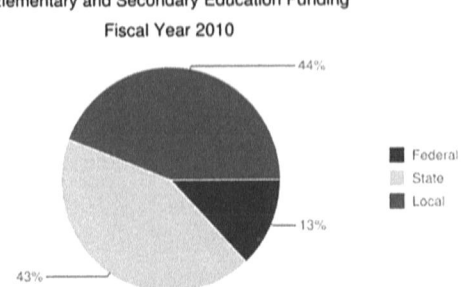

Elementary and Secondary Education Funding
Fiscal Year 2010

Figure 8.1 The Education Funding Pie, 2010
Source: National Center for Education Statistics, compiled by New America Foundation (2012)

greatly on property taxes districts with more expensive housing receive greater school tax funding than districts with less expensive housing.

States' contributions to education spending come through **state income taxes** and state **sales taxes**. Some argue that income taxes are preferable to sales taxes because they are progressive taxes, which is to say that the amount paid goes up as earnings go up, so the tax burden is made more equitable. Not everyone agrees with that idea. The sales tax is criticized because it is a regressive tax, meaning that the tax burden is higher on people with lower incomes. However, the sales tax is a good producer of revenue and it has the added benefit of adjusting nicely to increases in spending. State and local spending shares for public education were nearly identical in 2010 (Figure 8.1).

Why is there so much conflict over school funding? In addition to some people being more supportive of taxes than others, the presence of **forced-riders** is a significant source of conflict. Forced-riders are individuals who have to pay for something and do not receive direct benefits from it. With respect to school funding, forced-riders are those without children, and those who have graduated from school and have no children or no school-age children. Property taxes, state income taxes, and sales taxes all create forced-riders.

There is considerable variation in school funding across and within states. The across-state variation is a function of state wealth and taxation. Wealthier states generally spend more per student on education. There are also variations by school district within states. Some states redistribute to poor districts by giving them money to help make up for differences between poor and rich districts. Rich districts generally have higher property values and can raise more money for schools. Not all states redistribute in this manner, so in some cases there is large variation in the amount of money available for schools.

The national role in public education has expanded incrementally, with even presidential administrations that disparaged national government involvement championing a national role in some cases. These national forays into education are typically met with skepticism from state and local governments, who once managed education policy and funding with little national government involvement. The national government's entry into education is typically eased by the contribution of federal funding to local districts. Those "carrots" typically require states and local districts to do something they would not ordinarily do. In the late 1940s, the national government bolstered school lunches, which fed children and also increased the distribution of farm products. In 1959, the US Government responded to the Soviet's advances in space by investing in education in elementary, secondary, and post-secondary programs. The Johnson Administration's passage of the Elementary and Secondary Education Act of 1965 (ESEA) provided benefits for school districts throughout the nation, but its major intent was to increase funding in poor and urban areas.

Even with so long a presence in education, the US Department of Education was not created until 1979, and only then after considerable conflict. President Ronald Reagan promised to abolish the US Department of Education in 1980 and cut its budget dramatically in his first two years in office. In 1983, however, President Reagan responded to a blue-ribbon commission report that chronicled deficiencies in public education by allowing budgetary expansion. President George H. W. Bush further expanded the Department of Education when he took office in 1989, essentially undoing most of Reagan's decentralization efforts and establishing a larger national government role in education. Reagan and Bush are not unique; public education is a tremendous policy tool that executives seek to use to accomplish broad goals. Democratic presidents typically work in league with education associations and **teacher unions**, although the latter have lost influence in the Obama presidency, and try to accomplish their goals via education budgets. Republicans are less enamored of education associations and unions and more accommodating to charter and other private schools than are Democrats. The parties are similar in their attempts to use the Department of Education as a conduit for their goals.

8.3 Education Quality in the United States

Education is a large portion of state and local budgets, and many people choose where to live based on the quality of schools they expect in their neighborhood. Although people often express positive views of the quality of their children's schools, there is a broader sense of public concern that schools are failing, and that sense seems to be most pronounced in urban areas. It is difficult to get a single definition of "high quality" education. To some observers, quality is measured by the extent of parental choice. To others, it is the extent to which school finance is equitable. We focus on school performance as measured by standardized tests. There are difficulties with reliance on standardized tests, which often are criticized for ethnic, gender, and racial biases, but for our purposes we define quality in terms of comparison on two highly visible cross-national surveys of student performance. We rely on these because we think of education as something that provides a boost to a city, state, or nation's human capital, which is to say that education performance is important because it increases citizens' ability to be productive (Barro and Lee 2001).

US Scores Rising

With this backdrop, there is good news and bad news in the evaluation of school quality in the United States. The good news is that math and science scores for fourth and eighth grade students, last measured in 2011, have been rising. The bad news is that the rate of increase in the United States is not as great as the rate of increase among some other leader nations, and education spending in the United States is higher than that in other nations that are getting better returns on their investment.

The Trends in International Math and Science Survey (TIMSS) (National Center for Education Statistics (NCES) 2013) has now been conducted five times, in 1995, 1999, 2003, 2007, and 2011. The Progress in International Reading Literacy Study (PIRLS) was completed in 2001, 2006, and 2011 (NCES). Together, these studies survey academic achievement in their respective fields across a large number of nations. The US score for fourth grade math in 2011 was eleventh among the fifty-seven nations that participated. Statistically, the United States' fourth graders were among the top fifteen scorers, as their scores were higher, although not significantly, than in a handful of other nations. US fourth graders' scores increased 23 percent between 1995 and 2011, comparable to the percentage change in Hong Kong and Japan, but well behind Korea and the United Kingdom, all nations that lead the United States. The eighth graders ranked eighth, and were statistically among the top twenty-four nations. US average scores increased seventeen points between 1995 and 2011, but only one point between 2007 and 2011. All of the leading nations except Japan – which lost ground over the years of the study – had larger gains than the United States.[2] Trends in the PIRLS (reading) scores are similar. US fourth graders were among the thirteen highest scorers among the fifty-seven participating nations. Five systems had higher scores: Hong Kong, China; Florida, USA (Florida tested independently as a benchmark); the Russian Federation; Finland; and Singapore. Seven systems were not statistically distinguishable. Score increases in the

---

[2] NCES 2013, http://nces.ed.gov/timss/figure11_3.asp.

United States exceeded those of the leading nations in the 2006–2011 measure, but lagged the leaders by a large percentage in the 2001–2011 change measure (NCES 2013). PIRLS data are not provided for eighth graders.

Why does the United States lag nations that spend much less on education? There are a number of possible answers, some of which lead to drastically different policy choices. As discussed below, one claim is that the rise of national government involvement in education in a quest to equalize opportunities across racial, class, and economic divides led to higher spending on things that are not directly linked to education. Another claim is that schools spend too much time performing parenting and other tasks that once were not required of schools, and such parenting is expensive and takes away from the educational mission of the schools. Yet another claim is that the highly bureaucratic school systems that have grown over the years focus too much spending on administrators and teachers and insufficient resources on teaching students. Others claim that the schools should spend more to address the social and other problems that schools are forced to address, and increasing spending may help improve outcomes. There is no easy answer, but the search for high quality schools continues. We discuss some of the older and newer school reforms of the past decades with a view toward their effects on school quality.

8.4 Federal Education Policy after Sputnik

The late 1950s were a watershed for elementary and secondary education policy in the United States. **Sputnik** was a beachball-sized satellite that weighed less than 200 pounds. The Soviet Union successfully launched it in October 1957, and it orbited the earth in about 98 minutes (NASA 2013). The successful launch affected the United States greatly. Sputnik spurred the United States to become more active with their then-nascent space program. Aside from spurring the creation of the National Aeronautics and Space Administration (NASA), Sputnik created an understanding, correctly or not, that the United States was lagging behind the Soviet bloc in math and science training, and that spurred federal government investments in schools at all levels.

The **National Defense Education Act (NDEA)** was rushed through Congress in 1958 and provided public schools with an infusion of federal money to stockpile microscopes, chemicals, slide rules, and other supplies that were "scientific" in nature. The NDEA was reserved entirely for public schools, although private and parochial schools could borrow materials and books from public schools. Also, following the norms of the times, the NDEA was segregationist in its application. Funds were not provided to non-white schools.

The Elementary and Secondary Education Act of 1965 (ESEA)

In 1968, then-President Lyndon B. Johnson invoked President Franklin Roosevelt's "four freedoms" speech, describing them as ". . . a summary of our aspirations for the American Republic and for the world" and going on to claim:

> Today – wealthier, more powerful and more able than ever before in our history – our Nation can declare another essential freedom. The fifth freedom is freedom from ignorance. It means that every man, everywhere, should be free to develop his talents to their full potential – unhampered by arbitrary barriers of race or birth or income. We have already begun the work of guaranteeing that fifth freedom.

> Congress under the Johnson administration had moved more aggressively into financing public education with the passage of the **Elementary and Secondary Education Act of 1965 (ESEA)**. Although many now accept a role for the national government as a matter of fact regardless of our preferences, the Congressional action signaled a significant shift in spending by the national government. Elementary and secondary education was principally the concern of state and local governments prior to 1965; the Johnson Administration's actions greatly changed long-accepted relationships.

The initial goal of ESEA was to reduce the educational differences between the poor and the larger public and to improve the educational performance and training of school systems. ESEA was designed to help reduce differences in the quality and performance of schools. The Act initially had six "titles:"

Title I – Financial Assistance to Local Educational Agencies for the Education of Children of Low-Income Families

Title II – School Library Resources, Textbooks, and other Instructional Materials

Title III – Supplementary Educational Centers and Services

Title IV – Educational Research and Training

Title V – Grants to Strengthen State Departments Of Education

Title VI – General Provisions

Title I was the most controversial, and the remaining titles in some ways made passage of Title I possible, as they provided direct benefits to school districts, benefits that would accrue to school districts regardless of the district's or its families' economic resources. Title I set the stage for a federal role in redistributing education resources for the poor. Education had long been managed by the states and local governments and there were, and remain, substantial differences in education spending according to the wealth and tax efforts of states and localities. Title I was the first large-scale federal move into public school finance. The ESEA titles expanded the federal government role in education by providing benefits to states and school districts that expanded their programs and made them dependent on the national government for maintenance of that spending. In Title V, for example, states were granted money to hire various educational specialists, who may have been valuable, but whose services were paid by the national government, which rendered the state governments dependent upon Washington to support employees and tasks for which they had previously not been responsible.

Title I was the national government's most significant foray into public education. The Act has changed incrementally during the more than forty-five years of its existence. In its initial phase during the Johnson Administration's War on Poverty, the Act's primary goal was to lessen the differences in educational opportunities and outcomes between poor and non-poor Americans. Educational researchers demonstrated that children who lived in poverty and attended impoverished school systems did worse on achievement exams than did children from non-poverty backgrounds. The ESEA provided funding to the states, who then sent funding to school districts, with the goal of reducing school funding inequities. In the 1980s, the Reagan Administration revised ESEA to provide more local control over spending, reducing the power of the national government by reducing the restrictions on spending that were previously imposed on the states. Later in the decade, the Act was altered to place greater emphasis on skills like critical thinking and greater parental involvement. In 1994, the Clinton administration altered the Act with the passage of the **Improving America's Schools Act (IASA)**. IASA was created to provide education that was less focused on rote learning and standardized test taking and more focused on activities like reading novels, conducting experiments, and the like. It can be viewed in some ways as an incremental extension of the changes to ESEA begun in the latter years of the Reagan administration, although they were portrayed as a move away from the Reagan and Bush administrations' education focus.

No Child Left Behind

The 2001 **No Child Left Behind Act (NCLB)** passed under President George W. Bush was a significant change from the early ESEA, in part because it strengthened the role of the national government in public education by using the typical "carrot" of federal funding as an incentive for schools to achieve certain goals. The NCLB Act, which was passed with bipartisan support, established the goal of all children being able to meet state academic standards for reading and math by 2014. NCLB funded a set of federal programs designed to improve the performance of US schools. These policy changes included increasing standards of accountability for schools, school districts, and states, providing parents with more flexibility to choose their children's schools, and increasing schools' focus on reading and math. NCLB was divided into several areas, all intending to ensure that students reach national testing levels in math and reading.

NCLB is built on five main objectives: standards and assessment, accountability, **adequate yearly progress (AYP)**, corrective actions for chronically failing schools, and assurance of specific staff qualifications.

The "standards and assessment" objectives focus on the national government assuring that state governments adopt challenging academic standards for their students. Those standards must specify what children are expected to know and what they are expected to be able to do. States must have established standards for math, reading, and language arts by mid 2002, and standards for science by 2005–2006. The states were also required to give assessments in each area in some years, with students being tested a minimum of three times over the course of their K-12 academic careers. The AYP is the crucial test for states' schools: they were required to develop single state-wide accountability systems to apply to all public school students, and their AYP is determined by how well students meet those accountability measures each year. States report the AYP for four subgroups each year: economically disadvantaged students, students from major racial or ethnic groups, students with limited English proficiency, and students with special needs. Schools must, at a minimum, meet two requirements to demonstrate AYP. They must demonstrate that 95 percent of students take the assessment and each school as a whole and each subgroup of its students must meet the measurable objectives that were established by each state and must in addition meet some other standard – for example attendance or high school graduate rates – established by the state.

Schools that fail to meet AYP for two consecutive years are identified for corrective action, including parents being offered the chance to transfer to another public school in the district, with the transportation costs paid by the district. Schools must offer a choice program, that is, choice cannot be waived as a requirement for schools. If the school fails AYP for three years, supplemental education services are arranged for its students. If the school fails to make AYP for five years, the district must restructure the school, and if it fails for six years the school's governance must be altered.

NCLB required that teachers receive more specialized certification in their specialty areas. Those teaching in core areas are required to earn content-area certification. The general focus was away from teacher education from colleges of education and toward more disciplinary education. For example, a high school teacher specializing in science education would be required to take more courses in actual science classes like chemistry and physics and pass substance area tests and fewer courses in subjects like classroom management and other education school offerings.

The final prong of NCLB is an increased parental role. Parents were to be given more information about their children's performance and about the school's performance. Parents also must be notified when their children are taught for four weeks or longer by not-highly-qualified teachers. Parents have the right to demand information about teacher qualifications. Parents must be notified if children are identified as being in need of additional language preparedness instruction and parents may opt out of that language training.

The carrot that led to NCLB's passage was rises in federal government spending. Federal education assistance to the states increased over $13 billion between 2001, when it was passed, and 2004. Critics, however, claim that there are problems with the funding. Some claim that states that developed especially rigorous AYP standards were at greater risk of being penalized than states which developed less stringent standards, and even the states with weaker standards argue that the full costs of NCLB are not borne by the national government. Also, some states that had established state-wide high-stakes tests, like Florida, were nonplussed when they failed their AYP after assuring themselves and their citizens that their public school students were improving dramatically on the state-specific tests. This was particularly difficult in Florida in the first year of NCLB evaluations. Jeb Bush, who claimed to be the state's "education governor" and had initiated a number of education reforms that included the adoption of a high stakes test that is required for students to graduate from high school, was not pleased that the national policy initiated by his brother, the president, issued Florida a failing grade. This experience helped establish states' frustrations with NCLB: they simultaneously wanted to have the latitude to create their own tests and standards and to receive payments unhindered from federal regulations. The case of Florida's poor NCLB performance under the two Bushes illustrates that even two executives, brothers in fact, who supported a number of the state education reforms widely touted by conservatives, could arrive at widely disparate views of what constitutes successful NCLB performance.

NCLB pitted the national government against state education departments in some instances, and especially against state teacher unions. The drive for greater teacher accountability and increased emphasis on teacher substantive skills threaten long-standing education seniority systems which sometimes reward teachers as a function of time in service as opposed to quality of their teaching. Reviews of NCLB were mixed, with some supporters claiming that the changes had improved states' ability to innovate, to allow teachers to move into more flexible teaching arrangements, making it easier for charter schools to get started and to flourish, and for states and school districts to better account for student performance through the use of tests.

Critics of NCLB are just as forceful in their complaints. They point to the program's emphasis on high stakes tests as a disincentive for students to do work that moves far beyond the state or nation-mandated level for "excellence," and claim that the program gives teachers strong incentives to "teach to the test." NCLB and state programs explicitly tied school and teacher financial rewards and promotions to student perform-ance on tests, which critics claim leads to an inappropriate focus on the test by teachers and administrators, and in some cases leads officials to focus on specific groups of talented students to help raise schools' test scores. For example, some schools create specialized academies that focus on some academic subject or curriculum that some-times exists within the school. The school then focuses its energies on training the students who opt into that program and less on the less academically inclined students. With that model, the school can raise its average test scores without concern for the less talented students in their populations. Of course, NCLB supporters may claim this as evidence of the value of school choice: When parents are empowered to choose the schools their children attend, performance improves.

Critics sometimes claim that test-based performance education diminishes the schools' efforts to teach the most talented students, as they focus solely on teaching them to get good scores on the test, and little else. In Florida, for example, public school students' academic years are focused around the state's Florida Comprehensive Achievement Test (FCAT), parts of which they must take in grades 4, 8, and 10 (writing), grades 3 through 10 (reading and math), and grades 5, 8, and 11 (science). Students who fail at any level must retake the exam to be promoted to the next grade. Students must pass a comprehensive FCAT, first taken in grade 10, to graduate from high school. The tests consume good parts of the school year. Teacher salaries and school budgets are based on FCAT scores. The test is taken in February (writing) and April (reading, math, and science) of each year. Some critics complain that some teachers stop introducing material and focus on test materials a month or so before the examinations begin and sometimes fail to offer new material after the final examination in April, making the remaining five or six weeks of each academic year unproductive.

The Race to the Top

The Obama administration has maintained some elements of NCLB, but has done away with others. Rather than lessening the role of charter schools the administration has championed them and sought to expand their presence. Even though they were initially opposed to charter schools and other NCLB reforms, the American Federation of Teachers, the AFL–CIO affiliated union, is now agreeing to some NCLB-driven changes in teacher tenure and pay. The National Education Association (NEA) is less enthusiastic about the Obama administration record. While the Bush administration treated NCLB as an entitlement to the states, the Obama administration under Education Secretary Arne Duncan implemented the "**Race to the Top**" program, in which states competed for grants. The program is designed to give states incentives to adopt standards that would help students be equipped to do well in college, the workplace, and the global economy; to develop data systems and methods for meas-uring and evaluating outcomes; to recruit and retain strong teachers and principals; and to help improve weak schools. The Administration established guidelines and scored states on their success in meeting them. The most successful states received federal money, over $4.35 billion since the program was initiated in 2009. Eighteen states and the District of Columbia received the funds in 2009 and 2010 for developing plans to increase college and career readiness, recruiting and rewarding good teachers and administrators, turning around struggling schools, and developing methods to track students. Of course, the states that were most successful in getting the funds are most pleased with the program, but external observers, including some Republican officials, claim that the competition worked especially well inasmuch as the promise of funds led states to innovate as they sought to win the awards.

The Obama administration also granted **waivers** to nineteen states so that they would not be held to the most stringent reading and math performance standards demanded by NCLB. The Obama administration has pushed for some education reforms supported by conservatives: merit pay and charter schools. Some observers view the provision of merit-based pay for teachers as a key way to attract and reward the best teachers. Teacher unions oppose merit because it threatens the pay increases that accompany seniority. Teacher unions are likewise skeptical about charter schools, as they also threaten the longstanding relationships between unions and school districts. The Obama administration, under Secretary Duncan, has advocated these reforms consistently.

The Obama administration has also worked to address the problem of higher education affordability. The recession years have been particularly difficult for higher education, as state governments have cut budgets for public colleges and universities and institutions have increased tuition fees to make up for lost state revenues. Even as state economies improve, GOP-dominated state legislatures are proving unwilling to restore education appropriations, with some of them arguing that the rising price of Medicaid is squeezing out higher education funding. A 2010 study shows that US student borrowers graduated with an average of more than $25,000 debt that year, up 11 percent over the prior two years (Project on Student Debt 2011). The national government provides need-based **Pell Grants** to college students; they were increased to $5,550 in 2011. In addition, the Federal Family Education Program, which provided federal guarantees of loans made by private lenders, was abolished in 2012. The removal of the supports for private loans is unpopular with some Republican legislators and will likely be targeted for change.

The Obama and Bush education policies are fairly consistent. Both administrations sought to increase the quality of public education, but they used different mechanisms. The NCLB Act of 2001 was an example of top-down policymaking by the federal government. The Bush administration imposed the standards on states and rewarded them according to whether they met standards imposed by the national government. The Obama approach, some of which involved retaining the Bush NCLB model, but with the waivers noted above, differed in that it involved a competition for funds rather than a mandate. The states were not required to compete for the Race to the Top money, but in fact most did. The NCLB standards were imposed and states were assessed regardless of their willingness to compete. Neither administration adopted policies that were entirely "market" or "non-market" oriented. Instead, both administrations' policies included pieces of both approaches, and elements that were attractive to conservatives as well as liberals. The diminished influence of education unions is especially interesting in the case of the Obama administration's support of charter schools and merit-based raises. The unions have been a strong source of support for Democrats, and the loss of once-sacrosanct positions suggests that changes in popular opinion about teacher unions are affecting policymaking.

8.5 The Battle over Educational Content

The battle over local control of education is evident in the controversy over educational content. The history of local control of education, and of local responsibility for its finance, leads to questions about what should be taught in the schools. Although there are legal proscriptions against teaching religion in the schools, or in discriminating against students due to race, religion, or other traits, there remain large differences among the states and within areas of states regarding what should be taught in the schools.

The Anti-Evolution Movement

The 1925 **Scopes Monkey Trial** was perhaps the most famous fight over what should be taught in schools. The case was fought over the Butler Law, a Tennessee law that outlawed teaching evolution and required that a creation-based theory be taught in Tennessee public schools. The governor of Tennessee was not a creationist, but he also believed the Butler Law would not be enforced and did not fight it, recognizing that to do so would be politically damaging in the state's rural areas. The court case was brought on by the American Civil Liberties Union (ACLU), who viewed the requirement to teach creation as a threat to freedom of speech and sought a venue for the case. A group of citizens from Dayton, TN, a small mining town located between Chattanooga and Knoxville, sought a science teacher willing to be defendant in the trial. A 24-year-old biology teacher and football coach named John T. Scopes volunteered, noting that he was following the state-provided text, which included evolution as its basis. The Scopes case came during a time at which a number of southern states had passed laws prohibiting teaching evolution, and the Butler Law passed in Tennessee mainly because it came up for vote during an election year – state legislators did not want to run for office on grounds that they opposed teaching the Bible. The defense attorney for the trial was Clarence Darrow. William Jennings Bryan led the prosecution. Darrow and Bryan were among the most famous orators of the time.

The anti-evolution cause was promoted strongly by Williams Jennings Bryan, the populist who had been the Democratic Party's nominee for the presidency three times, in 1896, 1900, and 1908. Bryan's populism was a mixture of what would now be considered left-leaning ideas, such as an opposition to the trusts, monopolies, his support for women's suffrage and the rejection of the gold standard, and decidedly illiberal (in current contexts) support for prohibition and creationism in public schools. He was a pacifist Secretary of State under Woodrow Wilson, and resigned when Wilson's militarist position toward Germany preceding World War I conflicted with his beliefs.

Clarence Darrow shared some of Bryan's liberal leanings, but was opposed to the teaching of creationism. He was a well-known labor lawyer who had worked on a number of high-profile cases, which pitted him in support of labor rights and workers. His involvement in the Scopes case was driven by a belief in scientific explanations for life.

Darrow's questioning of Bryan ultimately undermined the argument for evolution. The essence of Darrow's argument, and Bryan's inability to defuse it, was that the creation story is based on metaphor, with Bryan admitting as much on the stand. Upon gaining that admission from Bryan, Darrow asked for and received an immediate direct verdict. The jury convicted Scopes of violating the law, and the judge ordered him to pay a fine of $100.

The debate over teaching evolution was quieted by the **_Epperson v. Arkansas_** (1968) decision, in which the Court ruled that the ban on teaching evolution was religious and thus contravened the Establishment Clause. The same logic which was used in **_Edwards v. Aguillard_** (1987), which struck down a Louisiana law that required instructors teaching evolution to also teach the "creation science" theory. More recently, the debate was reanimated only in the 1990s with the rise of conservative Christian political activists.

Contemporary debates over how to teach the topic of evolution illustrate the cyclical nature of some issues. Although the debate has long been concluded in most nations, the openness of the United States' system contributes to the re-emergence of the topic. In 1999, the Kansas Board of Education enacted a provision that removed the subject of evolution from that state's standardized tests in an effort to have school boards de-emphasize that from the public school curriculum in the state. The battle has continued in Kansas, with changes occurring when the balance of the board changes between pro-design and anti-design forces.

The Dover, PA Case

In 2005, the Dover, PA school board voted to require teachers to read a statement about intelligent design prior to discussing evolution in their classrooms. Eleven of the district's parents brought suit against the ruling, arguing that it violated the

Establishment Clause. At trial, US District Judge John E. Jones, III, a George W. Bush appointee, ruled in *Kitzmiller et al. v. Dover Independent School District, et al.* (2005) that intelligent design did not meet the standards of scientific inquiry, especially the norm of unbiased testing, and ruled further that members of the school board had lied about their religious motivations in creating the rule. Even with this stern ruling, the intelligent design forces continue to battle for what has been described in *Kitzmiller* as failing to meet scientific standards of rigor. Judge Jones wrote:

> After a searching review of the record and applicable case law, we find that while Intelligent Design (ID) arguments may be true, a proposition on which the Court takes no position, ID is not science. We find that ID fails on three different levels, any one of which is sufficient to preclude a determination that ID is science. They are: (1) ID violates the centuries-old ground rules of science by invoking and permitting supernatural causation; (2) the argument of irreducible complexity, central to ID, employs the same flawed and illogical contrived dualism that doomed creation science in the 1980s; and (3) ID's negative attacks on evolution have been refuted by the scientific community. As we will discuss in more detail below, it is additionally important to note that ID has failed to gain acceptance in the scientific community, it has not generated peer-reviewed publications, nor has it been the subject of testing and research.
>
> *Kitzmiller* (2005): sect. 5.

Even with so stern a decision, attempts to include creation-based explanations for the beginnings of life remain. In the 2011 campaign for the Republican presidential nomination, Texas Governor Rick Perry told a Portsmouth, NH fourth grader, "In Texas, we teach both creationism and evolution in our public schools."[3] In March 2012, the Tennessee legislature passed a bill calling for "balanced" teaching of the "controversy," as the evolution-intelligent design issue is now described.

Box 8.1 H. L. Mencken on the Scopes Trial of July 18, 1925

William Jennings Bryan, fundamentalist, and Clarence Darrow, agnostic and pleader of unpopular causes, locked horns today under the most remarkable circumstances ever known by American court procedure.

It was on the courthouse lawn, where Judge Raulston had moved so that more persons could hear, with the Tennessee crowds whopping for their angry champion, who shook his fist in the quizzical satiric face of Mr. Darrow, that Mr. Bryan was put on the stand by the defense to prove that the Bible need not be taken literally.

---

[3] *New York Times*, August 18, 2011, http://thecaucus.blogs.nytimes.com/2011/08/18/perry-parries-hecklers-in-portsmouth/.

Box 8.1 *(cont.)*

The youthful Attorney General Stewart, desperately trying to bring the performance within legal bounds, asked, "What is the meaning of this harangue?" "To show up fundamentalism," shouted Mr. Darrow, lifting his voice in one of the few moments of anger he showed, "to prevent bigots and ignoramuses from controlling the educational system of the United States."

Mr. Bryan sprang to his feet, his face purple, and shook his fist in the lowering, gnarled face of Mr. Darrow, while he cried: "To protect the word of God from the greatest atheist and agnostic in the United States."

And then for nearly two hours, while those below broke into laughter or applause or cried out encouragement to Mr. Bryan, Mr. Darrow goaded his opponent. His face flushed under Mr. Darrow's searching words, and he writhed in an effort to keep himself from making heated replies. His eyes glared at his lounging opponent, who stood opposite him, glowering under his bulging brow, speculatively tapping his arm with his spectacles.

No greater contrast in men could be imagined. The traps of logic fell from Mr. Darrow's lips as innocently as the words of a child, and so long as Mr. Bryan could parry them he smiled back, but when one stumped him he took refuge in his faith and either refused to answer directly or said in effect: "The Bible states it; it must be so."

Pressures on Teachers

Political scientists Michael Berkman, Julianna Pacheco, and Eric Plutzer (2008) conducted a survey of US high school biology teachers and reported that about 16 percent of them were creation-oriented in their teaching. About one-sixth of teachers professed a "young earth" belief about the earth's origins, meaning they believed the earth to be 10,000 years or less of age. A smaller bloc of teachers – about one in eight – reported they taught creationism or intelligent design in a positive light, and the teachers who were creation-oriented spent less time on evolution-related topics than other teachers. Berkman *et al.* also reported that many teachers who were not creation-oriented in their teaching spent less time on evolution than is suggested by the science community, due in part to concerns with violating community norms. Thus, the threat of conflict may have a chilling effect on science education; the activism of state boards of education in Kansas, Texas, and other states may increase educators' concern with violating community norms in their teaching.

The battles over teaching evolution illustrate how school curricula reflect the prevailing attitudes of citizens. Of course, there is at times conflict over curriculum contents, and this plays out on state boards that are responsible for curriculum development. There are a number of hot-button issues – evolution, history, and economics – that have been the focus of attention recently as textbook adoption committees seek to find materials they believe most accurately reflect the information useful for their academic communities. In some cases, as in the state of Texas, a supermajority on the elected committee that establishes the state's textbook standards pushed successfully to include creationism in the Board's discussions in 2010, but a new board without so strong a contingent of fundamentalists rejected those appeals and did not include them in supplements in 2011. Some of the battle over school content is about emphasis. For example, some board members want greater emphasis on the Reagan presidency, and greater consideration of conservative economists like Milton Friedman and Frederic Hayek in curricula. There is conflict over these demands. In some cases, as with the focus on intelligent design over evolution or on the denial of global climate change, scientific observers claim that there is a desire to misinform students. In some of the cases about focuses on different characters in history, like the de-emphasis of Thomas Jefferson's role as a founding father in favor of those who did not espouse the value of separation of church and state, it is not so much incorrect information as a shifted focus to one that is more congruent with those members' ideological predilections.

8.6 Delegation Problems in Public Schools

The public has high expectations for what occurs in schools. A recent search of "public schools Fox news" produced jarring headlines: "You can't celebrate America, school says;" "Public school art project desecrates American flag;" "Utah bill would dictate use of transgender bathrooms;" among other items of interest. The term "public schools MSNBC" returned nothing. But both "Fox News education" and "MSNBC education" returned a story from late 2013 about a fall in US education rankings versus the world. Thus, there is some agreement between ideological contenders that schools are slipping.

The Demand to Fulfill Multiple Roles

Public schools are expected to fulfill multiple roles. They are expected to act as surrogate parents, public safety officers, medical providers, nutritionists, sporting venue providers, music and theater complexes, and should also teach children. Complaints about the poor quality of schools often focus on the high investment in schools – states' per-pupil spending averaged $10,560 in 2011 (*Governing Magazine* 2013) – and recall from the discussion above that US students do not perform as well as students in other industrialized democracies who spend much less on public education.

Explanations for poor school performance are varied. Some critics fairly attribute school failings to the many tasks assigned to schools, but recognize that removing those tasks is difficult, especially given that they are interconnected. For example, when the problem that children are not getting breakfast becomes apparent, the most obvious way to address the problem is to provide breakfast. And, of course, if children are hungry at breakfast, they will likely be hungry at lunch, and need dinner as well. If the school manages to provide three square meals a day for children, that leaves them hungry for the weekend, holidays, and summer. In that case, the school is, again, the most obvious place to treat the problem. However, the school is neither the cause of hunger nor its ultimate solution, and by placing the burden of child nutrition on the school, the school's teaching function is weakened. It is an example of Sutton's Law, named after Willie Sutton, who was famous for robbing banks. One reporter claimed that when Sutton was asked why he robbed banks, he responded, "Because that's where the money is." Sutton denied the comment, but Sutton's Law says that, when confronted with a question, first go to the most obvious answer. Hence, if we ask why students are not performing well in schools, the obvious place to look is in the schools.

Principal–Agent Problems in Educational Performance

In a broader sense, the education performance problem may be seen as a principal-agent problem, and more specifically a problem of delegation. There is a large number of childhood problems and a variety of tasks that affect school-age children and their families. In attempting to address those problems, local, state, and national governments often delegate the schools and their agents, teachers, to address the problems. A teacher who must attend to his or her students being fed, clothed, inoculated, parented, and so on has a much more difficult task than one who needs only to teach the students. This delegation problem, in which much is delegated to the schools without realistic assessments on how to complete the task, may prove especially costly, especially for low-income schools where some of the problems may be most pronounced.

This variety of principal–agent problem need not be thought of as affecting just public schools, as virtually any school (and any job) can have forms of delegation problem. The problem may be most pronounced in public schools precisely because they are public and as a result are more directly governed by public officials. Private schools are subject to public safety and other legal regulations, but are able to control their curriculums, textbook choices, and other curriculum decisions more freely than are public schools. Private schools can discriminate on student quality. They may provide subsidies so that academically strong but economically disadvantaged students may attend; they may also charge a premium for academically weak but economically advantaged students to attend (Epple and Romano 1998).

Recall the discussion of the controversy over teaching evolution that resulted in the Dover, PA case (*Kitzmiller et al. v. Dover Independent School District, et al.* (2005)) (see section 8.5). In that case, a majority of the elected school board established a rule that science teachers must include information on intelligent design prior to discussion of evolutionary theory. The teachers refused to follow the Board's demand, and a court case followed in which the judge ruled in favor of the teachers. That court decision represents a circumstance in which an agent – the teacher – successfully refused to follow the decision of the school board – the principal. Converting elected leaders' policy goals into real-world policy outcomes, a process known as policy implementation, is a common problem in any policy arena. Given that legislators cannot implement policies directly, they must hire unelected bureaucrats for the task. Of course, this sets up a classic agency problem. The bureaucrats that are hired to implement a given public policy may not share their principals' policy preferences.

In this regard, education policy is no different. Elected leaders cannot directly educate children. Instead, they hire teachers to perform this duty. Thus, enter an agency agreement with teachers in which the official (the principal) hires an agent (a teacher) to accomplish what the elected officials' principals (voters) elected him or her to produce (education). If elected officials and teachers agree on how to educate students, there is no problem. If elected officials' and teachers' views on how best to educate students differ, there is conflict. We often see areas of conflict between decision-makers and educators. Elected leaders have been chosen by their constituents to make public policy. Teachers have been trained in the best methods and technologies on education. When such tensions are present, what is the nature of the conflict that elected leaders and teachers (bureaucrats) face?

To better understand this dynamic and the problems that it generates, we consider a simple spatial model from Huber and Shipan (2002).[4] Figure 8.2 represents a single dimension in policy space, in this case representing education policy. (This policy space could represent any policy that we desire, i.e. the model is generalizable beyond education.) You can think of left–right movement on this policy scale mapping onto doing "more" or "less" of the given policy. It is important for us because it allows us to locate our actors on this policy dimension.

Let's imagine a legislator, L (here, the elective official), located on this dimension. For convenience, while we refer to a single leader, we could imagine that she represents the median leader in a group. The location of L represents the legislator's ideal point, where she prefers policy to be set. Now imagine that a bureaucrat, B (here, the teacher), is located at some point to the right of the leader. Substantively, this means

---

[4] This section is a cursory summary of Huber and Shipan's (2002) model. The reader should see their text for a thorough discussion.

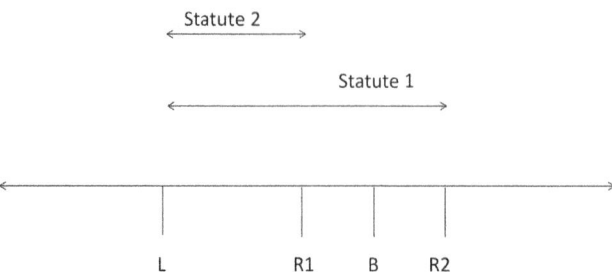

Figure 8.2 A Single Dimension in Policy Space

that the teacher wants to provide more of the policy than the leader prefers. Knowing that the teacher does not share her preference, what is the legislator to do?

If the legislator allows the teacher full discretion to deliver policy, then the teacher will deliver the outcome, R, and the legislator will suffer a policy loss, R–L. There are essentially two possibilities to avoiding this dilemma. First, the legislator could hire a teacher whose ideal policies are precisely equal to her own. Given the inefficiencies of screening and selection mechanisms designed to avoid the problems of adverse selection, selecting an agent who precisely shares the leader's preferences (who is, recall, the principal as in an agency model not as in head of a school) is challenging. Moreover, given the rules that constrain elective officials (e.g. civil service entrance exams and other rules that limit direct political control of bureaucrats, like tenure for teachers), selecting (or firing) agents purely on the basis of policy preferences is often illegal.[5] Second, the legislator could restrict the bureaucrat's discretion, limiting the set of policies from which the bureaucrat may select without sanction. The legislator can accomplish this by designing a statute that defines the bureaucrat's discretion, or allowable boundaries of policy delivery. In educational policy, examples of such discretionary statutes might include the legislature passing a bill that defines the total number of days that a school must instruct students, the minimum number of courses that schools must offer, or a list of textbooks from which teachers may select their course texts. If a teacher does not comply and attempts to enact policies outside the bounds of his discretion, he would invite scrutiny, investigations, and potential costs in the form of administrative punishment.

Consider the two statutes represented in Figure 8.2. If the legislator passes Statute 1, then the allowable policy set is fairly wide, ranging between the set of points between L and R_2. If the legislature passes Statute 2, then allowable policy is restricted to the set of points between L and R_1. What does this mean for the teacher? If the leader passes Statute 2, the teacher will not be in compliance with the law if he pursues his preferred

---

[5] Elected leaders can typically appoint agency heads and even second-tier agency officials. But, most bureaucrats are civil service employees, protected from political dismissals.

policy, B. As a result, the teacher risks detection and punishment for non-compliance. Under this statute, the best that the teacher can do is to locate policy at R_1. If the leaders pass Statute 1, the teacher can now pursue his own preferred policy and will locate policy at B. In either of these cases, the difference between the legislator's ideal point and the eventual point that policy is delivered, whether it is R_1 or R_2, represents a loss for the legislator. This loss is referred to as **bureaucratic drift**, or the tendency for bureaucrats (teachers in this case) to enact policies that deviate from those set by the political coalition that offered them.

You may be wondering, "If the legislator suffers a loss under both of these statutes, which allow the teacher discretion, then why not author a statute that grants the teacher zero discretion?" Such a statute would clearly force the teacher to locate policy at L. To understand the conditions under which a legislator may have incentive to not restrict a bureaucrat's discretion to zero, Huber and Shipan introduce another concept.

Converting a policy as expressed in a statute to an actual "real-world" outcome is the domain of the bureaucrat (the teacher). Teachers have professional expertise and skill and thus know more about how to teach students than legislators (recall our discussion from Chapter 1 on policy complexity). Because of this greater expertise, teachers are better informed than legislators about the likely outcomes that will occur if a specific policy is pursued. Thus, there exists an information asymmetry between legislators (leaders) and bureaucrats (teachers) on the relationship between policy outcomes. The uncertainty that exists between a policy and its outcomes is referred to as **policy uncertainty**. When the difference between a statutory policy and its implemented outcome is small, policy uncertainty is low. But when the difference between a policy and its implementation outcome grows, policy uncertainty increases. Of course, policy uncertainty varies over policy areas. As you might imagine, there are policy areas where bureaucrats do not possess a great informational advantage over legislators. If the legislature passes a law that says kindergarten classes must be no larger than twenty students, then the legislature has a reasonable expectation of how implementing this policy may affect class sizes. On the other hand, if the legislature passes a law that seeks to alter methods for teaching calculus in high schools, then the legislature may find itself at an informational disadvantage relative to the professional teachers who understand how to teach calculus. This notion of policy uncertainty must be included in the spatial model.

Consider Figure 8.3, modified from Huber and Shipan (2002). This figure is similar to Figure 8.2, with two additional pieces of information. To represent policy uncertainty, imagine that there is a relation that maps policy, in x, to outcomes, in y. This mapping identifies precisely in which direction and by what magnitude policy outcomes deviate from their intended policy effects. Huber and Shipan assume that policy deviations always occur to the left and are always one unit in magnitude. You could easily employ another choice to make a similar point. This means that any policy

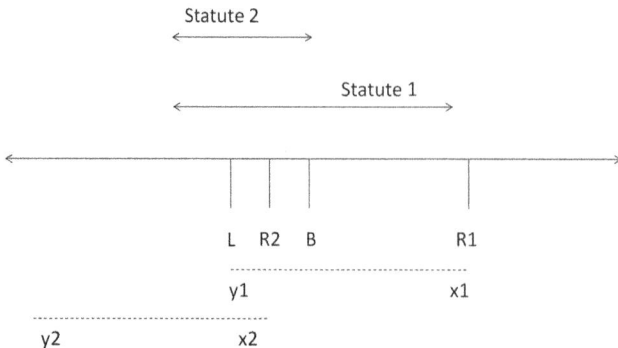

Figure 8.3 A Model of Legislator and Teacher Preferences with Uncertainty

enacted at x_1 will produce an outcome one unit to the left at y_1. Similarly, any policy enacted at x_2 will produce an outcome one unit to the left at y_2. Bureaucrats are assumed to be fully aware of this policy deviation, while legislators are assumed to have no information on this process.

Now we can return to the question raised above: why might the legislator not author a statute that allows the bureaucrat zero discretion? Imagine two possibilities for the legislator. One possibility is that the legislator lives in a world where policy uncertainty is equal to zero. Another possibility is that policy uncertainty is greater than zero and translates policy into one-unit deviation in outcomes. If policy uncertainty is equal to zero, then the legislator would want the bureaucrat to enact policy at L, fully expecting that the outcome will also be delivered at L. If policy uncertainty exists, then the legislator would want the bureaucrat to enact policy at x_2, expecting policy to be delivered at y_2. The problem is that the legislator may not know in which of these worlds she is living.

Let's assume that the legislator is completely uncertain about which of these worlds exists. As Huber and Shipan (2002) note, this suggests two errors a legislator may make. First, the legislator may give too much discretion to the bureaucrat. If the legislator believes she is living in the world where outcomes are delivered one unit to the left of the policy, then she would want the bureaucrat to deliver policy at x_1, which would yield the policy outcome y_1. To provide the bureaucrat with enough discretion to pursue policy at x_1, however, the legislature must adopt Statute 1 that allows enough discretion to pursue policy at x_1. Notice, however, that if the legislator was wrong in her belief about the world and policy is actually delivered where it is produced, then the bureaucrat can simply pursue their own preferred policy at B, which would generate a policy loss for the legislator. Second, the legislator may grant too little discretion to the bureaucrat. Now imagine that the legislator believes that the first state of the world exists – where there is no difference between adopted policy and its outcomes. If the legislator believes she is living in this state of the world, then she would want the bureaucrat to deliver policy at a point that would yield the policy outcome y_1. In this world, the Legislator might adopt the narrower Statute 2. Notice, however, that if the legislator was wrong in her belief about the world and policy is actually delivered one unit to the left, then if the bureaucrat adopts x_2, the actual policy outcome will be y_2. With this outcome, the bureaucrat suffers a policy loss, y_2–L. Had the legislator granted the bureaucrat additional discretion, by adopting Statute 2, then the Bureaucrat would have adopted B and the legislator would have suffered a smaller policy loss, L–B.

We can see from the model that the legislator's choice of bureaucratic discretion is not only a function of the bureaucrat's preferences (relative location), but also the level of policy uncertainty that the legislator possesses between policy and outcomes. Huber and Shipan's model provides insight into the question of why a legislator might not author a statute that allows the bureaucrat zero discretion. Their model suggests that given certain conditions a legislator may actually reap suboptimal policies if they do not allow the bureaucrat to capitalize on their policy expertise.

Returning to the practical case of the Dover, PA school district's demand that teachers make students aware of the literature on intelligent design, the teacher who refused to incorporate that into his lessons deviated from the statute and as a result was an example of bureaucratic drift in his shift from district policy. The legislators who promulgated the policy granted too little discretion to the teacher who, having better knowledge of the scientific status of evolution versus intelligent design (recall that the judge agreed that intelligent design is not scientific), succeeded in presenting his preferred view rather than the view the board wished to have taught.

8.7 The Push for Early Childhood Education

There seems to be policy congruence on support for early childhood education in the United States, although there is disagreement on how best to deliver that education. When the Head Start program received budget cuts of about $400,000 to its nearly $8 billion budget, critics were quick to complain about the impact on families and children that would occur. That is understandable: certainly, families accustomed to receiving Head Start benefits for their preschool children would lose the educational benefit for their children and the economic benefit to their family, as Head Start gives parents a place to put their children while they work or are otherwise out of the home. **Head Start** was created by the Johnson administration in 1965 and is designed to give preschool training for the children of people who live at or below the poverty line. Although Head Start has many supporters, it is unclear whether the program has lasting effects on children's ability to read or otherwise perform in ways that differ from children from similar economic circumstances who do not receive Head Start.

Head Start was the subject of a major policy analysis, plans for which were laid during the Clinton administration in 1996, and done between 2002 and 2006, with the final report published in 2010 (US Dept. HSS 2010). The study was designed well and made use of random assignment of children to treatment and control groups and exhaustive data analysis. The results showed no impact on participating students' academic, socio-emotional, or health status at the end of first grade. That is, students who selected into Head Start did not differ on these markers from students who did not select in. The Department of Health and Human Services allowed researchers longer than usual to complete the study as they worked hard to find a significant effect of Head Start.

Even with null research findings, there is public support for Head Start. Part of that is a function of public belief in the value of early education. Another part of it is a seeming disbelief that Head Start does not produce learning benefits. However, another possibly more important part is that Head Start provides large benefits to the *families* of children who are in Head Start, because it provides a source of day care, which is crucial for working people, and is a gateway into another set of benefits for impoverished children, like health care and meals. Eliana Garces and her colleagues (2002), in a study using non-experimental data, report significant **spill-over effects** for children who participated in Head Start, including greater likelihood of completing high school and attending college among whites and less likelihood of being charged with a crime or convicted among blacks.

Pre-kindergarten Expansions

There is other evidence of long-term benefits of pre-kindergarten programs other than Head Start. The state of Oklahoma created universal pre-kindergarten for its children in 1998. Initial program evaluations conducted by William Gormley and colleagues in 2001 and 2003 showed strong short-term effects which were more pronounced for low income, African-American, and Hispanic children than for whites (Besharov *et al.* 2012). Subsequent research showed little persistence of long-term gains, except for some evidence among boys who benefited from lasting effects on their math scores (Hill *et al.* 2012). Despite public enthusiasm of universal pre-kindergarten, policy analyses provide, at best, mixed evaluations of the program's value, especially with regard to its long-term effects.

Early childhood education is viewed as an opportunity to affect child development in the initial years and the hope is that the effects of interventions will be lasting. As a result, enthusiasm for early childhood education is high among the public, and some state governments have promoted its expansion actively. Some of the value of early childhood education is remarkable. Psychologists have long noted that differences in vocabulary vary greatly by income group, with the children of better-educated and more affluent people showing evidence of much better language knowledge than the children of less affluent and poorer educated people by as early as 18 months of age (Fernald *et al.* 2013). Early childhood educational interventions are one tool that may be used to improve those cognitive differences, as they will only worsen as children age.

Despite evidence of the value of early childhood interventions, there is not unanimity on how best to implement policies.

8.8 Education Reforms

The litany of complaints about the quality of public schools in the United States led to the birth of a reform movement that calls for, among other things, competition in schools. School districts are often described as monopolies, and it is only in the past twenty-odd years that they began to provide more parental choice in schools through the creation of magnet schools, various specialized schools like math and science or arts-intensive schools, and other innovations. The districts were in most cases led to create those specialized programs by public demand for choice in schools, and that demand for choice was brought about by complaints from critics of the existing education system. Public schools have been fairly rigid bureaucracies and are understandably protective of their resources. The school choice issue is in some ways simple: most people recognize the value of school choice, but they also recognize the organizational and other difficulties, like the desire to stay in neighborhood schools, the desire to stay near friends, and the like, that occur with school choice.

School Choice

School choice refers broadly to a set of policy proposals that allow parents or guardians to choose their children's schools rather than have them assigned to specific schools within specific school districts. In an idealized setting, school choice would be entirely open within a community, and schools would succeed or fail based on consumer preferences. If people were unconstrained in their choice of schools, real estate markets would be altered given that families' choices of housing are often driven by their desire to live near good schools. As noted in Box 8.2, state-assigned school grades are used by parents in Florida as a guide to their housing choice. There are other spillover effects of school choice as well. In some areas, choice is used to create specialized academic programs. In others, students cluster in certain schools to play particular sports. School choice is an appealing idea, but it at times introduces unintended consequences that introduce additional problems.

Box 8.2 Does School Quality Affect the Price of and Demand for Housing?

In a 2004 paper, economist David Figlio and school administrator Maurice Lucas assessed the effect of school quality grades on the price of housing in Florida. They report evidence that suggests that homebuyers did respond to state-administered school grades in their search for housing by seeking housing in better school districts. They not only show that schools with better grades fetched higher prices, but they also showed that the students who moved to those better-graded schools had higher grades, which suggests that parents searched for stronger schools based on the school grades (Figlio and Lucas 2004).

School choice is often a source of conflict because its backers and opponents sometimes base their support or rejection upon ideology or fear of change rather than on unbiased information. School choice proponents are often conservatives who base their rejection of traditional public schools on the observation that public school education is more expensive in the United States than in other nations, and that the results are poor compared to the number of nations. Some proponents of school choice are motivated by religion and seek choice as a way to remove themselves and their children from public institutions with which they may not share beliefs about curriculum.

School choice was first suggested by the Nobel prize-winning free market economist Milton Friedman in the 1950s and his wife and long-time collaborator Mary Friedman. Friedman initially proposed **school vouchers**, which would provide families with a voucher with which they could purchase school services on an open market rather than be limited to a school choice forced by what Friedman viewed as a monopoly provider, the single public school. Friedman was clear on what he viewed as the strongest barrier to school choice. He is quoted in a 1975 article in the *New York Times Magazine* as saying, "There is no doubt what the key obstacle is to the introduction of market competition into schooling: the perceived self-interest of the educational bureaucracy." School vouchers have proved controversial: their chief supporters are free-market conservatives and people who prefer parochial schools and their chief opponents are established school districts and teacher interest groups like unions, just as Friedman claimed nearly forty years ago, but other opponents voice concern about inequities that would be exacerbated by vouchers.

The principal equity concern about school vouchers focuses on information asymmetries. Vouchers make marketing central to a school's success, and marketing often focuses on emotional stimuli. Decision-making, in turn, is suboptimal. For example, reporters for the *Washington Post* reviewed the District of Columbia's federal voucher program and "found that hundreds of students use their voucher dollars to attend schools that are unaccredited or are in unconventional settings, such as a family-run K-12 school operating out of a storefront, a Nation of Islam school based in a converted Deanwood residence, and a school built around the philosophy of a Bulgarian psychotherapist (Layton and Brown 2012).

A recent series of reviews of a well-known public school voucher program in Milwaukee, WI suggest that the presence of vouchers does not affect student performance in schools. Three policy analyses of a five-year evaluation of the Milwaukee Parental Choice Program conducted by contractors affiliated with the School Choice Demonstration Program at the University of Arkansas were submitted for review in early 2012. The studies focused on performance on voucher (MPCP) and Milwaukee Public School (MPS) students' grade 4, 8, and 10 test scores; comparison of reading, math, and science scores for MPCP and MPS students; and completion and school persistence scores for MPCP and MPS students. An independent review of the studies reported no significant differences among students compared in any of the three studies. In the first study, there was some evidence of improved reading scores among eighth graders, but a reviewer noted that the change appears after only the final year of the study, with no differences in the prior years. Thus, there is little evidence for a meaningful effect on the largest, longest, and most evaluated school choice program in the United States (Cobb 2012).

Schneider *et al.* (2002) demonstrated the importance of parent information in school choice. Their research was based on studies of school choice programs in four areas in New York and New Jersey. They found that parents of all income levels sought information on schools, but that the information available to them and the quality of schools from which they could choose limited their choices.

Charter Schools

Another form of choice is the creation of charter schools. Charter schools are established by each state and as a result the details of their charters vary. They are publicly funded schools that are created as the result of petitions by parents, community groups, or teachers. Charter schools are relieved of some requirements of other public schools. The extent to which they are relieved of requirements varies by state, with some states waiving all requirements other than attendance and national government rules like the need to conform to the requirements of the Americans with Disabilities Act, to some waiving all requirements other than those that apply specifically to charter schools. To receive the charter, schools must consent to produce some agreed-upon outcome for which the school must demonstrate accountability. For example, there are charter schools designed to train high school students in specific job skills, schools that focus on the arts, and so on.

A US Department of Education-contracted policy evaluation of the effectiveness of charter schools reported no conclusive evidence of their positive or negative effects on learning (Gleason *et al.* 2010). The study focused on thirty-two charter schools in fifteen states. Participants in the 2,300 student study included random selection of students who had been included in the charter school, as well as students who had applied, but had not been drawn from the pool of randomly selected applicants. The results showed that students who received subsidized lunches, a measure used to capture family income levels, performed *better* as measured by improvement in test scores than children from more affluent homes. Overall, although there was no conclusive evidence that the charter schools provided better education than the non-charter schools, the positive outcomes appear to be clustered in schools in which children were lower income, in urban areas, and where the schools' scores had been below the median score in prior assessments. The researchers are careful to note that the results are correlational and not causal, but they nevertheless suggest that the charter schools may be helpful for less affluent students in urban schools than for more affluent students in suburban or non-urban schools.

Box 8.3 Two Views of Teaching Reform: Charter Schools and Teacher Unions

Critics of teacher unions sometimes claim that the process of removing poor teachers blocks efforts to reform the schools. They point to the "rubber rooms" where, until 2011, tenured New York City teachers whom the city wished to dismiss were assigned to non-teaching jobs at full pay, sometimes for years, as evidence of a public education failure. In 2010, NYC had over 300 teachers who were charged with incompetence and managed to dismiss only thirty of them over the year; their dismissals were tied up by legal challenges, union-bargained blocs to firing, and the like. The rubber rooms were closed in 2011, largely as a result of their being made examples of by their critics and the press. The change points to the widespread loss of support for the teacher union. Even the Obama administration's Race to the Top policy initiated in 2008 weakened teacher union protections.

Charter Schools and the Harlem Children's Zone

As we just noted, there is important variation in charter school performance. "No excuses" charter schools, for example, have shown some success (Thernstrom and Thernstrom 2003).[6] The Knowledge is Power Program (KIPP) is one example of a no excuses charter school. "KIPP schools emphasize traditional math and reading skills,

---

[6] The "no excuses" term was popularized by Thernstrom and Thernstrom (2003).

the development of a strong student work ethic, strict behavior norms, long school days and an extended school year" (Angrist *et al.* 2011: 1). Given the nature of these schools, skeptics have rightly asked if their success is a function of selection bias. The concern is that students, and parents, who attend these schools differ in important ways from students who do not attend these schools. In other words, those who voluntarily choose to attend a very strict school with longer school days and a longer school year are the same as those who choose not to attend such a school. Success at KIPP schools, then, may result from an omitted variable.

One strategy for addressing selection bias is randomization. Specifically, it is necessary to randomly assign some students to attend a KIPP school and other students to attend a different school. As it happens, the KIPP school in Lynn Massachusetts uses a lottery, a random assignment tool, to choose its students. (They only do this because they have too many applicants. The lottery is how they choose among the applicants.) Angrist *et al.* (2011) use this lottery to evaluate the KIPP school in Lynn Massachusetts. They find that the KIPP Lynn school improves students' reading and math scores, as well as their performance on the Massachusetts Comprehensive Assessment System test. The student gains are strongest for those with limited English proficiency and special education students. These results address some of the skeptics' concerns.

The Harlem Children's Zone (HCZ) is a program involving "no excuses" charter schools and community services. The Promise Academy is one of these charter schools, and one of the questions for public policy is whether this charter school improves educational outcomes. As before, the primary threat to causal inference is selection bias. Being a no excuses school, there is concern that those who attend are different in important ways from those who do not attend. And as before, researchers address this threat to inference by relying upon a lottery. The Promise Academy receives more applicants than it can admit. Dobbie and Fryer (2011) compare outcomes for those who attended the Promise Academy (the lottery winners) and those who wanted to attend, but were denied admittance (the lottery losers). Some of their results are presented in Table 8.2. They find that the Promise Academy improved elementary school students' math scores by 0.191 standard deviations and reduced their absences by 2.412 standard deviations. The effects are similar for middle school students. Their math scores improved by 0.229 standard deviations and absences were reduced by 2.199 standard deviations. In some ways, the significant reduction in absences is not surprising. After all, students will be kicked out of school if they miss too many days. The significant improvement in math scores is more noteworthy.

It is not entirely clear why the Promise Academy is so effective. It may stem from having better teachers or from the curriculum and no excuses approach (longer school days and a longer school year). Chetty *et al.* (2014a, 2014b), for example, find that some teachers have a more significant effect on student learning than others. One might

Table 8.2 Effects on Math Scores and Absences for Charter vs. Non-Charter Students

	Elementary School	Middle School
Math	0.191*	0.229*
	(0.116)	(0.037)
Absences	−2.41*	−2.199*
	(1.413)	(0.650)
N	748	1449

Note: * = p<0.05, one-tailed.

imagine that better teachers prefer a no excuses environment. At the same time, research on curriculum finds that the no excuses approach generally has a positive effect on student learning (Hoxby and Murarka 2009). Perhaps the answer is that both better teachers and the curriculum are driving these results.

The elementary school coefficients come from the two-stage least squares lottery model reported in Table 5 in Dobbie and Fryer (2011). The middle school coefficients come from the two-stage least squares lottery model reported in Table 3.

8.9 Higher Education in the United States

The value of post-high-school education is generally agreed upon, but there are conflicts over how best to provide that schooling, and how to pay for it. College is expensive. For the 2013–14 academic year, the College Board (2015) reports that a "moderate" budget for a public school averaged $22,826, and a moderate budget at a private college averaged $44,750. Those figures go well beyond tuition and include fees, books, housing, transportation, and more. In addition, many students receive financial aid to lessen costs, but the fact remains that large numbers of undergraduate students emerge from school with substantial debt. The College Board also noted that the average debt for recent graduates was $26,500 in 2013. Federal aid for undergraduate students through the Pell Grant program and others declined from $52 billion in 2010–11 to $47 billion in 2012–13, and the amount of federally insured loans likewise declined. Private loans are becoming more frequent, and they are more expensive than federal loans. Hence, the real price of school is increasing dramatically.

American universities were initially private and public schools were much younger than the best-established privates (with a few exceptions). Beginning with the **Morrill Act** of 1862, which granted 30,000 acres per senator and representative of each state to be sold to create an endowment to enable each state to create a land-grant institution, states have had public institutions of higher learning. The mission of those institutions was (and remains to be) to educate people in agriculture, home economics, mechanical arts, and other practical professions. **Land-grant schools** are often "aggie" schools whose original mission was to focus on more applied skills than were typically taught in university curricula. The land-grant ideal is still seen in some universities, many of which have strong agricultural outreach programs. A second Morrill Act was passed in 1890 to broaden the scope of the land grant to students living in segregated states. That expansion established the provision that racially segregated states must create schools under the act. Those schools were funded with grants rather than land, and the 1890 act led to the creation of **historic black colleges and universities (HBCUs)** that continue to exist today. HBCUs are sometimes criticized as historical artifacts, but they have strong supporters in state legislatures and among their alumni.

Concerns with Prices and Debt

The price of higher education is receiving attention among state legislatures as they debate the value and logic of state investment. Governors in some states, notably Texas Governor Rick Perry, are seeking "$10,000 degrees," which would guarantee students a degree in four years at a brick and mortar college. The price tag does not include housing or other add-ons, but is attractive to students (and parents) who leave college with debt and without jobs. The other prong of the $10,000 degree is that it must focus on items that lead to employment, and they are thus a state economic development tool.

Student Loan Debt and Higher Education: A Crisis?

As of 2015, a study by Experian suggests that US citizens hold a total of approximately $1.2 trillion in student loan debt.[7] This total is comprised of current and former students with varied backgrounds. Students included in this figure can range from someone who attended beauty school for one semester and dropped out to individuals who have completed their PhDs or MDs. At first glance, this number is staggering. Total US household debt, comprised of mortgages, auto loans, student loans, and revolving debt (e.g. credit cards), is approximately 11.5 trillion dollars. Student loans make up over 10 percent of this total, and the percentage is rising. The size and rate of growth of student loan debt, together with the rising default rate of student loans, is a growing concern among the public, the media, and elected officials. The presence of large amounts of student loan debt is thought to be a burden not just for the individual note holder, but also for the larger economy. Large student loan debt represents a drag

---

[7] See www.experianplc.com/media/news/2014/experian-analysis-finds-student-loans-increased-by-84-percent-since-the-recession-40-millio/.

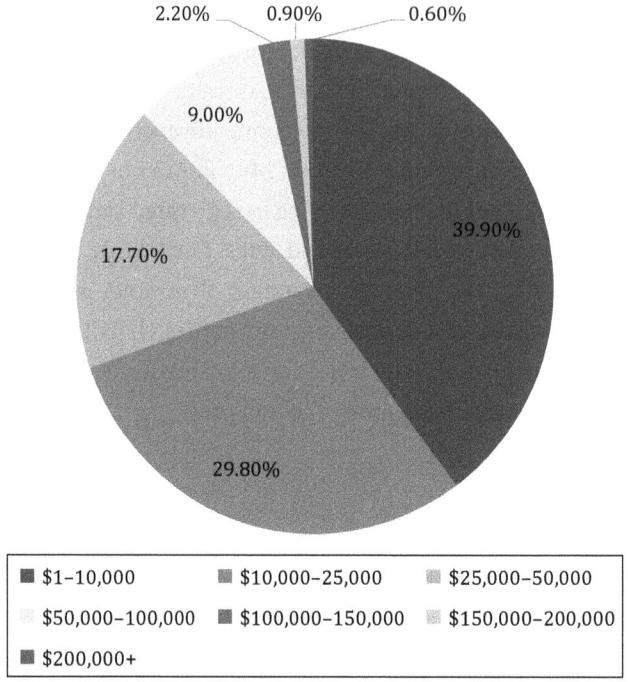

Figure 8.4 Distribution of Student Loan Amounts
Source: Federal Reserve Bank of New York (2014)

on economic growth. Graduated students, who would normally be spending income on setting up their households (e.g. buying a new car, TV, or townhouse), are instead sending in payments to their banks for loan processing. What is behind this surge in debt?

Consider how much the typical student holds in loans. Figure 8.4 displays the distribution of student loan debt by the size of the total loan amounts. The first thing to notice about the distribution is that it is positively or right-skewed (the underlying data used to generate the pie chart are right-skewed). This means that there are a few extreme outliers that hold very high levels of debt, in this case over $200,000. However, over 50 percent of students have debt totaling between $9,000 and $20,000. A skewed distribution suggests that measures of central tendency will provide very different impressions of the "middle" of the distribution. Recall from Chapter 4 that in a positively skewed distribution, the mean value of the distribution will be higher than the median, because of the few extreme high values. In the distribution above, the median student loan debt is around $10,000, while the mean student loan debt is around $25,000 – not a trivial difference when trying to understand what the typical student is facing. Therefore, you should always be careful, when consuming information on skewed distributions, to consider whether your information source is reporting the mean or the median. The second thing to notice is that the number of students that hold exorbitant sums of debt are truly outliers. This is not the typical case. But is does make for an eye-catching headline when the media runs a story about an outlier and leaves it to the consumer to wonder whether that case is typical. While the totals may not necessarily be as large as popular wisdom may suggest, there is no denying that student loan amounts have been rising.

What is behind this trend of rising student loan debt? Some have argued that the cost of college is driving the increase in student loans and default rates. And it is true that college costs have increased. Consider that over the thirty years between 1982 and 2012 the average cost of a four-year public college degree increased from $7,534 to $17,474 in constant, inflation-adjusted dollars.[8] This is equivalent to a 131 percent increase. This sounds like a lot. And it is. College tuition has risen for any number of reasons, including: to keep pace with inflation, to pay for an ever-growing administrative system, and to compete with other colleges for well-known faculty (Lorin 2014).

While these increases may be a part of the problem of increasing student debt, we cannot evaluate these increases in a vacuum. Let's consider them from the perspective of whether college graduates' incomes are keeping up with this rate of increase. Consider the median weekly earnings of full-time and salary college graduates. Between 1982 and 2012, their earnings have increased from $393 to $1,071 – a 172 percent increase. This suggests that the earning power of college graduates, which is correlated with their ability to repay student loans, has increased *faster* than college tuition at public colleges or universities.

So, if college graduates are actually earning more, why is holding student loan debt a potential problem? The answer is that it depends upon whether you are likely to reap the benefits of your degree. Not everyone who takes out student loans to attend college is able to capitalize on their educational investment. There are two important factors that hinder the ability to reap the rewards of higher education: failing to graduate; and earning a lower income than expected after graduation.

First, not all those who attend college finish. And not completing college diminishes their lifetime earning prospects. Those with only partial degrees earned only $697 in 2012, compared to $1,071 for college graduates. This amounts to only a 70 percent increase in income compared to 1981 for those who only obtained "some college education" (recall that tuition increased 131 percent). For students who never complete college, the cost of repaying student loans will simply be much more of a burden. Moreover, the retention rate among first-time degree-seeking undergraduates at degree-granting post-secondary institutions varies by institution. For 2013, these retention rates were 79 percent for public institutions, 80 percent at private/not-for-profit schools, and

---

[8] Source: US Department of Education, National Center for Education Statistics. 2015. *Digest of Education Statistics, 2013* (NCES 2015-011), Chapter 3.

only 51.4 percent at for-profit schools.[9] Notice the rather large gap between public and not-for-profit universities and for-profit schools. This gap is one of the growing difficulties with student loan debt. To be clear, for-profit schools are not just the large online universities with which you may be familiar. This classification also includes some beauty schools, barber schools, technical schools, culinary schools, and the like. While some of these schools may offer degrees, many only offer students certificates, which offer students lower return on this investment.

Second, not all student loans are necessarily wise economic investments. Students who go deep into debt may find themselves earning a lower income than expected after graduation. This could be due to their professional career choice or simply due to the state of the economy upon graduation. In either case, students may face a future stream of income that is not high enough to justify a rather large upfront loan obligation.

Along with increased loan obligations, we have also seen student loan defaults rising. Federal student loans are considered to be in default when a student has sent in no payments for 270 days. So who is not paying? Most highly ranked four-year public or four-year private schools have single digit default rates, on the order of 3 to 8 percent. Junior colleges or community colleges tend to have higher default rates, ranging as high as 23 percent. For-profit schools can have even higher default rates. Delinquent student loan recipients tend to be either those who *dropped out* of four-year public or four-year private schools or those who *graduated* from four-year for-profit schools.[10] To put this differently, loan defaults are particularly problematic among those who never finish, or those who finish from for-profit schools. This pattern may reflect lower economic security among those who drop out or attend for-profit schools, or it may be a case of adverse selection – despite what elected officials claim, college may not be for every student.

Online Education

Another development in higher education that may affect policy and planning is the emergence of **massive online open courses (MOOCs)**. MOOCs are now offered at MIT, Harvard, Stanford, and several other colleges and universities around the world. They provide open access to coursework and may prove to be especially valuable for non-degree-seeking students. Experience with them to date is that people seldom complete the courses, but their existence will prove to be a long-term concern for existing colleges and universities as they compete for students.

[9] Source: US Department of Education, National Center for Education Statistics. 2015. *Digest of Education Statistics, 2013* (NCES 2015-011).

[10] Source: www2.ed.gov/offices/OSFAP/defaultmanagement/cdr.html.

Affirmative Action in College Admissions

All competitive colleges use some sort of formula for determining whether an applicant should be admitted. The factors inputted to this formula, at a minimum, include your SAT scores and your high school grade point average. Some schools have also included race as an input, with African-Americans being given more points for admission than other racial groups. This is an example of affirmative action. Believing there is value in having a racially diverse student body but not wanting to explicitly include race in an admissions formula, the states of Texas and Florida guarantee admission to a state university if a student graduates in the top 10 or 20 percent of his or her class. Fryer and Loury (2008) call the Texas and Florida approach color-blind affirmative action and the more traditional approach sighted affirmative action. One question of interest is whether color-blind affirmative action is a more efficient policy. How does it affect educational outcomes, particularly for minority groups?

Both color-blind and sighted affirmative action assume some diversity contributes to the organization's mission. Color-blind affirmative action is a less efficient policy for achieving this goal. Fryer and Loury (2008) offer two reasons for why this is the case. First, high school grade point average is not the only factor that predicts college success, but it is the only factor used in color-blind affirmative action. Some other factors that predict college success include extra-curricular activities (e.g. band, debate, etc.), admissions essays, and high school quality. A sighted affirmative action policy takes these and other factors into account. Second, color-blind affirmative action creates incentives for individuals to focus less on learning and less on acquiring the range of skills and experiences that help them perform well in college and more on easy classes and high grades.

8.10 Conclusion

Education at all levels constitutes a large portion of the budgetary efforts of local, state, and, increasingly, national government. There is inherent conflict in how school will be paid for, what should be taught, and to whom. The conflict occurs as a result of delegation problems. Citizens delegate public education to local, state, and national government. Policymakers seek to manage educational content and methods, but do not have the expertise of educators and must temper policy decisions with the understanding that educators' expertise must be regarded. Educators must defer to community demands as well, which results in conflict between educators' expertise and public preferences. Educational reforms like charter schools are popular with the public and are part of an emerging pro-reform movement that will result over time in significant changes in the design and management of schools and education.

Public education is an important function in state and local governments. The school reform movement has been effective in changing the range of choices available to students. US students' test scores are improving, but still lag behind those of students in other industrialized nations. A substantial part of the problem with testing is a result of American students being more diverse than those from other nations. Much of the time and money investment in US schools focuses on guidance, social work functions, and nutrition, which reduces the time that teachers may spend on teaching.

The national government has a large and growing role in public education. The recent push for a national standard for education is under attack from critics who do not think it is sufficiently demanding and from those who view it as a threat to state and local control of education decisions.

The schools in some states are under pressure not to teach science rigorously, or at least to give non-scientific and pseudo-scientific claims some consideration in classroom instruction. Teachers are under pressure to teach material that appeals to the community norm without regard to its intellectual or scientific rigor. The courts have ruled that school boards cannot mandate that teachers treat unscientific information as credible, but teachers feel pressure and in some cases alter their teaching to meet community norms.

Schools at all levels are under pressure to perform strongly, and performance measures are used to determine school funding levels and teacher salaries in some areas. Schools are receiving federal government support to create early childhood education programs. They are experimenting with charter schools and a variety of different delivery models. Colleges and universities are under pressure to teach subjects that lead to job placements, and there is pressure to hold tuition down and to provide online education. Both public and private education are changing and new models and new technologies for teaching suggest they may be much different in the coming years.

Key Terms

The Enlightenment
Charter school
High-stakes test
Teacher testing and qualifications
Property taxes
Millage rate
State income taxes
Sales taxes
Forced-riders

Teacher unions

Sputnik

National Defense Education Act

Elementary and Secondary Education Act of 1965

Improving America's Schools Act

No Child Left Behind Act

Adequate yearly progress

Race to the Top

Waivers

Pell Grant

Bureaucratic drift

Policy uncertainty

Head Start

Spill-over effect

School choice

School vouchers

Morrill Act

Land-grant school

Historic black colleges and universities

Massive online open courses

CHAPTER EXERCISES

1. Should people whose children attend private or parochial schools pay taxes for public schools? Should there be a distinction between the tax treatment of private and parochial schools?

2. Should children who attend private or parochial schools take state-specific academic achievement tests, including high stakes tests that determine whether they move to the next grade along with the public school students who are required to take them?

3. Should teacher pay be determined by their students' performance on assessment tests?

4. Can university classes be taught effectively in massive online open courses?

5. Should college enrollment be provided to all qualified students at taxpayer expense, as is done in public schools? If so, should the funding organizations, for example, state governments, have a say in what courses of study students pursue?

REFERENCES

Angrist, J. D., Pathak, P. A., and Walter, C. R. 2011. "Explaining Charter School Effectiveness." National Bureau of Economic Research Working Paper 17332.

Barro, Robert and Lee, Jong-Wha. 2001. "International Data on Educational Attainment: Updates and Implications." *Oxford Economic Papers* 3: 541–563.

Besharov, Douglas J., Germanis, Peter, Higney, Caeli A., and Call, Douglas M. 2012. "Oklahoma's Universal Pre-Kindergarten." University of Maryland School of Public Policy, Welfare Reform Academy. Available online at www.welfareacademy.org.

Chetty, R., Friedman, John, and Rockoff, Jonah. 2014a. "Measuring the Impacts of Teachers I: Evaluating Bias in Teacher Value-Added Estimates." *American Economic Review* 104(9): 2593–2632.

2014b. "Measuring the Impacts of Teachers II: Teacher Value-Added and Student Outcomes in Adulthood." *American Economic Review* 104(9): 2633–2679.

Cobb, Casey. 2012. "Review of the SCDP Milwaukee Evaluation Report #29." National Education Policy Center, Boulder, CO.

College Board. 2015. Trends in Higher Education. Available online at http://trends.collegeboard.org/college-pricing/figures-tables/average-published-undergraduate-charges-sector-2015-16.

Dobbie, Will and Fryer, Roland G., Jr. 2011. "Are High Quality Schools Enough to Increase Achievement Among the Poor? Evidence from the Harlem Children's Zone." *American Economic Journal: Applied Economics* 3(2): 158–187.

Epple, Dennis and Romano, Richard E. 1998. Competition between Private and Public Schools, Vouchers, and Peer-Group Effects." *American Economic Review* 88(1): 33–62.

Federal Reserve Bank of New York. 2014. "Measuring Student Debt and Its Performance." Staff Report Number 668.

Fernald, Ann, Marchman, Virginia A., and Weisleder, Adriana. 2013. "SES Differences in Language Processing Skill and Vocabulary Are Evident at 18 Months." *Developmental Science* 16(2): 234–248.

Figlio, David and Lucas, Maurice E. 2004. "What's in a Grade? School Report Cards and the Housing Market." *American Economic Review* 94(3): 591–604.

Fryer, R., Loury, G., and Yuret, T. 2008. "An Economic Analysis of Color-Blind Affirmative Action." *Journal of Law, Economics, and Organization* 24(2): 319–355.

Garces, Eliana, Thomas, Duncan, and Currie, Janet. 2002. "Longer Term Effects of Head Start." *American Economic Review* 92(4): 999–1012.

Gleason, Philip, Clark, Mellissa, Tuttle, Christina Clark, Dwyer, Emily, and Silverberg, Marsha. 2010. *The Evaluation of Charter School Impacts*. NCEE Report 2010–4029. Washington, DC: US Department of Education. Available online at http://files.eric.ed.gov/fulltext/ED510573.pdf.

Gormley, William, Jr., Phillips, Deborah, and Gayer, Ted. 2008. "Preschool Programs Can Boost School Readiness." *Science* 320: 1723–1724.

Governing Magazine. 2013. "Per Pupil Education Spending by State." Available online at www.governing.com/gov-data/education-data/state-education-spending-per-pupil-data.html.

Hill, Carolyn J., Gormley, William T., and Adelstein, Shirley. 2012. *Do the Short-Term Effects of a Strong Preschool Program Persist?* Center for Research on Children in the US, Georgetown University, October.

Hoxby, C. M. and Murarka, S. 2009. "Charter Schools in New York City: Who Enrolls and How They Affect Their Students' Achievment." National Bureau of Economic Research Working Paper Number 14852.

Huber, J. and Shipan, C. 2002. *Deliberate Discretion: The Institutional Foundations of Bureaucratic Autonomy*. New York: Cambridge University Press.

Layton, Lyndsey and Brown, Emma. 2012. "Quality Controls Lacking for D.C. Schools Accepting Federal Vouchers." *Washington Post*, November 17. Available online at www.washingtonpost.com/local/education/quality-controls-lacking-for-dc-schools-accepting-federal-vouchers/2012/11/17/062bf97a-1e0d-11e2-b647-bb1668e64058_story.html.

Lorin, Janit. 2014. "College Tuition in the U.S. Again Rises Faster than Inflation." *Bloomberg Business*, November 13. Available online at www.bloomberg.com/news/articles/2014-11-13/college-tuition-in-the-u-s-again-rises-faster-than-inflation.

National Aeronautics and Space Administration (NASA). 2013. "Sputnik." Available online at http://history.nasa.gov/sputnik/.

NCES. 2013. "Trends in International Math and Science Study (TIMMS)." Available online at http://nces.ed.gov/timss/figure11_3.asp.

Project on Student Debt. 2011. "Student Debt and the Class of 2010." Available online at http://ticas.org/sites/default/files/pub_files/classof2010.pdf.

Schneider, Mark, Teske, Paul, and Marschall, Melissa. 2002. *Choosing Schools: Consumer Choice and the Quality of American Schools.* Princeton University Press.

Thernstrom, S. and Thernstrom, A. 2003. *Closing the Racial Gap in Learning.* New York: Simon & Schuster.

US Department of Health and Human Services. 2010. "Head Start Impact Study Final Report." Washington, DC. Contract 282-00-0022. Available online at

http://journalistsresource.org/wp-content/uploads/2011/08/1108HeadStartImpact.pdf.

9 Crime and Punishment

Outline

Questions

- Why are some individuals more inclined to break the law than others?
- Does getting "tough on crime" reduce crime?
- When the police aggressively pursue minor offenses, is there a reduction in major crime?
- What are the arguments for and against capital punishment?

Overview

- The primary analytic concepts we use to provide insight on crime policy are opportunity costs and expected utility.
- The primary measures of crime are the Uniform Crime Report and the National Crime Victimization Surveys.
- The choice to break the law is a function of the cost of crime, the probability of arrest and conviction, and the benefits of crime.

- Both human and social capital are significant influences on the choice to offend.
- The opportunity cost of crime helps explain why the poor and young are more likely to break the law than older and wealthier individuals.
- Tough on crime laws, such as "three strikes and you're out" and truth-in-sentencing, reduce crime, but create other social costs.
- The broken windows policing strategy aggressively targets minor offenses. Some research indicates that it reduced crime in New York City in the 1990s, but its success in other municipalities has not been significant.
- A larger police presence reduces crime.
- The legalization of abortion appears to have reduced crime.
- Capital punishment is supported by a majority of the public, but it has little effect on reducing crime.

Introduction

In 2000, a young man named Wes Moore was arrested for murdering a police officer. On the same day as Mr. Moore's arrest, another man, also named Wes Moore, received a prestigious Rhodes scholarship. It turns out that the two men have more in common than just a name. Both are from Baltimore, had run-ins with the law as youth, are African-American, and were raised by single mothers. Despite these similarities, their lives have turned out very differently. Why did one become a murderer and the other a Rhodes scholar?

The scholar Moore says that good fortune, particularly in having good mentors, was a crucial determinant in different roads they took in life. Fortune, no doubt, did play a role in each of their lives, yet there are other important differences between the two Moores that explain why one pursued a life of crime and the other a life of scholarly and business achievement.

The scholar Moore had two parents for the first three years of his life; the other Moore's father was never present in his life. The scholar Moore's parents both had college degrees; the other Moore's parents had only high school degrees. The scholar Moore's mother was closely involved in his life, sending him to a military school to avoid bad influences; the other Moore's mother was more interested in partying than in what was going on in her son's life. The scholar Moore's siblings were successful; the other Moore's siblings were criminals.

In this chapter, we discuss how the differences between the two Moores help us understand why some people choose to commit crime while others do not. Briefly, the choice to commit a major crime, like most other significant choices in life, is influenced by many factors. For example, being raised in a one-parent family is frequently cited as the greatest risk factor for turning to crime; although both Wes Moores were raised by single parents, we see that a single-parent childhood is not always a deter-minant of criminality. For a few years, the scholar Moore had two parents in his life. Of perhaps equal importance, the scholar Moore's siblings grew up with two parents, contributing to their social adjustment and ability to help Wes avoid crime. The other Moore's siblings did not provide such positive role models.

Both Wes Moores saw the psychic, social, and economic rewards from crime, but the social costs for the scholar Moore were much higher because of his mother's involve-ment in his life and his adolescence in military school. While a military school is not for everyone, its discipline and routine can be useful for some. Once the scholar Moore became comfortable with his new school, he pursued education with a passion. Educa-tion, we know, is one of the greatest deterrents to crime. It raises the opportunity cost of crime and provides one with the psychological resources to weather difficult times and identify creative solutions to problems. In contrast, the other Moore had fewer role models with a higher education, was not pushed to study as much, and, consequently, did not pursue academic learning with as much enthusiasm. Having siblings who committed multiple crimes and living in a high crime area – the military school was not in a high crime area – the other Moore did acquire an education, but it was more of an education in crime than in academics. In summary, their social environments significantly influenced what they were likely to see as something they could pursue with success. For the scholar Moore, it was education; for the other Moore, it was crime.[1]

In the rest of this chapter, we elaborate on these points by situating them within a theory of criminal behavior. Once we understand the major influences on the likeli-hood of committing crime, we discuss and evaluate a variety of the effects of various public policies. First, however, we begin with a discussion of crime itself: what it is, how it is measured, and some descriptive information on homicide rates to anchor the analysis. The chapter concludes with a discussion of capital punishment.

9.1 What Is Crime?

Crime is a violation of the law. Violations range from gravely serious, like murder and rape, to less serious forms of law-breaking, like not wearing a seat belt. Most crimes fall somewhere between the extremes: robbery, theft, drug trafficking, drug possession, etc. Although there are many types of violations of the law, we can usefully classify most of them into five types: violent crime, white collar/corporate crime, organized crime (including terrorism), property crime, and drug crime. Crime is enormously expensive. In the early 1990s, Miller *et al.* (1993) estimated that crime costs about

---

[1] The discussion in these paragraphs is based on the book, *The Other Wes Moore: One Name, Two Fates*, by Wes Moore. We highly recommend it to you.

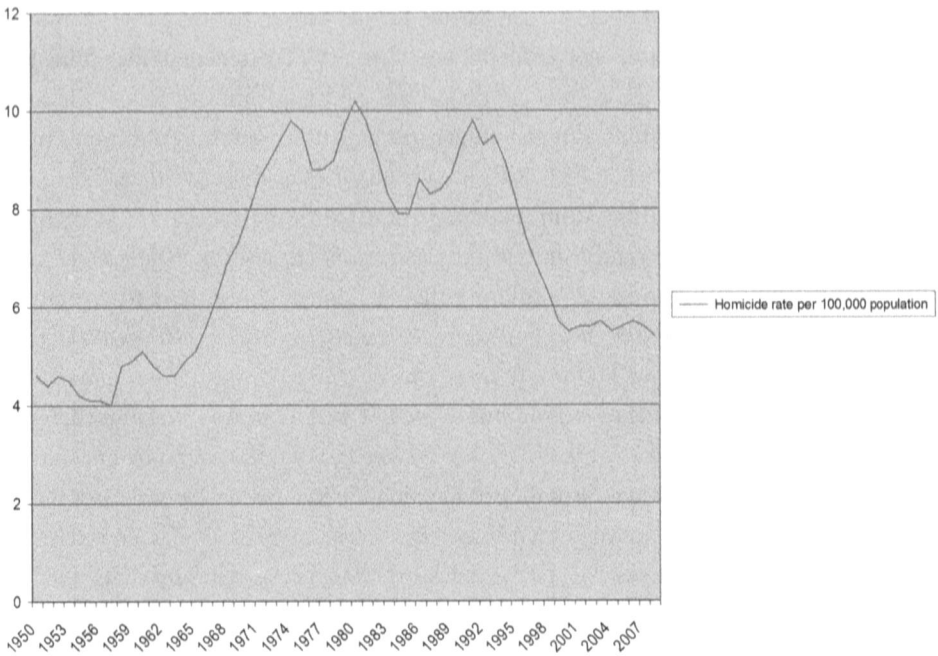

Figure 9.1 Homicide Rate Per 100,000 Population

$200 billion a year. Government expenditures on police and the criminal justice system cost at least another $75 billion. Even greater than the financial cost of crime is the toll it takes on quality of life. Perhaps one can be happy anywhere, but it is much easier to be happy in a safe and orderly environment than in an unsafe and disorderly one.

In this chapter, the question of central interest is: What public policies are useful for reducing crime? We begin with a brief discussion of measures of crime. These indicators of crime are of critical importance because policy evaluation is based on these measures. Understanding these measures, as well as their strengths and weaknesses, will help us to navigate policy evaluations. With this foundation laid, we turn to the central theoretical question: Why do some individuals choose to break the law? We present a general theory of criminal activity. Broadly stated, crime is a way to satisfy desires, whether they be financial or psychic. Armed with a general understanding of why crime occurs, we examine several strategies for reducing crime. We discuss these strategies and specific policies that flow out of them. In particular, we examine how well these strategies account for the variation in the homicide rate (see Figure 9.1).

Measuring Crime

In the United States, there are two major sources of crime data: the FBI's **Uniform Crime Report (UCR)** and **National Crime Victimization Surveys (NCVS)**. Since 1930, the FBI has generated an annual Uniform Crime Report with data voluntarily submitted to it by about 17,000 local law enforcement agencies. To generate the data, law enforcement agencies are given specific definitions and guidelines to follow. Because all agencies are nominally following the exact same guidelines and the data comes from official government agencies, the UCR is often thought of as objective data. This does not imply that the UCR is free from measurement error. Some agencies may interpret the FBI's guidelines differently or not report certain crimes for political reasons. Changes in administrative focus within a police district may also lead to significant fluctuations in reported crime data. For example, the city of Chicago showed a significant change in crime when a new police chief took over in 1961. Such large changes due to adjustments in administrative procedures are not very common, but they are still possible. Users of this, and any other data, always need to examine carefully the context around any significant changes. Another reason that UCR data may be imperfect is that some victims of crime do not report a crime to the police. Initially, the UCRs had better coverage of large, urban areas. The farther back in time one goes with this data, the less representative it is for the whole country. Over time, smaller municipalities have increased their reporting and the UCR now provides a more accurate picture of crime in the United States. However, as noted, the UCR is not free from error.

The National Crime Victimization Survey, managed by the Bureau of Justice Statistics, is an alternative measure of crime that has been used since 1972. The NCVS is a large survey of randomly selected American households regarding crime victimization. Household respondents are asked to report if they have been victims of assault, burglary, larceny, motor vehicle theft, rape, or robbery. NCVS surveys typically find more crime than what is reported in the UCR. Undoubtedly, some of the difference is due to crimes not being reported and some of it results from misreporting on the survey. The last point highlights the central concern with victim surveys: there is no independent check on what is reported. Nevertheless, most research suggests that there is not a significant degree of lying in these surveys.

General Demographic Characteristics of Victims and Criminals of Homicide

Crime is much more likely to strike some people than others. Table 9.1 shows homicide rates for the 1970s, 1980s, 1990s, and 2000s according to different age groups, races, and genders. These data are for homicides, but other crimes, such as property crimes, show similar patterns. As we see in the table, black males, particularly those between the ages of 18 and 24, are much more likely to be murdered than any other group. White women over 25 years of age are the least likely to be murdered. From this table, we can also discern that men in general are more likely to be murdered than women, and younger people are significantly more likely to be killed than older people.

Table 9.1 Who Is Killed? Average Homicide Rates Per 100,000 People, by Age, Race, and Gender, 1970s–2000s

	White Male			Black Male			White Female			Black Female		
Decade	14–17	18–24	25+	14–17	18–24	25+	14–17	18–24	25+	14–17	18–24	25+
1970s	11.6	23.3	9.5	75.8	181.8	98.8	1.2	2.6	1.4	8.8	28.5	20.2
1980s	12.5	25.3	9.7	84.4	180.8	79.4	1.2	2.5	1.3	6.9	21.5	13.5
1990s	19.7	31.0	7.2	169.4	296.0	54.0	1.4	2.5	0.9	8.0	16.4	7.2
2000s	8.3	24.0	5.5	60.3	199.8	39.5	1.0	2.2	0.8	4.0	11.4	4.0

Note: Data for the 1970s is 76–79. Data for 2000s is 00–05.

Table 9.2 Who Kills? Average Percentage of Homicides, by Age, Race, and Gender

	White Male			Black Male			White Female			Black Female		
Decade	14–17	18–24	25+	14–17	18–24	25+	14–17	18–24	25+	14–17	18–24	25+
1970s	3.9	13.6	23.7	4.0	14.8	24.8	0.4	1.5	4.0	0.5	2.5	6.3
1980s	3.5	13.9	26.3	4.2	15.6	23.8	0.3	1.3	3.8	0.3	1.9	4.9
1990s	4.9	14.1	21.2	7.9	23.7	19.0	0.4	1.1	3.0	0.4	1.3	3.1
2000s	3.1	15.1	23.2	4.5	23.3	21.3	0.4	1.3	3.5	0.3	1.4	2.6

Note: Data for the 1970s is 76–79. Data for 2000s is 00–05.

Table 9.2 shows demographic information about those who commit murder. The age group that kills the most are young people between the ages of 18 and 24, and men commit nearly 90 percent of all murders. White men over the age of 25 and black men aged between 18 and 24 commit the most murders of any group. In the next sections, we discuss factors that increase the likelihood of committing a homicide, and, conversely, policies that can reduce crime.

9.2 Why Do Individuals Engage in Crime?

Individuals engage in crime for reasons stemming from both nature and nurture. Those with mental illness are particularly likely to run afoul of the law (Lamb and Weinberger 1998). Others are raised in environments that encourage law-breaking. Some view criminal activity as an opportunity to "get ahead" financially. Some view it as a rite of passage or way to enter a social club (i.e. a gang). Criminal activity is a complex blend of economic, expressive, personal, and social factors. Its complexity notwithstanding, we will shed some light on general policies that usually affect the choice to break the law.

In a seminal article, the Nobel Prize winner Gary Becker (1968) argued that crime is a function of (1) the punishment associated with being arrested and convicted, (2) the probability of being arrested and convicted, and (3) the return or benefit from crime, which is also weighed by the probability of obtaining the returns. We should note that Becker's focus on benefits and costs does not imply that there is not a social dimension to criminal activity. What Becker's framework does is clarify that social factors, like attaining social prestige or social disapproval, and emotional rewards are benefits and costs just like material rewards and punishments. Non-pecuniary benefits of this sort are referred to as **psychic rewards**.

An Expected Utility Model of Crime

As discussed in Chapter 7, the expected utility of a choice is the probability of an outcome multiplied by the utility of an outcome summed across all possible outcomes of a choice. At a general level, we can represent the expected utility (EU) of a choice in the following way:

$$ExpectedUtility = \sum_{i=1}^{n} P(Outcome)i * U(Outcome)i$$

Where P equals probability of an outcome, U equals utility, and utility is a function of benefits minus costs. Many choices may usefully be summarized by two outcomes. This yields

$$ExpectedUtility = P(Outcome_1) {}^*U(Outcome_1) + P(Outcome_2) {}^*U(Outcome_2)$$

Analogously, the expected utility for a choice to commit a crime is:

$$ExpectedUtility\ (Crime) = Probability_{Not\ Caught} {}^*Utility_{Not\ Caught} + Probability_{Caught} {}^*Utility_{Caught}$$

To explain choices, we need to compare the expected utility of one option against the expected utility of another option. The decision-maker chooses the option with the greatest expected utility. Here, we want to compare the expected utility of not committing a crime with the expected utility of committing a crime. For convenience, set the expected utility for not committing a crime equal to zero.

$$ExpectedUtility\ (no\ crime) = ExpectedUtility\ (crime)$$
$$0 = Probability_{Not\ Caught} {}^*Utility_{Not\ Caught} + Probability_{Caught} {}^*Utility_{Caught}$$

This simple set-up leads to the following conclusions. First, anything that increases the first two terms ($Probability_{Not\ Caught}$ or $Utility_{Not\ Caught}$) makes the right-hand side greater than the left and therefore makes crime a more attractive approach. This is because the first term is a probability and all probabilities are non-negative, and the second term is the utility of not getting caught and is presumably utility enhancing and positive. Second, anything that increases the second two terms ($Probability_{Caught}$ or $Utility_{Caught}$) makes the right-hand side smaller and therefore makes crime a less attractive approach. This is because, even though the first term is a probability and is non-negative, the second term representing the utility of getting caught will enter this equation as a negative (since getting caught detracts from utility). More specifically, as a person believes it is more likely that they will get away with a crime ($Probability_{Not\ Caught}$ increases), they are more likely to choose crime. As a person believes that a crime is more valuable ($Utility_{Not\ Caught}$ increases), they are more likely to choose crime. Additionally, as a person believes that being caught committing a crime is very bad ($Utility_{Caught}$), they are less likely to choose crime. The following example illustrates these general conclusions.

Imagine you are late for class and cannot find any legal parking spaces. You have a choice, to park far away and be late to class, and suffer a penalty, –L, or to park illegally (do not break the law vs. break the law). The utility for being caught is the cost of the parking ticket, C. The utility for not being caught is, NC, the benefit you derive from attending class on time. The probability of not being caught is P and the probability of being caught is 1–P. If you decide to park legally, then you will do so far away and be late for class for certain. We can represent the expected utility of the "Parking Legally" choice as follows:

$$EU(ParkLegally) = Probability_{lateforclass} {}^*U_{lateforclass} = 1^*(-L) = -L$$

Notice that this outcome is certain. You know with certainty, probability=1, that if you pursue this option you will suffer a loss, –L, for being late. Now let's consider the expected utility of "Parking Illegally."

$$EU(ParkIllegally) = Probability_{Not\ Caught} {}^*Utility_{Not\ Caught} + Probability_{Caught} {}^*Utility_{Caught}$$

$$EU(Park\ Illegally) = P_{Not\ Caught} {}^*U_{Not\ Caught} + (1-P)_{Not\ Caught} {}^*U_{Caught}$$

$$EU(ParkIllegally) = P^*NC + (1-P)^* - C$$

We can see that the expected utility of parking illegally is driven by the probability of getting caught, the value of making it to class on time, NC, and the cost of the parking ticket, –C, if you are caught. If we set this equal to the Expected Utility(Park Legally), we get:

$$-L = P^*NC + (1-p)^*C$$

Under what conditions will it be worth parking illegally? The answer is when the expected utility on the right-hand side of the above equation (P*NC + (1–p)*C) is greater than –L. All else equal, if the cost of the parking ticket, C, is small to you, say $5, then you may well choose to park illegally. As the cost of the parking ticket increases – imagine it is $500 – then you are less likely to park illegally if all else is equal. Among other things, this explains why most people are less likely to park illegally in a handicapped spot than a non-handicapped spot; in the former, a ticket is more expensive.

Further, as the probability of being caught increases, you are less likely to park illegally. If you are able to sneak into a gated lot, you may believe your chances of receiving a ticket are lower and therefore are more likely to park illegally. In other words, you know that the parking officials concentrate most of their attention on non-gated lots.

Finally, if the utility of not being caught, L (attending class on time), is really high for you, then you are more likely to park illegally. Broadly speaking, the utility of not being caught is a function of the value you attach to the action minus any costs you incur from undertaking it. In our parking example, the utility of not being caught is a function of the value you attach to going to class that day. If you have an exam, then your utility for parking illegally and making it to class on time increases.

Prospect Theory and Crime

Another influential theory of choice is Prospect Theory. Prospect Theory incorporates aspects of human psychology into expected utility theory. Kahneman and Tversky (1979), the pioneers of Prospect Theory, put forward the following formula for the expected utility of a choice:

$$EU = \sum_{i=1}^{n} w(pi)v(xi)$$

This formula is very similar to the basic expected utility formula. The only differences are the addition of two new parameters, w and v. As before, p represents the probability for each possible outcome, i, and x_i represents each possible outcome. The parameter w is a weighting function, and the parameter v is a value function. Let's say more about the two new parameters. The value function, v, allows for deviation in utility from a reference point; it can vary by individuals. In other words, individuals may differ in the value, or utility, they assign to the status quo. Some people may like the status quo and have one value on v, while others dislike the status quo and have another value on v. Similarly, the weighting function, w, allows for variation across individuals in the probability, or weight, they assign to events. Some people, for example, may believe that a very unlikely event, like winning the lottery, is much more likely than it really is. Alternatively, one can think of the weighting function as capturing different attitudes toward risk. Some people are more risk acceptant than others, and this is a way to incorporate that knowledge about risk into an expected utility formula. In the context of crime, Prospect Theory suggests that people may have different reference points, and therefore different value functions and utility for a specific choice, and different attitudes toward risk.

Let's discuss our parking example in the context of Prospect Theory. If you park legally, you will be late but not suffer any fines. Your net utility is a loss of 1. If you park illegally, there is a 1 percent chance you will be caught, and if you are caught, your net utility will be –100 (the benefit of being on time minus the cost of the parking ticket). What do you do?

Now consider a different scenario. Your teacher does not penalize for being late. If you park legally, your net utility is 1. You do not lose anything from class and you are able to relax on your way to class. However, sometimes your teacher gives bonus points for those who show up on time. If you park illegally, you will make it to class on time and there is a 1 percent chance you will receive 100 bonus points. What do you do?

A majority of people tend to choose to park legally in the first scenario, while a majority tend to choose to park illegally in the second scenario. The reason for the different responses is that people tend to overweight low probability events. In the first scenario, they feel like they are in a domain of losses and act risk averse. In the second scenario, they feel like they are in a domain of gains and act risk acceptant.

In the context of crime, Prospect Theory suggests that those with fewer opportunities to succeed in life are more likely to be risk acceptant and opt for crime over the straight and narrow path. Next, we discuss factors affecting the values of these parameters in more detail.

Benefits and Costs of Criminal Success

Successful criminal action may produce some benefits for an individual. The primary benefit is the attainment of the criminal objective (e.g. acquiring a large amount of money from robbing a bank). In addition, there may be emotional (e.g. the short-term thrill associated with successfully undertaking a risky adventure) and social (e.g. prestige in a gang) benefits to crime. This does not mean crime pays. Successful criminal action produces costs for the perpetrator. These costs are primarily emotional. Again, we want to underscore that these costs materialize even if one is not caught; there are additional costs if one is caught, which we discuss in the next section.

One plausible explanation for how an individual assigns personal costs of successful criminal action may depend on his or her character. Character refers to a person's value system, which, in this context, can usefully be thought of as comprising two interconnected dimensions: rule-following and empathy. The more a person considers rule-following as central to their character, the less likely they are to break the law, all else being equal. For a strong rule-follower, breaking the law creates cognitive dissonance and entails an emotional cost. Empathy affects a person in a similar way. Empathy is the ability to "understand and share another person's experiences and emotions" (Merriam-Webster 2006). When we empathize strongly with another, we do not want anything negative or bad to happen to that person. Crimes often create a victim; in other words, crime often affects someone negatively. (Some crimes may be thought of as "victimless," like prostitution among consenting adults, gambling among consenting parties, and recreational drug use, although the claim that those crimes are victimless may be a source of disagreement among people.) Empathy, then, increases the cost of crime. More broadly, we can say that the cost of successful criminal action is guilt, a cost we impose on ourselves for doing something we believe to be wrong.

This discussion ignores individual calculations of whether a person considers the law just or does not consider the law just: Henry David Thoreau refused to pay his poll tax in 1846 because he detested slavery and, because taxes supported a government that allowed slavery, he refused to pay and accepted being jailed as a consequence of his refusal. He believed the law not to be just because it supported an unjust institution. In his essay *Civil Disobedience*, Thoreau carefully acknowledges that he accepts the government's right to assess taxes and is willing to pay the price by being jailed. As it happens, Thoreau expected to spend a long time in jail, but his relatives paid his fine and he was released after a night's stay. Thoreau did not appreciate their intercession, nor did he wish to support slavery. There are numerous situations in which people commit crimes from which they profit in some way – even if it is profiting by making a point – that do not reflect poorly on their character.

The character Raskolnikov in Dostoyevsky's novel *Crime and Punishment* illustrates how even a successful crime carries costs for the perpetrator. In the novel, Raskolnikov murders a mean, old pawnbroker and takes her money. He justifies his action by telling himself that he will do good with the pawnbroker's money and that the pawnbroker was not a pleasant person. Raskolnikov is not detected. However, he soon begins to suffer great guilt for his actions; in the language of our model, he pays a cost for the crime, even though he has not been arrested. Eventually, his anguish becomes so great that he turns himself in. Even when not caught, committing a crime punishes those who undertake such actions.

An understanding of character, particularly rule-following and empathy, helps us understand why many who steal are not poor. They typically do so with some sort of rationalization. They may persuade themselves that whoever owns what is being taken does not deserve it or that they will pay it back in the future. Common to these rationalizations is not appreciating how stealing harms others and oneself. It is in this sense that character is as central to understanding the appeal of crime as a person's life circumstances. Thinking about it from the opposite perspective may help. If a person believes that stealing is wrong and values a rule-following identity, the utility of committing crime decreases because, no matter what object is attained through the crime, there is an emotional cost.

A focus on character also helps explain why some commit the most horrible crimes, like murder. Murderers tend to have little empathy for their victim. This lack of empathy reduces the cost of a successful crime, thereby increasing the appeal of crime. A useful synonym for a person with little to no empathy is a sociopath. Sociopaths lack guilt for their crimes. It is no wonder that serial killers and mass murderers are, almost by definition, sociopaths. To deter sociopaths from committing crime, the probability of apprehension along with the penalty for being caught needs to increase. Sociopaths may suffer from mental illness or another disorder that induces sociopathic behavior. Before turning to those topics, we first address how a person's peer network affects the utility of crime.

While the object of crime and character receive significant attention, perhaps the most important factor affecting the overall utility of crime is a person's social context. Areas with a high crime rate make crime more appealing. In most cases, crime carries a social cost. However, when the number of criminals with whom one interacts increases, then the social cost of crime decreases. "Social interactions seem to create a sense of invulnerability and a willingness to violate social norms and take risks, as long as one is in the company of likeminded individuals. Bing [1991] quotes a young criminal, Bopete, as saying 'but when I'm with my homeboys, I don't think of dyin' never at all. Only when I'm alone'" (quoted in Glaeser *et al.* 1996: 511). The importance of social interactions on human behavior points to the role of gangs for understanding variation in crime across communities and time. We return to this point in the next section.

Once the costs of crime are factored in – fines, imprisonment, social ostracism, shame, and lost legal income – it is a rare individual who truly benefits from crime. Some factors, however, may make the benefits of crime more appealing. The first of these we already noted: the opportunity cost for that individual for engaging in crime versus legal employment. The less a person earns or the less likely they are to find a job, the more likely that person is to commit crime. This is not to say that all poor people commit crime. Most poor or unemployed people do not commit crime. However, poverty and unemployment increase the probability that a person will turn to crime. We even see this in countries' corruption levels; in low-income countries, public officials are more frequently found misusing public office for private gain.

In summary, the benefits of crime can be monetary, psychic, and social rewards connected with the crime. Depending on the individual, there may also be psychic or social costs to committing a crime and getting away with it. For example, even if a person is not caught, they may feel guilty about their actions, thereby decreasing the overall utility of committing a crime. We also noted that, in many cases, the social reward from crime is more important than any reward directly attached to the criminal enterprise. Although crime is an individual choice, the decision is influenced by a number of societal factors. These factors not only include the probability of finding employment and a person's amount of legal social capital, but also peer group.

Utility of Being Caught: Cost of Crime

Individuals who commit a crime experience three types of costs: punishment by the state, social costs, and economic opportunity costs. **Punishment by the state** represents the primary cost for one who is convicted of a crime. State punishments include fines, time in jail, time in prison, and capital punishment. An individual may also experience **social costs**, such as ostracism from a group or shame. Most public policies meant to curb crime focus on state sanctions, but social sanctions can be significant. Indeed, Nagin (1998) contends that social sanctions are a more important deterrent than imprisonment. As Aristotle postulated long ago, human beings are social animals, and this makes social sanctions especially significant.

For many people, **economic opportunity costs** are a more important deterrent than punishment or social costs. Economic opportunity costs are what a person gives up in legitimate income for the benefit associated with the crime. For example, a person could work at McDonald's and make minimum wage, $7.25 an hour.[2] In a twenty-hour week of work, he would bring home $145 minus taxes. Alternatively, an individual could try to make a living through crime, perhaps by selling illegal drugs. There is a significant amount of variation in how much money drug dealers make, but, for illustrative purposes let us assume that one could make $200 a week.[3] The opportunity cost of being a drug dealer is $145, the amount the person gives up in legitimate income by choosing not to work. Overall, then, we can say that selling drugs only makes the person about $55 dollars (the benefits minus the opportunity cost). Once you factor in the other costs of selling drugs (e.g. fines or time in prison), the little extra that can be made is hardly worth it.

Research indicates that economic opportunity costs exert a strong influence on criminal behavior. In reviewing this literature, McCarthy (2002: 426) observes that "rising wages explain a considerable amount of the decline in offending that occurs with age." That is, as people age, they usually make more money, which is one reason why older people are less likely to commit crimes. It does not pay very well, relative to

---

[2] This is the federal minimum wage in 2015. Twenty-nine states have higher minimum wages. Alabama has no minimum wage.

[3] Levitt and Venkatesh (2000) found that a gang of crack dealers in Chicago earned, on average, $11 an hour, about twice the minimum wage. Some "foot soldiers" made less, which motivated Dubner and Levitt to raise the provocative question, why do drug dealers live with their moms? The answer is that you can make more money as you progress through the ranks, with some gang leaders making thousands a month.

what they are able to make through legal employment. Further, research shows that the effect of legal employment on whether a person will continue to break the law or not outweighs a person's criminal history. There *could* be benefits to being caught committing a crime, but these would be minor, certainly relative to the benefits of committing a crime and not being caught.

Probability of Conviction

For deterring crime, what is even more important than actual punishment is a person's perception that they will be caught and convicted. Summarizing a number of research studies, McCarthy (2002: 425) notes that: "The results point to large deterrent effects emanating from the certainty of punishment (number of convictions over the number of arrests), and smaller, generally insignificant effects from the severity of sanctions (average sentence length)." If individuals think they will not be caught and convicted, then a harsh sentence associated with a crime has little influence on their behavior. As Becker (1968: 176) notes, those with judicial experience have understood this point for centuries. This implies that policies that increase the likelihood of apprehension and conviction may be more important for reducing crime than policies that increase the fine or jail time of a crime. Policies that increase the probability of apprehension and conviction include more police, better policing strategies, effective neighborhood associations, and more judges. We discuss these factors in more detail in the next section.

More generally, the attractiveness of crime increases as educational and social capital decrease and criminal capital increases. **Capital** is a resource used in pursuit of an end. The more of the resource one has, the better able one is to pursue the end. Perhaps the primary form of capital is money or wealth. If a business has a large amount of **financial capital**, it has a lot of money that it can invest to improve its product. In addition to money, the other common forms of capital are human and social. **Human capital** is an individual's skill set. Not all individuals are equally productive. Individuals with better skill sets are more productive than others. Of course, "better skill sets" depends on the context. For manual labor positions, the desired skill set may well be physical strength. For most white-collar positions, the desired skill set usually revolves around problem-solving skills. Normally, human capital is a function of education, job training, and health. That is, individuals with more education are more productive because they are better problem-solvers and can perform more specialized jobs; work experience naturally increases a person's ability to do a particular job, and healthy individuals are more productive than unhealthy people.

Social capital may be defined as social networks that have value (Putnam 2000). Value is an intentionally broad concept, as social capital is important in many contexts. Building on Tocqueville, Putnam (2000) thinks of social capital primarily as membership in groups – even groups as casual and recreational as bowling leagues.

As public associations increase, communal ties increase; these are a key factor for building and sustaining democracy. Knack and Keefer (1997) contend that social capital, in the form of trust and cooperative norms, is essential for economic growth. Coleman (1988) theorizes that social capital is a function of family structure and that it increases human capital, in the form of educational attainment.

Increases in human and social capital usually decrease criminal activity. More educated individuals tend to make more money and are better acculturated in society, both of which reduce the incentive to break the law. Individuals from stable two-parent families (social capital in the Coleman sense) are also less likely to offend. Membership in many public associations increases the social cost of criminal activity, thereby reducing crime. Human and social capital accumulation does not necessarily reduce crime. It depends on the specific skills a person is developing or associations of which they are members. That is, **criminal capital** is human or social capital that enhances a person's ability to profit from illegal activity. It is the criminal knowledge and skill set. One form of criminal capital is the number of people a person knows who are criminals. As a person becomes personally familiar with more criminals, they acquire more knowledge of how to conduct crime and may even believe that the social cost for engaging in criminal activity decreases. Supportive research indicates "illegal income increases with the number of connections with other offenders" (McCarthy 2002: 428). Finally, low social capital in the form of not trusting society to treat you fairly can significantly increase the choice to offend (de Mesquita and Cohen 1995). Lack of trust in the government and society does not make you commit crime, but it does reduce the deterrent effect of punishment.

9.3 Strategies to Reduce Crime

In the previous section, we explained how the decision to offend is a function of the benefits of crime, the costs of crime, and the probability of experiencing the benefits and costs. That discussion suggests a number of strategies, or policies, for reducing crime. We can classify most strategies into one of three categories: strategies that aim to reduce the benefits of crime, those that increase the cost of crime, and those that increase the probability of experiencing the cost of crime. We now turn to an examination of strategies in each of these categories.

Strategies that Reduce the Benefits of Crime

Strategies that aim to reduce the benefits of crime focus primarily on economic advancement (e.g. increasing the minimum wage) and education. Each operates by improving an individual's ability to gain wealth and happiness through means besides crime.

Economy

When it comes to understanding why some areas have more crime than others or why crime is higher in some decades than others, the condition of the economy comes to mind. The underlying argument is that crime is a way to make money and those with less wealth, or a sudden need for more money, have a greater incentive to turn to crime. Put differently, one can make money through work or through crime; if you do not have a job or cannot make very much through work, then you are more likely to turn to crime.

Some strategies or public policies that are intended to reduce crime by reducing the economic benefits of crime center on increasing economic growth and/or increasing the minimum wage. Increasing economic growth is a public policy proposal with which few are likely to disagree. Like many good things, it is much easier said than done. In this chapter, our focus is on crime; in Chapter 5 we discussed policies that affect economic growth.

Economic circumstances affect crime because the **opportunity cost of crime** is smaller for those with a smaller wage or who are unemployed. Kelly (2000) shows that poverty is a robust predictor of property crime: areas with greater amounts of poverty have significantly higher levels of property crime, even after controlling for population density. This is the case regardless of single-parent rearing, education levels, unemployment rate, the number of police in the area, and other factors. Grogger (1998) also provides evidence to support the opportunity cost hypothesis. He finds that the decrease in youth wages in the 1970s and 1980s was associated with an increase in crime. Further, research has shown that black males commit more crime than white males. Given what we just noted about the opportunity cost of crime, it follows to ask if this difference is partly a function of different earnings. Indeed, Grogger (1998: 784) finds that the black–white wage gap accounts for about "26% of the racial differential in crime participation rates."

The opportunity cost argument is also relevant for explaining why young people commit more crime than older people. Wages increase with age, for most people. Therefore, crime is less appealing as one gets older. Yet another implication of the opportunity cost argument is that **recidivism**, repeat offending, should decrease if the parolee is able to attain legal employment. Indeed, "work appears to be a turning point in the life course of criminal offenders over 26 years old. Offenders who are provided even marginal employment opportunities are less likely to reoffend than those not provided such opportunities" (Uggen 2000: 542).

While the wage rate and amount of poverty in an area are strong influences on crime, one economic factor that only has a minor effect is the employment rate (Gould *et al.* 2002; Cantor and Land 1985). This is best seen by examining the drop in crime in the 1990s. Besides being a time when crime declined, the 1990s was also a period of economic growth and decreased unemployment. Unemployment was about

6.8 percent at the beginning of the decade and had declined to around 4.8 percent by the end of it. Based on this significant reduction in unemployment, we might think that the unemployment hypothesis accounts for the significant decline in crime in the 1990s. However, summarizing the research on unemployment and crime, Levitt (2004: 171) writes, "the observed 2 percentage point decline in the US unemployment rate between 1991 and 2001 can explain an estimated 2% decline in property crime (out of an observed drop of almost 30%), but no change in violent crime or homicide." Unemployment seems to matter less than other economic factors because of unemployment insurance and the fact that most people who lose a job find another one before their economic situation turns dire.

It is also important to bear in mind that the economy indirectly influences crime. A strong economy can increase government revenue, government revenue allows for the hiring of more police, and more police can lead to less crime. To the extent that more police contributes to less crime (in the next section we note that this is the case), the influence of economic factors on crime may be quite substantial after all.

Education

Because crime is more appealing to those who earn less money, another strategy for reducing crime is to increase education. This is because education, by increasing a person's human capital, increases earning potential. Education, then, increases the opportunity cost of crime because education increases the ability to earn more money legally. Education may also increase patience and risk aversion, traits that militate against violating the law. Indeed, those with a high school education are much less likely to commit crimes (Lochner and Moretti 2004; Lochner 2004). Freeman (1996) shows that over half of those in prison have less than a high school education. Given this strong relationship between more education and less crime, policies that encourage students to stay in high school are some of the most effective strategies for reducing crime. Policies that promote marriage are one example; students are much less likely to drop out of high school if raised by two parents. Kelly (2000) shows that the factor with the most substantive influence on committing crime is whether a youth comes from a one-parent family. Matsueda *et al.* (2006) also show a strong relationship between family structure and the probability that a young person will commit crime.

Strategies that Decrease the Probability of Attaining Criminal Benefits

To decrease the probability of attaining criminal benefits, it is important to decrease criminal capital and anything that makes it easier for one to succeed at attaining criminal objectives. Two strategies for reducing the probability of attaining the benefits of crime include reducing the influence of gangs and modifying gun control laws. We address the latter at the end of the chapter.

Peer pressure is a powerful influence on behavior. Some peer groups encourage socially acceptable behavior (e.g. following the rules, working, studying for classes, etc.). Other peer groups encourage less socially acceptable behavior. Groups that encourage criminal behavior are referred to as gangs. The existence of gangs helps explain the significant variation in crime across otherwise similar neighborhoods. A poor neighborhood with a gang presence sees much more crime than a poor neighborhood without a gang presence. How, then, does one reduce the influence of gangs in a neighborhood?

Esbensen *et al.* (1999) report that youth join gangs for the following reasons: protection, fun, respect, money, and because a friend was in the gang. To reduce gang influence, then, it is important to improve public safety, cultivate rule-following and empathy in individuals, and improve economic conditions. More specifically, it is important to increase police presence in gang-affected neighborhoods, encourage school-based life skills programs, promote community organizing efforts, and support anything that encourages stable two-parent families. Gangs are much less likely to thrive in such environments (Wyrick 2006). When gangs do not thrive, criminal capital decreases; when criminal capital decreases, the probability of attaining criminal benefits decreases; when the probability of attaining benefits decreases, crime decreases.

Strategies That Increase the Cost of Crime

Strategies that increase the cost of crime include relaxing gun control laws, enforcing capital punishment, increasing sentencing (more people behind bars), and implementing public education programs about the harms and dangers associated with crime (particularly drug use).

Tough-on-Crime Policies

One approach to reducing crime is to be tough on crime. Being tough on crime typically entails implementing policies that make it easier to put people in prison and/or policies that increase sentence length.

The imprisonment argument of crime reduction has two components. First, imprisonment is thought to reduce crime through deterrence. As imprisonment rates increase, potential criminals hypothetically develop a stronger belief that they may be apprehended and sent to jail. Therefore, they should be less likely to commit crimes. Second, the imprisonment argument is thought to reduce crime by "draining the pool." With more people behind bars, there are fewer people to commit crimes. Crime data indicates that most people do not commit any serious crimes, some people only commit crimes rarely, and others commit crime frequently; imprisonment theory reasons that if you imprison someone guilty of committing a couple of crimes, you are probably incarcerating someone who is likely to commit more crime.

One such tough-on-crime imprisonment strategy is "**Three Strikes and You're Out.**" **Three strikes laws** require judges to give a mandatory extended sentence to anyone convicted of three serious offenses. Currently, twenty-four states enforce this and other habitual offender laws. The general theory behind these laws is that they send a signal to potential criminals, especially those who have committed two crimes, that there will be a high cost to criminal activity. These laws aim to reduce recidivism, or repeat offending, by putting people in prison. Three strikes laws intentionally take away a judge's discretion, for such discretion reduces the clarity of the signal that the public wants to send to criminals. However, critics argue that all offenses are not equal and that it is the *job* of a judge to examine the circumstances of an offense. Critics also suggest that it makes little sense to sentence every third offender to a long-term imprisonment because most people end criminal activity by their late 20s.

By equating dissimilar offenses, three strikes laws have led to some controversy. For example, in California, drug possession and shoplifting are technically on a par with murder and rape under the terms of the three strikes law. This has led to some individuals receiving a life sentence without the possibility of parole for committing three non-violent offenses (Bazelon 2010).[4]

Do tough-on-crime policies reduce crime? On the one hand, "the evidence linking increased punishment to lower crime rates is very strong" (Levitt 2004: 178). The US prison population started to increase in the 1980s and rose steadily throughout the 1990s (although it has leveled off in recent years). After analyzing this and other factors, Levitt (2004) concludes that the increase in imprisonment contributed to about a 12 percent drop in violent crime and an 8 percent decrease in property crime. On the other hand, Corman and Mocan (2005) find that the increase in prisoners from New York City accounts for only a 1 to 2 percent reduction in crime in that city during the 1990s. Western (2006: 185) also finds that the effect of tough-on-crime policies on reducing crime is small. Given the economic cost of jailing people, it is far from clear that these policies are worth it.

Truth-in-sentencing (TIS) laws, encouraged by the 1994 Crime Act, are another type of tough-on-crime policy. A **truth-in-sentencing** (TIS) law requires that a person serve at least 85 percent of their sentence. To date, these laws only cover violent offenses. The first thing we should note about these laws is that they are efforts by the principal, the public, to reduce agent discretion. In this case, the agents that are being corralled are parole boards and judges. In restricting these officials' ability to reduce sentences, even if the reasons are noble, the principal minimizes what they perceive as the agent's morally hazardous behavior. With that noted, a second aim of these laws is

---

[4] In *Ewing v. California*, the Supreme Court upheld the constitutionality of three strikes laws.

to reduce crime through deterrence. Research indicates that truth-in-sentencing laws do, in fact, reduce violent crime (Shepherd 2002). Moreover, other agents, namely police and prosecutors, see the signal the principal is sending with these laws and increase their efforts to arrest and prosecute offenders (Shepherd 2002). As it becomes clear to potential offenders that they will not be released after serving only a small part of their sentence, they are deterred from committing a crime covered by a TIS law. Unfortunately, someone bent on crime does not easily desist from all criminal activity. Although TIS laws reduce the amount of crime covered by the law, other types of crime, namely property crime, increase. That is, when a TIS law is enacted, some portion of criminals substitute property crime for violent crime. As we have noted throughout, public policies always involve trade-offs.

Two consequences of three strikes and truth-in-sentencing laws have been that serial, non-violent criminals get sentenced to crimes and spend years in state and county jails, which contributes to enormous numbers of incarcerated persons and high spending on prisons. Benson *et al.* (1995) show that language in the 1984 federal legislation that attended the Just Say No campaign enabled police agencies to confiscate property that was used in drug crimes, including cars, homes, and other valuable items that they could then sell to provide support for their agencies. Their cross-sectional study of arrests and sentencing in Florida during the early 1990s revealed a police focus on drug arrests rather than others – like other property crimes and some violent crimes – because police shifted their efforts to policing drugs in order to gain the benefits of forfeited property. Kuziemko and Levitt (2004) also report that the sentencing laws of the 1980s led to a large increase of imprisonments for drug crimes during the 1980s to 2000s, which resulted in shorter sentences for property and some violent crimes and, while the price of drugs rose as a result of the harsher sentences, the net cost of the intensified drug policing did not provide comparable benefits. The regression results in Table 9.3 show that each increase of a unit of the log of the

Table 9.3 The Impact on Violent and Property Crime of Imprisoning Drug Offenders Versus Those Committing Other Types of Crimes

	Violent Crime	Property Crime
Logged per capita Prison population	−0.103*	-0.248*
	(0.033)	(0.026)
Observations	612	612
Other covariates?	Yes	Yes
R^2	0.98	0.95

Note: * = $p<05$, two-tailed.
Source: Excerpted from Kuziemko and Levitt 2004, Table 3, p. 2058

population incarcerated for drug offenses reduced the size of the logged per capita prison population jailed for violent crime 0.10 percentage points (10 percent) and the size of the logged per capita property crime population by nearly 0.25 percentage points. In other words, as more people overall have been incarcerated, primarily for drug offenses, there has been a reduction of those incarcerated for violent and property crime. This suggests a crowding-out effect. Those in charge of the criminal justice system have a finite number of prison cells in which they can place people. If they are forced to place more drug offenders in prison, then some others will not end up in prison.

Public Education Programs

One of the most important strategies for increasing the cost of crime is persuading people that crime is a bad choice. It is helpful to remind people that there are not only potential financial costs, prison costs, and harm done to others, but also that crime makes you unpopular or uncool. Public education programs can highlight the harm associated with particular choices, such as drinking and driving, both to educate and to stigmatize particular choices. Through this combination of knowledge and stigmatization, these programs increase the cost of crime.

One famous public education campaign to reduce crime was Nancy Reagan's "Just Say No" campaign. In this case, drug use, which often leads to additional crimes, was targeted. Shortly after becoming First Lady, Nancy Reagan was asked by an elementary school student what to do if offered drugs. She responded, "Just say no." Soon, Just Say No clubs were appearing around the country. Some observers ascribe Nancy Reagan's efforts, as well as other public education campaigns, to a decline in drug use in the 1980s (Benze 2005). Other observers agree that illicit drug use has declined overall, and attribute much of that change to public education campaigns (but not necessarily "Just Say No"). However, in the years between 1990 and 2010, the use of marijuana among eighth graders increased, as it did among high school and college students, and the rate of cigarette smoking increased dramatically among eighth grade, high school, and college-age people (Johnston et al. 2011). The use of illegal drugs other than marijuana did lessen between 1997 and 2010, however, and researchers attribute that to longer-term messages indicating the dangers of drugs (Johnston et al. 2011).

Not surprisingly, illegal drug use contributes to additional illegal activity. Crimes increased greatly in the 1980s. Some observers claim that one of the primary causes of the 1980s crime increase was crack cocaine (Grogger and Willis 2000). Crack is a form of the stimulant drug cocaine that can be smoked. It is highly addictive and inexpensive. Crack cocaine was popular with males under the age of 25, and especially black males. In the mid 1980s, men committing homicides, particularly black males younger than 25, increased significantly – along with crack cocaine use. Goldstein et al. (1997) estimate that about 25 percent of all homicides in New York City in 1988 were related to the use of crack cocaine. Rather than being driven by crimes committed by crack users ("crackheads"), who more often would resort to property crimes like theft than to violent crime, a research panel from the US Sentencing Commission describes the violent behavior as a function of the creation of a "jittery" black market for the drug, a market that was characterized by rapid shifts in control and a preponderance of young dealers who were prone to violence. Crack cocaine became less popular in the 1990s, and the homicide rate for young males declined (Levitt 2004: 181).

While Nancy Reagan's "Just Say No" campaign succeeded in being a well-known catch phrase, there is no evidence that it produced lasting effects on the likelihood of its target population – children – choosing whether to use drugs. Mrs. Reagan's campaign consisted solely of her pronouncement in 1982 that a child should "just say no" if someone offered drugs. A series of poorly devised policies emerged from that utterance, and those policies, because of political popularity, gained legitimacy over policies that work, like those that involve long-term involvement with at-risk people. The Drug Abuse Resistance Education (DARE) program is one example of a public education effort aimed at reducing crime. Most rigorous research on DARE as it existed from its creation in 1983 until 2008 indicates that it is not effective. The DARE model is to appeal to authority figures, typically parents, teachers, and a DARE police officer assigned to an elementary school, and the behavior is to tell children that "drugs are bad" (Mr. Garrison from "South Park" is modeled on a DARE counselor), give them a t-shirt that is fitted for an adult (a shirt that will almost certainly be worn ironically by a person in high school or college), and declare a success. To successfully teach students to avoid drugs requires a longer-term investment than DARE. DARE has remained in schools despite being demonstrated to be ineffective largely due to successful lobbying by the interest group that supports it. In 2001, the Surgeon General of the United States labeled it as a program that "does not work."[5]

Birkeland *et al.* (2005) explain DARE's continued existence despite a long record of being revealed as a failure in meeting its stated goal of reducing self-reported drug use among the graduates of its elementary school programs as a function of the program's providing benefits that are not measured in evaluations. DARE was created in 1983 by the Los Angeles Police Department. The LAPD plan was for (usually) fifth or sixth grade students to meet with a police officer for one hour per week for one semester. During that time, the officer would inform them of the dangers of drugs, the risks and penalties of illegal drug use, and teach them methods for combatting peer pressure to use drugs. Birkeland and her co-authors (2005) argue that DARE continued to exist due to its having some salutary effects, mainly in having students meet with police officers. Beginning 2009, DARE revamped and provided a longer-term curriculum

[5] David Satcher, MD, PhD, Surgeon General of the United States, *Youth Violence: A Report of the Surgeon General* (Rockville, MD: Office of the Surgeon General (US), 2001), ch. 5, Prevention and Intervention, Box 5-2.

designed and taught by prevention specialists rather than by police officers, and the revised curriculum, which now involves students first in elementary and then in middle school, may improve the program's performance toward its stated goal of reduced drug use (Nordrum 2014).

Another public information program, Mother's Against Drunk Driving (MADD), has significantly increased the social cost of driving under the influence of alcohol and decreased the perceived benefit of doing so. The "Just Say No" campaign and MADD were both responses to new developments. New drugs are like new technologies: one cannot predict their creation or arrival. For this reason, public education campaigns will always be an important tool for combating crime.

Strategies That Increase the Probability of Experiencing the Cost of Crime

Strategies that increase the probability of experiencing the cost of crime include improving policing strategies and increasing the amount of police.

Policing Strategies: Fixing Broken Windows

In a celebrated article, James Q. Wilson and George L. Kelling (1982) argued that crime had increased because policing strategies had changed away from foot patrols and community control. The theory has become known as the **Broken Windows theory**.

They argue that when police foot patrols increase, the amount of fear a typical citizen feels decreases. People tend to feel more secure knowing that police are around. In addition, more foot patrols lead to higher levels of public order. This is the key benefit of foot patrols, for "disorder and crime are usually inextricably linked" (Wilson and Kelling 1982: 2). Breaking this link, then, is the key to reducing crime. They explain it this way: "Social psychologists and police officers tend to agree that if a window in a building is broken and is left unrepaired, all the rest of the windows will soon be broken ... one unrepaired broken window is a signal that no one cares, and so breaking more windows costs nothing" (Wilson and Kelling 1982: 2). Similarly, the presence of graffiti or panhandlers can signal that no one cares and the police are not around. In brief, to reduce crime, the Broken Windows theory advocates targeting minor offenses.

The Broken Windows theory has attracted much attention. It advances an intuitive argument for reducing crime, and many police chiefs and mayors have used it successfully. In 1990, William Bratton took charge of New York City's Transit Police. He implemented policies based on Wilson and Kelling's theory. He ended lax policies on fare dodgers and implemented mandatory background checks for every individual who was arrested. When Rudy Giulani was elected mayor in 1993, he applied the Broken Windows theory citywide. Crime dropped greatly in New York City in the

1990s, and Giuliani publicly credits the Broken Windows theory for it. "We have made the 'Broken Windows' theory an integral part of our law enforcement strategy. This theory says that the little things matter ... Obviously, murder and graffiti are two vastly different crimes. But they are part of the same continuum, and a climate that tolerates one is more likely to tolerate the other".[6]

Although Giuliani credits the theory for New York City's drop in crime, there are those who remain skeptical. The primary argument against him is that crime dropped in all major American cities during the 1990s and not all of these cities implemented a Broken Windows policing strategy (Levitt 2004). Donohue and Levitt (2001) and Levitt (2004) also contend that abortion is a central cause of the drop in crime across America in the 1990s; New York City may have experienced a larger decrease in crime than other cities because it had a higher abortion rate than most of the country. We will discuss this explanation in more depth in the next section. Finally, Levitt notes that New York City significantly increased its police force during the 1990s. This suggests that the drop in crime may be a result of more police rather than a different policing strategy. In summary, the three arguments against the Broken Windows explanation for New York City's crime decrease in the 1990s are that: (1) other cities also experienced a drop in crime; (2) abortion is the primary causal factor; and (3) more police contributed to the decline. Sampson and Raudenbusch (1999) note that disorder may not cause more crime, but may be caused by the same forces that cause crimes. If this is the case, then Broken Windows policing will not be effective, which is what they conclude in their research.

Corman and Mocan (2005) find much more support for the Broken Windows theory. First, they contend that although the Broken Windows strategy may not account for *all* cities' decrease in crime, this does not mean that it does not account for *any* city's decrease in crime. Corman and Mocan analyze New York City's crime data in the 1990s and find that measures for the Broken Windows theory are a significant influence on that city's decline in crime. Second, Corman and Mocan control for the size of the teenage population and still find support for the Broken Windows theory. Finally, while the Broken Windows strategy does not necessarily require more police, they find that in most cases it will lead to more police being hired. Foot patrols are labor intensive, which is part of the reason why law enforcement agencies have moved away from them.

Harcourt and Ludwig (2006) offer a novel approach to evaluating the Broken Windows theory. They examine data from the US Department of Housing and Urban Development's (HUD) Moving to Opportunity (MTO) program. MTO is a program that moves low-income families from public housing communities with high crime to

---

[6] Rudy Giuliani, "The Next Phase of Quality of Life: Creating a More Civil City," speech given on February 24, 1998, available online at www.nyc.gov/html/records/rwg/html/98a/quality.html.

communities with less crime and disorder. If the Broken Windows theory is correct, then we would expect that individuals moved from high disorder neighborhoods to low disorder neighborhoods should commit fewer crimes than before they were moved. Harcourt and Ludwig (2006) do not find support for this hypothesis.

More Police

Police are law enforcement agents. Through their presence and work, they aim to stop and deter crimes, thereby providing order to a community and enhancing the common good. Following this notion, when the number of police in an area increases, the probability of criminal success should decrease. Concerns about **endogeneity**, however, make it difficult to establish a causal relationship between more police and less crime.

In public policy, endogeneity means that a suggested cause may be the effect (i.e. X does not cause Y, but Y causes X) or caused by some other variable.[7] The problem is that if something is endogenous, then it is not a cause; causes are exogenous to the effect. For example, it is logical to hypothesize that higher campaign spending increases a candidate's expectations about winning an election. The problem is that expectations about winning likely influence how much one spends. In many situations, endogeneity is a chicken-and-egg question: Which comes first? More crime or more police? In other words, we tend to observe more police in areas with more crime. Indeed, in a survey of studies, Cameron (1988) finds that about 80 percent of the studies examining whether more police leads to less crime find either no relationship or the opposite relationship. Does this mean that the presence of more police causes more crime? Which is the cause of which? We want to know if more police reduce crime, or if expectations about crime affect the number of police.

The best way to address the question about the relationship between the number of police and the amount of crime is not through a cross-sectional analysis, but with an over-time analysis. Cross-sectional analyses compare crime rates in different areas at the same point in time. The implicit hypothesis is that areas with more police per capita will have lower rates of crime than areas with fewer police per capita. Above, we identified the problem with this approach: areas with more crime are likely to hire more police to address their crime problem. The studies that Cameron (1988) reviewed were primarily cross-sectional in design. It is not surprising that these studies failed to show a negative relationship between more police and crime. The question of interest is this: Does an increase in the number of police officers in an area lead to less crime?

---

[7] More generally, endogeneity means something determined within a system, where a system is a function. For example, y is a function of x and u. If x, the purported cause, is determined by something else in the system, y or u, then x is endogenous.

Levitt (1997) notes that the number of police officers in large US cities varies over time; in particular, in a mayoral or gubernatorial election year, there are more police officers on staff. The reason for this is obvious. Crime is often an important political issue, and incumbents want to demonstrate that they are aware of and responding to the public's concerns. "Given that police staffing increases in election years, then if police affect crime, a . . . relationship between election years and crime should emerge" (Levitt 1997: 278). This is precisely what Levitt finds for homicides. More police leads to a significant drop in the homicide rate. However, more police does not lead to a statistically significant decline in property crimes.

One limitation of Levitt's innovative study is that the data is aggregated at the annual level. We could have more confidence in this finding if we could examine daily fluctuations in the number of police and crime. Klick and Tabarrok (2005) undertook such a study. They note that when the Homeland Security Advisory System increases the alert level, Washington, DC increases the number of police on duty. If more police reduce crime, then we should observe fewer crimes on high alert days. After observing the daily variation in crime in Washington, DC, Klick and Tabarrok (2005: 271) conclude "that on high alert days, total crimes decrease by an average of seven crimes per day, or approximately 6.6%."

Other research employing advanced statistical procedures to isolate cause-and-effect also finds that an increase in the number of police in an area leads to a decrease in crime (Marvell and Moody 1996; Corman and Mocan 2000; Corman and Mocan 2005). Further, the increase in the number of sworn police officers appears to be one of the primary explanations for the significant drop in crime during the 1990s. Levitt (2004: 177) finds that in the 1990s the number of police officers per capita increased by about 14 percent. Corman and Mocan (2005: 260) find that New York City increased its police force by about 35 percent in the 1990s and that this increase accounted for about 20 percent of the reduction in motor vehicle theft and grand larceny.

Box 9.1 Wayward Police

In 2014 and 2015, several cases of police misconduct made national news. Principal–agent theory helps us understand why police sometimes misbehave. First, principal–agent theory tells us that the selection of agents – who becomes a police officer in this case – is essential to carrying out the principal's wishes. It is important, then, that those becoming police officers have excellent character and represent the public. Second, principal–agent theory tells us that agents are more likely to comply when they are more likely to be monitored. Body cameras should increase agent compliance. Research by Brehm and Gates (1997) tells us further that agent compliance depends critically on "peripheral" persuasion.

Box 9.1 (*cont.*)

By peripheral persuasion, they mean persuasion from one's peers. Agents learn from other agents "and look for 'social proof' for their own actions" (p. 48). This helps explain why we observe significant variation in police conduct across police precincts. Precincts take on a culture, a normal way of doing things, and it is difficult for a new principal to come in and change that culture when much of the interaction is between the agents. At the same time, it suggests that professionalization policies can, slowly, change cultures.

As we have noted previously, in public policy, there is almost always a trade-off. While more police may reduce crime, hiring more police costs money. In larger cities where the homicide rate is higher, it is likely that the benefits of more police would outweigh the cost.

Who Gets Punished?

Imagine that a person you know gets caught with a small amount of illegal narcotics at a concert. He is arrested, handcuffed, put into a bus with other people who have been caught with similar substances at the concert, is taken to jail, spends the night in jail, and is arraigned the next day and charged with felony possession of a controlled substance. If he is fortunate enough to have resources – his own, help from his parents, or help from his friends – he can post bond the next day and be released. If he cannot post bond, he may spend some time in jail as he awaits trial. (Bond is usually 10 percent of the bail amount; $5,000 bail would require paying a $500 bond, money that is put up by the bail bondsman and is not returned.) If he can afford a private attorney, he will hire one. An attorney usually gets a retainer of $1,500 to $2,000 to represent a person on a case like this. The attorney's billable rate is perhaps $150 to $300 per hour, depending on his or her skills and demands. If he cannot hire a private attorney, he may request a public defender. Public defenders typically have large caseloads and have little time to spend with each client.

How much money a person has to spend on their defense can have a large effect on how they are punished. If the person you know who's been arrested is fortunate enough to have money, or if his friends or parents have money, he can hire an attorney who has time to devote to his case. The attorney may be able to negotiate with the prosecutor for drug treatment and testing rather than a criminal charge (having a felony or misdemeanor conviction creates difficulties for people searching for jobs). If your friend does not have those resources, he may be more likely to end up with a felony charge, jail time, or probation. Having resources is a benefit to persons who are charged with crimes.

Research by Bruce Western (2006) illustrates in detail the problems that arise from being poor and black in the US criminal justice system. Western's research focuses on the rise of incarcerations that began following the 1970s crime crackdowns and were strengthened during the 1980s and 1990s with policies like three strikes and truth-in-sentencing. He finds that black men from cities are imprisoned disproportionate to their contribution to the population and that their imprisonment has created increasing problems for urban areas and black families. Western describes a string of relationships in which there is a crackdown on criminal behavior, more people are imprisoned, poor people are more likely to be imprisoned than non-poor people, black people are more likely to be poor than non-black people, more people in cities are arrested because of poor economic conditions and the clustering of black people in cities, the large number of young black men being in jail produces a situation with fewer men from cities having work experience or training, and the cycle continues. Thus, the ultimate pay-off of crime control is to create more need for jails as fewer people develop work skills, which leads them to resort to crime.

9.4 Abortion and Crime Rates

Most policies have multiple effects. Effects that are not directly intended are called **externalities**. They may be either positive (something people want more of) or negative (something people want less of). Evaluating public policies that have a positive direct effect and a negative externality, or a negative direct effect, and a positive externality is difficult as these effects are usually not commensurable. That is, the effects cannot typically be measured on the same scale. One policy that appears to have a positive externality with regard to crime is the legalization of abortion. In the following section, we are not taking a position on the abortion issue, only noting that research indicates a side effect of **abortion on crime**.

In a provocative, but carefully researched study, Donohue and Levitt (2001) contend that the legalization of abortion as a result of the 1973 *Roe v. Wade Supreme Court* decision is central to explaining the crime decline of the 1990s.[8] The theory behind this hypothesis is straightforward. Most abortions occur because the pregnancy is not wanted. Unwanted children are at a higher risk of committing crime. Therefore, abortion contributes to a reduction in crime.

What is the evidence for this theory? Most crimes are committed by young adults. For obvious reasons, very few crimes are committed by children aged 12 and under. If the abortion theory is correct, then (1) we should not observe any significant changes in crime between 1973 and 1985, (2) any changes that do occur should be connected

---

[8] Five states had legalized abortion in 1970: Alaska, California, Hawaii, New York, and Washington.

Table 9.4 Changes in Crime as a Function of Abortion Rates

Abortion frequency (ranked by effective abortion rate in 1997)	Effective abortions per 1,000 live births, 1997	% change in crime rate, 1973–1985			% change in crime rate, 1985–1997		
		Violent crime	Property crime	Murder	Violent crime	Property crime	Murder
Lowest	67.5	+31.8	+29.8	−21.1	+29.2	+9.3	+4.1
Medium	135.0	+28.8	+31.1	−19.7	+18.0	+2.2	−12.6
Highest	257.1	+32.2	+15.2	−9.7	−2.4	−23.1	−25.9

Note: Table 2 from Donohue and Levitt (2001: 400).

with the cohort born after the legalization of abortion, and (3) states with higher amounts of abortion should experience a greater decline in crime. With regard to the first point, we can note that the murder rate did not decline until after 1985. On a national basis, crime did not drop greatly until the mid 1990s. This would have been the time that the first cohort affected by *Roe v. Wade* would be 20 years old, the age at which most crimes take place (Cook and Laub 1998). Table 9.4 provides data on each of these points. First, as we just noted, there was not a decrease in crime between 1973 and 1985. However, if crime was dropping in this period, it would not mean that the abortion theory is wrong because it has no expectation for this time frame. We would simply need to observe a larger decrease in the subsequent period. Second, after 1985, we observe that crime rates began to drop. Third, and most importantly, regions that had the highest abortion rates saw the biggest drops in violence, property crime, and especially murder rates between 1985 and 1997. For better or worse, the legalization of abortion contributed significantly to the 1990s crime decline.

9.5 Capital Punishment

The primary arguments in support of **capital punishment** are twofold. First, capital punishment increases the cost of crime, thereby deterring criminal activity. The argument is that people commit crime in part because they do not think the consequences of being caught are very severe. Capital punishment is a severe penalty; therefore, if capital punishment exists, people should be deterred from committing crimes subject to this penalty. From a deterrence perspective, capital punishment is unique because it does not aim to deter an individual who committed a capital crime from committing more crimes; the individual is executed by the state. Rather, it aims to deter other people from committing similar crimes. Second, capital punishment is seen by some as a way to balance the scales of justice. It is retribution for a horrible crime. From this perspective, it does not matter if capital punishment deters crime, though of course that is the desired effect. What matters is that the execution provides some solace to the victim and signals society's sense of justice.

The primary arguments against capital punishment may also be grouped into two categories: (1) the sentence of capital punishment can be unfairly and incorrectly given out; and (2) capital punishment is not an effective deterrent to crime. Regarding the first argument, most research finds that "for crimes that are comparable, the death penalty is between three and four times more likely to be imposed in cases in which the victim is white rather than black" (Radelet and Borg 2000: 47). Regarding the effectiveness of capital punishment, critics point out that it does not deter additional crimes or homicides. Capital punishment is much more common in the South, but the South also has the highest murder rate. Critics contend that if capital punishment was an effective deterrent, the South's murder rate should not be higher than other parts of the United States where capital punishment is less common.

Levitt (2004) also offers reasons as to why capital punishment does not account for much, if any, of the 1990s crime decrease. First, the capital punishment deterrence argument assumes that criminals are instrumentally rational – that they think about the probabilities and consequences of their actions. If one observes an increase in capital punishment, then a potential murderer might conclude that there is a significantly higher probability of experiencing this fate. Capital punishment rates in some states did increase in the 1990s, but "the likelihood of being executed conditional on committing murder is still less than 1 in 200" (Levitt 2004: 175). In other words, capital punishment is a rare event and therefore not likely to significantly deter. Second, property crime dropped significantly in the 1990s and no one makes the argument that capital punishment deters property crime. Instead, it seems that something besides capital punishment accounts for the decline in crime in the 1990s.

Capital punishment is also monetarily questionable. It is a more expensive penalty than the alternative of life in prison without parole. Radelet and Borg (2000: 50) cite the findings of von Drehle (1988) as typical. He found that each electrocution cost about $3.2 million, while a life imprisonment sentence only costs about $600,000. The Death Penalty Information Center reports that between 1973 and 2010, 130 individuals have been released from death row after additional evidence established their innocence.

Punishment

Public opinion on capital punishment mirrors the points we just noted. When asked whether they are in favor of the death penalty for a person convicted of murder, a majority of Americans answer affirmatively (see Figure 9.2). In 2009, 65 percent of the

Are you in favor of the death penalty for a person convicted of murder?

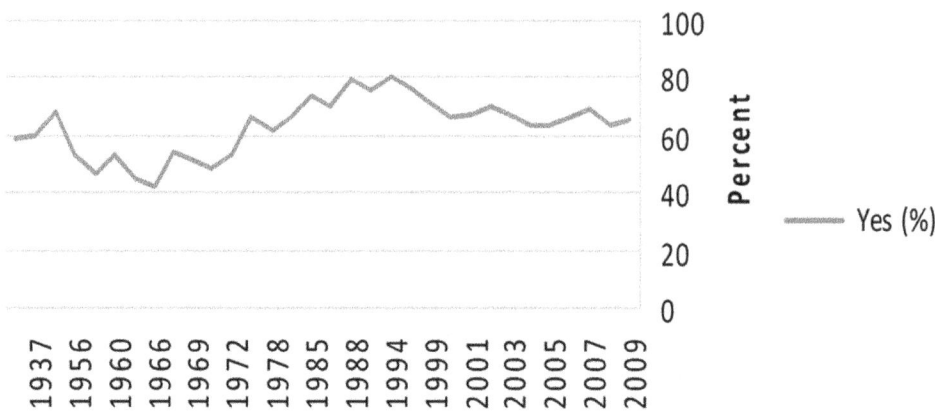

Figure 9.2 Support for the Death Penalty, 1937–2009

public supported the death penalty for homicide. This is down from a peak of 80 percent in 1994, but it is still a solid majority.

Public Opinion and Capital Punishment

However, when asked whether they are in favor of the death penalty or life imprisonment (with no possibility of parole), support for capital punishment decreases significantly. In 2006, the most recent year this question was asked, the life imprisonment choice is the plurality winner (see Figure 9.3).

Among those who support the death penalty, the primary reason given is that this punishment "fits the crime" (37 percent give this answer). They contend that the guilty person took a life and should now pay with their life. While deterrence is traditionally the primary argument for the death penalty, only about 11 percent support the death penalty because they believe it deters others from committing crime.[9] For those who oppose the death penalty, the primary reason given, by 46 percent of respondents, is that it is "wrong to take a life." Another 13 percent cite religious beliefs for opposing the death penalty. In 1991, 11 percent opposed the death penalty because they thought persons could be wrongly convicted. This figure rose to 25 percent in 2003. As we noted, many death row inmates have been exonerated. It seems the public is aware of the increasing number of exonerations.

[9] Data in this paragraph come from Gallup polls, which can be found at www.gallup.com/poll/1606/Death-Penalty.aspx.

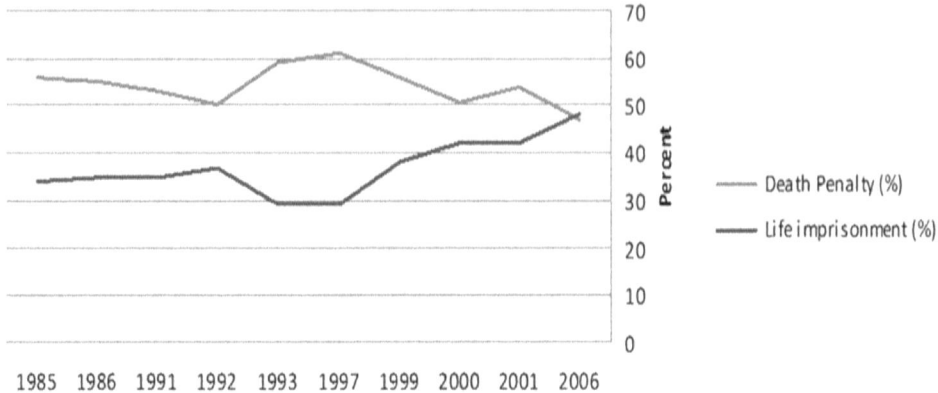

Figure 9.3 Support for Death Penalty vs. Life Imprisonment

We note that there are significant differences in opinion on the death penalty between Republican and Democrat Party identifiers. In 1988, about 81 percent of Republicans supported the death penalty for someone convicted of murder; this number was significantly lower for Democratic identifiers, at 63.6 percent. Over the last twenty years, this gap has increased. In 2008, about 84 percent of Republican identifiers supported the death penalty, while only 54 percent of Democrats did.[10]

Political scientists Frank Baumgartner, Susanna De Boef, and Amber Boydstun (2008) argue that support for the death penalty is diminishing due to reframing that has occurred in the wake of the Innocence Project's successes in revealing errors in death penalty convictions. They collected *New York Times* articles on the death penalty over the years 1960 through 2005 and charted the "net tone" of articles over that forty-five-year span. They find that the number of articles opposed to the death penalty increased over the 1990s, as did the number of articles that reported innocence or other reasons for exoneration. They also find evidence that the innocence argument dominates anti-death penalty reporting, getting more weight in the newspaper articles than charges of racial bias or other claims that also had been used. Baumgartner, De Boef, and Boydstun then study trends in public opinion toward capital punishment and report that a majority remains in favor, but that support is softening. They argue that how the death penalty is framed by the media has changed as a result of widespread findings that innocent people – mainly men, and disproportionately black men – have been sentenced to death.

---

[10] Data reported in this paragraph comes from the National Election Surveys for 1988 and 2008.

Principals, Agents, and Capital Punishment

Capital punishment cases can help us understand how judges respond to electoral pressures. Many question whether the prosecution in a capital punishment case is more likely to prevail when judges are subject to election. Judicial elections are becoming more contested (Hall and Bonneau 2006), perhaps giving judges an incentive to support outcomes that are likely to be popular with the public. Yet, the question may seem odd to some, as capital punishment cases are presided over by trial court judges; unlike appeals court judges, including the Supreme Court, trial court judges have much less judicial independence. They need to follow the rules. However, trial court judges do have influence over how the trial proceeds. They rule on pre-trial motions; the funding of expert witnesses, which allows certain specific lines of questioning; and in some cases appointing defense counsel. This influence over the process provides trial court judges with an ability to influence the outcome of the case, even though they themselves have no direct say in the outcome; the final outcome is determined by a jury.

Goelzhauser (2012) investigates whether there is a relationship between capital punishment conviction rates and judicial elections. He finds that there is a relationship. States in which judges are elected have more capital punishment convictions than states without judicial elections, a finding that holds despite the inclusion of a number of relevant control variables. What this research underscores is that judges are agents. They work for the public, and the public, or principal, has ways of influencing the agent's behavior. In this case, it is through the mechanism of elections. This example also highlights that the principal's preferences may not be ideal. That is, in some cases, people will be better off if the agent does not succumb to pressure from the principal. No one said, however, that democracy is a perfect system.

9.6 Should Municipalities Increase Restrictions on Owning a Firearm?

Some think that firearms increase the number of homicides, for the simple reason that they make it easier to kill. Most homicides in the United States involve a firearm, and firearms are easily available to purchase. For this reason, some speculate that tighter gun control laws will reduce the homicide rate. Advocates of less gun control have the opposite expectation. They contend that gun ownership can deter criminals. If more people had guns, people would think twice before harming someone else. The latter argument essentially says that guns do not kill people, people kill people. Ozzy Osbourne expresses the response of the other view: "I keep hearing this thing that guns don't kill people, but people kill people. If that's the case, then why do we give people guns when they go to war? Why not just send the people?"[11]

Both arguments are anchored in the theory of crime that we presented earlier. Proponents of gun control contend that a person will be less likely to attain the benefits associated with a crime if they do not have a gun, for a gun makes it easier to achieve their criminal end. Opponents of gun control also focus on the probability of attaining the benefits of crime, but they argue that a person will be less likely to seek out those benefits if they think that other individuals have guns.

In 1993, Congress passed, and the president signed, the Brady Handgun Violence Prevention Act.[12] Under the Brady Act, individuals desiring to purchase a handgun have to meet stricter background checks. For example, persons convicted of certain crimes are not able to purchase a handgun, nor are illegal aliens. On the one hand, it seems that the Brady Act has been successful, as about 3 percent of persons attempting to purchase a handgun are denied because they fail the background check associated with the Brady Act (Cook and Ludwig 2006: 714). Nevertheless, "Ludwig and Cook (2000) report no difference in homicide trends after the passage of the Brady Act . . ." (Levitt 2004: 174). Many attribute this ineffectiveness to the presence of an active black market for handguns. Research on the Brady Act, however, does not measure changes in gun *ownership*, but on legal handgun *purchases*.

One may also approach this question by examining the relaxation of gun control. Many municipalities, for example, permit the possession of concealed weapons. The motivation behind this policy is that a potential criminal will be less likely to commit a crime if they think that their target (or those nearby) possesses a weapon. In other words, hypothetically, laws permitting individuals to carry concealed weapons deter crime. Lott and Mustard (1997) find some support for this hypothesis. However, more recent and comprehensive research (Duggan 2001; Ayres and Donohue 2003) casts significant doubt on the findings of Lott and Mustard (1997).

Another way to examine this question is by looking at whether municipalities that have instituted gun control bans have seen a decrease in homicides and gun-related crimes. From 1976 until 2008, Washington, DC banned the possession of handguns. Over this period, homicide rates in DC rose and fell just like they did in other cities. That is, there is little evidence that the gun control ban in DC reduced crime. Similarly, in 1982, the city of Chicago passed an ordinance prohibiting the possession of firearms, yet its homicide rate has remained similar to other cities.

Although gun bans have not reduced crime, there is strong evidence that an increase of guns in an area contributes to more crime (Duggan 2001; Ludwig and Cook 2006).

---

[11] Reene Jana (1998), "Questions for Ozzy Osbourne," *New York Times Magazine*, June 28, 1998. p. 8.
[12] The Act is named after James Brady, who was shot during an attempted assassination of President Reagan by John Hinckley.

Specifically, increases in gun ownership are followed by increases in homicides, and decreases in gun ownership lead to decreases in murders. How can this be reconciled with the ineffectiveness of gun control bans? Black market activity plays an integral role. Gun control bans seem to have little effect on the number of guns in an area because most legally owned guns are owned by law-abiding citizens who will not go on to commit serious crimes. As this suggests, the over-abundance of guns in some areas does not rest with law-abiding dealers. It is specifically "underground" retailers that need to be targeted. Of course, this is easier said than done.

9.7　Conclusion

This chapter focuses on the expected utility model of crime. It is imperfect, particularly neglecting the strategic interaction between policy and citizens, but does provide significant insight on the causes of crime and strategies for reducing crime. Generally speaking, crime increases when one is less likely to be caught, the punishment is not severe, and the benefits of crime are great. In this context, we discussed how character affects crime. Those with greater empathy and a rule-following mentality, for example, commit less crime because they view the cost of crime as greater. We also discussed how an increase in one's criminal capital, which often comes from living in high crime areas, increases the expected utility of crime by making one both more likely to succeed at crime and by reducing the social cost associated with being caught.

We discussed a number of targeted strategies for how to combat crime: increasing economic opportunities, tough on crime laws, better policing, public education campaigns. We also noted that major crime rates may be significantly affected by other social policies, such as the legalization of abortion. Finally, we discussed capital punishment, its racial dimensions, support in the public, and effect on crime. In terms of who is sentenced to death, we noted that what is perhaps most noteworthy is the race of the defendant and the race of the victim. A black man convicted of murdering a white man is much more likely to end up on death row than any other racial grouping. We also noted that there is little evidence in support of the deterrent effect for capital punishment.

Key Terms

Crime
Uniform Crime Report
National Crime Victimization Surveys
Psychic rewards
Punishment by the state

Social costs

Economic opportunity costs

Capital

Financial capital

Human capital

Social capital

Criminal capital

Opportunity cost of crime

Recidivism

Three Strikes and You're Out

Three strikes laws

Truth-in-sentencing

Broken Windows theory

Endogeneity

Externalities

Abortion and crime

Capital punishment

CHAPTER EXERCISES

1. Why did crime in general, but homicides in particular, increase in the 1970s and 1980s and then decline in the 1990s?
2. What is the difference between jail and prison?
3. How do wage rates and economic growth affect crime rates?
4. What sort of policies might encourage students to stay in high school?
5. Why do you think some public education programs work to reduce drug use and others do not?
6. What part of the expected utility of crime equation does the Broken Windows argument influence?
7. What part of the expected utility of crime equation does the abortion argument influence?

REFERENCES

Ayres, Ian and Donohue, John J. III. 2003. "The Latest Misfires in Support of the 'More Guns, Less Crime' Hypothesis." *Stanford Law Review* 55(4): 1371–1398.

Baumgartner, Frank, De Boef, Susanna, and Boydstun, Amber. 2008. *The Decline of the Death Penalty and the Discovery of Innocence*. New York: Cambridge University Press.

Bazelon, Emily. 2010. "Arguing Three Strikes." *New York Times*, May 17.

Becker, Gary S. 1968. "Crime and Punishment: An Economic Approach." *Journal of Political Economy* 76: 169–217.

Benson, Bruce, Rasmussen, D., and Sollars, T. 1995. "Police Bureaucracies, Their Incentives, and the War on Drugs." *Public Choice* 83(1/2): 21–45.

Benze, James G., Jr. 2005. *Nancy Reagan: On the White House Stage*. Lawrence, KS: University Press of Kansas.

Birkeland, Sarah, Murphy-Graham, Erin, and Weiss, Carol. 2005. "Good Reasons for Ignoring Good Evaluation: The Case of the Drug Abuse Resistance Education (D.A.R.E.) Program." *Evaluation and Program Planning* 28(3): 247–256.

Brehm, John and Gates, Scott. 1997. *Working, Shirking, and Sabotage*. Ann Arbor, MI: University of Michigan Press.

Cameron, Samuel. 1988. "The Economics of Crime Deterrence: A Survey of Theory and Evidence." *Kyklos* 41(2): 301–323.

Cantor, David and Land, Kenneth. 1985. "Unemployment and Crime Rates in the Post-World War II United States: A Theoretical and Empirical Analysis." *American Sociological Review* 50(3): 317–332.

Coleman, James S. 1988. "Social Capital in the Creation of Human Capital." *American Journal of Sociology* 94(Supplement): S95–S120.

Cook, Philip J. and Laub, John H. 1998. "Unprecedented Epidemic in Youth Violence." *Crime & Justice* 24: 27–64.

Cook, Philip J. and Ludwig, Jens. 2006. "The Social Costs of Gun Ownership." *Journal of Public Economics* 90(1–2): 379–391.

Corman, Hope and Mocan, Naci. 2005. "Carrots, Sticks, and Broken Windows." *Journal of Law and Economics* 48(April): 235–266.

2000. "A Time-Series Analysis of Crime, Deterrence, and Drug Abuse in New York City." *American Economic Review* 90(3): 584–604.

De Mesquita, Bruce Bueno and Cohen, Lawrence E. 1995. "Self-Interest, Equity, and Crime Control: A Game-Theoretic Analysis of Criminal Decision Making." *Criminology* 33(4): 483–518.

Donohue, John J. and Levitt, Steven D. 2001. "The Impact of Legalized Abortion on Crime." *Quarterly Journal of Economics*. 116(2): 379–420.

Dostoyevsky, F. 2001. *Crime and Punishment*. Mineola, MN: Dover Publications.

Duggan, Mark. 2001. "More Guns, More Crime." *Journal of Political Economy* 109(5): 1086–1114.

Esbensen, F.-A., Deschenes, E. P., and Winfree, L. T. 1999. "Differences between Gang Girls and Gang Boys: Results from a Multi-Site Survey." *Youth and Society* 31: 27–53.

Freeman, R. 1996. "Why Do So Many Young American Men Commit Crimes and What Might We Do About It?" *Journal of Economic Perspectives* 10(1): 25–42.

Glaeser, Edward, Sacerdote, Bruce, and Scheinkman, Jose. 1996. "Crime and Social Interactions." *Quarterly Journal of Economics* 111(2): 507–548.

Goelzhauser, G. 2012. "Accountability and Judicial Performance: Evidence from Case Dispositions." *Justice System Journal* 33(3): 249–261.

Goldstein, Paul J., Brownstein, Henry, Ryan, Patrick J., and Bellucci, Patricia. 1997. "Crack and Homicide in New York City: A Case Study in the Epidemiology of Violence" in Craig Reinarman and Harry G. Levine (eds.), *Crack in America: Demon Drugs and Social Justice*. Los Angeles, CA: University of California Press, pp. 118–124.

Gould, Eric D., Weinberg, Bruce A., and Mustard, David B. 2002. "Crime Rates and Local Labor Market Opportunities in the United States: 1979–1997." *Review of Economics and Statistics* 84(1): 45–61.

Grogger, Jeff. 1998. "Market Wages and Youth Crime." *Journal of Labor Economics* 16(4): 756–791.

Grogger, Jeff and Willis, Michael. 2000. "The Emergence of Crack Cocaine and the Rise in Urban Crime Rates." *Review of Economics and Statistics* 82(4): 519–529.

Hall, Melinda Gann and Bonneau, Chris W. 2006. "Does Quality Matter? Challengers in State Supreme Court Elections." *American Journal of Political Science* 50(1): 20–33.

Harcourt, Bernard E. and Ludwig, Jens. 2006. "Broken Windows: New Evidence from New York City and a Five-City Social Experiment." *University of Chicago Law Review* 73: 271–320.

Johnston, L. D., O'Malley, P. M., Bachman, J. G., and Schulenberg, J. E. 2011. Monitoring the Future: National Survey Results on Drug Use, 1975–2010, Vol. I: Secondary School Students. Ann Arbor, MI: Institute for Social Research, University of Michigan.

Kahneman, Daniel and Tversky, Amos. 1979. "Prospect Theory: An Analysis of Decision under Risk." *Econometrica: Journal of the Econometric Society* 47(2): 263–291.

Kelly, Morgan. 2000. "Inequality and Crime." *Review of Economics and Statistics* 82(4): 530–539.

Klick, Jonathan and Tabarrok, Alexander. 2005. "Using Terror Alert Levels to Estimate the Effect of Police on Crime." *Journal of Law and Economics* 48(April): 267–279.

Knack, Stephen and Keefer, Philip. (1997). "Does Social Capital Have an Economic Payoff? A Cross-Country Investigation." *Quarterly Journal of Economics* 112(4): 1251–1258.

Kuziemko, Ilyana and Levitt, S. 2004. "An Empirical Analysis of Imprisoning Drug Offenders." *Journal of Public Economics* 88(9): 2043–2066.

Lamb, H. Richard and Weinberger, Linda. 1998. "Persons with Severe Mental Illness in Jails and Prisons: A Review." *Psychiatric Services* 49: 483–492.

Levitt, Steven D. 1997. "Using Electoral Cycles in Police Hiring to Estimate the Effect of Police on Crime." *American Economic Review* 87(3) 270–290.

    2004. "Understanding Why Crime Fell in the 1990s: Four Factors that Explain the Decline and Six that Do Not." *Journal of Economic Perspectives* 18(1): 163–190.

Levitt, Steven D. and Venkatesh, Sudhir Alladi. 2000. "An Economic Analysis of a Drug-Selling Gang's Finances." *Quarterly Journal of Economics* 115(3): 755–789.

Lochner, Lance. 2004. "Education, Work, and Crime: A Human Capital Approach." *International Economic Review* 45(3): 811–843.

Lochner, Lance and Moretti, Enrico. 2004. "The Effect of Education on Crime: Evidence from Prison Inmates, Arrests, and Self-Reports." *American Economic Review* 94(1): 155–189.

Lott, John R., Jr. and Mustard, David B. 1997. "Crime, Deterrence, and Right-to-Carry Concealed Handguns." *Journal of Legal Studies* 26(1): 1–68.

Marvell, Thomas B. and Moody, Carlisle E. 1996. "Specification Problems, Police Levels, and Crime Rates." *Criminology* 34(4): 609–646.

Matsueda, Ross L., Kreager, Derek, and Huizinga, David. 2006. "Deterring Delinquents: A Rational Choice Model of Theft and Violence." *American Sociological Review* 71(February): 95–122.

McCarthy, Bill. 2002. "New Economics of Sociological Criminology." *Annual Review of Sociology* 28: 417–442.

Merriam-Webster Online Dictionary. 2006.

Miller, Ted, Cohen, Mark, and Rossman, Shelli. 1993. "Victim Costs of Violent Crime and Resulting Injuries." *Health Affairs* 12(4): 186–197.

Moore, Wes. 2011. *The Other Wes Moore: One Name, Two Fates*. New York: Spiegel and Grau.

Nagin, D. 1998. "Criminal Deterrence Research at the Outset of the Twenty-First Century" in M. Tonry (ed.), *Crime and Justice, A Review of Research*. University of Chicago Press, pp. 1–42.

Nordrum, Amy. 2014. "The New D.A.R.E. Program—This One Works." *Scientific American*, September 10. Available online at www.scientificamerican.com/article/the-new-d-a-r-e-program-this-one-works/.

Putnam, Robert D. 2000. *Bowling Alone: The Collapse and Revival of American Community*. New York: Simon & Schuster.

Radelet, Michael L. and Borg, Marian J. 2000. "The Changing Nature of Death Penalty Debates." *Annual Review of Sociology* 26: 43–61.

Sampson, Robert J. and Raudenbush, Stephen W. 1999. "Systematic Social Observation of Public Spaces: A New Look at Disorder in Urban Neighborhoods." *American Journal of Sociology* 105(3): 603–651.

Shepherd, Joanna. 2002. "Fear of the First Strike: The Full Deterrent Effect of California's Two and Three Strike Legislation." *Journal of Legal Studies* 31(1): 159–201.

2002. "Police, Prosecutors, Criminals, and Determinate Sentencing: The Truth about Truth-in-Sentencing Laws." *Journal of Law and Economics* 45(2): 509–534.

Thoreau, Henry David. 2008. *Walden, Civil Disobedience, and Other Writings: Authoritative Texts, Journal, Reviews and Posthumous Assessments, Criticism*. New York: W. W. Norton & Co.

Uggen, Christopher. 2000. "Work as a Turning Point in the Life Course of Criminals: A Duration Model of Age, Employment, and Recidivism." *American Sociological Review* 65(4): 529–546.

United States Sentencing Commission. 2002. "Report on Cocaine and Federal Sentencing Policy." Available online at www.ussc.gov/news/congressional-testimony-and-reports/drug-topics/report-congress-cocaine-and-federal-sentencing-policy.

Von Drehle, D. 1988. "Capital Punishment in Paralysis." *Miami Herald*, July 10, p. 1.

Western, Bruce. 2006. *Punishment and Inequality in America*. New York: Russell Sage.

Wilson, James Q. and Kelling, George L. 1982. "Broken Windows." *Atlantic Monthly* 249(3): 29–38.

Wyrick, P. A. 2006. "Gang Prevention: How to Make the "Front End" of Your Anti-Gang Effort Work." *United States Attorneys' Bulletin* 54: 52–60.

10 Civil Rights

Outline

Questions

- What are rights?
- How can a majority credibly commit to protecting minority rights?

Overview

- The primary analytic concept we use to provide insight on civil rights is credible commitment.
- Rights grant individuals privileges and immunities.
- Rights depend on consent of the governed.
- A majority has a difficult time credibly committing to protect minority rights.
- Protests and institutional rules increase the probability that the majority can solve its credible commitment problem.
- The Citizens United Supreme Court decision has led to an increase in political campaign spending.
- Changes to the Fairness Doctrine led to the rise of AM talk radio.

- Electronic Health Records and behavioral marketing may be reducing individuals' privacy rights.
- Marriage rights, rights for disabled people, and women's rights have increased in recent years.

Introduction

A 63-year-old woman who decides to buy a condominium in a safe, modestly priced retirement community in central Florida may not be discriminated against because of her gender, religion, country or origin, the language she speaks, family status, or physical handicap. The US Fair Housing Act of 1968, amended in 1988, does not allow this type of discrimination. However, if she is an "out" homosexual she may be discriminated against simply because the law does not say home salespeople and landlords cannot discriminate against people due to their sexual preference. The Fair Housing Act of 1968 as amended in 1988 says nothing about sexual preferences. And if she has a minor child who wants to live with her she may be discriminated against for a second reason, for the law says real estate agents or landlords may discriminate against the young in areas that are intended for the elderly. The US Fair Housing Act of 1968, amended in 1988, says so. In one case, she has a right because of certain personal characteristics. In another case, she may be discriminated against because of something the law does not say. In the last case, she may be discriminated against because of something the law says.

Why are some civil rights protected under the law and others are not? The short answer is that civil rights are politically defined and, as such, the growth of civil rights follows the shifts in public opinion and politics over time. But this only conveys part of the civil rights story. Most stories of civil rights expansions include the new expansion of minority rights by a majority. But, under what conditions would a majority willingly designate new rights for a minority? And once they have done so, why would the minority have faith that the majority would not simply revoke these rights in some future round? In this chapter, we take up these questions.

We begin with a discussion of rights and the tension between majority rule and minority rules. The protection of rights is a credible commitment problem for the majority. We illustrate this with an extensive form game. In the process, we highlight a few ways for minorities to attain rights and how to make those rights more secure.

10.1 Rights: Natural, Civil, and Human

This chapter focuses on civil rights, but what are civil rights? We all have an intuitive sense of these rights. We have the right to voice our political opinions, whether they are for or against the government. We have the right to **due process** under the law, which among other things includes the right to a lawyer. We have the right to vote. We have the right to marry. These are only some of the civil rights we all have. To better understand these and other civil rights, we are going to take a step back and define some important terms.

It is useful to think of rights as contracts. **Rights** require others to either do something or not do something.[1] In this way, rights grant certain privileges and immunities. For example, the right to free speech requires others not to censor you. It is a privilege and you have immunity from prosecution. (There are limitations on this immunity, and other rights, which we come to later.) The right to due process under the law requires the police to allow you to have a lawyer present when you are being questioned. The right to vote requires that poll workers allow you to vote when you go to the polls. The right to marry prohibits the government from stopping two consenting adults from entering into this particular type of relationship.

Some political philosophers distinguish between natural and civil rights. **Natural rights** come from nature or nature's God and cannot be taken from a person. Because they do not emanate from government, they are **inalienable**. **John Locke**, an eighteenth-century British political philosopher, describes our natural rights as the right to life, liberty, and property. Locke's influence is seen in the US Declaration of Independence, where natural rights are described as life, **liberty**, and the pursuit of happiness. What Locke calls natural rights, others have called natural law, with natural law providing the fundamental goods and principles that contribute to human fulfillment (e.g. life, liberty, and property). Civil rights, in contrast, come from government. Because they come from government, or the consent of the governed, rights can be created and rights can be taken away.

Contrary to this view, we think the distinction between natural and civil rights is not so sharp. Thomas Hobbes, a seventeenth-century British political philosopher, also described the state of nature. For Hobbes, the state of nature was not as serene as Locke portrays. In fact, life in the state of nature is "solitary, poor, nasty, brutish, and short" (Hobbes 1991: 310). To gain rights and flourish as human beings, we need government. That is, all rights come from government. Individuals form governments to improve their lives. Government improves our lives when it protects the common good that is necessary for human flourishing, and central to the common good is the identification and protection of rights. There are two implications of these points. First, all rights, whether natural or civil, should be thought of as human rights (see e.g. Finnis 1980). We demarcate rights to contribute to human development and happiness.

---

[1] Consistent with this view, we see that the United Nations Declaration of Rights, as well as other international human rights documents, states rights in one of two ways. Either "Everyone has the right to . . . or No one shall be . . .".

Second, rights help specify the common good, and at the same time the common good gives a reason for why rights may be constrained (Finnis 1980). The right to life, for Locke and in American history, has limits. If a person is tried and found guilty of committing first-degree murder, then the state may execute him or her. Protecting the common good is a motivating principle behind capital punishment. Similarly, you may have heard that it is illegal to shout "fire" in a crowded movie theater when there is not a fire. This is an abridgement on your speech rights for the common good. Your Fifth Amendment rights are limited if you are in the military: "No person shall be held to answer for a capital, or otherwise infamous crime, unless on a presentment or indictment of a grand jury, *except in cases arising in the land or naval forces, or in the militia, when in actual service in time of war or public danger . . .*" (emphasis added). In practice, all rights have or can have limits.

Limitations on rights may occur for reasons that are less clearly motivated by the common good or even for selfish political reasons. Different jurisprudential philosophies often stem from different views of the common good or just different political interests. Consider a more recent example of rights limitations. The Civil War and the accompanying Fourteenth, Fifteenth, and Sixteenth Amendments ended slavery and made blacks full citizens of the United States, but a variety of laws were passed, primarily in the South, to limit the civil rights of black Americans. The Civil Rights Act of 1965 outlawed many of these practices. Among other things, this law ended unequal voter registration requirements and school racial segregation. One section of the 1965 Civil Rights Act required certain parts of the country, mostly in the South, to seek "pre-clearance" before changing their voting rules. In a sense, then, this law restored or protected certain voting rights for black Americans. In 2013, the US Supreme Court ruled, in *Shelby County, Alabama v. Holder, Attorney General of the United States* (679 F. 3d 848, 2013), that part of this act was unconstitutional because the coverage criteria was based on old data and Congress had not updated it. The practical effect of the ruling was to end the pre-clearance requirement. In a sense, this ruling allows for restricting voting rights. This begs an important question: How do you protect minority rights in a majority rule political system? Before discussing this question, we note that we are not addressing the ethics of limiting rights. Whether it is ethically wrong to limit any particular right in any particular case or grant some right that should not be granted is a subject for a different book.

10.2 Commitment Problems and Rights

Civil rights issues can be understood as a classic **commitment problem**. Problems of commitment arise when actors fail to achieve their objectives given their inability to make credible promises or threats. For example, in the case of the expansion of voting rights, how can the minority position holder believe that the majority position holder will respect the minorities' rights? How can the majority make its commitment credible when it makes the rules? A promise or threat is credible when it is in an actor's interest to follow through on it. Commitment dilemmas arise when an actor has either an immediate incentive to renege or when one or more actors' incentive to renege changes over time. Even if the terms of a deal are beneficial early on, one party may find that as time passes conditions change and they have an incentive to violate their promise. We refer to this latter situation as the problem of **time inconsistency**. As time moves forward, at least one party's incentive to renege on their promise or threat rises. In Chapter 13, we note that credible commitment problems are an important cause of military conflict.

We have already seen an example of the credible commitment problem in Chapter 2. Recall the Prisoner's Dilemma. The Prisoner's Dilemma arises because, despite their incentives to cooperate, once they are sequestered in separate rooms each party does not hold the other's promise to cooperate as credible. In the absence of this credible promise, each party defects and is rewarded with a lower outcome than they could have reaped had they cooperated.

Consider a few examples from everyday life. If you have dated someone exclusively, you have likely experienced the concern that a commitment problem fuels. Over the first few days, weeks, and months of the relationship, you may feel a deep abiding desire to be with your new dating partner. But as time goes on, and you begin to either learn new information about your partner or meet other people at your new job or in a class, you may begin to feel differently about the original dating agreement. With new information, your incentive to renege on your dating agreement changes. Such new information can arise for either party in a dating relationship. And when it does, and as the incentives to renege grow, one party may suffer the ultimate emotional loss of enduring a break-up. In the end, such relationship outcomes are an inefficient waste of time and energy. Such commitment problems extend to a variety of everyday situations. Individuals make promises to themselves about attempting to eat more healthfully, to spend less money, to watch less television, or to complete tasks more promptly. Each of these promises can be quite difficult to keep, given the ease with which your self-contracted promise can be broken. How, then, can commitment problems be resolved?

Solutions to Commitment Problems

To solve the reneging temptation, sufficiently high costs must be imposed on each of the parties to offset their incentive to violate the terms of the agreement. Such solutions to commitment problems are generally referred to as **commitment devices**. A commitment device attempts to "lock in" the parties to their agreement. Of course, the effectiveness of a commitment device varies with the level of costs generated by it. The most effective commitment device is one where the temptation is completely removed from the party or parties (we can think of this as imposing an infinite cost on the party). Less effective commitment devices are those that attach finite costs to reneging. They are less effective precisely because if the incentive to renege is sufficiently high, one party may prefer to pay even moderately high costs of breaking their promise.

With regard to the everyday commitment problems discussed above, what are some potential commitment devices? A long-standing institutional solution to the commitment problem of dating and relationships is marriage. When the financial and social costs of divorce are sufficiently high, married parties will have greater faith that their bond will remain unbroken long into the future. Of course, the costs generated by violating a marriage agreement (divorce) vary by culture and over time. In the United States, during the 1950s, the divorce rate was approximately 25 percent. However, in the late 1960s more women were entering the workforce and found themselves less reliant upon their husbands for financial support. Moreover, into the 1970s the social stigma of divorce waned. As a result, the costs attached to violating a marriage agreement decreased. By 1978, the divorce rate had risen to approximately 50 percent.[2] Marriage had become a weaker commitment device in securing a relationship's future.

Solutions to everyday commitment problems can be creative. People who are concerned that they are eating too much junk food may attempt to reduce their consumption by not walking down certain aisles in the food store where most junk food is sold. People who are concerned with spending too much money may cancel their credit cards. People who are concerned that they are watching too much TV may cancel their subscription. Each of these commitment devices is thought to raise considerably the costs of reneging on the promise. True – if you change your mind and want to watch television you can call to have the subscription reconnected, but this entails larger long-term costs than simply saying I'm not going to watch TV tonight.

The best commitment devices are those that remove the temptation altogether. History provides a famous account of a commitment problem from Cortez's 1519 to 1521 expedition into Mexico. Cortez faced a problem. Upon landing in the New World, he knew that his heavily outnumbered men may not be motivated to fight a brutal campaign against the Aztecs. Knowing that they could simply board their vessels and head back to Spain, his men were aware that they had a credible "exit strategy." Cortez was concerned that with this thought of an exit strategy in his men's mind they may be

---

[2] The divorce rate has since declined – but not necessarily due to its increased effectiveness as a commitment device. Most research suggests that the decline is due to more people marrying later in life, when they are more confident with their choices.

less motivated to secure victory in their campaign. To solve this credible commitment problem, Cortez burned all of his ships in front of his men – imposing on his men the ultimate commitment device. His men would now have to fight hard if they ever wanted to see Spain and their loved ones again.

Culture as well may also serve as a commitment device by raising the costs of reneging. We can interpret religious sanctions of punishment in the afterlife or cultural edicts against immoral acts in this light. These cultural practices raise internal psychological costs for violating agreements. Recall the discussion of crime in Chapter 9, in which people's psychological discomfort is cast as one reason they choose not to engage in crime. If you want to see who among your friends operates with a higher moral code, you can poll them to see which of them has ever left a tip at a restaurant that they *never intended to revisit*. There is no motivation under classic economic theory to suggest you should ever tip with no expectation of return – but many do. Why? Most will say that it is simply the "right thing to do." Of course, cultural mores vary across individuals and within and between societies making reliance upon them challenging in the absence of universal adoption.

Civil Rights as a Commitment Problem

Commitment problems are ubiquitous in the political and policy worlds. Wealthy aristocrats cannot credibly commit to social spending for the poor, who outnumber the rich. But, transitioning to democracy, where the median voter is poor, is a credible commitment by the rich to increased social spending. Similar conditions hold for any majority and any minority under democracy. Any majority that promises to respect the rights of any minority faces a standard commitment problem. The minority will always be left wondering, "Why should I believe the majority will respect my rights when abiding by their promise is costly to them?"

Consider the following problem. Figure 10.1 displays an **extensive form** representation of a simple game between a Majority and a Minority group. We use the extensive form of our game rather than the normal form that we introduce in Chapter 3 to allow for the fact that the sequencing of moves is a critical component of most commitment problems.

Imagine that a Majority can decide to commit to some level of respect for Minority rights. We call this level of rights the Status Quo, SQ. SQ is determined before the game starts. Now, imagine that the Minority can choose to either protest SQ or comply with it. If the Minority opts to comply with SQ, then the game ends and each party receives SQ. If the Minority opts for protest, then the game proceeds. Protests are not costless. After all, collective action is challenging for all of the reasons that we discussed in Chapter 3. In addition, protests can be costly in the form of lost lives, physical integrity, time, and economic productivity. So, if a Minority wants to protest

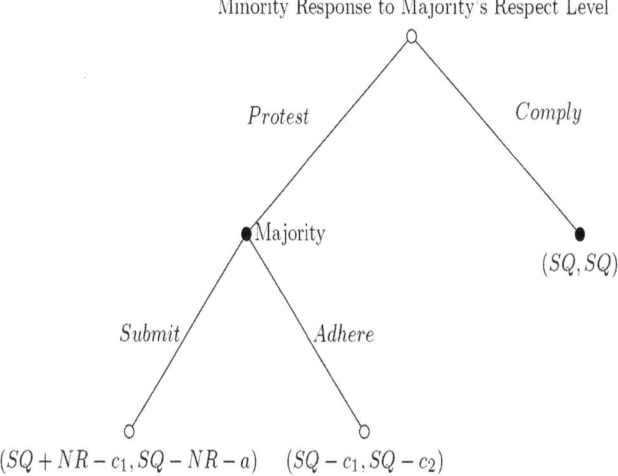

Figure 10.1 Civil Rights as a Credible Commitment Problem

to secure better rights, they must be willing to pay a cost, c_1. If the Minority opts for protest, then they may secure a rights package that consists of the SQ plus some new set of rights, NR, minus the costs of the protest, c_1.

Facing protests, the Majority now has a choice. The Majority can either submit to the protests providing some New Rights, NR, and paying an **audience cost**, a. An audience cost captures the notion that when the Majority is forced to backtrack on their well-publicized Minority policy, their supporters may punish them for their broken promise.[3] Alternatively, the Majority can Adhere to the Status Quo, Choosing to pay a cost, c_2, to put down or wait out the protests. The cost parameter, c_2, captures the notion that, in a democracy, putting down a protest or waiting it out costs the Majority in terms of prestige and reputation if the Minority chooses to comply eventually and perhaps in terms of financial sacrifice if the protests are long-running and comprehensive.

What can we learn about Civil Rights with this game? We are interested in finding any equilibrium solutions to our game. Recall from Chapter 3, a Nash Equilibrium is a set of strategies such that no player can unilaterally improve their position given the other player's action. For our extensive form game we must use a slightly different form of Nash Equilibrium, or a refinement. Our refinement is a subgame perfect Nash Equilibrium, or just **subgame perfect equilibrium** (SPE). An SPE reveals the strategy profile of each player for every subgame of the larger game tree that is also Nash Equilibrium.

---

[3] James Fearon (1994) coined the term "audience cost," but he bases it on work done by Thomas Schelling (1960, 1966).

We must use the method of backward induction to find the SPE for our extensive form game. To do this, we start at the end of the game and work backwards highlighting, for each node, each player's best choice given that they are at that point in the decision tree. We do this for each node in the tree until we reach the beginning of the game. When we are finished, we will have a game tree with several highlighted branches, representing best plays. It is important to note, however, that we are using parameters as pay-offs and the expected outcome of the game and the equilibrium strategy profiles will be conditioned on assumptions about the values of these different parameters. Given a set of parameter values, if we follow the connected highlighted paths to the end of the game we will find the expected outcomes of the game. Outcomes will depend upon assumed values of these parameters – so we will only consider a subset of these values.

Since the Majority determined the Status Quo, the Minority is Player 1 and the Majority is Player 2; recall that pay-offs are ordered (Player 1, Player 2). Now let's start at the lowest node, the Majority party choice. If the Majority finds itself at this node it will compare the utility of Submitting to the utility of Adhering. We can see from the game that these utilities are ($SQ-NR-a$) and ($SQ-c_2$), respectively. Under what condition will they submit to the protests of the Minority? The Majority will submit when ($SQ-NR-a$) > ($SQ-c_2$). This will be true when c_2 > ($NR-a$). In other words, when the cost of putting down protests or waiting them out outweighs the utility that the Majority gets from continuing to deny new rights and the expected audience costs of losing to the Minority, they will Submit and go along with granting the Minority an expansion of their rights. This insight accords with much of civil rights history in the United States. Whether workers' rights, women's rights, African-American rights, or most recently gay rights, we observe that the Majority most often adheres to the SQ until it becomes too costly to do so, either because the audience costs of giving in decrease, the costs of ignoring or putting down minority protests increase, or both. So, with this information, the Minority Party know where they are going to wind up if they opt for Protest over Comply – what should they do?

What of the minority choice? If the minority chooses to comply, then they will receive the Status Quo. If they choose to protest, then their pay-off depends upon what the majority is expected to do. Using the insight from above, we can see that the majority is expected to submit to protests when c_2 > $NR-a$. Let's assume that this is true. If c_2 > $NR-a$, then the Majority will submit to protest. From the Minority's perspective, they must now compare the utility that they expect to receive if they comply, SQ, to the utility they expect to receive if they protest and the majority submits to their protests, ($SQ+R-c_1$). You should be able to see that, given the condition, c_2 > $NR-a$, the Minority will prefer to protest when $NR > c_1$. In other words, when the minority has determined that the new rights that they expect to win through protest outweigh the costs that they expect to bear by participating in protests, then they will protest. So, there are two expected outcomes. If $NR > c_1$, then the Minority party will Protest and the Majority party will Submit and the SPE strategy profile is (Protest; Submit). If $NR < c_1$, then the Minority party will Comply and the Majority's node will never be reached (but if it were the Majority would choose Submit) and the SPE strategy profile is (Comply; Submit).

What about the other condition for the Majority, $c_2 < NR-a$? When this condition is met, the Majority is expected to adhere to SQ even in the face of protests. So the Minority must compare their utility of complying, SQ, with the expected utility of the majority adhering to the Status Quo in the face of their protests, $SQ-c_1$. Under this condition, it is easy to see that as long as protests are costly, $c_1>0$, then under this condition the minority will always prefer to comply and the SPE strategy profile is (Comply; Adhere). So when the Majority is expected to Adhere, Protest is simply too costly to justify it as a tactic. When $c_1=0$, an unlikely event, the Minority Protests and the Majority Adheres with a SPE strategy profile of (Protest; Adhere).

Until now, we have ignored the time inconsistency problem that makes civil rights a difficult commitment problem. Figure 10.2 at the right introduces another move after the Minority chooses to comply with the Majority's setting of the Status Quo. Now we allow the Majority to decide to adhere by their own status quo civil rights or to attempt to revert against the Status Quo, restricting minority rights further. This demonstrates why civil rights is a credible commitment problem. Notice that if we ignore the left half of the game, where minorities are allowed to protest, we can see that a majority always has an interest to revert against the status quo in future iterations $(SQ+NR)>SQ$. In other words, respecting minority rights is costly for the Majority. In the absence of protest, a future majority would always prefer revert or restrict minority rights.

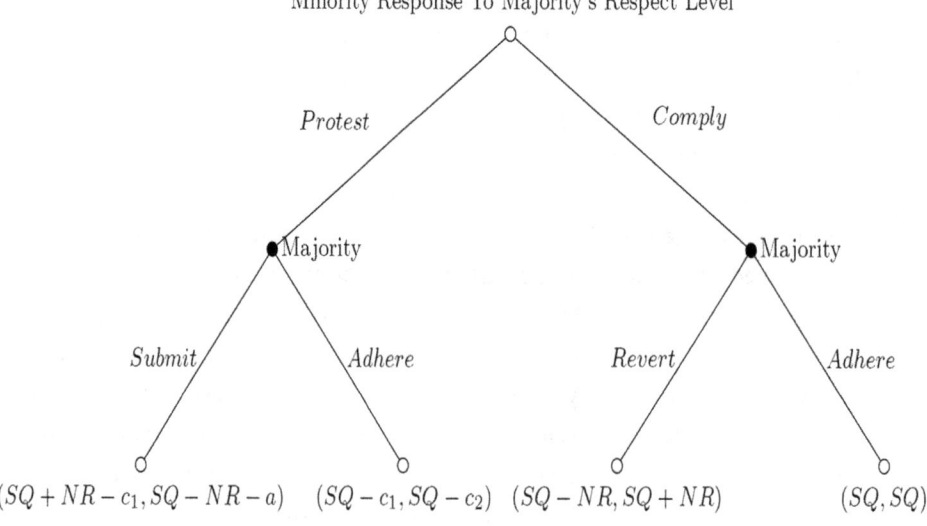

Figure 10.2 Civil Rights as a Credible Commitment Problem

Notice also that the strategy profile (Comply; Adhere) is not an SPE and is therefore never an expected outcome of this game.

We also see that again the operative constraint on minority protest is the expected cost of engaging in protest, c_1. If the costs of engaging in protests are sufficiently high, the Minority may choose to comply with the Majority's Status Quo even if that Status Quo is expected to be violated in the future. This suggests a particularly unstable outcome for minorities vis-à-vis the Majority. Absent some other commitment device, minorities must always be willing to bear large costs of protests to ensure their rights. However, Protest capacity is a transient resource. At some points in American history, citizens have been willing to take to the streets to protest what they believe to be unjust acts, while at other points they have been more apathetic. But if protest pressures are transient, then so too are the rights protections of minorities. Perhaps there is another way.

As we mentioned above, more effective commitment devices are those that present parties with large costs for reneging. The game that we just walked through suggests that, in the absence of protests, majorities have incentive to simply renege on their promises to respect minority rights. But what if reneging on those promises were made costly via another way, that is, absent protest? We could pass legislation. Would this work? Perhaps. After all, some of the most successful civil rights advances in the United States occurred at the hand of legislation in the form of the Civil Rights Acts of the 1960s. But legislation is also vulnerable to the whim of the majority. As new political coalitions are swept into power, newly defined majorities could attempt to redefine the rights of the minority. Less transient than legislation, however, is the Constitution. Once adopted, constitutional protections are more costly to change. Indeed, an amendment to the US Constitution requires two-thirds of each body of the House and three-quarters ratification of the states. By enshrining protections in the Constitution, majorities can more credibly commit to respect minority rights. The Thirteenth Amendment (abolished slavery), the Fourteenth Amendment (required states to grant the same rights as the national government), the Fifteenth Amendment (gave slaves the right to vote), and the Nineteenth Amendment (granted women the right to vote) to the Constitution can been seen as attempts to more strongly commit the United States to protecting minority rights. The first three, the Thirteenth, Fourteenth, and Fifteenth Amendments, were Reconstruction Amendments forced on the southern states as a condition of their being allowed to re-enter the Union following their secession. The Nineteenth Amendment was the product of a long push for women's rights that began in 1848 when Elizabeth Cady Stanton and Lucretia Mott organized the first women's rights convention at Seneca Falls, New York. The Reconstruction Amendments' passage followed a civil war.

Of course, constitutional protections are not perfect commitment devices. Their enforcement and protection very often fall to interpretation of the Supreme

Court and lower level courts. If a majority has politicized the courts, it may be able to encourage the Court to undo constitutional protections granted to minorities. For example, the voting rights of blacks received substantial expansion through the Voting Rights Act of 1965, which elaborated on the protections afforded by the Fifteenth Amendment via the passage of legislation that guaranteed that black voters were assured fair districts through a rule that affected a handful of southern states, as well as a few counties in Michigan, New York, and California. The US Supreme Court ruled in 2006 that those regulations were no longer to be enforced, thus weakening a commitment that had been promised in the past. Thus, things can change. Then, the question becomes: What incentives do members of the Court have to protect minorities? This is a case that we do not address here.

10.3 Political Speech

The First Amendment of the US Constitution guarantees that citizens in the United States have freedom of religion, freedom of speech, freedom of the press, freedom of assembly, and freedom to petition the government. As with other rights, these freedoms expand and contract over time as a function of majority rule and court decisions. Freedom of speech is most expansive during times of domestic and international peace. When domestic or international conflicts arise, the government sometimes attempts to rein in speech.

In the United States, there is a strong commitment to free speech, as there is in most Western democracies. In this section, we focus on three expressions of political speech that have been the focus of Supreme Court decisions, legislation, and public discussion in the recent past: campaign advertising, the fairness doctrine, and national security issues.

Box 10.1 *Citizens United v. Federal Election Commission* (2010)

Citizens United, a conservative interest group, wanted to air a film entitled *Hillary: The Movie*, which was critical of Hillary Clinton in the thirty days before the 2008 Democratic primary elections. A Federal District Court in Washington, DC ruled that doing so would violate a 2002 piece of campaign legislation. Citizens United appealed that and the case reached the Supreme Court in 2009. The Court decided in favor of the plaintiffs, which greatly expanded the speech rights of organizations and businesses and has profoundly affected campaign spending in the United States.

Campaign Speech

In *Citizens United v. Federal Election Commission* (558 U.S. 310 130 S. Ct. 876, 2010) the US Supreme Court ruled that the First Amendment forbids the regulation of independent political expenditures by businesses, labor unions, or associations. The *Citizens United* decision expanded the rights of independent groups to spend for political speech. In fact, independent groups can now make unlimited donations to political campaigns. The effect of the decision has been a great increase in campaign spending. At least one person has described it as among the most important speech cases in US history (Toobin 2012).

Disparate groups, among them the **American Civil Liberties Union (ACLU)** and the Heritage Foundation, met the Citizens United decision with favor. The ACLU focuses on civil rights generally and supports the expansion of free speech in most instances. They filed an *amicus curiae* (friend of the court) brief in support of the Court's decision, a 5-4 vote decided by the conservative bloc. The Heritage Foundation is a conservative, highly partisan organization that may support the decision for partisan reasons. The expansion of rights sometimes attracts groups that more typically are opposed to one another.

The decision was met with mixed reactions. Some groups opposed the expansion because of concern that businesses and individuals could now spend limitless amounts of money for political purposes without concern of regulation. The decision also makes more powerful the independent groups that are influential in electoral politics. Conservative groups and liberal groups alike are raising enormous amounts of money for campaigns and critics worry that the lack of limits on spending will make elections unfair.

The Fairness Doctrine

The Federal Communications Commission (FCC) established the **Fairness Doctrine** in 1949. It requires that broadcasters provide time for public service broadcasting and that they present opposing views so that the public has a diversity of opinion. The FCC ceased to enforce the rule in 1987 and struck it entirely in 2011. The establishment and subsequent abandonment of the rule greatly affected political speech.

The FCC created the Fairness Doctrine to ensure that US-based radio and television broadcast stations, which are considered a public trust and are regulated by the Commission, provide balanced and fair coverage of controversial issues. The FCC dropped the doctrine in 1985 as part of the Reagan administration's widespread deregulatory efforts, a decision that held up to legal challenge. The agency's rationale for the change was twofold. First, the agency argued that the growth of cable television had expanded the range of broadcasts to such an extent that the doctrine was no longer needed. Second, FCC administrators argued that the doctrine had exerted a **chilling effect** upon speech. A chilling effect is thought to lead to a reduction of speech that might have occurred. The federal courts agreed, and subsequent legislative attempts to reintroduce the doctrine were vetoed by President Reagan in 1987 and by President G. H. W. Bush in 1991. Subsequent administrations have likewise not reinstated the Fairness Doctrine.

The demise of the Fairness Doctrine helped resurrect AM radio, as well as the creation of profitable talk radio (Jamieson and Cappella 2008). The AM radio band is weaker than FM, and the sound is better on FM. Because of this, music broadcasters focused on the expansion of the FM band in the 1980s as they sought more affluent suburban markets. In turn, AM stations moved to broadcasting talk radio as an inexpensive and, it turned out, profitable source of revenue. There was little political talk radio before the Fairness Doctrine ended. The expansion of conservative talk radio especially flourished in the time that followed the Fairness Doctrine's cancellation. Conservative broadcasters like Rush Limbaugh and Glenn Beck have capitalized under the new system. Liberal radio broadcasters have not been so successful. However, the end of the Fairness Doctrine also led to more politicized television channels, with both liberal (MSNBC) and conservative (Fox News) stations experiencing commercial success.

The Fairness Doctrine ensured that political and other inflammatory speech could be tempered by an opposing view, but did so at a cost to freedom of speech. Some politicians and judges were quick to point to the threat it presented to freedom of speech, but reaped a political benefit from that expansion of speech rights. The doctrine's demise is positive in terms of its expansion of speech, but that expansion comes at a cost.

The fairness doctrine provided balance between sometimes extreme and controversial positions and gave the public the opportunity to hear, at worst, two opposing

Table 10.1 Should the Government Require All Radio and Television Stations to Offer Equal Amounts of Liberal and Conservative Radio and Television Stations to Offer Equal Amounts of Liberal and Conservative Political Commentary?

Yes	47%
No	39%
Not sure	14%
N = 1,120	

Source: Rasmussen 2008

biased arguments from which they could glean elements of truth or at least recognize distinctions in arguments. Political psychologists note the existence of a confirmation bias, that is, a bias toward confirming a person's existing beliefs (Boudreau and Lupia 2013). In a 2008 survey conducted by the conservative Rasmussen polling organization, 47 percent of respondents stated that government should require television and radio broadcasters to provide airtime to both liberal and conservative opinions; 39 percent disagreed and 14 percent had no opinion. Those data are old, but suggest some support for the fairness doctrine or something like it, but the policy has not been resurrected and there appears to be no support for doing so. Removing the fairness doctrine removes broadcasters' incentives to report unbiased news, and the quality of public information may decline. However, free speech advocates prefer that anyone can broadcast what they wish, within proscriptions of decency and the like, and many also assume that consumers are capable of deciding among broadcasters without FCC enforcement of the fairness doctrine.

National Security and Free Speech

The First Amendment grants freedom to the press, and the Fourth Amendment grants individuals protection from unreasonable government searches. The controversy surrounding Edward Snowden has raised questions about whether there should be limits on these civil rights. Snowden was a US Government contract employee who collected and gave to the media classified information about US surveillance programs. Can the media print or air national security information? Is it okay for the government to collect metadata on Americans? We begin with the latter question.

To what extent should citizens' activities be free from government surveillance? Recent revelations about the extent of government surveillance of US citizens via their use of Internet and cell phone communications have resulted in citizen fears about the rising security state. Citizens expect to be kept safe from violence and other security threats, but they do not want to be intruded upon. Recent survey research collected from a sample of 1,008 adults in June 2013 (Newport 2013) revealed overall public disapproval of the US Government's use of telephone and Internet records to compile logs of calls and other communications (Table 10.2). Fifty-three percent of American adults disapprove of the federal government's use of information in this way. The opinions vary by political party affiliation: Democrats (40 percent) are less likely to oppose the government's use of private materials in this way, but 63 percent of Republicans are, a likely reflection of partisan leanings (Gallup 2013). Fifty-six percent of Independents disapproved of the government's actions.

Table 10.2 Americans' Opinions Regarding Surveillance
Question: *As you may know, as part of its efforts to investigate terrorism, a federal government agency obtained records from larger US telephone and Internet companies in order to compile telephone logs and Internet communications. Based on what you have heard or read about this program, would you say you approve or disapprove of this government program?*

	Approve	Disapprove	No Opinion
National Adults	37%	53%	10%
Democrats	49%	40%	11%
Independents	34%	56%	10%
Republicans	32%	63%	5%

Given that a majority of the public disapproves of government invasion of citizen telephone and Internet records for purposes of surveillance, what is the appropriate trade-off between security and privacy? When Gallup interviewers asked the 53 percent of persons who disapproved of the government actions whether there were circumstances in which it would be acceptable for the government to act as it did, 21 percent claimed there would be circumstances under which it would be acceptable, 30 percent said there were no circumstances under which it would be acceptable, and about 2 percent gave other, unspecified reasons. Among the 37 percent who agreed with the government action, about 11 percent claimed it did not violate liberties, 23 percent claimed that halting terrorism warrants allowing intrusion, and 4 percent claimed other unspecified reasons. About 10 percent offered no opinion.

Taking this set of opinions into consideration, about 30 percent of US adults believe there is no circumstance under which they agree that the government should have the right to intrude upon their telephone and Internet security as it had. Some of the disapproval of the action has to do with partisanship, and some of it may be purely situational. For example, people may be more prone to accept government interference if the country was under attack, but not otherwise.

Citizens were also asked their opinions about the circumstances of Edward Snowden, a US Government contract employee who claimed to have leaked the information about federal surveillance of citizens while working for the government. He is living in Russia and is "a man without a country" given that he has a US passport and is *persona non-gratis* in the United States and among its allies. When one-half of the sample was asked whether they believed Snowden was right or wrong to leak the information, a plurality (44 percent) said "yes" and 42 percent said "no." About 39 percent of Democrats responded, "yes," which was lower than Independents (47 percent) and Republicans (49 percent). Although no majorities supported Snowden's actions,

59 percent of all adults agreed that the press was right to report the information, and there were majorities among Democrats, Republicans, and Independents.

This illustrates the complicated way in which citizens view their rights and the responsibilities of the press. On the one hand, they disagree with the government's surveillance of their records, they disagree that Edward Snowden was correct to reveal the information, but they support the press's decision to publicize the actions. This again illustrates the trade-off between the desire for protected speech, in this case the desire to be protected against the intrusiveness of government, and the desire for information. By revealing the extent of information collected by Edward Snowden, the press revealed what may have been national security secrets. Doing so may have affected the government's ability to monitor terrorists, which runs counter to the goals of most citizens.

10.4 The Right to Privacy

Privacy is the right to be left alone in the absence of some clear public need to know about an individual's private life, occupation, personal habits, or preferences. People vary in the extent to which they seek privacy in their lives, but few people want their lives to be open to the public without the ability to live outside of public view.

The US Constitution provides no explicit guarantee of privacy, although many people believe there to be. The US Supreme Court, in the *Griswold v. Connecticut* (381 U.S. 479 1965) decision, famously invoked the "penumbras, parameters, and peripheries" idea in Justice William Douglas' majority opinion. That is, Douglas wrote that the Constitution, with the Bill of Rights, provides zones that establish the right to privacy in marital relations.

Box 10.2 Prosecuted for Birth Control

Estelle Griswold was director of a Planned Parenthood League of Connecticut. She provided a married couple with information about birth control. She was arrested with a colleague under a Connecticut law that made counseling about birth control illegal. The Court ruled that, while there is not a written right to privacy in the Constitution, there are sufficient elements to warrant considering there to be one.

Source: *Griswold v. Connecticut* (1965)

Although the right to privacy has been extended beyond what was established in *Griswold*, there is constant tension between those who would expand those rights and those who prefer a stricter interpretation of the Constitution. For example, in *Roe v. Wade* (410 U.S. 113 1972), the Court affirmed that women had the right to privacy in determining whether to seek an abortion. The Court has grappled with the abortion issue constantly since, and Constitutional literalists, those who claim to read just the words of the document without expansive interpretation, like Justice Antonin Scalia and Justice Clarence Thomas, do not generally make interpretations of a right to privacy beyond those explicitly granted in the Bill of Rights.

In this section, we discuss two areas in which right to privacy is now emerging: medical records privacy and behavioral targeting. Medical records privacy issues arise alongside the increasing digitization of health care recordkeeping; a person's digital health care record is a trove of useful information for providers, but also contains abundant information for insurers, employers, and others who may have an interest in a person's health status. Behavioral targeting reflects newly emerging abilities to track individuals' purchase decisions by a number of means and to tailor sales pitches to them. Medical records privacy and behavioral marketing are examples of how information that is thought to be private may be used, often without the individual actively agreeing for them to be used as such, in ways that affect individual privacy.

Medical Records Privacy

In 2009, the Obama administration announced a plan to invest $15 billion by 2014 for the purpose of providing physicians, health management organizations, and hospitals incentives to develop systems of **electronic health records** (EHRs).[4] The administration signed the HITECH Act into law; it laid out the administration's plan for creating EHRs. His announcement was part of the economic stimulus program that was enacted to infuse money into the economy following the recession of 2008. Obama was following a prior commitment made during his predecessor George W. Bush's administration, in which the former president included the promise of making electronic health records available to most Americans by 2014.

There are strong medical practice justifications for creation of EHRs. There are managerial efficiencies that come from having records of treatments so that there is no overlap. When people's records are available to practitioners, there are fewer medical errors from conflicting drug treatments. Further, practitioners can be certain of what treatments people receive and are better able to coordinate their care with other providers. In addition, EHRs create a strong medical record that can be essential for maintaining a thorough medical history. Physicians and hospitals with EHRs are able

---

[4] The federal government's investment in EHRs was approximately $16.5 billion by the end of September 2013 (Levingston 2013).

Table 10.3 Practices with Electronic Health Records

Netherlands	99%
New Zealand	97%
Norway	97%
UK	96%
Australia	95%
Italy	94%
Sweden	94%
Germany	72%
France	68%
USA	46%
Canada	37%

Source: Commonwealth Fund, 2009 data

to work more efficiently given that they have information readily available and do not have to consult paper charts, and productivity among providers increases as a result.

EHRs are used widely in a number of nations: In the Netherlands, about 99 percent of physician offices use EHRs, and several nations that have constitutional or legislatively protected rights to privacy have high percentages of practices with EHRs. The United States, with no explicit right to privacy and in which the Obama administration has allowed private vendors to develop and sell unique versions of EHRs, many of which cannot communicate with rival software firms' versions, has a low rate of participation. As the Affordable Care Act becomes more entrenched and as EHRs become more able to communicate with each another, enrollments are expected to increase.

EHRs involve collecting and recording information about people that is personal and invasive. Much of the information is maintained in cloud-based storage, and because of lax regulations on privacy regulation in the United States, this is susceptible to being hacked and used for illegal purposes like identity theft. Additionally, there is concern that medical records may be sold to marketers who may use them to focus on items they wish to sell. For example, persons diagnosed with diabetes may receive ads for sugar-free sweets. There are concerns that insurers may use medical records and medical histories in their risk profiling of individuals or communities. For example, when a person buys life insurance, he or she typically has a brief physical examination that determines his or her height, weight, and blood pressure, is asked about the occurrence of cancer, heart attack, and other similar illnesses, and is asked if he or she smokes. The person being examined has an incentive not to be entirely truthful about behaviors correlated with risk, as risk affects the price of insurance. If insurers have access to EHRs, their risk of insuring people who will collect pay-outs before they are expected drops. Thus, EHRs may affect moral hazard and adverse selection in the purchase of insurance.

Other issues may arise with the existence of EHRs. Employers may gain access to potential employees' health records, which might affect the decision to hire a person or the decision to retain a person. For example, an employer may decide not to hire a person if the employer learns from a health record that the person has a high rate of absenteeism. People may suffer ostracism or other social distress if certain conditions were revealed by EHRs.

Electronic Health Records provide numerous benefits and are unlikely to cease to exist, but they present possibly severe threats to individual privacy. In the absence of laws to protect privacy, patients are often advised to ask for copies of their records if for no other reason than to determine whether they are correct. In the United States, the competition among software companies for business has created a large number of programs, so many that some hospitals must have multiple programs to process different health insurers' paperwork. That large number of programs complicates work for practitioners and payers, and also provides multiple points of access for information thieves. As the number of programs lessens as the market matures, it is possible that access to hackers and other misusers may decline.

Behavioral Targeting

Behavioral targeting refers to the use of personal information for the purpose of marketing. It involves some external agency's collection and compilation of a record of an individual's online activities. This includes everything they do online: their interests, preferences, communications, and the data collection can be longitudinal, that is, the agency may provide the end user over time information about one individual's online activities. The information may then be sold to marketers, or used by the group that collected the information, to deliver online advertisements that are tailored specifically for the user and that the advertisers expect to be more effective marketing tools. Behavioral targeting requires sophisticated use of big data extraction and analysis skills, which are being developed by scientists in the data industry and academic computer scientists. A 2010 report on the *Wall Street Journal* reported it to be extensive in the fifty companies studied for the piece. They reported that, on average, the companies had installed sixty-four cookies and other software-tracking devices. Websites like Google, Facebook, EBay, and others collect the information from users and sell them to marketers as a portion of their revenues, as do Internet service providers (ISPs). Google and Facebook are acknowledged to be the organizations that are most aggressive about collecting user information (Hoofnagle *et al.* 2012). A University of California, Berkeley Law School "Web Privacy Census" reports that all 100 of the top websites have behavioral tracking software installed. They track each "click" of a person's online activity.

For example, if you are logged into Facebook and click a "like," that cookie registers your like. If you like a service or product, that information is recorded and may be used for marketing. If you take a Facebook "quiz" like "What college major am I best suited for?" you will be pointed to an independent site which will ask you to respond to a few vaguely relevant questions, and each of your responses will be collected for marketing. The answer about the best major is irrelevant to the questioner, but the data you enter is valuable and may be used in-house, sold to another user, or both. This is not unique to Facebook: Google does the same when you, for example, enter addresses to which you are considering traveling, when you search for shoes, and on and on.

The privacy implications of behavioral targeting are clear: people use the Internet, possibly with the belief that they are doing so privately, but their moves are being tracked by the providers they use, and are then being sold downstream to marketing companies and companies who use them for advertising. Chris Hoofnagle and his co-authors describe behavioral advertising as "the offer you cannot refuse" (2012) because ISPs and websites track information without the explicit agreement of users, and actively work to develop new and more difficult-to-avoid methods to collect information to ensure they may continue to collect information when internet users delete cookies or otherwise attempt to halt data collection.

Although there are calls to limit providers' ability to collect user data, they are often rejected by policymakers on the grounds that, in a free market, users have the choice to participate or not participate in various free and paid online activities, and demands for regulation are described as paternalistic (Hoofnagle *et al.* 2012: 273). Supporters of regulations on the ability to collect data argue that users' inability to halt data collection indicates that, if the only way to avoid being tracked is to not be on the internet, which is thought of as a public good, regulation is not paternalistic. In the meantime, ISPs and websites are using increasingly sophisticated methods to track users' clicks, so the ability to remove oneself from view while using the Internet is nearly impossible.

10.5 The Right to Due Process of the Law

Due process is stated twice in the US Constitution. The Fifth Amendment forbids the government from withholding "life, liberty or property without due process of the law," and the Fourteenth Amendment, which was ratified in 1868 after the Civil War, says the same thing in reference to the need for all states to be faithful to the law. The Fourteenth Amendment was added to gain "full incorporation" of the clause in the states, which argued that it did not apply to all of their actions. The due process clause figures prominently in cases in which citizens are denied their rights by the national or state governments, and figured prominently in civil rights cases.

In this section, we discuss two issues that have recently been argued as due process issues. The first is the ongoing incorporation of same-sex marriage in the United States. The acceptability of same-sex marriage among the public has increased dramatically in the past decade. The cases in state and federal courts have addressed it as a due process issue, with proponents arguing in favor of equal treatment and opponents arguing that marriage does not fit as a due process right. The second due process issue we discuss is that for persons with physical and intellectual disabilities. Despite the existence of legislation guaranteeing access to schools, jobs, lodging, and the like, the legislation often remains unimplemented.

The Expansion of Marriage Rights

The US Supreme Court ruled that same-sex couples' right to marry is protected under the US Constitution. The Court's vote of 5–4 expanded rights for gay and lesbian people and punctuated a period of rapid opinion change among the American public. Data in Table 10.4 show large changes in public opinion toward gay and lesbian marriage in 1996, 2005, 2010, and 2015. In 1996, 27 percent of respondents reported that gay and lesbian marriage was acceptable to them; that had jumped to 60 percent in favor in a poll taken May 6 to 10, 2015, prior to the Supreme Court decision. This represents a large opinion change in a brief time, and it also represents twenty years of policy change as the United States made incremental policy shifts that led to the recognition of the legality of same-sex marriage.

Table 10.4 Public Opinion Toward Recognition of Same-Sex Marriage

Question: *Do you think marriages between same-sex couples should or should not be recognized by the law as valid, with the same rights as traditional marriages?*

	Should Be Valid	Should Not Be Valid	No Opinion
1996	27%	37%	3%
2005	37%	59%	4%
2010	44%	53%	3%
2015	60%	37%	3%

Source: Gallup 2015, www.gallup.com/poll/117328/marriage.aspx

The legal push for marriage equality began in 1972, when the US Supreme Court ruled that a gay couple in Hennepin County, MN, who claimed they had the right to marry, declined to decide on the merits of the couple's appeal of a prior decision that denied them the right to marry for want of a substantial federal question. That is, the US Supreme Court claimed that same-sex marriage was not an issue for the national government to decide. That led a handful of states to pass laws forbidding same-sex marriage in the 1970s. However, laws and court rulings in other states suggested that the marriage equality claim might succeed, so organizations and activists who supported marriage equality were engaged in the attempt to get change.

President Bill Clinton supported passage of the **Defense of Marriage Act (DOMA)**, which was a blow for supporters of same-sex marriage in the United States and a disappointment. In 1993, the Hawaii Supreme Court ruled that the state could not deny gay couples the freedom to marry, making Hawaii the first state to make legal same-sex marriage. That decision led anti-gay activists in several states to organize a multi-state campaign to make marriage for same-sex couples illegal in the states. States stepped up earlier attempts to pass laws defining marriage as strictly heterosexual. The newly empowered Republican House majority, which won election from the Democratic majority in 1994, then moved to protect traditional marriage, defined as marriage between a man and a woman. The idea caught on in the Republican primaries in 1996, and DoMA, which confined marriage to that between heterosexual couples, was passed by both houses of Congress in 1996, and was signed by Bill Clinton.

State DoMAs were for the most part symbolic until 2003, when Massachusetts became the first state to allow gay marriage. Before that, Vermont passed the nation's first civil union law in 2000. Same-sex marriage laws began to diffuse among the states after Massachusetts' passage of its law, and there has been a wave of federal court decisions invalidating some state objections to the laws. In 2013, the US Supreme Court ruled that, where same-sex couples are married in jurisdictions that allow gay marriage, the federal government must recognize their union and treat them equally for purposes of taxes, pensions, benefits, and the like. The case was decided in a 5–4 vote with Justice Anthony Kennedy writing the majority opinion. The opinion indicated that the decision was based mainly on the Fifth Amendment right to due process. Justice Kennedy also wrote the majority opinion on the 2015 case that made same-sex marriage legal.

There was considerable support for laws that make it illegal for homosexuals to marry in the United States. Prior to the Supreme Court's ruling legalizing same-sex marriage, thirteen states had either amendments or statutory rules that forbade same-sex marriage, generally using DoMA language. Thirty-six states, either by statute or by judicial decision, allow same-sex marriage. Thus, there is wide variation in state-level interpretations of marriage laws across the American states, with changes in state policy occurring over the course of time (Haider-Markel 2001). However, the 2015 Supreme Court ruling voids those state-level restrictions.

Table 10.5 Public Opinion Toward Gay and Lesbian Rights and Public Policy

Dependent variable: Log of Public Policy Index

	Coefficient	Standard Error
Opinion	0.86*	0.22
Government ideology	0.13	0.16
Voter ideology	0.35	0.23
Intercept	1.13	0.06

$R^2 = 0.69$

Note: * = p<05, two-tailed.

Source: Lax and Phillips 2009

Despite the growing legality of the practice, some oppose same-sex marriage on various grounds. Some churches moved rapidly to accept and others to reject the decision. The American and Southern Baptist churches, the Roman Catholic Church, the Orthodox Jewish Movement, Islam, and the Church of Jesus Christ of Latter Day Saints reject same-sex marriage. The Episcopalian, Reform and Conservative Jewish congregations, the Society of Friends, the United Church of Christ, and others have welcomed the practice. Buddhism and Hinduism have not taken a stand. Justice Roberts' dissent in *Obergefell v. Hodges* (2015) argued that the justices' ruling in favor of the plaintiffs was overreaching doing what the justices may have believed was the right thing to do, but, in Roberts' view, was not warranted on due process grounds.

Recent research documents the impact of public opinion toward same-sex marriage, civil unions, and other protections of the rights of gay people on public policymaking. Political scientists Jeffrey Lax and Justin Phillips found that opinion drives policy-making with regard to gay and lesbian rights in the states. They measured public opinion on eight items that pertain to gay and lesbian rights[5] and combined them to make an additive scale. Higher scores indicate stronger state policies toward gay rights. They report regression results (Table 10.5) that show that a one-unit change in the aggregate measure of policy-specific opinion (i.e. the values on opinion about gay and lesbian rights averaged over each state year) produces a 0.86-unit increase in the logged value of the state policy scores. It is statistically significant, and the relationship is stable even with tests for other independent variables; the authors control for government ideology (high scores indicate a more liberal state government) and voter ideology

[5] Lax and Phillips (2009) measure opinion toward parental adoption, civil unions, no prohibition against same-sex sodomy, employment non-discrimination for sexual orientation, housing non-discrimination for sexual orientation, health benefits for domestic partners, hate crime laws (sexual orientation), and allowing same-sex marriage in forty-eight states (AK and HA excluded).

(high scores indicate more liberal voters). The meaning of this is that state governments are responsive to citizen opinions in a policy-specific area. Earlier research on less specific measures of opinion suggested that state governments were responsive to voter demands (Erikson *et al.* 1993), but this research shows that citizens who have tolerant views toward gay and lesbian people receive policy that reflects that view; people who are intolerant of gay and lesbian rights are rewarded with less tolerant policy.

Due Process for People with Disabilities

People with disabilities are often at a disadvantage vis-à-vis their due process rights. Although governments, businesses, schools, and universities have done much to improve access to services and have followed some rules that require that disabled people have access to services, the accommodations usually are the result of lawsuits rather than something that institutions recognize as a problem and proactively address. Researchers note that disability is often considered from an "impairment" view that is created in the United States by the Social Security disability system, rather than a "rights" issue (Fleisher and Zames 2005). The rights perspective suggests that persons with disabilities deserve the rights of others, while the impairment view reflects the idea that disabled people are in a special class of citizenship in which special treatment is required given their circumstances (Stone 1989). The impairment model suggests that accommodations are nice, but optional given their cost, and the rights model suggests they are required as a condition of citizenship.

Providing the disabled access and service is expensive, especially where facilities must be retrofitted, or where special teachers or programs must be provided. The shift to a rights model has occurred over the past fifty years, and began about a decade after the major civil rights legislation was passed in the United States. Section 504 of the **Rehabilitation Act of 1973** established disability as a civil rights issue. It stated that no otherwise qualified person with a disability will be, because of that disability, denied privileges or benefits or denied access to facilities that are provided by or receive financial assistance from any US government agency. Disabilities are defined broadly, as physical or mental impairments that affect the ability to conduct life activities such as walking, seeing, speaking, learning, working, doing manual tasks, and breathing. In addition, the Rehabilitation Act required employers to make reasonable accommodation for qualified applicants to work in their industry, although small employers for whom the costs of providing the accommodation are released from that requirement.

Section 504 of the Rehabilitation Act was not implemented until 1977, and then because of pressure from a newly engaged disability rights community. The federal government was slow to implement the policy initially due to pressure from groups in business and in other areas like education that were concerned about the costs of the policy. In 1975, a related law, the **Individuals with Disabilities Education Act**

(IDEAS) passed, and in 1990 the **Americans with Disabilities Act (ADA)** passed. IDEAS required persons with disabilities to be provided with an **Individualized Education Program**, which requires that parents be allowed to engage with their child's school to develop an education program that both deem appropriate. The ADA extended Section 504 of the Rehabilitation Act of 1973 protections that had previously applied only to governmental agencies or those that received government funding to the private sector.

It is expensive to create facilities that accommodate the needs of people with disabilities. For example, in the 2008 amendments to the ADA, there are more than twenty specific rules that must be followed to build wheelchair-accessible dressing rooms in clothing stores. The rules involve the height of seats, the size of doors, the size of spaces, height of door hooks, the width of door swing, and more. These rules are necessary, but are extremely expensive to address in facilities in which they must be retrofitted. For example, New York City subways are not entirely ADA compatible, but newer facilities, like the newer MARTA trains in Atlanta, are. Disabilities rights attorneys, recognizing this, often focus on gaining assurance that newly constructed facilities will be accessible, as courts often rule against the right to access based on the price. It is also costly to provide specialized educational services, specially trained teachers, and so on for a small population.

Critics of laws like the ADA argue that private enterprises should be free to determine whether they wish to provide services or facilities that are readily accessible to disabled people. Economists estimate that hours worked by disabled persons *declined* after the implementation of the ADA, which counters the claim that productivity would increase following the law's implementation (Acemoglu and Angrist 2001). The authors explain the unexpected decline in light of the costs of hiring a person, arguing that the increased costs of hiring a disabled person experienced by employers reduces access to employment, the opposite of what was expected under the ADA.

There are also controversies over what constitutes disability. For example, the diagnosis of disability for students in colleges and universities has been a source of contention in some cases. Students who are diagnosed with disabilities that make it more difficult for them to learn at the typical pace of university courses, or who have learning disabilities that make it difficult for them to complete examinations in classroom settings, take notes, or who have other diagnoses of learning difficulties are provided access to disability learning centers, which are paid for by colleges and universities. Religious schools that take no federal money are not required to follow ADA guidelines for student disability.

Table 10.6 shows the most frequent diagnoses for college and university students in 2008–09, by type of institution. Two things stand out in this table. First, among the roughly 11 percent of students nationwide who were categorized as learning disabled in that year, the largest group was diagnosed with a "general learning disability." Two-year private for-profit schools and four-year private for-profit schools had the largest

Table 10.6 Diagnoses of College Students with Disabilities, 2008–09
Learning Disability Diagnosis

School Type	General Learning Disability %	ADD/ ADHD %	Chronic Health Condition %	Mental Illness or Psychological Condition %
Two-year public	31	13	10	15
Two-year private not-for-profit	28	13	9	11
Two-year private for-profit	46	13	5	11
Four-year public	29	23	11	16
Four-year private not-for-profit	36	26	11	13
Four-year private for-profit	29	22	9	14

Source: National Center for Educational Statistics, *Students with Disabilities at Degree-Granting Postsecondary Institutions* (2011), Table 4, http://nces.ed.gov/pubs2011/2011018.pdf

portions of students described as such in their student bodies. Also remarkable is the percentages of students diagnosed with ADD/ADHD. Each category of four-year school has more than 20 percent of its disabled students listed in that category. The ADD/ADHD diagnoses are interesting to note given the prevalence of college students using the stimulants prescribed for ADD/ADHD treatment as a method to improve their study habits and to "juice" themselves to perform well on exams and in classrooms.

Although there are legitimate ADD/ADHD diagnoses, a review of medical literature indicates that people are able to achieve false diagnoses of the disability (Sansone and Sansone 2011). College-age people with positive ADD/ADHD diagnoses are disproportionately white and affluent, and there is concern that they and their parents are seeking the diagnoses to help them with school. Related to this, there is extensive illegal sale of prescription stimulants on college and university campuses, and sales peak during exam times (McCabe *et al.* 2006). The illegal use of stimulants to improve test scores is a problem, in general, but for this chapter the concern is the issue of feigning disability for advantage in school. An ADD/ADHD diagnosis allows more time for exams, having a note-taker, and other benefits that are unavailable to other students. This is an interesting issue for colleges and universities and one that may expand over time as the number of students with such diagnoses increases.

The trade-off between the due process rights of disabled people and the rights of employers and others who are affected by the higher costs of accommodations and training illustrates the manner in which rights compete. Some critics argue that disability rights are often given less attention because disabled people are poorly organized politically, and their interests are often cross-cutting. That is, a disabled attorney is both disabled and an attorney, and she may consider her right to practice law outside the constraints of the ADA preferable to exercising her full rights as guaranteed by the law. However, the opposite view may hold: persons who support full incorporation of disability rights may expect those rights to be assured as a right of citizenship.

10.6 Gender and the Right to Equal Pay for Equal Work

Although the Fifth and Fourteenth Amendments to the US Constitution appear to secure the right for women and men to be paid equally, they have never been interpreted that way. The national government enacted the **Equal Pay Act** in 1963, and wage differential between men and women declined markedly, but the gap has not closed. The Civil Rights Act of 1964 forbids gender-based discrimination in wages, hiring, promotions, and benefits. The Act also created the **Equal Employment Opportunity Commission (EEOC)**, which is responsible for ensuring that there are no racial, gender, religious, national origin, religious, or retaliation-based barriers to employment (EEOC 2013). It did not address issues of sexual orientation. During the 1970s, the EEOC required that employers no longer specify the gender or race of the persons they wished to hire. In the early 1970s, newspaper want ads listed the gender, and in some cases, the race of persons the employer wished to hire. With the emergence of the EEOC, that was no longer allowed, although job sorting by gender and race still did, and does, exist.

Despite those and more recent federal actions, like Obama administration rules passed in 2009 to provide people with the right to know the salaries of others in their organizations, and a recent failed attempt to pass a law requiring employers to provide employee salary data to the Department of Labor, gender gaps in wages persist. Women historically worked in different industries than men, and have the major burden of childbearing and care, and, even where they are recently out of college make different career choices than men, but even where those considerations are controlled statistically, gender-based pay inequality exists.

In 2013, the median pay between women and men was 77 percent, meaning that women earned about 0.77 cents for each dollar earned by men (AAUW 2014). When controls are inserted for college major so that there are direct head-to-head comparisons, there was a 7 percent gap in women's earnings in 2012 that was unexplained by factors such as job choice, marital status, or the like. A similar analysis for men and women ten years out of college showed a 12 percent pay gap (AAUW 2014). Thus, there is clear evidence of a gap in women's and men's pay in the United States.

The United States is not remarkable in the extent of male–female pay gaps. In a 2013 report, Norway is reported to have the smallest gap in gender pay equity among wealthy nations. The United States ranks sixth in the world ranking of 136 nations (Hausmann and Tyson 2013). Although disparities exist in the United States, and although they diminished during the 1970s through the 1990s, they have begun to increase in the 2000s (AAUW 2014). The world data suggest that nations in which education is open make the greatest strides toward reducing the gap.

Some of the cause of the wage gap is linked to preferences: Women historically have chosen work that does not pay highly disproportionately to their percentage of the population, which results in a wage gap. However, there are also path dependencies that lead to work being valued differently in some cases, even when the skills, knowledge, and abilities required of jobs are identical and should be compensated equally. Although progress toward wage equality is slow, and it appears to have slowed slightly during the 2008 recession, there is reason to believe that it will continue, but that a portion of what is occurring now is a function of earnings histories. That is, people earn wages over a lifetime and the wage gap follows them over their earnings careers.

Recent evidence suggests that for young people, those "millennials" between 18 and 32 years of age, the gender gap in earnings is very small. An analysis of census data for 2012 shows women aged 25 to 34 to have hourly earnings of about 93 percent of what men of that age group earn (Pew Research 2013). Women in that age group are better educated than women of their mothers' or grandmothers' generations, and better educated than men of their age. However, they remain concerned that men earn more for their work than they do, and men do not share that concern. It remains to be seen whether the parity evident among persons of that age will continue in their age cohort, but the data are encouraging for people who wish to see gender equity in pay.

The right for equal pay for equal work is progressing. Proponents of the policy view it as a fundamental right of citizenship. Opponents rarely oppose the idea of equal pay, but oppose the economic and social regulation that is required to achieve the goal. In a free market, jobs should pay the market rate regardless of gender, race, sexual orientation, or other personal characteristics of the person seeking work. The continued existence of a pay gap between women and men suggests that something in the market is not working efficiently.

10.7 Conclusion

The promise of civil rights in a democratic system depends on the government's ability to protect citizen rights and citizen acceptance of government's commitment to ensuring those rights. There is often a tension between rights and liberty. The assurance of rights often comes at a cost to personal liberty and there is a constant balancing between the two in a democratic political system. Rights expand over time in democratic systems, leading some observers to worry that the eventual result of that expansion is the loss of freedom. The presence of checks and balances to the powers of any single institution of government makes broad expansion of power impossible, except under extreme circumstances. During the Great Depression, the national government's powers expanded considerably, as they did during the post-war War on Poverty. At present, the Congress and the Supreme Court are reducing some of the rights guaranteed in favor of a more limited government. For example, the Court has ruled in favor of the freedom to spend unlimited amounts of money for political campaigns, which did away with Congressionally imposed campaign limits. The commitment model presented in this chapter illustrates the trade-offs faced by the majority and minority when seeking to change that status quo position on rights. When opinion toward an issue – like same-sex marriage – changes, the costs of refusing to change become too high for the majority, and a change occurs.

Key Terms

Due process
Rights
Natural rights
Inalienable rights
John Locke
Liberty
Commitment problem
Time inconsistency
Commitment devices
Extensive form
Audience cost
Subgame perfect equilibrium
Citzens United v. Federal Election Commission
American Civil Liberties Union
Fairness Doctrine
Chilling effect
Privacy
Griswold v. Connecticut
Electronic health records
Behavioral targeting
Defense of Marriage Act

Rehabilitation Act of 1973

Individuals with Disabilities Education Act

Americans with Disabilities Act

Individualized Education Program

Equal Pay Act

Equal Employment Opportunity Commission

CHAPTER EXERCISES

1. Are there patterns to the expansion of rights and the expansion of liberties? Under what circumstances do governments most often support the expansion or contraction of one over the other?

2. Is the "Fairness Doctrine" a desirable public policy? What are the implications of not having the doctrine for speech? How would speech differ if the Doctrine were reinstated? Should it apply only to radio and television, or should it apply to print and online media as well?

3. Should spending in political campaigns be regulated or should individuals and groups be allowed to spend whatever they choose?

4. Should people be allowed to opt out of having their health information recorded as electronic health records?

5. Do female–male wage differentials exist due to generational trends, or are they due to deeper institutional issues? Can we conceive of differences in male and female earnings as a commitment problem on the part of employers and the government?

REFERENCES

AAUW. 2014. "The Simple Truth about the Gender Pay Gap." Available online at www.aauw.org/files/2014/03/The-Simple-Truth.pdf.

Acemoglu, Daron and Angrist, J. 2001. "Consequences of Employment Protection: The Case of the Americans with Disabilities Act." *Journal of Political Economy* 109(5): 1–43.

Boudreau, Cheryl and Lupia, Arthur. 2013. "Political Knowledge," in James Druckman, Donald P. Green, James H. Kuklinski, and Arthur Lupia (eds.), *Handbook of Experimental Political Science*. New York: Cambridge University Press, pp. 171–186.

Erikson, Robert, Wright, Gerald C., Jr., and McIver, John. 1993. *Statehouse Democracy*. New York: Cambridge University Press.

Fearon, James D. 1994. "Domestic Political Audiences and the Escalation of International Disputes." *American Political Science Review* 88(3): 577–592.

Finnis, John. 1980. *Natural Law and Natural Rights*. New York: Oxford University Press.

Fleisher, Doris Zames and Zames, Freida. 2005. "Disability Rights: The Overlooked Civil Rights Issue." *Disability Rights Quarterly* 25(4). Available online at http://dsq-sds.org/article/view/629/806 (online journal published by The Knowledge Bank, Ohio State University).

Gallup. 2015. "Marriage." Available online at www.gallup.com/poll/117328/marriage.aspx.

Haider-Markel, Donald. 2001. "Policy Diffusion as a Geographical Expansion of the Scope of Political Conflict: Same-Sex Marriage Bans in the 1990s." *State Politics and Policy Quarterly* 1(1): 5–26.

Hausmann, Ricardo and Tyson, Laura K. 2013. *The Global Gender Gap Report 2013*. Geneva, CH: World Economic Forum.

Hoofnagle, Chris J., Soltani, Ashkan, Good, Natianiel, Wasmbach, Dietrich J., and Ayenson, Mika D. 2012. "Behavioral Advertising: The Offer You Cannot Refuse." *Harvard Law and Policy Review* 6(2): 273–296.

Jamieson, Kathleen Hall and Cappella, Joseph N. 2008. *Echo Chamber: Rush Limbaugh and the Conservative Media Establishment*. New York: Oxford University Press.

Lax, Jeffrey R. and Phillips, Justin H. 2009. "Gay Rights in the States: Public Opinion and Policy Responsiveness." *American Political Science Review* 103(3): 367–386.

Levingston, Suzanne Allard. 2013. "Electronic Health Records' 'Make or Break' Year." *Bloomberg Businessweek*. Available online at www.businessweek.com/articles/2013-11-14/2014-outlook-electronic-health-records-make-or-break-year.

McCabe, S. E., Teter, C. J., and Boyd, C. J. 2006. "Medical Use, Illicit Use, and Diversion of Abusable Prescription Drugs." *Journal of American College Health* 54(5): 269–278.

Pew Research. 2013. "On Pay Gap, Millennial Women Near Parity – For Now." *Social and Demographic Trends* 1–16. Available online at http://pewsocialtrends.org/2013/12/11/on-pay-gap-millennial-women-near-parity-for-now/.

Sansone, Randy and Sansone, Lori A. 2011. "Faking Attention Deficit Disorder." *Innovations in Clinical Neuroscience* 8(8): 10–13.

Schelling, Thomas C. 1966. *Arms and Influence*. New Haven, CT: Yale University Press.

   1960. *The Strategy of Conflict*. Cambridge, MA: Harvard University Press.

Stone, Deborah. 1989. *The Disabled State*. Philadelphia, PA: Temple.

Toobin, Jeffrey. 2012. "Money Unlimited: How John Roberts Orchestrated the Citizens United Decision." *New Yorker*, May 21. Available online at www.newyorker.com/reporting/2012/05/21/120521fa_fact_toobin?currentPage=all.

11 Homeland Security

Outline

Questions

- How should a state allocate limited resources to defend against a strategic adversary like a terrorist group?
- How much will people trade off civil liberties for greater security?

Overview

- The primary analytic concepts we use to provide insights on homeland security are delegation and coordination problems.
- Bureaucracies are central to the implementation of public policy.
- Politicians take more of a fire alarm than a police-patrol approach to bureaucratic change and creation. At the same time, bureaucratic change and creation is a window of opportunity for advancing particular political interests.
- Key homeland security functions are protection, policing, mitigation, and resilience.
- Given that resources are limited and adversaries are strategic, the best way to allocate resources for protection is to apply risk management, which assesses each target's vulnerability, threat, and impact on society if destroyed and harmed.

However, in practice, pork-barrel politics is a more decisive influence on homeland security allocations.

- Many individuals perceive a trade-off between civil liberties and security. As threat perceptions and trust in government increase, individuals are more willing to give up civil liberties for greater security.
- The Patriot Act and Protect America Act both trade off civil liberties for security. They aim to increase security by expanding the use of National Security Letters, warrantless wiretapping, and data mining.
- Efficient emergency response is a function of planning, training, exercising, equipping, and public education. As recent events attest, the federal government has been deficient in each of these areas.

Introduction

Imagine you are a politician running for a national political office in 1992. The Cold War is over and the economy is coming out of recession. Would reforming homeland security or the intelligence community be a major part of your campaign? Probably not, even though there had been blue ribbon commissions calling for a reorganization of the country's intelligence community. Now imagine you are running for a national political office in 2002. Would reforming homeland security or the intelligence community be a major part of your campaign? With the terrorist attacks of 9/11 still looming large in people's minds, there is a good chance you would make it part of your campaign.

Imagine you are in charge of allocating resources across the United States to protect the country from a potential terrorist attack. What criteria will you use to divide the resources? Will you apportion the resources equally across the states, as the Constitution does with Senate seats, giving an equal amount to each state? Will you distribute the resources based on population, giving more money to California than Rhode Island? What about distributing the resources based on vulnerability and the potential harm that can result from an attack on a particular site? And how do you take into account that terrorists are likely to adapt to whatever strategy you choose?

Imagine you are the President of the United States. It is likely that your political prospects depend in part on the likelihood of a terrorist attack occurring. Should one occur, you may well be blamed for not protecting the country. Would you authorize the National Security Agency to collect data so that they can run computer algorithms that may help identify suspected terrorists?

Imagine you are creating a disaster response plan for your city. Who do you put in charge at the disaster scene? The police, because law and order is critical. The fire department, because there are fires and people who need to be rescued from buildings. There is often more than one reasonable choice. What do you do?

In this chapter, we discuss each of these scenarios in depth. In the process, we will enhance our understanding of how governments and bureaucracies work to gain particular knowledge about homeland security challenges and policies. First, we analyze the creation of the Department of Homeland Security. The creation of the Department of Homeland Security provides an instructive example of when and why bureaucratic creation and change occurs and underscores the important role that bureaucracies play in executing public policy. Second, we discuss how the government should allocate resources to enhance the state's security. Ultimately, homeland security depends on protecting the country from threats. To do so, the government needs to allocate resources. What guidelines should govern the distribution of resources for protecting the nation? We show that the most prudent policy is one that focuses on risk management, where risk is a function of three factors: threat, vulnerability, and consequences. Although a **risk management** approach is the optimal defense strategy, we note that in practice the distribution of homeland security resources is driven more by electoral concerns than risk management principles. Third, we highlight how principal–agent problems create a trade-off between national security and civil liberties. We show that this tension is not new in American history, and we discuss in detail current controversies surrounding the USA Patriot and USA Freedom Acts and warrantless wiretapping. Fourth, we discuss how coordination problems are at the center of emergency response.

11.1 The Department of Homeland Security: An Example of Bureaucratic Change

What Is Homeland Security?

Homeland security involves efforts to protect the state from external and internal threats. The **Homeland Security Act of 2002**, which created the **Department of Homeland Security** (DHS), expands on this definition. It says that the primary missions of the DHS are "to prevent terrorist attacks within the United States, reduce the vulnerability of the United States to terrorism; and minimize the damage, and assist in the recovery, from terrorist attacks that do occur within the United States" (Homeland Security Act 2002). Put simply, the mission of the DHS is to minimize the likelihood of major disasters, whether manmade or natural, in the United States, and when **disasters** do occur, to minimize the damage done through emergency response actions. To accomplish these tasks, the DHS focuses on protection, policing, mitigation, and resilience (see Figure 11.1). Broadly stated, policing and protection policies aim to reduce risk, while mitigation and resilience policies aim to reduce the extent of damage from disasters and attacks. We elaborate

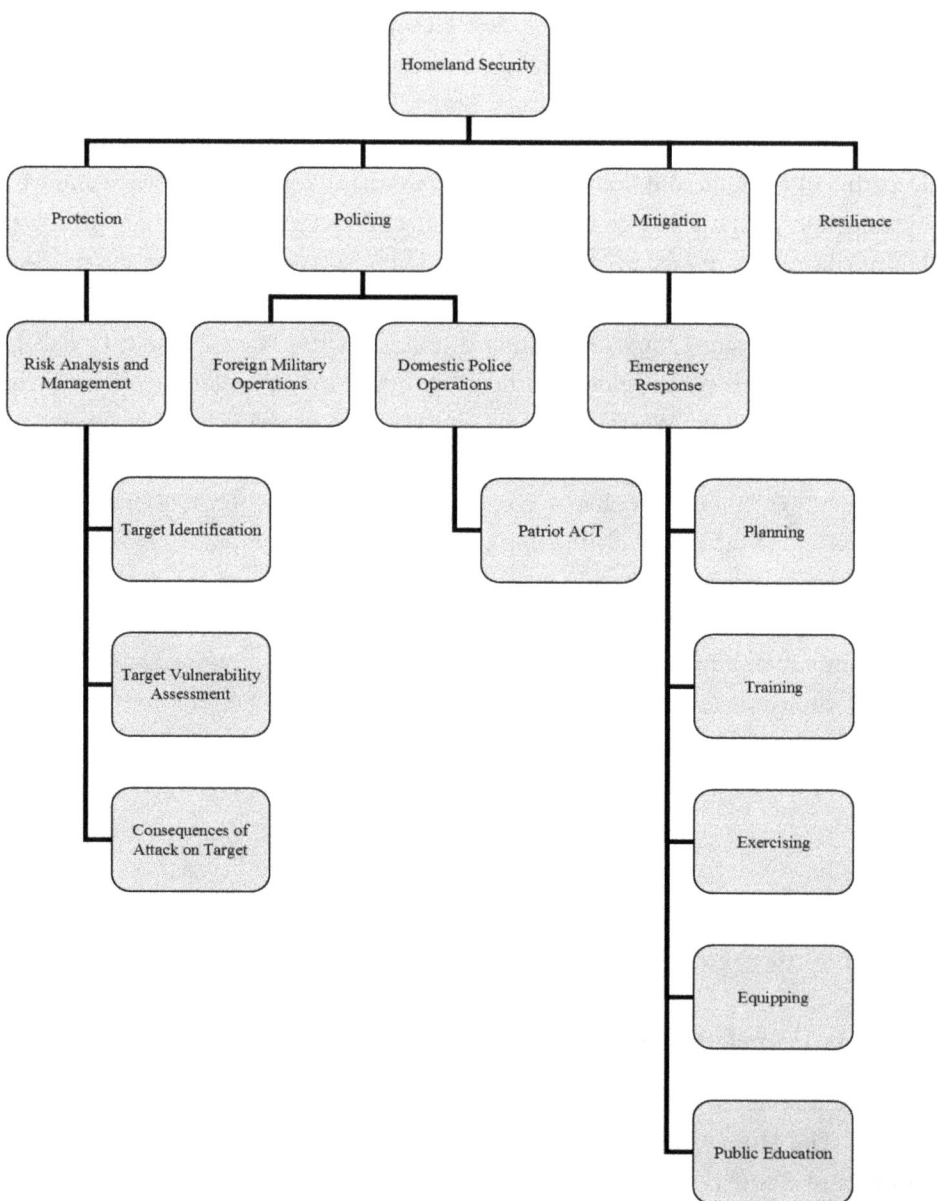

Figure 11.1 Major Functions in Homeland Security

on these tasks throughout the chapter, but first we discuss what a bureaucracy is and how bureaucratic change occurs.

What Is Bureaucracy?

If we want to understand public policy or politics, why do we care about bureaucracies? One might think that politicians produce policy. This view is partially correct.

By creating laws, politicians establish a broad framework that guides what the government does. Bureaucracies implement policy, and are themselves created by laws. More precisely, the **bureaucracy** is the set of institutions that "interpret, elaborate, and carry out public policy" (Moe and Wilson 1994: 4). In terms we have used throughout the book, bureaucrats are agents and politicians are their principals. To use a baseball metaphor, politicians establish the strike zone, while bureaucracies call the balls and strikes. In some situations, it might be more apt to say that politicians say that a game will be played and the bureaucracies determine how the game will be played. As the baseball metaphor implies, bureaucracies are not only integral to understanding public policy, but also have great influence on the implementation of policy. "A powerful, well-designed agency can turn policy goals into reality, while a weak, poorly designed one can get nowhere" (Moe and Wilson 1994: 4). In this section, we examine the creation of the Department of Homeland Security. In the process, we will illustrate both the importance of bureaucracies and how political forces shape bureaucracies.

During the Cold War, the United States organized its homeland security effort around the Soviet threat. Given the location of the United States relative to the Soviet Union, a major land attack was unlikely. Accordingly, the United States focused on air and missile attacks and set up the North American Aerospace Defense Command (NORAD) with the Canadian Government in 1958. With the end of the Cold War, threats to the United States changed from major war and communism to asymmetric warfare and terrorism (Cohen *et al.* 2006: 680). In turn, these threats called for a different type of homeland security effort. Instead of focusing on protecting the country from a major military attack from the Soviet Union, the government needed to shift its focus to protecting the country from smaller attacks by smaller groups. Such a shift would require a significant change to the design of the nation's homeland security bureaucracy.

Understanding Bureaucratic Change: Fire Alarms and Police Patrols

Bureaucratic change, however, is difficult. Bureaucratic change is about changing principal–agent relationships. At the polls, voters focus more on specific policy issues than bureaucratic reforms. How many candidates running for office, for example, campaign on reforming health policy or tax cuts versus reforming a bureaucracy? With little voter interest, members of Congress have little incentive to pursue bureaucratic reforms. Further, the interest groups that support reform are usually less organized than the entrenched interests benefitting from the status quo. After all, the status quo reflects the success these interest groups achieved at an earlier point in time. Because of these difficulties, the public and politicians take more of a **fire-alarm** than a **police-patrol approach** to bureaucratic change (McCubbins and Schwartz 1984). A police-patrol approach calls for being proactive, for patrolling the streets to address situations before they become big problems. A fire-alarm approach is reactive. Only when there is a fire, a major problem, is there activity. When there is a fire, or major disaster, a broad political constituency becomes activated, incentivizing politicians to pursue bureaucratic overhaul. Zegart (2006) echoes these arguments with respect to reforming the intelligence community and standard operating procedures within intelligence bureaucracies. She notes that prior to 9/11 many blue-ribbon commissions called for more attention to terrorist activity and a reorganization of the nation's intelligence agencies. In the late 1990s, however, there was little motivation among members of Congress or the public to change the intelligence community or homeland security status quo. The events of September 11, 2001 served as a fire alarm for the need to reorganize both the intelligence community and the nation's homeland security bureaucracy.

A goal of all presidents is to be seen as a strong leader, one who acts decisively to protect and promote the nation's interests (Moe and Wilson 1994: 12). Reform of homeland security began less than one month after the attacks of 9/11. On October 8, 2001, President Bush created a Homeland Security Office by executive order. The Homeland Security Office did not last long. A little over a year later, on November 25, 2002, President Bush signed into law the creation of a new federal department, the Department of Homeland Security. This is a very large and complex organization with a diverse set of responsibilities, including law enforcement, site protection, emergency response, and disaster relief (see Figure 11.1).

How did we move from a small Homeland Security Office in the White House to a large Department of Homeland Security bureaucracy? In a word, the answer is politics. Politicians are attentive to what their constituents care about. Most of the time, most people do not pay much attention to the bureaucratic organization of government. Crises, or major events, increase public attention, and when enough of the public is paying attention, Congress and the president are likely to take action. This theory of political responsiveness may tell us why Congress and the president felt compelled to do something, but it does not tell us why they created a new federal bureaucracy. Indeed, the Bush administration did not initially support creating a new Department of Homeland Security.

The Bush administration dropped its opposition and eventually supported the creation of the Department of Homeland Security because it came to believe that creating a new bureaucracy would, among other things, convey to the public that the administration was focused on providing the public good of security (Cohen *et al.* 2006: 680). In addition, the administration compromised with Congress on the union status of DHS employees. We now discuss these points in more detail.

Why would creating a new bureaucracy suggest that the administration was providing for the nation's security effectively? After 9/11, a majority of the public was either very concerned or somewhat concerned (as opposed to "not too worried" or "not worried at all") about another terrorist attack (Gallup 2001). When fear is high, there is a desire for something to be done, and creating a new bureaucracy is doing something. It allows politicians to go back to their districts and tell their constituents that they have done something to make them safer. In the 2002 midterm elections, the Democratic Party was seen as opposing the creation of DHS and suffered at the polls for this perception (Cohen *et al.* 2006: 695). Since some problems related to the 9/11 attack were caused by too much decentralization (e.g. not sharing information among different parts of the intelligence community), an increase in centralization through DHS suggested to people that something effective was being done. The final bill creating the Department of Homeland Security significantly centralized the nation's homeland security efforts, moving about twenty-two agencies into the DHS (Cohen *et al.* 2006: 691).

In addition to responding to the public's desire to do something regarding homeland security, the Bush administration embraced the idea because it advanced other political goals. In particular, it allowed for rent-seeking. **Rent-seeking**, a term coined by Anne Krueger in 1974, is a central idea in political economy. Rent-seeking is the pursuit of wealth outside of traditional economic exchange. In other words, a successful rent-seeker acquires wealth, but does not create any additional wealth. In contrast, an owner of capital or laborer earns wealth only through investing and creating products that, when sold, build wealth. Rent-seeking is a common political activity, with pork-barrel spending being the primary way in which it occurs. Pork-barrel spending means politicians are allocating resources more for political purposes (i.e. to help them win re-election) than economic or national security ones. The creation of the Department of Homeland Security provided ample opportunities for rent-seeking through pork-barrel spending.

The creation of the Department of Homeland Security led to increased spending on civil defense, police, and fire departments, among other agencies. Was the money allocated for homeland security done primarily with an eye to protecting the nation or for more narrow political purposes? In a study of how funds from the 2004 Homeland Security Appropriates Act were allocated, Coats *et al.* (2006) find evidence of some rent-seeking. They find that "a 1 percent rise in electoral votes per capita seems to increase homeland security spending per capita by 1.3 percent" (Coats *et al.* 2006: 283). That is, more money was allocated to states with more electoral votes than one would expect based on just threat factors like population size, wealth, presence of nuclear power plants, etc. Notwithstanding some evidence for rent-seeking, their research does not show a high degree of rent-seeking with this particular bill. In fact, one of their other measures of rent-seeking, the closeness of the election, was not statistically significant, and measures of threat were statistically significant.

To earn passage of the Homeland Security bill, the Bush Administration compromised with the Democratic Party. For Democrats, an important concern was giving union status for employees in the new Transportation Security Agency (TSA). The Bush administration agreed to do so. This was not a popular move with the president's core supporters, but a majority of the public supported it. In late September 2002, 45 percent of Republicans, 80 percent of Democrats, and 68 percent of Independents supported keeping union status for Department of Homeland Security employees (*Newsweek* Poll 2002). With only mild opposition from the president's base and the desire to be seen as a strong leader and advance other interests, President Bush acquiesced on union status for TSA employees.

The fire-alarm approach to the bureaucratic reorganization of US homeland security efforts is not unusual. The **Goldwater-Nichols Act of 1986** significantly reorganized the Department of Defense. As before, blue ribbon commissions and experts in the field had been calling for changes to the defense department, but without a catastrophe, change is usually slow to occur. In this case, the botched effort to rescue US hostages in Iran in 1980,[1] the bombing of the Marine barracks in 1982, and the poor execution of the Grenada invasion contributed significantly in motivating Congress and the president to act (Locher III 2001). The primary goals of the Goldwater-Nichols Act were to improve the military advice being given to the president, create unity of command for military operations, and improve the ability of the separate military branches (Air Force, Army, Marines, and Navy) to operate jointly.

To achieve the first goal, Goldwater-Nichols significantly strengthened the position of the Chairman of the Joint Chiefs of Staff (CJCS). The Chairman would now serve as the primary military liaison to the president. That is, all of the other military chiefs had to give their advice to the CJCS instead of directly to the president. For the second goal, Goldwater-Nichols created the combatant command structure, which is still in place.[2] It may be surprising to learn, but before the changes created by Goldwater-Nichols, theater commanders had to coordinate with the other military branches to obtain control over assets in their theater of operations. In other words, if an Army general planning and overseeing combat operations wanted to task Air Force planes, he had to ask the Air Force for permission. Now, combatant commanders have direct control over all military assets in their area of responsibility. The first three changes greatly clarify who is responsible for what. Third, Goldwater-Nichols aimed to rectify the services' poor ability to work with each other. During the invasion of Grenada, for example, Navy radios could not communicate with Air Force radios. Since Goldwater-Nichols, the military has increased training with the other branches and requires that senior officers serve in a joint position to be promoted further.

---

[1] For an excellent discussion of this event, see Mark Bowden's (Bowden 2006) "The Desert One Debacle."

[2] Currently, there are six combatant commanders, each with their own area of responsibility. That is, if the United States goes to war, the commander of that area will lead the military campaign. For more information, see the Department of Defense website: www.defense.gov/Sites/Unified-Combatant-Commands.

11.2 Homeland Security and Resource Allocation

To enhance homeland security, governments employ four sets of policies: protection, policing, mitigation, and resilience (Mueller 2010: 1). **Protection** is passive defense; it involves domestic measures that make it difficult for an attack to succeed. **Policing** is active defense; it involves domestic and foreign operations that reduce the ability of an adversary to carry out an attack at home. **Mitigation** involves policies that reduce the consequences of an attack. It falls primarily within the domain of emergency management. **Resilience** measures also reduce the consequences of an attack, but where mitigation efforts focus on how to respond to an attack, resilience efforts emphasize diversification of critical infrastructure and assets. All of these types of policies are important, but we will focus most of our attention on protection.

On the topic of prevention, the central question that governments face is this: Given a threat against any one of many potential targets, how should the government allocate resources to minimize the negative consequences of an attack? Perhaps one's first response to this question is to allocate resources to protect all potential targets. Resources, however, are finite and potential targets are plentiful. There are thousands of bridges and shopping malls, millions of buildings, and hundreds of millions of people. To fully protect every potential target would require resources far beyond what is possible. With this in mind, we can restate the question. Given limited resources, how should the government allocate its resources to enhance homeland security? One could choose to distribute resources evenly across the fifty states. Since there is likely some correlation between the amount of damage that could be inflicted and a state's population size, this distribution plan seems unwise. California surely has more significant targets than Rhode Island. One could choose to distribute resources on a per capita basis; thus, states with more people would receive more funds from the federal government than states with fewer people. A potential problem with this system is that states with more people are not necessarily the states with the most, or most critical, sites vulnerable to attack. More importantly, one of the central problems for homeland defense is that terrorists adapt. If terrorists want to attack airlines and the government successfully defends against such attacks, terrorism does not necessarily end. Rather, the terrorists are likely to switch targets (Enders and Sandler 2006). Such a switch is an example of **strategic adaptation**: one's actions are influenced by one's expectations of how others will respond.

Powell (2007: 528) shows that a government's best strategy is to allocate resources in a manner that minimizes a likely attacker's maximum pay-off, a **minimax strategy**. To do this, the defender should protect its most valuable targets in rank order. That is, as much as possible, the defender should protect its most valuable target, then its second most valuable target, then its third most, and so on. What targets are most valuable?

Value here is defined in terms of **risk**. A site's risk is the product of the consequences of an attack on that site times the vulnerability of that site to an attack times the threat of that site to an attack (Willis *et al.* 2005: 10). Thus, a government should allocate resources based on a risk management strategy that prioritizes potential targets based on their risk.

In general, there are two ways to protect potential targets within the United States. One can defend specific sites or one can defend the borders of the country, thereby offering some protection to all sites. With **site defense**, one reduces the likelihood of attack against a particular site. With **border defense**, one reduces the likelihood of attack against many sites. The problem with site defense is that terrorists are strategic and will search for less protected sites. The problem with border defense is that it gives the same amount of protection to all sites, but the consequences of an attack are higher for some sites than others. Perhaps not surprisingly, the best strategy is to allocate resources to both border and site defense. A precise division between border and site defense is difficult to determine. In general, as the number of high-value targets increases, border defense becomes a better strategy.

We just noted that the best defensive strategy is to allocate resources based on risk management that identifies potential targets and the risk to each target. In practice, federal funds are not allocated strictly on risk management. The law requires that a minimum percentage of federal funds go to each state (75 percent), even if this means diverting funds from sites with a higher risk. In 2006, there was some momentum to lower this minimum to 25 percent, but it was blocked in the Senate. As an example of homeland security funds not being allocated strictly in accordance with a risk management approach, consider that: "While the port of New York and New Jersey is widely regarded as at the highest risk, it received only $6.6 million in FY 2005, about equal to Memphis and far behind Houston's $35.3 million" (Cohen *et al.* 2006: 716).

More generally, we can note that government efforts to protect the homeland face the same sort of **agency problems** discussed in other chapters. As before, the principal is the public and the agents are elected officials. If a terrorist attack occurs, the principal wants to know if the agent did everything possible to prevent the attack from occurring. But the principal does not have all of the necessary information or expertise to make this assessment with complete certainty. The principal can hold the agent accountable, but only to an imperfect standard. Bueno de Mesquita (2007) shows that this imperfect standard leads the government to over-allocate to observable counter-terror efforts and under-allocate to less observable counter-terror efforts like intelligence resources.

Building on the above points, **Mueller** (2010) contends that government efforts at protection are often misguided and wasteful. He offers five policy suggestions (Mueller 2010: 6–9). First, "any protective policy should be compared to a 'null case':

do nothing, and use the money saved to rebuild and to compensate any victim." Mueller's logic is that the likelihood of any particular target being attacked is very small, terrorists often choose their targets in a random manner, and rebuilding is typically not that expensive. Second, "abandon, or at least greatly scale back, efforts to imagine a terrorist target list." There are just too many potential targets. Any list will leave off something and thereby alienate some politician. Third, "temper **worst-case thinking**." A central problem with worst-case thinking is that it creates a psychological effect that hinders clear thinking. If one starts with the premise of catastrophic costs, then "there is a tendency to conclude that no protection cost would be unbearable no matter how unlikely the prospect of an attack." Fourth, "consider the negative effects of protection measures: not only direct cost, but inconvenience, enhancement of fear, negative economic impacts, reduction of liberties." Fifth, "consider the **opportunity costs**, the trade-offs, of protection measures." Every dollar spent on a particular protective effort could be spent in some other way. What is the most effective use of that dollar? For Mueller, the small likelihood of an attack implies that most resources spent on protection would be better spent in some other manner. Whether this is the case or not, Mueller is correct to highlight the importance of opportunity costs.

Homeland Security as a Colonel Blotto Game

Colonel Blotto games illustrate some of the challenges in homeland security. A Colonel Blotto game is a zero-sum game in which players allocate limited resources over sites. Zero-sum means that whatever one player wins, the other player loses.

We will name the two players in this game Defender and Attacker. Defender wants to protect two sites from attack. Attacker wants to inflict significant damage on as many sites as possible. We will label the two sites C (perhaps for the state's Capitol) and E (for a critical economic site). For our initial explorations of this game, let us assume that Defender has three resource units, while Attacker has two resource units. At each site, the player with more resources wins. If they allocate equal resources to the same site, then Defender wins (there is a defensive advantage). For example, if Defender allocates all of her resources to Site C and Attacker allocates all of his resources to Site C, then Defender wins (Defender has three resource units at the place of attack, while Attacker only has two resource units). If Defender correctly guesses the site Attacker intends to attack, then Defender can successfully protect it. However, if Defender allocates all of her resources to Site C and Attacker splits his resources between Sites C and E, then Defender successfully defends Site C, the capitol, but loses at Site E, meaning attacker successfully harms Site E. What is the best strategy for Defender to pursue? That is, how should Defender allocate her resources to protect the two sites? How should Attacker allocate his resources so that he can successfully harm at least one site?

Do you think it is prudent for Defender to allocate all of her resources to one site, say the Capitol? No. Let's explain why. If Defender allocates all of her resources to one site, then she is likely to lose (i.e. at least one of her sites will be successfully attacked) two out of three times. For example, if Defender allocates all of her resources to Site C and Attacker allocates his resources to Site E, then Defender loses at Site E. Alternatively, if Attacker splits his resources, using one to attack Site C and one to attack Site E, then Defender successfully repels the attack at Site C but not at Site E. Defender only protects both sites if Attacker allocates all of his resources to Site C as well. Since Defender does not know Attacker's specific plans, it would not be prudent for Defender to put all of her eggs in one basket as it were and only protect one site.

The attacker will not split his forces. Here is why. If the attacker splits his forces evenly against a defender who is dividing her forces, then the attacker loses both battles. (Recall that we just established that the defender is dividing her resources.) Therefore, the attacker will not split his forces.

We have now established that Defender will split her forces and Attacker will not split his forces in the scenario under investigation. Defender will either allocate two resource units to Site C and one resource unit to Site E or vice versa. Attacker will either allocate all of his forces to attacking Site C and none to Site E or vice versa. This means that in some situations, Attacker will achieve a successful attack. For example, Defender suffers a loss if she allocates two resource units to Site C and one unit to Site E, while Attacker allocates two resource units to Site E and none to Site C. Of course, Attacker does not know to which site Defender will allocate two units, but if this game is repeated enough, Attacker is likely to correctly guess, even if by accident, the more vulnerable site at some point in time.

There are a number of important features about the Colonel Blotto game we just discussed and these types of allocation problems in general. First, the outcome is a function of a **strategic interaction**. A strategic interaction is any situation in which the outcome is generated by the calculated choices of at least two actors. In a Colonel Blotto game, for example, whether the Defender successfully defends her sites depends on both her allocation of resources to the sites and the attacker's resource allocations. Second, each actor has limited resources. Because resources are limited, choices have to be made. Third, Defender does not have a dominant strategy, that is, a strategy that is guaranteed to successfully defend all of her sites no matter what Attacker chooses. Instead, Defender's best reply to Attacker's expected choice is a mixed strategy. A **mixed strategy** assigns a probability to each option. It is like randomly choosing what site to defend or attack. This is viewed as the best strategy in order to keep the attacker guessing. Recall that if the attacker knows what the defender will defend, then the attacker will choose the most vulnerable site available. By playing a mixed strategy, the defender keeps the attacker guessing. In football, a mixed strategy would be to sometimes run the ball and sometimes pass the ball. Unfortunately, with a mixed strategy, there is always some possibility that the defender guesses incorrectly and the attacker successfully damages the defender. Powell (2007) offers a mathematical proof that a mixed strategy is the best choice for Defender under a very large set of conditions (e.g. Defender has more sites, some sites are more valuable than others, Defender and Attacker each have more resources). Fourth, even if Defender has a troop advantage, this advantage quickly decreases as Defender has to defend more sites, for then Defender is once again spreading out her resources. If Attacker is aware of his resource/troop disadvantage, and most attackers are aware, then Attacker has a strong incentive to create new targets for Defender to defend. Attackers, for example, want the defender to not only defend nuclear power plants and the capital, but a host of "soft target" sites, like shopping malls and other gathering places. Fifth, Attacker can try to reduce Defender's resource advantage by encouraging "lone wolves." Lone wolves are individuals who are not directed by an organization, but intend to commit a terrorist attack to support a group's goals. By being unaffiliated with the organization and not taking orders from anyone, they are difficult to track.

Security vs. Civil Liberties

Infringements on civil liberties in pursuit of, or at least in the name of, national security have occurred throughout American history. In 1798, as a result of the XYZ affair with France, the United States and France engaged in a brief naval war. Because of the war, the Federalists, the majority party at the time, were concerned about subversive activity by the French. They also wanted to suppress political criticism of the government. These concerns led to the passage of the **Alien and Sedition Acts of 1798**. These Acts comprise four laws. The Alien Friends Act gave the president the authority to determine if an alien was "dangerous to the peace and safety of the United States," and if so, he could deport the person. The Alien Enemies Act allowed the president to deport aliens if they came from a country at war with the United States. The Naturalization Act of 1798 increased the length of time to fourteen years that an alien had to reside in the United States before becoming a citizen. Most damaging to civil liberties was the Sedition Act. With this Act, it became illegal to publish "false, scandalous, and malicious writing" against the government. In light of these Acts, James Madison wrote to Thomas Jefferson: "Perhaps it is a universal truth that the loss of liberty at home is to be charged to provisions against danger, real or pretended, from abroad" (Padover 1953: 258).

In 1861, President Lincoln suspended *habeas corpus* for some parts of the Union. When a federal district court said Lincoln's order was illegal, he just ignored the court's decision. Lincoln justified his actions by saying that "measures otherwise unconstitutional might become lawful by becoming indispensable to the preservation of the Constitution through the preservation of the Nation" (Schlesinger 1973: 71).

In 1917 and 1918, the US Congress, at the urging of President Wilson, passed the **Espionage and Sedition Acts**. The Espionage Act made it illegal to pass on information that would negatively affect military operations. The Sedition Act outlawed "disloyal, profane, scurrilous, or abusive language" about the US Government or flag during war. It was upheld by the Supreme Court in *Debs v. United States* (1919), but was essentially overturned by the Court in 1969 in *Brandenburg v. Ohio*.

In response to bombings by leftist anarchists, called the Galleanists, Attorney General A. Mitchell Palmer ordered the arrest of about 10,000 alleged communists in 1920. These arrests became known as the **Palmer Raids**, and this episode is also known as the first Red Scare.

In 1942, President Roosevelt issued an executive order to place **Japanese-Americans in internment camps**. All told, approximately 120,000 Japanese-Americans living on the West Coast were placed in ten different camps. When these forced relocations were challenged in court, the Supreme Court ruled in favor of the government (e.g. *Yasui v. United States* (1943), *Hirabayashi v. United States* (1943), *Korematsu v. United States* (1944)). In 1988, President Reagan signed a bill apologizing for the internment. The apology attributed the government's actions to "race prejudice, war hysteria, and a failure of political leadership" (Senate Bill 1009, 1988).

Box 11.1 Questions on the Trade-Off between Civil Liberties and Security

1. Some people say it should be a crime for anyone to belong to or contribute money to any organization that supports international terrorism. Others say that a person's guilt or innocence should not be determined only by who they associate with or the organizations to which they belong.

2. Some people say the government should be able to arrest and detain a non-citizen indefinitely if that person is suspected of belonging to a terrorist organization. Others say nobody should be held for a long period of time without being formally charged with a crime.

3. Some people say that law enforcement should be able to stop or detain people of certain racial or ethnic backgrounds if these groups are thought to be more likely to commit crimes. This is called racial profiling. Others think racial profiling should not be done because it harasses many innocent people just because of their race or ethnicity.

4. Some people say high school teachers have the right to criticize America's policies toward terrorism. Others say that all high school teachers should defend America's policies in order to promote loyalty to our country.

5. Some people say that law enforcement should be free to search a property without a warrant solely on the suspicion that a crime or a terrorist act is

Box 11.1 *(cont.)*

being planned there. Others say that protection against searches without a warrant is a basic right that should not be given up for any reason.

6. Some people say that government should be allowed to record telephone calls and monitor email in order to prevent people from planning terrorist or criminal acts. Others say that people's conversations and email are private and should be protected by the Constitution.

7. Some say that people who participate in non-violent protests against the US Government should be investigated. Others say that people have the right to meet in public and express unpopular views, as long as they are not violating the law.

From this brief discussion, we can draw a few inferences. First, during times of war or when foreign threats are strong, the executive branch of government is particularly inclined to take actions to promote security and these actions curtail the civil liberties of at least some citizens. Second, the political party of the president does not seem to matter. Both Democratic and Republican presidents are willing to infringe on civil liberties in times of threat. Third, these restrictions on civil liberties have been supported by broad segments of the population, but not by everyone. Fourth, the legislative and judicial branches sometimes support these restrictions on civil liberties.

Public Opinion on the Civil Liberties vs. Security Trade-Off

As just discussed, since the terrorist attacks on 9/11 some civil liberties have been restricted. The public largely supports these restrictions, yet civil liberties are a core part of America's political identity. Why do people support curtailing civil liberties? For some insight on this question, we turn to a study by Darren Davis and Brian Silver (2004). The dependent variable in this study is support for civil liberties. This is the percentage of pro civil liberties responses on seven questions about the **trade-off between civil liberties and security** (see inset box for the questions).

To explain why some individuals are more willing than others to trade off civil liberties for security, we will focus on four of their key independent variables. The first predictor variable is called Sociotropic Threat. This is a measure of one's "generalized anxiety" or belief about the "threat to the country as a whole." The second predictor is Personal Threat. This is an individual's average score on five survey questions about their sense of threat (e.g. how concerned are you to go into tall buildings? How concerned are you to fly?). These two variables are positively correlated at 0.44,

Table 11.1 Multiple Regression Estimates on Pro-Civil Liberties Responses

	Coefficient (Standard Error)
Sociotropic Threat	−4.93* (0.98)
Personal Threat	−0.15 (0.50)
Trust in Federal Government	−3.59* (1.04)
Trust in Law Enforcement	−4.58* (1.09)
N	1309

Notes: * = p<05, two-tailed.
Model 1 From Table 3 of Davis and Silver (2004).

meaning higher values of sociotropic threat are associated with higher values of personal threat. The third predictor is Trust in Government, and the fourth predictor is Trust in Law Enforcement. In Table 11.1, we present coefficient estimates and standard errors from this multiple regression model.

In looking at Table 11.1, we observe that the coefficient on Sociotropic Threat (−4.93) is more than twice its standard error (0.98). This indicates that the variable is statistically significant at conventional levels: there is less than a 5 percent chance of observing this relationship by chance. We also observe that the sign on the coefficient is negative. This means that a one-unit increase in an individual's Sociotropic Threat score decreases their support for civil liberties by 4.93 percent (recall that the dependent variable is an individual's percentage score on support for civil liberties). The multiple regression estimates show that there is no statistically meaningful relationship between Personal Threat and support for civil liberties. (We know this because the coefficient is not twice as great as the standard error.)

Threat perceptions are not the only factor affecting opinions on the security–civil liberties trade-off. Trust in the government also matters. Davis and Silver (2004: 35) also find that: "The more people trust the federal government or law enforcement agencies, the more willing they are to allow the government leeway in fighting the domestic war on terrorism by conceding some civil liberties." We see this in the statistically significant and negative signs on the Trust in Federal Government and Trust in Law Enforcement variables in Table 11.1.

In additional models, Davis and Silver add a number of demographic (e.g. gender, age, education, where you live (urban/rural), etc.) and attitudinal (e.g. dogmatism, liberalism, etc.) factors. The basic findings on threat and trust in government and law enforcement do not change.

11.3 Principal–Agent Problems and Warrantless Wiretapping

Following 9/11, the security–civil liberty trade-off was illustrated in the debate surrounding the **USA Patriot Act**. The USA Patriot Act is an acronym for the *Uniting and Strengthening America by Providing Appropriate Tools Required to Intercept and Obstruct Terrorism Act of 2001*. In general, the Patriot Act enhanced the government's ability to gather information and obtain search warrants, "removed the major legal barriers that prevented the law enforcement, intelligence, and national defense communities from talking and coordinating their work," and increased punishments for those committing acts of terrorism (Department of Justice). The Patriot Act came about because after 9/11 many came to believe that the United States failed to stop the terrorist attacks because government agencies failed to connect the dots and could not obtain enough information on potential terrorists. These information problems stemmed from US law. When collecting information for criminal prosecution, the police need to have a "**reasonable suspicion**" that the individual is guilty. However, the law governing the government's surveillance of individuals required "**probable cause**," a higher standard of guilt. This higher standard was intended, as Congress did not want the government to infringe upon civil liberties.

The Patriot Act and 2008 amendments to the FISA law made it easier for the government to collect information on individuals. Previously, the government could only wiretap a specific phone or location. The advent of easily obtainable mobile phones and the Internet made specific wiretaps of little use. With the Patriot Act, roving wiretaps are now allowed. In addition, banks are now required to report suspicious money transfers, and countries with which the United States grants a visa-waiver must have biometric indicators on their passports (Campbell and O'Hanlon 2006: 123).

One of the more controversial aspects of the Patriot Act was its expansion of the use of **National Security Letters**. National Security Letters are "a type of administrative subpoena created in the 1970s which enabled the FBI to review in secret the customer records of suspected foreign agents. Changes under the Patriot Act allow the FBI to use the letters to scrutinize US residents and visitors who are not alleged to be terrorists or spies. Businesses that receive the letters are required to turn over electronic records about finances, telephone calls, email, and other personal information. The letters may be issued independently by FBI field offices and are not subject to judicial review unless a case comes to court" (*Washington Post*, Patriot Act Primer). Under the 2006 re-authorization of the Patriot Act, libraries are no longer subject to National Security Letters.

Given what we have just said about the Patriot Act, it should be no surprise that public opinion is divided on its merits. In an April 2005 CBS News poll, approximately 49 percent of respondents who were knowledgeable about the Patriot Act said that it was a necessary tool for the government to find terrorists, while 45 percent responded that it went too far. We again note significant differences between Democrats and Republicans on this topic. Nearly 88 percent of Republican respondents replied that the Patriot Act was necessary for finding terrorists, but only 23 percent of Democrats agreed (CBS News Poll, 2005).

The Foreign Intelligence Surveillance Act (FISA)

Another controversial area of the war on terrorism has been the expansion of electronic surveillance, specifically **warrantless wiretapping**. In 1978, Congress passed the **Foreign Intelligence Surveillance Act (FISA)**. FISA regulates how the government can conduct physical and electronic surveillance between "foreign powers" and "agents of foreign powers" in the United States. In practical terms, this means that FISA allows the government to wiretap the international phone calls of suspected foreign agents with a warrant. The motivations for FISA were twofold. First, American "courts had clarified that the Fourth Amendment and its warrant requirement applied to domestic security surveillance" (Wittes 2008: 224). Second, FISA was a response to the "electronic surveillance of political dissidents that came to light during the Watergate era" (Wittes 2008: 224).

FISA established the Foreign Intelligence Surveillance Court (FISC), a federal court that reviews government requests to obtain electronic surveillance warrants against suspected foreign enemies. The FISC only hears from government lawyers and witnesses and the defense cannot see or challenge a warrant application (Wittes 2008: 225).

With this background, we can better understand some of the controversy around the National Security Agency's warrantless surveillance programs. As part of the war on terror, the Bush administration "authorized the NSA to intercept international communications into and out of the United States" of any suspected terrorist (DOJ White Paper, p. 5). These communications include phone calls, emails, text messages, internet activity, or other forms of communication. The Bush administration has argued that these programs are legal based on the **Authorization for Use of Military Force Against Terrorists**, the joint resolution passed by Congress on September 18, 2001, which authorizes the president to use all necessary means to protect the country.

There are two primary concerns with the president's surveillance program. First, some of the surveillance taps into systems that reside inside the United States. This goes against FISA, which only allows the interception and monitoring of international communication. Second, the government is practicing **data mining**. Data mining involves collecting large amounts of information and then analyzing this information for patterns. The government appears to be gathering large amounts of information, analyzing this information with various computer algorithms, and then identifying potential targets based on the analyzed information. In other words, instead of identifying a target and then collecting information, which is what FISA calls for, the government is collecting information and then identifying targets. Since data mining, at the collection stage, does not focus on specific individuals, the government argues that it does not need a warrant, thus, warrantless wiretapping.

Regarding the first concern, Wittes notes that FISA was not created with modern communication technologies in mind. When FISA was created, almost all overseas telecommunication involved phone calls. Since it was easy to identify if a phone call was international or not, it was relatively straightforward to protect against purely domestic surveillance. With the internet, it is much more difficult to determine the location of the sender and recipient of an email. If the government cannot tap into the internet – note that FISA does not allow domestic surveillance – then it will be more difficult to gather information on foreign enemies. With the **Protect America Act of 2007**, Congress no longer requires that the government know ahead of time that a foreign agent is outside the United States; the government only has to believe that the agent is not within the nation's borders.

The data-mining concern is more difficult to address and goes to the heart of the national security versus civil liberty trade-off. On the one hand, the more information the government collects and analyzes, the better it can connect the dots and identify terrorists. On the other hand, the greater the probability that some people's civil liberties will be infringed upon. From the government's perspective, it does not need a warrant to practice data mining, as no humans are looking at the collected data until the algorithms identify potential targets. From a civil liberty perspective, it is danger-ous for the government to collect information on citizens and the algorithms that the government uses to identify potential foreign enemies are not known. More generally, the data-mining problem raises the security–liberty trade-off in a particularly acute way because of the difference between collecting information for criminal prosecution and collecting information for intelligence. To better understand the civil liberties–security trade-off and the concerns associated with warrantless wiretapping, we turn to a discussion of PRISM.

PRISM

PRISM is the US Government code name for the National Security Agency's top-secret mass electronic surveillance data-mining program. PRISM came into being after the passage of the FISA Amendments Act of 2008. Central to this Act was the granting of immunity to any private company that voluntarily cooperates with the US intelligence community. Cooperation means they allow the NSA to access their electronic records (e.g. email). In the summer of 2013 when Edward Snowden leaked information about the program, Microsoft, Google, Yahoo, and others were cooperating with the NSA. Whose email is the NSA reading? This is where PRISM becomes more controversial. The Fourth Amendment to the US Constitution prohibits the government from unreasonable search and seizure; to search an American's email or phone records, one needs a search warrant. The Fourth Amendment does not apply to foreigners, and the primary focus of NSA electronic surveillance is potential foreign terrorists. However, in the process of accessing the email and phone records of foreigners, the NSA will collect information on some Americans, specifically any American who has some contact with someone in another country. It is unclear whether the incidental collection of data on Americans is a violation of the Fourth Amendment.

The PRISM program illustrates several of the principal–agent dynamics discussed previously. The NSA is the agent. It works for the president, who works for the American people. The primary principal, then, of interest is the American people. They want a job done – protecting the US homeland from terrorist attacks – and they want the job done in accordance with their preferences. It is difficult, however, for the American people to monitor the NSA. Its programs are often classified. Indeed, until the Snowden leaks, the American people did not know about PRISM. What the public does is monitor through its elected representatives, Congress and the president. The president and FISA court are in fact aware of and monitoring the NSA's PRISM program; in Congress only the members of the House and Senate Intelligence committees have knowledge of PRISM. This does not resolve the matter, for how do we know that the agents (primarily the president and Congress) are acting in accord with the principal's preferences when the principal is unaware of what the agent is doing and therefore has not expressed a preference? Situations of this sort – that is, situations in which the principle has not expressed a preference on a specific policy and is probably unaware of the policy – arise routinely in all areas of public policy. The problem for the principal is to mitigate the moral hazard problem: the agent acting differently from the principal desires because the agent is partially protected from the costs of its actions.

We have discussed three general approaches to reducing the moral hazard problem: clearly defined standard operating procedures, careful screening of agents, and outcome-based incentive schemes. While all three methods apply to this example, the most important is standard operating procedures. Recall that standard operating procedures are specific sets of guidelines on what to do. Laws are essentially standard operating procedures. That is, writing and creating laws is one of the principal's primary ways for controlling agents. Here, the agent of interest is the executive branch. How should they be controlled?

One way for a principal to control an agent is to create laws that increase reporting. Reporting requirements are like a police-patrol. If something inappropriate is occurring, the report readers (Courts, Congress, special interest groups) can raise questions and draw attention to the concern. This is the approach recommended by Wittes (2008) to address the civil liberties–security trade-off connected to warrantless wiretapping and data mining. "Computerized filtering of data" is not the problem, according to Wittes (2008: 251), "but humans acting upon that filtering." Insofar as this is accurate, then more and broader reporting may effectively address moral hazard concerns.

USA Freedom Act

In June 2013, Edward Snowden, an NSA contractor, gave classified documents to journalists. Subsequently, some of the information in these documents was published, revealing for the first time the extent of the government's data-mining programs. Of particular concern to many is that Snowden exposed that the NSA was collecting phone data on American citizens. For his actions, some have called him a patriot and whistleblower, while others view him as a traitor. The US Government has filed criminal charges against him. To avoid being brought to trial in the United States, he is residing in Russia.

In June 2015, Congress passed and the president signed into law the USA Freedom Act. This law is at least partly in response to Snowden's revelations and modifies the USA Patriot Act. The central difference between the Patriot and Freedom laws is that the USA Freedom Act establishes limits on the bulk collection of telecommunication metadata on US citizens. This means the government can only collect phone data for a specific investigation. It cannot collect data on all people in the country as a whole, at least not without the approval of a judge or the FISA court.

11.4 Disaster Response as a Coordination Problem

If a major terrorist attack or natural disaster does occur, then the Department of Homeland Security oversees the government's response. The **Federal Emergency Management Agency (FEMA)** is the lead organization within the DHS for coordinating disaster response activities. Emergency response involves three sets of actions: preparation for an emergency, response to an emergency, and recovery from the emergency (National Response Framework, 2008)

As most adults recognize, "prior proper planning prevents poor performance." What constitutes prior proper planning? As far as emergency preparation goes, proper groundwork involves planning, training, exercising, equipping, and public education. Planning involves determining what needs to be done, when, where, and how. If a hurricane hits a major city, what will the people need? How do we get needed supplies to the people? A good plan, while necessary for an effective response, only goes so far. It is also important for emergency responders to train; for them to train most effectively, they need to be equipped appropriately. Finally, public education is very important for an effective emergency response. Each person should know what to do if a disaster strikes. Where do they go? What sort of supplies should they have?

As we know from Hurricane Katrina, federal, state, and city governments did not plan and execute very well. Secretary of Homeland Security Chertoff (2005) observed that "80 percent or more of the problem lies with planning." Similarly, the General Accounting Office (Walker 2006: 5) concluded that: "Although the NRP framework envisions a proactive national response in the event of a catastrophe, the nation does not yet have the type of detailed plans needed to better delineate capabilities that might be required and how much assistance will be provided and coordinated." The confusion about who was in charge in the aftermath of Hurricane Katrina underscores that planning was poor and not sufficiently detailed.

Coordination is a significant analytic problem in many emergency response situations. When an emergency occurs, questions often arise about who is in charge, who is doing what, who knows how to do what, and where are the appropriate tools and supplies. For example, when the hijacked airplanes crashed into the World Trade Center on 9/11, the New York City police and fire departments both needed to respond. They did. But coordination between them was not great. "The New York City Police Department (NYPD) had a helicopter circling overhead, but the fire chiefs had no direct link to the police assessments" (Kettl 2003: 255). The lack of information associated with the poor coordination is part of the reason some New York City firefighters went up the towers without orders.

Coordination problems arise because there are different preferences and the absence of clear rules. Particularly in the context under discussion, one's preferences are strongly influenced by one's work group. In other words, in an emergency, the police tend to have law and order preferences, while the fire department tends to have rescue preferences. For everyone to act coherently, it helps to have an institutional solution to this sort of coordination problem. An institutional solution is an agreed-on set of procedures that everyone will follow. The agreed-on procedures include designating who is in charge, how communication will occur (e.g. what radio frequencies to use), and where people should initially report.

Coordination problems are common. In a coordination problem, the actors agree that disagreement is the worst possible outcome, but the actors have different preference rankings on which outcome is most preferred. Some examples of coordination problems include the side of the road on which to drive, the language used for international air traffic control and communication, etc. What coordination problems have in common is that both players view disagreement as much worse than any agreement between them. For example, as far as travel and safety are concerned, it does not matter if we drive on the right or left side of the road. All that matters is that

Sven

		Streep	Schwarzeneggar
Olga	Streep	2, 2	4, 1
	Schwarzeneggar	1, 4	3, 3

Figure 11.2 Coordination Game on Which Movie to See

we agree on which side of the road to drive. A simple example illustrates the problem and ways to solve it.

Olga and Sven are trying to decide which movie to see this weekend (see Figure 11.2). Sven would like to see the new Arnold Schwarzeneggar movie, but Olga would like to see the new Meryl Streep movie. Equally important, they value being together, even if it means seeing their least preferred movie, more than being apart. In this game, there are two equilibria: either they agree to see Streep or they agree to see Schwarzeneggar. Which do they see? Olga and Sven need an institution, a rule, for determining how they should coordinate. One possible institution is that they alternate on who decides. This week Sven decides and next week Olga decides.

In addition to the creation of an institution, focal points can mitigate coordination problems. A focal point is something easily identifiable for the actors involved. In the Olga and Sven example, a focal point might be the start time of the movie. If Olga and Sven want to be in before midnight and the Streep movie starts at 8pm while the Schwarzeneggar movie does not have any show times before 10pm, then the movie start time serves as a focal point and helps them coordinate on which movie to see.

What is important about focal points is that they can arise naturally, that is, without communication. Focal points are great for resolving coordination problems, but they are not always present. In many contexts, they presume similar backgrounds or preferences. Actors with very different life experiences may not agree on what is a focal point. Olga, for example, might be a night owl, while Sven is a morning bird. If that is the case, then the movie start time is not a focal point.

To further understand how focal points arise, consider a situation in which two people become separated at Disney World. If they have similar backgrounds, then each may know that the other person will go to the front-left of Cinderella's castle and wait. However, if they have different backgrounds, then one may think the best place to meet up is at the front gate, while the other thinks the best place to meet is at the front-left of Cinderella's castle. In the former situation, the front-left of Cinderella's castle is a focal point. In the latter situation, there is not a focal point. When focal points are not present, an institution (i.e. a rule or plan) is the best solution to the coordination problem.

Similarly, in many emergency response situations, first-responders have different preferences, owing to their different backgrounds and job functions, about what to do and when to do it. In most emergency situations, a focal point is not likely to be present. What is necessary for successful coordination and response to the emergency is an institution, an agreed-upon plan or set of rules for what to do.

Prior to 9/11, and even today, some communities have made more progress than others on addressing coordination problems. Arlington County Virginia is one such community. Arlington County is the home of the Pentagon. When they were attacked on 9/11, the emergency response was exemplary (see e.g. Kettl 2003). This is because they had "an integrated command structure, mutual aid agreements with surrounding communities, a solid emergency team, an assistance program to back up employees amid the incredible stress of their work, and constant drilling in the years leading up to the terrorist attack" (Kettl 2003: 255). The integrated command structure and constant training are critical. There is often some plan prior to an emergency, but the chaos and stress of an emergency makes it difficult for the plan to be executed appropriately. However, it is much easier to get everyone coordinated or re-coordinated when there is an integrated command structure. Similarly, individuals from different groups must train with each other in order for everyone to become familiar with the myriad idiosyncrasies that every group has.

Even with excellent coordination, a good plan, and a well-trained and equipped force, responding to an emergency is difficult. Training is not likely to inoculate most people from the emotional nature of an emergency, and when emotions run strongly, more often than not, decisions are less sound. In a sense, emergencies are like the fog of war. Events do not typically go as planned in war and it is often difficult to know what exactly is happening, but a well-prepared force is much better able to deal with uncertainty and operate effectively in the fog.

Emergencies are by definition temporary. Recovering from an emergency, however, can take a long time. Where response actions focus on the short term, providing food and temporary shelter, for instance, recovery actions focus on the long term, such as fostering economic development so that there are jobs and finding permanent housing options.

Recent federal disasters highlight the importance of addressing principal–agent problems. Few emergency situations were as poorly overseen as Hurricane Katrina. While the federal structure of the US Government increases the number of coordination problems in disaster response, there is no reason these problems could not have been better addressed, prior to or during the emergency. One problem with the federal response to Hurricane Katrina was poor leadership, which hampered federal and state coordination. The head of FEMA at the time, Michael Brown, had very little if any experience in emergency management.[3] It is not unique that political connections

---

[3] With the creation of the Department of Homeland Security, the Director of FEMA became known as the Undersecretary for Emergency Preparedness and Response and Director of FEMA. Currently, the position is titled Administrator of the Federal Emergency Management Agency.

more than expertise aided Brown in attaining his position. (He was a close friend of an important campaign consultant to President Bush.) Nevertheless, Brown's selection shows how a focus on political connections over expertise is an example of adverse selection. Adverse selection is when the principal chooses an agent that imperfectly mirrors and implements the principal's preferences. Less than two weeks after Katrina made landfall, Brown was relieved of his oversight duties. Given the political fallout, it is perhaps not surprising that executive and Congressional screening for becoming director of FEMA has focused on having emergency management experience. Better screening, to prevent adverse selection, has contributed to better leadership. Coupled with improved coordination, which has happened partly because of the better leadership, federal emergency responses have been better since Hurricane Katrina.

11.5 Conclusion

The mission of the Department of Homeland Security (DHS) is to reduce the likelihood of and damage from terrorist attacks, natural disasters, and other emergencies. To reduce the likelihood of an attack, the DHS engages in protection and policing activities. To best protect the US homeland, DHS practices risk analysis and management. This involves identifying targets, assessing their vulnerability, and gauging the consequences to the country from damage to these targets. With a sound risk assessment, authorities can better manage limited resources to protect the most important targets. Risk analysis and management can also help reduce the damage from a natural disaster, as funds can be allocated to the most critical assets in an area. Policing activities are also important for limiting the ability of terrorists to cause significant harm in the United States. These activities can involve both foreign military operations and domestic police activities. Both of these activities, particularly the latter, sometimes involve a trade-off of civil liberties for national security. Aspects of the Patriot Act that involve warrantless wiretapping exemplify this trade-off.

In addition to protection and policing, the DHS is the lead agency for coordinating the federal response to attacks, natural disasters, or large-scale emergencies. In other words, the DHS is responsible for mitigating the effects of an attack or natural disaster and developing plans to make the country more resilient so that damage from attacks and disasters is not too extensive. As the poor response to Hurricane Katrina showed, effective emergency response requires detailed plans and extensive training.

From a larger perspective, principal–agent, coordination, and strategic distribution problems are at the core of this chapter. Principal–agent and coordination problems motivated the creation of the Department of Homeland Security. The disaster of 9/11 gave Congress and the president a strong incentive to address coordination problems between national security and law enforcement agencies. Moreover, the agents, Congress and the president, wanted to demonstrate to the principal, the US public, that they were working to improve their performance so that the principal would not remove them from office. To signal to the principal that they were reforming, they passed new laws and created the Department of Homeland Security. In other words, the Department of Homeland Security did not come about because experts believed it was the best way for the government to organize its national defense agencies. Rather, it came about because the agent was responding to the principal's demands to do something.

In this chapter, we also analyzed a strategic distribution problem: How should the government allocate scarce resources to protect itself from terrorist attacks (and natural disasters)? The distribution of resources always creates political controversies because the distribution of power is never equal. Figuring out how to protect the homeland is even more challenging because the adversary reacts to whatever distribution is chosen. This led us to the conclusion that perfect protection is not possible. Instead, the government should follow a risk minimization strategy and allocate resources to the most important sites first.

Principal–agent problems are at the heart of the debate on warrantless wiretapping. To the extent that the NSA's post 9/11 electronic surveillance is inconsistent with the public's desires on how to balance civil liberties with security, we have a moral hazard problem. If there is a moral hazard problem, a useful approach is to better control the agent through better and more specific laws.

We also noted that coordination problems are at the core of emergency management. Disaster response, like major military operations, involve many different groups, and for these groups to operate effectively they need to coordinate their activities. When coordination is poor, communication is confused or absent, people and supplies are not where they should be, and mistakes increase. To successfully address coordination problems, it helps to create new institutions. These new rules and norms clarify the chain of command and how things should be done. Yet, without practice of working together and effective leadership, institutions that should solve coordination problems will not be effective.

Key Terms

Risk management
Homeland Security Act of 2002
Department of Homeland Security
Disasters
Bureaucracy
Fire-alarm approach
Police-patrol approach
Rent-seeking
Goldwater-Nichols Act of 1986
Protection

Policing

Mitigation

Resilience

Strategic adaptation

Minimax strategy

Risk

Site defense

Border defense

Agency problems

Mueller

Worst-case thinking

Opportunity costs

Strategic interaction

Mixed strategy

Alien and Sedition Acts of 1798

Habeas corpus

Espionage and Sedition Acts

Palmer Raids

Japanese-American internment

Trade-off between civil liberties and security

USA Patriot Act

Reasonable suspicion

Probable cause

National Security Letters

Warrantless wiretapping

Foreign Intelligence Surveillance Act

Authorization for Use of Military Force Against Terrorists

Data mining

Protect America Act of 2007

Federal Emergency Management Agency

Coordination

CHAPTER EXERCISES

1. When and why are new bureaucracies created?
2. Why would the Senate be more likely than the House of Representatives to block a change in the minimum amount of funds allocated to each state?
3. Besides homeland defense, what other political scenarios are like Colonel Blotto games?

4. Do you think data mining is an effective way to prevent terrorist attacks, or do you think the government should identify targets first, and then collect information?

5. Do you think Edward Snowden is a patriot or a traitor? Why?

REFERENCES

Bowden, M. 2006. "The Desert One Debacle." *Atlantic Monthly* 297(4): 62.

Bueno de Mesquita, E. 2007. "Politics and the Suboptimal Provision of Counterterror." *International Organization* 61(01): 9–36.

Campbell, K. M and O'Hanlon, M. E. 2006. *Hard Power: The New Politics of National Security*. New York: Basic Books.

Coats, R. Morris, Karahan, Gökhan, and Tollison, Robert D. 2006. "Terrorism and Pork-Barrel Spending." *Public Choice* 128(1-2): 275–287.

Cohen, D. K, Cuéllar, M. F., and Weingast, B. R. 2006. "Crisis Bureaucracy: Homeland Security and the Political Design of Legal Mandates." *Stanford Law Review* 59(3): 673–759.

Davis, D. W. and Silver, B. D. 2004. "Civil Liberties vs. Security: Public Opinion in the Context of the Terrorist Attacks on America." *American Journal of Political Science* 48(1): 28–46.

Enders, W. and Sandler, T. 2006. *The Political Economy of Terrorism*. Cambridge University Press.

Kettl, Donald. 2003. "Contingent Coordination: Practical and Theoretical Puzzles for Homeland Security." *American Review of Public Administration* 33(3): 253–277.

Krueger, Anne. 1974. "The Political Economy of the Rent-Seeking Society." *American Economic Review* 64(3): 291–303.

Locher III, J. R. 2001. "Has It Worked? The Goldwater-Nichols Reorganization Act." *Naval War College Review* 54(4): 95–116.

McCubbins, M. D. and Schwartz, T. 1984. "Congressional Oversight Overlooked: Police Patrols versus Fire Alarms." *American Journal of Political Science* 28(1): 165–179.

Moe, T. M. and Wilson, S. A. 1994. "Presidents and the Politics of Structure." *Law & Contemporary Problems* 57: 1–44.

Mueller, J. 2010. "Assessing Measures Designed to Protect the Homeland." *Policy Studies Journal* 38(1): 1–21.

Powell, R. 2007. "Defending against Terrorist Attacks with Limited Resources." *American Political Science Review* 101(3): 527–541.

Wittes, B. 2008. *Law and the Long War: The Future of Justice in the Age of Terror*. New York: Penguin Press.

Zegart, A. B. 2006. "An Empirical Analysis of Failed Intelligence Reforms before September 11." *Political Science Quarterly* 121(1): 33–60.

12 Immigration Policy

Outline

Questions

- How does immigration policy work in the United States?
- Who is immigrating to the United States?
- How many people are immigrating to the United States?
- Why do people immigrate to the United States?
- Does immigration benefit the United States?
- Do immigrants assimilate?
- How does immigration affect US security?

Overview

- The primary analytic concepts we use to provide insight on immigration policy are comparative advantage, collective action, and commitment problems.

- The United States admits a certain number of legal immigrants each year for political and economic reasons.
- Immigration and visas are both well liked by most segments of the business community, but criticized by many in society at large.
- Since 1875, the US Government has restricted immigration in a variety of ways. The 1965 Immigration Act is particularly noteworthy as it ended a system of national origin quotas, though it maintained a ceiling on the number of legal immigrants allowed into the country.
- A set of push and pull factors help explain immigration to the United States. Push factors include political repression, political violence, and poverty in one's home country. Pull factors include political freedom and economic opportunity in the United States.
- Fundamental principles of international trade apply to immigration. Immigration is a substitute for labor. As such, labor-intensive states tend to export labor and capital-intensive states tend to import labor. This accurately describes the relationship between Mexico and the United States.
- Cost-benefit analysis shows that immigration tends to economically benefit the overall economy, but may hurt particular groups in society.
- In support of the melting pot thesis, past and current immigrants tend to learn English and are very patriotic. At the same time, most immigrants, even if their families have lived in the United States for decades, tend to identify with their ethnic group.
- Public opinion on immigration is as much a function of perceived economic threat as cultural threat.
- Reforming immigration policy in the United States is very difficult because of political entrepreneurs and credible commitment problems.

Introduction

In celebration of the 4th of July, America's Independence Day, federal courthouses across the United States induct new citizens. In Detroit, for example, ninety-five immigrants from thirty-eight different countries became US citizens on July 4, 2010. "I realized my dream: a better opportunity for my family," Jose Torres, an immigrant from Mexico, says about what Independence Day means to him (Donnelly 2010). Seventy-four people became US citizens at the annual naturalization event at Thomas Jefferson's Monticello home in 2008 (Brulliard 2008). Among the group were Ali Hussain Al Asady, a refugee from Iraq, and Sawsan Mohamed El Fatih Zeyada, a refugee from the Sudan. Olga Bussineau, a 57-year-old immigrant from Mexico, perhaps sums up the view of all of the new citizens: "I love America. It's a beautiful land."

These brief examples of immigrants to the United States shed light on a number of immigration questions. Why do people immigrate to the United States? There is more than one reason, but for many it is an opportunity to make a better living or a place of political refuge from the violence and persecution in their home country. Who is immigrating to the United States? People come to the United States from all over the world, as the example about Detroit's new citizens highlights, yet a particularly large number of immigrants come from Mexico. Does immigration benefit the United States? Most immigrants are gainfully employed and enhance the economic strength of their new country. Do immigrants assimilate? It takes time, of course, for people to adapt to a new country and, for many, to learn a new language. Yet, most immigrants eagerly do so, and the children of immigrants are especially likely to be regular Americans.

In this chapter, we focus on three aspects of political economy to clarify immigration public policy. First, we use the theory of comparative advantage to explain why the United States is a net recipient of migrants. Economic motivations are not the only reason people come to the United States, but they are an important one. Second, we present a cost-benefit analysis to understand the overall effects of immigration on the US economy. There are not only costs and benefits in general to immigration, but some groups within the United States experience greater benefits (or costs) than others as a result. In the aggregate, immigration is a net benefit for the United States. Third, we discuss how collective action, political entrepreneurs, and credible commitment problems help explain the intensity of the debate on immigration policy. Before delving into these topics, we present some important descriptive information concerning immigration in the United States. Specifically, we give a brief overview of how immigration works, the history of immigration policy in the United States, how many people are immigrating to the United States, and how this has changed over time.

12.1 How Legal Immigration Works

An **immigrant** is a person who leaves one country, which we will call the home country, to become a permanent resident in another country, the host country. A host country allows immigrants for economic and ideological reasons. Most immigrants come for economic reasons. That is, employment opportunities and wages are better in the host than in the home country. Host countries also admit immigrants primarily for economic reasons. Host countries need labor of a particular type (sometimes manual labor, sometimes more specialized skills) and immigrants fill that need. Countries also admit immigrants for ideological reasons, such as granting asylum to someone for political reasons or allowing in humanitarian or political refugees. During the Cold War, for example, the United States granted asylum to individuals fleeing the Soviet Union and admitted humanitarian and political refugees from Laos and Vietnam.

When non-citizens come to the United States, the Immigration and Naturalization Service (INS) classifies them as either immigrants or non-immigrants. Immigrants have the right to live and work permanently in the United States; once here they are officially designated as permanent residents. The identification card for a permanent resident is green in color; thus, the description of a non-citizen acquiring a **green card**. Non-immigrants can only live and work in the United States for a temporary time and for a specific purpose; they are in the United States on a visa. Most non-immigrants are tourists and students. Students who wish to study in the United States must apply for and receive an F1 visa to do so. They must be in school to keep their visa.

Becoming a Legal Immigrant

Non-citizens may become legal immigrants through one of four paths: the family-based system, the employment-based system, asylum and refugee status, or through a diversity lottery. The **family-based system** awards immigration status to family members of US citizens, with immediate family members having precedence over siblings and their children. Most new permanent residents in the United States enter through the family-based system (see Table 12.1).

The **employment-based system** also includes a number of priority levels. For example, priority one workers are classified as those with "extraordinary abilities," while priority two workers are defined as having "exceptional abilities." Most workers in both of these categories have advanced degrees; they are likely to be researchers, physicians, or executives. Although most US immigrants do not fall into these first two employment categories, they do constitute a large percentage in some fields. It is estimated that about 55 percent of PhD natural scientists younger than 45 were not born in the United States (Freeman 2006: 147). Priority three workers are the most common. They are what many might think of as regular workers: individuals with specialized skills, but lacking an advanced degree, who are of limited supply in the United States. Priority four workers include translators who work for the US military and individuals who work for US embassies abroad. Finally, to qualify for a priority five immigration status, a person has to invest at least $1 million and create at least ten new jobs. Not surprisingly, people with $1 million to invest are relatively rare.

Family ties and economic motivations are not the only reasons people seek to immigrate to the United States. Some seek to become US residents to escape political or religious persecution in their home country. These are **refugees** and **asylum seekers**. A refugee is a person fleeing their home country because of a well-founded fear of persecution, usually for political or religious reasons. An asylee, or asylum seeker, is a person requesting refugee status in another country. If granted asylum, then an individual is allowed to become a permanent resident. If the asylum request is

Table 12.1 Persons Obtaining Legal Permanent Resident Status by Type and Major Class of Admission: Fiscal Years 2000–2009

Type and Class of Admission	2000	2002	2004	2006	2008
Family-based system	581,442	670,556	632,170	802,577	716,244
Employment-based preferences	106,642	173,814	155,330	159,081	166,511
First: Priority workers	27,566	34,168	31,291	36,960	36,678
Second: Professionals with advanced degrees or aliens of exceptional ability	20,255	44,316	32,534	21,911	70,046
Third: Skilled workers, professionals, and unskilled workers	49,589	88,002	85,969	89,922	48,903
Fourth: Special immigrants	9,014	7,186	5,407	9,539	9,524
Fifth: Employment creation (investors)	218	142	129	749	1,360
Diversity	50,920	42,820	50,084	44,471	41,761
Refugees	56,091	115,601	61,013	99,609	90,030
Asylees	6,837	10,197	10,217	116,845	76,362

Source: US Department of Homeland Security

denied, then the person has to leave the host country. The central difference between a refugee and an asylee is their geographic location when they apply for residency. A refugee applies for residency while living outside of the host country, while an asylee applies for residency once present in the host country. Persons obtaining permanent resident status as refugees or asylum seekers have increased throughout the 2000s, even surpassing the number of new residents through the employment-based system in 2009. This change is because it is more difficult to obtain an employment visa since 2001 and the United States has been admitting more refugees from Iraq in recent years.

Finally, non-citizens can become legal immigrants through the **diversity lottery**. The diversity lottery awards up to 50,000 visas annually. To be eligible, a person must be from a country that sends few (defined as fewer than 50,000 non-refugee immigrants in the last five years) immigrants to the United States. Broadly stated, the diversity lottery awards visas to people from Europe (except Great Britain and Poland, as many immigrants come from those countries) and Africa.

Immigration and Citizenship

Do immigrants, that is, legal permanent residents, have to become US citizens? No, as the name suggests, permanent residents can remain residents of the United States forever (permanently) without becoming citizens. Legal permanent residents differ from citizens in a couple of ways. Permanent residents do not have the right to vote, hold government jobs, or sponsor other immigrants. They may also be expelled from the United States if they commit a felony. To become a US citizen, legal permanent residents go through the **naturalization** process. This involves living in the United States for at least five years, taking a citizenship test (in English), and swearing an oath of allegiance to the United States. Not surprisingly, those who speak English better are more likely to become citizens, as are those who own homes or are married to a US citizen. Between 1995 and 2005, an increasing number of legal immigrants have chosen to become US citizens (Passel 2007). Indeed, Mexican immigrants have significantly increased their rate of naturalization since 1995, though they are still less likely to naturalize than a non-Mexican born immigrant.

Non-Immigrant Visas

A **visa** is a government-issued authorization that allows a person to enter a country and stay for a limited period of time. In the United States, visas are generally given to persons for employment, education, or tourism. There are multiple classes of visas; here, we briefly describe some of the more common ones. A-class visas are for ambassadors and other foreign government officials. B-1 visas are for individuals traveling to the United States for business. For example, if executives at Toyota are thinking of opening an automobile factory in the United States and they want to scout for locations in the United States, the Toyota executives would obtain B-1 visas. B-1 visas are also used for individuals traveling to the United States to attend a business conference. Tourists to the United States obtain B-2 visas. J1 visas are for cultural exchange. Two of the most common types of people receiving J1 visas are international students studying in the United States and au pairs. The last type of visa we will mention is the H-class. These visas give non-native individuals the right to work in the United States for a temporary period of time. (Note that the B-1 visa does not allow an individual to obtain employment in the United States, only to travel to the United States for business purposes. H-class visas allow individuals to obtain employment.) H-1B visas are given for white-collar jobs (e.g. computer programmers and professors), H-1C for nurses, H-2A for agricultural workers, and H-2B for non-agricultural workers.

The government only gives out a finite number of H-class visas each year. Currently, the annual quota on H-1B visas is 65,000, though individuals working at universities or government research laboratories are exempt, as are up to 10,500 applicants from Australia; in addition, for the last several years, the government has authorized an additional 20,000 H-class visas for individuals with advanced degrees. Since the early 2000s, the 65,000 quota has filled up quickly. That is, the government receives many more than 65,000 requests for H1-B visas, and the available visas have been awarded within the first six months of the fiscal year. As the number of visa petitions exceeds the number of available visas, it is clear that US businesses desire an increase in H-class visas. This is a particularly strong sentiment in Silicon Valley, where many computer programmers obtain employment. They note that there are greater complementarities between capital and skilled labor than between capital and unskilled labor. That is, capital is more productive when there is an abundance of skilled labor. High technology and service industries, for example, rely much more on skilled labor than on unskilled labor. These industries are most profitable when there is an abundance of capital to invest and plenty of skilled labor to employ. Based on this argument, many high-tech businesses call for more H-1B visas. (As an aside, in a land-abundant economy, such as the nineteenth-century United States, there are greater complementarities between unskilled labor and land than between skilled labor and capital. This suggests that the most beneficial immigration policy for the United States in the nineteenth century was to admit unskilled labor, which it did.)

Box 12.1 H1-B Worker Shortage or Replacement Workers?

In October 2014, Walt Disney World tech employees in Orlando, FL were replaced by workers from India with H1-B visas. The 250 displaced workers first were required to train the new Disney employees. There are reports of similar occurrences in other US companies.

There is constant pressure to increase the number of H1-B visas granted; there are now 85,000 per year. Those who seek the increases claim that they are hiring people with skills that are in high demand that are not being met by US workers. Critics say that the H1-B visas are displacing US workers.

US companies are under pressure to be as profitable as possible, and outsourcing technical work is one way to maintain profitability. Policymakers must confront the issue of H1-B visas to balance the interests of workers and businesses.

However, many criticize the use of H1-B visas for taking jobs away from Americans and reducing wages; accordingly, they call for a decrease in the annual quota. There is a fair amount of evidence to support the latter charge (see e.g. Borjas 1995: 15). However, there is not a lot of sound research on the charge that the use of H1-B visas reduces job opportunities for Americans. One informative piece of research is by Wadhwa *et al.* (2007), who find that there is not a shortage of engineers with a bachelor's degree in the United States, thereby implying that the number of H-1B visas does not need to increase. They also note, however, that about 60 percent of engineering doctorates are awarded to non-Americans and that most successful high-tech companies are started by individuals with advanced degrees. They conclude that the United States needs to make it easier for foreign students to stay in the country after obtaining their degree (Wadhwa *et al.* 2007).

12.2 History of Immigration Policy

The United States did not regulate immigration until 1875, when it passed a law prohibiting new Asian laborers. In the 1880s, Congress passed a series of laws further limiting Chinese immigration. Beginning around 1881, however, the United States experienced a large influx of immigrants. Nearly 25 million immigrants entered the country between 1881 and 1920 (US Department of Justice, "Immigration and Naturalization Service" (1993, p. 25); US Department of Commerce, "Bureau of the Census" (1975, pp. 8, 14; 1993b, p. 50)). With relatively high unemployment after World War I, opposition to immigration increased. This motivated Congress to impose restrictions. The **1921 Emergency Immigration Restriction Act** restricted immigration across the board by establishing quotas for each country and region. The quotas were based on the percentage of ethnics already in the United States from that country. For this reason, the system created by the 1921 law is sometimes called the **national-origins system**. The chief effect of these policy changes was to reduce immigration from Asia. There were about half as many immigrants from Asia in the 1920s as there were in the 1910s (see Table 12.2). Immigration from European countries also dropped significantly in the 1920s, but this was more a result of economic growth in Europe, outside of Germany, which still sent many immigrants to the United States during this period.

The national-origins system changed in 1965. Two factors motivated the change to the country's immigration laws. First, unemployment was low and economic growth

Table 12.2 Persons Obtaining Legal Permanent Resident Status by Region: 1900–2009

Region	1900s	1920s	1940s	1960s	1980s	2000s
Europe	7,572,569	2,560,340	472,524	1,133,443	668,866	1,420,935
Asia	299,836	126,740	34,532	358,605	2,391,356	3,407,648
America	277,809	1,591,278	328,435	1,674,172	2,695,329	4,337,617
Africa	6,326	6,362	6,720	23,780	141,990	763,988
Oceania	12,355	9,860	14,262	23,630	41,432	65,229
Not specified	33,493	930	135	119	305,406	201,135

Source: US Department of Homeland Security

was high. Second, the Civil Rights Movement was calling Americans to be true to its founding principles and national ideals. Significant restrictions on immigration seemed inconsistent with American principles, motivating changes to the country's immigration laws. Under the new law, the **Immigration and Nationality Act Amendments of 1965**, family ties were made a central factor for determining admittance and specific country quotas were abolished. With the end of the country quotas, a significant change in the national-origins of immigrants to the United States occurred after 1965. Immigrants from Asia increased by about 390 percent from the 1960s to the 1970s and continued to increase throughout the 1980s, 1990s, and 2000s (see Table 12.2). In the 1950s, for example, only about 6 percent of immigrants came from Asia, but in the 1980s, Asian immigrants accounted for about 37 percent of all immigrants. The ending of the national-origins system also led to a sharp increase in immigrants from the Americas, particularly from Mexico and Central America. From the mid nineteenth century until the early part of the twentieth century, most immigrants to the United States came from Ireland and Italy; in the last two decades, most US immigrants have come from Mexico.

As in the 1920s, public opinion in the 1980s started showing concerns about the new immigrants. Opinion on the new immigrants was salient enough to again prompt the federal government to change its immigration policy. The result was the **1986 Immigration Reform and Control Act (IRCA)**, which made two significant changes to US immigration policy. First, for the first time, it made it illegal for employers to knowingly hire **illegal immigrants**. Second, it granted amnesty to about 3 million illegal aliens in the United States. Both of these policies had significant ramifications and contributed to the more recent illegal immigration problem in the United States. In the words of Massey *et al.* (2002: 3), the IRCA "offers a textbook example of how ill-conceived policies cannot only fail to achieve their manifest goals but unleash a host of unintended consequences and amplify them to the fullest." What were these effects?

The illegal immigrants in the United States in 1986 were largely seasonal workers from Mexico. They would come for a few months to work in the agricultural fields and then go back home. Preventing employers, who needed labor, from hiring illegal immigrants drove the problem underground, creating more black market activity and, temporarily at least, harming production. In response to business calls for more labor, in 1990 Congress voted to increase by 150,000 the total number of immigrants allowed into the country. Of course, this was far below what was needed for the agricultural sector alone, but the large increase only a few years later is a signal of the pressure business groups were placing on Congress to allow more immigrant labor into the country.

The 1986 IRCA law legalized about 2.3 million Mexicans. In doing so, Congress hoped to curb future illegal immigration. It failed to do so for three reasons. First, observers noted that those who were legalized "had relatives in Mexico, and legalization would dramatically increase the odds that these relations would them-selves migrate to the United States without documents" (Massey *et al.* 2002: 91). Second, it set a precedent for legalization. One message illegal immigrants could take from the 1986 law is that if they were in the United States at the right time they could be made legal. This was a clear incentive for some to immigrate. Third, the law did not address the reason Mexicans were migrating to the United States in the first place: economic opportunity. In fact, with continuing and in some cases increased subsidies to agriculture, there were plenty of agricultural jobs in the United States. That is, it is not just the 1986 IRCA law that has contributed to illegal immigration, but other policies as well, such as agricultural subsidies (a form of protectionism), for these help keep the agricultural industry competitive on world markets.

The effects of these policies are illustrated by the variation in US immigration over time (see Table 12.2). In the 1900s, over 8 million people legally immigrated to the United States. With the start of the Great Depression in 1929, immigration to the United States decreased significantly. Only about 700,000 people immigrated to the United States in the 1930s. For national security reasons, the United States admitted relatively few immigrants in the 1940s, but with the end of World War II, immigration started to increase again. It was not until the 1990s, however, that the United States was admitting about as many immigrants as it did in the 1900s, though as a percentage of the population, immigration today is much smaller than around the turn of the twentieth century. Nevertheless, the United States still admits many more immigrants than any other country. Finally, we note that there has also been a significant change in immigrants' gender. Prior to the mid twentieth century, most immigrants were male. Now, an immigrant to the United States is equally likely to be a man or a woman.

How does this discussion relate to the analytic problems discussed in this book? One important connection to make is that the national-origins system and the Immigration and Nationality Act Amendments of 1965 are institutional solutions to a coordination problem. With regard to the 1921 law, the coordination problem was that a majority of citizens believed some immigration is a good thing, but they disagreed on which and how many should be admitted. Finding a compromise is often difficult, but compromises are more likely when there are easy-to-understand criteria. The national-origins system was just this. Tying immigration levels to the existing ethnic composition in the country seemed to many to be a straightforward and simple plan. Indeed, the 1921 law passed by a voice vote in the House of Representatives and a 78–1 vote in the Senate. In the mid 1960s, because of the Civil Rights Movement, the dominant frame of reference changed from ensuring ethnic homogeneity to recovering the ideal of America, one element of which is that the United States is a country of immigrants. With this new focal point, maintaining country quotas on immigration was untenable.

12.3 Why Do People Immigrate?

To understand why people leave one country to go and live in another country, it is helpful to think of factors that push people out of their home country and factors that pull people into a specific new country. Some of the primary push factors are political repression, political violence, and economic hardship. In some cases, only one of these factors will explain why an individual left his or her country and in other cases all three sets of factors will be relevant. Political repression, for example, helps explain why the United States has received many immigrants from Cuba. After the communist revolution in Cuba in 1959, political repression against supporters of the Batista regime led many to flee Cuba for the United States. Political repression restricts or denies a person's voice in politics. Political violence is the threat or imposition of bodily harm. In recent years, many immigrants to the United States from Central America have been motivated by political violence in their home countries. Economic hardship is perhaps the best-known reason for leaving one's country. The large influx of Irish immigrants to the United States in the nineteenth century was largely motivated by economic push factors. The Great Famine in Ireland (1845 to 1852) led many Irish to go elsewhere to feed their families.

Box 12.2 The 2014 Child Immigration Crisis

In the summer of 2014, there was a very large increase in the number of unaccompanied migrant children apprehended at the US southern border. What led to this change? It appears that a central part of the story is a 2008 law, the William Wilberforce Trafficking Victims Protection Reauthorization Act. This law prohibits deporting children if they are likely to be subject to violence in their home country. The goal of the law is to protect children subject to trafficking. An unintended consequence of the law is that some families saw it as a way for their children to flee the violence of their home countries. Guatemala, Honduras, and El Salvador have very high violent crime rates. Through word-of-mouth networks, people learned of the US law and some families concluded that it was better for their children to migrate than to live in the violence of their country. This episode shows both how policies in one country affect what happens elsewhere and how push and pull factors operate together.[1]

---

[1] For details on unaccompanied children at the US border, see www.cbp.gov/newsroom/stats/southwest-border-unaccompanied-children.

Push factors only tell one side of the story: that people want to leave their current country. If there are no better options, however, then they will stay put. Immigration, then, also requires examining pull factors. Pull factors include political freedom, connectedness, and economic opportunity. The United States scores well on each of these pull factors. As political freedom and economic opportunity are straightforward, we will say a word about connectedness. Connectedness is anything that greatly reduces the transaction costs of moving to and living in a new country. Distance is one aspect of connectedness; all else equal migrants choose the closest new country in which to settle. The presence of ethnic kin is another important connectedness factor. Immigrants, like any other group, tend to cluster, as doing so greatly reduces the transaction costs of moving to a new country. Since the economy tends to be the most important pull factor, we will say more about it.[2]

International trade and the **Heckscher–Ohlin theorem** is discussed in Chapter 13. That theorem tells us that a country tends to export products that make intensive use of its abundant factor. It also says that countries tend to import products that make intensive use of its scarce factor. Also remember that abundance and scarcity are relative concepts. With two countries and two products, Country 1 must be abundant in factor A and scarce in factor B, while Country 2 must be abundant in factor B and scarce in factor A. Now consider the United States and Mexico (or any other country in Latin America). From an international economics perspective, trade and immigration are similar. A labor-abundant country can export goods that make intensive use of labor or export people. Similarly, a labor-scarce country can import goods that make intensive use of labor or import people. Now relative to the United States, Mexico is labor abundant and relative to Mexico, the United States is capital abundant. In the context of immigration, the Heckscher–Ohlin theorem tells us that Mexico is likely to export people to the United States. And this is exactly what we see.

In addition to the economic "pull" factors encouraging immigration into the United States from Mexico, Central America, and elsewhere, there are "push" factors. By push factors, we mean policies in the sending country (Mexico in this case) that inadvertently incentivize immigration. Cortina (2014) documents the effect of one such policy. With the adoption of the North American Free Trade Agreement (NAFTA), the Mexican Government created a program named Procampo to help modernize its agricultural industry. Individuals who applied for the program would receive a cash transfer. The goal of the program was for individuals to use the cash to invest in their farms and increase their agricultural productivity. With the idea that each individual farmer would know best what she or he needs to do, cash was viewed as the most efficient means of attaining the goal. But all policies tend to have unintended

---

[2] For an in-depth discussion of how policies in the United States can create unintended consequences and pull immigrants into the country, see Massey *et al.* (2002).

consequences. Not all individuals have the same economic incentive to migrate. Poorer individuals, for example, have a greater incentive to migrate from Mexico to the United States, if they can pay for the upfront costs of migration. The Procampo program, with its cash transfer, may well have inadvertently helped foster migration. Cortina (2014: 115), for example, finds that those who "received Procampo were more likely to migrate to the United States in comparison to those that did not receive cash transfers" and that "this effect was notably stronger among the poor than among the wealthier."

The lesson of the Procampo program is not that social welfare in Mexico increases migration. In fact, one of Mexico's other social welfare programs, Progresa, has been found to reduce migration out of Mexico (Stecklov *et al.* 2003). Why have these programs had different effects? Procampo is an unconditional cash transfer program, while Progresa is a conditional cash transfer program. Among the conditions in the Progresa program is attendance at health and nutrition programs. If you do not attend, then you do not receive the money. There is no increased incentive to migrate with this sort of program. The lesson of these programs is that program design and context matters.

Box 12.3 Vietnamese Manicurists: Replacement or Displacement of Jobs?

In 1987, there were 3,900 Vietnamese manicurists in California. In 2002, there were nearly 40,000. Were non-Vietnamese manicurists replaced (i.e. did they lose their jobs) or displaced (did they choose to go elsewhere for work)? Overall, the number of manicurist jobs increased substantially (even controlling for population growth). The increase in jobs, as well as data on inflows and outflows from the job, indicates that non-Vietnamese were displaced. This indicates that there is not a fixed number of jobs over which people compete; jobs can be created. In this case, Vietnamese manicurists made many innovations to increase demand for their services. Nevertheless, for those displaced, there may be extra costs to searching for non-manicurists jobs or difficulty in finding one (see Federman *et al.* 2006).

12.4 Economics of Immigration: Wages, Welfare, and Taxes

Now we are in a better position to understand how immigration affects the host state's economy. Immigration benefits the overall economy, but just as is the case with trade, some individuals and groups in the receiving country will suffer economically. First, immigrants provide needed labor or skills. People emigrate from one country to another because there are more or better job opportunities in the host country. If a host country has jobs available, and the existence of immigration is one telltale sign that there are such jobs, then the host's economy has room to grow. That is, a lack of labor, or in some cases a shortage of labor with particular skills, is restricting a state's economic growth. By providing needed labor and skills, immigrants increase economic production, which leads to less expensive products for society as a whole. Those who benefit the most from immigrants' labor and skill are those who use their services. Immigrants who produce products that are consumed by all, benefit all. Immigrants, however, are generally working in low-skill service industries (e.g. agriculture, hotel housekeeping, in-house maids, and restaurants). The major consumers of the products in these industries are those with more capital and human capital. One group that benefits from this sort of immigration is high-skilled women (Cortes and Tessada 2011). High-skilled women include lawyers, physicians, and others in professions that require advanced education. Despite having demanding and well-paying jobs, most women do a disproportionate amount of housework. Not surprisingly, this is a group eager to consume the services of low-skilled immigrants interested in housework. One effect of this consumption is that these women tend to produce more, increasing their own wealth as well as the overall economic pie (Cortes and Tessada 2011). Overall, then, immigration benefits those who are relatively better off in society (e.g. a middle or upper-class person can now hire a maid at a cheaper price). Second, immigrants contribute to the host state's economy through their purchasing power. In other words, immigration can generate increasing returns to scale by expanding the size of the state's economy.[3] Third, immigrants tend to be more risk acceptant or industrious than the average individual, and these character traits lead to more entrepreneurial efforts, particularly when property rights are well protected as they are in the United States.

Although immigrants benefit the overall economy, and some groups within society in particular, there are costs to immigration. First, immigration may affect the wages of native workers that compete for the same jobs. Since most immigrants of late to the United States have had less skill, only natives with less skill are likely to see an effect on their wages. Borjas (1995) contends that immigration between 1960 and 2000 has led to a decline in wages for the less skilled, but not the skilled; his research finds that this effect is rather small (Borjas, 1994, 2003). As is often the case, an assessment depends on determining the proper comparison. Borjas (2003) compares the wages of the less skilled with all other workers. In contrast, Card (2005) contends that the appropriate comparison is between high school drop-outs and those who only have a high school education. There has been no change in this wage gap since 1980, though there has been a large increase in the wage gap between those with a high school education and

---

[3] Helpman and Krugman (1985) is the pioneering work on increasing returns to scale in international trade.

those with a college education.[4] Cortes (2008) helps reconcile these findings. She compares the wages of low-skilled natives with limited English proficiency and of Hispanic origin with all other low-skilled natives. She finds that the former group has experienced a wage decrease, while the latter has not. The reason is straightforward. Low-skilled natives with limited English proficiency compete directly for jobs with immigrants with limited English proficiency; as a result, there is a decrease in wages in this group. However, most low-skilled Americans are not competing with immigrants for jobs. In turn, immigration has had little effect on wages for most Americans.

Immigration may carry with it other costs. Are immigrants more likely to use welfare than natives? The answer depends on their skill level and reason for immigrating. Immigrants with white-collar skills are much less likely to be on welfare than Americans born in the United States. In contrast, "refugee groups tend to exhibit much higher rates of welfare participation than non-refugee groups" (Borjas 1994: 1702). Garand *et al.* (2015) report Mexican-American immigrants to be more likely to participate in welfare programs. The primary refugee groups in this period are from Cambodia and Laos, where welfare participation in 1990 was around 45 percent. Immigrants from India, Japan, South Africa, and most of Europe had welfare participation rates much lower than the average American household. In the aggregate, however, the rate of welfare use among immigrants is higher than among those born in the United States. In 2002, about 22 percent of all immigrant households received some type of welfare, while only about 15 percent of non-immigrant households received welfare (Borjas 2008). Nevertheless, the use of welfare by immigrants does not necessarily mean that they impose a net cost on the receiving state, for immigrants pay taxes. Borjas (1994: 1707) cautions that calculations about the net benefit or cost that immigrants impose are very sensitive to the assumptions one uses about tax rates and the costs of public goods that they consume. With respect to welfare, taxes, and overall economic effects, Borjas (2008) concludes that immigration is a net wash for the US economy.

Many Americans believe low-skill immigration increases crime. Based on the economic model we presented previously, there are some reasons to believe this and some to doubt it. Poorer people tend to have lower opportunity costs for committing crime; they are more desperate to feed their families. Many immigrants are also young males, a group that commits a disproportionate amount of crime. However, those who choose to immigrate tend to be more industrious than others, a trait associated with a lower propensity to commit crime. Immigrants also face greater costs for crime if they are caught (deportation). Almost all rigorous research on immigration and crime finds a negative correlation: increased immigration is associated with less crime. In a

---

[4] The primary reason for the increase in the wage gap between low-skilled and high-skilled workers is technology (see e.g. Acemoglu and Autor 2011 for a discussion).

comprehensive review of the research, the National Academies summarize the relationship between immigration and crime throughout American history this way: "Then, as now, immigrants are less crime-prone than native-born Americans" (Waters and Pineau 2015: 318). The one partial exception to this research consensus is by Spenkuch (2013). His research shows a negative relationship between immigration and violent crime, but a positive relationship between immigration and property crime. One cannot conclude from his research, however, if immigrants are responsible for the change in property crime or if it is native-born Americans living in the same country. In other words, ill-will or job displacement may lead native-born Americans to commit more crimes in heavily populated immigrant areas. While we cannot conclude with confidence who is responsible for the increase in property crime in Spenkuch's research, we can note that all the other research on this topic finds immigrants, especially first-generation immigrants, commit less crime than native-born Americans.

12.5 Immigrants and Assimilation

Do immigrants assimilate to their new country? On the one hand, the United States is known as the great **melting pot**; there is considerable ethnic diversity in the United States, yet only minor ethnic conflict, and nearly everyone speaks the same language. While almost all ethnic groups in the United States have experienced some discrimination, particularly African-Americans, individuals from all ethnic groups have achieved fame and fortune. On the other hand, some degree of ethnic segregation has been a part of America since its founding. In a celebrated 1963 book, Nathan Glazer and Daniel Patrick Moynihan noted that there was a world **beyond the melting pot**. The major ethnic groups in New York City, they argued, maintained a degree of ethnic consciousness and distinctiveness. Even if their families have lived in the United States for many decades, even centuries, most people identify themselves with the ethnic group from which they are descended (e.g. Irish-American, Italian-American, Puerto-Rican-American, African-American, etc.). However, maintaining, even championing, one's ethnic identity does not mean that immigrants do not assimilate, if by assimilation we mean English proficiency, patriotism, and political connectedness. We discuss how recent immigrants score on these measures of assimilation.

An important indicator of assimilation is proficiency in English. One reason to think that recent immigrants will learn English as fast as previous immigrants is economic. Immigrants who become proficient in English tend to earn much more than immigrants who do not speak English very well. As one of the central reasons for emigrating to the United States is economic, it is likely that recent immigrants will learn English. To be sure, there are some ethnic enclaves, like Miami's Little Havana or East Los Angeles, where English is less of a benefit than in most parts of the country. Nevertheless, even in counties that are 75 percent Hispanic, Hispanics proficient in English earn about 11 percent more than those who are not (McManus 1990). A little over 40 percent of Mexican immigrants in the United States for less than five years spoke only Spanish in 2000. "Among Mexicans who had lived in the United States more than 20 years, only 7 percent of men and 10 percent of women remained monolingual" (Katz *et al.* 2007: 175).

What is perhaps even more important than the English proficiency of first-generation immigrants is the English proficiency of second-generation immigrants. Although the average immigrant to the United States has less education than the average American, children of immigrants stay in school longer than children born to parents who were born in America (Card 2005: F317). Similarly, second-generation immigrants are slightly more likely to have a job than second-generation natives. Based on a comparison of second-generation immigrants' educational attainment since 1970, Card (2005: F320) concludes that recent immigrants are assimilating faster than previous immigrants.

Attitudes, particularly patriotism and support for economic individualism, are other indicators of assimilation. The former is straightforward. On the one hand, the more you love something, the better you know it, and the better you know something, the more aware you are of imperfections. At the same time, the more you love something, the less the imperfections bother you. For this reason, greater degrees of patriotism are associated with higher levels of assimilation. Economic individualism is also viewed as a central trait of the American culture. Highlighted by immigrants coming to America for a better life, the Horatio Alger stories in the mid nineteenth century, and the United States championing capitalism against the Soviet Union's promotion of communism during the Cold War, many have identified economic individualism as part of what it means to be an American. Are recent immigrants, especially Mexican-Americans, less supportive of economic individualism and less patriotic than Anglo-Americans? Research by De la Garza *et al.* (1996) indicates that there is no difference between these groups in their support for economic individualism or patriotic feelings. In fact, they find that "Mexican-Americans at all levels of acculturation who are United States citizens express patriotism at levels equal to or higher than do Anglos" (De la Garza *et al.* 1996: 346).

However, Huntington (2004) has argued that there are important differences in the assimilation of Mexican immigrants, and those from Latin America more broadly, pre-1990 and post-1990. Since 1991, seven Latin American states have made dual-citizenship legal. For example, an immigrant from Mexico to the United States may become a US citizen, but retain Mexican citizenship as well. In light of dual citizenship laws, a natural question arises: are dual citizens less connected to the United States? **Traditionalists** contend that dual-citizens have divided loyalties. By not making a choice on their preferred citizenship status (one can always renounce citizenship in a country), dual-citizens imply that they want membership in whatever country best meets their needs at the moment. Such a position may reduce one's commitment to one or both countries (Geyer 1996; Renshon 2000). In contrast, **transnationalists** argue that dual citizenship conveys a welcoming attitude, and that encourages assimilation. Transnationalists also note that globalization makes it easier to maintain relationships in multiple countries and that one can be loyal to multiple groups simultaneously.

Research on the political connectedness of Latin American dual-citizens in the United States supports the traditional view. Dual-nationals are less likely to participate in US elections, feel less psychologically connected to the United States, and are less proficient in English than immigrants that are not dual-nationals (Staton *et al.* 2007). While there are relevant differences between new immigrants with single and dual citizenship, the long-term effect of dual-citizenship is less clear. Most first-generation immigrants, for example, are not proficient in English. Over time, dual-citizens and their children may be no different than other immigrants and their children. Of course, only time, and research, will tell.

12.6 Illegal Immigration

It is estimated that there were about 11 million illegal immigrants in the US in 2008 (Preston 2008; see also Hoefer *et al.* 2006). As large as this number is, most analysts think that it has decreased in recent years. We discuss the reasons for that decrease below. The Pew Hispanic Center estimates that about half of all illegal immigrants come from Mexico, with another quarter coming from other parts of Latin America.[5]

Becoming an Illegal Immigrant

One can become an illegal immigrant in three ways: overstay a visa, enter the country illegally, or commit visa fraud. A little less than one-half of all illegal immigrants earn that status by overstaying a visa. For example, a person may be admitted into the United States on an H-1B visa to work as an electrical engineer for three years. If the visa is not renewed and the person is still in the country after three years' time, then he or she is an illegal immigrant. Visa overstays account for all of the 9/11 hijackers who were illegal immigrants. Two of the hijackers were in the United States on overstayed visas and a third had violated the terms of his visa; in addition, two of the other hijackers had previously overstayed a visa in the United States. Despite the large number of visa overstays, a number in the millions, the Department of Homeland

---

[5] See www.nytimes.com/2008/07/31/us/31immig.html?partner=rssnyt.

Security's ability to track those entering the country on a visa still needs much improvement (see e.g. www.gao.gov/new.items/d0482.pdf).

Illegal entry, a misdemeanor offense, is the other primary way of becoming an illegal immigrant. Slightly more than one-half of all illegal immigrants enter the country illegally, as opposed to visa overstays who enter legally but become illegal if they do not adhere to the terms of their visa. Most illegal entrants come from Mexico, and the most common method of illegal entry is to cross through the desert in the South-western United States (i.e. the desert in Arizona, California, New Mexico, and Texas). A relatively small number of people, however, enter the United States illegally by crossing into the country from Canada. In a celebrated case in 2005, the United States and Canada arrested about thirty people who were responsible for smuggling over 100 people into the United States from Canada.

Although it does not comprise a large percentage of the illegal immigrant popula-tion, visa fraud is common enough to deserve note. Visa fraud occurs when one gains entry into the United States under false pretenses. The movies *Green Card* (1990) and *The Proposal* (2009) depict the most common form of visa fraud: **green card marriage**. These are marriages designed to allow someone to enter the country, though the couple has little intention of living together (although of course in the movies love blossoms). In some cases, one person receives money for the marriage and in other cases one person is simply duped into believing that the person loves them.

Why Is There Illegal Immigration?

Like legal immigration, illegal immigration is driven primarily by economic motiv-ations. Previously, we noted that states tend to export the factor in which they are relatively abundant. Thus, labor-abundant countries export products that are labor-intensive or labor itself, and labor-scarce countries tend to import labor-intensive products or labor. Relative to each other, Mexico is labor abundant and the United States is labor scarce. In other words, there is a need for more labor in the United States, and that is why there are so many illegal immigrants in the US trade, that is, the importing of labor-intensive products from other countries allows US consumers to acquire more at a lower cost. Importing labor, legal and illegal, does the same thing. With additional, needed labor, US companies and farms can produce more, bringing down the cost of their products for US consumers and export markets. Officials estimate that about 60 percent of all agricultural workers in the United States are illegal immigrants.[6] Do countries that export labor, like Mexico, receive anything in return? Mexico, like all states that have immigrants living abroad, receives remittances from its people working in other countries. Remittances are the money immigrants

---

[6] See www.nytimes.com/2010/07/10/us/10enforce.html.

send back to their home country, usually to their families; it is a major source of foreign income in Mexico.

The economic motivation for legal and illegal immigration accounts for the recent decrease in illegal immigration to the United States. The Department of Homeland Security estimates that the number of illegal immigrants in the United States dropped by about 800,000 from January 2008 to January 2009.[7] Similar decreases were observed with the 1991 recession. This decrease in immigration and fewer jobs in the United States has led to a 23 percent decrease in Mexican remittances between 2009 and 2014 (World Development Indicators).[8] Nevertheless, because of slowing economic growth throughout most of the world, including Mexico, illegal immigrants already living in the United States have less incentive to leave as their job prospects may not be much better in their home country. That is, fewer people are illegally entering the United States at present, but there has not been a large exodus of the already present illegal population.

Addressing Illegal Immigration

Since 2001, the United States has taken a number of measures to address concerns about illegal immigration. The government has instituted new travel procedures for those entering the country, began constructing a border fence, and increased enforcement of laws against hiring illegal immigrants.

New Requirements to Enter the Country

One of the more significant changes in US public policy since 2001 has been increased border enforcement. In 1997, there were approximately 6,300 border patrol agents on the Southwest border. In 2010, there were nearly 17,000 border patrol agents on that border.[9] In addition, as part of the 2004 Intelligence Reform and Terrorism Prevention Act, the United States created the **Western Hemisphere Travel Initiative**. This law requires that all persons entering the United States from other Western Hemisphere countries present a valid passport. No longer can Americans travel to Canada or Mexico without a passport, for they will not be able to re-enter the United States without proof of citizenship. More importantly, individuals on various watch lists will have a much more difficult time entering the United States legally as everyone entering the country now has to present official identification, making it easier for law enforcement to identify individuals of interest.

---

[7] See www.dhs.gov/xlibrary/assets/statistics/publications/ois_ill_pe_2009.pdf.

[8] See http://data.worldbank.org/indicator/BX.TRF.PWKR.DT.GD.ZS and World Bank 2012.

[9] See www.politifact.com/truth-o-meter/statements/2010/jul/02/barack-obama/us-has-more-border-patrol-agents-border-mexico-eve/.

Border Fence

Because most illegal entrants are from Mexico and enter the United States from the South, some have called for the construction of a fence along the 2,000 miles of the US-Mexican border. Indeed, in 2006, the **Secure Fence Act** overwhelmingly passed both Houses of Congress and was signed into law by President Bush (the vote in the House of Representatives was 283–138 and the vote in the Senate was 80–19). It calls for the construction of 700 miles of fence along the US-Mexican border. As with all public policy issues, there are benefits and costs associated with the border fence. The largest potential benefit is a decrease in illegal immigration. The fence will make it more difficult to cross into the United States, though it is not an insurmountable barrier. Of course, it is not clear that illegal immigration itself is economically costly, given how it increases economic productivity. Rather, the cost of illegal immigration is more closely connected to a violation of justice and/or security. To the extent the border fence reduces illegal immigration, it is beneficial in reducing these concerns. These potential benefits, however, are not without costs. The clearest cost associated with the border fence is economic. It is expensive. So far, the government has spent over $2 billion dollars to construct about 700 miles of fence, with an average cost of about $3.9 million per mile.[10] Further, the Government Accountability Office has estimated that it will cost about $6.5 billion over the next twenty years to maintain the fence.[11] There are also concerns about the environmental impact of the fence, particularly along the Rio Grande river, and its impact on the US relationship with Mexico, where the fence is not popular.

Given the benefits and costs of illegal immigration, are the benefits and costs of the border fence worthwhile? In political economy terms, we want to ask if this policy is efficient. If, for example, the border fence costs X and substantially reduces illegal immigration, but the net costs of illegal immigration are less than X, then we would say that the policy is not efficient. It costs more than what illegal immigration costs. Given the multi-billion-dollar cost of the fence, the efficiency of the policy is doubtful.

Work Force Audits

In addition to new policies to reduce the number of illegal immigrants entering the country, the government attacks illegal immigration through **work force audits**. In these investigations, the government matches the social security numbers on a business payroll with a list of social security numbers on all W-2 certificates. When there are anomalies, the government orders the business to fire the individual with the falsified social security number and may impose a fine on the business.

---

[10] See www.gao.gov/products/GAO-09–244R; and www.gao.gov/new.items/d09244r.pdf.
[11] See www.cbsnews.com/stories/2009/09/17/national/main5317298.shtml.

These audits beg the question of why a business hires illegal immigrants in the first place? The answer is twofold. First, hiring illegal immigrants can increase a business's profit, by increasing productivity if there are not enough available workers or through lower wages. Second, businesses do not necessarily know if someone is an illegal immigrant, particularly if the immigrant provides a social security number.

12.7 Immigration and Public Opinion

Two sets of factors influence most individuals' views of immigration, economic and psychic. **Economic factors** are monetary influences on opinion, while **psychic factors** are all of the non-monetary influences on a person's opinion. We begin with a discussion of economic factors.

Previously, we noted that immigration is like free trade. It is akin to an export, where the product exported is labor itself. All people in the importing state, the state receiving the immigrants, benefit from having less expensive products, but some people may see their salaries decrease or lose their jobs. Like trade, immigration leads to aggregate benefits and concentrated costs. Which people in a state are likely to benefit from trade and immigration and who is likely to suffer more costs? Answering this question will help us identify who is likely to support and who is likely to oppose (legal) immigration.

Recall that the Heckscher-Ohlin theory tells us that states that are relatively abundant in capital (call them rich states) are likely to export capital-intensive products and import labor-intensive products. Poor states, that is, states that are relatively abundant in labor, tend to export labor-intensive products and import capital-intensive ones. The **Stolper–Samuelson theorem** tells us that individuals working in the abundant factor benefit from trade, while individuals working with the scarce factor experience the costs of trade. In rich states (i.e. states relatively abundant in capital), individuals with large amounts of capital benefit from trade, while laborers suffer the costs of trade. In contrast, in poor states (i.e. states relatively abundant in labor), laborers benefit the most from trade, while individuals with large amounts of capital experience the cost of trade.

If the Stolper–Samuelson theorem is accurate, then in a relatively rich country like the United States, we should observe that individuals abundant in capital are more likely to support free trade and immigration than laborers. This is exactly what public opinion indicates (Scheve and Slaughter 2001). In addition, when we extend the analysis beyond the United States and examine opinion in both capital- and labor-abundant countries, we not only observe that high-skilled individuals in wealthy countries are more supportive of immigration than low-skilled individuals in those countries, but also that high-skilled individuals are more supportive of immigration than high-skilled individuals in poor countries. Further, low-skilled individuals in poor countries are more supportive of immigration than low-skilled individuals in wealthy countries, all of which is consistent with the Stolper–Samuelson theorem (O'Rourke and Sinnott 2006).

Economic concerns are not the only influence on one's views toward immigration. Non-monetary factors like cultural threat and chauvinism also affect opinions. Cultural threat is a person's view about changes to the world around them. If you view these changes negatively, then they are classified as a threat. Chauvinism is support for your country even if you believe it is pursuing policies that are wrong or that you cannot be a member of a country if you are not fully assimilated into it. Not surprisingly, individuals who are more chauvinist are more likely to oppose immigration. Similarly, as one's sense of cultural threat increases, opposition to immigration increases. Indeed, the empirical support for this cultural threat hypothesis on immigration is very strong (Brader *et al.* 2008; Citrin *et al.* 1990; Citrin *et al.* 1997; Fetzer 2000; Hainmueller and Hiscox 2007; Kinder and Kam 2009; McLaren 2001; McDaniel *et al.* 2011).

To further illustrate the effects of economic and cultural threat on immigration opinions, we discuss a study by Malhotra *et al.* (2013). In this innovative research, they examine public opinion on H-1B visas. US companies use H-1B visas to hire highly skilled foreign workers (e.g. engineers, computer programmers, see Box 12.1). By examining who opposes and who supports increasing the number of H-1B visas, we can gain a better sense of the factors influencing opinion on immigration. Thus, the dependent variable in this study is a person's opinion on this question: Do you think the United States should increase, decrease, or keep about the same the number of H-1B visas? Respondents had to choose from these options: increase a great deal, increase a little, keep about the same, decrease a little, or decrease a great deal.

To explain variation in opinion on this question, we will focus on three predictors. The first predictor is Economic Threat, which they code as whether or not an individual works in the high-technology industry.[12] The next two predictors assess one's sense of Cultural Threat. The variable Way of Life is a person's response to this question: How threatened do you think the American way of life is by foreign influence? Higher values on this variable indicate that one believes foreign influence is more threatening. Next, they asked individuals to evaluate if Indians are capable, polite, hardworking, hygienic, and trustworthy. One's average score on these evaluation questions forms the variable Negative Indian Traits. Based on our previous discussion we expect that individuals who work in the high-tech industry believe foreigners are threatening the American way of life and view Indians more negatively

---

[12] We note that the authors examined a number of different measures of the key concepts.

Table 12.3 Multiple Regression Predicting Support for H-1B Visas

	Coefficient (Standard Error)
High-technology worker	−0.07* (0.04)
Threatened by foreign influence	−0.30* (0.03)
Negative Indian traits	−0.12* (0.05)
N	868

Note: * = p<05, two-tailed. Model includes controls for unemployment, age, age squared, gender, marital status, education, white, income, party identification, and high-technology county.

will be more likely to oppose increasing the number of H-1B visas. The results of the multiple regression analysis are presented in Table 12.3.

Table 12.3 shows support for both the economic and cultural threat expectations. We reach this conclusion by examining the sign and statistical significance on the coefficients. In terms of the sign, we see that each is negative. In words, this means high technology workers are less supportive of H-1B visas than those not working in the high technology sector. Those who believe the American way of life is threatened by foreign influence are less supportive of H-1B visas than those who do not believe foreigners threaten the American way of life. And those who have more negative views of Indians are less supportive of increasing H-1B visas, which go primarily to Indians. As we have noted in several places in this book, the signs on the coefficients are only relevant if they are statistically significant as well. If the coefficients are not statistically significant, it means that we are just as likely to observe this particular number by chance. Put differently, if a coefficient is not statistically significant, then we cannot say that the effect of that variable on the outcome is any different from zero. Previously, we have used the twice as great rule of thumb to determine statistical significance. In Chapter 3, however, we noted that for directional hypotheses, if the coefficient is at least 1.65 times greater than the standard error, then the coefficient is statistically significant at the 5 percent level, assuming a sample size greater than 120. Each of the coefficients in Table 12.3 is more than 1.65 times greater than its standard error, so we conclude that each is statistically significant. This gives us some confidence that there really is a negative association between the predictors and the outcome.

Substantively, a one-unit increase in each predictor leads to a percentage decrease in support for H-1B visas. So, high technology workers are 7 percent less supportive of H-1B visas than workers not in this area. And individuals that believe the American way of life is threatened by foreign influence are 30 percent less supportive of increasing H-1B visas. That is a large effect; it is larger than any other effect in the model (including the control variables). To summarize, the analysis presented in Table 12.3 shows support for the economic threat hypothesis. Individuals who believe they may lose their jobs, or suffer a loss in wages, are less supportive of immigration. This applies to low- and high-skilled Americans. However, non-economic factors, what we have termed psychic or cultural, have an even larger effect on an individual's opinion about increasing immigration.

12.8 Collective Action, Credible Commitment Problems, and the Immigration Reform Debate

The analytic problems discussed in this book shed light on the intensity of the immigration reform debate. Most citizens are not significantly affected negatively by immigration. Illegal immigrants help keep labor costs low, benefitting consumers of their labor. Some illegal immigrants receive welfare, but they also pay taxes, including social security taxes in some cases, though they will not receive social security benefits. Given that the overall economic effects of immigration are either positive or not negative, why is there so much debate on immigration and why is the debate so intense?

Three analytic concepts help explain the intensity of the debate on immigration. First, there are unequal benefits and costs associated with immigration. Second, **political entrepreneurs** have seized upon the issue and framed it in a way that makes compromise more difficult. Third, **credible commitment problems** also make it difficult to find a compromise.

Immigration leads to unequal benefits and costs, and this affects collective action on the topic. A majority of Americans gain economically from illegal immigration, but each person in the majority gains relatively little. In contrast, those who lose from illegal immigration lose a lot; they lose their jobs. Those who lose from illegal immigration, then, are more likely to act collectively. They have a greater incentive to organize and they are relatively smaller, making it easier for them to organize. Nevertheless, a focus only on the economics of illegal immigration probably does not account for all of the intensity of the debate. Those who lose from illegal immigration are not so large and economically powerful to warrant a debate so intense. Something else is going on. The debate is intensified because political entrepreneurs are using illegal immigration to rally people for broader political ends.

A political entrepreneur is a person who identifies or frames an issue such that it motivates people to engage in political action. In other words, a political entrepreneur's work to make an issue salient in order to solve the collective action problem. In return for solving the **collective action problem**, the political entrepreneur receives selective benefits, such as fame or campaign donations to help the entrepreneur attain an important political office. To make an issue salient, political entrepreneurs have an incentive to frame an issue in moral terms. Doing so makes it affect more people and it reduces an individual's resolve not to act. That is, political action is viewed as less costly, for one derives emotional benefits from acting on behalf of justice.[13]

Credible commitment problems are also present in the debate on immigration reform. A credible commitment problem is present when the incentives to uphold an agreement will change in the future. Here's an illustration of the problem. For some in the United States the most preferred policy on immigration is to provide a path to citizenship for illegal immigrants. For others, the most preferred policy is to build a border fence. Supporters of legalization contend that a fence is costly and not necessary if a path to citizenship is established. Supporters of the fence respond that legalization without a fence will lead to an endless stream of immigrants and that the absence of a fence makes it easy for potential foreign terrorists to enter the country. If legalization occurs first, then those who want a fence have little leverage to obtain their policy outcome. In other words, from the perspective of those who want a fence, a policy with a path to citizenship before a fence represents a credible commitment problem. If the other side gets what it wants, they have less reason to honor any commitment to give the other side what it wants.

In addition, reaching an agreement is difficult because of the expectation that immigration will continue in the future. As outlined in this chapter, the United States has always allowed in immigrants – more at some times in the nation's history and less at others. Given its prosperity and appeal to many, it is likely that many will continue to want to emigrate to the United States. In political economy terms, with regard to immigration and the laws that regulate immigration, there is a long shadow – that is, the consequences of any deal reached today may extend for a long time into the future. Of course, it is always possible to pass a new law, but as this chapter shows, new laws that significantly change old laws do not come about very often. Thus, because of the expectation that immigration will continue, getting the law to resemble one's preferences is very important.

In summary, unequal benefits and costs for winners and losers from immigration as well as political entrepreneurs framing the topic in terms of justice to rally people to action help explain the intensity of the debate while the credible commitment problem and long shadow of the future on immigration help explain the challenge in finding an acceptable compromise.

---

[13] Policy entrepreneurs are related to political entrepreneurs, but focus on getting policy ideas before the public and policymakers despite being non-officeholders (Roberts and King 1991).

12.9 Should the United States Repeal the Fourteenth Amendment?

The first sentence of the Fourteenth Amendment states: "All persons born or naturalized in the United States, and subject to the jurisdiction thereof, are citizens of the United States and of the State wherein they reside." Put plainly, the Fourteenth Amendment grants citizenship to anyone born in the United States. The Fourteenth Amendment was enacted after the Civil War, in 1868 to be precise. Its primary purpose was to guarantee the citizenship of freed slaves and their children, thereby repealing the Dred Scott Supreme Court decision of 1857. Recently, this amendment has become part of the debate on immigration in America, with some calling for its repeal.

Those who want to change or repeal the Fourteenth Amendment make three arguments. First, it encourages illegal immigration. Children born to illegal immigrants are legal US citizens. To guard against deportation, the parents of the child can petition to stay in the United States to raise their American child in America. Second, in 2008, approximately one in twelve births in the United States, or 340,000 new babies, were born to illegal immigrants. Critics of the Amendment contend that it is unjust for a baby to be given citizenship when the parents came to the United States illegally. Third, the principle of *jus soli* (the right of the soil), or birthright citizenship, is held by a minority of states, almost all of which are in North, Central, or South America. (Mexico also practices birthright citizenship.) In addition, other states, including Ireland in 2005, New Zealand in 2006, and Australia in 2007, have recently changed their laws to deny birthright citizenship.

Those who support maintaining the Fourteenth Amendment as is also make three arguments. First, the United States receives many more immigrants, legal and illegal, than other states; as a result, to end birthright citizenship would greatly increase the number of undocumented persons in the country and it would be a bureaucratic nightmare to deal with the non-citizens. Another issue, where would you send the children of non-citizens?

Second, the argument that "anchor babies" encourage illegal immigration is fatuous. Illegal immigration is primarily a function of economic opportunity. Indeed, most children born to illegal immigrants have been living in the United States for a number of years, and many children born to an illegal immigrant are married to an American citizen. If the goal is to discourage illegal immigration, then resources could be used more effectively to secure the borders or investigate firms that may be employing illegal immigrants. To change the Fourteenth Amendment, one has to pass a new Constitutional amendment: that will be very difficult to accomplish as approval by two-thirds of the House and Senate as well as three-quarters of the State Legislatures is needed. At this point in time, it is very unlikely that such an amendment would pass.

Finally, many Republican supporters of the Fourteenth Amendment note that it is politically unwise to alienate Hispanic voters as they will soon be the largest minority group in the United States. Opposing the Fourteenth Amendment may provide some short-term political gain for some politicians, but the long-term political costs are likely to be severe.

12.10 Conclusion

A country's immigration policy aims to promote its economy, security, and values. Immigrants often provide needed skills and labor for a region's economy, thereby contributing to economic growth. Immigrant manpower and skills, particularly fluency in other languages, can also contribute to national security. Immigration may realize a state's values when the state admits political asylum seekers, those fleeing persecution, or simply those looking for new opportunities.

Three aspects of political economy improve our understanding of immigration policy. Trade theory and comparative advantage based on the Heckscher-Ohlin theory explain why some countries export people and some countries import people. In addition to this basic economic principle, we noted that other political (repression, violence, policy) and economic (poor economy or healthy economy) factors push and pull some individuals to migrate from one country to another. In this chapter, we also described some of the economic costs and benefits of immigration, and noted that the net effect on immigration in the United States is slightly positive. Finally, we explained how concentrated costs associated with immigration and political entrepreneurs highlighting cultural threat have led to collective action on immigration, and how this collective action, coupled with problems of credible commitment, have made the policy debate on immigration reform very contentious and difficult to resolve.

Key Terms

Immigrant
Green card
Family-based system
Employment-based system
Refugees

Asylum seekers

Diversity lottery

Naturalization

Visa

1921 Emergency Immigration Restriction Act

National-origins system

Immigration and Nationality Act Amendments of 1965

1986 Immigration Reform and Control Act (IRCA)

Illegal immigrant

Heckscher–Ohlin theorem

Melting pot

Beyond the melting pot

Traditionalists

Transnationalists

Green card marriage

Western Hemisphere Travel Initiative

Secure Fence Act

Work force audit

Economic factors

Pyschic factors

Stolper–Samuelson theorem

Political entrepreneur

Credible commitment problem

Collective action problem

CHAPTER EXERCISES

1. What are the benefits of legal immigration? What are the drawbacks?
2. How might the four procedures for becoming a legal immigrant (family-based, employment-based, refugee/asylum, and diversity lottery) be used to restrict immigration from a particular country?
3. Why is amnesty (granting legal status to illegal immigrants) considered by some to be a policy that can reduce future illegal immigration?
4. In combating illegal immigration, which is more important – cutting off the supply (through measures like the border fence) or cutting off the demand (through measures like work force audits)?
5. Do you think that the term "melting pot" is an accurate way to describe the United States? Why?

REFERENCES

Acemoglu, Daron and Autor, David. 2011. "Skills, Tasks and Technologies: Implications for Employment and Earnings," in Orley Ashenfelter and David Card (eds.), *Handbook of Labor Economics*, Vol. 4, Part B. Amsterdam: Elsevier, pp. 1043–1171.

Borjas, G. J. 1994. "The Economics of Immigration." *Journal of Economic Literature* 32(4): 1667–1717.

1995. "The Economic Benefits from Immigration." *Journal of Economic Perspectives* 9(2): 3–22.

2003. "The Labor Demand Curve Is Downward Sloping: Reexamining the Impact of Immigration on the Labor Market." *Quarterly Journal of Economics* 118(4): 1335–1374.

2008. "Immigration." *The Concise Encyclopedia of Economics*. Library of Economics and Liberty. Retrieved August 12, 2010 from www.econlib.org/library/Enc/Immigration.html.

Brader, Ted, Valentino, Nicholas A., and Suhay, Elizabeth. 2008. "What Triggers Public Opposition to Immigration? Anxiety, Group Cues, and Immigration Threat." *American Journal of Political Science* 52(4): 959–978.

Brulliard, Karin. 2008. "Bush Welcomes New American Citizens." *Washington Post*, July 5. Available online at www.washingtonpost.com/wp-dyn/content/article/2008/07/04/AR2008070402260.html.

Card, D. 2005. "Is The New Immigration Really So Bad?" *Economic Journal* 115(507): F300–F323.

Citrin, Jack, Green, Donald P., Muste, Christopher, and Wong, Cara. 1997. "Public Opinion toward Immigration Reform: The Role of Economic Motivations." *Journal of Politics* 59(3): 858–881.

Citrin, Jack, Reingold, Beth, and Green, Donald P. 1990. "American Identity and the Politics of Ethnic Change." *Journal of Politics* 52(4): 1124–1154.

Cortes, Patricia and Tessada, José. 2011. "Low-Skilled Immigration and the Labor Supply of Highly Skilled Women." *American Economic Journal: Applied Economics* 3(3): 88–123.

Cortes, Patricia. 2008. "The Effect of Low-Skilled Immigration on US Prices: Evidence from CPI Data." *Journal of Political Economy* 116(3): 381–422.

Cortina, Jeronimo. 2014. "Subsidizing Migration? Mexican Agricultural Policies and Migration to the United States." *Policy Studies Journal* 42(1): 101–121.

De la Garza, R. O., Garcia, F. C., and Falcon, A. 1996. "Will the Real Americans Please Stand Up? Mexican American and Anglo Support for Core American Values." *American Journal of Political Science* 40(2): 335–351.

Donelley, Francis. 2010. "Immigrants Celebrate America." *The Detroit News*, July 3.

Federman, Maya N., Harrington, David E., and Krynski, Kathy J. 2006. "Vietnamese Manicurists: Are Immigrants Displacing Natives or Finding New Nails to Polish?" *Industrial & Labor Relations Review* 59(2): 302–318.

Fetzer, Joel S. 2000. *Public Attitudes toward Immigration in the United States, France, and Germany*. New York: Cambridge University Press.

Freeman, R. B. 2006. "People Flows in Globalization." *Journal of Economic Perspectives* 20(2): 145–170.

Garand, James C., Xu, Ping, and Davis, Belinda C. 2015. "Immigration Attitudes and Support for the Welfare State in the American Mass Public." *American Journal of Political Science*, doi: 10.1111/ajps.12233.

Geyer, Georgie Anne. 1996. *American No More: The Death of Nationality*. New York: Atlantic Monthly Press.

Glazer, Nathan and Moynihan, Daniel P. 1963. *Beyond the Melting Pot: The Negroes, Puerto Ricans, Jews, Italians and Irish of New York City*. Cambridge, MA: MIT Press.

Hainmueller, Jens and Hiscox, Michael J. 2007. "Educated Preferences: Explaining Attitudes toward Immigration in Europe." *International Organization* 61(2): 399–442.

Helpman, Elhanan and Krugman, Paul R. 1985. *Market Structure and Foreign Trade: Increasing Returns, Imperfect Competition, and the International Economy*. Cambridge, MA: MIT press.

Hoefer, Michael, Rytina, Nancy, and Campbell, Christopher. 2006. "Estimates of the Unauthorized Immigrant Population Residing in the United States: January 2005." Office of Immigration

Statistics, Department of Homeland Security. Available online at www.dhs.gov/xlibrary/assets/statistics/publications/ILL_PE_2005.pdf.

Huntington, Samuel P. 2004. *Who Are We?: The Challenges to America's National Identity*. New York: Simon & Schuster.

Katz, M. B., Stern, M. J, and Fader, J. J. 2007. "The Mexican Immigration Debate: The View from History." *Social Science History* 31(2): 157–189.

Kinder, Donald R. and Kam, Cindy D. 2009. *Us against Them: Ethnocentric Foundations of American Opinion*. University of Chicago Press.

Malhotra, Neil, Margalit, Yotam, and Mo, Cecilia Hyunjung. 2013. "Economic Explanations for Opposition to Immigration: Distinguishing between Prevalence and Conditional Impact." *American Journal of Political Science* 57(2): 391–410.

Massey, Douglas S., Durand, Jorge, and Malone, Nolan J. 2002. *Beyond Smoke and Mirrors: Mexican Immigration in an Era of Economic Integration*. New York: Russell Sage Foundation.

McDaniel, Eric L., Nooruddin, Irfan, and Shortle, Allyson F. 2011. "Divine Boundaries: How Religion Shapes Citizens' Attitudes towards Immigrants." *American Politics Research* 39(1): 205–233.

McLaren, Lauren M. 2001. "Immigration and the New Politics of Inclusion and Exclusion in the European Union." *European Journal of Political Research* 39(1): 81–108.

McManus, Walter S. 1990. "Labor Market Effects of Language Enclaves: Hispanic Men in the United States." *Journal of Human Resources* 25(2): 228–252.

O'Rourke, Kevin H. and Sinnott, Richard. 2006. "The Determinants of Individual Attitudes towards Immigration." *European Journal of Political Economy* 22(4): 838–861.

Passel, J. S. 2007. "Growing Share of Immigrants Choosing Naturalization." *Pew Hispanic Center Report*.

Preston, Julia. 2008. "Decline Seen in Numbers of People Here Illegally." *New York Times*, July 31. Available online at www.nytimes.com/2008/07/31/us/31immig.html?_r=2&partner=rssnyt.

Renshon, Stanley A. 2000. "Dual Nationality + Multiple Loyalties = One America?" in Stanley Renshon (ed.), *One America? Political Leadership, National Identity, and the Dilemmas of Diversity*. Washington, DC: Georgetown University Press, pp. 232–282.

Roberts, Nancy C. and King, Paula J. 1991. "Policy Entrepreneurs: Their Activity Structure and Function in the Policy Process." *Journal of Public Administration Research and Theory* 1(2): 147–175.

Scheve, Kenneth F. and Slaughter, Matthew J. 2001. "Labor Market Competition and Individual Preferences over Immigration Policy." *Review of Economics and Statistics* 83(1): 133–145.

Spenkuch, Jörg L. 2013. "Understanding the Impact of Immigration on Crime." *American Law and Economics Review* 16(1): 117–219.

Staton, J. K., Jackson, R. A., and Canache, D. 2007. "Dual Nationality among Latinos: What Are the Implications for Political Connectedness?" *Journal of Politics* 69(2): 470–482.

Stecklov, Guy, Winters, Paul, Stampini, Marco, and Davis, Benjamin. 2003. *Can Public Transfers Reduce Migration? A Study based on Randomized Experimental Data (ESA Working Paper no.03–16)*. Rome: The Food and Agriculture Organization of the United Nations.

US Department of Justice. 1993. "Immigration and Naturalization Service," p. 25.

US Department of Commerce. 1975. "Bureau of the Census," pp. 8, 14; 1993b, p. 50.

Wadhwa, Vivek, Gereffi, Gary, Rissing, Ben, and Ong, Ryan. 2007 (Spring). "Where the Engineers Are. Issues in Science and Technology." Available online at www.issues.org/23.3/wadhwa.html.

Waters, Mary and Pineau, Marisa Gerstein (eds.). 2015. *The Integration of Immigrants into American Society*. Washington, DC: National Academies Press.

World Bank. 2012. "World Development Indicators." Washington, DC: World Bank. Available online at http://data.worldbank.org/data-catalog/world-development-indicators.

13 Foreign and Defense Policy

Outline

Questions

- Why is there variation in defense policy across presidential administrations?
- Do negative domestic political conditions cause states to go to war? Do leaders "wag the dog"?
- What are the central causes of war between countries?
- What sorts of policies can promote peace between countries?
- Why is trade policy so controversial?
- Why are some politicians more likely than others to support protectionist policies?

Overview

- The primary analytic concepts we use to provide insight on foreign policy are principal–agent theory, bargaining theory, comparative advantage, and collective action.

- Leaders respond to their winning coalitions. As the composition of the winning coalition changes, government policy changes. It is the change in the composition of winning coalitions that accounts for variation in defense policy.
- Negative domestic political conditions may make leaders more hawkish, but they cannot cause war, for war is a strategic process that involves at least two states.
- Because different winning coalitions represent different interests, the impact of domestic political conditions varies across leaders. For example, Democratic presidents are more hawkish when unemployment is high, while Republican presidents are more hawkish when inflation is high.
- War results from bargaining failures over perceived disagreements. Bargaining failures result from incomplete information about resolve, capabilities, or an inability for at least one side to credibly commit to abide by the terms of a deal.
- In crisis bargaining, costly signals reduce uncertainty and may reduce conflict escalation. The expected cost of war has a significant influence on the outcome of crisis bargaining.
- The principle of comparative advantage explains the benefits and costs of trade.
- Collective action and institutional incentives account for support for protectionism and free trade.

Introduction

With each new president, American foreign policy undergoes some significant changes. Shortly after his inauguration in January 2009, President Obama made changes to US foreign policy. He shut down overseas secret prisons and worked to end significant military involvement in Iraq by 2011. Similarly, when President Clinton took office in January 1993, he immediately ended the Mexico City policy, which prohibits foreign aid to foreign groups that provide assistance with abortion. President George W. Bush reinstituted the policy when he took office in 2001. President Obama terminated the policy when he took office in 2009.

American foreign policy, however, does not completely change with each new president. Throughout the Cold War, both Democratic and Republican presidents organized their foreign policies around containing communism. Since its creation in 1949, no US president has proposed ending, or even fundamentally altering, the NATO (North Atlantic Treaty Organization) military alliance. In the otherwise partisan 1980s and 1990s, presidents from both parties supported the extension of Most Favored Nation (MFN) status to China.[1] In Congress, both Republican and Democratic

---

[1] Most Favored Nation (MFN) trade status means that the tariffs applied by the United States to one state apply to any state to which it accords MFN status. In other words, a state with MFN status will not have higher tariffs on its goods relative to any other state trading with the United States.

representatives and senators object to closing military bases. Indeed, there is perhaps no better way to unite senators and representatives from different parties than to propose closing a military base in that state. The reason is straightforward: closing a military base means job losses for one's constituents.

What accounts for the change and continuity in American foreign and defense policy? To answer this question, we focus in this chapter on three central policy problems: principal–agent, bargaining, and collective action problems. Principal–agent relationships help us understand key changes in continuity in American foreign policy. We show, for example, that leaders respond to their **winning coalition**, the group of people central to a leader attaining and retaining office (Bueno de Mesquita *et al.* 2003). When the composition of the winning coalition changes, either because a new president was elected or a leader's base of support changes, government policy is more likely to change. Still, different political groups in society, like Republicans and Democrats, agree on some issues some of the time. Different winning coalitions, then, do not always lead to policy change. Continuity in policy is also accounted for by the distribution of political preferences in the country. About one-third of the electorate identifies itself as Democrats, one-third as Republicans, and one-third as Independents. With this distribution of political preferences, a candidate needs the support of many independent voters to win the presidency. So long as the preferences of independents are stable, American foreign policy will be relatively stable.

Electoral motivations and the size and composition of winning coalitions also influence the use of military force abroad. By 2006, American public opinion had turned against the war in Iraq, yet President Bush ordered an increase in US troops in Iraq. If electoral concerns, which are often reflected by the state of public opinion, influence presidential decisions, why did President Bush send more troops to Iraq? In this chapter, we show that this policy, popularly called "the surge," was very popular with the president's winning coalition, and it is a response to the institutional incentive for the president to achieve a policy success.

Bargaining theory, and the size and composition of the winning coalition, have perhaps surprising implications for when the United States uses major military force abroad. Contrary to popular views, poor domestic political conditions very rarely lead to the use of military force abroad. The reasons are straightforward. It is better for a president to directly address his or her domestic political problems – perhaps pushing for a tax cut or extending unemployment benefits. And other states know that the president has an incentive to use military force when the economy is not performing well; as a result, they avoid major entanglements under these conditions.

Bargaining theory and coalition composition also help us solve another puzzle: Why do states engage in war when both sides would be much better off resolving their disputes peacefully? The Persian Gulf War illustrates the puzzle. In January 1991, a UN coalition led by the United States had about 500,000 troops in the Persian Gulf.

President George H. W. Bush demanded that Saddam Hussein evacuate his army from Kuwait. Despite the large amount of troops on his border, Saddam Hussein stood firm. The choice was disastrous for him. The UN coalition attacked on January 17, 1991, and after only forty-three days, Saddam Hussein and the Iraqi Army were evicted from Kuwait. Approximately 40,000 Iraqis died in combat (compared to about about 370 Americans). Subsequently, severe sanctions were imposed on Iraq to contain Saddam Hussein from rebuilding his military. Clearly, it would have been better for Iraq to yield prior to war. In this chapter, we explain why the two sides had such difficulty reaching an agreement short of war.

In this chapter, we also discuss some of the central economic and political aspects of international trade. Why do countries engage in trade? Does trade harm the economy? We also address a question coming from the opposite perspective: Why is there not more support for free trade? Why are protectionist policies so common? We use two analytic concepts to provide some insight on these questions: comparative advantage and collective action.

13.1 Principal–Agent Theory

The public elects the leaders of the government. Every two years, members of the House of Representatives are elected. Every six years, members of the Senate are elected. Every four years, we elect a president. However, the public does not implement public policy. Elected officials and government bureaucrats do that. In a representative democracy, as in the United States, the public is in charge. But the public only establishes the parameters that guide policy choice and implementation, and these parameters sometimes allow for significant discretion on the part of elected officials or government workers. To better understand the relationship between the public and elected officials, as well as the public's influence on public policy, we turn to a discussion of **principal–agent theory**.

Agents are subordinates or representatives. **Principals** are bosses, the person, or group, for whom the agent works. For example, a member of the House of Representatives is an agent representing a particular Congressional district. The people in her district are the principal. Principal–agent relationships do not apply just to politics. If you have a job and are not self-employed, then you work for someone. You are an agent and your boss is the principal. Further, an individual may be an agent in one context and a principal in another. You may have a boss, a principal, and you may oversee others, that is, have agents that you manage. Similarly, in one context, the President of the United States is an agent of the people of the United States. In another context, the president is the principal who directs and manages individuals in the federal government. In this latter context, cabinet secretaries, such as the Secretaries of State and of Defense, are agents representing the president.

Adverse Selection and Moral Hazard Problems

Principal–agent relationships have two key features. First, in at least some important situations, there is an asymmetry in preferences between the principal and agent. What the principal wants the agent to do is not the same thing that the agent wants to do. The problem with a difference in preferences is that it creates different motivations to pursue tasks. At the most basic level, a principal may want an agent to work, but the agent may prefer shirking (not working). When a principal chooses an agent with different preferences, it is called **adverse selection**.

Second, there is an asymmetry in information between the principal and the agent. Principals have agents for reasons of efficiency, expertise, or more often than not for both efficiency and expertise. In terms of efficiency, agents help a principal get the job done quicker and better. Imagine that the president did not have agents to assist him running the federal government. Then, the president would be bogged down in managing each department of the government: the State Department, the Defense Department, the Energy Department, the Treasury Department, etc. There is not enough time in the day to supervise closely all of these agencies. Without agents, a principal would get much less accomplished. In terms of expertise, agents usually know more about their particular job than does the principal. The Secretary of Treasury, for example, typically comes from the corporate or financial world and has more detailed knowledge of economics and finance than the president. Even if a particular agent is not more knowledgeable than the principal upon taking a job, she is likely to become more familiar with the details of the job because she is focused on that one job, while the principal's attention is dissipated across a range of agents. For reasons of efficiency and expertise, then, there is an asymmetry in information between principals and agents.

The problem with this information asymmetry, or to be more precise an information disadvantage, is that it makes it difficult for a principal to monitor the performance of an agent effectively. How does one effectively monitor if one does not know what should be monitored? In turn, monitoring limitations contributes to a problem of moral hazard. A **moral hazard problem** is a situation in which an actor who is at least partially protected from risk acts differently than if she were not protected from risk. Risk may usefully be thought of as the probability of suffering harm or failing. A risk-acceptant person is more willing to choose a course of action that has a specific probability of failing (such as 20 percent) than a less risk-acceptant person. The classic moral hazard situation involves an insurance company and a driver. A risk-averse driver knows that an accident is possible and would like insurance to avoid expensive car repairs. Insurance companies make money from extending insurance policies. With insurance, however, there is less of an incentive for the driver to be risk-averse while driving. For example, once covered a driver may be more likely to talk on a cell phone while driving. In other words, with insurance the driver is more likely to engage in morally hazardous conduct, that is, conduct that may make an accident more likely. If the insurance company could monitor the driver's actions perfectly, then the moral hazard problem would be solved, but it is not possible to monitor an individual's every action.

Standard Operating Procedures, Screening, and Outcome-Based Incentives

What can a principal do to address the adverse selection and moral hazard problems? Principals can never completely solve these problems. They are an inherent feature of life. But these problems can be ameliorated with three types of strategies: careful screening of agents, outcome-based incentive schemes, and standard operating procedures.

Principal–agent problems, particularly adverse selection, are mitigated when the principal chooses agents that closely mirror the principal's preferences. When the principal and agent have the same, or nearly the same, preferences, adverse selection is less of a problem, as the agent is likely to do what the principal desires. **Screening** out individuals with significantly different preferences, then, is a major goal of the principal when choosing agents. In employment situations, the most common screening mechanism is a background check on criminal history. Principals want to guard against theft and it is reasonable to think that one with a history of criminal conduct is more likely to repeat such conduct. In a similar way, elections, both primaries and general elections, help screen out less competent candidates. Of course, there is no guarantee that one can screen out incompetent candidates or choose the best candidate, but the screening aspect of elections is one reason democracy as a political system tends to produce more public goods than other types of political systems.

Outcome-based incentive schemes are central to reducing moral hazard problems. For example, an insurance company will adjust its rates based on the size of the deductible. As the deductible increases, a driver has less incentive to engage in hazardous driving, and therefore the overall rate will decrease. Of course, incentive structures are only second-best solutions. (Discussion question: What is the best solution and why is that rarely, if ever, attainable?) The driver would prefer a smaller deductible for the same overall price and would like to promise the insurance company that he will not engage in inappropriate behavior. The insurance company would like to believe the driver, but with little ability to monitor fully and the driver having an incentive to act recklessly, the insurance company will not accept such a promise. In brief, information asymmetries leave us with the second-best solution of outcome-based incentive schemes.

A third strategy that principals employ to mitigate the problems of adverse selection and moral hazard is the creation and implementation of **standard operating procedures (SOPs)**. SOPs are specific guidelines or instructions on what to do in a given situation. With SOPs, a principal can have greater confidence that the agent is doing what he wants the agent to do. They also make monitoring the agent's performance easier, for it is easier to assess if a checklist is followed than if the best possible choice was made in a situation. However, SOPs come with a cost. They reduce agent discretion. Since not all situations are the same, it is very difficult to have a checklist to cover every contingency. Many jobs, then, are accomplished best when agents are given the discretion to make decisions on their own.

During the Cold War, it was often observed that US soldiers were better than soldiers from communist states as US soldiers were given more discretion to make decisions on the battlefield. Nevertheless, SOPs are especially common in the military as human life is often at stake in a choice situation. Before soldiers fire their weapon, they will usually have to run through a checklist of sorts to ensure that they meet the rules of engagement. We can also note that voters often follow an SOP when they vote. If the economy is doing well, retain the incumbent, otherwise vote for the challenger.

13.2 Principal–Agent Problems and Foreign Policy

As noted earlier, the President of the United States is an agent of the public. Does this relationship have the key features of principal–agent relationships discussed earlier? In some situations, it seems that the preferences of the president are different from the preferences of the median voter. No president after all perfectly caters to public opinion. In addition, the president tends to have much more information than the public about foreign events and available options. Information asymmetry on foreign policy, then, commonly characterizes the relationship between the president and the public. Given that the public is at an information disadvantage, what can the public (the principal) do to ensure that the president (the agent) carries out its wishes, particularly on matters of war and peace?

Gambling for Resurrection

In an influential article, Downs and Rocke (1994) apply principal–agent theory to foreign policy. They note that the best way for the public to control the president is to focus on outcomes. For example, with regard to war, the public should not re-elect a president when a war is going poorly. If a war is going well, then the public should re-elect the president. What if the president in the first situation, when war is going badly, is well intentioned in trying to act on the public's preferences, but the president in the second situation went to war for more nefarious reasons? Should we still boot the one from office and re-elect the other? Yes, for two reasons. First, it is not possible to know the intentions of either president with complete confidence. Second, election is the primary incentive the public can give to a candidate. If the public re-elects a president when war is going badly, then there is little incentive for future presidents to focus on attaining a positive outcome. Similarly, if the public fails to re-elect a president who triumphs in war, then there is little incentive for future presidents to focus on winning wars, all else being equal. (Discussion question: What does all else being equal imply? What is the other major area of policy? What should the public do when a president is successful in one area, but not in another?) In summary, the public focuses on outcomes to provide incentives for future presidents.

Downs and Rocke (1994) make another interesting observation. Presidents likely understand that they are judged by how well a war is going (as well as the state of the economy and other factors). When a war is going poorly, then the president has an incentive to "**gamble for resurrection**," that is, adopt extreme measures in the hope that things will turn around. If the military situation does not improve, the president is no worse off for gambling for resurrection. After all, the reason he is adopting more extreme measures is because he was not likely to be re-elected with a losing military conflict. However, if the military situation significantly improves, then the president has a much better chance of retaining office. In other words, while one might expect that a president would abandon a losing campaign, the insight from Downs and Rocke (1994) is that presidents are more likely to increase involvement in a war when it is going poorly.

Public Opinion and Foreign Policy

Principal–agent theory helps us understand partisanship in Congress on foreign policy and the continuity and change in American foreign policy over time. Political candidates desire to win office, and if elected, to remain in office. To win office, candidates need to persuade people to vote for them and mobilize them to turn out. This is where political parties enter the picture. Parties help persuade and mobilize the public (Aldrich 1995). Because of the importance of political parties for persuading and mobilizing other voters, candidates often cater to the views of their core constituents, the **party activists**. Political scientists typically define party activists as individuals who actively participate in political campaigns, with active participation defined as engaging in at least four of the following six activities: voting, attending political rallies, wearing a campaign button, displaying a campaign sign or bumper sticker, working for a political party or candidate, engaging in efforts to influence others' views, and donating money to a political party or candidate (Carmines and Stimson 1989: 93). Democratic politicians pay closer attention to the views of core Democratic constituencies, and Republican politicians pay closer attention to the views of core Republican constituencies. By examining the foreign policy views of Democratic and Republican voters and activists, we can better understand the change and continuity in American foreign policy over time.

In the mid 1980s, one important foreign policy issue concerned the extent to which the United States should support opponents of the communist regime in Nicaragua (called Contras). In a 1985 Gallup poll asking about support for a trade embargo against the Nicaraguan regime, about 65 percent of Republican respondents approved of the embargo, while only about 26 percent of Democratic respondents approved. In the 104th Congress (1994 to 1996), the Republican leadership attempted to pass a bill to amend title 10 of the US code regulating military personnel. The proposed amendment would limit the ability of American troops to serve under UN command. Reflecting the view of their electoral bases, 97 percent of Republican legislators voted for it, but only 43 percent of Democratic legislators supported it. With many Congressional districts strongly favoring one party over another, it is not surprising that votes in Congress on this topic split along party lines. In other words, while all representatives pay attention to the views of their constituents, the distribution of preferences in a particular district tends to favor one party over the other. When Republican and Democratic voters hold sharply different views, it is no surprise that voting in Congress on a similar issue is partisan, a majority of Democrats voting differently from a majority of Republicans. Souva and Rhode (2007) show that this pattern occurs across a number of foreign policy issues since the 1970s.

Public Opinion and Defense Spending

Over the last several decades, perhaps no issue has better distinguished Democratic and Republican identifiers and party activists than defense spending. Party identifiers are those who publicly list a party label. They are unlike party activists in that they do not necessarily engage in any political activity on behalf of the party or a candidate. Since the early 1970s, Republican identifiers have been much more supportive of increasing defense spending than Democratic identifiers (see Table 13.1).[2] Fordham (2007) shows that before the Vietnam War, Democratic identifiers were more supportive of increasing defense spending than Republican identifiers. In 1976, the difference in support between Republican and Democratic party identifiers was about 11 percent. This increased to nearly 20 percent in 1980 and 1984. The gap was smallest in 1992 (the Soviet Union dissolved in 1991) and 2000. The gap between Republican and Democratic activists is even larger. It has not fallen below 18 percent since 1972, and it reached a peak in 2004. In that year, 88 percent of Republican activists

[2] This table is based on Fordham (2007). His table covers 1972 to 1990. We extend it to 2008.

Table 13.1 Support for Military Spending among Party Activists and Identifiers

	Identifiers			Activists		
Year	Republicans (%)	Democrats (%)	Difference (%)	Republicans (%)	Democrats (%)	Difference (%)
1972	30	22.7	7.3	28.8	6.6	22.2
1976	83.1	72.1	11.0	91	72.7	18.3
1980	73.5	54.0	19.5	76.3	35.0	41.3
1982	40.7	20.0	20.7	50.0	25.6	24.4
1984	43.7	22.8	20.9	53.1	13.5	39.6
1986	37.1	22.0	15.1	45.8	12.2	33.6
1988	43.0	21.0	22.0	37.5	16.5	21.0
1990	21.9	17.5	4.4	41.6	6.3	35.3
1992	21.8	14.3	7.5	30.0	6.0	24.0
1994	38.8	16.7	22.1	55.0	5.3	49.7
1996	42.7	24.1	18.6	61.5	10.7	50.8
2000	30.2	22.4	7.8	44.4	18.5	25.9
2004	70.3	28	42.3	87.9	13.9	74.0
2008	60.9	39.2	21.7	83.3	20	63.3

Source: American National Election Studies

supported increasing defense spending, but only about 14 percent of Democratic activists did. This is reflective of the larger polarization on the Iraq War.

In light of these views on the military for each party's core constituents, it is not surprising that President Nixon stepped up the military effort in Vietnam, that President Carter cut defense spending (for the first couple of years of his term in office), that President Reagan sought large increases in defense spending, that President Clinton cut defense spending, and that President George W. Bush proposed to increase defense spending, even prior to the attacks of September 11, 2001.[3] As we will

---

[3] In February 2001, a Gallup survey found that 21 percent of Democratic identifiers said the United States was spending "too much" on the military, while only 9 percent of Republicans had that view. And, consistent with surveys on support for the "surge" in Iraq in 2007, in a February 2007 poll, Gallup found that 18 percent of Republican identifiers said the United States was spending "too much" on the military, while 58 percent of Democratic identifiers said that.

see in the next section, a similar story emerges when we examine support for the Iraq War and the surge in Iraq in 2007. The principal's preferences, that is, the public's view, influence what the agent does, but they do not strictly determine the agent's actions.

13.3 Principal–Agent Theory and the Iraq War

How well does principal–agent theory account for President Bush's choices on Iraq? According to principal–agent theory, the agent should not stray too far from the principal's preferences. In Figure 13.1, we observe that a majority of the public (about 66 percent) supported President Bush's handling of Iraq in March 2003. Going back to October 2002, support for President Bush's actions on Iraq was never below 50 percent. This support was even higher among Republican identifiers. Now, principal–agent theory does not predict that politicians blindly follow public opinion. What public opinion does is serve as a constraint on the president's actions. Politicians that act against the majority's opinion on salient issues are very unlikely to retain office. Indeed, because of this electoral check, politicians are not only limited by public opinion, but also try to mold it.

With regard to public opinion, one of the central analytic questions is whether it influences the president (and other politicians) or they influence it. The short answer, of course, is that it is both. Presidents respond to public opinion and, by means of the

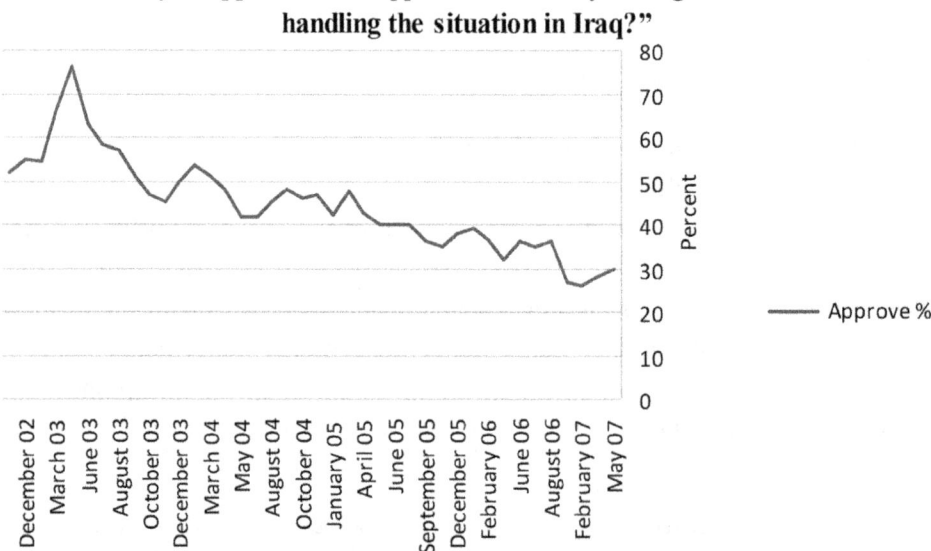

Figure 13.1 Support for President Bush's Handling of the Iraq War
* USA Today/Gallup Polls. Data available at www.pollingreport.com/iraq4.htm.

bully pulpit, can influence it. Notwithstanding the sometimes reciprocal influence, the causal force of opinion on politician choice is usually stronger than politician framing on opinion. This is so for three reasons. First, opinions on current events are ultimately based on an individual's **core values** (Hurwitz and Peffley 1987), which are difficult for politicians to manipulate. Core values are an individual's primary beliefs. In the domain of foreign policy, core issues include one's view of the morality of warfare and belief in the superiority of one's country (Hurwitz and Peffley 1987). In the short term, politicians are not likely to change a person's core values; instead, what they try to do is influence which core value receives emphasis. Second, while an agent can sometimes manipulate the principal's beliefs, there are bounds on what can be achieved. Baum and Potter (2008: 43) label this the **elasticity of reality**. It would have been much more difficult, for example, for the Bush administration to mobilize public opinion against a state with which the United States had no history of conflict and was not in violation of any UN Security Council resolutions. Reality notwithstanding, there is an even more important constraint on what the agent can get away with. Third, politicians can only manipulate opinion to a small degree because of opposition parties and the media. At the beginning of a conflict, Baum and Potter (2008) observe that there is often an information gap between the administration and the public, with the latter not being well informed. Over time, however, this information gap decreases, owing to the efforts of the media to focus on a conflict and opposition candidates to accentuate any negatives. More generally, we can observe that the truth tends to come out, and this provides a constraint on how much an agent can manipulate a principal.

With the absence of weapons of mass destruction in Iraq and deteriorating stability prior to 2007, public support for the Iraq War and President Bush's policies naturally declined. Shortly before the 2006 Congressional elections, support for President Bush's management of the Iraq War was around 30 percent. Not surprisingly, the president's party suffered greatly at the polls. The Democratic Party gained thirty-one seats in the House of Representatives and five seats in the Senate, taking majority control of each institution. These facts highlight two general analytic points. First, when performance is poor (or at least when expectations are worse than expected), the principal punishes the agent, which in this context means that the president's party experienced significant electoral losses. As we noted previously, this outcome-based incentive scheme (how well do you fare in the next election) is the principal's primary method for reducing moral hazard by the agent. Second, the public responds rationally to new information (Shapiro and Page 1988). It would be particularly odd if public approval of the president did not decline when the central motivation for going to war turned out to be not relevant, American troops were in a war longer than initially indicated by the president, and violence greatly increased in Iraq after the February 2006 Samarra Mosque bombing.

Recall that one of the central claims of principal–agent theory is that a leader responsible for getting his state into a war that is not going well will "gamble for resurrection." That is, the leader will act aggressively to salvage the war, even to the point of ignoring the majority opinion in the country. This is precisely what President Bush did in late 2006 and early 2007 with the so-called surge in Iraq. Although public support for President Bush and his handling of the Iraq War was very low and 61 percent of respondents to a Gallup survey in January 2007 opposed increasing troops in Iraq, he increased the number of American troops in Iraq in order to turn the tide, and perhaps pull out a draw.[4]

The **surge** was the popular name for President Bush's new strategy for Iraq. Announced in January 2007, the policy called for an additional 20,000 troops to go to Iraq, primarily to Baghdad where the violence was the worst. More important than the increased number of troops, President Bush's "A New Way Forward," the official name of the strategy, called for a change in counter-insurgency (COIN) strategy. The new COIN strategy placed more emphasis on protecting the civilian population. The primary way in which it aimed to do this was to hire Sunni tribesman as security agents. Essentially, the plan called for co-opting them so that they did not support Al Qaeda. At the time of writing, public support for the surge has increased. Only time will tell if that significantly affects President Bush's standing in history.

13.4 Diversionary Foreign Policy

President Clinton's order to launch cruise missiles against targets in Sudan and Afghanistan on August 20, 1998 during the midst of the Monica Lewinsky scandal raises a general question of whether negative domestic political conditions increase the likelihood that a president will use military force abroad.[5] Diversionary theories of conflict answer this question affirmatively. According to **diversionary theory**, domestic political problems, usually associated with poor economic conditions, provide an incentive for the use of force abroad as a way to divert the public's attention away from domestic problems and increase public approval through a rally-around-the-flag effect. The **rally-around-the-flag** effect refers to an increase in presidential popularity when the country is attacked or attacks another country. The theoretical argument in support of a rally effect is that in times of crisis, such as a common threat, people feel a need for solidarity with those around them and so they unite around something in common, the flag. Further,

---

[4] It is also worth noting that a majority (67 percent) of Republican identifiers supported the "surge" (www.gallup.com/poll/26080/Public-Opposes-Troop-Surge-61-36-Margin.aspx). Gambling for resurrection is less likely to occur when one's own party opposes an action.

[5] The 1997 movie *Wag the Dog*, starring Dustin Hoffmann and Robert Deniro, outlines diversionary theory.

diversionary theories typically focus on economic conditions because these are known to influence presidential popularity and the likelihood of re-election.

The diversionary theory of force begs a question: Why does the president not choose policies that will directly address the problems leading to the domestic dissatisfaction? If possible, a president will likely choose this course of action. In some contexts, however, a president may not be able to take direct action or such actions will not have an effect in the needed time frame. The federal government can address economic problems through changes to monetary policy, fiscal policy, or both. Monetary policy is about the supply and cost of money. In the United States, and in most advanced economies, monetary policy is controlled by the Federal Reserve. Fiscal policy is about government borrowing, spending, and taxing. Since the president has little control over monetary policy, he is likely to focus on fiscal policy when there are economic problems. However, fiscal policy, whether in the form of tax cuts or spending, requires the support of Congress. If Congress opposes such endeavors, then the president has a greater incentive to engage in diversionary foreign policy actions.

In an innovative argument, Fordham (1998) argues that the domestic political conditions that are likely to trigger diversionary motivations differ for Democratic and Republican presidents. Democratic and Republican presidents, he notes, do not have the same economic constituencies (they also have different social constituencies, but his argument and most diversionary theories focus on economic conditions). The Democratic Party is closely connected to organized labor and is viewed as more friendly than the Republican Party toward workers. For this reason, Hibbs (1977, 1987) argues that Democratic politicians are more likely to battle unemployment than inflation. In contrast, the Republican Party is more closely connected to big business and wealthier Americans; as a result, inflation is a greater threat to Republicans' core constituents than it is to the core of the Democratic Party. Based on their constituency preferences, Fordham (1998) concludes that Republican presidents are more likely to use force when unemployment is high, while Democratic presidents use force when inflation is high.

Is diversionary theory a useful explanation for US foreign policy actions? The short answer is no, but diversionary arguments may apply better for other countries. The central logical problem with most diversionary theories is that they do not fully incorporate strategic interaction. Two types of strategic interaction are usually missing: the president's interactions with leaders of other countries and the president's interactions with other political leaders within the United States, especially Congressional leaders.

The use of force involves two countries: the initiator of force and a target of the military action. The popularity of American presidents is well known in other countries. Leaders in other states, then, should know when an American president has a diversionary incentive to use force, and therefore, likely targets should be particularly cooperative at these times. Smith (1996) and Fordham (2005) call this **strategic conflict avoidance**. If the strategic conflict avoidance argument is accurate, then we should find few opportunities for the use of force when diversionary incentives are highest. Fordham (1998) finds support for this hypothesis. Likely targets avoid or are more appeasing of a country experiencing diversionary incentives.

A second form of strategic interaction involves the president and key Congressional leaders. Although the president does not need Congressional approval to use force abroad short of war, it is politically better for a president to have Congressional support than not. Howell and Pevehouse (2005) observe that when Congress opposes the president, it is more difficult and costly for the president to mobilize public support and, if the use of force turns out to be prolonged, then the political opposition is mobilized and ready to challenge the president. Based on this insight, Howell and Pevehouse (2005) find (a) that presidents are less likely to use force when Congress opposes it and (b) little support for diversionary incentives. That is, poor domestic political conditions are not associated with a greater use of force abroad, but Congressional support for the president does increase the probability of using military force.

Research on public opinion suggests that the conditions necessary for a diversionary use of force to produce a rally effect are unlikely to occur. To understand this, we need to first note that when forming foreign policy opinions most people generally look to the views of elites whom they trust. Next, rally effects occur, in part, because there is a dearth of opposition information. At the beginning of a military campaign, the administration has an information advantage in getting its message out. Over time, other views come out, and when these views are not consistent with the administration's story, public support goes down. In other words, debates between elites, especially in different political parties, counteract incentives to rally-around-the-flag. Research on how an elite consensus influences public opinion, then, supports Howell and Pevehouse's argument that a president is more likely to use force when supported by Congress. Further, this implies that diversionary uses of force are unlikely. As Baum and Potter (2008: 49) write: "The non-traditional, aggressive, or unilateral missions leaders might initiate to 'wag the dog' in turn are the very types of conflict most likely to provide cues (such as partisan elite discord) that tend to turn the public against a military engagement."

13.5 Bargaining Failure and War

If diversionary theory does not explain why war occurs, what does? Before offering a coherent explanation of conflict, we should note that diversionary theory captures a central insight about war: it is political. The German military theorist Carl von Clausewitz best expresses this point. In war, "the political object is the goal, war is the means of reaching it, and means can never be considered in isolation from their purpose."[6] In other words, Clausewitz is telling us that the beginning, execution, and ending of war are inextricably tied up with politics.

Imagine two actors, A and B, disagree on something, such as territory, policy, or the nature (composition) of a state's regime. (Why the actors disagree is not important at this stage of the analysis, though reducing serious disagreements is an important way to promote peace.) They can resolve their disagreement through negotiations or using military force (i.e. going to war). Using military force is costly in terms of money and potentially lives; in other words, both the winner and loser of a violent conflict suffer costs. It is important to keep in mind that the cost of going to war is distinct from the outcome. Indeed, because war is costly, there is always a negotiated settlement, a bargain, that leaves both states better off than going to war. At the end of a war, there is often a clear victor, such as one actor now being in control of the disputed territory, but to achieve this outcome both the victor and vanquished experienced costs. Therefore, at the end of the war, each actor can look back and recognize that any agreement short of war that cost less than what that actor spent would have been better for it. Of course, the actors do not know how much the war will cost. That is a key point. But they do know that war is costly and each has expectations about how much the war will cost them. This creates a **bargaining range**, a set of agreements both sides prefer to war, because the agreements are less costly than war. So long as war is costly, and it always is, there is a bargaining range (Fearon 1995). A numerical example clarifies the logic of the situation.

Imagine that two individuals are negotiating over control of $100. They can either reach an agreement on how to split the money or fight (i.e. go to war) to see who gets it. However, if they choose to fight, they each have to pay a cost of $20. Let's assume for now that they are equally matched so that the outcome of a fight is 50-50. With these parameter values (the probability of victory, cost of war, and value of the issue in dispute), each individual has an expected value for fighting of $30.[7] Any offer from the other person that is less than $30 should be rejected, for one has a higher expected value for going to war. More importantly, our two negotiators should accept any offer between $31 and $69 dollars. This is because going to war only has an expected value of $30 for each person. As a result, any offer between $31 and $69 makes both individuals better off than going to war. As should be clear, the bargaining range exists because fighting is costly. This returns us to the question we left off with. Given that war is costly and that there is always a negotiated settlement that leaves the bargainers better off than going to war, why does war occur?

---

[6] Clausewitz 1976: 87.

[7] Expected utility of fighting = Probability of Winning * Utility of Winning + Probability of Losing*Utility of Losing − Cost of Fighting = (0.5*100) + (0.5*0) − 20 = 50 − 20 = 30.

One explanation for bargaining failure, and therefore the occurrence of war, is **asymmetric information with an incentive to misrepresent**. For simplicity, we call this the information problem. How does it work? There may be conflicting expectations about the precise outcome because of uncertainty about how strong each side is or about each side's resolve. Each of these factors affects the cost of fighting, and therefore what an actor asks for in negotiations. For example, if State A thinks it has a 70 percent chance of winning, it may demand the whole territory, but if State B thinks State A only has a 50 percent chance of winning, then State B will be unlikely to accept State A's offer. Disagreements about which side is more likely to prevail in conflict are more likely to occur when states have relatively equal amounts of power (Reed 2003) or one side thinks the other side is not likely to devote all of its resources to a conflict, while it is willing to make such a sacrifice. This last point highlights the importance of resolve, which is how committed an actor is to a particular course of action. While two or more actors may only sometimes disagree about relative power, they are likely to often have uncertainty about just how committed the other side is to a particular course of action or the other side's intended military strategy.

Reiter (2003) provides a number of illustrations of these points. One might have expected, for example, for France to accede to German demands in 1940. After all, Germany had just routed Poland, demonstrating their military prowess. Reiter recounts how the French observed Germany's military strategy against Poland and revised their defense plan as a result. Instead of focusing on their border with Germany, the French military came to believe that Germany was more likely to attack through Belgium, as that area was more conducive to tanks than the forests of the Ardennes. By shifting their forces toward the Belgian front, the French likely thought they could reach an agreement with Germany. However, the Germans understood French expectations and saw their preparations. They countered by initiating a small attack on Belgium, luring French forces in, and then launching their main attack through the Ardennes. "This successful change in German strategy prevented a possible war-avoiding settlement," Reiter (2003: 35) notes, "as the two sides did not agree on the potential outcome of a German–French campaign (each was confident of victory)." Uncertainty about capabilities, resolve, and military strategy is all too common in international relations.

If asymmetric information about military capabilities, strategy, or resolve can cause war, why do states not reveal all of their capabilities and strategies? The answer is simple: revealing all of one's information may result in a worse offer from the other side. As Clausewitz observed centuries ago, "In the whole range of human activities, war most resembles a game of cards" (Clausewitz 1976: 86). When playing cards, you do not show your entire hand to the other players. You conceal your cards and sometimes bluff; this is the incentive to misrepresent in order to get the best deal possible. Since the other side knows you have an incentive not to reveal all of your information, they are unlikely to believe any claims that you have revealed everything.

In our earlier example about the French and Germans in 1940, the Germans could also not reveal their plan to launch a surprise attack through the Ardennes, for then the strategy would not succeed. Similarly, the Japanese could not tell the United States that they were planning to attack Pearl Harbor in 1941. Japan knew that, to succeed, the attack had to be a surprise (and they had to find the American aircraft carriers in port). In summary, conflicting expectations about who might prevail in a conflict occur because of *uncertainty about capabilities, strategy, or resolve and an incentive to misrepresent* these factors.

Second, two sides may fail to reach a negotiated settlement because of a **credible commitment problem**. This problem exists when at least one actor has an incentive to renege on an agreement. Incentives to break one's promise usually occur because of a change in capabilities, but a change in preferences or resolve may also lead to an incentive to break one's word. More generally, a credible commitment problem is a time-inconsistency problem. At present, both sides may want to reach a deal, but at least one side believes that the other side will not honor its word in the future because of an expected change in capabilities or resolve.

Is a credible commitment problem the same as a trust problem? They are similar, but not identical. On one hand, a commitment problem is the same as a trust problem. In both situations, one person thinks someone else will not honor his word. On the other hand, there is a slight difference in the cause of this expectation. Trust problems result from beliefs about a person's character. Commitment problems result from beliefs about the incentives working on the other person. If at least one actor believes another will not honor its promise, then a negotiated compromise will not happen and fighting will likely occur.

Strategies for Promoting Peace

The goal in understanding the proximate causes of conflict is to devise strategies for promoting peace. What insights on promoting peace do we gain from seeing war as the result of a bargaining failure? Negotiated agreements are more likely to occur when there are institutions that increase the *credibility of information*, institutions and other mechanisms that enhance the *credibility of promises*, and factors that *increase the cost of war for both sides*.

First, institutions that make communication more credible reduce uncertainty about resolve and capabilities. In turn, with less uncertainty, expectations about the precise outcome of a conflict are able to converge. The great challenge is finding ways to enhance the credibility of one's speech; remember there is an incentive to misrepresent. What one needs to do is send a **costly signal**. A costly signal is an action that imposes a cost on oneself, the sender. By imposing a cost on yourself, you signal to others that you are not bluffing.

A significant body of research indicates that democratic political institutions enhance the ability of leaders to send costly signals (Fearon 1994; Schultz 1998, 1999). Because of credible opposition parties, the leader of a democracy is much less likely to bluff than the leader of a non-democracy, for a democratic leader is easier to hold accountable. Also, the transparency associated with democratic societies (freedom of assembly, media freedom, etc.) makes it easier for potential adversaries to gauge public support. Knowing this, democratic leaders are less likely to bluff. In other words, on average, democratic leaders are better able than autocratic leaders to generate **audience costs**, the cost imposed on a leader for backing down from a public threat.

Second, and most importantly, when there are mechanisms that increase the credibility of promises, typically by reducing the benefits of reneging, agreements are more likely to occur. Domestic and international institutions can increase the credibility of promises. In a democracy, for example, a leader is more likely to pay a cost for breaking an agreement with another state. This is because opposition parties have an incentive to highlight the promise breaking for their own political ends. In contrast, most dictators have few people to whom they answer; this makes it easier for them to renege on a deal. Alliances can also help reduce credible commitment problems. If a state has strong allies, then an increase in power in one's rival is less concerning for the alliance keeps war too costly for the rival.

Third, when the cost of war increases, there is a larger bargaining range. In other words, the ability to inflict damage on the other side reduces the overall benefits of war. In this respect one common explanation for the absence of World War III between the United States and the Soviet Union is the presence of nuclear weapons. Both the Soviet Union and the United States possessed secure second strike capability. This means each side had enough nuclear weapons and had those weapons dispersed in such a way that the other side could not knock them out with a surprise attack. Thus, since both sides had secure second strike capabilities, there is the promise of **mutual assured destruction (MAD)**. In turn, MAD guaranteed that any direct war between the Soviet Union and the United States would be very costly, making it easier to find some sort of compromise.

Finally, we might notice a relationship between these strategies for promoting peace and political ideologies. Conservatives in the United States, for example, tend to focus on peace through strength. To the extent that strength reduces another actor's incentive for reneging on an agreement or it increases the bargaining range between actors, the strategy of peace through strength can contribute to peace. Liberals in the United States tend to favor building institutions that promote transparency and conflict mediation. These strategies are also useful for reducing the likelihood of bargaining failure. Transparency and accountability institutions enhance one's ability to send costly signals, thereby clarifying one's resolve. Mediation may also clear up confusion about the actor's capabilities and resolve or provide a credible third party that can help enforce an agreement.

In summary, we can reduce the probability of bargaining failure, and therefore the likelihood of war, with institutions that facilitate the communication of costly signals, third-party guarantees and institutions that enhance the credibility of such guarantees, and increasing the cost of war for both sides.

Crisis Bargaining

To better understand the strategic nature of foreign policy, how domestic politics influences international relations, and how costly signaling can help resolve disputes short of war, we present a simple crisis bargaining game. The game is based on Schultz (1998).

As shown in Figure 13.2, there are two actors, United States and Target, and three decision nodes. To give the game concreteness, imagine that there is a good in dispute and that at present the challenger possesses it. The good may be a piece of territory or something more abstract like a policy. Policies, in this context, include violation of the non-proliferation treaty, violation of Chapter VII Security Council resolutions, human rights practices, etc. If a policy is in dispute, assume the United States wants to change Target's policy.

The United States moves first and has to choose between making a challenge (a threat) or doing nothing. If the United States does nothing, then the game ends and each actor receives its status quo pay-off. The status quo for Target is possession of the good or continuation of the policy; for the United States, it is not possessing the good and not changing the policy. If the United States makes a challenge, then Target has to choose how to respond. Target can either resist the challenge or concede to the United States' threat. If Target concedes, the game ends and the United States receives the good or policy change, while Target gives up the good or changes policies.

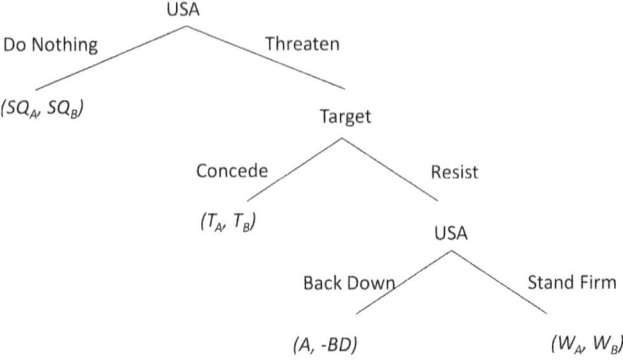

Figure 13.2 Crisis Bargaining Game

However, if Target resists the United States' challenge/threat, then the United States has to choose between standing firm and backing down. If the United States backs down, the United States receives a penalty for making a public threat and not following through, while Target maintains the good in dispute. If the United States stands firm, it means there is military conflict, the outcome of which is determined by the balance of power, war expectations, and war costs.

While the outcome of this game, as in any formal model, depends on the specific parameter values, we will describe several plausible scenarios both to illustrate how to identify the game's equilibria (i.e. its predictions) and key points. Each scenario is defined by a specific preference ordering of the possible outcomes for each player.

In Scenario 1 (Figure 13.3), the United States' preference ordering indicates that war is more costly than audience costs. While the president may receive a penalty for going back on his word, the president believes that going to war would result in an even greater penalty. This may be because war is expected to be costly or that the issue is not salient enough for the public to embrace the cost of war.

To solve the game, we employ backwards induction and identify all subgame perfect equilibria. A **subgame perfect equilibrium** is a set of strategies in equilibrium for all subgames. The subgame perfect equilibrium is a refinement of the Nash Equilibrium solution concept; what it does is eliminate non-credible choices.

In Scenario 1, at its last decision node, the United States chooses "Back Down" over "Stand Firm." This is because its war pay-off is smaller than its pay-off for backing down. Now we move backwards, up the game tree, to identify Target's choice. If Target chooses to concede, it receives Threattarget. If it chooses to Resist, it receives Back Down, because we know that the United States chooses Back Down at its decision node. Since Target prefers Back Down to Threattarget, Target chooses to Resist. Now

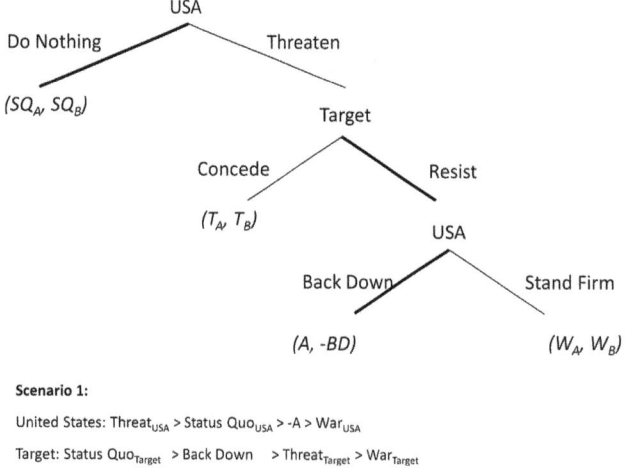

Scenario 1:

United States: Threat$_{USA}$ > Status Quo$_{USA}$ > -A > War$_{USA}$

Target: Status Quo$_{Target}$ > Back Down > Threat$_{Target}$ > War$_{Target}$

Figure 13.3 Scenario 1: Crisis Bargaining Game with Player Choices Highlighted

we move backwards again to identify what the United States does at its first decision node. Here the United States chooses between Challenge and Doing Nothing. If it challenges, it will receive its back-down pay-off (we know from the backwards induction we just performed), which is worse than what it gets from the status quo. Thus, in Scenario 1, the United States will choose to do nothing, and each player receives its status quo pay-off. Formally, the subgame perfect equilibrium is United States (Do Nothing, Back Down), Target (Resist).

Why does the United States not challenge Target in Scenario 1? After all, the status quo is not its most preferred outcome. The key factor driving the United States' choice not to challenge is the relationship between –A and W1. In Scenario 1, the US prefers the –A pay-off to the W1 pay-off. In other words, the United States views war, W1, as too costly. Since Target knows that the United States is not likely to follow through on its threat, it will resist. Knowing this, the United States would prefer not to suffer audience costs, –A, so it does not challenge. Simply put, the United States' threat is not credible, and it is not credible because it is not willing to go to war to back up the threat.

Now consider Scenario 2 (Figure 13.4). The only difference between Scenarios 1 and 2 is that the United States now prefers its war pay-off to its back-down pay-off. Let us solve the game using backwards induction. The United States, at its last decision node, chooses to Stand Firm. Knowing that the United States will stand firm, Target chooses to concede. Knowing that Target will concede, the United States, at its first decision node, chooses to Threaten Target. Each player will then receive its Threat pay-off. The subgame perfect equilibrium is United States (Threaten, Stand Firm), Target (Concede).

Why does the United States threaten Target in Scenario 2? Here, the United States believes that its audience cost penalty, backing down from a public threat, is greater than its cost for going to war. Since Target knows that the United States will face great

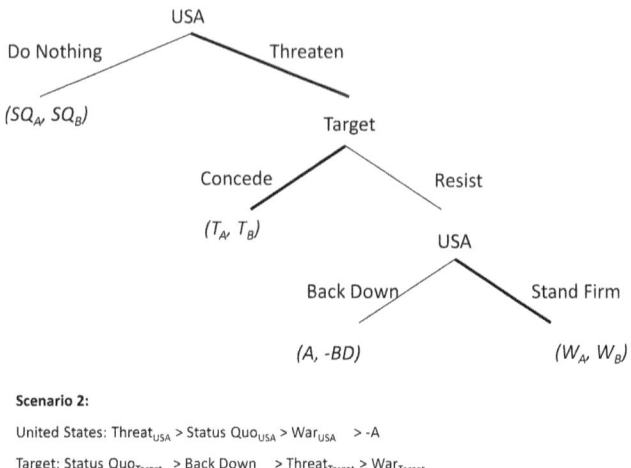

Scenario 2:

United States: Threat$_{USA}$ > Status Quo$_{USA}$ > War$_{USA}$ > -A

Target: Status Quo$_{Target}$ > Back Down > Threat$_{Target}$ > War$_{Target}$

Figure 13.4 Scenario 2: Crisis Bargaining Game with Choices Highlighted

audience costs for backing down and that Target does not want war, the United States' has a credible threat and Target concedes. In other words, the United States' threat is a costly signal of its resolve to go to war, and it is a costly signal because of the penalty it will suffer for not following through on its action. It is important to note that a threat in and of itself is not costly. Sometimes a threat is just a bluff, or in the language of game theory, cheap talk. What makes a threat a costly signal is whether one will be penalized for not following through on one's word. It is this penalty for not following through that makes a costly signal informative. If one is not resolved to go to war, then one is unlikely to send such a signal.

The crisis bargaining game and the two scenarios discussed here highlight several key points about foreign policy. First, states do not always get what they most desire. Recall that in Scenario 1, the United States preferred its threat outcome to its status quo outcome, but it did not choose to threaten because it knew that Target would resist and it would ultimately back down. More generally, states do not always get what they want because of strategic interaction. This leads to a second key point.

Second, states do not simply act; they interact. Interaction means that one actor's choices are influenced by what it thinks the other actor(s) will do. Failing to consider what others will likely do in response to your actions is likely to produce negative results for you. In the same way that the best chess players understand the current state of the board and can think several moves ahead, the best foreign policy analysts and practitioners anticipate others' reactions to their moves before making a choice. Strategic interaction and anticipatory decision-making of this sort may result in one not attaining one's most preferred outcome, but it also reduces the probability of one attaining one's least preferred outcome.

Third, domestic politics influences international interactions. Recall that in Scenario 2, the United States has a credible threat. What makes the threat credible is the domestic political penalty the United States will suffer if it backs down from its threat. In this scenario, domestic politics actually helps the United States signal more effectively and attain a better outcome for itself. In other words, a state's domestic political institutions and context provide useful information about that state's resolve, and knowing something about another state's resolve helps reduce information problems and bargaining failures that lead to war. Of course, not all domestic political institutions or contexts reduce the probability of war, only institutions that reduce information problems. In general, democratic political institutions are better at reducing information problems than autocratic political institutions, which is one reason why pairs of democracies are less likely to experience significant military conflict than other pairs of states.

Fourth, relative power influences foreign policy and international interactions. Remember that the central difference between Scenarios 1 and 2 is that the United States preferred war to backing down in the latter. This may be for one of two reasons.

War is preferred either because audience costs are extremely high or because the cost of war is small, all else equal. In general, when one state is much stronger than another, it has a better chance at prevailing in a military conflict; it will also suffer fewer costs from the war compared to the other state. A strong relative power advantage, then, makes military threats and war more attractive, all else equal. Moreover, other international factors affect a state's cost of war. States that have significant assistance from allies will generally experience a lower war cost than if they did not have allies. Similarly, international backing for one's position, such as a UN Security Council resolution, can increase one's resolve and lower one's war cost. In brief, relative power, alliances, and support from international institutions affect the cost of war. Anything that lowers the cost of war makes it relatively more likely and anything that increases the cost of war decreases its probability.

13.6 International Trade

International trade is one of the most contentious public policy topics. People object to international trade for a variety of reasons, including the belief that it harms the economy, harms the environment, and creates dangerous dependencies. In contrast, supporters of trade are puzzled about why there is so much protectionism. The concepts of comparative advantage and collective action provide some insight here. In brief, trade produces aggregate benefits, but concentrated costs. Couple the aggregate benefits and concentrated costs with political institutions and we can fairly accurately explain why some politicians are more supportive of trade than others.

The primary principal that governs international trade is **comparative advantage**, a concept first articulated by David Ricardo. A state has a comparative advantage when the **opportunity cost** of producing a product is cheaper in that state than in another state. Opportunity cost is what you give up when you pursue one option versus another. The key insight of the principal of comparative advantage is that a state is better off putting its resources to use producing what it is most efficient at producing and importing other goods. Even if a state is more efficient than all other states at producing all possible products, it will be better off channeling its resources into the product that it is *most* efficient at making, and then trading for other products. In other words, comparative advantage tells us that it is beneficial to specialize in order to increase production and profit, while trading for products that some other state specializes in producing.

Tables 13.2 and 13.3 illustrate these points. We have two countries, North and South, and two products, computers and t-shirts. In Table 13.2, we observe that South produces both products more efficiently. That is, it takes fewer labor hours to produce t-shirts in South (10 hours) compared to North (15 hours) and fewer labor hours to

Table 13.2 Labor Hours to Produce T-Shirts and Computers

	T-shirts	Computers
North	15	30
South	10	15

Table 13.3 Opportunity Cost of Producing T-Shirts and Computers

	T-shirts	Computers
North	1/2 computer	2 t-shirts
South	2/3 computer	1 1/2 t-shirts

produce computers in South (15 hours) compared to North (30 hours). This means South has an absolute advantage at producing both products. The counterintuitive insight from Ricardo (and Adam Smith before him) is that both countries have a comparative advantage in one product. It still makes sense for South to trade even though it produces both products more efficiently. Table 13.3 helps explain why.

Table 13.3 shows the opportunity cost for producing each good. North gives up half a computer for each t-shirt it produces. In other words, the labor used to produce a t-shirt could also be used to produce a computer. If we moved all of the t-shirt labor hours to the computer industry, how many more computers could we produce? It depends on the number of labor hours, but for each hour it would be half of a computer. For comparison, South gives up two-thirds of a computer for each t-shirt produced. The country with the lower opportunity cost has a comparative advantage in producing that good. North has a comparative advantage in producing t-shirts, and South has a comparative advantage in producing computers.

Trade increases aggregate (world) wealth, but it is not without costs. The central problem with trade is that the benefits are dispersed, but the costs are concentrated. With trade and the concomitant specialization it entails, everyone benefits a little from having cheaper products, but some people may experience large costs as they may lose their job and have to change industries. Given what we have said about comparative advantage, each country does best when it specializes in the production of the product it is most efficient (has the lowest opportunity cost) at producing and trades for the other one. Let us say that North will specialize in the production of t-shirts and South in the production of computers. This means that the computer workers in North lose their jobs in the computer industry, though there will now be more jobs available in the t-shirt industry. Similarly, the t-shirt workers in South will lose their jobs and will have to find employment in the computer industry. One implication of international trade is that it works best and will be more widely supported if a state has a robust job retraining policy. For this reason, it is useful to think of trade as a new technology. When a new technology, like the automobile, is developed, people in the industry using the old technology, the horse and buggy for example, lose their job, but new jobs become available to manufacture the new technology. Still, this means the horse and buggy driver has to change jobs. The benefits and costs of new technologies are similar to those associated with free trade.

The factors that affect the products a country produces allow us to better understand why some states are much more likely to export airplanes and others to export textiles. In other words, comparative advantage in international trade is largely a function of **factors of production**. Factors of production are what is necessary to produce a product. Most economists identify three types of factors of production: land, labor, and capital (as noted in other chapters, capital includes financial capital, human capital, and social capital). We can communicate the essential ideas, however, by only focusing on two: labor and (financial) capital.

Let us assume that there are only two industries, textiles and airplane manufacturing. The textile industry is labor-intensive, while the airplane industry is capital-intensive. **Labor-intensive** means that the ratio of labor to capital is greater to produce textiles than it is to produce airplanes, while **capital-intensive** means that the ratio of capital to labor is greater for airplanes than for textiles.

Which type of product should a country produce for export? The **Heckscher–Ohlin theorem** helps answer this question. It says that if there are two factors of production, a country will export products based on the intensive use of its abundant factor and import products based on the intensive use of its scarce factor. Thus, countries that are relatively wealthy will export capital-intensive products and import labor-intensive products, while countries that are relatively poor will export labor-intensive products and import capital-intensive products. For example, relative to the United States, Mexico is labor abundant and relative to Mexico, the United States is capital abundant. The Heckscher-Ohlin theorem tells us that Mexico will export products that are based on the intensive use of labor and the United States will export to Mexico products that are relatively more capital abundant. Analogously, another way to export capital-intensive products is to export capital. Businesses do this by investing in the economies of labor-intensive states, including the building of manufacturing plants in those states. This type of investing is called foreign direct investment.

There are two general political economy models for explaining who benefits and who loses from trade within a country, and consequently public opinion on trade. According to the **Stolper–Samuelson model**, individuals working in the abundant factor benefit from trade, while individuals working with the scarce factor experience the costs of trade. In rich states (i.e. states relatively abundant in capital), individuals with large amounts of capital benefit from trade, while laborers suffer the costs of trade. In contrast, in poor states (i.e. states relatively abundant in labor), laborers benefit the most from trade, while individuals with large amounts of capital experience the cost of trade. For example, in the United States, the Stolper–Samuelson model says that those who are relatively better off should support free trade and laborers should be relatively more opposed to free trade.

The **Ricardo–Viner model** focuses on industries (or sectors) instead of factors of production. According to the Ricardo–Viner model, workers in more competitive industries will benefit from trade, while workers in less competitive industries will suffer from trade. Competitive, in this context, means the industry is likely to see its exports increase with fewer restrictions on trade. Unlike Stolper–Samuelson, the Ricardo–Viner model does not expect class conflict over trade. Rather, both owners and laborers in a highly competitive industry benefit from trade and both owners of capital and laborers in a less competitive industry suffer from trade. Political conflict on trade policy, according to Ricardo–Viner, will occur between different industries. In the United States, for example, the Ricardo–Viner model expects that those in the automobile industry, both the wealthy upper-management and the factory workers, will oppose free trade as their vehicles were viewed by many as less appealing than Japanese-made cars.

Ricardo–Viner and Stolper–Samuelson have different expectations about who benefits and who loses from trade because they make different assumptions about how mobile factors of production are. In the Stolper–Samuelson model, factors of production are perfectly mobile. This means that a worker who loses a job in one industry can easily find a job in another industry. Similarly, capital that is used in one industry can easily be transferred to another industry. Sometimes this is the case. If a job does not involve any particular skills, then it is not difficult to change jobs. When jobs are more skill-based or capital is more specific to an industry, Stolper–Samuelson is less useful. For example, if workers in the automobile industry lose their jobs and they cannot easily obtain new positions in growth areas, like nursing, then we would say that the factors of production, labor in this case, are not very mobile. In this case, the Ricardo–Viner model better explains who benefits and loses from trade. Hiscox (2002) finds that each of these models is accurate, contingent on the degree of factor mobility.

Collective Action, Institutions, and Protectionism

Protectionism is any policy meant to restrict trade or alter who is trading what to whom. Protectionism has two general forms: tariffs and non-tariff barriers. **Tariffs** are taxes on imports. Because they increase the price of goods, they alter trade flows. **Non-tariff barriers** include a large number of policies. Some of the most common non-tariff barriers are quotas, subsidies, labor standards, environmental standards, human rights standards, and currency manipulation. Each of these policies either specifically restricts how much can be traded between countries (e.g. quotas, labor, environmental, and human rights standards) or alters the price of goods traded (e.g. subsidies, currency manipulation).

Collective action theory tells us that smaller and more heavily invested groups are more likely to organize. With trade, this means that, on average, those who lose from trade are more likely to organize. Recall that those who lose from trade tend to be smaller in number, lose a lot, and are highly concentrated in an industry or factor of production. Each of these factors makes it easier for them to organize. Businesses supporting trade also organize, and they typically have more resources at their disposal. Which set of interest groups, call them labor and business for convenience, wins the policy battle determines if there will be protectionist policies. It is more accurate to say that the labor versus business battle determines the degree of protectionism in a country, for presently all countries in the world have some protectionism.

Political institutions influence the outcome of the protectionist battle significantly. One set of institutions that matters here is the size of one's political constituency. In the United States at the national level of government, some politicians are beholden to Congressional districts (Members of the House of Representatives), some to states (Members of the Senate), and one person to the entire country (the president). In general, and on average, those who represent smaller constituencies are more likely to yield to protectionist sentiments. Of course, this depends on whether a particular constituency, a district for example, is likely to benefit from trade or not. Assume for the moment that some people in any constituency will be harmed from trade. As we increase the constituency size that set of people has less influence, and it is for this reason that, on average, those who represent smaller constituencies are more likely to yield to protectionist pressures. It is not surprising, then, that presidents tend to be more supportive of free trade policies than members of the House of Representatives. This is not to say that ideology does not affect votes, only that institutions matter a lot. This is easiest to see among members of the Democratic Party. Both Presidents Clinton and Obama have been more supportive of free trade than Democratic members of the House of Representatives, whether in 1994 or 2015. The institutions that govern the size of the constituency to which the elected official is responsible help explain this difference.

Fast Track trade authority is another important institution for understanding trade policy. With Fast Track, first passed in 1974, Congress gives the president authority to negotiate a trade agreement and then vote the agreement up or down. When Congress passes Fast Track authority, it restricts its own powers. Fast Track prohibits introducing amendments and prohibits filibusters. As amendments and filibusters are two of the primary ways in which members of Congress stop a bill from becoming law, Fast Track authority greatly increases the likelihood that Congress will approve a trade deal. Even with Fast Track, members of Congress still vote on trade bills. Given the points we made earlier, we should be able to predict Congressional votes with a political economy model. Some research has done just this and finds that "Legislators appear to anticipate the economic effects of trade and aid policies on their districts and vote accordingly. In particular, Stolper–Samuelson models of trade and aid preferences receive important corroboration" (Milner and Tingley 2011: 62).

13.7 Conclusion

In this chapter, we focus on two types of strategic interactions to explain foreign and defense policy: principal–agent and state-to-state interactions. Principal–agent interactions are useful for explaining the broad contours of foreign policy. In many situations, it is useful to think of the president as an agent and the principal as the president's winning coalition. When typical Democratic and Republican identifiers have similar foreign policy views, then there is significant continuity in American foreign policy. However, when Democratic and Republican identifiers have different foreign policy views and the presidency changes from Democrat to Republic, or vice versa, then we are likely to observe significant changes in American foreign policy. We illustrated these points with a discussion of US defense spending over the last fifty years. Moreover, since agents respond primarily to their principal, they may undertake actions with which many in society disagree. This characterizes President Bush's decision to implement "the surge" in Iraq in 2007. It was popular with his winning coalition, but not with the broader public.

State-to-state interactions are useful for understanding the causes of war and how to promote peace between states. War occurs when two states are unable to find a mutually acceptable bargain. In turn, the inability to find a mutually acceptable bargain turns on asymmetric information or credible commitment problems. Domestic and international institutions that increase accountability and transparency help reduce these bargaining problems. In addition, we showed that increasing the cost of war can make it easier to find a resolution to a dispute. The crisis bargaining game presented in this chapter illustrates these points.

The principles of comparative advantage and collective action help us understand key aspects of trade policy. First, the principle of comparative advantage tells us that trade produces aggregate benefits – it helps a country's overall economy – and concentrated costs – some people will lose their job as a result of free trade, though new jobs will also be created, but maybe in a different part of the country. Second, the problem of collective action tells us that those who lose from trade have a greater incentive to mobilize than those who gain from trade, but protectionist pressures can be muted by institutional configurations that make political representatives accountable to larger and more diverse groups. The larger the constituency, the more likely the beneficiaries of trade will outnumber the losers from trade. Thus, institutions and collective action help explain why there are calls for protectionist policies, but also why free trade preferences typically prevail in the political arena.

Key Terms

Winning coalition

Principal–agent theory

Principals

Adverse selection

Moral hazard problem

Screening

Outcome-based incentive scheme

Standard operating procedure

Gamble for resurrection

Party activists

Core values

Elasticity of reality

Surge

Diversionary theory

Rally-around-the-flag

Strategic conflict avoidance

Bargaining range

Asymmetric information with an incentive to misrepresent

Credible commitment problem

Costly signal

Audience cost

Mutual assured destruction

Subgame perfect equilibrium

Comparative advantage

Opportunity cost

Factors of production

Labor-intensive

Capital-intensive

Heckscher–Ohlin theorem

Stolper–Samuelson model

Ricardo–Viner model

Protectionism

Tariffs

Non-tariff barriers

Collective action

Fast Track

CHAPTER EXERCISES

1. In general, what groups comprise the winning coalition for a Democratic president? For a Republican president? Does the coalition change when a new president is elected? Who forms the winning coalition in a monarchy? In a military regime? In a single-party communist state?

2. Are politicians more responsive to party activists or the mass public? Explain.

3. Why are Republican Party identifiers more likely to support increasing military spending than Democratic Party identifiers?

4. How do politicians attempt to manipulate public opinion? What constraints exist to limit the ability of politicians to manipulate public opinion?

5. Why is diversionary theory a poor explanation for the outbreak of a large-scale war?

6. Why do some actors resort to force to resolve their disputes?

7. From one perspective, trade creates mutual gains. From another perspective, trade creates mutual dependency. Is trade harmful to a country's security? Explain.

8. One central feature motivating collective action is group size. But in the US political system for the last fifty or so years, protectionist sentiment has been stronger in the Democratic Party than in the Republican Party. Why is this? What does this tell us about the theory of collective action?

REFERENCES

Aldrich, John H. 1995. *Why Parties? The Origin and Transformation of Political Parties in America*. University of Chicago Press.

Baum, Matthew A. and Potter, Phillip B. K. 2008. "The Relationships between Mass Media, Public Opinion, and Foreign Policy: Toward a Theoretical Synthesis." *Annual Review of Political Science* 11: 39–65.

Bueno De Mesquita, Bruce, Morrow, James D., Siverson, Randolph M., and Smith, Alastair. 2003. *The Logic of Political Survival*. Cambridge, MA: MIT Press.

Carmines, Edward G. and Stimson, James A. 1989. *Issue Evolution: Race and the Transformation of American Politics*. Princeton University Press.

Clausewitz, Carl von. 1976. *On War*. Michael Howard and Peter Paret (eds. and trans.). Princeton University Press.

Downs, George W. and Rocke, David. 1994. "Conflict, Agency, and Gambling for Resurrection: The Principal–Agent Problem Goes to War." *American Journal of Political Science* 38(2): 362–380.

Fearon, James D. 1994. "Domestic Political Audiences and the Escalation of International Disputes." *American Political Science Review* 88(3): 577–592.

  1995. "Rationalist Explanations for War." *International Organization* 49(3): 379–414.

Fordham, Benjamin O. 1998. "Economic Interests, Party, and Ideology in Early Cold War Era US Foreign Policy." *International Organization* 52(2): 359–396.

  2005. "Strategic Conflict Avoidance and the Diversionary Use of Force." *Journal of Politics* 67(1): 132–153.

Fordham, Benjamin O. 2007. "The Evolution of Republic and Democrat Positions on Cold War Spending – A Historical Puzzle." *Social Science History* 31(4): 603–636.

Hibbs, Douglas. 1977. "Political Parties and Macroeconomic Policy." *American Political Science Review* 71(4): 1467–1487.

1987. *The American Political Economy: Macroeconomics and Electoral Politics*. Cambridge, MA: Harvard University Press.

Hiscox, Michael J. "Commerce, Coalitions, and Factor Mobility: Evidence from Congressional Votes on Trade Legislation." *American Political Science Review* 96.03 (2002): 593–608.

Howell, William G. and Pevehouse, Jon C. 2005. "Presidents, Congress, and the Use of Force." *International Organization* 59(1): 209–232.

Hurwitz, Jon and Peffley, Mark. 1987. "How Are Foreign Policy Attitudes Structured? A Hierarchical Model." *American Political Science Review* 81(4): 1099–1120.

Milner, Helen V. and Tingley, Dustin H. 2011. "Who Supports Global Economic Engagement? The Sources of Preferences in American Foreign Economic Policy." *International Organization* 65(1): 37–68.

Reed, William. 2003. "Information, Power, and War." *American Political Science Review* 97(4): 633–641.

Reiter, Dan. 2003. "Exploring the Bargaining Model of War." *Perspectives on Politics* 1(1): 27–44.

Schultz, Kenneth A. 1998. "Domestic Opposition and Signaling in International Crises." *American Political Science Review* 92(4): 829–844.

1999. "Do Democratic Institutions Constrain or Inform? Contrasting Two Institutional Perspectives on Democracy and War." *International Organization* 53(2): 233–266.

Shapiro, Robert Y. and Page, Benjamin I. 1988. "Foreign Policy and the Rational Public." *Journal of Conflict Resolution* 32(2): 211–247.

Smith, Alastair. 1996. "Diversionary Foreign Policy in Democratic Systems." *International Studies Quarterly* 40(1): 133–153.

Souva, Mark and Rhode, David. 2007. "Elite Opinion Differences and Partisanship in Congressional Foreign Policy, 1975–1996." *Political Research Quarterly* 60(1): 113–123.

Index

CPSIA information can be obtained
at www.ICGtesting.com
Printed in the USA
LVHW061614110723
752105LV00007BA/168